Paul Berry was Vera Brittain's close friend for twenty-eight years and was her Literary Executor. He was the joint editor of *Testament of a Generation: The Journalism of Vera Brittain and Winifred Holtby*. He died in 1999.

Mark Bostridge's books include the bestselling *Letters from a Lost Generation*, the award-winning *Florence Nightingale. The Woman and Her Legend*, and *The Fateful Year. England 1914*.

Vera Brittain
A Life

Paul Berry and Mark Bostridge

With a new introduction
by Mark Bostridge

Virago

VIRAGO

This edition published 2022
Published by Virago Press 2001
First published in the United Kingdom in 1995
by Chatto & Windus Ltd

1 3 5 7 9 10 8 6 4 2

A CIP catalogue record for this book
is available from the British Library.

ISBN 978-0-34901-501-9

Printed and bound in Great Britain by Clays Ltd, Elcograf S.p.A.

Papers used by Virago are from well-managed forests
and other responsible sources.

Virago
An imprint of
Little, Brown Book Group
Carmelite House
50 Victoria Embankment
London EC4Y 0DZ

An Hachette UK Company
www.hachette.co.uk

www.virago.co.uk

In memory of my beloved sister, Monica
PB

To my mother and father and Ian
with love
MAB

'I tried very hard to write the truth but . . . the real truth is so often one of the most difficult things to discover, let alone to tell and impress upon others.'

Vera Brittain, 1933

Contents

List of Illustrations

Introduction to the 2022 Edition

> '*Since her death in 1970, Vera Brittain's standing as a writer, pacifist and feminist has reached heights unequalled in her lifetime. She herself had always put her trust in the judgement of posterity, and once compared her work for peace to a small voice, speaking against the tide of its time, which comes to prominence later.*'

This was the opening to the original edition of *Vera Brittain: A Life*, published by Chatto & Windus more than a quarter of a century ago, in 1995. By the mid-1990s, the revival of Vera Brittain's reputation was well under way. As she had anticipated, posthumous interest in her life and work stemmed from a new generation's discovery of *Testament of Youth*, her classic memoir of the First World War. A bestseller on its original appearance in 1933, *Testament of Youth* became a bestseller once again following its triumphant republication in 1978 by Virago Press.

Brittain's widower, Sir George Catlin, in his early eighties and living in retirement in the New Forest, had his reservations about allowing his late wife's name to be associated with a company trading under the 'deplorable title' of Virago, which he felt carried the damaging implication of '(!!Lesbian)'. But the book received renewed acclaim: for its moving depiction of the cataclysmic impact of war on the men and women of 1914, and for the self-depiction of the young woman at the centre of the story, who emerged from a conventional background to become a major campaigning force for peace and women's rights, as well as the author of some twenty-nine books.

Further reissues of Vera Brittain's work by Virago have included *Testament of Friendship*, her biography of Winifred Holtby; the sequel to *Testament of Youth*, *Testament of Experience*, covering the years 1925 to 1950; as well as novels and a new edition of her war poetry.

In 1979, *Testament of Youth*'s newfound fame was cemented by an award-winning BBC Television adaptation. The success of the five-part series was founded on the dramatization by Elaine Morgan, which brilliantly captured the essence of the original book, and on Cheryl Campbell's luminous and intelligent performance in the central role. The following year, Kenneth MacMillan's ballet *Gloria* took its theme from the book, offering a tribute to the millions who died in the Great War, and to the women who mourned them.

In 1998, as the First World War slipped out of living memory, the publication of *Letters from a Lost Generation* (which I co-edited) – the wartime correspondence between Vera Brittain, her brother Edward, fiancé Roland Leighton, and two close friends, Victor Richardson and Geoffrey Thurlow – became a focal point of Britain's commemoration of the eightieth anniversary of the Armistice. Adapted for Radio Four, these letters offer revealing first-hand accounts of what it was like to be a Voluntary Aid Detachment nurse serving at a field hospital near the Western Front; or a young subaltern, straight out of school, fighting in the trenches of northern France, or the mountainous regions of northern Italy.

As another major anniversary of the war approached, the centenary in 2014 of its outbreak, *Testament of Youth* was being adapted for the big screen. James Kent's feature film, starring Alicia Vikander as Vera Brittain, was released at the beginning of 2015. Due to the restraints of screen time, it was a freer adaptation than the 1979 television version. However, just as the TV series had before it, the film introduced a host of new people to the book. This time, though, rather than being those with a direct link to the war, or ones who'd grown up living in the shadow of it, these readers were often men and women in their late teens or twenties, with little knowledge of the 1914–18 conflict. They were shocked to discover the way in which war had erupted across the lives of young people, not so dissimilar to themselves, a hundred years earlier.

This edition of *Vera Brittain: A Life* coincides with the publication of *Between Friends*, a new selection of Vera Brittain's correspondence with Winifred Holtby. Holtby was Brittain's great friend, a fellow writer and reformer, famous for her novel *South Riding*. It was their friendship which rescued Brittain from near breakdown following the war. For fifteen years Winifred became an essential part of Brittain's life until her premature death, in 1935, from kidney disease, at the age of thirty-seven.

The biography remains after all this time the fullest and most authoritative account of Vera Brittain's life. At certain points it significantly alters the picture presented by Brittain herself in her autobiographies. However, I must admit that my immediate reaction on returning to the book now is to reflect that it's something of a miracle that it ever came into existence.

Going back and re-reading a book you've written after a long gap – and this was my first book – is like encountering an old friend again following years of separation or estrangement. You circle him or her a bit warily, remembering the good times, but maybe more insistently the stresses and strains of the relationship. *Vera Brittain: A Life* was at times a very difficult book to write. To a large extent this derived from problems associated with its dual authorship. Paul Berry desperately wanted to write Vera Brittain's biography. That he'd failed so far to do so when I was imposed on him by Chatto in 1986, to help 'finish' a book that turned out not to exist, was partly due to his being too close to the subject. Paul, a distant relation of Winifred Holtby's on his mother's side, had been a good friend to Brittain, from their first meeting in 1942 to her death nearly three decades later, and became almost a surrogate son. He was one of her literary executors and after her death in 1970 pursued the aim of reviving her reputation, with extraordinary dedication and loyalty to her memory. But these qualities, admirable in themselves, didn't help him in the writing of the biography that had been authorised by Brittain's family and estate. For he found himself torn between that loyalty and the desire to produce a book that wasn't a hagiography – one that would be as honest about Brittain's faults and failings as it would her virtues and achievements.

I was brought in to break the logjam. A friend of two of Vera Brittain's grandchildren from my school and university days, I'd also worked briefly for Shirley Williams, Brittain's daughter, while she was President of the Social Democratic Party (SDP). Still only in my mid-twenties – 'you mean you're writing someone's *authorised* biography?', I remember my dentist exclaiming incredulously – I was at an age when matters of candour didn't much trouble me. I certainly influenced Paul, four decades my senior, in the direction of a much more candid approach.

It was impossible not to love Paul. He was a saintly man of great integrity. He was also a very brave one. As a pacifist during the Second World War, he had chosen to join a London bomb-disposal squad, a compromise between being a conscientious objector and enlisting in the Army (Brittain drew on his experiences for Adrian, the protagonist of her novel *Born 1925*).

Over a period of eight years we worked together on the biography. A reviewer later described the book as 'fastidiously researched', which undoubtedly it was (there's a whole other book going on in the reference notes at the back). But the endless researching was also a way of putting off the fateful day when we would have to decide how we were going to combine our very different approaches and styles in the writing of the final draft. In the end, with Paul ill and fearing that he wouldn't live to see the biography published, I took the book and drastically rewrote our earlier attempts. Although we were reconciled long before his death in 1999, there was always the unspoken accusation between us that I had stolen his book – and his Vera Brittain – away from him. Yet he had given the biography something infinitely precious: that stamp of authenticity that can only come from close personal knowledge of the subject.* The book benefits immeasurably from this.

The archival resources at McMaster University in Hamilton, Ontario, Canada, which had purchased Brittain's papers in 1971, were enormous. Paul and I amassed further material in the course of our research – later donated to Somerville College, Oxford, to form an archive there – only adding to the weight of our task. We were able to interview many 'witnesses', individuals who possessed first-hand memories of events covered in the book. Among these was Major Daniel, who'd been at Uppingham School with 'The Three Musketeers', Edward, Roland, and Victor. He told Paul that he'd observed Roland Leighton, after that final Speech Day in the summer of 1914, taking his seven prize books back to his dormitory in a wheelbarrow. Paul also conducted a telling interview with Cicely Williams, a Somerville contemporary of Vera Brittain's, who later became a distinguished paediatrician and nutritionist. She had so disliked Brittain's first novel, *The Dark Tide*, which lampooned the college and various university figures, that she and a friend burned a copy, page by page, in her mother's backyard. As so often throughout her life, Vera Brittain's outspokenness did not win her popularity.

One of my memorable meetings was with an elderly gentleman in his late seventies, Malcolm Bendon. As a child in 1916 he'd lived in Sandgate in Kent, and he recalled, as if it were yesterday, the two young officers – Edward Brittain and Geoffrey Thurlow – who were billeted on his family. Geoffrey especially stood out for his sense of humour, and because Mr Bendon's elder sister developed a crush on him. Another elderly 'witness' I went to talk to was Donald Soper (by that time,

---

* I have written more fully about our collaboration, as well as the problems associated with my search for the truth about the death in Italy in 1918 of Vera Brittain's brother Edward, in my book *Vera Brittain and the First World War. The Story of Testament of Youth* (2014).

Lord Soper). He remembered the charismatic appeal of Canon Dick Sheppard, leader of the Peace Pledge Union, the largest peace society in Britain in the thirties, and that extraordinary mass meeting, just outside Dorchester in the heat of the summer of 1936, which played a vital role in persuading Vera Brittain to become a pacifist. With his snowy white hair and resonant, yet perfectly modulated voice, which spoke with such authority, he seemed the epitome of holiness and a man very close to God.

No biography is ever definitive. New material, new revelations are liable to turn up. Different generations will interpret parts of a subject's life in new ways, or will emphasise aspects of it that have previously been overlooked or ignored. In 1995, the tragedy of Edward Brittain's final hours on the Asiago Plateau, and the uncovering by the military police of his homosexual relationships with men in his company (described in chapter 3) raised barely a flicker of interest. Twenty years and more later, with the LGBT movement in full flow, the story has been explored on television, radio, and in print (also in Pat Barker's 2012 novel *Toby's Room*, in which the fate of Toby Brooke, an officer at the front, mirrors Edward's experience).

New pieces of information are constantly surfacing. Recently I was contacted by someone who'd come across the diary of one of Vera Brittain's school contemporaries at St Monica's, in Kingswood, Surrey. An entry from 1911 describes the schoolgirls being taken to a suffrage meeting in Tadworth village. This was 'the very mild and constitutional suffrage meeting' that Vera Brittain mentions in *Testament of Youth* as her 'practical introduction to feminism', alongside her more significant reading that year of Olive Schreiner's *Woman and Labour*, the 'trumpet-call' to action.

I'd always assumed that the speaker at the meeting was a female suffragist. According to the diary, though, the 'very amusing' and 'energetic' lecturer was a man: Bernard Langdon-Davies (1876–1952), a Liberal Party activist and subsequently a conscientious objector during the First World War. Often life-writing seems like the largest of jigsaw puzzles, where only one thing is certain: that the collecting of an infinite number of pieces could go on forever.

In April 2021, Shirley Williams, Vera Brittain's daughter, died at the age of ninety. As an MP, Labour Cabinet minister, the co-founder of the SDP, Britain's first new political party in over eighty years, and latterly as leader of the Liberal Democrats in the House of Lords, she had more than fulfilled her mother's hopes for her. The former British diplomat, Stephen Wall, summed up Shirley's wider contribution to British politics when he wrote that her life was a striking illustration of the fact that in politics the exercise of principle can be just as potent as the pursuit of power.

Shirley had been very supportive of this biography, recognising that a well-researched life had an important role to play in the development of her mother's posthumous reputation. She was discomfited by the discovery of the circumstances surrounding her uncle Edward's death, but ultimately did nothing to prevent us from publishing our account. She offered factual corrections and interpretative suggestions on a number of subjects, which were gratefully accepted. Overall I admired her tacit acceptance of the idea that we should be guided in what we wrote by the surviving documentary evidence. This held true even in areas like her parents' 'semi-detached' marriage, where our frankness must occasionally have given her pause.

Shirley left behind over sixty-five boxes of unsorted material, from her own and her mother's life. Shirley's papers have been donated to the British Library, while anything relating to her mother, including a rich trove of original photographs, has gone to the Somerville archive. Among these photos was an album of First World War snapshots, most of them small and blurry. Three were of especial interest. They show Vera Brittain as a VAD outside some wooden huts. In one she stands beside a parasol erected on a wooden bench, presumably to allow a patient to sun himself, smiling at the camera. This is Étaples, probably in the summer or early autumn of 1917.

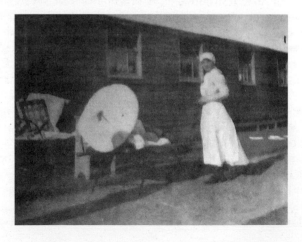

The huts may even be the German ward at the 24 General, where Vera Brittain nursed German prisoners of war, and where she was struck by the tragic and fundamental absurdity of a situation in which she might be trying to save the life of a man whom, a short time before at Ypres, Edward Brittain had been trying to kill. This was an important staging post on her path towards internationalism and, eventually, along a more arduous stretch of road, to pacifism.

The photo is a reminder that there were sunny, carefree moments even in a camp described by Brittain as resembling at times 'a Gustave Doré illustration to Dante's *Inferno*'. It also brings to mind the significant discovery concerning the German ward that came to light after the publication of this book. In 1999 the historian Douglas Gill published an article revealing the discrepancies he'd uncovered between the records kept by the base administrative staff at Étaples and Vera Brittain's account in *Testament of Youth* of nursing German prisoners.* Contrary to Brittain's narrative of German prisoners dying in large numbers at the 24 General, the official records for the hospital, consulted by Gill at the National Archives, show a very low mortality rate: as low as 2 per cent for Vera Brittain's prisoner-patients at the time she nursed there. Her chilling recollection of the plight of dying German patients is therefore largely fictional. But it fits with *Testament of Youth*'s overarching anti-war theme and highlights the way in which the autobiography sometimes reflects the disillusionment of the twenties and early thirties, and Brittain's determination to prevent another generation from drifting towards world conflict, rather than a strictly accurate representation of what she experienced during the war itself.

That experience in 1917 of nursing German prisoners of war, as well as of encountering ordinary Germans – 'sullen and depressed, from shame, poverty and malnutrition' – in 1924, on a visit to Cologne, must have still resonated with Vera Brittain two decades later, when she was one of the very few British voices to speak out against the Allied policy of the saturation bombing of German cities during the Second World War. Today the indiscriminate bombing of the German civilian population in night attacks that flattened cities at a vast cost in human life remains a morally questionable one. And Vera Brittain's arguments (outlined in chapter 14) that strategically the policy was

* Douglas Gill, 'No Compromise with Truth. Vera Brittain in 1917', *Krieg Und Literatur*, V, 199, 67—93. The records of the 24 General are held at the National Archives, WO 95/4085.

bound to fail, that it would neither hasten German military or industrial collapse, nor break enemy morale, have largely been upheld by modern historians.

In 2014, the city of Hamburg, reduced to rubble in the bombing raids of 1943, with more than 35,000 people killed – including thousands of forced foreign labourers and more than 5,000 children – unveiled a plaque in the Hammerbrook district to commemorate its 'Firestorm'. In poignant recognition of Vera Brittain's efforts to prevent the suffering of war's innocent victims, and as a gesture of reconciliation during the centenary year of the outbreak of the Great War, the surrounding embankment of the canal was named in her honour: the *Vera-Brittain-Ufer*. Similar recognition was made in Berlin, another city devastated by the RAF in 1943–44, where a *Vera-Brittain-Ufer* was opened on the banks of the River Spree, opposite Berlin's Cathedral.

As I write this, the world is watching in horror as Vladimir Putin unleashes his terrible war on Ukraine. So many of the tropes of wartime, all too familiar to Vera Brittain and her generation, are being repeated on a scale not seen since the Second World War. There are emotional scenes at railway stations as families are separated, with men going off to fight. There is the desperate fleeing from their homeland of millions of displaced Ukrainians. And there are Russia's airstrikes on civilian targets, including schools and hospitals, causing the deaths of hundreds of men, women, and children. In the midst of television reports of carnage and destruction, there was also a heartening interview with two young Ukrainian doctors, one of whom had only days earlier lost a close friend in a Russian attack. They spoke of their work in treating injured Russian soldiers, and their expressions of care, rising above any considerations of the 'enemy' or of nationhood, summoned up the spirit of the Red Cross motto, *Inter Arma Caritas* ('In War, Charity'), to which Vera Brittain so fervently subscribed (and which, incidentally, provided the epigraph to her poem about 'The German Ward', written in 1917).

Can war ever be 'humanised' or its impact limited? In a sense this is what world governments have been attempting to do ever since 1945, notably in the protocol of the Geneva Convention, currently being violated by Russia, which outlaws attacks on civilians.

Ultimately, as a pacifist, Vera Brittain took a more defiant approach. 'We cannot humanise war', she wrote in 1943, 'we can only end it. The sole remaining alternative is to end ourselves.'

Readers of this biography will come to understand how her own life had brought her to this inescapable conclusion.

Mark Bostridge
March 2022

ONE

'A Bad History of Inheritance and Environment'

'. . . In my heart I know that I am merely the scion of my father's Staffordshire family – which is old enough, but respectable with the terrible respectability of the middle-classes, & [which] has slowly through the years grown rich from the profits of a paper-mill.'

Vera Brittain to George Catlin, 10 February 1924

'Yes, basically she was very conventional and I think one of her troubles was that she was ashamed of this.'

Clare Leighton, 1976

I

In old age Vera Brittain looked back with a certain pride on her North Staffordshire origins. She had left the region before her second birthday and her subsequent visits had been sporadic, but she had often returned there in her imagination. As a girl she had sometimes accompanied her father to the Brittain paper mill at Cheddleton, and picnicked on the banks of the Churnet, or fished for minnows in the stream at Trentham where two of her aunts ran a small school. In later life distance lent enchantment to her 'ugly old Staffordshire', and memories of the semi-rural, semi-industrial landscape, and tales of some of her more colourful ancestors left their imprint on the three longest of her autobiographical novels, *Honourable Estate* (1936), *Account Rendered* (1945), and *Born 1925* (1948). 'The old Staffordshire ghosts will always dominate', she told an interviewer four years before her death, admitting that her recollections of the county were so deeply rooted that they obstinately displaced later experiences whenever she started writing a novel. Hers was the Staffordshire of Arnold Bennett's 'Five Towns', the air heavy with smoke, the countryside densely clustered with the huge bottle-kilns of the Potteries. In one passage, strikingly reminiscent of Bennett, from an article entitled 'Memories of a Staffordshire Londoner', she recalled the view from her youth across the Potteries Ridge:

A pall of smoky mist perpetually dimmed this vast industrial slope, with its pithead and potbank chimneys ... I can still picture the setting sun on summer evenings, a huge, empyreal reflection of the furnaces, like an angry ball of flame descending upon a smouldering world.

As a child Vera's imagination had often been stirred by her father's stories of the Meighs of Ash Hall, relations on his mother's side, 'some of whom possessed a strong vein of eccentricity'. Job Meigh, Vera's great-great-grandfather, was a cobalt manufacturer with the Hanley firm of Hicks, Meigh and Johnson, and a deputy lieutenant of Staffordshire. In 1837, the year of Queen Victoria's accession, he began to build Ash Hall, a mock Elizabethan mansion on a hill overlooking the village of Bucknall, just outside Hanley. Completed in 1841, its ornate black and gold gates stood at the entrance to a red gravelled drive and were flanked on either side by monkey puzzle trees. Pinnacles, turrets, mullioned windows, and the Meigh family crest, granted to Job Meigh in 1840, dominated the red sandstone façade. Ash Hall still stands today, an entertaining monstrosity amidst a sprawling mass of postwar housing, its red sandstone long since darkened by the smoke that once blew across the fields from Hanley.

Meigh himself was every bit as picturesque as his grandiose ancestral home. According to family legend he was a tyrannical ogre who terrorized his wife, family, and large retinue of servants with violent swings of mood. When he was returning home with his wife one day, a furious quarrel arose, and in a fit of uncontrollable temper he pitched her out of the dog-cart he was driving and on to the frozen road, causing her injuries from which she never recovered. It is presumably with unconscious irony then that Job Meigh is commemorated on a plaque in Bucknall Parish Church as 'a devoted husband'. In old age he attempted to halt the ravages of time by dyeing his hair with a substance which turned it bright green when washed. The Meighs were litigious as well as eccentric. Their association with Bucknall Church ended in a bitter and protracted dispute with the church authorities when they claimed exclusive right to the pew which they had used for many years. Job Meigh's grandson, William, Vera's great-uncle, spent nearly a thousand pounds in the mid-1880s in an unsuccessful legal action after the churchwarden allowed several other parishioners to occupy the Meigh pew during a crowded harvest festival service. For many years afterwards, a church inscription triumphantly recorded 'the democratic victory of the church authorities over the Meighs'. After their defeat the family never attended Bucknall Church again.

In marked contrast to the Meighs, Vera's Brittain forebears were 'staid

Midland yeomen', who had been living on the borders of the Pottery towns since at least 1538 when records begin. References to branches of the family, then usually spelt 'Bretton', are to be found in the parish registers of the villages to the south and west of Newcastle-under-Lyme, like Betley and Chapel Chorlton, throughout the seventeenth and eighteenth centuries. Early in the eighteenth century the name begins to appear in the registers of Newcastle itself. These distant ancestors were, for the most part, small bankers, land agents or manufacturers on a modest scale, chiefly hatters and nailers. One of them, Richard Brittain, a hatter, achieved local prominence in 1741 as Mayor of Newcastle.

The foundations of the family's fortunes were laid in the second half of the nineteenth century by Thomas Brittain Senior, Vera's great-grandfather. He had started his business career at the age of twenty-one in 1824, working at the Kinnersley Bank, a private bank in Newcastle, of which he eventually became manager. In 1854 he assumed control of the Ivy House Paper Mill in Hanley when its owner, George Henry Foudrinier, was declared bankrupt. The following year, on the death of Mr Kinnersley, Thomas Brittain negotiated the bank's takeover by the National Provincial Bank, and purchased the Ivy House Mill.

The purchase of the paper mill was a shrewd investment. The pottery industry had been interested in paper-making since the 1780s when tissue paper first began to be used in the process of transfer printing from designs on copper plates on to earthenware. Although initially frowned upon by Staffordshire potteries, who preferred traditional hand-painted work, transfer printing had gradually made itself indispensable to the industry, and the Foudriniers, an inventive and industrious family of Huguenot origin, had played a decisive role in making it popular. Acquiring a derelict corn mill on the north bank of the Caldon Canal at Ivy House, Hanley, they had set about developing a high grade tissue paper for transfer printing which was widely employed throughout the ceramic industry.

Thomas Brittain was a cautious man who over the years developed a sound financial acumen. When he died in 1894, he had amassed a personal fortune of £131,000 (making him in modern terms a millionaire several times over). For more than thirty years, Mill 630 at Hanley, the trade mark which the Ivy House Mill continues to use to this day, remained an exclusively family business. Thomas took his son, Thomas Brittain Junior, into partnership, and a few years later, in 1870, a nephew, Frederick Haigh, 'a man of indefatigable energy and resourcefulness', was brought into the firm.

In 1863 Thomas Brittain Junior, reportedly a man of 'noble character', married Elizabeth Charlotte Meigh, the granddaughter of the eccentric cobalt manufacturer. They lived at Park Fields, an attractive white-fronted house overlooking sloping green fields, at Tittensor near Barlaston, the village about four miles south of Stoke-on-Trent, famous for its associations with the Wedgwood family. It was here that Vera's father, Thomas Arthur Brittain, the oldest of eleven children, all but one of whom survived infancy, was born on 6 April 1864. Arthur, as he was known in the family, was a difficult, obstinate child, frankly declared to be unmanageable by his mother. On account of this and the rapidly expanding family of young Brittains at Park Fields, he was brought up from an early age by his father's parents at their home, Field House (also known as The Cloughs), 'a three-storied house of sulphur-coloured brick flanked by a Spanish fir', on a hill top between Keele and Newcastle. He spent just one unhappy term at Malvern School in the summer of 1878, where he rebelled against the rigours of the school's discipline, before being sent to the High School at Newcastle, a short journey from his grandparents' home. It was to be the young Vera's proud boast that while her father had been at the High School, Arnold Bennett had been a pupil nearby at the Middle School; at best a tenuous link, but in a family largely devoid of literary or artistic connections, one that she valued highly.

In the autumn of 1882, at the age of eighteen, Arthur Brittain started work at the Ivy House Mill. Three years later his father, Thomas Brittain Junior, was dead at forty-six. His sudden death came as a serious blow to the now thriving business. Old Mr Brittain was in his eighties and had allowed his son to assume control of the company. In order to retain the business in family hands, he turned to his son-in-law, Joseph Cecil Clay, a Shrewsbury banker, who had married his daughter Emily, and persuaded him to join the firm. With Clay's 'sound wisdom and financial experience', production at the mill continued to expand. When it became clear that additional premises were required, Frederick Haigh negotiated a partnership with Jeremiah Steele, the proprietor of a small paper mill at Cheddleton, near Leek on the banks of the river Churnet. In 1889 the Ivy House and Cheddleton mills combined, and in the following year they were incorporated as a limited liability company known as Brittains Limited, with Arthur Brittain, at twenty-six, the youngest of the four founding directors.

Brittains' 'exquisite fine papers' had earned them an international reputation by the early years of this century. 'Duplex' paper, introduced in 1895, enabled potters to enrich the decoration of china and earthenware with multi-coloured designs, a process that would eventually prove the basis for the bulk of pottery decoration throughout the world. Brittains were in the vanguard too of the manufacture of gauze tissue for typewriter carbons, and also produced speciality papers. In the 1870s, Oxford University Press had difficulty in obtaining paper of the thin, tough, opaque quality which they needed for their small Oxford Bible, and applied to Brittains, who were able to develop the paper at the Press's Wolvercote Mill. Over the years this Oxford India Paper won the Press many *Grands Prix*, and added significantly to Brittains' prestige.

Within fifty years of entering the paper business, the Brittains had established themselves locally as a family of some standing and influence. They were undoubtedly 'dowdy and stolid', but combined with this a strong conviction of their own superiority, and an unshakeable belief in the power of money. Elizabeth, Arthur Brittain's widowed mother, whom Vera could dimly recall in her large mob cap and black knitted shawl, was an especially forbidding and uncompromising woman. On one occasion she had discovered her unwedded cook in labour and had turned her out of Park Fields at midnight, leaving the hapless servant to give birth in a hansom cab on the way to the workhouse. She had never been close to her eldest son, but had expected him nonetheless to further her own dynastic ambitions by marrying an heiress of county rank. It was, therefore, with a mixture of considerable disapproval and disappointment that she and other members of the family viewed Arthur Brittain's decision in 1890 to marry Edith Bervon, the daughter of a local musician, 'without money or pedigree'.

The origins of the Bervons are obscure and Vera herself was never able to come to any definite conclusions about them. Their dark hair and olive skin lent some credence to the theory that there had been French or Spanish blood in the family at some time, and this colouring together with their hooded eyelids encouraged the notion that they might also have inherited some Jewish blood, though Vera invariably denied this. Vera's maternal grandfather, John Bladder Inglis Bervon (as a professional singer he quickly dropped his second name), was a gifted though impoverished musician. Born in Birmingham in 1837, he had married Emma Jane Hampson of Narborough in Norfolk while in his mid-twenties. He possessed a fine baritone and, as the review cuttings in his scrapbook indicate, was a considerable singer in his early career. He gave many concerts, sometimes with his wife, a mezzo-soprano, and took operatic roles as Count di Luna in *Il Trovatore* and Count Arnhem in *The Bohemian Girl* with the English Opera Company in Belfast in 1860. The Bervons lived for a time in Scarborough, but by the late 1860s had settled in the North Wales seaside resort of Aberystwyth where Inglis Bervon was employed as organist at the newly consecrated parish church of St Michael. Edith Mary Bervon, the third of six children – two boys, four girls – was born in Aberystwyth on 19 November 1868.

Inglis Bervon was charming but feckless, a generous-hearted man whose life centred on his music. At Aberystwyth during the summer months he instituted a series of concerts at which the 'elite of the musical world' performed to the delight of large and 'fashionable' audiences. He had a casual disregard for money and undertook such activities free of charge, despite the difficulty of supporting a large family on his meagre church salary. During Edith's childhood the family moved several times in order that her father might find more lucrative work. In 1871 they left Aberystwyth for Forden in Montgomeryshire. A few years later they were uprooted again, this time to Stafford where Inglis Bervon took up an appointment as organist and choirmaster at St Mary's Church. Here he supplemented his salary by composing psalm and hymn tunes and organ voluntaries which he later published, and, more profitably, by giving singing lessons. Evidently he made a success of teaching for in 1884 he left Stafford to set up a practice as 'Professor of Music' in Hanley. He was recognized 'as one of the best voice trainers in this part of the country', the *Staffordshire Sentinel* reported in a glowing tribute after his death, 'and many of our best local amateur *artistes* have benefited from his tuition.'

Among his pupils was Arthur Brittain, who on meeting Edith, 'a graceful and exceptionally gentle girl of twenty-one', was immediately attracted to her. He set his heart on making her his wife, despite the unwavering opposition from his family, and according to information which Vera later managed to prise from her mother, 'moved heaven & earth to get her'. Edith, by all accounts the prettiest of the Bervon sisters, seems to have been less certain that this impatient and headstrong young man was the husband she wanted. But the prospect of escaping 'from the poverty & sordidness which surrounded her for a life of steadily increasing comforts' was an undeniably attractive one, and when Inglis Bervon died suddenly of a heart attack at the age of just fifty-three, a week before Christmas 1890, leaving an estate valued at little more than £250, the necessity of making a good marriage must have appeared even more imperative. With her mother and sisters pressing her to accept him, Edith Bervon agreed to become Arthur Brittain's wife.

They were married in April 1891 in a service at Christ Church, Southport, witnessed by only the bride's mother and a friend of the bridegroom's. The bride suffered a bad attack of pre-wedding nerves. 'Please don't excite yourself . . . as I am afraid you will make yourself ill . . .', Arthur Brittain scribbled in a note to her, while waiting for the buttons on his morning-coat to be altered. To cheer her he wrote that he was arranging for the bell-ringers 'to give us a merry little peal as we come out of the church . . .'.

The conspicuous absence of any Brittains from the ceremony coupled with the fact that it took place in Lancashire, well beyond Staffordshire's borders, leads to speculation that like the marriage of Stephen and Jessie Alleyndene, Arthur and Edith's fictional counterparts in *Honourable Estate*, this wedding may have taken place in secret. A secret marriage would certainly account for the unrelenting hostility of the Brittains towards Edith and her family. After one formal visit from Elizabeth Brittain to the widowed Mrs Bervon, the Brittains ostracized the Bervons completely, and more or less cold-shouldered Edith too. The insult cut deep and in later years Edith Brittain seldom spoke of her early life.

The young couple's first home was at Atherstone House in Sidmouth Avenue, Newcastle-under-Lyme (now 9 Sidmouth Avenue), a three-storeyed, semi-detached villa with an attractive black and white frontage which overlooked the extensive private grounds of Pitfield House. A shady, tree-lined street, Sidmouth Avenue had been built in the 1870s on land which had formerly belonged to Viscount Sidmouth. Situated at the smarter end of Newcastle, it was occupied by the professional class and well-to-do businessmen. To enforce privacy and emphasize its splendid isolation a gate stood at the entrance to the avenue, cordoning it off from social inferiors.

Arthur and Edith Brittain's early years of marriage were blighted by misfortune. In May 1892 their first child, a boy, was stillborn. Shortly afterwards, Arthur Brittain developed appendicitis. A bungled operation, and a lifelong inclination to malinger, left him as a semi-invalid for nearly a year. However, a baby girl born at Atherstone House on 29 December 1893, during her father's absence at a Christmas pantomime in Hanley, was robust and healthy, which must have more than compensated for any initial disappointment about the child's sex. A month after her birth, at St George's Church in neighbouring Queen Street, she was christened Vera Mary.

II

In the summer of 1895 Vera, at little more than eighteen months, moved with her parents to Glen Bank, a large white-painted semi-detached house set back from the Chester Road in the silk manufacturing town of Macclesfield in Cheshire. Dating from the middle of the century, the property's one and a half acres included an orchard, paddock, gardener's cottage, and coach house. At sufficient distance from her in-laws for Edith Brittain to be free of their snubs, Macclesfield was also close enough to the Cheddleton Mill to allow Arthur Brittain to make his daily journey to work there.

Vera was almost two when her brother, Edward Harold Brittain, was born on 30 November 1895. For the next nine years, until they were sent to day schools, the two children led an isolated existence circumscribed by a governess, servants (a housekeeper-cook, two maids and a gardener), and well-intentioned parents who possessed an inherent belief in the prerogatives of class and money. In this claustrophobic environment, Vera and Edward formed a close and intimate dependence upon one another. From an early age this dependence was founded upon the compatibility of their almost diametrically opposed temperaments. 'I often picture the little scene as I first saw him & his dear little sister', their governess recalled almost twenty years later, after Edward's death, '– two sweet little mites in white silk frocks at Mrs Archer Smith's party! & I was so struck at the time by their devotion to each other.'

In looks they were alike. With her dark hair, which in youth had an auburn tinge, hazel eyes, and diminutive stature – she grew to five foot three inches – Vera physically resembled her Brittain ancestors. Edward, with his dark brown hair and brown eyes, also inherited a strong likeness to his father's family, but as a well-built young man of over six feet he had the physique and height of his taller Bervon relations. He had their less intense and more easygoing manner, too, which provided the foil and counterbalance to his sister's more volatile and confrontational personality. For in disposition as well as appearance Vera acknowledged that she had inherited many Brittain characteristics.

Harsh and intolerant of each other as well as outsiders – 'a hard, undemonstrative, quarrelsome family, united only by weddings and funerals' – her father's younger brothers and sisters were habitually referred to by Vera as 'my unaltruistic collection of relatives'. Feuding perpetually among themselves, constantly removing and reinstating one another in their wills, they were fascinated by money for its own sake. Despite their wealth they lived in spartan, comfortless surroundings, and their austere clothes and Staffordshire accents made them alarming and uncongenial figures to Vera as a child. Few of them were welcome at Glen Bank. While Norman, later a director of the paper mill, and Edith, Arthur

Brittain's two oldest siblings, remained on good terms with their brother, William, a solicitor eight years Mr Brittain's junior, fell out with him in youth and never spoke to him again (it was William's proud boast that he never forgave anyone with whom he had a disagreement). Tom, the youngest brother, considered the fool of the family, was shipped off to Canada as a lumberjack. When this and a brief foray into sheep-farming in Australia failed, he turned to diamond-mining in South Africa, and to his family's amazement and envy, returned to England a rich man.

Frank, Mr Brittain's second brother, was also in South Africa, farming and big-game shooting, when war broke out at the end of 1899. Enlisting with the Natal Carabineers, he was involved in the fighting for the defence of Ladysmith, but died of enteric fever, half an hour before the relief of the town in February 1900. Among Vera's first conscious memories was the sight of the banners and streamers hanging from Macclesfield's windows to celebrate the relief of Ladysmith, and of waiting for Uncle Frank who never returned. He remained no more than a name to her until in Durban on a lecture-tour, sixty years later, she received a letter from an old woman whose father, a farmer, had befriended the young British immigrant. Over tea at Vera's hotel she told her how her father had insisted on towing Frank Brittain's self-made cabin to their farm, and had invited him to live with them as one of the family. She gave Vera a photograph of him with other patients in hospital, 'looking very ill and very sad'.

As she grew older Vera was often to reflect on the apparent indifference and neglect of the older generation of Brittains towards each other. Only for Muriel, the baby of the family, did Mr Brittain retain any real affection, and even they were destined to quarrel in the Twenties after her marriage to Henry Leigh Groves, heir to a wealthy brewing family, over an episode mysteriously alluded to in the family as the 'Cat's Tongue' incident. From the early Twenties the Groves lived at Holehird, near Windermere in the Lake District, a neo-Gothic house with a 552-acre estate, including an alpine garden and orchid houses. One of the few Brittains to possess a sense of fun, Muriel was a consummate practical joker, and as a girl Vera offered easy and rewarding prey. 'Ghosts' made out of broom-handles and melon rind smeared with phosphorus to make them glow were among the tricks with which she terrorized her young niece.

Aside from their mutual antagonism, many of the Brittains also shared a tendency to nervous instability and severe depression. The Meighs were assumed to be the source of this 'insane, suicidal element'. Her great-great-grandfather, Job Meigh, Vera told Winifred Holtby in 1933, 'was certainly mad by modern standards for the latter half of his life, & would probably have been certified today.' Aunt Lily, one of her father's sisters, was 'a mental defective', and spent most of her life confined under restraint. So great was the stigma attaching to mental disturbance that her nephews and nieces were forbidden even to mention her name.

Both Arthur Brittain and his sister Edith were to end their lives by suicide. Nor did the next generation escape affliction. Among her cousins Vera could number several instances of mental illness. The most tragic of these was the only child of Edith Brittain's marriage to Will Hole, Philippa, who suffered periodically from mental instability after her mother killed herself in 1925 by jumping from a mountain in Wales. A selection of her rather sentimental verse was printed privately in the Twenties, and during her more serious bouts of insanity, she would sometimes issue invitations to tea under the name of Mrs T.S. Eliot. She was also responsible for sending a series of poison-pen letters to Vera after the publication of *Testament of Youth*, denouncing Vera's mother for refusing to acknowledge her 'Welsh-Jewish blood', and 'attributing monstrous sex irregularities' to Vera's parents and other relatives.

In later years, Philippa Hole was saved from long spells in psychiatric institutions by Muriel Groves, who hid her at Holehird. Sometimes members of the family staying in the house would catch a glimpse of a woman wandering, Mrs Rochester-like, along the corridors of an upper floor. On one occasion in the Forties, Vera's daughter Shirley pointed her out to Muriel, who looked straight through the solid retreating figure of Philippa Hole and retorted, 'Nonsense, it's your imagination. There's nobody there.'

Vera acknowledged that she had inherited 'the melancholy pessimistic strain' in the Brittain family and sometimes spoke in dramatic terms of the curse of hereditary insanity hanging over her head. She was 'only too aware', she wrote in her late thirties, 'of a bad, bad nervous inheritance' which occasionally resulted in 'childish and ridiculous' outbursts when she was ill or overwrought. Her experiences in the First World War compounded this tendency and for much of her life she was conscious of a conflict within herself between spontaneity and self-preservation. She always had to fight hard for what little confidence she achieved, and even in old age the predominant impression she created among those meeting her for the first time was of a woman who seemed to be in a state of almost perpetual worry.

Vera depicted her childhood as outwardly serene and uneventful, as indeed it appears to have been. But her inner imaginative life was a more turbulent world, full of unexplained fears waiting to torment her. Fear of thunder, of sunsets, of the dark, and of the full moon were among the 'strange medley of irrational fears' which she later mentioned. In an autobiographical incident from an unfinished novel written in the Twenties, Vera portrays herself at four years old, cowering in fright from the 'tremendous & glittering moon':

> The little girl in the big arm-chair had gazed at it, tense with fear, till at last it grew into a face with two wicked eyes & an evilly grinning mouth. Unable to bear it any longer, she hid her face in the cushions, but only for a few moments; the moon had a dreadful fascination which impelled her, quite against her will, to look up at it again. This time the grin was wider than ever & one great eye, leering obscenely at her, suddenly closed in a tremendous & unmistakable wink. Four-year-old Virginia was not at any time remarkable for her courage ... Flinging herself back into the chair, she burst into prolonged & piercing screams.

Vera may have borne the indelible character of her father's family, but it was her mother's sisters and younger brother whom she saw more often as she was growing up, and whom she found infinitely more sympathetic. Her Bervon aunts, in contrast to the cold, forbidding women of the Brittain family, dressed attractively and fashionably, and spoke quickly in pleasant, lilting Welsh voices. All three of them, in their different ways, were resourceful and despite their impecunious beginnings ended their days in comfortable affluence. After studying at the South Kensington College of Art, Lillie, like her older sister Edith, made a good marriage to Arthur Bentley-Carr, a stockbroker cousin of the Duchess of Windsor's second husband, Ernest Simpson. Marrying comparatively late in life (the twelve-year-old Vera was her bridesmaid) she was said to have 'snared' her husband by subtracting several years from her true age. Florence and Isabel (Belle), the oldest and youngest sisters, remained unmarried, and both were forced to earn their own livings to support themselves and their widowed mother.

Florence, Vera's godmother and later her headmistress, had been employed in various unspecified 'practical capacities' (possibly as a lady's companion) for some years before meeting Louise Heath-Jones at the turn of the century. Their 'remarkable friendship' – a business partnership as well as an intimate companionship – lasted for more than thirty years in the course of which they established and ran a private girls' school, St Monica's, at Kingswood in Surrey. When Florence Bervon died in 1936, Vera eulogized her as 'one of the pioneer women who achieved economic independence long before careers for both sexes became a matter of course.'

Aunt Florence may have earned Vera's respect, but it was Aunt Belle, more happy-go-lucky and adventurous than her sisters, who won her affection. Belle had been a governess to an English family in India before returning to England shortly before the outbreak of war, brimful of stories of suttee and other native customs, to live with her mother in Purley in south London. In the Twenties, after her mother's death, she opened a tea-shop named The Golden Hind on the sea-front at Deal in Kent.

Completing the Bervon family were Vera's two uncles, though Vera knew only William, the younger son, as the older, Charlie, had emigrated to New York some time before her birth. With Uncle Bill, who was just thirteen years her senior, Vera formed a close attachment and he proved a loyal ally in her adolescent rows with her parents. During the war when his 'indispensable' work at the National Provincial Bank in the City prevented him from enlisting despite his repeated attempts to do so, his 'gallant letters' cheered Vera's nursing in Malta and France. When he died suddenly at the age of forty-five in 1926, weakened by his years of wartime overwork, she mourned him as yet another personal casualty of the war 'which cost my uncle his life as surely as if he had been in the trenches . . .'.

Dominating Vera's childhood was her irascible but loving father. Neurotic and temperamental, the slightest departure from routine could set his nerves jangling and the house reverberating to the sound of his unpredictable outbursts. 'Fancy him going off in a rage like that', the four-year-old Edward remarked to his mother at breakfast one morning as his father pushed him aside and stormed off to the office because his coffee was cold. He could be heard on occasion taking out his frustration on the drawing-room piano, playing 'Onward Christian Soldiers' at fortissimo. Despite his sudden swings in mood, he could also be an attentive parent, taking pride in his children and fond of petting and spoiling Vera whom he nicknamed 'John' 'or 'Jack', suggesting the disappointment he had felt that she had not been a boy.

A deeply ingrained conservatism was the hallmark of Arthur Brittain's character. The processes and profits of paper-making provided the focus of his life, and he was impervious to anything that lay outside the boundaries of his family and business. At Brittains, like his father and grandfather before him, he exerted a strongly paternalistic style of management, and hoped one day to hand down the business to his own son. 'Never a Trade Union man near the place', was his proud boast, though he maintained good relations with his workforce, was generally solicitous of their welfare, and regarded himself as an enlightened employer.

'We knew him as "Arthur Band Box" ', remembered one nephew, 'since he was so fussy about his dress and presentation.' With his crisp moustache and well-cut clothes, he bore 'the imprint of suave prosperity'. He rated his suits methodically – 'Best', 'Second Best', 'Third Best', and so on – and extended the same precision to his financial affairs, keeping meticulous accounts, and secreting large sums about the house to protect himself and his family against unexpected contingencies. The one adventurous streak in his nature was reserved for his driving. A keen motorist, he was among the first Staffordshire businessmen at the beginning of this century to travel to work by car. He owned a Wolseley Eight and then a two-seater De Dion Bouton which was kept in a specially designed garage with a wood-block floor and hot pipes to keep it dry. His reckless driving must have sometimes given his wife qualms. A letter from the ten-year-old Vera to her mother gives an excited account of one afternoon's drive to Buxton, the spa town ten miles to the east of Macclesfield:

> Yesterday we went to Buxton in the motor . . . and it was all misty as soon as we began to mount the hills and soon it got so misty that we could scarcely see three yards in front of us . . . We had a sugary bun in Buxton, and it was the nicest ride we ever had. Coming back the mist had quite cleared away, except on the horizon, and we tore down those hills in one place as though we were in the fifth speed instead of the third so you'll be glad to hear that we are all alive and kicking. Yesterday also we took little Titoos for a ride . . . Titoos said it was like being in an open train on the sea, and she simply loved it.

The hazards of motoring caught up with Mr Brittain a few years later when he was involved in an accident in the bleak countryside between Staffordshire and Derbyshire. He was pinned in a ditch under his car and for several days lay in a critical condition in a tiny moorland inn on the Staffordshire side of the county boundary.

Edith Brittain possessed 'incredible energy & a charming face', but retained an aura of disappointment about her, as if life had not quite lived up to her expectations. Her 'fatalistic pessimism' left her always ready 'to distrust the best and believe the worst.' A nervous woman, prone to what she called 'the horrors' (the result, so it was said, of having been locked in a dark cupboard as a child), she was of a gentler, more equable temperament than her husband. Her early married life had been fraught with tensions. The genteel poverty of her upbringing had not prepared her for the task of adapting to the highly ritualized conventions of prosperous middle-class life in a provincial community. A middle-class wife of the late Victorian and Edwardian era was expected to organize her household in such a way as to advertise and demonstrate to the neighbours and the world at large the social standing of the family. She ignored the complex and subtle gradations of the social code at her peril. It was bad enough for Edith Brittain to be criticized by her mother- and sisters-in-law, who told her that with a full-time nursemaid to look after her children it was inappropriate for her to be seen pushing her own perambulator; but even more humiliating was the experience of the first dinner party she gave in Macclesfield when she was severely taken to task by the bank manager's wife for having 'mixed her sets' in her selection of guests.

In time Edith Brittain became as practised as any at maintaining the façade of crushing respectability, and a stickler for the observation of social niceties. But it was achieved at the expense of considerable effort and the loss of some spontaneity and warmth. Her finely chiselled features stare out uneasily from a carefully posed studio portrait, taken towards the end of the 1890s by the Manchester firm of Lafayette, 'Photographers to the Queen'. There is an air of discomfort about the way in which she wears her dress of fine lace over floral silk with its complicated frills and accompanying feather fan. The daughter of one of her friends remembered her from about this time as being 'a very pretty woman' who 'always seemed . . . to wear pretty clothes'. To this friend Mrs Brittain admitted that she sometimes 'felt overdressed but that Mr Brittain liked her to be well turned out'.

In these early years Edith Brittain sought consolation from the petty snobberies of her surroundings in the love of music which she had inherited from her father. She was a competent pianist with a strong soprano voice, and musical evenings were a regular feature of family life at Macclesfield. Mrs Brittain would run through her repertoire of lachrymose ballads while Vera and Edward, from about the ages of seven and five, would sometimes be allowed to stay up to play piano duets to their parents' guests. Vera was an able accompanist, though her hands were always too small to stretch an octave easily. Edward on the piano and later the violin was considered to be the promising musician.

Although by the standards of the time Mr and Mrs Brittain were comparatively accessible parents, much of Vera and Edward's childhood was spent in the charge of a succession of nursemaids, and later a governess, in the nursery at the top of the house. They were especially fortunate in their governess, Miss A.M. Newby, a plump, rubicund woman in her thirties who joined the household when Vera was five and remained for the next six years. Vera refers to her as being 'adored' and 'devoted and intelligent', and the examination papers set by Miss Newby show her to have been a capable and conscientious teacher who taught reading and writing and then moved on to provide her pupils with a basic grounding in history, geography, French, drawing and painting.

The letters dutifully written by Vera to her mother whenever Mrs Brittain was away from Glen Bank visiting friends or relatives, give an impression of a secluded and stultifying routine, relieved only by occasional excursions into the outside world, including seaside holidays with Edward and Miss Newby at Colwyn Bay. The arrival of a travelling circus in Macclesfield elicited special pleading from Vera in a letter to her mother of 1903:

> We want to go to the Italian circus very much, please do let us go. It is a shilling each admission and Towby has plenty of money left over from the house-keeping. It is quite clean and there is nothing objectional [sic] about it, a gentleman told us . . . Please send a post-card as soon as you get this saying whether we may go or not . . . There is nothing nasty about it, no freaks or menageries . . . only acting dogs, ponys, goats, etc.

Another of Vera's letters from the previous year describes the rumpus that ensued when a mouse was discovered in the nursery. 'I saw a mouse in the place & Edward saw it in the nursery . . . and Spot came running . . . and he caught it and killed it.' A postscript by Miss Newby emphasized the part played by the intrepid younger brother in protecting his sister and governess. 'We had a great fright over the poor little mouse this morning', she reported to Mrs Brittain. 'Vera *shrieked*, I picked up my dress and rushed away, and Edward was very bold and took the poker and tried to kill it.'

Edward was his sister's sole companion and confidant and their lack of contact with other children fostered Vera's natural introspection. Looking back at the end of her life she commented ruefully upon 'the pitiful verbosity of my lonely youth'. Most evenings when they were supposed to be asleep, Vera would regale Edward with stories of 'a semi-ornithological community known to us both as "The Dicks".' While Edward was absorbed in early attempts at making music on his small violin, Vera was developing her talent for story-telling by writing short literary epics. Between the ages of seven and eleven she produced five 'novels', written in special notebooks, patiently constructed for her by Miss Newby out of off-cuts from the paper mill (sadly Miss Newby did not live to see her charge's subsequent literary fame; she died in April 1933, four months before the publication of *Testament of Youth*). As soon as she had been able to hold a pen Vera had been quite clear about where her ambitions lay. 'I cannot remember a time when I did not consciously intend to become a writer; my mind began to invent stories from the moment that it was capable of formulating a coherent idea.'

The Brittains, to Vera's everlasting regret, were not a bookish family. While Mrs Brittain's reading extended to a love of Dickens and the latest work of popular fiction from Boots' library, her husband rarely ventured any further than the newspaper, and the local paper at that. In later years Vera would often dwell on the misfortune of having been brought up in a household which, she once claimed, contained 'precisely nine books': six yellow-back novels, including Wilkie Collins's *Poor Miss Finch* ('a sensation novel for Sunday reading') and several of Mrs Henry Wood's romances, Longfellow's *Complete Poems*, Matthew Arnold's 'Sohrab and Rustum', and a copy of *Household Medicine*. To satisfy her hunger for books Vera had desperate recourse to her parents' limited library, supplementing her reading with a few of L.T. Meade's children's stories, and classics like *Uncle Tom's Cabin* and *The Wide, Wide World*, which she received as presents for Christmas and birthdays. By the age of ten she had devoured the romantic novels and the poetry and had turned as a last resort to *Household Medicine*. Despite her close perusal of the volume, however, she could not remember that 'it provoked in me any troubled meditations, or even led to my asking uncomfortable questions.'

Vera's childhood 'novels' – in the order in which they were written, 'The Five Schoolgirls', 'Edith's Trial', 'The Feud of the Cousins', 'A Mistaken Identity', and 'The Breaking-in of Dorothy' – are, like the sensational romances which evidently inspired them, 'full of misunderstandings and catastrophes, of early deaths, agonized soliloquies and death-bed scenes and repentances'. The *dramatis personae* of these juvenile productions were all taken 'frankly and rapturously from real life'. In Macclesfield lived a family with five daughters whose ages ranged from about fifteen to twenty-six, and it was around the imaginary lives of these five young women that Vera 'wove my dreams and built my stories'. The family were not among the Brittains' calling acquaintances, and Vera never spoke to any of the girls, but she often persuaded Miss Newby to take her for walks through the section of the town where they lived in the hope of meeting them.

The stories are copiously illustrated with the longest running to some 45,000 words. The characters are well-defined and the plots, with their obvious borrowings from the conventions of Victorian melodrama, sweep along at a great pace. An obsession with death, especially violent death, is a common theme and her heroines are usually portrayed as noble and self-sacrificing. The most surprising element in all five 'novels' is the intensely religious sentiment which permeates them. In the account of her childhood in *Testament of Youth*, Vera chose not to emphasize any strong religious influence. She mentions in passing that at Macclesfield the family and servants assembled for prayers before breakfast, but implies that this was merely following the example set by her father's family, rather than the expression of a devout conviction. More telling perhaps is her admission that when at the age of five or six she called Edward 'a little fool', her nursemaid terrified her with a vision of the devil waiting to catch her round the corner by prophesying, 'Now you'll go to hell'. The nursemaid was applying with literal logic Christ's injunction in Matthew 5, 'That whosoever is angry with his brother without a cause ... and ... shall say, Thou fool, shall be in danger of hell fire', and it seems likely that she may have subjected Vera and Edward to similar stern doses of biblical doctrine.

Certainly Vera's juvenilia make liberal use of quotations from hymns, including her favourite 'Abide with me', the Anglican Prayer Book, and Bunyan's *Pilgrim's Progress*. The latter obviously exerted a powerful hold on the child's burgeoning imagination, though strangely Vera omitted it from the list of books she had read when young. In 'The Breaking-in of Dorothy', the last of her five stories, written at the age of eleven, many of the chapter headings like 'The Pilgrim's Progress', 'The Valley of the Shadow of Death', and 'The Celestial City' are direct derivatives. Like Bunyan's pilgrim, Dorothy's path to her salvation leads her through Vanity Fair, and after her friend Edith's death, Dorothy's 'weak mind was not strong enough to bear her up for despair, Giant Despair had taken hold of her.'

Her parents looked indulgently upon these early efforts as 'an example of amusing if quite unimportant precocity'. But they may also have considered that like Vera's heroine, Ruth Alleyndene in *Honourable Estate*, who is given to histrionic recitations from the Bible alone in the schoolroom, their daughter was 'inclined to be fanciful and a good deal too introspective', and that she needed the company of other girls of her age. In 1905, therefore, when the family left Macclesfield for the fashionable Peak District resort of Buxton, it was in order that eleven-year-old Vera and nine-year-old Edward could attend private day schools as a preliminary to being sent away to boarding schools.

III

In social terms, the move to Buxton in Derbyshire signified a step up in the world for the Brittains. At the beginning of the twentieth century Buxton was still enjoying its heyday as a spa town. In the 1780s, the fifth Duke of Devonshire, taking advantage of Buxton's natural spring waters, had developed it as a rival to Bath, with its own colonnaded Crescent and Assembly Room. But it had been the arrival of the London and North Western and the Midland Railways in 1863, bringing in their wake a period of renewed building activity, which had established Buxton as an exclusive retreat of leisured society on a modest though prosperous scale. Thousands came each year to receive the benefit of hydropathic treatments at the Thermal and Natural Baths and to take the waters from St Ann's Well in the Pump Room. In the afternoons they promenaded, or were wheeled in their bath chairs around the Pavilion Gardens and listened to the band in Milner's glass and iron pavilion, built in the style of the Crystal Palace. Buxton was continuing to add to its attractions at the time of the Brittains' arrival. Frank Matcham's sumptuous Opera House, with its Baroque-style interior, had been erected at the east end of the pavilion in 1903, while the vast Empire Hotel was slowly rising to accommodate the heavy influx of summer visitors.

Lying in a shallow basin at an altitude of one thousand feet, which makes it the highest as well as one of the coldest market towns in Britain, Buxton is surrounded by scenery of impressive beauty and grandeur. On fine days Vera and Edward would escape from the cultivated prettiness of the town's parks and gardens to walk with their pug dog, Koko, among the wild-growing rhododendrons on the hillsides of the Goyt Valley; or to bicycle over the moors to Corbar Woods. During the freezing winters, which some years lingered on until May, tobogganing was a popular pastime among Buxtonians, and the long straight descent down Manchester Road from Corbar Hill was closed annually for this purpose.

It was in Manchester Road that Arthur Brittain took the lease of the family's first Buxton home, High Leigh. The family remained there for almost two years before moving in 1907 to Melrose, a larger 'tall grey stone house', dating from the 1880s, close to the Empire Hotel, in the more select residential area known as The Park.

With the departure of Miss Newby on their move to Buxton, brother and sister were separated for the first time in their lives. Edward was sent to Holm Leigh, a small preparatory school, while for two years, until she was thirteen, Vera attended Buxton's Grange School, which advertised itself as 'a high-class school for the daughters of gentlemen'. Under Alice Aldom, Vera's first headmistress at the Grange, the school's academic aspirations were as low as its social pretensions were high (Vera's untidy handwriting was stigmatized as being 'exactly like a cook's'). But Miss Aldom's successor, Lena Dodd, a graduate of Cheltenham Ladies' College, appears to have raised the school's sights. Vera was described on her first report card as 'a very intelligent pupil' and she soon made her mark as something of a prodigy. At the end of her first term Vera emerged successfully from the University of Cambridge's Preliminary Local Examination with passes in Dictation, English Grammar and Composition, Arithmetic, History, Geography, French, Freehand Drawing, and Religious Knowledge. Her proud parents had her certificate framed and hung on the wall of their High Leigh dining-room.

Edward started at Uppingham School in Rutland in the spring of 1908. Although Mr Brittain had rebelled against the discipline of his own public-school education, he was keen for his son to enjoy its advantages, and Uppingham, where a considerable proportion of boys were drawn from the families of prosperous industrialists, must have appeared particularly suitable. Transformed from an obscure country grammar into a major public school by its pioneering Victorian headmaster, Edward Thring, Uppingham had become the model of a 'muscular Christian school'. Since Thring's day, however, there had been a marked decline in standards. According to Uppingham's historian, the last years of the old century and the first years of the new had seen 'all that was worst in public school athleticism, militarism, and morality come to Uppingham'. Games, especially cricket for which the school was nationally renowned, seemed to the artist, C.R.W. Nevinson, who was there in the first years of the century, to be 'the main object of the school'. Nevinson also recalled Uppingham's mood of 'appalling jingoism' during the South African War. The large and enthusiastically run Officers' Training Corps had placed Uppingham in the forefront of public-school militarism, and regardless of whether a boy belonged to the Corps or not, the atmosphere of militarism was pervasive. No one was allowed to take part in any inter-house athletic or sporting contest, or win a school prize, without having first passed a shooting test.

In spite of these excesses, the school's basic strength derived from its adherence to Thring's dictum that every boy should learn to do something well, and for Edward this meant an opportunity to develop his musical gifts. Uppingham's music department, led by the youthful Robert Sterndale Bennett, grandson of the distinguished composer, was among the finest in the country. By Edward's time there were six or seven music teachers, but it was under the inspiring direction of Sterndale Bennett himself that Edward took up the viola and organ, in addition to piano and violin, and began to compose songs and short concertos. From the Lower School in the autumn of 1909 he moved to The Lodge where he was one of thirty boys. He was 'a good and desirable boy', the headmaster wrote at Christmas 1910 when Edward was fifteen.

Vera was to regard her brother's life at Uppingham with unconcealed envy. 'For girls – as yet – there is nothing equivalent to public schools for boys', she wrote several years later without a trace of irony, 'these fine traditions & unwritten laws that turn out so many splendid characters have been withheld from them – to their detriment.' The nearest equivalent among girls' schools would have been Cheltenham or Roedean. For Vera to have been sent to either of these, however, would have been looked upon by her father as a needless extravagance. Instead in 1907 she had been sent away to St Monica's, the 'select' girls' school at Kingswood in Surrey where her aunt, Florence Bervon, was Co-Principal. Given the haphazard nature of girls' education at this time, it was to prove a fortunate choice.

It was also, as Vera later admitted, a safe one. St Monica's had been founded in 1902 by Louise Heath-Jones. Florence, the eldest and most formidable of Edith Brittain's sisters, had joined her two years later, and Lillie Bervon, one of Vera's younger aunts, had taught drawing and dancing there for a time before her marriage. Responsibility for the administrative running of the school and for the girls' welfare fell to Miss Bervon, who possessed neither academic qualifications nor training, while Miss Heath-Jones, educated at Cheltenham and Newnham College, Cambridge, took charge of the curriculum and supervised the teaching.

'The Ladies' were both about forty and complemented each other perfectly. Miss Heath-Jones, tall, gaunt and restless, with pebble spectacles and large hands, was nervously brilliant and an idealistic Anglican. Miss Bervon, shorter and plump, while at the same time statuesque ('she reminded me of a public building', said Clare Leighton, who knew her after the war), was more practical and down-to-earth. Although it was still in its infancy, St Monica's was already highly esteemed and boasted an impressive list of patrons, including the Bishop of Gibraltar and Canon Scott-Holland of St Paul's. The main school building was an imposing red-brick mansion, magnificently set in six acres of grounds, with views overlooking the Chipstead Valley from a south-facing terrace. The 'bracing, sunny and dry climate' around Kingswood, potential parents were informed, 'is strongly recommended by medical men for growing and delicate girls'. Even more bracing, in the stuffy and restrictive world of much of girls' education at this time, were St Monica's objectives: to provide 'a many-sided education, to inculcate habits of thought and appreciative study, healthy pleasure in outdoor pursuits and to provide the regular discipline of school games, to develop the power to use leisure well, and to take an intelligent interest in the current topics of the day.'

The school roll numbered between ninety and a hundred pupils, but the character of St Monica's was homelike rather than institutional. What remained in Vera's memory were 'its tasteful decorations and gracious gardens, its appetizing meals and large staff of servants . . .'. Pictures of famous women adorned the walls of the dining hall, while the bedrooms, occupied by up to eight girls, were simply and attractively furnished. Not that the girls were pampered. Fires were not allowed in the bedrooms and 'sometimes in the depth of winter', recalled Lady Bateman who was at St Monica's a decade later, 'the water froze and we had to break the ice before washing.'

A large number of Vera's school contemporaries came from wealthy upper-middle-class families and were destined for London or Edinburgh society. Their parents' primary concern was that they should return home after four years, equipped with all the accomplishments of ladylike refinement that would help them to make a good marriage. Training in suitably feminine pursuits and skills featured prominently in the curriculum. 'Special courses are given to the elder girls in Cooking, Dressmaking, and Hygiene', the prospectus disclosed. 'All learn to use their needle and to knit.' Each evening Florence Bervon, stately and well-corseted, 'rather like Queen Mary in appearance', summoned one or two girls individually to her drawing-room. Ostensibly the interview was to discuss the girl's progress, but it also provided a useful opportunity for an impromptu lesson in deportment. Mary Campbell, a pupil in the Twenties, remembered knocking nervously on Miss Bervon's door one evening, and entering hesitantly, pausing to get her bearings. "That's certainly not the way to enter a room', came Florence Bervon's brisk reprimand from her armchair by the window. 'Go out and come in again properly.'

On more traditional lines, there were drawing, handwork and elocution lessons, together with theatricals and Miss Heath-Jones's special innovation, 'The Drawing-Room' where, before a school audience, the girls played piano, violin, or cello solos, recited or sang. At one of these performances Vera played the first movement of the 'Waldstein' Sonata: 'Miss H-J said in report today that it was a pleasure to hear me . . . I also had to sing solos which come in the various part songs we had.'

In moments of self-deception, Miss Heath-Jones would declare that she 'did not turn out the fashionable girl'; but the reality of the situation, given the social expectations of parents for their daughters and the school's dependence, at least in its early years, on such a wealthy clientele, was that she had no alternative but to do precisely that. As Vera would later recognize, Miss Heath-Jones 'was far in advance of the teaching standards of the day and the pre-war type of school she had elected to control.' Forced to steer an uneasy course between academic and social priorities, she nonetheless gave the academic side of the curriculum a strikingly enlightened stamp. The school motto of 'Service and Sanctification', emblazoned on a blue and white badge, suggests that the ultimate aim of the Principals for pupils who showed potential was to provide an education that would prepare them for lives of public service and duty. 'To us women comes the cry for larger opportunity for wider freedom', reads a signed notice by both women in the school magazine, 'but it is foolish to demand these good things if we have not educated ourselves in character and brain to use them.'

Four resident staff taught English, mathematics, science (even in its most rudimentary form still a comparative novelty in girls' schools), nature study, history and, for more advanced pupils, a little elementary Latin. Lessons in conversational and written French and German were given by qualified nationals. Religious instruction was 'under the care of the Principals'.

Miss Heath-Jones's own lessons in history and scripture left a lasting impression on Vera. In an autobiographical sketch of 1935 she recalled how 'the barriers which then rigidly divided history, literature, economics, politics and religion into watertight compartments tumbled down before me for ever . . .'. As preparation for public examinations, the classes, deviating wildly from the syllabus, were to prove scrappy and inadequate, giving Vera cause to complain that while she had been given 'a very great amount of useless information', the 'simple and important things' had been left to her imagination. Later, though, she would come to appreciate Miss Heath-Jones's lessons as 'teaching in the real sense of the word – the creation in immature minds of the power to think . . .'. In one conspicuous departure from the teaching practice of the day the girls were encouraged to read newspapers – though in the form of carefully selected cuttings – and debate current affairs.

The competition from her classmates was more exacting than she had encountered at the Grange School, but Vera was nonetheless consistently at the top of her form. 'We had report today', runs a letter to her mother when she was sixteen. 'I had a very good one. Among other things I had 89 for piano, 82 for French, 80 for German, and I was top of everything except that I was bracketed with Magda Salvesan for Sewing.'

Vera felt at some disadvantage in the company of girls with imposing social connections. This was to some extent counterbalanced by a confidence in her intellectual superiority, but her position as Miss Bervon's niece (and her goddaughter) added to her discomfiture, and it did not help that she was 'one of those unhappy children whose lives are made a torment by being constantly held up as an example to their fellows'. While she aroused some violent crushes at St Monica's, other girls actively disliked her, and 'there was very little of that halfway house of ordinary popularity'. Denied the company of other children from an early age, she experienced difficulty in forging lasting friendships. She was respected for her intelligence and admired for her prettiness, but some found her lack of easy-going humour and her caustic tongue formidable stumbling blocks. Although not malicious, she gave short shrift to the foolish, and possessed a disconcerting habit of analysing faults and failings – her own as well as those of others – with unvarnished honesty.

Vera's closest friends were Stella Sharp, the good-natured, fair-haired daughter of a vintner from Chelmsford, and Cora Stoop, a small, dark, half-Dutch girl from a wealthy Byfleet family ('Betty' and 'Mina' in *Testament of Youth*). Her relationships with them and other members of her year were passionate, but also at times painful and confusing. In the hothouse atmosphere of boarding-school life, emotions among adolescent schoolgirls frequently ran high. Their intense friendships, 'GPs' or 'Grand Passions' as they were known in St Monica's slang, were accepted as an important part of the pattern of growing up. Indeed, schoolmistresses of the time regarded a romantic friendship, more commonly the admiration of a young girl for an older prefect or teacher, as a useful means of instilling both loyalty to the school and the virtues of discipline and self-control. However, if a strong emotional attachment threatened to disrupt the school routine and a girl's progress, a headmistress might decide to intervene.

Stella Sharp had arrived at St Monica's in the summer term of 1910 and, as Vera recorded in her diary summary of the 'Chief Events of the Year', 'for some reason or other interested me very much'. They shared the same dormitory, 'a ripping one', were both in the tennis and cricket teams, and Vera soon discovered that to know Stella was 'to trust her & to trust to love'. Unfortunately, after a few months, Stella's untidiness and slapdash ways brought her and her highly charged friendship with Vera to the attention of Miss Heath-Jones. In front of the whole school Stella was severely berated 'for slackness, unsteadying & lack of responsibility.' Stella 'tried to control herself . . .', Vera dramatically reported in her diary, 'but the expression on her face & the way in which she said "Present" gave me a queer feeling in my throat.' After telling Stella that 'the best friendships always began with the two people being very wrapped up in each other', Miss Heath-Jones sent for Vera to talk about 'friendship and Stella's weaknesses'. In the course of their interview Vera's 'self-control gave way all of a sudden',

> & I cried for all I was worth, & then told her . . . of all my hopes & ideals, all the thoughts that had weighed upon my mind, kept me awake at night & unbalanced my brain. I told her of all the shadows of the greater things of life & my wish to write about them. I told her that Stella was necessary to me not only because I loved her but because she understood these things. Miss Bervon came in in the middle & to my great joy they understood as I never hoped they could do . . . They realised about Stella & saw that she was necessary to me, & I went up into their bedroom, & afterwards had tea alone with them in the drawing room. They . . . said I could go into the garden for half-an-hour & have Stella. So the dear girl & I talked over everything. My sense of relief was too great for words.

This need for Stella as someone to whom Vera could turn for emotional support and understanding established a pattern that was to repeat itself in Vera's adult friendships with women. While the quaintness of the idiom and the frenzied emotional pitch conspire to make this episode appear more than a little ridiculous, underlying it is an expression of serious intent. Vera's four years at St Monica's were to strengthen her growing perception of herself as a writer.

Shortly after arriving at St Monica's, Vera had dashed off another novel – 'a tale of those I knew at school, a few of whom I loved' – but it was her reading at sixteen of Shelley's stanzas on the death of Keats, *Adonais*, which finally determined her 'to become the writer I had dreamed of being since I was seven years old'. The poem's 'exquisite grief', its mixture of polemic and elegy, fed her morbid streak, and inspired her to try her hand at writing verse of her own. 'Vera should write some day' was the verdict of her midsummer report for 1911, and later that term Miss Heath-Jones appointed her Editor of the school magazine. Throughout the holidays she compensated for the usual shortage of contributions by writing practically the whole of the magazine herself, substituting a 'passionate four-page editorial' for the single column of earlier years. Reports of the term's cricket matches – Vera had been Vice-Captain of the cricket XI that baking hot summer – and of picnics on the Epsom Downs, mingled with pieces on the current industrial unrest and the Parliament Bill debates while Miss Heath-Jones looked benignly on the mounting printer's bill.

Another mistress, Edith Fry, hired by Miss Heath-Jones on a part-time basis in 1910 to take over the teaching of her history and literature lessons, was to exercise a strong influence on Vera as she reached late adolescence. A tiny, sparrow-like woman in her late twenties, Miss Fry was a graduate of Royal Holloway College. 'I never met anyone who so attracted me, both intellectually & otherwise', Vera recorded in her diary. 'She . . . has one of the most fascinating, clever and sympathetic faces that I ever saw, & searching deep blue eyes.' Vera's friendship with Stella Sharp might be frowned upon as unhealthy and verging on the obsessive, but a crush on a teacher was tacitly accepted as bearing all the hallmarks of 'disciplined love', leading, it was hoped, to greater emotional and intellectual maturity on the part of the pupil. Vera herself attributed a major role in her transition to adulthood to Edith Fry's stimulating tutelage. Miss Fry encouraged her to read more widely and critically than before. Carlyle, Ruskin, Dostoevsky, and H.G. Wells's *A Modern Utopia* ('which opened for me a new world of experience') were all eagerly consumed:

> My . . . writing tends towards a purpose now – I want to write, but I will not reveal what until the time shall come. I believe that this is greatly due to Miss Fry's teaching, and her understanding of Carlyle and Ruskin, about whom she taught us, so differently to the dull, hackneyed type of 'literature' that so many English mistresses make use of today.

A more controversial addition to the reading list was William Morris's Utopian *News from Nowhere*. An embryonic Fabian, Miss Fry was strongly sympathetic to Morris's social and political ideas, ideas which Vera decidedly did not share. Her essays on Morris show her to have had no time for his challenge to Edwardian bourgeois orthodoxy, and reveal her unquestioning acceptance of conventional social and political beliefs. She attacks his socialism ('When competition ceases, most of a country's energy ceases with it'), and rejects his thesis that the cause of crime is to be found in class distinctions, arguing that its roots are to be found in original sin.

Rather less conventional were her remarks on feminism in an essay on Thomas More's *Utopia*:

> [Women's] rights are a burning question not only in their own, but in male minds, and not infrequently their voices are heard in our streets demanding of the age a speedy reparation for the injuries done to them by the 'centuries that are gone'.

In the summer of 1911, a few months before Vera wrote these lines, Miss Heath-Jones had lent her a copy of *Woman and Labour*, the recently published, pioneering feminist work by the South African writer, Olive Schreiner. Its impact on Vera was at once profound and far-reaching; writing in 1926, she would liken her introduction to Schreiner's ideas to a conversion experience. *Woman and Labour*, she wrote, 'sounded with a note that had the authentic ring of a new gospel.' If, as Deborah Gorham has argued, Vera was 'born feminist', in the sense that she 'responded with a spontaneous sense of outrage' whenever she was confronted by the limitations placed on women's role in society, then *Woman and Labour* allowed her to articulate that outrage and gave expression to her feminism.

It is impossible to know precisely at what age Vera first became aware of the differences in treatment meted out to men and women. One of her most insistent childhood memories was of her feelings of anger at being made to travel in a second-class carriage with her mother and Edward while her father ensconced himself in a first-class compartment on the same train. Undoubtedly she must have realized from her earliest consciousness that the care and attention lavished on Edward's upbringing and education was far in excess of that given to her own. 'Girls did not mean so much to their parents in those days . . .', was her blunt comment many years later.

Her four years at St Monica's had coincided with the Women's Social and Political Union's increasingly violent campaign for women's suffrage under the charismatic leadership of Emmeline Pankhurst. 'The name of Mrs Pankhurst was a familiar echo in my school days', Vera wrote in a commemorative article after Pankhurst's death, 'an echo that grew louder as her exploits gathered publicity.' At her mother's tea parties during the school holidays, Vera listened in critical silence to the sweeping indictments of Mrs Pankhurst and her 'screaming sisterhood' as news of window-smashings, church-burnings, imprisonments, hunger strikes and forcible feedings reached Buxton. Over their teacups Buxton matrons attacked the detested 'suffs' in a 'vocal variety of witch-burning'.

Louise Heath-Jones was 'an ardent if discreet feminist'. From the girls' parents she was careful to conceal her feminist leanings, but to a few senior pupils, including Vera, she talked freely about the pioneers of women's education, of Emily Davies, the founder of Girton, and of Dorothea Beale, her own Principal at Cheltenham. She occasionally took older girls to suffrage meetings of the more moderate kind, and in the summer before she left the school, Vera accompanied her to a constitutional suffrage meeting in Tadworth. It was, however, a comparatively mild affair and left little impression.

Woman and Labour, Vera was to write later, 'supplied the theory that linked my personal resentments with the public activities of the suffragettes.' Appearing just as the militant campaign was reaching a new crescendo of violence, and dedicated to Constance Lytton, one of its most committed participants, the book examines the relationship of women to work, war and, in a penultimate chapter on 'Sex Differences', to men. What seized Vera's attention, however, were not Schreiner's musings on sexuality, nor her impassioned argument for women as natural peace-makers, one day to provide an important reference point in Vera's own pacifism. Rather it was Schreiner's championing of a woman's right to work which spoke directly to her, and which would continue to speak to her in adult life when she took up the cause of a feminism of equal rights. Condemning the middle-class woman's parasitical dependency on men in modern industrial society, in which she exists through the 'passive performance of sex functions only' with a consequent impairment of her intelligence and vitality, Schreiner stakes the claim of women everywhere to 'take all labour for our province'. 'Give us labour and the training which fits us for labour!' is the theme reiterated throughout. 'We demand this, not for ourselves alone, but for the race.'

However, the direct relevance of Schreiner's ringing rhetoric to Vera's own situation in her final school year cannot have been immediately apparent. For while Vera wrote of her longing for 'independence' and a 'wider life' – and while she had certainly been encouraged by her teachers to think in these terms – the future offered little hope of attaining them. She may indeed, as she later claimed, have been fired with the ambition to go to university from the moment she discovered 'that such places existed', but it was not a realistic prospect for a young woman in Vera's position. Higher education for women in the years leading up to the First World War was still most commonly thought of as a form of teacher training for middle-class women who were unlikely to marry, and who faced the necessity of supporting themselves.

Clearly Vera did not fit into this category. She was pretty, from an affluent background, and likely to make a good marriage. Moreover, with fees at an Oxford women's college – and Vera never seems to have shown the slightest inclination to go anywhere but Oxford – running to as much as £35 a term, Mr Brittain may have baulked at what he saw as an unnecessary additional expense. As far as he was concerned her formal education was complete. Nor would he agree to Vera joining Stella Sharp at a finishing school in Brussels, from which Stella would return in 1912 to be presented at court. He was an overprotective father – his recurrent fear whenever Vera visited London in the years before the war was that she might be abducted by White Slave Traders – and worried about Vera travelling abroad without parental supervision.

Instead a compromise was agreed upon which postponed the inevitable homecoming by allowing Vera an extra term at St Monica's in the winter of 1911. That December, a few weeks short of her eighteenth birthday, Vera returned to Buxton and to 'provincial young ladyhood'.

IV

For the time being all thought of Oxford remained no more than a distant dream, and Vera had no alternative but to return home to 'come out' in provincial society. Throughout much of 1912 and 1913 she would be occupied in undergoing this strange form of social baptism which marked the end of her childhood and advertised her marriageable status. Initially at any rate, she entered with enthusiasm into the whirl of the Buxton season, making her debut at the High Peak Hunt Ball on 9 January 1912.

During the interminable winter months there were carefully chaperoned dances at the Peak Hydro, in local halls and private houses, with pink and silver programmes and pencils dangling on coloured cords, supper intervals, and a succession of young men. For Vera, with her hair 'up' and looking demure and pretty in the regulation white satin and pearls, it was gratifying never, for want of a male partner, to have to sit out or dance with other girls. 'I am really beginning to love dancing for dancing's sake', she wrote in her diary after staying up until two at the Cottage Hospital Ball, five days after her nineteenth birthday. 'I danced every one, including three extras, and could have gone on for hours.' She acted in amateur theatricals and played bridge, naively enthusing about one 'most thrilling afternoon' when her mother gave 'a truly fashionable bridge party'. She tobogganed, played tennis and joined the Buxton Golf Club. She had music lessons for which her father bought her a new piano; and she paid calls and took part in the Sunday church parades in the Pavilion Gardens. 'I put on my new white serge and the Paris hat with the white tulle bows, white shoes & stockings & a low necked blouse, and looked quite a dream', she recounted after one such parade in May 1913. 'The people in the Gardens after Church stared like billy-oh.'

The impression this gives of a high-spirited, fun-loving girl suggests that Vera was not quite as she depicted herself twenty years later in *Testament of Youth*, a young woman singlemindedly in revolt against the mores of her own society. Yet, as the diary, which she began to keep in voluminous detail in 1913, makes clear, beneath the gregarious, carefree surface a deeper compulsive force was driving her 'to get seriously to thought and work, and leave behind me for a time that other side of myself, the frivolity so dear to me.' At the end of her debutante year, she was ashamed to reflect on how little she had read or written. The endless round of social engagements was settling into a monotonous routine. And she was beginning to feel stifled by the snobbery and narrowmindedness of Buxton itself.

For the rest of her life Vera would be especially outspoken in her condemnation of Buxton and the values she believed it stood for. To her it epitomized 'the mean, fault-finding spirit' of the British provincial town, and she showed it no mercy. In two novels, *Not Without Honour* where it appears as Torborough, and *Honourable Estate* where it is disguised as Sterndale Spa, she subjected it to a critical exposé; and in *Testament of Youth*, without cover of fictional guise, she continued to lambast it for its 'carping pettiness'. 'My picture of Buxton is not in the least exaggerated', she told the noted suffragist and internationalist, Helena Swanwick, in 1933, defending the portrayal of the town in her autobiography. 'If anything it was more snobbish, more obscurantist, than I have shown it.' It was not simply the rigid lines of social demarcation that Vera found difficult to bear (Mrs Harrison, for instance, with whom Vera was friendly, had been blackballed from the tennis club because it was considered that in marrying a hotel proprietor she had married beneath herself); it was also the collective lack of any spirit of enquiry, the closed minds which rejected, with automatic suspicion and contempt, any independence of thought or initiative. When the idea of moving south was mooted, Vera could only

> cry with relief at the bare thought of leaving this hateful artificial place, & these cold, emotionless, unimaginative people, for a softer climate, warm bright country & people who love & understand . . . Even as a child, when I heard we were coming here I shrank from the thought & knew then that we should never like Buxton with its cold austerity & its provincial narrow inhabitants.

Even today, eighty years on, it is still possible to catch a hint of the kind of hostility which the Brittains themselves aroused among some Buxtonians. An elderly resident whose parents knew Arthur and Edith Brittain ('they had a mill or something') dismissed them as social climbers who had tried to break into the 'inner circle'.

At home at Melrose, as 1913 wore on, Vera found herself increasingly at odds with her parents' expectations. Arthur and Edith Brittain were disturbed and genuinely bewildered by their daughter's expressions of wilful independence, her refusal to give up the idea of going to Oxford, and her lack of inclination to settle down and marry. Vera had left St Monica's, her head filled with Olive Schreiner's feminist arguments, and Miss Heath-Jones's discussions of the 'Woman Question', and she had no intention of resigning herself to the life of the dutiful, stay-at-home daughter, dependent on her father, and content to wait for the first suitable man to present himself as a prospective husband. To her music master, who was horrified when she announced her intention of earning her own living, Vera retorted 'very heatedly' that she had more brains than her brother and she intended to use them. After all, she confided to her diary in January 1914, in terms that were distinctly Schreineresque, 'I may leave no more impression behind than the most abject parasite that ever lived on someone in this country – but I am determined anyhow to have a good attempt . . .'.

Her father's response to such notions was to patronize her, often provoking stormy altercations. 'He is such a very Early Victorian person', she complained. He regarded her as a plaything or toy to be spoiled and petted, 'not as a sensible human being who *counts*', she wrote angrily after one row in which he had told her that it was ridiculous for 'a little slip of a girl' to argue with him about matters she did not understand. '. . . He has nothing but contempt for me & my knowledge', she continued, 'just as he has at heart for all women because he believes them for some unknown reason to be inferior to him . . .'.

Vera's relationship with her mother was often close and yet overlaid by strains produced by differences of temperament and fundamentally opposed outlooks. Vera's ambivalent feelings towards her mother stemmed from the fact that she was struggling both to acknowledge the parts of herself that were like her mother while at the same time separating herself from what she saw as her mother's limitations.

Temperamentally Vera was her father's child and Edith Brittain was often at a loss as to how to deal with her impatient and headstrong daughter. Nor, as a product of a conventional Victorian upbringing, did she find it easy to empathize with Vera's desire to be independent. 'She was brought up in an age which taught that a wife was *always* subservient to a husband', Vera recognized, '& must never disobey him even though he were in the wrong.' Mrs Brittain could only sigh and declare that she would much rather have 'an ordinary daughter', someone to help her with the house 'and be like other girls'. Despite St Monica's best efforts, however, Vera showed little aptitude and even less inclination for cooking or household duties (at twenty-one, embarking on her wartime nursing career, she would attempt to boil an egg by bringing a saucepan of water to the boil, turning off the gas, and leaving the egg in cooling water for three minutes). Try as she might, Vera could never match her mother's exacting standards of household management. Economy and punctuality were the watchwords of Edith's domestic regime. Nothing was allowed to go to waste: eggshells were scrupulously saved for clearing soup, and the waste cuts from the mill served as a fairly rudimentary supply of lavatory paper. Even the servants lived in fear of the annual spring-clean. It was too much for Mr Brittain's nerves and he would depart to Brighton for a holiday until it was over.

In crueller moments Vera might lament her mother's lack of intellect ('we certainly don't get our brains from her'), and resist her over-solicitous concern for her welfare. But she remained acutely aware of Edith's dissatisfaction with her as a daughter. In a letter to her own daughter, Shirley, forty years later, Vera spoke of the burden of parental expectations which can weigh a child down. She herself had been

conscious all my life that I had disappointed *my* mother, because, as she once told me what she really wanted was the kind of daughter who was happy just to stick around the house and do the flowers – and if you had turned out to be the flower-doing kind I didn't want you to feel that you had disappointed *me*.

For her part Vera was sometimes exasperated by her mother's social ambitions and her preoccupation with domestic trivia. Initiated by her into the afternoon routine of paying calls and leaving cards, in later life she could still recall with a shudder her mother's feelings of humiliation whenever the silver salver in the hall remained unadorned by visiting cards from the ladies of Buxton's 'self-appointed elite'.

Into this stuffy environment, Edward's arrival home at the beginning of his school holidays, with his 'bright sane personality', brought his sister a welcome breath of fresh air: 'No tongue can tell the difference it makes to me when he is not here'. At eighteen he was in his final year at Uppingham, where his charm and 'power of making himself agreeable to anyone' had made him universally popular. More placid than his sister, and with a keen dislike of confrontation and argument, he frequently counselled Vera to adopt a less defiant stance in her clashes with her parents. Three years later, during the war, when Edward was on extended leave from his battalion and living alone with his parents in their London flat, Vera recalled with wry amusement the advice that he had once so freely dispensed:

Yes I know what it is like in the flat; now perhaps you will realise what I had to put up with for two years, & not even in London, but in Buxton. Mother used to tell you I was 'difficult' or 'discontented' & 'trying' & you really used to think there was a good deal in what they said, but now – do you wonder? The only variation of the present life was that Father instead of going to Harrods, used to sit in front of a blazing fire & smoke till the room became unendurable, & instead of talking about the War used to talk about the weather!

Edward was unwavering in his devotion to Vera, as she was to him, though at times she found him a bit priggish, and said that he reminded her strongly of Tom Tulliver in George Eliot's *The Mill on the Floss*, who thought himself unable to do anything but what was right.

Although he admitted to feeling sometimes very ambitious, Edward lacked his sister's drive and determination. He once told her that he had never fully used his talent and ability, and believed that it was his 'special prerogative to be 2nd or 3rd in everything I do'; and his mother agreed that while Vera would be successful in anything she undertook, Edward would 'always just miss'. Music remained his motive force and he appeared to have fulfilled his early promise. One evening, at their friends and neighbours, the Ellingers', Vera provided the accompaniment on the piano as Edward played the first two movements of a Beethoven sonata, and Mrs Ellinger, Vera reported, 'said great things about Edward's violin playing'. At another 'At Home' he played a composition of his own which Vera praised for its 'modernness'. Music, she wrote in her diary, provided a relief for her 'often overburdened feelings', but she also believed that maintaining her proficiency as a pianist was the best means of staying intimate with Edward.

Edward's desire to please extended to his plans for the future. He had hopes of entering the Indian Civil Service, but was prepared to acquiesce in his father's wish that his only son should join him at the paper mill, which would also please his mother by keeping him at home. To Vera's consternation, it was the automatic assumption that Edward, despite being younger and less academically gifted, would in any case go on to university after leaving Uppingham. She bore him no personal animosity because of this, but had to admit that it reinforced her feminist convictions. As she was later to tell Roland Leighton, 'I have been impressed in this home of mine with the disadvantages of being born a woman until they have eaten like iron into my soul . . .'.

V

Religion and sex were the 'vague, inchoate problems' which troubled these last years of Vera's adolescence, as they must have done for so many of her generation. Overstimulated at home and at school with regard to religious observance and belief, she had been left in almost total ignorance about even the most elementary aspects of sexual behaviour.

Warnings about not going 'too far with men', of not being seen talking to her brother's friends, and of not travelling alone with strange men in railway carriages, had instilled in Vera by the age of eighteen a state of half-knowledge and prudish suspicion of the opposite sex. The role of the Madonna in Alice Buckton's mystery play, *Eager Heart*, which she had played in her final Christmas at St Monica's – carrying a small torch inside her shawl to make a halo on the 'baby's' face – had aroused her maternal instincts, but no man had ever played a part in the 'ardent, impersonal dreams' of her schooldays. When at nineteen she prevailed upon her mother 'to disclose a few points on sexual matters which I thought I ought to know', she found the information 'intensely distasteful' and 'most distressing'.

In Buxton she had quickly discovered that men found her attractive. Petite, with large limpid eyes, she looked young for her years and outwardly, at least, gave the appearance of fetching vulnerability. With a generous dress allowance from her father of £30 a year, she could afford to indulge her love of clothes, though she sometimes felt that in Buxton society it required more than a little courage to look really chic.

She flirted, and there were plenty of young men eager to press their suit, even if most of them proved to be conversationally inept on closer acquaintance. After one dance at the Palace Hotel in early 1913, Maurice Ellinger, the son of their neighbours and one of Edward's schoolfriends, 'murmured something that sounded like darling, and tried to put his arms round my neck.' With mock-seriousness Vera protested in her diary that 'they have no right to behave so to a girl much weaker and smaller than themselves!' The theatre correspondent of the *Buxton Advertiser* admired her from more of a distance. Of her performance as Lady Ethel in an amateur production of *Raffles*, he wrote that she looked so bewitching in her white frock that it was a wonder that all the male members of the cast had not succumbed to her charm.

The proposal of marriage which Vera received in September 1913 from 'a large, athletic young man with limited brains and evangelical principles' is a depressing reminder of how many a young woman of this period must have found herself married to the first man who decided, on the most cursory acquaintance, that she would make a suitable wife. The Spaffords were a Buxton family with textile interests in Manchester. They also lived in The Park and the Brittains met them fairly regularly at dances, musical evenings, and the progressive bridge table. Bertram Spafford was nine years older than Vera and, a keen tennis player, he sometimes partnered her in club matches. He told her that he had often watched her in church when she was a child, and had always liked her. Vera found his bumbling attentions an amusing diversion, though she later confessed that she had been a 'hard-hearted little brute' for leading him on. Throughout the summer he had been following her about and pretending to meet her accidentally in town. Then on 22 September she received the following letter:

My Dear Vera

The night I took you down to dinner at your house 16 months ago, I first knew I loved you – and since then you have been everything in the whole world to me. I was intending to wait until I could afford to ask you to be my wife, before I told you this; but I realised last time you went away the awful risk I was running of losing you and I can't face this possibility.

Is there the faintest chance of you caring for me even a little – and will you give me a chance of winning you, by waiting for me for a year, because by that time I shall be able to come forward and ask your father to let us be engaged openly.

Sincerely yours

Bertram Spafford

You are of course free to show this to your parents.

Vera's 'immediate and only reaction', she later remembered, 'was a sense of intolerable humiliation and disgust'. That same day she gave him her forthright and unequivocal refusal:

Dear Mr Spafford

Your letter came as a great surprise to me and I was very sorry to receive it.

I cannot for a moment entertain the idea of accepting your proposal, and I must beg you to consider this as final, as I have no doubt whatsoever of my feelings on the subject. I do, and always have, regarded you merely as an acquaintance, and to the best of my knowledge have always treated you as such.

I regret the necessity of hurting your feelings in this matter and trust that you will forget about it as soon as possible.

Believe me,

Yours sincerely

Vera M. Brittain

'Dear Mrs Vera Spafford', Edward teased, '. . . Don't be too hard on the wretched man.' Mr Brittain, however, considered the manner of Spafford's proposal to be presumptuous, and the next time Vera met him at a bridge evening she mischievously went out of her way to be as alluring as possible; but later, after she had seen him leaning mournfully over his garden gate, she wondered whether his feeling for her might not have run deeper than she realized.

Insofar as any man was the focus of Vera's attention at this time, it was the Reverend Joseph Ward, the young curate of St Peter's in the neighbouring town of Fairfield. Every Sunday, from the late autumn of 1913 to the summer of the following year, Vera, sometimes accompanied by her mother or Edward, would walk the three miles into Fairfield, and be spellbound and uplifted by the fiery rhetoric of Mr Ward's rationalistic sermons.

Towards the end of her time at St Monica's, Vera had been assailed by religious doubt and speculation. She had suffered 'sleepless nights for weeks on end' after reading Mrs Humphry Ward's controversial bestseller of 1888, *Robert Elsmere*, the story of a clergyman in the Oxford of Newman and the Tractarians, who rejects the superstition and dogma of the Anglican Church for a life of social service in the East End of London. The book had aroused doubts in her mind about orthodox Anglican observance. She did not know what label to attach to herself – agnostic, deist, or even heretic – but she had arrived at a repudiation of the miraculous elements underpinning the Bible. Christ was possibly the greatest man who had ever lived, but his divinity, 'though greater in degree & realization', was fundamentally the same as the rest of mankind's.

Mr Ward was a real-life Robert Elsmere. He had been schooled in the 'Higher Criticism', and confessed that he had thrown much of the old theology overboard. His sermons, which emphasized the social relevance of Christ's teaching, had won him an enthusiastic following among the members of his working-men's Bible Class – leading Mr Brittain to denounce him as 'a pleb talking to plebs' – and his services were packed with the poor of Fairfield to whom, Vera observed, he appeared as a spiritual leader. His superiors, threatened by his radical views, regarded him as dangerous and subversive, and mounted a campaign which eventually hounded him into resignation.

Mr Ward's story, which unfolds in Vera's diary with all the immediacy and in-built suspense of fiction, was in fact to provide the basis, a decade later, of her second novel, *Not Without Honour*. By the time she portrayed him as its hero, Albert Clark, she had come to recognize 'this brilliant man' for the 'part-charlatan, part-exhibitionist' that he was. Nevertheless, 'a nucleus of very real influence remained.' When he preached on overcoming the world by faith, for instance, his words took on a heightened significance for her, as he spoke of breaking away from convention, and forming one's own personal Utopia.

Away from the pulpit, Mr Ward was no less a source of interest for Vera. Her intense, almost reverential, absorption in him reflects her later response to two other men whose spiritual qualities strongly influenced her, Dick Sheppard, founder of the Peace Pledge Union, and the Quaker, Corder Catchpool. Her relationship with Mr Ward, though, undoubtedly contained elements of a discreetly flirtatious character. For once deliberately courting her husband's disapproval – '. . . it would be a good thing if he were tumbled out', Arthur Brittain had shouted after attending one of Mr Ward's services – Mrs Brittain encouraged Vera's preoccupation with the Fairfield controversy. She invited Mr Ward and his wife to tea, and although Vera was at first 'hot & shy', Mr Ward's charm and sense of humour soon made her feel 'strangely happy & content all the time he was near me'. Flattered by Vera's attention, Mr Ward attended both nights of the production of *Raffles* in which she appeared. He also supported her ambition to go to Oxford, and told her how he had walked seven miles to obtain the Euclid lessons which enabled him to begin his theological training at Cambridge.

By late 1913 a combination of circumstances had at last set in motion the events that would take Vera to Oxford. Vera later wrote that her mother's growing sympathy for the idea, coupled with the opinions of an old family lawyer, favourably inclined towards higher education for women, had succeeded in wearing down her father's resistance to the idea. But it was John Marriott, visiting Buxton for a series of Oxford University Extension lectures at the Town Hall in the spring of 1913, who confirmed her in her determination to go to Oxford and showed her how she might set about achieving that goal.

Marriott, the bluff, hearty lecturer in Modern History at Worcester College, Oxford, had been lecturing for the extension delegacy for fifteen years and had been its secretary since 1895. He was one of the most popular of its speakers, lucid, 'careful not to soar too far above the heads of his audience', and possessed of a dramatic manner of delivery. His Buxton talks on the 'Problems of Wealth and Poverty' had not been well attended. 'Unintellectual Buxton all over', Vera had scoffed in her diary, though she herself had been absent from the first of the series, having been otherwise engaged at a dance. At subsequent lectures, though, she was the outstanding contributor. Complimented by Marriott on the standard of her weekly essays, she was soon reflecting on how 'the smallest intellectual success always brings me back to the longing for the harder, less comfortable but more idealistic life that I would choose . . .'. When Marriott required a bed for the night after one lecture, Vera persuaded her mother to allow him to stay at Melrose.

In *Testament of Youth* when Vera paid tribute to John Marriott as the '*deus ex machina* of my unsophisticated youth', responsible for her final victory over her family's opposition to her attending university, she may have been overstating his influence on her parents for dramatic effect. Marriott himself wrote, with a defensive air, in his own memoirs that '. . . *The Testament of Youth* [sic] contains so many references to me that my friends declare themselves frankly bored by them.' Nonetheless, his 'genial matter-of-factness' undoubtedly made an impression on Mr Brittain. Taken off-guard by his discovery that 'a professor' carried his golf clubs with him, Arthur Brittain was content to bask in the reflected glory of Marriott's praise of his daughter.

Encouraged by Marriott to compete for an essay prize in connection with that year's Oxford Summer School, Vera entered and won. For two weeks that August she attended the Summer School itself. Chaperoned by Miss Heath-Jones and Miss Bervon, she lodged at St Hilda's, attended lectures in the university's Examination Schools, and dined with Marriott at his North Oxford home. Marriott encouraged her to try for Lady Margaret Hall, the most 'ladylike' of the four women's colleges, but it was Somerville which attracted Vera most. Famous for its academic excellence, Somerville possessed the virtues in Vera's eyes of being both non-denominational and of actually looking like a college. The other women's colleges, she thought, looked 'like recently erected hotels or high-class boarding-houses.'

Her preliminary interview with Somerville's intimidating Principal, Miss Penrose, was far from auspicious. As Vera flitted across the lawn of the Fellows' Garden on a warm summer's evening, dressed in inappropriately 'gay attire', Miss Penrose's eyes widened in disapproval, 'and disbelief in my intellect'. She advised Vera to apply to read English, and on no account to take the Scholarship. As it was, Vera would have to take two examinations: the college entrance examination in March and the Oxford Senior Local, for university entry, the following July. It was only later, after returning to Buxton, that Vera decided, with some persuasion from Edward, to sit the Scholarship anyway. If she was going to accept the challenge she might as well aim for the highest stakes.

Back home, Vera finally received her father's permission and he agreed to pay for the coaching in mathematics and Latin that she would need for the

Oxford Senior. Reluctant to ask him to meet the additional expense of tuition in English literature, Vera planned to prepare herself for the Somerville exam. 'Violent in speech though always generous in action when once convinced of its necessity', Mr Brittain was proud of Vera, though more than a little bemused by his daughter's academic ambitions. He remained fixed in the view that all women dons were dried-up and cold-blooded, and worried about the possible effects of such influences upon Vera's marriage prospects. Ultimately, though, he could never forgo an opportunity to play the indulgent father.

'In a small narrow place like this, one half thinks me too go-ahead for words, & the other absolutely mad & a perfect fool', Vera wrote in October, summing up the mixture of bewilderment and disapproval with which her mother's Buxton acquaintances had greeted the news of her exam. She had quickly embarked on the intense regimen of study that was to occupy her for the next few months. From six in the morning until lunchtime each day she worked on the Augustans and the Romantics for the Somerville Scholarship in a small, chilly sewing-room at the back of the house. Then after lunch and a game of tennis or golf, she returned less eagerly to grapple with a few mathematics problems or a Latin unseen, supplemented by an hour's tuition at Mr Lace's, a local crammer.

Her first paper during four days of exams and interviews at Somerville in March was almost her last. Horrified to discover that she had prepared herself for the literature essays along entirely the wrong lines – having read too much criticism and too little of the prescribed texts – she sat petrified for half-an-hour, intending to admit defeat and to ask Miss Penrose to send her home that afternoon. But once her initial panic had subsided, she decided to remain and answer the questions as best she could.

She had only a week to wait to discover that her persistence had paid off. On 25 March she received a letter from Miss Penrose, congratulating her on having been awarded a College Exhibition of £20 a year for three years, one of only two awards made that year in English.

She had, of course, still to overcome the hurdle of the Oxford Senior that summer before the place at Somerville was definitely hers, but even that daunting prospect could not detract from her feelings of triumph and justifiable pride. Whatever the shortcomings of her performance, she could only assume that some traces of native intelligence had managed to shine through. 'The more I think about it the more amazed I feel'. Her mother had become 'quite flustered in her delight', and to her surprise her father 'seemed quite overjoyed'. Adding to her own joy was the fact that Edward too would be going up to Oxford that coming Michaelmas term of 1914.

'Oxford is heaven on earth except for the climate which gave me this cold . . .', he had written to her the previous December, after winning a place at New College. 'I drink to next year when I expect we shall enjoy ourselves there.'

Her confidence boosted, Vera resumed her work for the Oxford Senior with fresh enthusiasm. Intermittently, though, in the next few months, thoughts of a very different nature were often to be uppermost in her mind.

At Christmas 1913, after enduring an evening in the company of some superficial and dull-witted men, Vera had written of her longing to meet 'a good strong splendid man, full of force & enthusiasm, & in earnest about his life!' Only one man would ever live up to these exalted expectations. On 16 April, three weeks after the result of her exam, she came in purposely late for dinner. At the table was a schoolfriend of Edward's, the recent winner of the Senior Open Classical Postmastership at Merton, Oxford, who had been invited to stay a few days over the Easter holidays. His name was Roland Leighton.

TWO

Roland

'I want to love! I want something great and pure to lift me to itself! . . . I am so cold, so hard, so hard; will no one help me?'

'There is another love, that blots out wisdom, that is sweet with the sweetness of life and bitter with the bitterness of death, lasting for an hour; but it is worth having lived a whole life for that hour.'

Olive Schreiner, *The Story of an African Farm* (1883)

I

Roland Aubrey Leighton was one of life's Principal Players. At Uppingham he had blazed a meteoric trail. In his final year there he combined the responsibilities of Captain of his school house, The Lodge, Captain in Classics, Praepositor, Editor of the school magazine, President of the Union Society, as well as Colour-Sergeant of Uppingham's Officers' Training Corps, the institution that so largely determined the school's ethos. A brilliant post-Oxford career was envisaged for him by family, schoolmasters and contemporaries as a poet and diplomat, or perhaps as Editor of *The Times*. 'I know I haven't got the stuff in me of which Bystanders are made', he wrote home from France in 1915 when war had indefinitely postponed the fulfilment of that promise. 'I must be the Principal Player or nothing.'

His self-assurance and assumption of pre-eminence derived in no small part from his mother's love for him which stopped just short of idolatry. Born on 27 March 1895, Roland was the oldest surviving child of Robert Leighton, a writer of boys' adventure stories and an authority on dog-breeding, and Marie Connor Leighton, a prolific romantic novelist and author of sensational melodramas for the Northcliffe Press. Marie had married at seventeen after a brief, disenchanting debut as an actress on a provincial tour. Her first baby had been accidentally smothered by a nurse, and, overcome with grief and remorse, Marie had vowed when Roland was born that she would atone for her 'many sins of selfishness' by devoting herself to him. She dressed him expensively in velvet suits and silk blouses, letting his yellow curls grow long, and spoiling him wildly. He alone of her children, she believed, had inherited something of the colour of her Celtic and Cornish ancestry rather than the fusty Scottish puritanism of the Leightons. He was her shining knight, her Lochinvar, and only he, she claimed, understood her incurably romantic mind 'that always has what you may call the apple blossom feeling in it.' As he grew older, Roland began to respond with extravagant gestures of his own. At the age of ten he gave his mother some scarlet silk stockings for her birthday and thereafter habitually lavished gifts on her, indulging her passion for Parma violets and pink carnations, and sending her hot-house flowers throughout the winter. 'My letters to her are always love-letters really', he was to tell Vera. 'It is because we understand each other so well I suppose: there is a much deeper affection between us than you would expect in mother and son.'

The special closeness of this bond led Mrs Leighton to neglect her daughter, Clare, and younger son, Evelyn, Roland's junior by three and six years respectively. Both adored and worshipped their elder brother too much to hold this against him, though Clare's suppressed resentment surfaced years later when she came to write her candid portrait of her mother under the suitably flamboyant title, *Tempestuous Petticoat*. It had taken several drafts, she admitted in old age, to write out her feelings of bitterness at her mother's blatant favouritism. Evelyn broke decisively with his parents. A naval cadet at Osborne in 1914, he took the navy '*in loco parentis*' from the age of sixteen' and in adult life could rarely be persuaded to talk of his family.

Marie Leighton was like a character straight from the pages of one of her own novels and every inch the figure of a romantic novelist. 'Our mother lived upon romance', wrote Clare, 'and wove it into her most prosaic daily duties.' Swathed in sables and ermine regardless of the season, with petticoats protruding from under her dress, Marie had wispy straw-coloured hair invariably surmounted by an elaborate hat which looked as if some exotic bird had escaped and landed on her head. Irrepressibly vital, capricious, and extravagant, she was courted by a band of ageing male admirers ('Mother's Old Men' as Roland unflatteringly called them) whose regular visits her long-suffering and faithful husband patiently endured. Robert Leighton, some years older than his wife, with red hair and moustache, possessed 'the kindest manner in the world', but tended to be cut off from the rest of his family by deafness. Descended from a family with strong literary credentials – his father was the Scottish poet Robert Leighton, author of such vernacular poems as 'The Bapteesement o'the

Bairn' – he had been responsible for accepting Robert Louis Stevenson's *Treasure Island* (then called 'The Sea Cook') for serialization in the children's magazine, *Young Folks*. As Editor of the magazine, he had published poems in 1885 by the teenage Marie Connor. So impressed had he been by their quality that, against the rules of the firm, he had invited her to visit him at his office. He had lost his job as a consequence, but had fallen in love with his young contributor, and they had eloped to Scotland.

Bound by ties of work from the beginning, the Leightons' literary output was enormous. In all Robert Leighton would publish some fifty books, Marie eighty. They collaborated on twelve more, including *Michael Dred, Detective*, the earliest story in which a detective is unmasked as the murderer, and *Convict 99*, their greatest success, which ran for nearly a year as a serial and went into several editions when published in book form in 1898. Alfred Harmsworth, later Lord Northcliffe, was the guiding hand on both their early careers. In 1896 Robert became the first Literary Editor of the *Daily Mail*, the foundation stone of the Harmsworth newspaper empire; and Marie's serial stories appeared for many years in the *Mail* as well as in *Answers*, the striking, orange-coloured weekly paper which she helped to inaugurate, and which at its height recorded net sales of more than a million copies. Harmsworth personally supervised each episode of the stories, sometimes arriving by hansom at the Leighton house late at night, to demand a more exciting cliffhanger to a story.

The Leighton household in St John's Wood, and later at Heather Cliff on the coast at Lowestoft, the house to which the family moved in the summer of 1913, was dominated by books and writing. All three children had been practically born in the inkwell as Mrs Leighton struggled to finish her latest serial, rushing to marry off her heroine to the hero as her first labour pains began. While at one end of the long study table, Clare remembered, her mother would be painstakingly plotting murders and arson, at the other her father's imagination would be roaming the prairies of Canada in search of Indians for adventure stories like *Kiddie of the Camp*. Everything revolved around Mrs Leighton's work, as her writing earned far more than her husband's, and largely supported the household: this fact alone, Roland liked to claim, had made him a feminist. Roland too was a writer of sorts. The wreck of a toy typewriter bore testimony to his childhood literary ambitions. In adolescence he had turned to poetry, and the few poems which he allowed to survive, transcribed in his small, precise handwriting into a pocket notebook, reveal the influence of W.E. Henley, and of Henry Newbolt, whose jingoistic doggerel he apparently knew by heart.

After the sterile propriety of the Brittains' Buxton existence, the

Leighton family's Bohemianism was to prove an intoxicating revelation for Vera. It was also to provide her with a window on a world which she had as yet only dreamed about, of publishers and their deadlines, of tales of famous writers like George Meredith, whom Marie Leighton had befriended in his last years, and Hall Caine, who had first brought her story-telling talents to Harmsworth's attention. Even the Leightons' carefree way with money and their constant state of 'literary poverty' seemed at first to have a certain glamour attached to them.

In 1913 Marie Leighton's long series of writing contracts with the Harmsworths' Amalgamated Press had been abruptly terminated. 'The Serial, which is now running in *Answers*, is, in my opinion very poor stuff', a disgruntled reader wrote about one of her final contributions. 'Every instalment has at least three remarkable coincidences, and the authoress seems to be covering very much the same ground as in her last effort. Forced to depend on less remunerative book contracts, Mrs Leighton was concerned that the family's depleted finances might prevent Roland from going to Oxford and realizing 'his really remarkable abilities'. In some desperation she turned to her old employer, now Lord Northcliffe, writing him an 'audacious letter' to plead for her son's future.

> I wanted mainly to ask you whether there would be any promising opening in the business for our Roland. He is the boy, who at three years old, one day when you were at Abbey Road, asked you on his own account to have a cigarette, and he is now eighteen and a half and without exaggeration singularly brilliant . . . He is now trying for an Oxford scholarship, but even if he gains one, the cost of his going to Oxford could not be less than two hundred and fifty a year over and above the help of the scholarship – and, as things are at present, we could not manage that . . . I am wondering if there might be any opening for him. He would make an exceedingly good secretary. He has personal style, distinction, culture and taste.

Northcliffe's reply has not survived. But in any case all discussion of Roland's future was postponed by the outbreak of war, little more than a year later.

Vera had first met Roland Leighton the summer before his visit to the Brittains. She and her mother had spent a few days at the end of June 1913 attending Uppingham 'Old Boys' week, and Edward had brought Roland into dinner with them. 'I like him immensely', Vera had written in her diary, 'he seems so clever and amusing and hardly shy at all.' Over the next few months Vera heard Edward talk a good deal about his new friend, whom he regarded with not a little awe and whose friendship was a source of pride to him. For as well as being Captain of their house and Uppingham's most brilliant scholar, Roland also had a reputation for aloofness. Roland, Vera was to write when she had come to know him better, possessed the kind of 'reserved conceit – or conceited reserve – which never boasts, but subtly reveals itself in those attributes which make the boys call him "The Lord" . . .'. He was of stocky build, his dark-brown eyes and dark, well-defined eyebrows providing a striking contrast to the pallor of his skin and his thick and bristly fair hair which he brilliantined down. Although he was fifteen months younger than Vera, she was never to think of him as such for he had the carriage and confidence of someone older. 'At nineteen', she wrote in her mature account, 'Roland looked twenty-four and behaved with the assurance of thirty.' He was impressive, she admitted, rather than handsome.

She had seen little of him the evening of his arrival at Melrose in April 1914. He had sat beside her at dinner without uttering a word, and after the meal she had rushed off into town to review a one-act play for the *Buxton Advertiser*. It was only the next morning, after she had hurriedly copied out her piece with Roland standing at her elbow, dictating what she had written, that they had time to talk and discuss 'various matters such as literature and religion'. By the evening of the following day, after 'a most interesting conversation, a good deal of which was about our ideas of immortality', Vera decided that 'he is interested in me now, though I can't make out whether he likes me very much or dislikes me very much.' On a ten-mile walk across the moors to Goyt Valley on Sunday afternoon, with Vera's young neighbour Maurice Ellinger tagging along, she was unable to resist mocking him for his conceit, and for his condescending remarks expressed in the superior tones of the 'Quiet Voice'. He became depressed and remained silent for half the walk. Later they returned to their speculations about religion and immortality.

While Edward was at organ practice on the Monday morning, Vera and Roland talked away more hours, sitting on a tree stump in Corbar Woods. When Vera left the next day for a short holiday in the Lake District with her aunt and uncle, the Groves, Roland found it difficult to hide his disappointment that he would be spending his last days in Buxton without her. A parcel from him quickly followed Vera to Windermere. Inside was a copy of the novel which he had often talked about in the course of his stay, Olive Schreiner's *The Story of an African Farm*. Inscribed on the flyleaf were the words, 'V.M.B. In gratitude for much. R.A.L.' The accompanying letter read:

Dear Vera

– Edward has commanded me to address you in this way. I hope you do not object – Here is The Story of an African Farm . . . When you have read it let me know what you think of it, and whether you agree with me that Lyndall is rather like you – only sadder perhaps and not so charmingly controversial.

I am so very sorry that you had to go away just as I was learning to renounce the Quiet Voice and had begun to feel less shy. It sounds very selfish of me to say this; but I have enjoyed my visit to you (as you put it) immensely. Now that the greater attraction has taken herself off I shall be free to devote myself to the neglected Edward. Not that he seems to mind very much.

He had made her promise that he would see her again at the Uppingham Speech Day in July. Despite its proximity to her Oxford Senior exam, Vera had resolved to attend 'at all costs'.

In the intervals between more bouts of Latin and mathematics, *The Story of an African Farm* enthralled Vera. 'It is a great book', she wrote in her diary, 'and it has made my head almost ache with thinking.' Writing to Roland to thank him warmly for his gift, she admitted that it had impressed her 'very much', adding that 'it is the kind of book that makes an incident in the story of our "soul's years" . . .'. For the present, Olive Schreiner displaced George Eliot as Vera's literary mentor and idol; and *African Farm* took the place of *Woman and Labour* as Vera's personal 'Bible'.

The source of *African Farm*'s appeal is not difficult to trace. Schreiner had begun writing it when she was barely twenty, and as one critic has pointed out, 'Its power is fuelled by the idealism, the vague but intense yearning, the urgent questioning, the obsession with romantic love and loneliness and suffering and death, which characterize the sensitive and intelligent adolescent's dealings with life.' The novel centres on the lives of three children, growing up on a Karoo farm in the 1860s against a background of religious bigotry. More than anything else the book is about dreams, specifically children's dreams, and those of the orphan Lyndall and of Waldo, the son of the overseer of the farm, take the reader right to the heart of the novel. Waldo dreams of studying the rocks and fossils as a scientist in a search for absolute truth. Lyndall, 'the first wholly serious feminist heroine in the English novel', has a vision of an independent life and free choice for women. Here for Vera was the later theorizing of *Woman and Labour* presented within the framework of an alluring fiction. In *African Farm* she also found the flavour of real life. 'Nothing is nicely wound up', she explained to Roland, 'and everything left in the unsatisfactory state things are always left in this world.'

In later years Vera would shy away from associating herself too closely with *The Story of an African Farm*: it represented an absorption in herself and an obsession with her own suffering that she had long since outgrown. Yet for both Vera and Roland the novel was to become the leitmotif of their relationship, and in a way the lives of its characters were to stand in for the shared experience of which subsequent events would so cruelly deprive them. Its tragic conclusion would foreshadow their own doomed love affair.

Vera was alive, too, to the resemblance that Roland saw between herself and the heroine of his – and his mother's – favourite novel. Apart from their shared outlook, there were other obvious similarities. Lyndall is very small with beautiful eyes. She is the focus of male attention: her lover rides one hundred miles to see her, and Gregory Rose leaves everything to follow her, dressing in women's clothes so that he may nurse her on her deathbed. 'I think I am a little like Lyndall', Vera confessed to Roland, 'and would probably be more so in her circumstances, uncovered by the thin veneer of polite social intercourse.' 'But', she continued a trifle disingenuously, 'how you should think me like her, and why you see any resemblance, I cannot imagine.' For Marie Leighton, conscious of what she called her son's 'Lyndallesque Romanticism', Roland's gift could mean only one thing. If he had sent Vera *The Story of an African Farm*, Marie would later say,

> then she can't be the ordinary sort of girl . . . She can't be of the great army of those who play games and are always taking bodily exercise, and yet never by any chance do anything more useful than arrange cut flowers . . . She must be a personality – one of the few girls who can think and are not afraid to do it; one of the few who know what real romance is . . . And if she is this – then he is not wholly mine as he was a few weeks ago. He will never be wholly mine any more.

Lyndall, and by association Roland Leighton, were never far from Vera's thoughts as the July Speech Day approached. One sultry July evening, she gazed out of her bedroom window and, in a conscious echo of Lyndall, longed for something to worship. 'I spend much time wondering', she recorded in her diary, 'whether I, who so desire to stand alone, shall ever find something or someone the reverence of which is not dependence.' In a conversation with Bertram Spafford, her unsuccessful suitor of the previous autumn, with whom she had been indulging in a 'heartless, retrospective flirtation' for most of the summer, her identification with Schreiner's heroine was stronger still. She could only marvel at Spafford's perseverance in pressing his suit, and despise her own callous indifference to his feelings. She also perceived, though, that his notion of a wife was as a cushion, or a hot-water bottle, something for a husband to soothe himself with at home. Informing him that she no longer wished to be the object of worship, she wrote in her diary that '. . . I know that until I have loved someone purely, passionately and selflessly, my character-building will lack something always.'

'I am coming to Speech Day right enough', Vera had assured Roland on 24 May; 'in fact if I can summon up enough courage to face your confessedly merciless criticism of feminine attire, I may even wear a new frock for the occasion!' On 10 July she and her mother travelled to Uppingham where they were to stay in the cramped quarters of the school's Waterworks Cottage. It was Edward's farewell Speech Day, but it was on Roland's account even more than her brother's that Vera had come: '. . . My interest in him seems to have increased without seeing him, and there is nothing strange in my being attracted by so marvellous an intellect and a not-easily-understandable personality.' Vera and Roland talked briefly in the quad that evening. As soon as she saw 'his plain intelligent face and dark expressive eyes again, I knew I had not overrated their attraction for me . . .'. He had broken the Uppingham record for school prizes and was the next day to receive the seven main ones, including those for Greek and Latin prose, and the English essay. She would look out for any atom of conceit at the prizegiving, she warned him, and squash it immediately.

'Of the functions which mark the social life of a public School during the year', the Uppingham magazine reported, 'Speech Day lays claim to the first place, and nowhere, we venture to think, is the occasion more enthusiastically and pleasurably honoured than is the case at Uppingham.' The weather that July was sunny and cloudless and 'a large and notable' gathering of parents were present for Speech Day. A service in the chapel opened the proceedings, followed by the Corps review. Close to 350 boys mustered on the school's Middle Field to take part, among them Roland, Edward, and their mutual friend, Victor Richardson, dubbed by Marie Leighton 'The Three Musketeers'. Vera admired the 'fine sight' of the Corps as they stood to attention for inspection. At midday, school and guests filed into the Memorial Hall for the presentation of the prizes, presided over by the Headmaster, the Reverend Mackenzie. The climax of his speech epitomized 'the confusion of patriotism and religion' so characteristic of Uppingham. Quoting the words of a distinguished Japanese General, Count Nogi, the Headmaster asked the assembled school to pay particular attention to his final precept, 'Be a man – useful to your country; whoever cannot be that is better dead.' Within just a few weeks his words would assume a fatally prophetic quality.

Roland received only 'a very average amount of applause' as he went up to collect his prizes. According to Edward, few understood him and most thought him arrogant and incapable of expressing emotion; but Vera empathized with his rejection of popularity as commonplace. Major A.C.E. Daniels, one of Roland's younger house contemporaries, recalled nearly seventy years later that when the prizegiving was over, Roland collected together all his book prizes in their distinctive Uppingham binding, and trundled them back to his dormitory in a wheelbarrow.

Wearing a rose-trimmed hat and a pink dress, Vera claimed all Roland's attention at the Headmaster's garden party, and quite managed to pierce his reserve. She pressed him to say 'if he really thought me like Lyndall and why he did. He replied, in spite of my saying that the Lyndalls of this world are few and far between, that he hoped and really thought I was . . .'. Disappointed not to meet Mrs Leighton, about whom she had heard so much, Vera learnt that she had been unable to witness her son's triumph as she was finishing a book. Roland, along with Edward and Victor, and like thousands of other public school boys, would shortly be leaving for the OTC Summer Camp at Mychett's Farm near Aldershot. 'I said goodbye to him with more indifference than I felt', Vera wrote of their parting at The Lodge gates the next day. 'I could not help wondering whether and when I shall see him again. He seems even in a short acquaintance to share both my faults and my talents and my ideas in a way that I have never found anyone else to yet.'

She wondered too, as she left Uppingham with her mother on 13 July, whether she would ever see 'its long straggling street and romance-tinged quads' again. But she never was to return. 'Somehow I have never felt able to go back there', she told Maurice Richardson, Victor's younger brother, over forty years later, '. . . there are too many ghosts for me . . .'. Instead in her writing through the years, she was to invest the place and that final Speech Day before the war with an almost mythical quality. In her last essay of any significance, written for a book commemorating the fiftieth anniversary of the Armistice in 1968, she invoked the memory of Uppingham as a symbol of a vanished world of prewar innocence. 'The echo of a boy's laughing voice on a school playing field in that golden summer' gradually becomes one of many voices:

> . . . the sound of the Uppingham School choir marching up the chapel for the Speech Day service in July 1914, and singing the Commemoration hymn . . . There was a thrilling, a poignant quality in those boys' voices, as though they were singing their own requiem – as indeed many of them were.

No portent of impending disaster had reached Buxton on Vera's return, though she was immediately cast into a depression by the realization of how easy it would be for her to fail her exam. The prospect of Oxford was beginning to look even more attractive with the added enticement of Roland Leighton's presence there. Already on 20 July, however, as her father drove her over to Leek to sit her Oxford Senior, the world of Vera's upbringing was beginning to fall apart. A fortnight later, at midnight on 4 August, Britain was at war with Germany.

II

Like most people that summer, Vera had remained oblivious to the rumblings of war until comparatively late. She had barely even noticed the newspaper columns devoted to the worsening diplomatic situation. On 25 July the first mention in her diary of the 'European crisis' caused by Austria's ultimatum to Serbia takes second place to a discussion of that day's tennis match and a description of the weather. However, by the first week of August the tone of the entries has changed to mounting excitement mixed with incredulity and bewilderment. 'Armageddon in Europe', she declares on 3 August, commenting on the swift passage of events which are too 'thrilling' for her to sleep. Soon the diary swells with all the bombastic rhetoric of a *Times* leader: 'The great fear now is that our bungling Government will declare England's neutrality. If we at this critical juncture were to refuse to help our friend France, we should be guilty of the grossest treachery . . . Germany has broken treaty after treaty and disregarded every honourable tie with other nations.' Her diary is also awash with rumour, the inevitable by-product of war. She reports at various times that the Emperor of Austria-Hungary is dead, that German Zeppelins are massing to destroy Paris, and that 100,000 Russians have passed through Stoke on their way to the front.

Buxton had immediately succumbed to war fever. Pandemonium had broken loose on Bank Holiday Monday, the 3rd, with panic-buying of food and newspapers. It was still in a state of uproar on the evening of the 4th when a restless Vera persuaded her parents to accompany her into town for word of the latest developments. Large crowds gathered in front of the Town Hall and Post Office where mobilization orders had been posted; Territorials and reservists, already in uniform, were taking leave of their wives and families and preparing to depart; 'suppressed excitement was everywhere in the air'. News was circulating, which the following morning's papers would confirm, that Germany, acting in defiance of Britain's ultimatum, due officially to expire at midnight, had invaded Belgium. 'Nothing like it, they say, has been known since the time of Napoleon, and even Napoleon did not make war on his neighbours at so mad a rate.'

War swiftly disrupted the normal pattern of life at Melrose. For a short while Vera abandoned her books to undertake 'the only work it seems possible as yet for women to do', knitting bedsocks and sleeping-helmets for soldiers. There was domestic upset. Mrs Kay, the cook, continually dissolved into tears at the thought of the imminent departure of her four reservist sons, and was unable to prepare meals. Mr and Mrs Brittain were full of pessimistic forebodings for the safety of Miss Heath-Jones and Miss Bervon who had been travelling on the Continent that summer, and Edward's early arrival home from the hurriedly disbanded camp at Aldershot increased their worry. He was already expressing his eagerness to volunteer, urged on by his sister. On 5 August Vera had shown him an appeal in the papers for young unmarried men between the ages of eighteen and thirty to join the army. 'He suddenly got very keen', she reported later, and rushed into Buxton with Maurice Ellinger in an unsuccessful attempt to enlist. The vague rumour of a temporary commission in the Notts and Derby Regiment encouraged him to send a letter of application to their Territorial Headquarters at Chesterfield. They had no more vacancies for recruits, but were sufficiently impressed with Edward's qualifications to forward his letter to the War Office. At eighteen, though, he still required his father's consent before he could take the matter any further, and this Arthur Brittain at first angrily withheld. Their father, Edward rather priggishly explained to Vera, 'not being a public school man or having any training, could not possibly understand the impossibility of his remaining in inglorious safety while others, scarcely older than he, were offering their all'. '. . . I would not have his decision back or keep him here', Vera wrote in her diary that evening.

A month later the row still raged, with Vera and her mother siding more openly with Edward against Mr Brittain. 'After dinner we all discussed again Daddy's refusal to let Edward go into the Army, and the unmanliness of it, especially after we read in *The Times* of a mother who said to her hesitating son "My boy I don't want you to go, but if I were you I should!" ' It was a question of honour, Vera maintained, and if her father was unwilling then it would be left to Edward and herself to live up to the name of 'Brittain'. She viewed with contempt what she saw as the contrasting response to the call of duty on the part of Bertram Spafford. He had told

Vera that he was concerned about the effect that enlisting might have upon his business. Watching him push his mother in her bath chair through the Pavilion Gardens she contemplated 'his obvious strength and suitability for military work', and branded him a 'shirker'.

The shallow patriotism and jingoistic euphoria of Vera's initial response to the war may appear distasteful now, but in view of her class, background, and education such reactions are scarcely surprising, and are indeed representative. For all her developing feminist consciousness and her forcefully expressed desire to escape from the provincial society in which she had been raised, she remained entrammelled by that society's conventional ideas of class, politics and nationalism. She revered the custom and tradition of her brother's public school education, and implicitly accepted the values of militarism and 'appropriate' gentlemanly behaviour which Uppingham stood for. She paid lip-service to ideals of duty and heroism, of the kind to be found in classics of the Edwardian schoolroom like Charles Kingsley's *Heroes*. And above all she failed to appreciate the effect that the public world could have upon the personal lives of individuals. 'Current events', she reminisced twenty years later, after the lesson had been painfully learned, '. . . represented something that must be followed rather reluctantly in the newspapers, but would never, conceivably, have to be lived'. 'Unsophisticated', 'idealistic', and 'pathetically unaware' were the words which Vera later used to explain her generation's susceptibility to war propaganda; a generation for whom the experience of war before 1914 was, like Vera's, no more than the haziest childhood recollection of the South African campaigns.

What is therefore surprising, and in a sense regrettable, is that in *Testament of Youth* Vera is unwilling to explore the roots of her own idealism in 1914 in anything more than a superficial manner. She recoils from probing too deeply her own motivation. 'Women are just as liable as men to be carried away by the war-time emotion and deceived by the shining figure of patriotism', she admitted in 1934. Yet one searches in vain in *Testament of Youth* for any indication of the role played by Vera in spurring Edward on to enlist. 'Kitchener's finger pointing from numerous hoardings left me quite unmoved by its hysterical monotony', she wrote of the Great War's most famous image of propaganda, two years before her death. Behind that denial, one assumes, lay the burden of a legacy of guilt.

Where the prevailing militancy of the diary is offset in these early months of war is in Vera's compassion for its victims and her horror at the cost in human lives. 'I am incapable of feeling glad at such a wholesale slaughter of the Germans . . .', she wrote on 8 August after reading reports of 25,000

Germans killed in the attack on Liège. Three weeks after the outbreak of war she can write:

> It was very hard to believe that not far away men were being slain ruthlessly, and their poor disfigured bodies heaped together and crowded in ghastly indiscrimination into quickly provided, common graves, as though they were piles of mindless vermin, and had not each a personality and a soul . . . The destruction of men, as though beasts, whether they be English, French, German, or anything else, seems a crime to the whole march of civilization . . .

This compassion for war's victims would deepen when as a VAD she began to nurse the wounded and dying. But even then her attitude to the war would continue to be dominated by her allegiance to the men she knew at the front. Her need to go on rekindling the belief that they were fighting for a noble and worthwhile end would inevitably blur her perceptions, and not for many years would she be able to discriminate between her respect and admiration for their courage, and her idealism about the war itself.

Preoccupied with bandaging classes and practising for the First Aid exam, along with her mother and other Buxton ladies, Vera had given little thought to the result of her Oxford Senior. Indeed her hopes of going to Oxford had receded slightly during these stirring days, and at one point she seems to have accepted quite philosophically that in wartime the strain on the family finances might be too great to send both her and Edward to university. But when on 27 August she heard at last that she had reached the required standard in the Oxford Senior, it was a bitter blow to be immediately informed by her father, 'fulminating furiously against the Government, the Germans, the financial situation at the mills', that it was now out of the question that she should go. Edward spoke up in her support and announced that in that case he would not go either, and even her mother agreed that her father's behaviour had been 'abominable'. As usual, though, Mr Brittain's anger quickly showed signs of abating and, confident of the outcome, Vera wrote that same day to Roland Leighton to tell him that he could expect to see something of her at Oxford in October.

A few days earlier she had received a letter from Roland recounting his frustrated attempts to join the army. Every bit as keen to volunteer as Edward – and 'engaged in cultivating a moustache' to improve his chances of being accepted – he had so far failed to win a commission in the artillery, infantry or Army Service Corps on account of his poor eyesight. In a further letter of 28 August he congratulated Vera on her exam success. He was glad, 'so very glad', and admitted that it was more than likely that October would find him also in Oxford, willing to run the gauntlet of Somerville's chaperonage system in order to see her.

She was delighted by the news partly because she considered that his intellect would have been wasted in the army, but still more so because she longed for the opportunity of three years at Oxford to get to know him better. In spite of all the obstacles thrown in their paths, she fondly imagined that 'our destinies have been shaped in such a way as to bring us ... to Oxford together. It is as though chords begin to sound faintly which have never even vibrated before'.

But it was not to be. Determined to serve his country and desperately concerned that he should not be found wanting, Roland continued exhaustively to pursue what military connections he could. For a short time that September he acted as Lowestoft's Assistant Recruitment Officer. Then at the beginning of October, aided by a medical certificate of fitness from a family doctor, which made no mention of his short-sightedness, Roland at last succeeded in enlisting as a second lieutenant in the 4th Norfolks.

His commission had not been confirmed when he wrote to Vera to tell her the news, but his letter nevertheless filled her 'with a kind of inexplicable mute despair'. He did not intend to go to Oxford for the present, he told her, and was not certain that he would go at all. It was not a decision he could regret, however, 'except for the incidental pleasure' of meeting her there. '... I don't think in the circumstances I could easily bring myself to endure a secluded life of scholastic vegetation. It would seem a somewhat cowardly shirking of my obvious duty.'

From a modern viewpoint, Roland Leighton seems to epitomize the spirit of the schoolboy volunteers of the generation of 1914. Trained at Uppingham to worship the twin gods of Patriotism and Duty, he responded eagerly to the excitement of war. He continued in the second part of his letter: 'I feel ... that I am meant to take some active part in this war. It is to me a very fascinating thing – something, if often horrible, yet very ennobling and very beautiful, something whose elemental reality raises it above the reach of all cold theorizing. You will call me a militarist. You may be right.'

Vera's reply reflects her ambivalent attitude. While unable to endorse fully the claims of war, she can at the same time echo Roland's sensuous rhetoric about its glamour:

> I don't know whether your feelings about war are those of a militarist of not; I always call myself a non-militarist, yet the raging of these elemental forces fascinates me, horribly but powerfully, as it does you. I find beauty in it too;

certainly war seems to bring out all that is noble in human nature, but against that you can say that it brings out all the barbarous too. But whether it is noble or barbarous I am quite sure that had I been a boy, I should have gone off to take part in it long ago; indeed I have wasted many moments regretting that I am a girl. Women get all the dreariness of war, and none of its exhilaration.

Roland's decision succeeded in dampening much of Vera's enthusiasm for the coming term. 'It is strange how what we both so worked for should now seem worth so little', she wrote a little mournfully. Almost as disheartening was the fact that Edward too had decided to postpone indefinitely his going up to New College. Arthur Brittain had renounced his opposition to his volunteering and Edward had appeared before the OTC nomination committee. It could only be a matter of time before he was commissioned.

'It will be strange', Roland admitted to Vera on 7 October, as he prepared to pack up and migrate with his battalion to Norwich, 'to think that the day after tomorrow you will be at Oxford and beginning a new life – and alone.'

III

The exigencies of wartime had already begun to transform Oxford when Vera started her undergraduate career at Somerville on 9 October 1914. That autumn the incessant sound of bugles competed with Oxford's bells. Half the men had gone from their colleges. In their place were companies of soldiers, young cadets, and subalterns in training who occupied their lodgings and took over the University Parks for their drill. Belgian, French, and Serbian refugees were much in evidence, and the Town Hall and Examination Schools had been swiftly converted into hospitals.

In spite of these external reminders, Vera maintained a sense of detachment from the war. There was as yet no friend or close relative at the front for her to worry about, and studying hard that first term she had little time to follow press reports of the Fall of Antwerp or events on the Ypres Salient. The excitement of new experience pushed the war further into the background. Against her expectations she quickly overcame her disappointment at Roland and Edward's absence, and to her own astonishment immersed herself in college life. 'I live in an atmosphere of exhilaration', she wrote after less than a week, 'half delightful, half disturbing, wholly exciting.'

Somerville's assortment of buildings symbolized its transition from hall to college (as it began to call itself in 1894), and its slow progress towards full recognition by the university. Walton Manor, a large grey house standing in three acres of garden and fields yellow with buttercups, had provided a hall of residence for seven of the original twelve women students when Somerville first opened its doors in October 1879. Gradually more distinctively collegiate buildings had been erected around this nucleus. The West building, comprising further residential accommodation, had been completed by 1895, and a library opened nine years later. The urgent requirement for a hall large enough to hold the entire college (whose numbers had risen rapidly to 104 by 1914) was answered when Somerville's crowning glory, the Maitland Hall, was proudly unveiled in October 1913. It served as the scene for one Commemoration Dance a few months before the outbreak of war. By the following summer it had been taken over as a military hospital reserved for officers.

Architecturally, Somerville was beginning to exist on a par with the men's colleges. Academically, it equalled and frequently surpassed the record of its male equivalents. Yet Somerville and the four other women's societies continued to be denied admission to degrees. As far back as 1884 a university statute which opened to women the examinations of Honour Moderations and Finals in Mathematics, Natural Sciences, and Modern History had effectively been the first public acknowledgement of the presence of women within the university. But discrimination against female students had persisted. Officially women could attend public lectures, but only if closely chaperoned. In 1896 a proposal before the University Congregation to award women degrees was decisively rejected. More than a decade was to pass before the status of women at Oxford became once again a matter for serious debate. In Joanna Richardson's phrase, women were tolerated but discounted until 1907 when the university installed its new Chancellor, Lord Curzon. A fervent believer in reform, Curzon proposed that women should be offered the titular degree without the constitutional privileges. The Hebdomadal Council agreed with him in principle, and in 1909 passed a resolution in favour of an early discussion on the subject. By 1914 even the more reactionary members of the university had come to realize that the day for awarding women full intellectual recognition could not long be postponed.

When, in 1920, the first batch of women MAs and BAs finally received their degrees to loud applause in the Sheldonian, it was to a large extent the result of the foresight and determination of one woman, Emily Penrose, Principal of Somerville since 1907. The first woman to reach the standard of a First in Greats, Miss Penrose had previously been Principal of both Bedford and Royal Holloway Colleges, London, where she had developed her exceptional gifts for administration and finance. She had quickly grasped that the strongest argument in favour of degrees for women would be the number of women qualified to receive them, and had therefore refused to accept students who were unwilling to take the full degree course. It came as an unwelcome shock to Vera to discover on her first day that in order to take the degree course in English she would have to sit Responsions Greek that December, and then Pass Moderations, which comprised papers in mathematics as well as Classics, the following June. This meant that she would not begin to study English literature until her second year and, worse, that she would have to get her Greek up from next to nothing to Responsions standard in under two months. However, with Roland's example of academic application and stamina to live up to, she soon accustomed herself to the idea and looked forward to the challenge.

Vera's arrival at Oxford thus coincided with a crucial period in the history of the women's colleges. With the question of degrees pending it was all the more essential that the woman student should avoid drawing attention to herself. 'Fearful of losing the battle at the last fence', the authorities demanded that she should keep her head down, work hard, and above all maintain the highest standards of propriety and social decorum. Chaperonage at lectures had been abolished, but 'Chap' rules continued to be applied at social functions until long after the argument over degrees had been won. 'Mixed parties' were scrupulously regulated, and even the male undergraduates who attended the May Morning celebrations at Magdalen Tower were required to bring a chaperon if they wished a woman to accompany them. At one of the first lectures Vera attended, a school acquaintance of Edward's insisted on speaking to her, 'in spite of my informing him that I must be treated as if I were in quarantine'. Stricter rules applied within Somerville's own walls where only male relatives were permitted. In the convent-like atmosphere a handsome brother's visit to his sister could create a flurry of excitement among the other girls, as Vera discovered when Edward called to see her, shortly before being gazetted to the 10th Sherwood Foresters. He was staying in Oxford for a few weeks that November to begin his OTC training under New College's auspices. 'He came up yesterday morning to tell me about it', Vera wrote to her mother on 18 November, 'looking so nice in his officer's uniform, and he created great interest in the minds of those working at their windows by walking up and down with me in the garden; the appearance of anyone in khaki at Somerville is a great source of attraction.'

Vera's letters to her mother revel in her new life. One drawback for someone raised on the comforts of Buxton and St Monica's was Somerville's spartan living conditions. The lack of hot baths, the freezing rooms and draughty corridors, the peeling yellow and brown paintwork, and the poor cooking (the perpetual smell of burnt fat seemed to hang in the air), provided a depressing contrast to the domestic regimes presided over by her mother and Miss Bervon. But Vera's own room in the Maitland building was a light and sunny one, overlooking the garden, and with Mrs Brittain's help she quickly set about making it her own. Its appearance was much improved by the arrival of her piano from home. She covered her cushions in a 'pattern of black stuff' sent by her mother which 'everyone admires', and she planned matching black curtains lined with rose-pink silk. Confined to bed for a day with a cold, she was pleased to have the opportunity to show off her 'attractive little eiderdown' to visitors which, she told her mother, 'is considered very smart'.

The grind for exams did not prevent Vera from becoming an enthusiastic participant that year in college and university activities. She joined the Oxford Society for Women's Suffrage as 'a small side of the enormous question of Feminism'; she contributed a review of the second volume of Compton Mackenzie's *Sinister Street*, with its romantic evocation of a serener Edwardian Oxford, to a competition in *The Fritillary*, the inter-collegiate women's magazine; she played lacrosse and tennis, and acted in college theatricals (the following term her performance as Victoria, a precocious ten-year-old, in Stanley Houghton's one-act comedy, *The Dear Departed*, practically brought the house down); and she joined the Bach Choir. Competition among Somervillians for a place in the choir was fierce – 'you have to pass a singing test before they will have you' – as it represented a link with the university proper.

A Hallowe'en party with chestnuts, stories, and strange incantations, and the inevitable cocoa evenings with their discussion 'on religion, genius, dons and Third Years', regularly kept Vera up into the early hours. Like most freshers she was relishing her first real taste of independence. In one letter home she attempted to communicate to her mother the thrill of a trip to the theatre to see Gilbert and Sullivan's *Iolanthe* 'on the cheap, which is half the joy', 'cutting' dinner and eating doughnuts and chocolate while waiting in the 'Early Doors' queue. It is difficult to imagine Edith Brittain being much amused.

Vera's reserve and her habit of holding forth 'in my customary dogmatic fashion' on subjects like religion (a sensitive topic in a non-denominational college) were an impediment to close relationships with the young women of her year. She consoled herself with the thought that she had come to college to work and to observe people for her writing, and that in order to do so she must remain to some extent apart. Rejoicing in the knowledge that she was considered the 'lion' of her year, she soon discovered that she had also acquired the reputation of being 'insufferably conceited, hard and cold'. College, she noted, 'thought me pretty and talked a good deal about my eyes, but wished I would not make my mouth sneer when I talked!' 'I wonder if I shall ever have the warmth under the hard crust aroused here', she wrote in her diary on 12 November. Five weeks into term she was able to record some progress in the Somerville convention of 'proposals', the ritual by which one girl announced her intention of calling another by her Christian name: she could now address Miss Wood as 'Katherine', and Miss Wadham as 'Dorothy'. She was also on friendly terms with a small group of first-years which included Una Ellis Fermor, her fellow English exhibitioner, later a distinguished Elizabethan scholar, Marjorie Barber, the daughter of a Congregationalist solicitor from Blackheath, Norah Hughes, a Winchester girl who had rebelled against the 'cathedral set' to go to university, and Vera's closest Somerville friend, a half-Belgian girl called Teresa Schenzinger. Vera, however, found Somerville's 'feminine atmosphere' hard to tolerate: '. . . strange how one can feel as I do about some women & be an ardent feminist still! . . . A feminine community is always appalling to anyone like me who gets on so much better in the society of men . . .'. Even in later years, Vera's feminism would be based on a desire to enter the world of men equally rather than on any great sense of identification with other women.

The idiosyncrasies of Somerville's dons afforded a rich fund of amusement for undergraduates. 'The Pen', 'The Darb', and 'The Lorie', affectionate shorthand for Emily Penrose, Helen Darbishire, and Hilda Lorimer, were the central figures of Vera's first year. With the Principal, Miss Penrose, Vera was never to feel at ease. Strikingly tall and spare in build ('I like her *Bones*', the artist De Laszlo remarked after painting her), Miss Penrose suffered from an awkward shyness which, as Vera Farnell, the Modern Languages tutor, commented, 'it took courage and determination to penetrate.' She was also equipped with a smile that came and went with startling suddenness, a razor-sharp mind, and the kind of family back-ground (she was related to the Arnold and Huxley families) that Vera always held in exaggerated awe. Miss Darbishire, the English tutor and a Milton scholar, was a gentler, outwardly more sympathetic personality, who inhabited a remote and gracious world 'from which she emerged with something of an effort.' Evidently so, as she was once encountered in a tutorial, wearing a red velvet gown with a fur ruff.

Miss Lorimer, an authority on Homeric archaeology, was the source of the greatest fascination for Vera, so much so that she planned one day to portray this 'indomitable little figure' with her frosty blue eyes, harsh Scottish accent and acerbic manner, in a novel. What set her apart from the other tutors was the breadth of her interests: not only Classics, but social service, poetry, plants and birds ('The Lorie Bird' was a common sight on her Sunday ornithological expeditions, cycling around Oxford with her binoculars). A 'past mistress of scorn', Miss Lorimer would sit in tutorials, making cutting remarks about Vera's Greek while calmly continuing with her 'everlasting knitting'. Her contempt led Vera to fear that she might be one of Miss Lorimer's yearly dislikes, which drove her on to prove herself. At the end of term, Mr May, her Greek coach, gave Vera the best report he had ever given any girl, and the transformation in Miss Lorimer's attitude was at once apparent. 'From thinking me lazy and somewhat ineffectual, I believe she really considers me worth something now . . .'.

While she had succeeded to a great extent in shutting out world events, Roland's letters, which had begun to arrive quite regularly from Norwich, served to remind Vera that the war which so many had prophesied would be over by Christmas was now unlikely to be so shortlived. There was still little chance, owing to his short sight, that he would get a frontline posting, but his battalion, though deficient in uniforms and rifles, was now up to full strength. Having rejected the option of 'scholastic vegetation' in wartime, Roland had spent two months in the unintellectual atmosphere of army life, suffering from mental starvation. He longed for the opportunity for 'half-an-hour's talk with someone with some personality and temperament'. Vera responded to his letters by playing down the excitement of Oxford. She was grateful to be in an environment where she was expected to work, rather than being thought a fool for wanting to do it; but she viewed her new life as only a temporary seclusion in an ivory tower.

Elsewhere there are indications that Vera was already finding it more difficult to shrug off the war. 'A splendid sermon at the University Church from the Bishop of Oxford', she told her mother on 29 November, had helped to stop her 'feeling useless and unnecessary to the present scheme of things.'

> He spoke especially to students . . . and said that the part of those who could not fight or take an active part in the war was to keep up as high as possible England's standard of intellectual and moral life so that those defending her might feel she was worth fighting for. He said that if one assumes we're fighting for righteous and honourable ideals abroad it was our duty to see that we did not let those ideals slip at home.

On 9 December Vera sat Responsions and the next day left Oxford for the vacation. Christmas was a muted affair, lightened for Vera by the news that she had passed her exam, but overshadowed by the fact that Edward, who had returned home from camp at Frensham for the holiday, expected to be sent out to France in the spring.

The last days of the old year brought Vera a meeting with Roland Leighton which was to move their friendship steps closer to love. In writing to thank the 'sinfully extravagant' Roland for his gifts of books and 'a beautifully French hand-painted card', Vera had mentioned that she would be in London for a few days at the end of the month, staying with her grandmother, old Mrs Bervon, at her house in Purley. Coincidentally Roland planned to be in London too, lodging with his mother in rooms at Titchfield Terrace, just off Regent's Park. Before long they had arranged to see each other. On 30 December, the day after her twenty-first birthday, Vera and Edward travelled to Charing Cross and, under the watchful eye of Aunt Belle, lunched with Roland at the Comedy Restaurant.

Five months had elapsed since they had last met, yet despite the letters they had exchanged in the interval, Vera and Roland remained tongue-tied throughout lunch. When the conversation warmed up, Roland invited Vera, and her aunt as chaperon, to see Herbert Tree's adaptation of *David Copperfield* at His Majesty's Theatre the following evening, and handed Vera a note from his mother, pressing her to come to tea the next afternoon. At dusk Roland and Vera lingered behind Edward and Aunt Belle as they walked back to the station along a darkened Regent's Street, the lights dimmed for fear of Zeppelin raids.

'In the vestibule of the Criterion', Marie Leighton wrote later, 'I saw someone very small, very slight, very delicate-faced and yet very resolute . . . Not one of us breathed a word as to what we had really come there for – namely to examine each other . . .'. It was a definite meeting of opposites, the intensely cerebral Vera ('She's quite human after all', exclaimed Mrs Leighton, 'I thought she might be very academic and learned'), whose shy appearance belied the forcefulness of her personality, with the equally strong-willed but flamboyant romantic novelist, even now dressed in a long black velvet coat and low-cut blouse, both trimmed with fur, and adorned by a hat decked out in feathers. For Mrs Leighton, accompanied by her daughter Clare, 'a sixteen-year-old flapper', it was also her first encounter with the girl whose very existence threatened to supplant her from her treasured first place in her son's affections. But if, as Clare Leighton maintained, she would grow to resent Vera 'for intruding upon Roland' there was no sign of it that afternoon. On the contrary, the two women quickly established an easy rapport, and Mrs Leighton told Roland afterwards that she had found Vera utterly charming. Vera, alternately longing for and dreading the meeting, and without the support of Edward who had left the previous evening to rejoin his regiment, had at first been nervous. 'But when I saw her brown eyes, so like Roland's, but with a merry twinkle which his promise but have not yet acquired, I knew I should love her, and not be in the least afraid of her.' The verdict, recounted Mrs Leighton, was 'an all-round satisfactory one'.

With Aunt Belle still discreetly in tow, Vera and Roland dined at the Florence Restaurant before going on to the theatre. Roland had presented Vera with some pink roses whose sweet scent, she was to recall years afterwards, seemed to bestow a benediction on the evening. Only his eyes betrayed any hint of his emotions and at one point during dinner Vera thought she saw him giving her a look which 'was nearer admiration than anything I have ever seen from him before'. Although there had been no declarations of love, and words which only skirted around the subject of their relationship, the experience of the past two days had confirmed 'that the feelings which, ever since I had known him I had thought might quite possibly arise between us, were no longer a dream but a reality'.

The reality, though, was also that Roland might be exposed to mortal danger in the months to come. He had warned that he intended to go on trying to transfer to a frontline regiment. He had no wish to die but admitted that if he had to, he would wish to be killed in action. 'I know you're the kind of person who would risk your life recklessly', Vera told Roland that evening.

'I was talking to someone a short time ago & I said I thought you were the kind who believes in the "one glorious hour of crowded life" theory; is it true?' He answered 'Yes I think it is', & I said 'I know you'll offer to ride with dispatches in front of blazing fire or something of that sort.' He thought he probably would.

At Charing Cross again that night as he saw Vera and her aunt on to their train they shook hands, and she made him promise that he would come to see her to say goodbye before going to the front. They lapsed into an uncomfortable silence, and as the train moved he took her hand in a long, warm grip.

'I am very fond of her, and I am afraid she is getting very fond of me too', Roland confided to Victor Richardson. In the letter which followed Vera back to Buxton, Roland thanked her 'very very much' for their two days together, adding that 'I think I shall always remember them in their wonderful incompleteness and unreality.' If she read between the lines she could find some more revealing expression of the emotions which had eluded him when they had been together. He had seen the New Year in, standing by the fountain in Piccadilly Circus: 'When twelve o'clock struck there was only a little shudder among the crowd and a distant muffled cheer and then everyone seemed to melt away again, leaving me standing there with tears in my eyes and feeling absolutely wretched.'

For Vera the passing of 1914 was marked by the momentous realization that she had fallen in love with Roland Leighton. 'I felt on Thursday evening', she told him on her return to Buxton, 'that I was just beginning – that you were allowing me to begin – to know the real you a little.' Her ambition and desire for independence were suddenly eclipsed by her feelings for him and by the dream that she might one day be the mother of his child. 'Beside these newly-born dreams', she rhapsodized in her diary, '. . . my old dreams and aspirations grew pale, as would the moon's cold splendour beside the passionate flames of the sun.'

A fortnight later they met again when, at Roland's instigation, Vera colluded in a minor deception. Constrained by convention, their opportunities for being alone had so far been pathetically few. Taking advantage of Vera's journey back to Somerville for the new term, Roland, now stationed at Peterborough, wrote suggesting that they meet in Leicester where she could change trains en route to Oxford. Inventing some plausible excuse for not going by the usual route via Birmingham, which was accepted without suspicion by her parents, Vera met him on Leicester station. After lunch he insisted on accompanying her to Oxford. Their journey in an empty first-class carriage, with Vera undoubtedly uneasy about such an audacious breaking of the rules, was marked by long silences and a sense of 'profound unsatisfactoriness'. The spectre of the war hung menacingly over them, contributing an underlying seriousness to their conversation, and making difficult any discussion of the future. At last as Oxford came into view he took her gloved hand and kissed it. 'Taken by surprise I resisted a little but quite unavailingly in his strong grip, and after all I did not really want to resist.'

At Somerville she was warmly congratulated by Miss Penrose on an outstanding performance in Responsions, and started classes with Miss Lorimer for Pass Mods. The events of the vacation made the resumption of college life seem at first rather dismal by comparison. But she soon recovered some of her exuberance of the previous term. Letters from Roland arrived more frequently now, and throughout January and February she followed with quiet dread his renewed attempts to be sent to the front. 'I would give anything to be allowed to go to France', he reiterated on 31 January from Lowestoft where he was preoccupied with drilling his platoon in abandoned schools, and staging 'sham fights' along with his corporal, the future novelist, R.H. Mottram, author of the *Spanish Farm* trilogy. 'Doesn't Lyndall say somewhere that you can get anything you want if only you want it hard enough? I feel so ashamed of myself for still being one of the "gentlemen in England now abed".'

In the last week of term Vera fell ill with a bad attack of flu and became so weak that she had to be collected by her mother, and taken home three days before term ended. Recovering in bed a week later she opened a letter from Roland which had been forwarded from Somerville, only to read the words: 'I think I have succeeded at last . . . If all goes well, I stand a good chance of getting out to the front – either straight to Belgium or else via the Dardanelles – in about ten days time.' He had manoeuvred a transfer to the 7th Worcestershire Regiment, but he was staying in London for his final leave, in order to say goodbye. Panicking that she might already have missed him – his letter had taken three days to reach Buxton – she was relieved when he telephoned that evening. In the confusion of conflicting arrangements Arthur and Edith Brittain, more than a little bemused by all the fuss, finally proposed that Roland be invited to spend the night at Melrose.

Alone with Roland in the morning-room, and later on a long walk across the moors in a fierce snow storm, Vera struggled to keep her tears in check and yet characteristically could not refrain from facing him directly with the consequences of his actions. She sometimes wished, she told him, that she had never met him and that he had not come to take away her impersonal attitude towards the war. But almost as soon as she said this she realized that she could not mean it. The war

seemed, I said, to have come just in time to make it possible that I should live ever after under the shadow of it, with all my future darkened by that Shadow of Death which I must always think of now as hovering close behind the footsteps of him & of Edward. 'Ah don't say that', he said. 'Don't say it will all be spoilt; when we return, things may be just the same.' '*If* you return,' I could not help saying. ' "When," not "If",' he insisted, but I said I did not imagine for a moment he was going out without realising fully all that it might mean. He answered very gravely that he had thought many times of what the issue might be, yet he had a settled conviction that he was coming back – not quite whole perhaps, but he hoped I should not like him less if he was, say, minus an arm.

After dinner as they sat before the fire in the drawing-room, their renewed discussions about the possibility of a Hereafter seemed to take on a terrible urgency. Their fragmented conversation touched upon marriage. As the fire slowly died he took her hand and kissed it 'as he did in the train before – but this time there was no glove upon it.'

It had all happened so quickly. They had met on no more than five occasions, but the war had dramatically accelerated the development of their relationship. This was first love – for both of them – but a first love bitterly intensified by danger and the threat of loss. In the months ahead it would be through their letters, frank, articulate, and sensitive, that their knowledge of one another would grow; so much so, that when they met again they would find it difficult to equate the images created by their words with the tangible reality. For Vera, it would be as if she had invested Roland with something of the 'intangibility' of 'the things of my imagination'.

Stunned and sick at heart as she returned home from the station after seeing Roland off on the morning of 19 March, Vera had a premonition that her life was never going to be the same again. And in a sense she was right. The shadows were closing in.

IV

I had another violent fit of desperation this morning. I suppose I must get used to them, but they alarm me a little & make me wonder what I may do if Roland dies. At present my one desire in life is to see him again. I think of how little there is of any tendency for the war to end, of how he is in the trenches day in & day out . . . of the long long weary months ahead, & wonder how I shall ever bear them . . .

So runs Vera's diary entry for 19 April 1915, three weeks after Roland had gone to the front. The wearing suspense of waiting for news of him and the anxious scanning of casualty lists had already become an accustomed way of life, and not even the arrival of his letters, usually in distinctive green army envelopes, could silence her anguished speculation for long. In the five or six days that his letters took to reach her (as opposed to the quicker two-day service from England to France) she sometimes imagined that there had been time for him to be killed a hundred times over, and it particularly unnerved her to think that he might never read the letter she sent him in reply. '. . . You know that I always write as often as I can', he wrote one afternoon that May after receiving 'such a sad, disappointed' letter from her, 'and let everyone else except Mother wait'. Vera had quickly taken to writing 'love-letters' of her own to his mother. It was to Mrs Leighton, rather than her own mother, that she turned most frequently for support, consoled by the older woman's 'strong unconquerable spirit'.

In moments of despair she searched feverishly for some semblance of a philosophy to cling to. One quotation from their beloved *Story of an African Farm* which emphasized endurance and offered a kind of masochistic relief, was to become her credo in the dark years ahead: 'The lifting up of the hands brings no salvation; redemption is from within, and neither from God nor man: it is wrought out by the soul itself, with suffering and through time.'

Roland's last letter before his departure, signed with 'Love and Hope' and enclosing the gift of an amethyst brooch (Vera had given him a fountain pen, 'an appropriate gift from one would be scribbler to another'), had confidently assured her that his return would always be a question of ' "when" and not "if" '. Late on the night of 31 March his battalion had made a calm crossing from Folkestone to Boulogne, where they had spent most of the next day in a rest camp, before travelling on by rail and a five-mile march to billets in a village three miles south of Béthune. In his letters Roland was forced to be circumspect as to his exact whereabouts; but the battalion diary of the 7th Worcesters reveals his movements. For most of April the battalion held a portion of the line, a few miles from the Franco-Belgian border, in Ploegsteert Wood, 'a vast wood of tall straight trees', known colloquially among British troops as Plug Street Wood. At the end of the month they moved to more conventional trenches, little more than a mile further south at Le Touquet. Here they remained until the middle of June when they began the move southwards into the Somme country.

On 11 April, as he prepared to take his platoon for their first forty-eight-hour stint in the trenches at seven o'clock that evening, Roland wrote to Vera from a billet at Armentières. 'The trenches run right into town on one side', he explained, 'and I could hear the rifle fire last night as I lay in bed'. Almost as an afterthought he added, 'I wonder if I shall be afraid when I first get under fire.'

From the start Vera begged him that she should not be spared any of the details of trench life, no matter how gruesome. His first letters describe his surroundings and daily routine with an almost military precision. The whole place, he related, was like a small town, 'honeycombed' with passages and dug-outs. 'These have some most amusing names written up over them, e.g., Westminster Bridge, The Bridge of Size and Tiers, Ludgate Hill,

Marble Arch, Dean's Yard, Southend Pier, the Junior Carleton . . .'. Every four days the battalion was relieved by the 8th Worcesters to enjoy a much-needed four days' rest in billets a few miles behind the lines. There was little opportunity while in the line for sleeping, washing or shaving. The removal of any article of clothing or footwear was forbidden, and so mud was scraped from the boots with a bayonet, and each foot tied up in a sack before climbing, boots and all, into the sleeping-bag. 'I shall be glad of the rest, as it has been a tiring four days here', Roland told Vera at one point during the early weeks. 'I was up nearly all last night mending the barbed wire entanglements in front of our trenches, and this morning can hardly keep my eyes open.'

Ploegsteert Wood, the scene of fierce fighting the previous November when the British had wrested it from German control, was still exposed to regular shell and rifle fire from the German lines, seventy to 180 yards away. Stray bullets from snipers, Roland informed Vera, were always flying overhead, especially at night, 'but no one minds them'. In the daytime you remained relatively safe as long as you kept your head beneath the parapet. It was at dusk, when the battalion generally moved in and out of the trenches, that the danger intensified, and on his first night in, a bullet had sailed uncomfortably close to Roland's head. More to be feared, though, was bombardment by heavy shell fire which, he admitted, was 'a most nerve-wracking job'. Writing to Vera on 3 May Roland reported that his trench had been the recipient of thirty-eight 3.5 shells only that morning which had fallen within thirty or forty yards of his platoon, but which had miraculously failed to hit anyone. 'When the shell hits the ground it makes a circular depression like a pudding basin about a yard and a half across by 18 inches deep . . . The explosion blows a cloud of earth and splinters of shell into the air, so that when they fire a salvo (all four guns together) the effect is rather terrifying and you wonder if the next one will come a yard or two nearer and burst right in the trench on top of you.' After two months of listening to the 'crooning whistle' of shells passing overhead – the sequence of boom, scream and crash as they exploded – he pronounced himself 'quite expert' in the nuances of shell sounds.

Keeping to his promise, he attempted to relay the inescapable sights of death and the dying. The discovery of the body of a British soldier which had lain hidden in the undergrowth since the early part of the war produced this particularly grisly description: 'The ground was slightly marshy and the body had sunk down into it so that only the toes of his boots stuck up above the soil. His cap and equipment were just by the side, half-buried and rotting away . . . You do not mind my telling you these gruesome things do you? . . . It is of such things that my new life is made.' When the first of his men was killed he wrote of finding him 'lying very still at the bottom of the trench with a tiny stream of red trickling down his cheek on to his coat', but then thought himself cruel for bringing the horrors of war closer to her, and added, 'At least, try not to remember: as I do.'

The lighter side of army life was also represented. In billets at Pont de Nieppe at the end of May, Roland arranged a concert for his company. 'You would have been amused to see me', he told Vera, '. . . singing a duet with a French girl to the strenuous accompaniment of a somewhat heavy-handed corporal at the piano.'

Ever the fastidious stylist, in his letters to Vera Roland juxtaposed pastoral scenes with elements of the destructive force of war, to strikingly ironic effect. 'I am sitting . . . writing this', he wrote on 20 April from a bench just outside his dug-out, 'while the sun shines on the paper and a bee is humming round and round the bed of primroses in front of me. War and primroses! At the moment it does not seem as if there could be such a thing as war.' Later in the same letter he remarks that 'Everything is in such grim contrast here', and nowhere is the contrast more starkly presented than in the following passage written a month later:

> I am writing this in the officers' hut [on a farm in the reserve line] . . . It is rather more luxurious than might be expected and actually has four wooden chairs and two small tables and an old shell-case full of apple-blossom on one of them! There is an apple-tree that I can see from the window now, standing in the middle of a field yellow with buttercups. It is raining slightly and for the moment is very still. You could walk across the field and think you are in England, except that English fields are not pitted here and there with shell holes and the trees haven't usually got telephone wires looped from one to another in unexpected places.

Of course the most bitter irony was that Roland, who had had such dreams of accomplishing some heroic feat in action, should do little more than spend day after day sitting in a ditch. After a week in the trenches he confessed that there was nothing 'glorious' in trench warfare. 'It is all a waiting and a waiting and a taking of petty advantages – and those who can wait longest win.' A month later he writes with tired resignation that he has still to see any 'real fighting'. He merely takes the occasional shot 'at a more or less docile and usually invisible enemy who is content to do the same . . .'. Only once is he driven to expressing anger when he reads reports of anti-German rioting in London, 'just because the *Lusitania* goes down and something a little nearer than Flanders comes home to them. Why not all this before?' These are just the first discordant notes in a mounting scale of disillusionment.

Vera's constant fear was that the experience of the horrors of the trenches would lead to some dramatic transformation in the Roland she loved. As her awareness of her love for him deepened with each communication from the front, so too did her consciousness of how the nearness of death seemed to break down the 'reserves and conventions' which had previously inhibited them. 'I never thought I should ever say to anyone the sort of things I write to you', she confessed to Roland. A letter from him signed 'with much love' had led her to offer him 'as much love as you wish' in return. She always let him set the note of their correspondence and was quite ready to echo it if it was a deep one. When, in one letter, he told her that he had just been kissing her photograph, the news brought tears stinging to her eyes. Was she then to envy the photograph, she asked him. 'When all is finished and I am with her again', he replied, 'the original shall not envy the photograph. The barrier which she seems to have found was not of reserve but rather of reverence.'

Her response to the war, now so vividly depicted in Roland's letters, continued to be ambivalent. There remains a tension between her horror at the waste of life and her own magnetic attraction to the glamour of war and need to go on believing that all the suffering is for some worthwhile purpose. Roland's first letter from France fills her with 'a queer exultation' and she writes in her diary, 'If only I could share these experiences with him I should glory in them'. Yet a few sentences later in the same entry, she is once again commenting on 'this reckless waste of life' in connection with the fighting at Neuve Chapelle, which the newspaper dispatches portray as a victory, but which she realizes was nothing less than an 'awful disaster'. When Roland wrote to her that war after all is 'for nothing – for an empty name, for an ideal perhaps . . .', he received a heartfelt reply:

> The terrible things you mention & describe fill me, when the first horror is over, with a sort of infinite pity I have never felt before. I don't know whether it is you or sorrow that has aroused this softer feeling – perhaps both . . . Is it really all for nothing . . . ? Last time I saw you it was I who said that and you who denied it. Was I really right, & will the issue really not be worth one of the lives that have been sacrificed for it?

However, almost at once this perception clouds over, and she admits in her diary, 'I am not sure that I agree myself in all I said to him.'

By the time she wrote those words, Vera had decided to volunteer as a nurse. 'Suffering myself', she told Roland, 'makes me want nothing so much as to do all I can to alleviate the sufferings of other people'. Nursing was to be an act of solidarity with Roland and a means of countering the endless mental torture of speculation about his fate with mind-numbing physical chores. At first she merely intended to work at Buxton's Devonshire Hospital in the long vacation, but shortly after returning to Somerville in the last week of April, she began to consider applying for a year's leave to train as a Voluntary Aid nurse. Oxford and the intellectual life appeared increasingly an irrelevance, and the university was in a state of abeyance as its male population dwindled still further and the staple events of its summer calendar – Eights Week, cricket, and honorary degrees at Encaenia – were cancelled for the war's duration. Somerville itself had been subject to an 'emergency migration' to Oriel College. A deputation from the War Office at the end of March had found the college buildings to be 'in every way suitable for the purposes of a Military Hospital', and students returning for the new term found that a move to the St Mary Hall Quadrangle of Oriel had already taken place (the *Oxford Magazine* remarked with some mirth that Dean Burgon, the Oriel Fellow who had been a ferocious opponent of women's education, 'must be turning in his grave'). About half the undergraduates were accommodated here; the others were distributed among five 'outhouses'. Reporting to Roland the order to evacuate Somerville as 'the Principal's official communiqué' – her letters to him were now sometimes peppered with military discourse – Vera wrote that 'I am to be – I had almost said "billeted" – in rooms at a place called Micklem Hall'. An oak-beamed house, parts of which dated back to medieval times, Micklem Hall was situated just off St Aldate's. Years later in her short history of Somerville, Vera Farnell commented on the eight lucky students who were installed in the grandeur of the Hall. Vera thought otherwise. She found her room dark and dingy and alive with black beetles and cockroaches, but at least, in a very small way, it brought her closer to the conditions of discomfort in which Roland existed. She was 'joyful to be told that the sacrifice of one's comfort and convenience is of use'. She was also pleased to have escaped 'the chattering, pervasive femininity' which had quickly overtaken St Mary Hall, and to have the company of one of her set, Marjorie Barber, who was sharing her lodgings.

It sometimes seemed impossible to continue calmly working for Pass Mods when there was no certainty about the future. 'Horror piled on horror, until one feels that the world can scarcely go on any longer', Vera wrote on 7 May, after studying reports that the Germans had won back Hill 60, and being informed by Roland that he was within the sound of the guns at Ypres. Instead of doing her work, she told him, 'I sit dreaming over it, thinking of you among barbed-wire entanglements . . .'. Fortunately Miss Lorimer, whose favourite brother had been killed fighting in Persia in 1914, was supportive. Free from the insularity of many of the other dons, she viewed sympathetically Vera's plans to nurse, and was herself to spend part of the war as an orderly in a hospital at Salonika. They covered the syllabus for Pass Mods by confronting the war's campaigns through the struggle for Troy in the *Iliad*, and its sorrows by means of a passage on death in Plato's *Phaedo*. 'But for this extraordinary linking of the old story with the new', Vera wrote in the Fifties after Hilda Lorimer's death, 'I don't think I should ever have got through my exam . . .'.

Rupert Brooke's war sonnets, *1914*, published in book form for the first time that May, a few weeks after his death in the Aegean, also helped to strengthen her spirit and revive her patriotic idealism. Vera was introduced to them by the English tutor, Helen Darbishire, who read them aloud to her and Marjorie Barber one evening in her room at Micklem Hall. The effect on Vera of the sonnets' romantic heroism was to be deep and lasting, and her diary was soon studded with references and quotations from them. She found them 'all sad & moving, in spite of their spirit of courage and hope . . .', and thoughts of Brooke inevitably mingled with those of Roland, to whom she enclosed copies of four of the sonnets in her next letter.

A couple of days before the Brooke reading, Vera had broached the subject of going down for a year during an interview with Miss Penrose. Although she proposed notice only provisionally, her mind was already more or less made up. College, as she had told Roland two weeks earlier, seemed 'too soft a job' in wartime, 'even though one suffers more in a fairly inactive existence than in the other sort. I want physical endurance; I should welcome the most wearying kinds of bodily toil'. For this reason she had elected to nurse rather than apply for a Civil Service post, more obviously suited to her abilities. Her need to empathize with Roland made her choose the option which, if she ever succeeded in getting to a frontline military hospital, would bring her as close to the dangers of the conflict as it was possible for a woman to be. The Principal accepted her proposal without demur, and surprised Vera by her understanding. The mass exodus of students from Somerville to take up war work was not yet a threat. The large-scale involvement of women in the war effort was still a thing of the future, and there had been a limited response among Somervillians to the call of King and Country. The records of the Junior Common Room reveal that by Easter 1916 Vera was one of only five undergraduates absent for war work. Nine months later this trickle had been transformed into a steady flow, leading the President of the Board of Education, H.A.L. Fisher, to publish an open letter to Miss Penrose, emphasizing that the 'true path of duty' for women students was to remain in college.

On 15 June Somerville's Minutes of Council record the suspension of Vera's exhibition for a year. On 17 June Vera took Pass Mods. Ten days later she exchanged the black and white subfusc of the Oxford student for the starched blue and white uniform of an auxiliary VAD nurse, and started work at the Devonshire Hospital in Buxton.

The VAD scheme had been established in 1910 to provide aid to the sick and wounded in the event of a military invasion. At the outbreak of war, the Voluntary Aid Detachments had 74,000 members, and their numbers increased dramatically less than a year later when it was expanded to deal with the severe shortages in the supply of professional nurses created by the devastating effects of trench warfare. Unlike other war work for women – in the munitions factories or the Women's Army Auxiliary Corps, for instance – VADs were almost exclusively drawn from middle- and upper-class families. It was therefore an entirely respectable occupation for a girl of Vera's background, and Mrs Brittain had happily cooperated in making arrangements for her at the Devonshire. Vera's ultimate objective of a transfer to a military hospital would be less easy to achieve. Despite making enquiries of the British Red Cross Headquarters soon after she started nursing, it would be some months before she succeeded in enrolling as a VAD under contract.

Built as a riding school and stables for the sixth Duke at the end of the eighteenth century, the Devonshire had been converted into a convalescent hospital in the course of the nineteenth. Its outstanding feature, dominating Buxton's skyline, is the circular area of half an acre covered by the world's largest unsupported dome. Around this circumference footsore and resentful nurses, forbidden to cross its diameter, made continual journeys. Vera's day was a long and arduous one, beginning just before 8 am (Melrose was a few minutes walk away, hardly the half-mile route march she describes in *Testament of Youth*) and continuing until lunchtime, then recommencing at 5 pm and finishing at 9.15. Her duties comprised mainly menial tasks, bed-making, dusting, washing floors, preparing meals, but also some patient care, bandaging and treating basic wounds. Constantly seeking to emulate Roland's sacrifice, she managed to bring to the most monotonous of jobs a high level of commitment, and had to be admonished by the trained nurses not to overwork. 'Oh! I love the British Tommy!' she enthused in her diary after her first day on the wards. '. . . And when I look after any one of them, it is like nursing Roland by proxy.'

Her hours off between shifts allowed her to spend time with Edward when he came home on embarkation leave at the end of July. His war, which had begun at such a pitch of enthusiasm, had been filled with false hopes and disappointments. His last leaves, as Vera put it, were legion. He had been expecting to be posted to France with his battalion since the spring, and was about to be disappointed again. To a large degree he blamed his failure on the 'shittishness' of his 'damned C.O.' who had taken an inexplicable dislike to him. At the end of the war's first year, only Roland of Uppingham's 'Three Musketeers' had succeeded in getting to the front. Victor Richardson had almost died in February from cerebrospinal meningitis, and was still convalescing. 'The course of war seeking never did run smooth in the Triumvirate', wrote Roland, in one of a series of letters to Edward, urging him not to be discouraged.

'The earthly and obvious part of me longs to see and touch you and realize you as tangible', Vera had written to Roland at the end of July, awkwardly expressing her physical desire for him, awakened, so she later claimed, by the 'knowledge of masculine functioning' which nursing had given her. She can hardly have failed to notice the tone of cynical detachment which had begun to creep into his letters: 'And so perhaps the real may be disappointing after all, in daylight, face to face. It is often so with dreams: but it is better to have dreamt than not, especially I suppose when one may never perhaps get further than dreaming.' Hopes of seeing him again face to face had been dashed before, when his leave had been cancelled at the last moment. It was with some agitation therefore that she received a wire from Mrs Leighton on 18 August, telling her that 'Roland comes home today'.

v

Amid the bustle of St Pancras Station on 20 August they found one another and again shook hands. In his crumpled tunic and shabby Sam Browne belt, he looked older, thinner and preoccupied, and she noticed sadly that he had acquired 'the premature air of having knocked about the world'. After lunch they travelled by taxi to Camberwell where Vera was interviewed for a transfer to the 1st London General Hospital for that October. Later they embarked on a shopping expedition for Roland to buy mouth organs for his men. That evening they took the train to Buxton.

Despite months of intimate correspondence, their four days together were marked by a resumption of the stiff formality and embarrassed shyness of their previous meetings. Roland's natural reserve was accentuated by an acute sense of dislocation which the tedious sequence of tiring journeys across the country to visit their families can only have exacerbated. His return home from the trenches must indeed have seemed to him like coming to another planet, with precious little time to readjust before he went back again. For Vera too there was the necessary adjustment from the epistolary Roland to this flesh and blood approximation. She had written to him with feeling, and entirely without regard to any social niceties, of her desire to kiss and be kissed by him; but sitting opposite him in an empty railway carriage the thrill of being once more in his presence combined with 'a kind of dread', and she was unable to defy convention and take the physical initiative. Instead, on the return journey to London the next day to have lunch with Edward and Victor, before going to the Leightons at Lowestoft, she goaded him into kissing her, which he did 'with boyish shyness and awkwardness'.

His proposal of marriage as they travelled up to Buxton that first evening was similarly reticent, and something of an anticlimax. They had been debating the way in which society, even in wartime, insisted upon labelling a relationship like theirs. When he asked her whether it would help if they became engaged, and then more directly, 'Shall we be?' she prevaricated. She had never intended to marry until she could be financially independent of her husband; nor did she wish to be a hindrance to his career in any way should he survive the war. Furthermore, having been together on no more than seven occasions, she questioned the strength of his feelings for her. 'Do you really care for me like that?' she asked him. 'Yes, like that,' came his terse reply.

They reached Buxton with their tempers frayed from their constant sparring on the subject, and retired to bed with Roland still denied an answer. 'She says she can't make up her mind, the little fool,' Mrs Brittain was overheard to exclaim angrily the next morning. 'That's just like Vera. You never know where you are with her.' But later that day they decided to announce to Roland's mother, tongue-in-cheek, that they were engaged 'for three years or the duration of the War', a reservation which, Vera hastened to inform her diary, had no foundation in fact. There could be no question, though, of Vera observing convention to the extent of wearing an engagement ring. Her 'best self' recognized a ring as a 'symbol of the old inequality & therefore hateful to me'.

It was dusk when they arrived at Lowestoft to a darkened house. Heather Cliff's position, perched, as its name suggests, on the edge of a cliff at the far end of town, made it a conspicuous landmark for ships at sea, and a potential target for Zeppelin raids. The black-out regulations had to be strictly observed. Mrs Leighton's eccentric style of dress had led local people to suspect her of being a German spy, and some even claimed to have seen signals being flashed from the windows of the upper floors.

Out of the dimness emerged Marie Leighton, husband Robert and their two younger children, Clare and Evelyn. The family surveyed Vera with curiosity. Robert Leighton was especially taken with her and, in a gesture of gentlemanly courtesy, presented her with a rose at breakfast the next morning. But as always, everything centred on his wife. On two consecutive evenings she regaled Vera into the early hours with a stream of anecdotes about Roland's childhood, and talked freely of all that he meant to her, dabbing at her eyes with a handkerchief as she did so. Unaccustomed to such displays of emotion within her own family, Vera could only reproach herself for her own unmoved self-possession. The two women had built a friendship on their shared adoration of Roland; the problem of which of them was to have the greater stake in him had yet to arise. The subject of their conversation, meanwhile, hovered wearily in the background, or lolled childishly on his mother's bed, aloof from their discussion.

Vera's diary account of her stay reveals just how baffled and frustrated she was by this aloofness of Roland's. His detachment, and the expression-less mask he so often retreated behind that weekend, made her despair that she might ever now get the chance to understand him better. Their one moment of real intimacy occurred as they sat alone on the cliff path, the afternoon before their departure. Silently drawing her closer to him, he rested his head against her shoulder for a while, and then kissed her.

However, it was only as they were actually parting the next day that she became fully conscious for the first time of the depth of his feelings for her. As she had to report for duty to the Devonshire the next morning, and he was not returning to France until the end of the week, they had arranged that he should see her off at St Pancras. Once again a crowded station provided the backdrop for their farewell. He kissed her and then almost furtively wiped his eyes with his handkerchief. This display of emotion came as something of a revelation to Vera. 'I hadn't realized until then that this quiet & self-contained person was suffering so much.' As the train began to move she had time to kiss him 'which I had never done before', and murmur 'goodbye'. She stood by the door and watched him walk back through the crowd. 'But he never turned again. What I could see of his face was set and pale.'

Roland arrived back at the front on 27 August. 'The worst part of leave is having to go back again', he wrote to Edward as he rejoined his battalion at Coigneux. Vera meanwhile resumed her chores and her anxious waiting. At home her parents took the news of her engagement calmly, though her father greeted it with characteristic pessimism. Where in prewar days he might have enquired about Roland's financial prospects, he now simply retorted that the whole idea was ridiculous since Roland was clearly not going to come back. Thwarted in his desire to receive Roland's request for his daughter's hand in person, Arthur Brittain drew himself up to the full stature of paterfamilias, pronounced him 'a thoroughly honourable English gentleman of the highest honour and integrity', and welcomed him 'into our family circle'. It was left to Marie Leighton to put her finger on the nub of the matter. Assuring Edith Brittain that her son loved Vera 'with a love which is of the mind as well as of the heart, and which therefore ought to last', she concluded by commenting, 'Of course it is the war that has hurried the matter into definiteness'.

With the memory of Roland's physical presence fading fast, Vera's letters were filled with an insatiable longing for him:

> I thought when I saw you off in March that nothing in the world could make me feel more deeply than I did then. I was mistaken. I thought that if you had kissed me once and we had even that much of fulfilment, that I should be more resigned to whatever cruel thing fate had in store for me. There again I was wrong. Resignation is a thing of the devil; it can't come until one has abandoned the hope that hurts so. So now, because you have kissed me . . . I feel an insane impatience quite unlike anything I have known before.

She tried to recall 'his quiet smile . . . the occasional contemptuous curl of your lip . . . & the way my absurd hands can be covered over quite by yours.'

Having recovered his emotional poise, Roland injected a new note of tenderness into his letters to her. In the first two weeks of September, from billets at St Leger and then back in trenches at Hébuterne, he was writing almost every day. Like Vera he found it disorientating to return to the written word as the means of communication; but like her, too, he was aware that the written word was often a safer vessel for the expression of feelings than the spoken. 'I do wonder if I am like my letters in the same way in which you are like yours', he wrote on 3 September. 'We both seem less reserved in our letters, more like our real selves. In fact you pretend to understand my letters better than myself, don't you? Am I such a fearsome person in real life after all?' Continuing this theme a week later, he imagined her standing in the doorway to his dug-out and pondered what his reaction might be. 'I shall probably feel like a very shy child at a party; and just look at you; and you would probably look at me and through me with your "wet" eyes (I do like that adjective of Clare's); and there would be a hopeless inadequacy about it all. I'm sure that we should both forget that we had ever been so intimate in our letters.'

As preparations gathered pace for the joint British and French offensive that was to go down in history as the ill-fated Battle of Loos, Roland was confident that at long last the time of testing had arrived, and that the 7th Worcesters would play a full part in the fighting. He had only time to scribble a few lines on 23 September to inform Vera that the posts were about to be stopped, signalling that the storm collecting over the Western Front was about to break. It had already broken, with terrible casualties, when Vera in a hurried note summoned up the courage to speak plainly of her feelings. 'If this word should turn out to be a "Te moriturum saluto", perhaps it will brighten the dark moments a little to think how you have meant to Someone more than anything ever has or ever will.' Mentally she prepared herself for the worst.

In the event it proved a false alarm. After five suspenseful days she could breathe again. News came from Roland that his regiment had not after all been involved in the Loos attack. 'Don't say you hope the next alarm will be real', she begged him. One consequence of the renewed fighting and the heavy influx of wounded into London was that Vera's posting to the Camberwell Army Hospital looked imminent. 'I am expecting to be called to London any day now', she wrote on 1 October.

She had applied to Red Cross Headquarters back in June with her old schoolfriends, Stella Sharp and Cora Stoop, in the hope that the three of them might nurse in a hospital together. Cora had quickly cried off as soon as their plans had begun to take shape, pleading glandular illness as her excuse – though Vera suspected that it had rather more to do with her romance with an artist who had not enlisted – but Stella had remained keen. The intensity of their teenage friendship had long since evaporated. Reliable, passive, complacent Stella was sometimes to prove a source of irritation to Vera. But her sunny temperament more often had a cheering effect on the life they shared as VADs over the next eighteen months. On 18 October they reported to the 1st London General, Camberwell. The main hospital building, red-brick and gabled with an adjoining chapel, still stands today. Situated in Cormont Road, then one of the few dignified streets in an otherwise run-down district of south-east London, it had been commandeered from St Gabriel's College for Ladies, a teachers' training college. Opposite lies a park, known as Myatt's Fields, where, in a long white hut, Vera attended her first ward of sixty acute surgical cases.

The strict regimentation of the Army Hospital, one of four Territorial General Hospitals established in the capital, came as a shock after the good-humoured atmosphere of the Devonshire. The hours were longer, the work more strenuous, the mutilation of bodies more grotesque and sickening; added to which, the professional nurses, 'stern disciplinarians' who, to Vera's initial horror, appeared to have acquired a 'bright immunity from pity', viewed the assistance of the semi-trained VADs with suspicion, and denied the necessity of volunteers being 'taught things'. At this stage of the war, any drudgery seemed divine, every task had a 'sacred glamour' attached to it, but in 1934 she recalled this early experience of nursing with barely suppressed indignation:

In spite of the knowledge of wounds and surgical nursing which some of us who were reasonably quick on the uptake acquired quite rapidly, our duties during the first six months consisted of sweeping and dusting, cleaning lockers, making beds, washing convalescent patients, sorting laundry, preparing dressing trays, scrubbing mackintoshes, clearing up after dressings, and washing and sterilizing bowls and instruments. Even in a ward of 'light medicals', we were never left on day duty for so much as five minutes without a sister or staff nurse remaining in charge.

She quickly inured herself to the 'butchers' shop appearance' of the wards and the 'holes in various parts of people that you could put your fist into'. But the task of holding a head or a leg, or the stump of an amputated limb for the sister to dress while the man 'moans & tries to squirm about', was at times almost too distressing to bear. 'I am sometimes tempted to shut my eyes', she told Roland, 'but never let myself. Most of the patients can't bear to see their own wounds, & I don't wonder.' Through more than three years of nursing the seriously wounded, Vera never ceased to be moved by pity for the shattered bodies and minds of these 'poor, poor souls'; nor, unlike the trained Queen Alexandra nurses, did she ever successfully develop the ability to conceal her feelings.

Off duty there were no comfortable lodgings to return to. A tram ride or, if she was unlucky, a two-mile trek in all weathers through some of the seedier parts of Camberwell – where 'they throw everything out into the street, from dead cats to the remains of their suppers!' – took her back to the VAD hostel on Champion Hill, a grim building equipped with only one bathroom for its twenty inmates.

Deprived of comfort and exhausted by the end of each long day, Vera still managed to write to Roland as often as three or four times a week. 'I am sitting on my bed writing on a box lid; it's the only place', she told him from her chilly cubicle at the hostel on her first evening at Camberwell. 'I hope you are all right. Nothing else matters if you are only that.' His replies now were shorter and punctuated by long gaps. Towards the end of September he had ruefully conceded that 'you have written to me so many more times than I have written to you lately.' On 18 October he apologized for his cruelty in leaving her letterless for so long: 'You must be wondering what has become of me by now. Such a very long time without a murmur of any kind . . . I am getting absorbed in my little world here. It is the only way to stifle boredom and regrets.' Feeling shut out and ignored, Vera responded acerbically, warning him against becoming too immersed in his world out there. To this he made no reply. She continued to write, only to have each letter in the ensuing few weeks meet with the same silence. His family too appeared to have been forgotten by him. Eighteen years later, Vera would pose a dramatic question, as she searched for the explanation for Roland's silence. Did it lie in the growing estrangement of his feelings for her, or in the 'terrible barrier' of knowledge about the war which seemed bound, sooner or later, to come between the men at the front and those at home who loved them?

Part of the answer lies in Roland's remark about becoming absorbed in his own world as a means of survival. His short spell of leave had pained and distressed him, and his mother had recognized the serious effect which this brief glimpse of home might have on his state of mind. It is not difficult to understand how he might have decided that the only way to make his existence tolerable was to try to block out memories of everything and everyone left behind him in England, and to live only for the immediate present. This was a common enough response of those exposed to conditions on the Western Front, even for a matter of weeks. It was what one French combatant described as the *automatisme anesthésiant* of the trench experience, a withdrawal into oneself and a gradual numbing of emotion. Daily life was reduced to the level of a series of reflexes in which the instinct of self-preservation and, in the case of a conscientious officer like Roland, the welfare of one's men, overtook all other concerns. The individual, in André Bridoux's striking phrase, was crushed 'by the necessity of the hour'.

There is, however, something else which may account for Roland's growing detachment. The gulf between his first-hand knowledge of the war and the sentimentalized conception of it to which Vera and his family still clung, was deepening and becoming unbridgeable. The blind incomprehension of the civilian population to the barbarity of trench warfare has become almost a commonplace in the literature of the First World War. In Roland's and Vera's widely opposed responses to the war sonnets of Rupert Brooke, we find a graphic illustration of this division of soldier from civilian. She had sent him a copy of *1914* in August. He had read it immediately, straight through, and had commented that while he had once talked of 'the Beauty of War . . . it is only war in the abstract that is beautiful', manifestly a critical reference to Brooke's heroic abstractions. It was in a letter to Vera of 11 September, however, written a fortnight after his return to France, that he made his most powerful and damning rejection of Brooke-style rhetoric. Nowhere is Brooke's name mentioned, but the echoes of his third sonnet, quoted with bitter irony, make the intention plain. In the course of superintending the building of some dug-outs, Roland had chanced upon the remains of some dead Germans, 'the fleshless, blackened bones of simple men who poured out their red, sweet wine of youth . . .'.

> Let him who thinks that War is a glorious golden thing, who loves to roll forth stirring words of exhortation, invoking Honour and Praise and Valour and Love of country . . . let him look at a pile of sodden grey rags that cover half a skull and a shin bone and what might have been Its ribs, or at this skeleton lying on its side . . . and let him realize how grand & glorious a thing it is to have distilled all Youth and Joy and Life into a fetid heap of hideous putrescence. Who is there who has known & seen who can say that Victory is worth the death of even one of these?

Vera's dependence on precisely the kind of rhetoric Roland is attacking here severely limited the impact of his letter to her. Indeed, Samuel Hynes has recently commented on how depressing it is to see how little Vera understood what Roland was telling her. Three days after she copied this passage into her diary, she was quoting, quite without irony, from Brooke's 'The Soldier'. Later still, she tells Roland that Brooke's lines about pouring out the red, sweet wine of youth keep coming into her head as she contemplates the wounded in her ward. Her writing provides other evidence of the way in which a sanitized and romantic image of the war served as an embrocation for her mind. In her poem, 'To Monseigneur', written in November 1915, she employs a chivalric metaphor, imagining Roland as her 'pure and stainless knight' and calling him 'Roland of Roncesvalles'.

If the possibility that Roland's personality might be irretrievably damaged or altered by the war was among Vera's worst nightmares, then the letter from him, which finally broke his silence in the second week of November, must have amply confirmed her fears. He informed her of his promotion to acting adjutant before going on to comment on his 'metamorphosis' into 'a wild man of the woods, stiff, narrowed, practical'. His next letter, little more than a week later, was scarcely more reassuring. 'Do I seem very much of a phantom in the void to you?' he asked. 'I must. You seem to me rather like the character in a book or someone whom one has dreamt of & never seen. I suppose there exists such a place as Lowestoft and that there once was a person called Vera Brittain who came down there with me.'

Her initial reaction was one of anger. His words, couched in the autocratic tones of the 'Quiet Voice', seemed inadequate recompense for all the weeks of worry and of being ignored. And yet when she put pen to paper she felt forced to temper the strength of her outburst lest her letter prove to be the last he ever read. 'I literally dare not write you the kind of letter you perhaps deserve, for thinking that the world might end for you on that discordant note.' Nonetheless her reply was laced with brutal frankness. One passage in particular must have struck home. The war, she reminded him, 'kills other things besides physical life, and I sometimes feel that little by little the Individuality of You is being as surely buried as the bodies are of those who lie beneath the trenches of Flanders and France'.

Throughout the rest of November the matter remained unresolved. Postal disruptions and Roland's transfer for temporary duty to the Somerset Light Infantry, some miles from his own battalion, impeded the flow of letters between them, and it was not until 27 November that a letter arrived from him in answer to hers. The distant and superior adjutant had been replaced by a Roland she hardly recognized, penitent, full of remorse, and 'almost humble'. 'No', she assured him later, 'you haven't lost the personality of Pre-War days. Roland Leighton's is at its deepest an individuality founded on a rock . . . He had only forgotten Himself a little and was yielding the substance to the shadow . . . But he has remembered now.' She had nearly wept over his letter and confided to her diary that it had driven her almost mad with longing for him. The news a few days later that he might be getting leave at the end of December put her 'into the seventh heaven at once'.

Out in France the cold snap of winter had begun to bite. At Hédauville, where Roland was in the trenches with the Somersets, the charred and pitted landscape was blanketed in a thick covering of snow. The only sound was of a few heavy trench mortars bursting with a crump further down the line. '. . . Otherwise nothing but silence and whiteness.'

Roland's letters, though, were once more warm and vital, and full of sympathetic concern for Vera. But they also possess an oddly dispassionate quality, as if he were looking in at their relationship from the outside. In one he thinks of her going out into a cold world every morning 'to a still colder and monotonous routine of fretful patients and sanguinary dressings and imperious sisters . . . and then late to bed, to begin all over again tomorrow.'

And if one does not even get a letter occasionally from someone who despite his shortcomings perhaps understands & sympathizes it must make it all the worse . . . until one may possibly wonder whether it would not have been better never to have met him at all or at any rate until afterwards. I sometimes wish for your sake that it had happened that way.

The prospect of leave does not fill him with unalloyed pleasure:

My leave, of course, is not definite at all yet and may not even come off for some long time. But I have hopes; and anticipation is very sweet, and better often, one thinks, than the realization. It was so last time, I remember.

Had he fallen in love with her as the embodiment of his favourite fictional heroine, Lyndall, she had asked him, prompting from Roland the following analysis:

'Well, after all, your real love was just a character in a book, n'est-ce-pas? And She whom you took to Lowestoft the first time was simply a flesh and blood approximation to Lyndall?' Is this true – or rather, do you think that it is true? It is quite possible to love an ideal crystallized in a person, and the person because of the ideal: and who shall say whether it is not perhaps better so in the end? Though it must be very trying to be the incarnation of an ideal – very trying. Apropos of which I may remark that the unfortunate Olive Schreiner is too often made responsible for things over which she had no control whatever.

If his remarks preoccupied her at all, they are unlikely to have done so for long. For at the beginning of the third week of December, Roland wrote confirming the dates of his leave as 24 to 31 December. He was back with his own regiment in trenches at Hébuterne and having to endure the onslaught of heavy rain which was turning the ground to mud 'in various stages of solidity or stickiness'. 'And shall I really see you again, and so soon?' she replied excitedly. An unusually accommodating Matron granted Vera Christmas leave, and with barely more than a week until Roland's return, she began to make arrangements to meet him.

She would be spending Christmas itself in Brighton. A row between Mr Brittain and his fellow directors – on the subject of whether the mill should make cigarette papers, a move he was determined to oppose – had developed into a permanent rift, and had been used as a pretext for manoeuvring him out of the company. Taking early retirement, he and Vera's mother had left Buxton at the beginning of December, and fulfilling a long-held wish, had migrated south, to settle temporarily in the comfort and affluence of the Grand Hotel on Brighton's seafront. At about the same time the Leightons, with their income steadily diminishing, had left the Lowestoft house for a modest cottage at Keymer, seven miles from Brighton. This put them in easy reach of the Grand Hotel, where it was planned that Roland, after spending Christmas Day with his family, would be reunited with Vera on Boxing Day. '. . . After all', Vera told Roland, 'it is only fair that your family should have you to themselves for a little, without being interrupted by an interloper, whatever her claims may be.'

On night duty on Christmas Eve, Vera filled the men's Christmas stockings. Directly after breakfast the next morning, she travelled down to Brighton and awaited a telephone call or telegram from Roland to tell her that he had arrived. By ten that night when no message had come, she went to bed, disappointed but assuming that his crossing had been delayed, or communication difficult.

At Keymer the Leightons sat up over their Christmas dinner. Shortly after midnight, Robert Leighton entered the room with a crumpled piece of pinkish paper in his hand.

The next morning, Vera had just finished dressing when she was called to the telephone.

> Believing that I was at last to hear the voice for which I had waited for twenty-four hours, I dashed joyously into the corridor. But the message was not from Roland but from Clare; it was not to say that he had arrived home that morning, but to tell me that he had died of wounds at a Casualty Clearing Station on December 23rd.

VI

On 6 February 1916, six weeks after Roland's death, one of his fellow officers, Captain Harry Adshead, wrote to Vera. The previous day he had ridden out to Louvencourt to see where Roland was buried.

> . . . I went up the road – past a few small farms and cottages until I was just out of the village and there I came to four cross roads – on the right hand corner is

a big wooden crucifix – one so often sees them in this part . . . On the opposite corner to this is the little cemetery. A cemetery only since the war began. It is a small piece of ground . . . about 100 yards long and 50 yards wide and the graves of French soldiers, on the other side the graves of our own men . . . And the last grave is his. Just a little mound of earth quite freshly turned – a little wooden cross at its head, with thin strips of metal bearing the inscription 'Lieutenant R.A. Leighton 7th Bn. Worcestershire Regt. – December 23rd, 1915.' And so he lies. And only transport wagons and ambulances and soldiers pass that spot.

Slowly, details of the circumstances surrounding Roland's death had filtered back to his family and Vera. On the evening of 22 December, two days after Christmas had been celebrated in billets at Courcelles, the 7th Worcesters had relieved the 4th Oxford and Bucks Regiment in trenches at Hébuterne. Roland's platoon had been ordered to repair the barbed wire in front of the trench, and Roland had gone ahead to inspect it and to see that all was safe before the rest of the wiring party followed. It was a moonlit night with the Germans only a hundred yards away, and he had no sooner reached the gap in the hedge on the concealed path leading to No Man's Land than he was shot and mortally wounded. A cry went up, 'Mr Leighton's hit, sir, and it's serious.' According to Roland's Colonel, who was some distance away, he was hit by 'a few rounds from fixed rifles', but Roland's batman wrote that 'it was a sniper who shot him', and this is confirmed by the official report that 'Sergt Day, Medical Officer, and Capt Adam did excellent work bringing him in during heavy sniping'. He was brought to the dressing station, given a large dose of morphia to deaden the pain, and then taken to the Casualty Clearing Station at Louvencourt, ten miles away, where he was operated on the next morning. His chances of survival were slight. Although the bullet had entered the right side of the abdomen making only a small wound, the exit wound was 'a very big and nasty one' which had penetrated the base of his spine and showed signs of 'gas gangrene'. On coming round from the operation he received Extreme Unction from the Jesuit Chaplain who, unknown to Vera or his family, had received him into the Roman Catholic Church that summer. At eleven o'clock that night he died peacefully. 'He seemed to have used up all his reserve of strength and he just went out.' He was twenty years old.

Agonizing questions gathered around Roland's death. Was there, perhaps, a curious rashness in his leading a patrol to mend the wire beneath so bright a moon? Was it folly, Vera asked herself, or the act of heroism to which Roland had so long aspired? He could hardly have been unaware of the risk involved. An ominous remark to Edward, the previous spring, about 'nearly coming to a bad end' while inspecting forward wire entanglements shows that he had already come close to being killed in this way.

It quickly became clear that no military purpose had been served by his death. In his nine months at the front Roland had seen no action. The diary of his battalion emphasizes how 'exceedingly quiet' the part of the line around Hébuterne had been throughout the last three months of the year. Figures for officer casualties confirm this uneventful scenario. Since April they had totalled just three: one killed, one died of wounds (Roland), and one from sickness. Only the passage of time and the easing of her sorrow would allow Vera to conclude that Roland's death had in fact been painful, unnecessary, and utterly devoid of 'heroic limelight'.

Of his recent conversion to Roman Catholicism Roland had said nothing. Yet his Company Commander testified to how religious, 'almost devotional', he had become in the weeks before he died. Mrs Leighton was hurt and bewildered that her son should have excluded her from all knowledge of his new-found faith. But Vera accepted it with philosophical calm. She had certainly long been aware of his attraction to Catholicism, and was glad that he had died with the hope of a life hereafter. 'This is not the kind of thing that distresses me or ever has . . .', she informed a correspondent some years later, 'I think that even the people nearest to one are not entitled to know everything about one's innermost mind'. Unlike Marie Leighton, though, who soon after Roland's death embraced Catholicism for fear that the boundaries of faith in the next world were unbreachable, Vera could not become a convert. The foundations of her adolescent agnosticism went too deep.

Hardest of all for Vera to bear in the months immediately following Roland's death would be the absence of any last message from him 'to inspire the long dreary years ahead'. Tantalizingly, the only word left by him which related to her came in the form of one of his poems, found amongst his bloodied and mud-stained clothes and possessions which had been returned from France. Headed 'Hédauville, November 1915', it dated from the period of their estrangement:

> The sunshine on the long white road
> That ribboned down the hill,
> The velvet clematis that clung
> Around your window-sill,
> Are waiting for you still.
>
> Again the shadowed pool shall break
> In dimples round your feet,

And when the thrush sings in your wood,
Unknowing you may meet
Another stranger, Sweet.

And if he is not quite so old
As the boy you used to know,
And less proud, too, and worthier,
You may not let him go –
(And daisies are truer than passion-flowers)
It will be better so.

In *Testament of Youth* Vera referred to this poem as strangely prophetic, and printed it as the epigraph to the final chapter of the book to symbolize her meeting and marrying George Catlin after the war. Yet she remained puzzled by it. 'What did he mean, I wondered, as I read and re-read the poem . . . What could he have meant?'

It is of course possible to place another gloss on what Roland is saying. Rather than foreseeing his own death and predicting that Vera will meet someone else, he could be gently suggesting that their own relationship is cooling and that Vera will eventually find happiness elsewhere. The calmness with which he imagines her with another lover suggests a loss of intensity in their own relationship, and the ambiguity concerning what has happened to him – death or disaffection – adds to this. He seems to be saying goodbye to their life together, as a romantic and, perhaps, unreal experience.

This is pure speculation, but other factors lend it some support. For both Vera and Roland the enforced separations of wartime had severely strained the building of a solid relationship to follow their initial attraction. They had tried to get to know each other through letters, but each had discovered, after months apart, that the object of their love was becoming increasingly a figure of their imagination. As Vera had written to Roland, shortly after their final meeting,

When I get your letters I feel as though I know & understand you much better than when I meet & see the actual you. You yourself always puzzle me. Reverence-reserve-indifference – in their actual manifestation they are so alike.

It was easier for Vera to dream of a future that they might share; for Roland at the front, it must have been a case of trying to find a way of dealing with the stern realities of the present, which perhaps inevitably excluded Vera.

This interpretation of 'Hédauville', taken in conjunction with the ambivalent tone of Roland's last letters, must leave open to question the true nature of Roland's feelings for Vera at the end. As Vera wrote when personal tragedy struck again, twenty years later, 'Next to the loss of their own future fulfilment . . . the worst thing about the dead is the questions you want to ask them that they will never answer.'

Whether she ever asked herself that particular question, it is impossible to say. In later life she maintained that the cruellest thing about Roland's death for her was the shattering of all her hopes. She recovered from the anguish of personal loss, but never quite overcame her sense of frustrated longing. A letter to George Catlin in the early Fifties attempted to explain the significance of the ghostly figure who had sometimes seemed to come between them:

> I doubt if anyone can feel twice that first vehemence of early passion if it is brutally frustrated almost before it finds expression. The more romantic and unsophisticated it is, the greater is the frustration, even though unsophisticated, romantic, physical enchantment is seldom a quality which survives more than a few weeks of marriage. Unless it becomes something else, the marriage soon fails – as Roland's and mine might have failed. But frustrated, it leaves a cruel vacuum.

THREE

'I, Too, Take Leave of All I Ever Had'

'There comes a terrible moment to many souls when the great
moments of the world ... enter like an earthquake into their own
lives ...'

George Eliot, *Daniel Deronda* (1876)

'There must be something beyond this life, this tragedy ...'
Geoffrey Thurlow to Edward Brittain, 22 January 1916

1

At twenty-two the first note of personal tragedy had entered Vera's life. For
nine months she had lived in fear and half in expectation that Roland would
be killed, but faced with the brutal fact of his death she could find no
strength of purpose with which to combat her sense of blank hopelessness.
Brighton seemed to wear an air of heartless indifference now as she
wandered aimlessly along the seafront, repeatedly turning the few bare facts
of Roland's end over and over in her mind. In the Grand Hotel strangers
stared inquisitively at her mourning. The prospect of remaining there for
the rest of her leave was too much for her, and she escaped to the Leightons'
cottage at Keymer where she was joined by Edward and Victor. Deprived of
Roland's commanding presence, they looked 'like courtiers without a king'.
With the melancholy strains of the Morning Hymn on the gramophone all
three of them broke down in tears.

Vera returned to Camberwell on 3 January 1916. Stella had relayed a host
of sympathetic messages from the staff. Matron had murmured, 'Poor dear
little girl', and Mrs Leggatt, who had been on duty with Vera on Christmas
Eve, 'was very tearful when she heard and said, she hoped you would come
back as it was the best thing and you were such a little brick'. Stella herself
had endeavoured to instil some courage and hope. 'Thank goodness you are
you and too brave to allow yourself to think there is nothing left worth living
for', she had written on 27 December. 'I know he was absolutely the only
man, the only bit of comfort is that you have met him and so have not entirely

missed the best thing . . . You must come through alone and your natural heroism is the only thing that will help you.'

Going back on night duty, however, while her grief was still so raw, imposed an intolerable strain. All eyes were upon her, furtively glancing to see how she was coping with her bereavement, while the cries and groans of the patients during the long night hours pushed her to the limits of her endurance. Vera had never felt so isolated and miserable, and on half-days roamed the streets of Camberwell unaccompanied. At the first opportunity in mid-January she went back down to Keymer. Grief had distanced her emotionally from her own mother. With Marie Leighton, who was close to mental and physical breakdown, she could share a greater degree of intimacy, and each possessed a deeper understanding of the other's loss. She arrived at an opportune moment to comfort her. Roland's kit, so redolent of the charnel-house atmosphere of the front, had been returned to his family. While Mrs Leighton wept over these last tangible remains of her son and demanded that the clothes be removed from her sight, Clare and her father made preparations to bury them in the garden after first melting the frozen earth with kettles of boiling water.

Broken and distraught though she was, Marie Leighton had thrown herself into work on a new book. *Boy of My Heart*, a short memoir of Roland, was her emotional valediction to the son she had worshipped. 'This is a book of absolute fact not a work of fiction', Hodder and Stoughton, its publishers, testified when the book appeared anonymously in June 1916, '. . . a record exact and faithful, both in large things and small, of the short years of a boy who willingly and even joyously gave up his life and all its brilliant promise for the sake of his country.' Vera figures in this story of Mrs Leighton's 'Little Yeogh Wough' (her baby talk for 'Little Hero'), her identity thinly concealed by the substitution of 'Brennan' for her surname, but she is incidental to the book's main theme of suffocating mother-love. Far too sentimental for modern taste, *Boy of My Heart* sold well: it perfectly matched the mood of its time (this, after all, was the year of the infamous letter, quoted in Robert Graves's *Goodbye to All That*, from 'a little Mother' celebrating the sacrifice of her sons in battle). Even so, some contemporaries squirmed with embarrassment at its tone. The *Times Literary Supplement* found the story moving, but admitted that 'the reader has an uncomfortable feeling that he is unduly prying into experiences much too intimate for publication', a view echoed by Geoffrey Thurlow, Edward's friend from his battalion, who had not known Roland. 'How Mrs Leighton could have published that book I cannot understand', he remarked, 'tho' I understand her writing it.'

Vera is not on record as having expressed any opinion of *Boy of My Heart*, though it may be significant that she put aside for the time being plans of her own to write about Roland, preferring instead to dwell on the pain of her loss in a series of short poems which were later to form the basis of *Verses of a VAD*. It was becoming difficult to ignore Marie Leighton's growing determination to be as possessive of Roland in death as she had been in life. Barely a month after his death, she had persuaded Clement Shorter, the editor of the *Sphere* and an old ally of hers from her Northcliffe days, to publish one of Roland's love poems to Vera, the villanelle 'Violets from Plug Street Wood', in the magazine, encouraging the entirely false impression that its romantic sentiments were meant for her. Nearly ten years later Vera was to make the possessiveness of a mother for her dead son the subject of an unwritten novel entitled, 'The Mother of Michael's Child'. By then political differences and Mrs Leighton's disapproval of Vera's independent lifestyle had marred the closeness of their relationship, and had begun to tarnish the ideal of authorship which Mrs Leighton had once represented for Vera. In the character of Eve Trelawney, 'the celebrated sensational story writer . . . a woman like a tank', she bitterly exposes Marie Leighton in all her human frailty:

> She is full of preconceived ideas and prejudice which form part of her personal philosophy, and which neither experience, reason, nor argument can change . . . The things she despises include women, especially unmarried women . . . education of any kind . . . neatness, elegant clothes, and . . . other people who succeed. Is very military, thinks the L[eague] of N[ations] folly. Estimates everything by its sex-value. Sees herself as the heroine of every episode. Her one passion besides herself is Michael, whom she has desired to *possess*, body and soul, ever since he was a tiny child.

The storyline of the novel is easily summarized. Michael Trelawney and Sylvia Lane meet at college and fall in love just before the outbreak of war. They become engaged, Michael is sent to the front, and while he is on leave in the autumn of 1916 they marry. A few months after he returns to France he is killed in action. Sylvia discovers that she is pregnant, and Mrs Trelawney 'spreads her tentacles over her because she is going to be the Mother of Michael's Child'. The rest of the book was to have dealt with Mrs Trelawney's struggle to possess Sylvia and her son, with Sylvia torn between Eve's Bohemian values and artistic temperament and the more conventional outlook of her own mother (dramatizing that familiar obsession of Vera's). In life, though, unlike fiction, there was not even the happy prospect of Roland's child as consolation. For Vera it was to be a source of regret for years to come that she and Roland had not consummated their relationship, and that she had not conceived his child.

By the end of January, after a few weeks of struggling with the hospital routine, she had made up her mind to leave when her contract came up for renewal in April. No longer was there the thought of Roland's hardships to spur her on. The uninspiring tasks which she had once undertaken with such dedication were now carried out cursorily or not at all. Suffering, she noted regretfully, was having a bad effect on her character. She reacted with open defiance to any criticism of her work, rejected any show of sympathy from fellow VADs, and rounded on Stella for her cheerfulness. 'In the utter blackness of my soul I seem to be touching the very depths of that dull lampless anguish which we call despair', she wrote in her diary. '. . . Little, sweet phrases from His letters keep coming always into my mind – and I just cry and cry.' The news that she was to be transferred to day duty produced another bitter outburst in a letter to her mother. 'Last time I was on day duty He was alive so it didn't matter what it was like, but now it will be detestable and I shall hate living among that common crowd.' On Sunday mornings she took to escaping from a new batch of chattering VADs, 'with their strange accents and stranger underclothes', by attending High Mass at St James's, Spanish Place, the Roman Catholic church whose beauty had attracted Roland long before he became a convert. She could not adopt his faith, but sitting in the midst of the early Gothic splendour of St James's she felt at peace with herself and closer to Roland. She needed all the inner strength that she could muster, for on 7 February, after many delays and false alarms, Edward finally received his orders to join the 11th Sherwood Foresters out in France. On 'a grey, unutterably dismal' afternoon three days later, Vera and Mrs Brittain saw him off at Charing Cross.

With Roland dead and Edward's departure opening up another period of prolonged anxiety for her, Vera might well have given way to complete despair. What helped to save her was the friendship and support of the third member of the Uppingham Triumvirate, Victor Richardson. Stationed at the Woolwich Arsenal where he had been assigned to comparatively unexacting guard duties after recovering from meningitis, Victor was free to meet Vera regularly in London for dinner at the Trocadero where he provided a sympathetic ear for her problems. In letters too, touchingly self-deprecating and 'maturely selfless', he treated her with a remarkable degree of compassion and consideration (unfortunately her side of the correspondence has not survived). Their common theme is the love and esteem they both felt for the memory of Roland, and for Edward. His friendship with them, Victor confessed, 'is the most valued thing I have ever had, or ever will, and now that you are His representative it seems natural to talk to you about it'.

That Victor Richardson should have emerged only at this point into the foreground of Vera's life was entirely characteristic of this modest and self-effacing young man. '. . . I am a very ordinary and matter-of-fact person', he insisted in one of his first letters to her. At The Lodge he had been content to let himself be overshadowed by Roland and Edward, and although he had won a university place at Queens' College, Cambridge, which like the two other schoolboy soldiers he never took up, he was a less spectacular student than either of his friends. He also came from a more ordinary and less affluent background. Frank, his father, was a popular but poorly paid junior partner in a well-established dental practice in Hove. A neighbour's daughter remembers Victor as studious, 'and very sensitive compared to his younger, more stolid brother, Maurice'. While Victor was at Uppingham his mother had died with tragic suddenness of cerebrospinal meningitis, the illness to which Victor himself succumbed less than three years later, and which he only survived after several days of acute anxiety.

'Very nice but a little dull and commonplace so far' had been Roland's verdict on Victor when he spent a few days with the Leightons at Lowestoft at the end of August 1914. This, though, was the supercilious voice of the former school Captain speaking, and in fact Roland had come to rely heavily on Victor's judgement and loyalty. For his part Victor placed Roland on a pedestal and was repaid for his devotion with Roland's deepest confidences. 'Tah' (or 'Tar'), as Victor was known to his friends, was Roland's 'Father Confessor', completely dependable and trustworthy, as his other nickname, 'The Brighton Block', implies. It was natural that Roland should have turned to Victor rather than Edward to talk about his relationship with Vera; and natural too that after Roland's death Victor should have attempted to fulfil the same role of confessor to Vera. 'You can imagine the pride I have always felt', he told her, 'at being considered worthy by Him to receive His confidence about the greatest thing in His life'.

It was Victor who went to considerable lengths to unravel the patchy and conflicting accounts of Roland's final hours which Vera continued to receive, months after the event. By telling her that the wire in front of the trenches had to be kept 'in good order under all circumstances' and that it was the job of a first-class officer to ensure the safety of his men by doing so, he convinced her that Roland's life had not been recklessly thrown away. Nothing was of more paramount importance to Vera now than to believe that Roland's death had been in the service of some greater cause. She told Edward that

Tah says [Roland] always used to say that our one hope of salvation as a nation lay in a Great War, and if He had said this to me I should certainly have agreed with Him. I do condemn War in theory most strongly . . . but there are things worse than even War, and I do believe even wholesale murder to be preferable to atrophy and effeteness. It is better to do active harm and definite wrong than to drift and make no effort in any direction . . . And when the War in question is a War *on* War, all the usual objections are changed into the opposite commendations.

Victor's powers of empathy enabled him to adapt to her prevailing mood. At times he offered solace in her bereavement. 'I understand only too well the desolating loneliness you must feel . . .', he wrote after one of their meetings. 'I could see last Wednesday how terribly you felt the parting.' At others he stiffened her resolve, by letting her know, for instance, that the Triumvirate's private name for her had been 'The Invincible'.

Her decision to give up nursing had Victor's full support as well as her father's warm approval. Arthur Brittain had always considered it beneath his daughter's station in life to be doing menial work, and had immediately promised her £50 – more than twice the annual salary of a VAD – to save her from any financial worry. But she remained in a quandary about her future. She hated to admit defeat and felt that in some way she was breaking faith with Roland, but the supply of nurses exceeded the demand and there was 'very little doing' at Camberwell while they awaited the next 'big push'. She could not help thinking too that she might make a more useful contribution to the war effort in some capacity which would give wider scope to her abilities – 'if only I knew what'. A clerical job at the War Office was one idea, perhaps, Victor suggested, as a preliminary to returning to Oxford in the autumn, and she got as far as making plans to rent a room in Bayswater. However, an interview with a War Office official seems to have put paid to that plan, and a visit to Somerville at the beginning of March confirmed in her own mind that she could not return there until the war was over.

She prevaricated a while longer, and finally settled on what was in effect a compromise. She could not bear that anyone should think she had chosen the soft option and so would be continuing as a nurse. But instead of remaining indefinitely at the 1st London General, she would join Stella and add her name to the list of those volunteering for foreign service. In weeks, or more probably months, she could expect to be sent to any one of several destinations: Egypt, Salonika, Malta or, as she fervently hoped, France. She silenced her natural rush of fear at the element of risk involved by telling herself that a woman on active service should not shirk foreign duties any more than a man.

Edward's letters offered the reassuring news that after an uneventful month in trenches in the region of the Somme town of Albert, he was in good spirits. His old battalion, though, the 10th Sherwoods, had been having 'a stiff time' that February under heavy German bombardment at Ypres, in the course of which Edward's great friend, Geoffrey Thurlow, had suffered shell-shock and a slight face wound. Vera had met Geoffrey when he spent a weekend with Edward at Buxton in October 1915, and had been 'very taken with him'. Although he was shy and so quietly spoken that it was sometimes difficult to catch what he said, she had had 'a vague impression all the time of there being a great deal somewhere behind – a quiet strength absolutely trustworthy'. Geoffrey was the third of her brother's friends with whom she would establish her own independent friendship. In early March while he was recovering in Fishmongers' Hall Hospital near London Bridge, she visited him with her mother. Huddled over a small gas stove to ward off the chill, one of the after-effects of shock, he was once again shy and ill at ease in their company. 'I was quite alarmed', he admitted to Vera later. 'Don't you hate meeting strange people?' In spite of his inhibitions he talked intently of the German attack in which most of his men had been killed, of being virtually surrounded, and agonized again over his decision whether to retreat or face certain death. 'His manner was very serious and he worked his fingers nervously and looked terribly sad when talking about the front.' Herself the victim of an anxiety state, Vera responded instinctively to Geoffrey's mental anguish and distress.

Of the four men who haunt the pages of *Testament of Youth*, Geoffrey Robert Youngman Thurlow is perhaps the most tragically unforgettable. His quiet sensitivity was allied to good looks which Vera clearly found attractive. She described him as 'strange, though very pleasant looking', with close-set blue eyes, a decided chin, and wavy brown hair. Born in Chingford in Essex, the youngest child of elderly parents, a retired printer and his wife, Geoffrey had attended nearby Chigwell School. There, according to a school notice published after his death, 'conduct and character rather than intellectual force won for him a position among his schoolfellows . . .'. A 'non-militarist at heart', he had not rushed to enlist in the first months of the war, but had gone up to Oxford in the autumn of 1914. While Vera had been studying for Responsions and Edward drilling in the Parks with the OTC, Geoffrey had been at University College. After only a term, he had felt compelled to put aside his personal objections to the war for patriotism's sake, and volunteer. 'Those days at Oxford', he was to reminisce when back in the trenches, 'often make life out here pass more quickly'. Gazetted a second lieutenant in the 10th Sherwood Foresters he had quickly befriended Edward. Their friendship, displaying the deep affection and selfless regard characteristic of many of the relationships of men within the same platoon or company, remained unbroken even when Geoffrey was sent out to France ahead of Edward with the 10th Sherwood Foresters in October 1915.

On 5 March, three days after her visit and unaware that it was Geoffrey's twenty-first birthday, Vera went again to Fishmongers' Hall, but she did not stay long as he was allowed only two visitors and his mother and sister, Cecilia, arrived for tea. Before she left, however, he invited her to go to a concert with him at the Queen's Hall during his convalescent leave. For Geoffrey this was a bold gesture, and it would in fact be another four months, after several more meetings, before he felt able to call Vera by her first name and drop 'the stiff and formidable Miss Brittain'. After he was passed fit by an army medical board and returned to France in August they would write frequently to one another with an increasing sense of intimacy and understanding. On her part also there was to be growing respect for a natural peace-lover who was forced to overcome his 'funk' in order to fight. He was not of 'any earthly use as an officer', he confided to her in one letter, being 'disgustingly windy' and lacking in courage. 'I only hope', he wrote in another, 'that I may be given strength of both mind and body – if Fate wills it – to last.'

At the beginning of June Edward returned to England for five days' leave. Cramming into this short period a weekend with Geoffrey in Macclesfield where the Brittains, despairing of Brighton hotels, had rented a furnished house, and visits to the Leightons at Keymer and Victor at Purfleet, he had little time to spend alone with Vera. During his forty-eight hours in London, however, he revealed to her that his leave was preparatory to a new 'show'. 'He spoke in veiled but significant language of a great battle – another Big Push – soon to take place, and knew that he was to be in it. He said it would be somewhere in the region of Albert, where he is now.'

'There seems to be an air of expectation about all the world, and a sense of anguished foreknowledge of the sacrifice that is to be made . . .', Vera wrote to Edward, now back at the front, at the end of June, as the 1st General received orders to prepare for a great rush of wounded. On 1 July, Vera and Stella emerged from Southwark Cathedral where they had attended a performance of Brahm's *Requiem*, and were met by the sight of newspaper boys and placards proclaiming 'GREAT BRITISH OFFENSIVE BEGINS'. Of Edward there would be no word for three terrible days. Victor was with her over the weekend, giving what comfort he could, and the arrival of the first convoy of patients at the hospital at least kept her mind on her work. On 4 July she found a note in the hospital letter rack. '. . . I was wounded in the action this morning in the left arm and right thigh not seriously. Hope to come to England. Don't worry. Edward.'

The next day, as Vera was preparing surgical dressing trays for the critical cases in her overcrowded ward, a VAD from the officers' ward across the road burst in to tell her that, by some extraordinary coincidence, Edward was among the wounded officers who had arrived during the night. Over the next three weeks, she was at his bedside as often as her nursing duties would permit, and learned of his experiences on the first day of the Somme 'by degrees'.

Edward had led the first wave of attack of his company, following three other New Army battalions, early on the morning of 1 July. While they were waiting to go over, the wounded from the first part of the attack began to crowd into the trenches. Then part of the regiment in front, the 9th Yorks and Lancs, began to retreat, throwing Edward's men into panic. He had to return to the trenches twice to exhort them to follow him over the parapet. About ninety yards along No Man's Land, Edward was hit by a bullet through his thigh. He fell down and crawled into a shell hole. Soon afterwards a shell burst close to him and a splinter from it went through his left arm. The pain was so great that for the first time he lost his nerve and cried out. After about an hour and a half, he noticed that the machine-gun fire was slackening, and started a horrifying crawl back through the dead and wounded to the safety of the British trenches. 'He says what made more impression on him than anything was seeing the dead hand of a man whose flesh was beginning to turn green and yellow, though he had only been killed that morning.'

The first day of the Battle of the Somme has come to epitomize all the waste, carnage, and confusion of the First World War: an insignificant amount of territory was gained at an unprecedented cost in British lives. Yet completely absent from Vera's diary account of Edward's experiences is any sense of 'indignation, anger, bitterness, cynicism, any suspicion that men have been sacrificed for little or no gain . . .'. Indeed she writes at one point, quite without irony, of 1 July 1916 as 'one of the greatest dates in history'. Her focus is narrowly confined to her brother's heroism. There is no place to question the uses to which it had been put. It would take almost another two decades for Vera to repudiate decisively the myth of martial heroism which had dominated her earlier responses to the Somme. Standing at the British memorial to the Missing of the Somme on the

Thiepval Ridge in August 1933 she would contemplate with a sense of shock 'some of the most representative results of my generation's pursuit of "heroism in the abstract" ' – the 73,367 names of 'men whose bodies, on that one battlefield alone, had never been found or even identified.'

Official endorsement of Edward's heroism arrived at the end of August when he received a telegram to say that he had been awarded the Military Cross, 'for conspicuous gallantry and leadership during an attack'. But it was only with difficulty that he could be persuaded to speak of the Somme again. Only slowly would the recognition dawn on Vera that 1 July had changed him completely and aged him by ten years. Edward possessed no warring side to his nature, Victor had explained. '. . . He is sustained by Duty alone.'

To Vera's great relief, convalescence and training would keep Edward in England for almost a year. For much of that time she herself would be abroad on active service, as in the middle of September she was recalled from leave to be informed that she had been posted to Malta. Consoling herself with the thought that in spite of the distance, no separation could be so very great, 'so long as those who were separated were still on earth', she set sail with Stella Sharp and a closely supervised contingent of VADs on the *Britannic* on 24 September.

II

Vera's eight months in Malta were the adventurous interlude which involuntarily broke the spell of the intense grief which had enveloped her since Roland's death. The voyage out, however, merely confirmed all her fears of foreign travel. Despite the magnificent sights on offer, including a few hours in Venice and a glimpse of the Greek island of Skyros where Rupert Brooke is buried, she lived in constant terror of being torpedoed by a German submarine. 'How we ever got safely through the Aegean Sea . . . is a mystery to me still', she wrote to her mother months later when both the *Britannic* and the *Asturias*, another converted hospital ship which had brought out the second Malta detachment, had been sunk with loss of lives. Life at sea quickly became monotonous. 'Discipline is very strict on board,' she reported to her mother three days after they sailed. 'We haven't to do anything in particular, and are not allowed to speak to any officers. It is a little annoying to be regarded as a designing female when one hasn't the least desire to speak to them . . .'. Worse was to follow when they reached

Mudros, the port at Lemnos, where they trans-shipped to the *Galeka*, a small liner which would take them into Malta's Grand Harbour at Valletta. Vera was one of sixteen VADs who fell ill in an epidemic of food poisoning. For twenty-four hours she lay 'boiling and panting' in the cramped and stuffy conditions of the VADs' quarters in the hold. On the afternoon of 7 October, deafened by the clanging of feast-day bells and dazzled by the glare of the light, she was carried off the *Galeka* on a stretcher and taken to Imtarfa Hospital, seven miles away in the centre of the island. There she remained for three weeks until judged fit enough to be discharged and begin work at St George's Hospital, about two miles west of Valletta, just above St George's Bay.

It was an inauspicious introduction to Malta, and yet the freer, less stressful life there was to prove a vitalizing, therapeutic experience after the starchy protocol of the 1st London General. A two-storeyed converted army barracks built of stone, St George's stood on a peninsula of land jutting out into the sea. The five wards on which Vera began her duties each contained fourteen service men suffering from eye disease or malaria, or sometimes from both. An army nursing sister was in charge, assisted by two VADs and a plentiful supply of Maltese orderlies. Vera was allowed considerably more latitude than she had had in England. VADs were in charge when the Sister was off duty, they wrote reports, took temperatures and pulses, and distributed medicines. The facilities were makeshift, but Vera was stimulated by the challenge of having 'to manage as best you can' with one cold tap and one sink, and to boil kettles on temperamental Primus stoves 'instead of walking to a gas ring'. The nurses ate in a mess tent at tables for five or six people. It did not matter if you were late, the dress regulations were relaxed (a blue crêpe-de-Chine mess dress, a daring fourteen inches above the ground, in addition to a white drill coat and skirt, and a Panama hat for outdoor wear), and the informal atmosphere was a welcome contrast to the Camberwell Dining-Room where Matrons had solemnly dispensed meals to subdued young nurses seated at long tables. 'I am ever so much happier in my work here than I ever was at Camberwell', Vera enthusiastically informed Edith Brittain. 'I wouldn't be on home service again for anything.'

The naval officers who formed part of the island's garrison took advantage of the sudden influx of young women to boost their social life, and VADs received a profusion of invitations to tea, tennis, and other more official gatherings. The week after her arrival Vera attended a garden party at the Governor's palace. A naval sub-lieutenant, whom she discovered to be the brother of a girl she had known at St Monica's, was keen to partner her in tennis matches. But although she enjoyed the occasional game and welcomed the exercise, she had 'a feeling all the time that it is not appropriate to the present state of affairs'. She preferred to take the halfpenny train ride into Valletta, to visit, with one or two others, the uninhabited parts of the island. One afternoon she was introduced to a young woman who was a cousin of Dorothy Sayers. Sayers had been a third-year student at Somerville when Vera was there in 1914–15, and her cousin gave Vera an open invitation to visit her whenever she was at a loose end. Often she simply spent her free time sitting in solitary meditation down on the rocks by the bay. She found it difficult to be among people who remained untouched by 'all the unhappy things in this war' and was surprised that it was still true of so many. Stella Sharp, gregarious and with no such misgivings about enjoying herself, had by now lost patience with her old schoolfriend's melancholic introspection, and had abandoned her to sample the diversions offered by naval society. 'I can never get over the case of Stella', Vera wrote later, resentful at the loss of her companion, 'who all through the war hasn't had one single thing to regret'.

As Christmas approached she prepared to mark the first anniversary of Roland's death. 'Fancy it being a year since He died!' Vera wrote to her mother on learning that Edith Brittain had thoughtfully sent flowers to the Leightons in Roland's memory. 'It is very absurd of people to say that time makes you forget; in a way you make yourself used to being without a person, just as I suppose you would manage with your left hand only if you lost your right, but I miss Him as much as I ever did & always shall; whenever I meet with something new or exciting or strange I always feel so sad . . . for there was a special interest attached to telling Him things that there never can be for anyone else . . .'.

Yet increasingly Malta itself was bringing her repose and reconciliation. When, in her teens, Olive Schreiner's childhood belief in the Old Testament dogma had died, Schreiner had built a new kind of pantheistic faith on her contemplation of the 'beneficent tenderness' of the natural world. Less consciously, Vera was discovering a strangely reinvigorating affirmation of life in the beauty of the Mediterranean island. She delighted in the Eastern mosques and minarets standing up against the sky, so that 'when one has looked for a little while one half expects to see camels driven by Arabs going across the desert spaces', in the brilliant light, and the glorious sunrises and sunsets. The flowers too were a source of wonderment, and she requested that a sketch book in which to paint them be sent from England. In her letters she describes 'bright golden flowers like cowslips only three times the size' standing on her bedside table in a blue pot 'just like the shape of the water pots in Ancient Palestine', and enthuses over the bougainvillaea, the golden oxalis, the red campions, and 'a little orange flower like a beautiful dandelion'.

Valletta's Indian and Egyptian street markets were a trap for the compulsive shopper, and Vera posted a steady flow of gifts home. To her mother she sent an Indian silk shawl, 'as I don't believe you have anything presentable enough to wear with evening dress or in the presence of company'; her father received a black and white matchbox inlaid with gold, Edward a cigarette case, and to Mrs Leighton she dispatched a blue and white Indian tablecloth. She was able to buy 'the most exquisite Egyptian cigarettes for 7/6 a hundred', and early in December she sent a supply to Edward with a bar of the famous Maltese nougat. With an incongruous sense of etiquette she questioned the propriety of including her brother's two friends on her Christmas-present list. 'I should so much like to send Geoffrey and Victor cigarettes', she appealed to her mother, 'but [I am] not quite sure whether it would be correct to do so. I wish you would let me know what you think about this.' Even in the midst of war, the inhibiting strictures of Vera's upbringing died hard.

Delays to the mail from England were a regular occurrence, allowing Vera little peace of mind. Her parents were in London in the autumn of 1916, where they were experiencing a renewed wave of Zeppelin attacks. 'I feel so far away & cut off from news', she told her mother, '. . . you'll not forget that there are cablegrams, will you?' Mrs Brittain's parcels always contained something to reinforce her morale: sweets, magazines like the *Saturday Review*, the *Sphere*, and the *Tatler*, a photograph of Edward which regrettably failed to catch 'the sparkle in his eyes which I am so fond of', but which she was pleased to have as it showed him wearing his MC. There was also the inevitable moan. 'It is no good your fixing a definite time at which to expect me home any more than if I were a man in the Army', Vera responded irritably after her mother had raised the question of her prolonged absence. Mrs Brittain had wanted her daughter at home to help cope with the latest domestic upheaval. After settling for a few months in a flat in Oakwood Court in Kensington, her parents moved to a smaller flat in the same block complaining, with some exaggeration, that London rents and food prices would soon lead to their utter impoverishment. It was better to be poorer in London, Vera reminded them, 'than to be prosperous in the horrid north'.

Throughout the winter and well into the spring of 1917, Edward remained out of harm's way at Brocton Camp in Staffordshire, employed in training and home duties. Vera's worst fears for the time being were for

Geoffrey, and for Victor who had recently gone out to France. When on her first trip into Valletta in mid-October she had resumed the anxious business of looking through the already out-of-date casualty list from the *Weekly Times* for Geoffrey's name, she had had no inkling that there was Victor's name now to look for too. Shortly afterwards, a letter from Edward had arrived, containing the surprising news that Victor had managed to effect a transfer to the 9th King's Royal Rifle Corps, and had left England just six days after her. 'Glad in a way he is out', commented Geoffrey, 'as he was so keen and the "gap" [in experience] of which Edward spoke may now be filled up . . .'.

She soon heard from Victor himself. His cheerful letter, dated 31 October, was sanguine to the point of disbelief about his first few weeks of trench life. 'The trenches are wonderfully clear even in bad weather & the dugouts very comfortable', he told her, 'though some people might dislike their earthy smell. Altogether life out here is very enjoyable & a welcome change from England.'

> I have so far [he continued] come across nothing more gruesome than a very few very dead Frenchmen in No Man's Land, so cannot give you very thrilling descriptions . . . Really I am beginning to agree with the Rifleman who when some dear old lady said 'What a terrible War it is', replied 'Yes Mum, but better than no War'.

His tone grated on her. The childlike ingenuousness which she had previously found so appealing now betrayed a note of unqualified militarism which at the very least she found distasteful. One might regard the war as a necessary evil in which every individual was duty-bound to play his or her part, but Victor's words smacked of exultation. 'Vera says that Victor Richardson loves war and says "Any war is better than no war . . ."', Geoffrey reported to Edward. 'Well! If he is not a hypocrite I admire him and wish I had his martial temperament!' Vera could not remain so passive, and delivered a stinging rebuke in her next letter to Victor. Evidently she did not measure the full force of her words for his hurt reply in early December indicated the extent to which he believed she had misjudged him. 'You seem to think that I have become a quite horrible individual', he began, and a little further on he confessed that 'It is quite awful to feel the silent contempt of those whom one regards as one's dearest friends'. But he did not believe that she 'quite understood the way I look at things'.

> After all if I stopped to consider the deeper meaning and significance of these things my life would be one long misery . . . Reflect that in one minute's time

one may be . . . blotted out for eternity. Why! one simply can't afford to let one's mind dwell on these things. One could not carry on.

. . . As regards suitability for this kind of War – very few men are suitable . . . One has to try therefore to convince oneself – and if possible other people – that one is at any rate a decent imitation of a soldier.

Geoffrey Thurlow's frequent declarations of his own cowardice and unsuitability as an officer sounded more sympathetic to Vera's ear than Victor's bravado. 'You say that you are not callous enough for a nurse', he had written to her a month before she sailed for Malta. 'Personally I'm far too timid for this life and whenever a shell comes near me I'm absolutely petrified within and without.' Beneath the shy exterior she had discovered someone of warm understanding with a sensitive mind, capable of responding to beauty even in the terrible conditions of the Western Front. 'I remember vividly the sunset the first day I was in the line . . .', he wrote in February 1917.

After a hot bombardment of 2 hours in the afternoon, the day ended with signs all around of the recent destruction. Looking back, silhouetted against a blood red sky were 5 trees with their branches mutilated and torn and beyond them the grey mists of evening. Strange how beauty follows on the heels of destruction.

Vera's parents had also warmed to Geoffrey. Arthur Brittain corresponded with him while Edith Brittain sent packages containing cakes, almonds and raisins, and told him that if she had had the chance to say goodbye to him in person when he returned to the front, her farewell would have included a kiss ('No!' he responded nervously, 'I dislike any form of kissing and only do it at home on a kind of sufferance, so from that point of view it was as well!').

But Geoffrey remained chiefly Edward's friend. Imperturbable and phlegmatic with a strong core of self-containment, Edward concealed from most people whatever fears and agitation he may have had. But better than anyone he understood and sympathized with Geoffrey's vulnerability to the strains of war, and shared the knowledge that at the front they were all potential victims of 'life on its way to death'. Their time together in England in 1915, training in the same battalion, had created a bond between them. They had formed a close-knit alliance against some of their older fellow officers, who regarded their youthful presence with suspicion, and had provided one another with mutual reassurances against fear and loneliness. When Geoffrey was sent out to France first, he felt suddenly bereft without

Edward's comradeship. 'I often long for you to be here tho' it is mere selfishness I know', he told him in November 1916. 'Daniels' only literature is that Horror *John Bull* and his sole topic of conversation is farming . . .'.

Edward kept all of Geoffrey's letters (the other side of the correspondence has not come to light). Vera wanted to include quotations from them in *Testament of Youth*, but could not bring herself to ask the Thurlow family for their permission to publish them. Written nearly eighty years ago, Geoffrey's letters illuminate in stark personal terms the anguished existence of a sensitive young man plunged almost straight from school into war. Repeatedly he wrote of his panic before going into battle, and his torment still echoes painfully down the years. 'I'm not the slightest use out here – far too windy . . . I only pray I don't make a fool of myself'. He had come to the conclusion 'that my most suitable war vocation would be a Padre's servant for verily I am far too windy for anything else.' Every casualty list, he told Edward, contained the name of someone he knew, and the odds on survival had become a pitiless lottery of diminishing hope. For Geoffrey the only consolation seemed to lie in the possibility of an afterlife. 'Don't you often speculate on what lies beyond the Gate of Death?' he asked Vera in Malta, and writing to Edward shortly before going into action, he anticipated 'our next meeting, Here or in the Hereafter'.

Since few in his battalion cared for 'aught save cards, whiskey', and what he referred to euphemistically as 'other things', it was a relief to be able to correspond with Edward about literature. 'I'm reading a great deal lately when we get time', he reported to him from France, 'and find Shakespeare quite refreshing after the toils of war'. Long afterwards, his sister, Cecilia, recalled to Vera 'one picture' she had never forgotten from a hot summer's day in 1915 of Edward, who was staying with them, and Geoffrey, 'sitting out of doors at tea time, Edward repeating lines from Rupert Brooke – from "The Soldier" and "The Dead" – which his sister had sent him, "for ever England".' Geoffrey's own copy of *1914* was blown up in his dug-out at Ypres. Cecilia replaced it and when, after Roland's death, Edward sent Geoffrey copies of his poems, 'Vale' and 'Ploegsteert', he pasted them in his 'beloved Rupert Brooke, now much war worn and shabby and yet all the dearer for that.'

Early in 1917 Geoffrey sent Edward a copy of William Hodgson's valedictory poem, 'Before Action', written two days before Hodgson died in a hail of machine-gun fire on the first day of the Somme. In his final verse the young poet crystallized for Geoffrey his own desperate prayer:

> I, that on my familiar hill
> Saw with uncomprehending eyes
> A hundred of Thy sunsets spill
> Their fresh and sanguine sacrifice,
> Ere the sun swings his noonday sword
> Must say goodbye to all of this; –
> By all delights that I shall miss,
> Help me to die, O Lord.

III

In early February 1917 Vera was moved to St George's only surgical block. None of the patients was seriously ill, and she took advantage of her additional leisure to catch up on her reading, immersing herself in the books that Edward had sent from England, Hardy's *Selected Poems* and Masefield's *Gallipoli*. As a sober contrast to Masefield's heroic romance she also read the recently published Report of the Commission on the Dardanelles, although as ever she inclined more to the heroic view of events. While the Report made 'tragical reading', she could not help thinking that it must have been 'a very fine and wonderful thing' to have 'fought so gallantly for such a forlorn hope', and wished that Roland, if he had to die, could have been killed defending Gallipoli's beaches.

With the arrival of the warmer weather in the middle of March she succumbed to the temptation of tennis, regularly partnering Stella against two of the medical officers, and following their matches with tea, vermouth and whisky in the officers' mess. But all the while she was troubled by a sense of foreboding. At any time now Edward would be passed fit and sent back into that 'terrible spring', and Victor's and Geoffrey's letters had begun to strike a common note of impending calamity at the front. Her correspondence with Victor had been intermittent since the New Year, hampered by delays in the post and also, perhaps, by a failure to return to their old familiarity after her outburst of the previous autumn. Nonetheless, he had continued to exhibit plenty of what he called 'the spirit which is going to win the War', so much so that a letter of 24 March, in which his tone had changed sharply to cynical resignation, came as an unpleasant shock. He intimated that they were on the verge of an attack and signed off with the words, 'Well, Vera, I may not write again – one never can tell – and so, as Edward wrote to me, "it is time to take a long long adieu".' Geoffrey's news was equally depressing. At the beginning of April he reported with unfeigned relief that he was being sent back to base for a month to attend a Corps School of Instruction. He had already set out for the school when he received orders to turn back and take his place with the battalion for the oncoming attack.

With so much time at her disposal the suspense of waiting for news was intolerable. Vera warded off the uncertainty by writing long letters to Edward. After two and a half years of war and with no end in sight, she freely admitted to him that her patriotism was running a little threadbare. 'The longer the War goes on,' she wrote on 17 April, 'the more one's concern in the whole immense business seems to centre itself upon the few beings still left that one cares about, and the less upon the general issue of the struggle.'

The following evening as she was making her rounds of the wards, a cable from her father arrived informing her that Victor had been dangerously wounded. 'There really doesn't seem much point in writing anything until I hear further news of Victor', she wrote distractedly to her mother the next morning, 'for I cannot think of anything else . . . I knew he was destined for some great action, even as I knew beforehand about Edward, for only about a week ago I had a most pathetic letter – a virtual farewell.' She cabled home immediately asking for more news and received a reply from Edward four days later: 'Eyesight probably gone. May live.' To her mother she rushed off another letter:

> I am quite broken hearted about Victor; I don't know whether to hope he will live or not; I am not sure whether I would rather be dead than blind, and he would so hate to be dependent on other people . . . I am so glad that Edward is to be in England till June; he will be more comfort to Tah than anyone else. I am waiting to write to Miss Dennant [Victor's aunt] till I get your letters, also to know if Tah is conscious enough to be written to, even though someone else must read it out; not that I should know what to say, for I don't suppose he knows his sight is gone, does he? I wish I was in England if there is anything at all I could do for him. If you can see him you will of course give him my love & tell him my indescribable respect, won't you.

On 9 April Victor had led his men in an attack on a heavily defended German entrenchment at Vimy Ridge, three miles north of Arras. Although hit in the arm he continued to press forward until he fell unconscious from a bullet wound in the head. His left eye was shattered and had to be removed. On a superficial inspection the right eye appeared undamaged, but a closer examination revealed that the optic nerve had been severed. Scarcely conscious, he lay for ten days critically ill in a Rouen hospital until he was strong enough to risk a cross-Channel journey to the 2nd London General Hospital in Chelsea for specialist treatment.

Edward was at Brocton Camp in Staffordshire, and on a brief leave the weekend after Victor arrived back in England he saw him twice on the Saturday and twice on the Sunday. 'This morning', he wrote after his last visit, 'he recovered consciousness for the first time and recognized my voice, took hold of my hand, and made about half a dozen remarks. He said he was as "right as rain". His father came soon afterwards but he had dozed off again.'

Vera was still coming to terms with the seriousness of Victor's injuries when on 1 May she received two more cables from England. The first told her that Victor's sight was now hopelessly gone, the second – delivered an hour later – informed her that Geoffrey had been killed in action on 23 April at Monchy-le-Preux, three miles south-east of Arras, in an attack on the Scarpe. Early in the action Geoffrey went out on top of the trenches, Edward told Vera later,

> and was soon hit in the left lung by a sniper. He was brought into the trench and put on a stretcher where he died in about a ¼ of an hour. Daniels [his Company Commander] says that he did not suffer any pain, and as his death was probably caused by haemorrhage I believe that there would be only a feeling of slight suffocation.

When the fighting was over, his body had disappeared, and was never found.*

Stupefied, Vera sat all day on the rocks by the sea in front of the Night Quarters, feeling all the time that she was not alone, but that Geoffrey was there, and that if she looked up she would see him standing beside her. Her overseas contract had already expired. She had intended to sign on again and remain in Malta, or transfer with the rest of the medical staff to Salonika (there had been rumours for some time that submarine warfare was making Malta impracticable as a hospital base). Suddenly, though, she decided to return home '& if he wishes it, to devote my life to the service of Victor, the only one (apart from Edward, who is different) left of the three men I loved. For I loved Geoffrey . . .'. She remembered all the times when Victor had been her mainstay after Roland's death, during the first weekend of the Somme – and resolved to stand by him and share the difficult days ahead.

---

* Although Geoffrey has no known grave, his name is honoured on three war memorials, at Chigwell School, University College, Oxford, and at the Faubourg d'Amiens Cemetery where he is one of 2,652 British soldiers commemorated on the Arras Memorial.

She was prepared, if necessary, to give up all thought of satisfying her own ambition to repay him a little for his sacrifice. At the back of her mind may have been a tinge of guilt at her past treatment of him. A stronger motivating factor, as she had indicated to her mother, was that Victor 'has always been so much a survival to me of a part of Roland'. In Victor's 'accurate, clear & reverent' memory of him, Roland seemed to live still.

It was a brave decision, and not one about which she apparently had second thoughts, although she was left with plenty of time to reconsider. It was three weeks before she received permission to begin her journey to England. The threat from submarine warfare had made travel by sea too perilous and she was to return by a complicated overland route which would take in Rome and Paris. In the meantime, Edward kept her informed of Victor's progress. '... I don't think there is the very least doubt that he will live', Edward wrote on 7 May. Victor had been told that it was unlikely that he would ever see again, but remained 'marvellously cheerful' and talked about entering the Church.

On 22 May Vera left Malta on the first stage of her return journey. Arriving back in England on 28 May, she spent the next ten days in constant attendance at Victor's bedside as he struggled to learn Braille. Although they talked at first about nothing more consequential than the hospital routine and the visits of his friends, his mental faculties did not appear to be in any way impaired. The matter of their future together does not appear to have been spoken about directly, though her very presence there must have signified to Victor something of her intention. However, Vera had made clear to Mr Richardson and Miss Dennant that she was willing 'to offer him a very close & life-long devotion if he would accept it ...', and one of Victor's childhood friends, who visited him in hospital, remembers hearing 'of his engagement, as we took it, to her'.

But on 8 June there was a sudden change in his condition. In the middle of the night he experienced what he described as a miniature explosion in his head, and subsequently became extremely distressed and disorientated. By the time Vera, his father and aunt had reached the hospital he had, as she wrote in *Testament of Youth*, 'meandered off through the grotesque by-paths of delirium'. He regained his composure while they were with him, but died early the following morning. He was buried near his mother at Hove.

In later years Vera was readily to concede that she was temperamentally far too ambitious and egotistical for marriage with a blinded and disabled Victor ever to have succeeded. But at the time she felt only an acute sense of bitterness for having been robbed by his death of the chance to serve a fellow human being. Seven years later she offered the following, faltering, explanation to her future husband:

> As for Victor – well, I am glad if that pleased you. At least you know that I am not really so cruel as I sounded about the war cripples. But as for being capable of it – capable of making up for what he had lost, I mean – I don't know; I only know that I meant to try, & that his death left me with a feeling of despair at not even being allowed to do, if not the best (was it?) at any rate the hardest thing I ever thought of doing . . . Not even to be permitted to 'do good' – that seemed too bitter an humiliation.

IV

'We started alone, dear child, and here we are alone again' were Edward's mournful words to Vera on learning of Victor's death. Everything, he wrote, that had seemed of value in life had tumbled down like a house of cards. In the short space of eighteen months the war had deprived him of his three closest friends, and their deaths had intensified his long-held premonition that he too would be killed. On weekend leave at Oakwood Court at the beginning of June he had been distant and withdrawn, solemnly and repeatedly playing Elgar's 'Lament for the Fallen' at the piano. He had reverted to his normal cheerful self by the time he returned to France at the end of the month, almost a year to the day of his action on the Somme, but immediately faced a series of misfortunes which further depressed him. At Boulogne his newly acquired trench equipment, including his revolver, went missing, and his loss was compounded by finding himself posted to the 2nd Sherwood Foresters where he knew no one, and where he had no time to acquaint himself with either his men or the terrain before being sent on a perilously dangerous early morning attack. The Company Commander got lost in the dark, nobody had the slightest idea where they were, and Edward and his platoon trudged apprehensively along interminable trenches. The incident unnerved him and it was with considerable relief at the end of July that he rejoined the 11th Sherwood Foresters. On 13 August, in a promotion that was less a recognition of distinguished service and more a reaction to the decimation of the battalion's officers, he was made Acting Captain.

A few weeks of civilian life had been sufficient to convince Vera of the impossibility of remaining in England as long as the war lasted. Resisting her parents' pleas that she remain at home, she had applied once more for overseas service, requesting that she be posted to France to be near to Edward. No longer fired with patriotic fervour nor entertaining thoughts about the nobility of any cause, she had privately dedicated herself to fulfilling her own 'small weary part in this War' until the bitter end.

At the beginning of August she joined a small draft of nurses who were being sent out to France to replenish the staff of a large military hospital. With some trepidation she set foot on French soil at Boulogne. 'It was the land of her beloved dead . . .', she was to write later in an unpublished novel.

She found in its atmosphere something vital & compelling, something restless & urgent, which was utterly different from anything she had noticed in countries farther afield. France was a living entity whose heart was heavy with dread & whose whole being was one vast suspense: one could feel the enemy on her soil & with her air breathed in her silent expectation of his next violent act.

Writing to Mrs Brittain on 3 August, she informed her that they would be travelling on to 24 General Hospital the next day. 'The place begins with the first letter of your Christian name', she told her, wary of the censor's watchful eye. 'Edward was there on June 30th & I came through it on May 27th.' In case her mother remained unable to guess her destination, she provided a further clue in the form of an acrostic: 'Even the austere people like every sort!'

They were headed for Étaples, some fifteen miles south of Boulogne, and they arrived there on the third anniversary of the outbreak of war. Lying upstream from the lively resort of Le Touquet Paris-Plage, along a spreading coast where sand dunes pushed back the sea, this little fishing port was the site of one of the British Expeditionary Force's base camps. Étaples Base, about a mile out of the town, provided hospitals, prisons, stores, railway yards and port facilities, as well as infantry depots through which, it has been estimated, more than a million officers and men had passed by September 1917, for regrouping and training on their way to the front. At the far north end of the camp was the Bull Ring, the infamous area of training grounds where troops were put through a harsh and demoralizing course of training, said to have been 'like passing through hell for two weeks'. Within two months of Vera's arrival at Étaples the base would erupt into a week of rioting during which the nursing staff were strictly confined to their quarters.

The northern end of the camp also contained a series of eight hospitals, differing in size. 24 General was on the brow of a hill, extending in long lines of wooden huts at right angles from the road, and interspersed with tents and marquees. The sisters' quarters, a collection of bell tents and some canvas and wooden shanties known as Alwyn huts, were separated from the main body of the hospital by a main road along which a heavy traffic of transports and ambulances constantly passed in the direction of the line. '... To have real Active Service conditions at last pleases me immensely', Vera wrote to her parents. At the end of the hospital furthest from the sisters' quarters were a group of marquees reserved for the nursing of prisoners. Ward 29 was the German ward.

Rumours that 24 General specialized in German prisoners had been circulating among the new batch of VADs since their arrival at Boulogne. At first surprised to discover that the rumour was in fact true, Vera was then shocked to find herself allocated to Ward 29. 'It was with very mixed feelings that I followed my guide to the German ward', she remembered in one of her earliest pieces of mature journalism, written the following year on her return from France.

> ... To the majority of British people who have never been out of England since the war began, the word 'German' has gradually come to indicate not so much an individual as the personification of those powers of evil against which an heroic Army is striving to prevail. To have shared this vague impression, & then suddenly to be cast into the midst of a number of persons whose hostile nationality this term describes cannot help but be a slightly alarming experience.

The great autumn offensive which would result in the taking of the Passchendaele Ridge, in early November 1917, was just beginning, and in the onslaught of work which followed Vera soon ceased to trouble about her patients' nationality. 'Am frantically busy ... convoys pouring in', Vera informed her mother within a few days of arriving at the base. She was trying to regain and add to the surgical knowledge which had grown somewhat rusty during her time in Malta. 'Every serious wound was represented there', she recalled, 'such as "G.S.W. [gunshot wound] – penetrating" of chest or abdomen, badly smashed heads and amputated limbs ... At one time more than half our cases were empyemas.' The small operating theatre attached to the ward sometimes dealt with as many as fifteen to twenty serious operations in a day. 'In the ward I'm in I can't possibly use less than one apron per day', Vera told Edith Brittain. The surgeon was always keen for Vera to see everything she could, and when she went to the theatre to restock the ward with the eusol, carbolic, and methylated spirits which were stored there, she often waited 'to see a limb amputated or a bullet extracted from the depths of a German brain.'

She felt none of the antipathy she had expected towards the German rank and file. 'You will be surprised to hear that at present I am nursing German prisoners . . .', she wrote to her parents. 'I cannot, however, really say I dislike nursing [them], though I should have expected to had I thought of it. To begin with, the majority are more or less dying; never even at the 1st London during the Somme push, have I seen such dreadful wounds.' She found it impossible not to admire their stoical fortitude, or fail to be moved to pity by such sights as a middle-aged Bavarian man slowly bleeding to death from his subclavian artery. 'One can only feel that, like all of us in this present unhappy world, they are the poor victims of that intolerable caste and system we are fighting to destroy.' She never overcame her dislike, though, of the officers, of whom there were half-a-dozen or so in the ward at any one time. Separated from the men by a green baize curtain, and invariably less seriously wounded, they were generally arrogant and punctilious, and resentful of their position as prisoners.

Vera mixed more freely with the other VADs than she had in Malta. More than half of them, she noted approvingly, were 'ladies' and free from 'the dreadful habit of talking shop'. They shared 'little after-supper tea-parties', and took part in amateur theatricals for one of which Vera wrote 'a little skit . . . in which the characters are an absurd Sister & a perfect little idiot of a V.A.D. . . .'. Vera reserved her warmest remarks in her letters home for the Sister who had taken over the chargeship of the German ward soon after her arrival. Some day, she told her mother, she hoped that she would meet Sister Moulson, 'though you would probably think her rather mad, as so many people do here.'

A member of Queen Alexandra's Imperial Military Nursing Service, Faith Moulson was in her early thirties and had been in France since 1914. One of five sisters, all of whom remained unmarried, she was descended through her mother from a long line of bishops, including her great-grandfather, Bishop French of Lahore, and her uncle, the Bishop of Manchester, while on the Moulson side she was connected to the acting profession through a distant relationship with the Thorndike family. There was an element of the dramatic in her manner and mode of speech. Barking orders at the patients and orderlies in an unhesitating and vehement German and taking 'a vigorous though half-scornful control of everything and everybody', Faith Moulson bore the fitting, though unofficial, title of 'Ober-Schwester'. At first Vera had strong doubts as to whether she could be happy under this regime: on one occasion a stunning rebuke from Sister

Moulson had sent her from the ward in tears. Yet before long she had conceived an intense admiration for this 'brilliant personality', whom she discovered to be not only highly efficient as a nursing sister, but also 'intellectually gifted apart from her profession'. And as Vera's novel from her Étaples experience makes clear, Faith Moulson also fulfilled a deeper need:

> She suddenly felt sure that . . . she would meet some individual of an unusual type, with whom she would become intimate, and whose intimacy would influence her life . . . and her instinctive mind had no doubt that the impending personality . . . would be that of a woman . . . Beyond one or two superficial school friendships and the warm regard of a don . . . women had not affected her at all up to the day she entered hospital.

Not the least of Faith Moulson's attractions for Vera was her calculated delight in shocking people with outrageous remarks. She seemed to radiate unconventionality (her nickname for Vera was 'Brittannia'). Hand in hand with Vera's respect for her intelligence went a fascination with her appearance. She was impressed by Faith Moulson's slender figure and dark good looks, and wrote about them in a manner strongly reminiscent of the passionate attachments of her schooldays: 'The white forehead, over which the dark hair, parted in the middle, waved so attractively, & the delicately pencilled brows, were worthy of an artist's portrayal of some medieval saint.'

Initially Vera was 'rather shy of going out with a striped sister', but soon they became constant companions off duty, often taking the short walk through the pinewoods to Camiers for tea, or driving out in a fiacre 'through beautiful countryside' to Paris-Plage where they ate 'a very good omelette, & chocolate & red-currant jelly'. Here was someone to whom Vera could unburden herself of her concern for Edward, while the older woman confided the history of a recent unhappy love affair with a surgeon at her previous base hospital. Their working relationship, however, was abruptly terminated in the middle of September when Vera was moved from the ward after a 'bewildering rumpus' involving one of the German prisoners, a young medical student who sometimes assisted at operations.

The German ward was to play a pivotal role in the development of Vera's pacifism in the course of the next twenty years. She had begun 'to think on definitely pacifist lines – though I did not then recognise them as such.' Nursing German prisoners had provided her with two powerful insights. From the outset she had been struck by the tragic and fundamental absurdity of a situation in which she might be trying to save the life of a man whom, a short time before at Ypres, Edward had been trying to kill. Furthermore her efforts as a nurse to ameliorate the suffering of her prisoner patients had reinforced the conviction she had held from the early days of the war, that a dying man has no nationality.

Such sceptical reflections about the war, and her own, hitherto unquestioning, role in it, received added impetus two months later, in the first week of December 1917, when she was once again transferred to a new ward, this time to a British hut specializing in acute medical cases. There she watched with a mixture of horror and outrage as the first victims of mustard gas from the Battle of Cambrai arrived on the convoys. A letter home to her mother, which she afterwards categorized as her 'first angry protest against war-time hypocrisy', drew attention to their terrible plight:

> I wish those people who write so glibly about this being a Holy War . . . could see a case – to say nothing of 10 cases – of mustard gas in its early stages – could see the poor things burnt and blistered all over with great mustard-coloured suppurating blisters, with blinded eyes . . . , and always fighting for breath . . . saying that their throats are closing & they know they will choke. The only thing one can say is that such severe cases don't last long; either they die soon or else improve – usually the former; they certainly never reach England in the state we have them here, and yet people persist in saying that God made the War, when there are such inventions of the Devil about . . .

Later she was to regard this as the period when she 'definitely ceased to regard the War as an instrument of God or even of human justice.'

With hindsight, one can see Vera taking her first significant steps at Étaples towards the internationalism which she was to espouse on so many lecture platforms for much of the interwar period. The seeds of her future pacifism had been sown. But she was as yet a long way from taking a formal position against war: indeed it is difficult to understand how at this stage she could possibly have done so. As a nurse serving close to the front line it would have been virtually impossible for her to formulate a reasoned antiwar point of view, let alone act on it by refusing to participate further in the war effort. The extent of her wartime ignorance of all the variegated strands of pacifist and antiwar opinion is perhaps surprising, but also particularly telling in this respect. She simply did not possess either the language or political knowledge necessary to turn her flashes of outrage into a sustained argument against the war.

The mature Vera might well have dismissed this as another illustration of her generation's lack of political consciousness which had contributed to the country's drift into war. In later years, however, she could sometimes be driven on to the defensive by the holier-than-thou attitude adopted by some veteran peace campaigners of the Great War towards relative latecomers to the peace movement like herself. In 1933, for instance, she was quite taken aback by Helena Swanwick, a founder of the Union of Democratic Control and a woman she had come to admire greatly, who suggested, after reading *Testament of Youth*, that she and Vera 'shouldn't have had a word to say to each other' had they met during the war. 'If we had heard of and understood the point of view that you represented before it was too late', Vera replied, obviously disconcerted, 'some of us – Edward, for instance, and probably myself – would doubtless have accepted it gladly.'*

The autumn of 1917 had been a harrowing time for Edward. 'You have no idea how bitter life is at times', he had written from the mud and cold of the Ypres Salient. As a company commander in the second half of September, he had spent only three and a half days out of the line. In October he enjoyed a brief respite on administrative duties, but later that month he was back in action and experienced a close brush with death in the hazardous process of making a dash from one support line to another. Two of the companies of the battalion had lost nearly all their officers. 'I ought to have been slain myself heaps of times', Edward told Vera, 'but I seem to be here still.' His family's hopes that he would survive the war were boosted when, in November, the 11th Sherwood Foresters were posted to join the Allied reinforcements on the little-heard-of and relatively quiescent Italian front in the Alps above Vicenza. After the humiliating rout of the Italian army at Caporetto that October, in which the entire Italian war effort had almost disintegrated, the job of breaking the Austrian offensive had suddenly assumed a new and pressing importance.

But with the battlefield in the grip of winter, and the precipitous mountain roads obliterated by snow and ice, there was little prospect of an Austrian attack across the mountains of the Trentino before spring, and early in January Edward was granted leave. Vera, who had by now been on continuous ward duty in France for just under six months, also obtained permission for leave to be with her brother. It was to be the last occasion on which the family was all together, but the reality fell short of the happy reunion that Vera had anticipated.

She arrived home, flushed and feverish, a few days after Edward, at the beginning of the third week in January, and the doctor immediately ordered her to bed where she remained for a week. It was, she wrote later, 'an

* Significantly, though, Edward was ambivalent about his sister nursing Germans. Writing to Vera on 14 September 1917, he commented that 'personally I think I prefer that you should be nursing our own men though of course the one is service as much as the other.'

uncomfortable leave'. Arthur and Edith Brittain, like many other civilians who had suffered the effects of years of 'diminishing hope' and 'of waiting for news which was nearly always bad when it came', were beginning to show signs of breaking under the strain. Nonetheless, Vera could not help but be irritated to find that conversation dwelt not on 'life or death, victory or defeat, national survival or national extinction', but on the price of butter and the incompetence of servants. Food and servant shortages had thrown Mrs Brittain's domestic ritual out of gear, and with an ailing daughter to tend to on top of all this, she easily became agitated. 'I hear they have shut up three rooms in the flat, which is a good thing', Edward subsequently commented to Vera with wry humour, 'but the work connected with the flat still forms the gist of most of mother's letters.' Arthur Brittain had had little to occupy his time since his retirement two years earlier. Sitting around the flat all day – 'and discussing (chiefly with himself) ineffably fatuous opinions about the war' – he brooded depressively about his health, while still managing to dress with almost foppish care, always wearing spats and usually sporting a butterfly tie.

The mood at Oakwood Court was lightened by a visit from Maurice Richardson, Victor's younger brother, who stayed with the Brittains for two nights during Vera and Edward's leave. Four years younger than Edward, Maurice Richardson hero-worshipped him as a recipient of the MC, and his admiration would lead him in March 1918 to enlist in the Sherwood Foresters (although he arrived in France only a few days before the Armistice was signed). He remembered Edward as 'not easy to get to know on first sight, but intensely loyal to his friends.' During his stay he accompanied Edward as he shopped at Selfridges for gramophone records to take back with him to Italy 'to cheer up his men', and felt flattered when Edward adopted his choice of 'Roses of Picardy'.

Three days were all that remained of Edward's leave once Vera was fit enough to rise from her sick-bed. In their short time together they snatched a few visits to theatres and concert halls, and on 25 January Vera travelled with Edward to Waterloo to see him on to his return leave train. With reason enough by now to be superstitious of station farewells, she left before the train departed: 'The sorrow of parting had become almost a mechanical sorrow.' Not once during his stay had Edward given any indication to his family of the strain he must have been under; the only telltale signs were in the greying hair around his temples, and in the lines etched deep on his forehead. He did indeed look at least a decade older than his twenty-two years, as Victor had remarked after the Somme.

In Italy the British Division had moved to the so-called Asiago Sector.

Here, despite the severe cold, there was dazzling scenery to admire while they awaited the arrival of milder weather. 'There have been wonderful sights to see', Edward reported to Vera on Easter Sunday 1918, '. . . huge peaks covered with tall pine trees – marvellous roads with hairpin bends and everything solid rock where the snow lies until June.'

Thankful to be back at Étaples and reunited with Faith Moulson, Vera was assigned to a light medical ward. For close on two months the pace of work slackened. Then on the morning of 22 March she came on duty to discover that her ward had been converted overnight into a surgical ward of which she was in sole charge, and that there were forty wounded men, at least ten of whom were awaiting emergency operations. The previous day, Ludendorff, the German commander, had begun a final desperate bid for victory against the Allied armies in the West. A creeping barrage of unparalleled intensity had been followed by a ferocious assault with specially trained bomb-throwers, flame-throwers, and machine-gunners. In the face of this overwhelming offensive, the British Fifth Army had broken.

For three weeks the exhausted doctors, nurses and VADs of 24 General worked frantically to cope with the never-ending rush of convoys, each transporting a new supply of casualties from further up the line, 'to be dispatched, a few hours later, to England after a hasty wash and change of dressing, or to the cemetery after a laying-out too hurried to be reverent . . .'. And all the time at the back of everyone's mind lay the 'secret, incredible fear' that the Allied forces might be in the process of losing the war.

The enemy approach, heralded by muffled gunfire and thudding shells, as one by one the towns marking the advances of the past three years were retaken by the Germans, instilled new panic among the hospital staff; and a series of nightly air raids on Étaples deprived them of their few hours of sleep. Vera was to regard it as little short of miraculous that she herself did not succumb to fear. Conscious all the time that her self-control was held nervously in check, she had been frightened that in the midst of danger she might suddenly give way to hysteria. In fact she soon learned that in facing the danger head on, all fear disappeared. The 'born coward' had immunized herself from fear by obeying the maxim, 'Always do what you are afraid to do'. It was a lesson she was to follow for the rest of her life.

By the second half of April it was becoming evident that Ludendorff's offensive was going to fail. The Germans, it seemed, could not now win the war. Vera, though, would not be in France to witness the Allies' recovery. At the end of March, while the fighting was still at its height, she had received a letter from her father informing her that as her mother had entered a nursing home with 'a complete general breakdown', it was her duty to leave France immediately and return to Kensington.

She had some difficulty stifling her resentment. The servitude of women to their parents was seemingly inescapable and, not for the first time, she envied Edward's freedom from such obligations. But there could be no question of applying for leave in the middle of a push. 'Father appears to imagine that it rests entirely with *me* whether I come home to-morrow or in 6 months', she wrote to her mother, 'but of course you understand differently.' She was left with no alternative but to break her contract, making her feel like 'a cowardly deserter'.

Arriving home at the end of April to find the flat empty and her father in a local hotel, she immediately rescued her mother from the needless expense of a Mayfair nursing home, brought her back to Oakwood Court and took charge of the household. However, after the 'strange exultation' of the life-and-death pressures of a military hospital, Vera could not accustom herself to the dull monotony of the daily trivialities of civilian life, and railed bitterly against them. Her parents appeared to regard her as a heaven-sent convenience upon whom duty laid the combined functions of nurse, companion and maid-of-all work. As soon as Mrs Brittain showed signs of improvement – her 'turns' were usually short-lived – and a new maid had been engaged, Vera began to consider her future. She could not reconcile herself to remaining at home indefinitely, but having broken her VAD contract there was little prospect of resuming her service abroad. In the absence of anything else to do, she thought again of returning to Oxford before the end of the war. 'I quite expected you would find Oxford rather an annoying and unsatisfactory place just now', Edward wrote towards the end of May, suggesting that Vera had gone so far as to apply to Somerville for reinstatement, 'but I think you are doing the best thing to go up again in October . . .'. Once again, though, the idea came to nothing. A life of intellectual occupation seemed as irrelevant to the greater concerns of the world in 1918 as it had done three years earlier.

The sultry weather exacerbated her black mood and she attempted to lose herself in the 'lurid' novel, based on her war experiences, which she had been writing on and off for almost a year. She was also impatiently awaiting the publication of her first book, *Verses of a VAD*, a small volume of the verse she had written since 1914. 'I am so glad you liked the poem on the German ward . . .', she had told her mother in September 1917. 'Am in the middle of one or two others but they don't get finished very quickly in these disturbing days. Should like to publish soon.' By October Marie Leighton had shown a typescript of the poems, which she 'liked very much', to Erskine Macdonald, whom Vera later described as an 'experimental publisher', but who in other circles was perceived as something of a rogue. He had been persuaded to publish her book by the offer from Arthur Brittain of 'ten reams of antique printing paper' without charge, but Vera had been unprepared for Erskine Macdonald's procrastination. In March 1918 she reported that 'I have just written to Erskine Macdonald to jog his unbusinesslike memory'; the following week she asked Mrs Brittain if she 'would do something to buck up Erskine Macdonald'. Two months later the book had still not appeared, and it was Edward's turn to express his exasperation. 'What is Erskine Macdonald doing with your poems? I should think it's about time they came out.' He did not live to see them in print.

Edith Brittain was staying with her mother in Purley, and Vera and her father were just finishing tea on the afternoon of Saturday 22 June when their prosaic routine was shattered by a War Office telegram informing them that Edward had been killed in action on 15 June. 'My son has given his life in a noble cause, and has now joined those other dear fellows who have so nobly sacrificed their precious lives in the service of our Country . . .', Arthur Brittain replied to one letter of condolence, his copperplate script showing clear evidence of a trembling hand. 'My dear, dear Vera', wrote Marie Leighton with dramatic intensity on receiving the news, 'What can I say to you? . . . There's no need for me to say that we all send deep and great sympathy. But as for me – I knew him so well, lately, and loved him so much! It's horrible. I think of his dark handsome head falling back – oh are you sure, quite sure? Isn't there any possibility of a mistake?'

However, the letters which arrived from Italy a fortnight later, from Edward's second-in-command, his batman, and a non-combatant friend working with the Red Cross, merely confirmed the facts of how he had died. At three o'clock on the morning of 15 June, under cover of darkness, the Austrians had launched a surprise and initially successful attack with a heavy bombardment of the British front line along the bottom of the San Sisto Ridge. Five hours later, the enemy had penetrated the left flank of Edward's company and had begun to consolidate their positions. Edward had led his men in a counter-offensive and had regained the lost positions, but while 'keeping a sharp look-out on the enemy', a short time later, he had been shot through the head by a sniper and had died instantaneously. He had been buried in his blanket with four other officers in the small cemetery at Granezza, four thousand feet up in the mountains.

Obsessively, and with almost lacerating masochism, Vera was

determined to learn every possible detail about Edward's last hours; only after having at least attempted this could she begin to grieve. On the list of wounded she noticed the name of Colonel Charles Hudson, Edward's twenty-six-year-old Commanding Officer. Hudson had sustained serious injuries when a bomb exploded on his foot while driving the enemy from the Allied right flank, a decisive action for which he was awarded the Victoria Cross and the Italian Silver Medal for Valour (making him one of the most heavily decorated officers of the entire war, as he was already the holder of the DSO and MC). He had been in the battalion since 1915, being promoted to command in November 1917 when the 11th Sherwood Foresters were ordered to Italy, and Vera had often heard Edward speak of him, though with more respect than affection. She was certain that Hudson would be able to tell her anything that remained to be learned of Edward's fate, and after making enquiries through the office for information about the missing and wounded, she tracked him down to an officers' hospital in Mayfair.

Hudson, who died in 1959, left an account in his war memoirs of Vera's first visit to him in hospital in which the picture he gives of her outspokenness and frayed nerves rings very true:

> I tried to give as much comfort as I could to the poor girl by telling her that since he was shot through the head he could have suffered little pain, but at this she flared up and said she was tired of hearing this story. Why was it that all her friends and acquaintances killed in the war had been shot through the head? Did I think that because she was a woman she was too weak minded to be told the truth, or so gullible that she could not recognize such nonsense?*

Hudson found it 'quite impossible' to convince Vera that he had nothing to add to information she had already received. She sensed his embarrassment when talking about Edward and felt 'that he knew far more than he chose to reveal.' Before long she had convinced herself that Edward had performed some act of gallantry for which Colonel Hudson was attempting to deny him the credit he deserved.

For weeks after Hudson's discharge from hospital Vera pursued him relentlessly with more enquiries, 'still passionately determined to learn whatever of the truth remained undisclosed.' But it was all to no avail. By

---

* Vera's scepticism may have arisen from the survival of Edward's chequebook, which he presumably carried in the breast pocket of his uniform. The last used counterfoil records a payment of 15s 6d on 14 June – the day before his death – and there is a bullet-hole through the remaining cheque and chequebook cover, making it probable that Edward received a bullet through his chest as well as, or instead of, his head. This chequebook was preserved among Vera's wartime relics at the time of her death, though it is possible that it only came into her possession after Edith Brittain's death in 1948.

now a new note of embarrassment had supervened in their conversations. Did he, she wondered, suspect her of having romantic designs on him? This was certainly the opinion of Hudson's sister who remembered that 'he had a hell of a time shaking her off'. In September she went to Buckingham Palace to see him receive his VC. At home afterwards, in a poem entitled 'To a V.C.', she tersely reminded him that:

> 'Tis not your valour's meed alone you bear
> Who stand the hero of a nation's pride;
> For on that humble Cross you live to wear
> Your friends were crucified.

It was, she thought, the end of a frustrating and futile encounter.

v

The publication of *Testament of Youth* fifteen years later, in the summer of 1933, established Vera's reputation as a writer and made her a bestselling author on both sides of the Atlantic. It also released an avalanche of correspondence from her readers. Among her letters in June 1934, almost a year after the book's appearance, was one with a Camberley postmark, but on this occasion it was not another of the fan letters with which she had become so familiar.

After the Armistice, Charles Hudson had drifted out of Vera's life. He had remained in the army, serving in North Russia in 1919 and in the Malay States in the Twenties, before becoming Chief Instructor at the Royal Military College at Sandhurst in Camberley in January 1933. The appearance of *Testament of Youth* had led him to write to Vera to confess that, as she had intuitively believed in 1918, he had deliberately withheld certain facts of a personal nature about Edward and the circumstances surrounding his death. He emphasized that his only consideration had been to spare her further anguish and distress, and suggested that if she still wished to have the information it would be best if they met for a private talk. However, he stressed that what he had to tell her could only cause further heartache and reopen old wounds. It was 'a matter which even after all these years' he could not bring himself to write about.

Since reading *Testament of Youth* Hudson had thought of contacting Vera, but had 'refrained from doing so for fear of doing more harm than good.' A visit to the Toc H hostel in Manchester, where the original wooden cross from Edward's grave had been erected after its return from Italy, had changed his mind. Standing in the room dedicated to Edward's memory, he had felt impelled to get in touch with Vera again.

Hudson must also have been prompted by a strong desire to put the record straight, and with good reason. Vera's account in *Testament of Youth* of their relations in 1918 was suffused with bitterness – at one point she described him as '. . . a stiff young disciplinarian, impregnated with all the military virtues but limited in imagination and benevolence . . .' – and although Hudson denied that he had been hurt by these 'somewhat bitter references', his son Miles has confirmed that Hudson always considered that the book had 'grossly traduced' him.

'It is quite possible that had my brother survived the War he might have told me whatever facts you have to relate', Vera wrote to Colonel Hudson, agreeing to a meeting on 9 July. They arranged that he should drive to her house at Glebe Place in Chelsea, where she could 'guarantee an uninterrupted talk in my study' after the children were in bed.

If Vera made any record of their conversation that evening, it has not survived. Fortunately Colonel Hudson's memoirs contain the gist of what he must have told her. On or about 12 June 1918, Hudson had received 'a most disturbing letter' from the Provost Marshal, the head of the Corps of Military Police, back at the Base. The Provost Marshal's letter informed him that a letter written by one of the battalion's officers while on leave in England to another officer in the battalion, had been censored at the Base. The context of this letter made it 'unmistakably plain' that the two officers 'were involved with men in their company in homosexuality.' The recipient of the letter and the more senior of the two officers, a company commander, was Edward Brittain. At this distance in time it is impossible to identify the other officer with any certainty.

The Provost Marshal instructed Hudson that as further enquiries were being made he was to avoid letting the officers concerned know that they were under investigation. But according to his memoirs, Hudson was inclined to treat Edward more sympathetically. On 14 June, the day before the Austrian offensive on the Asiago Plateau commenced, he had a conversation with Edward in which he gave him a strong warning, 'in spite of the injunction I had received.' Edward, he wrote later,

had been in the battalion in very early days but had been wounded soon after we went to France. A man of about my age [Edward was in fact more than three years his junior], musical and a product of Oxford [*sic*], he was a man of far higher culture and intelligence than the usual run of officer. When he returned to the battalion he found himself serving under me as his C.O. He had been meticulously correct in his attitude but firmly refused to meet me on a human and friendly footing. I had been puzzled by his manner but now I thought I knew why. I had the strongest objection to spying upon any officer, as the Provost Marshal's letter implied that I should. He had been loyal to me, and it seemed disloyal to him to play cat and mouse with him. In my talk to him I had said, 'I did not realize that letters written out here were censored at the Base.' He had turned white, but made no comment and I knew that I had said enough to warn him. After that it was up to him.

Edward was the only officer killed in the action on 15 June. After the battle in which he himself had been so seriously wounded, Hudson was informed that Edward had been found by his men shot through the head, and a terrible thought had crossed his mind. Faced with an enquiry and, in all probability, the subsequent disgrace of a court martial when his company came out of the line, 'had he taken his own life in desperation, knowing he would be accepted as a battle casualty?'; or had he, perhaps, deliberately courted death by presenting himself as an easy target for the sniper's bullet?*

Vera admitted that Colonel Hudson's disclosures had caused her 'some subsequent very distressful hours'. She had not been shocked by what he had told her about her brother's sexuality, 'and had in fact guessed it beforehand, for I know only too well what my brother had been through, and can readily understand what effect the loss in quick succession of all his friends combined with the strain of his daily life might have had upon one of his temperament.'

But I did find almost unendurable the thought of how bitter his last days must have been, and I reproach myself very much for not writing to him oftener and helping him more, especially during the spring of 1918. I used to think that being on duty for 14 hours at a stretch for weeks together during the German offensive was a good excuse for writing to nobody, but now this seems to me incredibly selfish when his problems were so much worse than my own.

In her letter to Hudson, however, Vera firmly rejected the notion that

* According to the *Manual of Military Law* (HMSO, 1914), sodomy or an act of gross indecency between men was punishable by a maximum penalty of ten years' penal servitude. Any officer found guilty of such an offence before a court martial would have been cashiered and handed over to the civil authorities. Published references to cases of this nature are rare, though Raymond Asquith unsuccessfully defended an officer on five charges of homosexuality in 1916. The officer in question was cashiered with one year's imprisonment. The social disgrace, especially for an officer like Edward, as a holder of the MC and member of a conventional provincial family, would have been especially severe in its consequences.

Edward might have intentionally sacrificed his life either by going ahead alone and shooting himself, or by going into action, seeking to be killed. She stood by the veracity of the three accounts of Edward's death which she had received in 1918, all of which had described him as having been killed by a sniper's bullet in full view of his men. Enclosing extracts from these letters, she told Hudson that Edward's part in the attack 'was much as I described it in my book . . .', and assured him that 'the only consideration in his mind during those hours' had been 'his immediate duty of saving the position.'

> An officer of his experience would, I imagine, fully realise the risk of jumping on the parapet, but it does seem probable that in the excitement of an unfamiliar attack he really did it to rally his men and for no ulterior motive. So I really do think that you can put out of your mind any lingering last suspicion of self-reproach or personal responsibility that you still may have.

Privately Vera could not be so certain. Doubts about Edward's death lingered on in her own mind and, as so often, it was through her writing that she attempted to come to terms with them. At the time of Hudson's unexpected reappearance, she was in the early stages of writing *Honourable Estate*, her lengthy 'novel of transition' covering the years 1894 to 1930. In the wartime section of the book, Richard Alleyndene, the younger brother of the heroine, Ruth, goes into the Gallipoli campaign seeking to be killed in order to avoid a court martial for homosexuality. When the fighting is over he is found 'shot through the neck with his jugular vein severed'. His farewell letter is delivered to his sister by an American lance-corporal to whom he had entrusted it the day before he died.

The letter describes in detail the horrors of war and the degradations of army life. 'After a few weeks nobody seems to care 2d about pictures or decent books', Richard Alleyndene declares, 'it's all cards and girls and whisky and what sort of harlot you're going to pick up when you next get a pass'. He and an old schoolfriend had decided when life became really intolerable 'that the only thing to do was to be everything we possibly could to one another.'

> There was no trouble at all to begin with, but soon after we got here . . . some swinish fellows began to talk. A few days ago the C.O. sent for me and told me that next time we are out of the line there will probably be an inquiry – which of course might mean a court-martial and expulsion from the Army. Well, I don't intend to let it come to that . . . I can't confront Father and Mother with the fact that their son is what they would call vicious and immoral instead of a virtuous patriotic hero.

There is, however, a significant difference of detail between Richard Alleyndene's situation as portrayed here and that of Edward Brittain. Whereas Edward had apparently been discovered exploiting the mutual bond of respect and trust that existed between an officer and his men, by having homosexual relations with men in his company, Richard Alleyndene's homosexual relationship is clearly in the tradition of the public school romantic friendship which Vera defends, in a rather strained argument, as being justified in wartime because of the unavailability of any women except prostitutes. The idea that Edward had behaved in any way that was accounted discreditable, or that his homosexuality was anything more than a passing phase, an outgrowth of his Uppingham education, was one that Vera seems to have found extremely difficult to entertain.

It was also painful for her to acknowledge to herself that there had been a darker side to his character which he had felt forced to conceal even from his beloved sister. His self-containment, she had long realized, had made him difficult to know well, though occasionally in letters written to her during the war, he had dropped his guard sufficiently to reveal evidence of deeper problems beneath. In one he had confessed 'that women are a great problem to me. I meet very few, of those I dislike almost all, and I don't think I understand any of them.' A common difficulty, one would think, for a man educated exclusively among his own sex, but then there is a stronger hint about his sexuality in another letter of 1918 in which he parries some remark of hers about his marrying with the comment that that is 'a most improbable occurrence'. But in 1939 she was nonetheless shocked to learn from her mother that Edward had been implicated at Uppingham in acts of what in public school jargon was known as 'beastliness'. Mrs Brittain had told Vera ('which she had never told me before'),

> that when she was going through Edward's belongings after his death, she came across . . . a private diary of his which made it quite clear that he had been concerned ('of course, probably only as an onlooker', she said, poor dear) in homosexual doings at Uppingham – she burnt it . . .*
>
> I always suspected Col. Hudson a little, but this seems to justify him. There was no evil in Edward; he was just deeply romantic about his friends, as musicians are. Uppingham was obviously no Nonconformist chapel, & in the

---

* This probably relates to the expulsion from Uppingham in June 1913 of Maurice Ellinger, the Brittains' Buxton neighbour and Edward's closest schoolfriend after Roland and Victor, for engaging in homosexual activities. At the time Vera, in greater ignorance of sexual matters than her brother, had turned to Edward for an explanation. 'There is only one unpardonable sin at a public school – immorality', he had told her, 'and this is the only thing for which a boy is not given another chance.' Maurice Ellinger, who had also been a teenage admirer of Vera's, tragically attempted suicide in 1915.

Army homosexuality is the only outlet for the romantic. Personally, I think the harm it does is probably much exaggerated ...

Once again, Vera's remarks about Edward are noticeably defensive, but there is no doubting his tendency to imbue his friendships with a romantic glow. One of his favourite collections of war poetry was Robert Nichols's *Ardours and Endurances*, a popular success of 1917, which was Edward's final birthday gift to Vera in December of that year. Like so many of Nichols's readers, Edward clearly responded to the book's 'homoerotic warmth', finding a reflection of his own experience in the narrative sequence of the poems in which the poet enjoys deep friendships with two soldiers in turn. The deaths in action of first one and then the other 'leave him devastated, and an irredeemable loneliness dominates the rest of the volume.' The deaths of Roland and Victor, and of Geoffrey, the loss that probably affected him the most, must have had a similarly devastating effect on Edward, as Vera had pointed out to Colonel Hudson. It is tempting to deduce from the evidence of the ardent quality of some of Geoffrey's letters to Edward (especially from the closing tag of many of them, 'Him that thou knowest thine') that their relationship may have gone beyond the bounds of chaste friendship. Here, though, it is probably as well to heed the warning note sounded by one critic, Martin Taylor, that sentiments that appear overtly homosexual to modern sensibilities may, in the context of their time, have been nothing of the kind. Certainly Geoffrey had been Edward's 'beloved friend', and there was touching confirmation of this when, while clearing the Oakwood Court flat in the autumn of 1934, Edith Brittain came across the tunic in which Edward had been killed. Inside the top pocket, preserved as a memento, was a letter from Geoffrey.

For Vera, Colonel Hudson's revelations about Edward's last days had invited 'such fundamental doubts and speculations which can never now be answered ...'. A few years before her own death, the subject was revived painfully for her when a young psychologist, who had developed something of a fixation with Edward from his reading of *Testament of Youth*, started to harass Vera for access to her First World War letters which she was then intending to bequeath to the Imperial War Museum in London. He had, it appears, guessed that Edward had had homosexual tendencies and wanted to use the letters in a study of his character, which he intended to relate to the general subject of sexual inversion. Vera became worried that the letters might one day fall into his hands, and warned her literary executor that he was 'a scientist of a rather crackpot variety' who was unlikely to respect the privacy of certain matters alluded to in Edward's correspondence. 'One of

Edward's correspondents, (whom I suspect was periodically homosexual)', she elaborated, 'wrote him several letters marked *"Private"*. I have always observed this request for privacy, but I doubt if Dr [X] would, since as a scientist he would feel it essential to know *everything*, in spite of the wishes of the writer!' Here, it can be safely assumed, is a reference to the correspondence which had entrapped Edward in June 1918. But it must remain forever a tantalizing glimpse. At Vera's death it was discovered that the letters had been destroyed.

VI

'It seems to me that the War will make a big division of "before" and "after" in the history of the world', Vera had written from Malta in 1916. The line between before and after was drawn irrevocably in her own life on 15 June 1918 when Edward's death removed the last and most important of the young men dear to her. Nothing would ever console her for his loss. She would miss him 'at every turn of the road'. Fifty years later there remained a quiet but ineradicable grief.

Late in August 1918, *Verses of a VAD* by Vera M. Brittain ('V.A.D. London / 268, B.R.C.S') belatedly appeared, 'ushered unobtrusively into an indifferent world', and on to a market long since saturated with war poetry. A foreword by Marie Leighton emphasized that most of the poems had been written on active service 'under conditions of strain and turmoil', and appealed for 'considerateness and tender sympathy' in judging the work 'of a young girl . . . who in her personal destiny has suffered as, I hope, very few have suffered.'

Predominantly elegiac and documentary in tone, the collection contains Vera's personal lamentations for the dead as well as several hospital poems, most notably 'The German Ward', an attempt to convey what she had learned from nursing enemy prisoners ('that human mercy turns alike to friend or foe / When the darkest hour of all is creeping nigh'). In 'To My Brother', included at a final stage in the book's preparation, Vera tries to tell Edward, 'as I could never quite tell him in words or in letters', how much she admired him for his courage and endurance. 'To My Brother', with its profusion of militaristic imagery, its martial excitement, and its hero-worship is essentially a pro-war poem. Any glimmerings of latent pacifism on Vera's part have been snuffed out by the need to show Edward her respect for his heroism. Written four days before he was killed, and

135

inscribed on the flyleaf of a copy of *The Muse in Arms*, an anthology of war poetry, which she sent out to Italy, it tragically arrived too late for Edward to read.

In their over-reliance on stock poetic emotions and language, and their striving for self-conscious effect, some of the *Verses of a VAD* tend towards the banal. Yet in the simpler, more restrained poems a voice of authentic experience and testimony is sometimes to be heard. The reviewer in the *Times Literary Supplement*, in one of the few notices which the book received, commended Vera on 'her well-finished and exact workmanship', noting that 'she only yields to the need of expressing, simply and clearly and with restraint, an exceptionally poignant personal sorrow for losses in the war . . .'.

By the time the war ended on 11 November 1918, Vera had become a 'complete automaton', existing in a state of numb disillusion, with little interest in either the present or the future. 'I ended the First World War with my deepest emotions paralysed if not dead', she was to write many years later. 'This would not have happened if I had had *one* person left. It was Edward's death rather than Roland's which turned me into an automaton . . . I could have married Victor in memory of Roland, and Geoffrey in memory of Edward, but the War took even the second best. It left nothing. Only ambition held me to life.'

FOUR

Lament of the Demobilized

'Now if we go back we will be weary, broken, burnt out, rootless, and without hope . . . and the generation that has grown up after us will be strange to us and push us aside. We will be superfluous even to ourselves . . .'

Erich Maria Remarque, *All Quiet on the Western Front* (1928)

I

In September 1918 Vera re-enlisted as a VAD, but having broken her agreement in returning from France to look after her parents, she was ineligible for an overseas appointment until she had served a further probationary period at home. Her first posting to St Thomas's Hospital filled her with fury. After the responsibilities and camaraderie in military hospitals abroad, she resented the supercilious attitude of the qualified nursing staff in a civilian hospital which consigned even an experienced VAD like herself to the perpetual drudgery of cleaning, dusting and polishing.

At the end of September she was transferred to Queen Alexandra's Hospital, Millbank, where in the more relaxed environment of a military hospital her bitterness abated, to be replaced by alternating bouts of somnambulistic lethargy and bleak despair. That winter a worldwide influenza epidemic reached its height, and in the United Kingdom over 200,000 people died. 'I have a "sense" (instinctive not rational) of being back in October 1918,' Vera wrote many years later as the V-2 rockets fell on London during the Second World War, causing heavy casualties. 'Our last minute horror was then the influenza epidemic. I cared so little whether I lived or died that I nursed case after case, first in St Thomas's and then at Millbank, & helped to lay out corpses which began to turn blue even before life left them, without ever getting more than a slight temperature & a sore throat.' She attributed her immunity to the fact that she was so fatalistically unafraid.

At Queen Alexandra's, on the morning of 11 November, Vera heard the crash of the maroons marking the first Armistice Day, but continued mechanically washing the dressing bowls, bitterly reflecting that the end of the war had arrived too late for all those closest to her. She completed her six-month contract at the beginning of April 1919, and at the end of the month went back up to Oxford. The determination to complete her university education was her lifeline to overcoming her postwar despair and isolation, but in returning to Somerville at twenty-five, after a four-year absence, she failed to anticipate the pitfalls and difficulties that lay ahead.

In 1914 she had intended to read English, but like many Great War survivors Vera had emerged with an overwhelming sense of obligation to the fallen generation. On her return to Somerville she decided to change to history in an attempt to understand 'why it had been possible for me and my contemporaries through our own ignorance and others' ingenuity, to be used, hypnotised and slaughtered'; she still idealistically believed that mankind could learn from the mistakes and disasters of the past.

If she had imagined that her war service and seniority would give her a certain cachet, an implicit prestige, then she received a rude awakening when the Principal, Emily Penrose, in a 'brief and laconic' interview brushed aside what Vera described as an 'emotional plea for one word of welcome, of encouragement'; Miss Penrose greeted her as though she had last taken leave of Vera for the Easter vacation rather than four years previously.

Somerville remained temporarily accommodated in the St Mary Hall Quadrangle of Oriel College – its own buildings were not derequisitioned by the War Office until July – and Vera found herself separated from the rest of the second year in lodgings in King Edward Street which she shared with five other senior students. With one of them, Nina Ruffer, an unassuming third-year reading anthropology, Vera soon became friendly. Sir Armand Ruffer, Nina's father, had been torpedoed and drowned in the Mediterranean in the spring of 1917 while Vera was in Malta, and it was this wartime link which first drew the two women together. Vera also felt a bond of understanding with Hilda Lorimer, her Classics tutor in 1915, who had herself only recently returned from working in a hospital in Salonika. They met occasionally for tea in Miss Lorimer's room, and although they had little opportunity for intimate conversation, Vera remembered with gratitude Hilda Lorimer's support for her decision to take up nursing, and her insistence that she should return to Somerville after the war 'because at College, more than anywhere else, one was likely to make the friendships that supported one through life.'

Nina Ruffer, a sufferer from heart disease, died suddenly from pneumonia that summer vacation while Vera was waiting to join her at a summer school in Cambridge; and when Vera returned to Oxford in October for the Michaelmas term, it was to a much bleaker existence. Her new room in Keble Road was pleasant, and her landlady told her that she could have 'a fire every evening if I don't light it before 5 . . .', but she experienced greater loneliness and desolation than before amid a crowd of first- and second-years at Somerville, most of whom were barely out of school. Writing to her mother, Vera tried to put on a brave face about her situation: 'Don't worry because I don't like college as much as I perhaps should have if I had come up before the War. Don't you know that the only people who ever do well at a University are the ones who aren't altogether happy there?'

She felt forced to disguise her own unhappiness so as not to add to her mother's worries. That autumn Arthur Brittain went down with a bad attack of flu. His recovery was made more protracted by the depression from which he had rarely emerged since Edward's death. Edith Brittain was also struggling to come to terms with her grief for Edward. In June, acutely aware of her mother's feelings as the first anniversary of Edward's death drew near, Vera had written to her suggesting that 'If I were you I should certainly go to the Melba concert next Sunday – Edward would like it, & I am not sure moreover that on the whole we don't allow ourselves to be too upset by "anniversaries".'

Vera's own state of mind was increasingly precarious. In the aftermath of Nina Ruffer's death she had begun to suffer from hallucinations, which suggest that she was on the verge of some kind of nervous breakdown. 'I *had* to see myself through it', she recalled several years later,

> because there was no one else to do so, no one even with sufficient perception to see that I was ill and not merely disagreeable . . . I could not sleep, and when I did I had dreadful nightmares, and then I suffered for months from the délusion that my face was disfigured; it always looked disfigured when I saw it in the glass, until I got into such a state where I almost screamed if I went into a room where there was a mirror . . .

The form that this disfigurement took was of a dark shadow lying across her chin, closely resembling an incipient beard. If, as seems most likely, Vera was suffering from survivor's guilt, then the 'beard', it has been recently suggested, may possess an especial significance. It may symbolize the guilt that Vera felt in seizing the intellectual and professional opportunities that could no longer be taken by her dead male contemporaries. Whether or not this is so, signs of Vera's strain would persist, at times worse than others, for more than a year. 'Such a state of mind is nearly intolerable', the historian Jay Winter has written, 'because it is infused with a burden of guilt which makes life a type of walking death, or which requires total identification with the dead who continue to live inside the survivor.'

For her tutorials that term in modern European history – by 'modern' the Oxford History School meant the period from 1789 to 1878, ending with the Congress of Berlin – Vera had assumed that she would have the undivided attention of C.R.M.F. Cruttwell, the Dean of Hertford College. She was a little resentful, therefore, to be told that she would be sharing her tutorials with a Miss Holtby, who had returned to college that October after serving for a year with the Women's Army Auxiliary Corps.

Winifred Holtby was nineteen when she originally went up to Somerville at the beginning of Michaelmas term 1917. The novelist, Constance Savery, vividly remembered meeting her there when

> On the first day of my first term I went in accordance with custom to report myself to the Principal. Another student ... was waiting outside Miss Penrose's study door. She was tall and dignified, a Norse goddess – if one can imagine a Norse goddess impeccably clad in the long sweeping garments of 1917, with a little eye-veil on her elegant small hat. A raw and scared schoolgirl, I waited humbly beside her, and was intensely relieved – and slightly incredulous – when her greeting made clear to me that she was only a Fresher, like myself, bound on the same errand. It was my first sight of Winifred Holtby. I can see her still exactly as she stood in the dark passage; a royal figure.

In the summer of 1918 Winifred had enlisted in Queen Alexandra's Women's Army Auxiliary Corps. Her first appointment was the supervision of the domestic staff in a luxurious Officers' Club in Mayfair, but in September she had embarked for France and the more challenging role of hostel forewoman at a WAAC camp near Abbeville.

During her year at Somerville, Winifred's cheerful good humour, kindness, and inexhaustible vitality had made her one of the most popular first-year students. When she returned in 1919, Constance Savery nostalgically recalled how 'Winifred Holtby burst in on us again, gay, radiant, friendly as of old', while Hilda Reid commented with pithy admiration that 'Winifred came back to a hero's welcome'.

There could scarcely have been a greater contrast between Vera's recollections of her pernickety parents, and lonely, class-dominated upbringing, and Winifred's memories of her adventurous, carefree childhood on her father's farm in the heartland of the Yorkshire wolds. In her novels, stories and articles, and in her letters and conversation, Winifred frequently recalled her early years in Rudston, a straggling village six miles from Bridlington. Writing in 1932 to the South African novelist and biographer Sarah Gertrude Millin, she confided that 'Quite half my life is there, and all my "roots" '.

After the Bosville Macdonalds of Thorpe Hall, the Holtbys were the most important family in Rudston, and before mechanization revolutionized every aspect of agricultural activity, the farms and farming were the hub of village life. The Holtby farm provided work for a large number of men and boys, and domestic employment for cooks, maids and washerwomen. It was a busy, stimulating world for an observant child.

The Holtby household was dominated by Winifred's mother, a dynamic, matriarchal figure. Kathleen Byass, a Somerville undergraduate, whose East Riding family had a passing acquaintance with Winifred's parents, described Alice Holtby as an exceptional woman, 'tall, massive & handsome & immensely kind'. All and sundry came within the scope of her philanthropic activities. With ample accommodation and a large domestic staff, she welcomed a steady procession of relatives and friends to Rudston House, and at Christmas as many as seventeen aunts, uncles and cousins sat down to a lively family dinner. Winifred inherited much of her mother's vitality and public-spirited concern for others, and shared with her less assertive father, David Holtby, a sense of humour and fun, and a delight in the absurdities of life.

Alice Holtby had been approaching forty when Winifred was born on 23 June 1898. Her older daughter, Grace, was docile and apathetic, and Alice Holtby's ambitions had focused principally upon Winifred, a precocious exuberant child with an irrepressible imagination. She could write, Winifred said, before she could read with comfort, 'and at the ages of three and four I was as implacable a narrator of impossibilities as the Ancient Mariner'. The two daughters of a local vicar shared the Holtby governess, and at Winifred's instigation the four girls compiled a magazine of poems and stories in a half-finished exercise book. With her cousins Edmund and Dolly Holtby from Dowthorpe Hall (the prototype for 'Maythorpe' in *South Riding*), young friends from neighbouring families, and the village children, the farmyard provided an ideal playground for hide-and-seek, and harumscarum climbs to the tops of strawstacks. At other times Winifred accompanied her father's old shepherd on long pony rides round the 940-acre farm, and the fields, she said, assumed more definite personalities than any of the people she knew. With friendly confidence she mixed easily and naturally with people of all ages from all walks of life, and she remembered with amusement and affection an old, itinerant Irishman who turned up at the farm year after year for harvest work, or when ill and destitute to be nursed back to health by Mrs Holtby.

When Winifred was eleven her mother sent her as a boarder to Queen Margaret's School in Scarborough, a Church of England school intended principally for the daughters of clergymen and professional people. The education was good, and Winifred was quickly recognized as an outstanding pupil, but the school was out of sight of the sea in a sunless situation, the heating facilities were inadequate and the sanitary arrangements rudimentary. Many years later Winifred declared that 'when I first went to school, life seemed to me as it might do if I suddenly woke up today in one of the more primitive societies . . .'.

When she was thirteen she was shopping with the School Matron in Scarborough and could scarcely believe her eyes to see in a bookshop window a privately printed collection of her childhood verse. Her mother had surreptitiously collected what Winifred later dismissed as her 'priggish, derivative and nauseatingly insincere' poetry and had paid £10. 15s for the production of five hundred copies of a pink and pale green forty-eight-page booklet tied with a purple ribbon entitled *My Garden and Other Poems*.

Winifred wrote poetry spasmodically all her life, but as an adolescent she was more absorbed with the exciting possibilities of amateur theatricals. As author, producer and performer, each Christmas she inflicted upon a long-suffering audience of relatives, neighbours and maids a series of melodramatic epics. Grace liked dressing up and romantic love scenes, their male companions preferred heroics and masculine daredevilry, while Winifred injected strong doses of audacious drama. *Grizelda's Vow* contained nothing more alarming than a murder or two, duels and a suicide, but after an explicit performance of *A Living Lie* with an elopement, leprosy, adultery, and a grand homicidal finale with the heroine murdering both her husband and lover before committing suicide, Mrs Holtby put her foot down. The following year she insisted upon an innocuous drawing-room comedy from French's published plays for amateur dramatic societies.

Among the many visitors to Rudston House were the two sons of a Driffield bank manager. The older brother, Harry Pearson, a tall, slim, religiously-minded boy two years Winifred's senior, also had ambitions to become a writer. He had, she said, 'a quite singular facility for words', and their mutual interest established a bond of compatibility and friendship.

George de Coundouroff was a Russian boy who had been sent to

England to study agriculture. Alice Holtby invited him to stay at the farm during the school holidays, and he soon became the Holtbys' unofficially adopted son. When he was sent to Russia in 1917 as an interpreter with the Allied Intervention force, Alice insisted that his pregnant wife, Edith, should live at Rudston. After George was reported missing, Edith de Coundouroff and her daughter, Margaret, remained with the Holtbys for the next twenty years. Edith's life cannot have been easy, and it is impossible to overestimate the importance of her selfless and loving support. She helped to soften the blow of Grace's untimely death in 1928, and of David Holtby's five years later, and by being with Alice Holtby she made it possible for Winifred to continue living in London with an easier conscience.

During the war conscription had dramatically reduced the number of farm workers available, and at the end of 1918 there was an orchestrated agitation for higher wages and a half-day on Saturdays. David Holtby was nearly sixty, he had no son and heir, and the unrest and intimidating prospect of an agricultural strike precipitated his early retirement. When Winifred returned to Yorkshire in August 1919 after being demobilized, it was not to Rudston but to Cottingham, four miles north of Hull, and to 'Bainesse', an imposing suburban residence with a large kitchen garden and a tennis court. She did her best to adapt to her new surroundings, but the Rudston farm and village activities dominated her imagination for the rest of her life.

She was at home for little more than a month before returning to Somerville. She was just twenty-one and, looking back, described herself as 'a creature of completely uncritical piety and sentimental conviction'.

II

Vera first met Winifred at a shared tutorial with Mr Cruttwell, and 'We did not,' she later wrote with disarming sincerity, 'to begin with, like each other at all'. Lonely, unhappy, and defensively conscious of being nearly five years older, Vera later wrote that 'Winifred's high-spirited presence overwhelmed me like a powerful gust of crude north country wind'. She described Winifred in 1919 as tall with an aquiline nose, strongly moulded chin, and slightly waving fair hair, and with 'perpetually parted lips and wide-open china-blue eyes full of an eager vitality'. In *Testament of Friendship* she discreetly referred to Winifred's choice of clothes at Somerville as 'colourful rather than judicious'. In her novel of college life she felt less inhibited in describing the sartorial idiosyncrasies of Daphne Lethbridge, whom she acknowledged to be in part a pen portrait of Winifred. She recalled that at their first meeting Winifred was wearing an orange crêpe-de-Chine blouse, brown velvet coat and skirt, and vivid green hat, and commented with lugubrious humour that 'Altogether she gave the impression of a rather uncontrolled kitchen garden'. She criticized also 'the crude yellow dress which made her so unattractively conspicuous', the curiously inappropriate green evening dress with wide patterned sash of orange and scarlet, and the magenta evening cloak which clashed badly with her fair hair.

Kathleen Byass was a third-year undergraduate when Vera returned to Somerville, and remembers her, by contrast, as being 'always very well dressed in a town fashion while the rest of us were mostly extremely dowdy!' 'She was very much more sophisticated and experienced . . . [than] all of us younger & very inexperienced girls straight from boarding school.'

Small, dark-eyed, and pale with slightly hollow cheeks, Vera was confidently aware of being attractive and strikingly pretty. She dressed expensively with meticulous care, and frequently chose black, enhanced with a colourful sash or an artificial flower. Black suited her, and suggested, too, that her war dead were not forgotten, though for one Somerville dance she wore 'a delphinium-like dress of soft blues and mauves', and at Eights Week appeared cool and composed in white georgette.

The unconcealed hostility which marred the first weeks of her relationship with Winifred was due, according to Vera, to 'our foolish rivalry'. As an exhibitioner, and a first-year student of outstanding promise, Somerville had regarded Vera as a possible First, and she was to sustain their expectations as the joint winner in 1920 of the Edith Coombs Prize for History. Hard-working, and with the ability to present facts and complex issues in highly readable and cogent form, Vera quickly devised an effective 'scaffolding' method for the preparation of her essays, which she subsequently adapted for her articles and books. Winifred, by contrast, had difficulty in marshalling her facts and arguments, in spite of the fact that she too had shown early promise, having achieved a distinction in History Previous, the preliminary Oxford examination, at the end of her first term. Winifred later admitted that when 'my immensely long, muddled and emotional history essays were condemned, I accepted the condemnation. It was, I recognized, just. But I set myself with diligence and distress to remedy my shortcomings . . . Term by term I set to to produce from my fuddled, nebulous and fragmentary impressions of the past, something more neatly and concisely designed to satisfy my tutors.'

At Winifred's tutorials, the more tactful dons, like Dr A.L. Smith, the

Master of Balliol, to whom both Vera and Winifred were sent in their final year, commented on a 'praiseworthy effect', or murmured a few words of appreciation for the amount of work she had done; but the thirty-two-year-old Charles Cruttwell was more outspoken. He had recently returned to Oxford after a spell in the military intelligence department of the War Office, and two years at the front which had left him permanently scarred, 'a wreck of the war'. Army service had made him an intimidating disciplinarian, although in other ways he was markedly eccentric, wearing his hair, for instance, in a distinctly unmilitary bob. Despite his half-humorous ferocity of speech, he could be an excellent tutor. Vera found his lectures that term on 'Nationality and Self-Determination' enlightening, and was also perhaps more inclined to be sympathetic towards him as a war survivor. Winifred, on the other hand, confessed later that he had 'put her off' as he reminded her too much of an army colonel. Cruttwell too was sharply divided over the quality of their work. While he thought Vera the ablest woman student that he had ever taught – and in her novel of university life, the character whom she frankly admitted to be an 'idealized self-portrait' produces essays which are 'monotonously excellent', or 'clear, acute, logical' – Winifred's work provoked his scathing criticism. He denounced her style as laborious, her subject matter as confused, and her spelling abominable. In her end-of-term report, Vera received 'a lengthy eulogy' from Cruttwell, but as she wrote to her mother, 'He didn't give a bit of a good report to the girl I coach with & yet she always strikes me as being quite good.'

Academically Vera won a head start over Winifred, but as far as personal popularity was concerned, she came nowhere near to matching her. Intense and outspoken, Vera lacked the qualities which make for easy, spontaneous rapport. She was well aware of this deficiency, and there was defensiveness – as well as a clear echo of Roland – in her tendency to dismiss popularity as 'commonplace and vulgar'. She was both pained and angered by the way in which her war experience appeared to be ignored in postwar Oxford, but she alienated her fellow Somervillians by talking constantly about her war service, of nursing the mutilated and dying, and about the deaths of her fiancé, brother and friends. She spoke disparagingly about people who hadn't travelled. 'She overlooked the fact that almost all the students had been too young for active service, and that the war had brought continental travel virtually to a standstill.'

It is not now possible to know whose idea it was to inveigle Vera into proposing the motion at a meeting of the newly formed Somerville Debating Society 'That four years' travel are a better education than four years at

University'. As the Secretary of the Debating Society it fell to Winifred to issue an official invitation, which probably explains why Vera held her responsible for the subsequent debacle. Male undergraduates were invited to the more important Somerville debates, but this one was to be a purely domestic event.

Cicely Williams, a friend of Winifred's from her first year, had initially felt sorry for Vera, but became irritated and impatient with her obsessive preoccupation with her war service. 'The debate was conceived as a jolly good idea to take her down a peg or two', she commented, but stressed that it was intended only as an amusing, high-spirited prank. With no premonition of the machinations afoot, Vera accepted the Debating Society invitation with alacrity. It was, she wrote, the chance she had been waiting for 'to tell her daily acquaintances what she thought of their attitude towards the acute problems of existence.' She told Edith Brittain, with overbearing confidence, that she proposed to make 'a most revolutionary speech, ardently supporting travel & violently attacking the University, so if any dons are present they will probably get a shock.'

Vera was a practised debater, having already taken part in debates with other VADs, while off duty in Étaples. In proposing the motion she drew heavily on her personal experiences, and dwelt in detail upon the enlightenment and understanding she had derived from her nursing service in Malta and France. She described her life abroad as 'a kaleidoscope of experience', and scornfully contrasted it with 'the narrow monotony of an academic career'. Her whole speech, she wrote later – but one has the suspicion that it was histrionic exaggeration – 'was a stinging indictment of her fellow-students' limitations'.

When the debate was thrown open Winifred sprang exuberantly to her feet. Aware that her tutorials with Vera had been awkward and constrained, her friends had urged her on as their spokeswoman in exposing Vera's supercilious disdain. Uncharacteristically, she launched a direct personal attack.

'The proof of the pudding's in the eating,' she concluded. 'We can only discover the comparative value of travel and a University career by looking at the kind of person they both produce. Now take the case of the honourable proposer; she regards herself as a person who's travelled and who doesn't think anything of education in comparison . . . Now, I don't see the object of going in for something that's only going to make one unhappy, and a general cause of depression to the people one associates with . . . In the words of Rosalind in *As You Like It:* "I had rather have a fool to make me merry than experience to make me sad; and to travel for it too!" ' Winifred set the tone for the whole evening. Her friends were elated, 'and the members of the Debating Society,' Vera said, 'proceeded to lose their manners with their heads'.

The debate ended with the proposal overwhelmingly defeated, and with Vera devastated and angry, and bitterly humiliated by the contempt of her college contemporaries. She stood silently by her chair as her tormentors left the hall, but afterwards, alone in her room, 'I lay on the cold floor and wept with childish abandonment'.

The antipathy between Vera and Winifred culminated after the debate in what Janet Vaughan, the Treasurer of the Debating Society, described as 'a terrific row', which lasted for two days. To help resolve a disruptive and unpleasant situation, Janet decided to bring Vera and Winifred together so that they could talk freely and frankly, and hopefully settle their differences.

Vera recognized that she had a strongly combative disposition. Her confrontations were an uncomfortable emotional strain, but paradoxically also provided an impetus and a surge of vitality. With Janet Vaughan's encouragement, she made a formal request for a meeting with Winifred as the Secretary of the Debating Society. On the Sunday evening, two days after the debate, Vera went to Winifred's room, and in a fictional reconstruction of their conversation – which she acknowledged to be 'substantially correct' – angrily informed Winifred that it was obvious that the debate had been arranged specifically to let her know how much she was disliked.

'You think you can use your Debating Society to tell people what you think of them when they make you feel uncomfortable,' she said, 'and you daren't say what you mean to their faces. But you won't get your society to prosper if you're going to make the proposer's chair a stool of repentance.' She dismissed as 'the gross impertinence of someone unspeakably ill-bred' the fact that Winifred had repeated in public a remark Vera had made privately that the only possible attitude to take towards life in general was one of cynicism. Taken aback at Vera's denunciation, and acutely aware of her distress, Winifred murmured she was sorry, offered a few consolatory words of regret, and promised that the Debating Society would send an official letter of apology.

Some years later, when Vera was writing her account of the debate for *Testament of Youth*, Winifred explained how this incident had appeared to her: '. . . the whole episode was such a shock to me that I hesitated afterwards to disclaim any motive, however bad. I had meant the whole thing to be a "rag" – as we WAACs had instituted rags in the Army – dozens of rough & tumble (& no doubt coarse, clumsy & vulgar) teasings – to rub off what seemed to me something of your superiority towards all my fellow-students who had not been to the War.' Winifred had regarded her war work as, if anything, an indulgence: 'I had been so infinitely happier both nursing & in the WAAC than I had been in that ghastly year at Oxford in 1917, that it never occurred to me that Army life was anything but a fortunate privilege, & superiority based upon it an intolerable form of snobbery, until I heard your story.'

However, the debate was not the only occasion when Vera's simmering resentment of Somerville's disregard for her war service threatened to sour a college relationship. Somerville's brilliant History tutor from Northern Ireland, Maude Clarke, and Vera were almost exactly the same age, and Vera could neither forget nor forgive that while she had thrown 'four years into the melting pot', Maude Clarke has been pursuing her academic career at Lady Margaret Hall. Cicely Williams maintained that in an outburst of frustration at the 'serene detachment' with which the tutor appeared 'to view the tragedy that had dislocated our lives', Vera confronted Maude Clarke and told her that but for the war she might well have achieved similar academic distinction. This may be so, as Vera was later to include an identical incident in her Oxford novel.

Maude Clarke was in any case the main butt of Vera's resentment as she poured out her postwar bitterness in 'The Lament of the Demobilised', published in the 1920 edition of *Oxford Poetry*:

> 'Four years,' some say consolingly, 'Oh well,
> What's that? You're young. And then it must have been
> A very fine experience for you!'
> And they forget
> How others stayed behind – and just got on –
> And we came home and found
> They had achieved, and men revered their names,
> But never mentioned ours;
> And no one talked heroics now, and we
> Must just go back and start again once more.

The Somerville debate had taken place towards the end of the Michaelmas term, and Vera and Winifred saw little of each other, outside tutorials, before returning home for the Christmas vacation. Winifred, unaffected and compassionate – she once wrote that she could never retain a good hate – realized from the intensity of Vera's almost neurotic outburst that her façade of superiority concealed a disturbed and unhappy woman, and in January, when Vera was in bed with a chill, she appeared at her door with a bunch of grapes. 'It was', their contemporary Mary Macaulay (later Lady Ogilvie) remarked, 'the beginning of a marvellous friendship.'

It was indeed; and yet, as Vera admitted in *Testament of Friendship*, 'Passionately as I desired Winifred's friendship, the building of it was her achievement rather than mine.' She was always to acknowledge that their friendship owed most to Winifred's forbearance, understanding and solicitude. At the outset their work gave them a common meeting ground, and they soon discovered that they shared an ambition to write. Before long they were going on walks together outside Oxford, as far afield as Wood Eaton or Marston Ferry. As early as February 1920, Vera was informing her mother that she was 'very fond' of the girl who shared her tutorials. So fond, in fact, that when she was not studying, she spent most of her time in Winifred's room in College, '& never see Keble Rd between 8.0 in the morning & 11.0 at night. So I think on the whole it would be better to address my letters to Somerville College . . .'. At the beginning of their third year, in the autumn of 1920, they both moved into rooms in Bevington Road, a five-minute cycle ride from Somerville.

Winifred's friends agreed that her need to be needed was one of the most conspicuous facets of her personality. She possessed an almost obsessive conviction of being a debtor to life. She had inherited her mother's concern for other people's misfortunes and her public-spirited philanthropy, and had grown up keenly aware of her good fortune in having a happy, comfortably-off home life. At Somerville no one needed her more than Vera. Since Edward's death, Vera had felt herself to be entirely alone, without anyone to understand her anxieties or fears, or to help her overcome her postwar neurosis. The delusions which had plagued Vera since Nina Ruffer's death had by now grown to alarming proportions. Winifred's 'patient, eager understanding' played its part in her slow journey to recovery, and when Vera was experiencing a particularly bad night she would sometimes sleep on the couch in Winifred's room.

There was rancour, though, among other Somervillians as her growing friendship with Vera absorbed increasing amounts of Winifred's time. Winifred's good nature had made her among the most popular of the postwar students, and her solicitude for others had established her as the immediate focus for anyone 'with a want, a grievance, or a dilemma.' Hilda Reid, who had returned to College after taking a year out because of illness, had been one of Winifred's closest first-year friends, and had therefore perhaps the most cause to resent Vera's intrusion. She believed Winifred to have been captivated by Vera's smallness and by her deceptive aura of vulnerability, and thought that Winifred supplied the humour and emotional support that Vera so obviously lacked. 'Winifred felt that Vera was her responsibility. It was almost a maternal possessiveness. Vera made her feel like a carthorse trampling all over a shrinking violet.' Cicely Williams remembered Winifred 'was such fun, such stimulating company, everyone was delighted to see her', and Cicely was not at all amused when Vera came along 'and gobbled her up.'

Dorothy Sayers had gone down in 1915 before Winifred arrived, but struck up a warm acquaintance with her during the years 1922 to 1925 when they were both on the Committee of the Somerville Students' Association. After Winifred's death she wrote of her keen and satirical intellect, and added that 'she united, in alliance as rare as it is precious, a most lovable and generous personality, which no one who had ever met her, were it only for a few moments, could ever forget.' Was she thinking perhaps of Vera when she concluded that 'all who were unhappy or oppressed found in her an eager and unfailing champion'?

The early months of Vera's friendship with Winifred Holtby coincided with what Vera was later to describe as her 'unbalanced excursion into spurious romance'. Vera's prettiness was obviously attractive to some of her male contemporaries at Oxford. 'If she dropped a glove when cycling', Hilda Reid recalled, 'there was always someone to pick it up, which never happened to the rest of us.' At one of the Somerville debates to which men were invited, some time in the spring of 1920, Vera was introduced to Robert ('Roy') Anthony, a St John's undergraduate, who was taking the shortened Modern History course for war-service candidates. Anthony had been up at Oxford in 1914, and had gone down after a year to serve with the Royal Lancashire Regiment in France, where 'he had had the luck to be wounded twice in such a way as to take him out of action for a time.' He was a year younger than Vera, and Hilda Reid remembered him as 'a nice little thing' who was much impressed by Vera's maturity and intelligence.

At the end of April Vera received a letter from Roy Anthony, addressed to 'Dear Miss Brittain', saying that he had been reading *Verses of a VAD*. They were, he told her, 'the saddest poems I have ever read, as well as some of the most charming', and he added that 'I know I'm only more or less of a stranger, but I felt I must just say how sorry I am for you, and though I know such a thing is impossible, how much I wish I could do anything at all for you in any way.' Pity is an insubstantial basis for love, but Roy Anthony had already lost if not his heart, then at least his head to a woman who seemed 'to have been harder hit in the war than anyone I have ever met.' 'Don't think me mad', he pleaded in a postscript, 'but I had to do something to relieve my feelings.'

Vera was flattered and intrigued, and the two began to see each other. Towards the end of that summer term, Roy Anthony proposed to her in an unchaperoned interlude in the bicycle shed during a Somerville dance, and Vera accepted. To her contemporaries the engagement was less a matter for congratulation than for amused speculation. 'We all joked about it', Cicely Williams remarked, 'and warned each other that bicycle sheds were dangerous places'. Hilda Reid mischievously recalled that there had been a full moon that night shining from behind a row of poplar trees, and insisted that the irresistibly romantic setting and Vera's sense of the dramatic had played a major part in her engagement.

Vera, however, quickly regretted it as an 'error of judgement'. In July she and Winifred escaped from Oxford to spend a fortnight's holiday together in Cornwall. From their cottage at West Pentire near Holywell Bay, Vera put an end to what was by now 'an intolerable situation'. She packed and posted back to Roy Anthony the photograph he had given her, and asked him to return hers.

Roy Anthony accepted Vera's decision with reluctance. He acknowledged 'without thanks' her letter and parcel, and expressed his conviction that

> you would have been wiser to have waited a bit and let us talk over everything. I feel just as convinced as I always did that despite our differences and the lack of passionate love on both sides we should have got along well together in harness.
>
> Also I think you are a little hard on me in describing me as having deceived you, or been dishonest about my feelings. After all, it was not as if, even on the first night of all, I had not confided to you my doubts as to whether I was really in love . . . However, it is useless to reproach you. You have acted as you think best for yourself, and the affair is ended now – perhaps it has taught us both something.

Her 'ludicrous little engagement' was a humiliating experience which Vera found distressing to remember and painful to write about, and in *Testament of Youth* she passed over the episode quickly, blaming herself for the unhappy fiasco, and preserving her erstwhile fiancé's anonymity. While the absence of Vera's correspondence with her mother for this period makes it difficult to be entirely clear about her motives, her involvement with Anthony does mirror in a number of ways her initial encounter, a few years later, with the man she would eventually marry, George Catlin. There is the same flattering interest in Vera's writing from her suitor, the same sympathy for her bereavements; and there is also a similar disclaimer, on both sides, of passionate love. However, the overriding consideration, as Cicely Williams observed, is likely to have been that Vera was 'set upon making a good marriage'. She was twenty-six, and the social pressures and parental expectations for a woman of her background were simply too great to be ignored.

At West Pentire Vera was discovering how much she could depend on Winifred's stabilizing friendship. They spent long hours preparing their special subjects for the following term (Vera had opted for International Relations, Winifred for the reign of Richard II), each afternoon they went for long walks along the cliff tops, and they talked without interruption. In August Vera was invited to stay at 'Bainesse' in Cottingham. There she met Winifred's parents for the first time.

'Surely now . . . I may begin . . . to find at least *one* human creature among my own sex whose spirit can have intercourse with mine', Vera had written on going up to Somerville in 1914. In Winifred Holtby she had at last found someone who would amply fulfil that description.

III

At the close of *The Crowded Street* (1924), Winifred Holtby's second novel, the heroine, Muriel Hammond, decisively rejects her life as a provincial wallflower, downtrodden by her mother, for 'an idea of service – not just vague and sentimental, but translated into quite practical things.' Muriel's transformation is the result of her friendship with the brilliant and mercurial Delia Vaughan who tells Muriel that 'Your life is your own . . . nobody can take it from you . . . But the thing that matters is to take your life into your own hands and live it.' Emboldened by this vision of an independent life, Muriel rejects a proposal of marriage from the local squire, and goes to London to share a flat with Delia.

Muriel is far too passive and conventional a character to be a self-portrait of Winifred, but there can be little doubt that in her portrayal of Muriel and Delia's friendship, Winifred was paying tribute to the part she believed that, from 1920, Vera had played in directing and encouraging her own interests and energies. Fifteen years later, as she lay dying, Winifred would express her recognition of this fact by telling Vera, 'I'm intensely grateful to you – you're the person who's made me.'

It was Vera, Winifred claimed, who had made her a feminist. Until she met Vera, Winifred appears to have been either unaware or unconcerned about the campaign for equal rights for women. Brought up in a family in which it was taken for granted that her mother was the ultimate authority, she had never recognized that there might be handicaps and disadvantages to being a woman. She confessed that no strong personal impetus, pressure from school, or family tradition had impelled her to undertake a university education, and that she had gone to Oxford because her mother had wished her to. Vera pointed out to Winifred how fortunate she was, and that the majority of middle-class women had no alternative but to make an early and, if possible, socially advantageous marriage. She told her of her own difficulties in overcoming parental opposition to go to Oxford.

At Somerville, Vera was a forceful and articulate feminist, and she irritated some of the other students who were too preoccupied with their studies to become embroiled in political argument and feminist polemic. Their apathy in turn antagonized Vera, and in analysing the areas where support for the feminist movement was at its weakest, she would later scornfully indict 'the contemptuous indifference of women undergraduates at Universities.' Although so 'war-absorbed' in February 1918 that she appears to have been completely unaware that women over thirty had been granted the vote, Vera's feminism had found a new focus in postwar Oxford when she entered the debate on the issue of 'Degrees for Women'. Being conspicuously in the vanguard of the University campaign for the right of women to degrees, Vera had contributed a provocative article in late 1919 on 'The Point of View of a Woman Student' to the *Oxford Outlook*, an undergraduate publication recently founded from Balliol by Beverley Nichols and N.A. Beechman. 'To us the Degree is not a mere "titular distinction"', she had written. 'It is the symbol of that abolition of unreasoning sex prejudice, of traditional fear and unsubstantiated distrust which we look for from the coming years.'

Recognizing the topicality of the subject, the enterprising editor of a local paper, the *Oxford Chronicle*, invited Vera to contribute an innocuous weekly report on the day-to-day activities of the women's colleges. She was to write general articles for the paper throughout her first year, but on this occasion her assignment was vetoed by the five Principals of the women's colleges meeting in solemn conclave. '. . . Not by Miss Penrose I am glad to say', Vera wrote indignantly to her parents, 'but by Miss Jex-Blake of Lady Margaret Hall who is known by everyone to be behind the times and who said she didn't consider it suitable for a student to do such work!! Miss Penrose doesn't agree with her but of course they are bound to act together.'

In response to an article in *The Times*, Vera took up her pen 'with partisan fury', and optimistically predicted that 'Our hour has been long delayed, but we are beginning to believe that it is near at last.' On 11 May 1920 the statute providing that women at Oxford be matriculated and admitted to degrees was passed. It came into force on 7 October. One of the first tasks at hand was the matriculation of nearly a thousand women, and appropriately Vera and Winifred were among them.

On a warm autumn day a week later, the first degree ceremony in which women participated was held in the Sheldonian Theatre. The men were the first to receive their degrees, and with her shrewd feminist eye Vera subsequently pointed out that 'no one noticed the establishment of a precedent, destined to continue for several years, by which all the men were admitted to degrees, however minor, before all the women, however impressive.'

During her year in the WAAC Winifred had had no direct contact with the war, but it is nonetheless surprising that until she met Vera the enormity of the slaughter on the battlefields of France and Belgium seems scarcely to have touched her imagination. But Vera, talking about Roland, Victor, Geoffrey, and Edward, brought home to Winifred in stark personal terms the brutality and insanity of war. Among Winifred's papers when she died were studio portraits which Vera had given her of her fiancé, brother, and two friends. It was to be as if Vera's dead became Winifred's own.

Vera's bereavements also confirmed to Winifred how fortunate she had been that her own childhood friend, Harry Pearson, should have survived four years of war. She declared that when the Great War broke out 'the first thing it made me do was to fall in love' as Harry at nineteen joined a West Yorkshire regiment. Badly wounded in the shoulder in 1916, he spent much of his convalescence with the Holtbys at Rudston and here he wrote Winifred a series of love poems. Fundamentally their relationship appears no more than an adolescent crush precipitated by the war, and she breezily dismissed them as sentimental. The war accentuated Harry's religious torment and lack of motivation, and, abandoning his Cambridge scholarship, he led an erratic and often impecunious existence. Believing that by rejecting his poems she had unintentionally contributed to his disintegration, Winifred accepted that part of her 'debt' was to give him whatever practical support she could as he drifted unpredictably in and out of her life. At the beginning of her third year at Oxford, however, it looked as if Harry might disappear from her life for good, when he became engaged to a pianist on a boat to South America. The news rocked Winifred's confidence, and disillusioned her about her 'power of holding others'; but, before long, Harry's engagement proved as ephemeral as so many other aspects of his life.

Initially Vera's hopes for a lasting peace were focused upon the political innovations and idealism of the League of Nations Union. The Peace Conference in January 1919 had unanimously adopted a resolution for its creation, and to a war-weary world it promised a new dawn of international collaboration. The war was over, but the blockade against Germany was relentlessly enforced until she had fulfilled the disarmament terms of the Versailles Peace Treaty, and this resulted in hardship and starvation. In view of Vera's experience of nursing German prisoners at Étaples, it is significant that the only time she is mentioned by name in the minutes of Somerville's Junior Common Room meetings occurs on 29 April 1920, when she successfully proposed that the money from the sale of the new college photograph should be given to the Starving Europe fund.

The League of Nations only slowly established itself as the most influential antiwar group in Britain, and at Somerville Vera was primarily concerned with the campaign for degrees for women, and in assessing the policies of the three political parties. 'She was very politically minded', remembered Lady Ogilvie. 'Most of us thought that sooner or later she would stand for Parliament', a view confirmed by Victor's brother, Maurice Richardson, who, while an undergraduate at Cambridge, visited Vera in Oxford and found her 'humourless and very political'. Vera decided to join the Liberal Party.

Winifred, in a burst of originality, was for one term a member of all three parties, and to the hilarity of her friends she attended a Conservative dinner, a Liberal dinner, and a Labour tea. After her flirtation with all three political parties she eventually decided to throw in her lot with the Liberals, but her experiment had taught her that 'perhaps the most important thing to remember about any party programme is that it has to be administered in an imperfect world, by men and not by angels'.

Ambition and a desire for fame were the dominant forces of Vera's postwar personality. In what she was later to call 'that egotistical little poem', she gave a significant indication of her drive and dogged determination:

> Because I dare to stand outside the gate
> Of that high temple wherein fame abides,
> And loudly knock, too eager to await
> Whate'er betides,
>
> May God forgive, since He alone can see
> The joys that others have but I must miss:
> For how shall compensation come to me
> If not through this?

Verses of a VAD had played a part in making Vera known beyond the confines of Somerville. Dons and undergraduates were aware of her modest publication. In the autumn of 1919, at the time when she was feeling at her most isolated from other Somervillians, she had been invited by Miss Blackwell 'to a social circle of more or less Literary people which she and her brother the publisher are having every Saturday evening & which I feel inclined to join.' For the rest of that winter and throughout the following year, Vera regularly attended the Blackwells' Saturday evenings. She told Edith Brittain that Basil Blackwell, then in his early thirties, had 'taken a great fancy to me & is very much disposed to help me in the future', though in case her mother scented romance she quickly added that '. . . He is married & has 2 little children so don't get excited . . .'.

In the summer of 1920 Basil Blackwell asked Vera to become an editor, with C.H.B. Kitchin and Alan Porter, of his annual selection of *Oxford Poetry*. The publication in the Michaelmas term of 1920 included poems by Vera ('The Lament of the Demobilised', 'Boar's Hill', and 'Daphne'), together with several other names destined to achieve distinction: Robert Graves, Edmund Blunden, L.P. Hartley, Roy Campbell, and Louis Golding. Vera, as co-editor, also found room for an uncharacteristically sombre effort by Winifred entitled 'The Dead Men'.

'Daphne' with its vision of a Winifred-inspired character, 'golden and fair / and undaunted', was also the name that Vera originally gave the novel which she began to plan, between 1919 and 1921, while still at Oxford. Taking Somerville as the model for her fictional 'Drayton College', the book set out to attack the cloistered, feminine world of an Oxford women's college, and to present a feminist exposé of university life. Vera structured the novel with herself as the principal character, Virginia Dennison. Winifred, being physically and temperamentally her opposite, made an admirable foil as Daphne Lethbridge; and by inventing a disastrous marriage for her with a male chauvinist Oxford don, Vera provided herself with the ideal setting for disseminating her feminist beliefs.

Slowly Vera's sheaf of notes accumulated. She drafted a blow-by-blow account of the debate at which she had been humiliated; wrote descriptions of dances, cocoa parties, and of Eights Week, tutorials and theatre excursions; and, on rashly dangerous ground, she recorded the traits, idiosyncrasies and conversations of tutors and lecturers like Maude Clarke, Lewis Namier, and Charles Cruttwell. Two years later Somerville would be startled to discover that Vera's time at college had not been entirely absorbed by her academic studies.

Winifred confided to Jean McWilliam, her WAAC friend from

Huchenneville days, that 'I can't think why I was cursed with this inordinate desire to write', but the desire for fame and prestige played only a small part in her irresistible ambition. She knew herself 'always to shrink from unpleasantness', and well aware that her mother expected her to take an academic appointment after leaving Somerville, she was loath to precipitate a parental crisis by announcing her intention of attempting a precarious writing career. Vera had no such reservations, and impressed upon Winifred that everyone was responsible for his or her destiny. If she was certain of her calling to be a writer, she told her, it was her duty to take up the challenge, and she constantly reminded her that:

> If thy faith be entire
> Press onward, for thine eye
> Shall see thy heart's desire . . .

For the setting of the novel, originally called 'Anlaby Wold', which she began at Somerville, Winifred turned inevitably to Yorkshire. Her story was to start before the war, with a girl of eighteen who had married a much older man for the sake of a farm that had been in the family for five hundred years. Too late she rebels against her circumstances, and falls in love with a young socialist agitator campaigning in the villages against the very system which she and her husband represent.

Their working partnership was to be the cornerstone of the Brittain–Holtby friendship. Each was the other's most invaluable critic. They discussed their books and journalism, and gave each other advice, encouragement, and tracked down relevant information. Having already published articles and poems, Vera felt herself to be several jumps ahead of Winifred, and at first mortified her 'by analysing and criticizing my ideas before they became books; by suggesting how and what and why I should write. It really drove me crazy until I had to set a complete taboo upon the discussion of my work save after it was done.' She gratefully acknowledged, however, that Vera's criticism of her finished work was 'most helpful . . . and I think has been of more value to me than anything'.

IV

Trinity 1921 was Vera and Winifred's final term, and as they frantically revised for their Finals they had little time for their novels. Vera was accustomed to academic success, and as Finals approached she hoped that on a good day with straightforward examination papers she would live up to her tutors' expectations. But by switching from English to Modern History on her return to Somerville she had placed herself at a considerable disadvantage by having only two years for a three-year degree course. She was also handicapped by her critical attitude to the Modern History syllabus. Why, she asked, should Modern History at Oxford stop short in the middle of the Victorian era? And she made it clear that the remote irrelevancies of early English history bored her 'to the limit of impatience'. As she toiled over Pavel Vinogradov's dreary history of *The Growth of the Manor*, and a dry-as-dust treatise on *Feudal England*, she was driven to distraction. Years later, recalling the abstruse complexities of 'Scutage' – the history of money paid by feudal landowners in lieu of personal services – she paused to speculate whether 'some incisive and lucid writer has at last let in light on its tangled obscurities'.

Winifred accepted the deficiencies of the syllabus with greater equanimity. She had quickly overcome her initial difficulties, and it was, she said, 'almost more than my moral equilibrium will stand' when her tutor at St John's praised her paper on 'Hobbes' Theory of the Natural'. On one occasion, commiserating with Vera as she struggled with a particularly intractable essay, Winifred remarked that it must be difficult not having written one for four years, and blithely shrugged off Vera's suggestions that she might also be having problems. 'Oh no . . .', she replied. 'One's memory keeps quite good, you know, so long as one's well under twenty-five'. Vera was not amused but relented, and Winifred's faux pas became a private joke.

Vera's viva was a tragicomedy. Fortified for the ordeal by a large dose of brandy given to her from a flask by one of her fellow-examinees, she faced the examiners in a mild alcoholic haze and believed that all hopes of a First disappeared in 'that rag-time performance'.

In spite of her unruly sentences and an inability to spell, Winifred's knowledge and originality had created a sharp division among her examiners. As she waited with Vera in the Examinations Schools she was well aware that she was being vivaed for a possible First. 'I went for my viva on Thursday', she told Jean McWilliam on 25 July. 'At the time I loved it. Only when it was all over I realized what had happened. I had been viva'd for forty minutes . . . and I made a perfect fool of myself. I never thought the viva would matter much, and I suppose I lost my head, only in a funny sort of way. I enjoyed myself and laughed, and made the examiners laugh sometimes; but I never gave them a single piece of useful information, though they gave me chance after chance to do so, and I knew most of the things, really. So I shan't get a First; but I had a good run for my money.'

With their exams behind them Vera and Winifred devoted much of their time to the production of the 'Going Down Play', which, until 1933, was an established Somerville tradition marking the end of the academic year. Vera had performed in amateur theatricals at St Monica's and in Buxton. She loved acting 'so much that I feel I must do it'. The 'GDP' in 1920 had been a parody of the Barrie play, *The Professor's Love Story*, combined with an updated version of *The Sleeping Beauty*. The plot recorded the experiences of the Somervillians who had lived in exile in Oriel during the war, and anticipated the conferment of degrees on women, which was to take place the following term. Winifred had played Merton New, a male under-graduate, while Vera had taken a supporting role.

For the 1921 'Going Down Play', *Bolshevism in Baghdad: A Psycho Analytic Experiment*, Vera took a leading role as Miss Cleopatra O'Nesbitt, 'the most charming of the four dons' who founded a college for the numerous wives of the Caliph of Baghdad. She asked her mother to send her white satin dress, as 'I have got to try and look like Cathleen Nesbitt as Cleopatra', and described her part as 'a romantic combination of the Queen of Egypt with our History tutor [Maude Clarke], who as a young Oxford don was being sent to convert the Baghdad Bolsheviks to political sanity.'

Among the Caliph's wives was Hilda Reid, demure and decorative as a 'waterlily', while with great versatility Janet Vaughan doubled as the Minister of Finance and the back half of a camel. Winifred was the joint author, and again chose to play the male lead as the Caliph. The Eastern location provided an excuse for a colourful spectacle, and the stage blazed with an assortment of Arabian garments of blue, jade and scarlet hastily run up 'out of bedspreads and a half a yard of butter muslin'. Winifred wore 'the most heavenly orange trousers'. The dons politely said that they loved it, and 'the Pen', Winifred reported, 'said it was "most amusing, really most amusing", so I suppose that is some compensation for hours of strenuous labour.'

Immediately after their vivas in the last week of July, Vera and Winifred left Oxford to spend a few days at Oakwood Court with Vera's parents. They had already agreed, several months earlier, to share a flat together in the New Year and to launch themselves on an 'adventurous, experimental London life . . .' as journalists and writers.

The highlight of their holiday was a visit to the Leightons' 'queer little jumbled house, hanging on the side of its twin in St John's Wood'. Mrs Leighton was like no one Winifred had ever met, wonderfully alive, and 'her eyes are blazing with vitality and humour and interest'. Robert Leighton was stone deaf and they listened entranced to his monologue of reminiscences of George Meredith. O. Henry, Andrew Lang and Thomas Hardy, and of George Eliot at nearly sixty coquettishly wearing straw hats with blue flowers, and blue ribbons tied under her chin.

At the end of July, Vera and Winifred travelled to Yorkshire, and here at the Holtby household in Cottingham they waited for their results. 'Not very nice,' Winifred whispered to Vera when the telegram at last arrived in the middle of a tennis party, 'both Seconds'.

It was, Vera admitted, a bitter blow. 'The results are most extraordinary', she told her mother. 'Of the 6 Somervillians who were supposed to be probable Firsts, 5 got Seconds & the 6th . . . only got a Third! . . . We're lucky to have Seconds with these examiners . . .'. In an attempt to mitigate her parents' disappointment she told them that she had specialized too much on European History to be good all round, but confessed that except when writing letters home she didn't even pretend to be philosophical. Later on she realistically accepted that 'I was never, I think, even within jumping distance of a First of which Somerville had hopefully believed me to be capable'.

In *Testament of Youth* she revealed that the ten examiners were equally divided as to whether to award Winifred a First, and that 'After the Viva the anti-feminist chairman [Professor H.W.C. Davis] had given his casting vote against her.' Her publisher, Victor Gollancz, cautiously suggested the removal of the anti-feminist tag. But Vera maintained that Professor Davis had been an opponent of degrees for women, and was widely credited with prejudice against women students, and particularly against giving them Firsts. 'It was believed by pretty well everyone in Oxford at the time that practically any chairman but Professor Davis would have given her a First'.

Vera and Winifred agreed that their failure to obtain Firsts absolved them from any obligation to try for academic appointments. Soon after they went down, Winifred received the offer of a History tutorship at St Hugh's, but resolutely refused. She was, she said, 'longing to get my teeth into some *work*', and too much Oxford would make her think the world was made for the benefit of historical research. Vera toyed briefly with the idea of applying for a London University lectureship, and Mr Cruttwell's testimonial indicates that she could have had a successful academic career.

'I was greatly impressed with her ability,' he wrote, 'the extent of her knowledge and her mastery over the subject. She has a shrewd enquiring and well-balanced mind with real literary gifts. I consider her to have definitely first-class abilities. She should make a stimulating lecturer and an inspiring and sympathetic teacher.'

Emily Penrose confirmed Mr Cruttwell's judgement, but made it clear that she was well aware where Vera's real ambitions lay. 'Miss Brittain's work,' she testified, 'has been excellent throughout and has gained in depth and maturity during her absence on war service ... her essays have been uniformly good, well-constructed and interesting, showing independent thought and much literary ability and taste.'

FIVE

'Very Small, Very Dear Love'

'The wonder always is that you do love me, that you see more in me
than what most people see – which is a combination of egotistical
bitterness plus a kind of insincere prettiness plus an intermittent (and,
as they think, designing) attraction for men.'

Vera Brittain to Winifred Holtby, 30 July 1926

I

At the end of August 1921, Vera set out with Winifred on a six-week holiday
in Italy and France. Vera had twice visited the Holtbys at Cottingham, and
Winifred had stayed with the Brittains in Kensington, but apart from a few
weekends in a small country cottage on Boar's Hill this would be the longest
period that they had spent alone together since their spell in the Cornish
cottage the previous summer. It was, Vera wrote, 'the most perfect holiday
of all my experience and, I believe, of Winifred's.' Their principal purpose
was to visit the remote military cemetery at Granezza, four thousand feet up
on the Asiago Plateau, where Edward lay buried, and to make a pilgrimage
on the return journey to Roland's grave at Louvencourt.

They set out, Winifred said, 'armed with small suitcases' (she promptly
dropped hers in the Grand Canal when they arrived in Venice), 'thin purses,
and the E.V. Lucas *Wanderer* books'. After stopping briefly in Milan they
travelled to Venice and succumbed at once to the magic of its winding
canals, the Piazza San Marco, the gondolas, and the open-air cafés. They
stayed in a low-ceilinged room at the top of a stone-built *pensione*, up two
flights of gloomy stairs smelling of seawater and incense, which at night
were eerily illuminated by two flickering candles in snake-shaped holders.
Parts of Venice, Vera told Winifred, reminded her of Valletta, but its beauty,
they agreed, was the beauty of a mausoleum, its brilliance, the brilliance of
decay.

Carrying a bunch of red roses they set out by gondola at five in the
morning on 7 September for Bassano, a small hill town at the foot of the

Tyrol 'where there is a wonderful view of Mt. Grappa – the chief Italian defence during the war.' From 'a dear little fat hotel-keeper' they hired a chauffeur-driven Fiat, and he insisted magnanimously on accompanying them to interpret in voluble French as the chauffeur spoke only Italian.

Even for those with the strongest nerves the ascent to the Asiago Plateau is an alarming experience. Driving in the open car along unwalled, zigzag roads, with the mountainside towering above and the Brenta Valley fading out of sight in a blue-green haze below, Vera was petrified. They drove through pine woods and 'barren slopes strewn with white rocks', noticing shell holes and trenches which did not seem untidy like those in France, 'for the hills themselves are full of jagged points and holes, and the little white cemeteries are hardly distinguishable from the stone-covered hillside.' At last, 'after a climb that seemed to have lasted for hours', they reached the highest corner of the plateau before stopping beside the low-walled cemetery of Granezza. Here, raised sharply above the road, in a small natural amphitheatre, with pine woods climbing upwards to the skyline, they counted fewer than sixty graves, each with its own white oblong headstone (in all 142 bodies would eventually be interred at Granezza, including those of three unknown British soldiers).

An atmosphere of quiet serenity hovered around this cemetery on Europe's highest battlefield. Placing her roses on her brother's grave, Vera sat beside him in silent remembrance. It was, she wrote in an unpublished article, 'strangely difficult to bid farewell to the graves of the British soldiers, strangely difficult to overcome the fantastic longing to keep them company in their loneliness.'

Four days later, Vera and Winifred arrived in Florence and were delighted by the 'embarras de richesses' they found there. Above all, they decided that the Palazzo Vecchio and the Loggia Lorenzo, 'which rise from the Piazza into the dark blue sky', were the 'loveliest things' in Florence. One evening they called on Maude Clarke, their young History tutor, who was staying in Florence with a party of undergraduates. Vera's relations with Maude Clarke had been difficult, and when Vera and Winifred appeared unexpectedly, bubbling over with enthusiasm, and carrying their Baedeker, Maude Clarke could not resist the supercilious remark, 'Doing Italy with a guide book like tourists? How quaint.'

After ten days in Florence they embarked on a four-hour charabanc drive to Siena. Their precipitous journey to the Asiago Plateau had taught them that 'our hair rises rather easily', and so Winifred booked tickets for them to travel by night. From Siena they moved on to Assisi where they found their hotel besieged with pilgrims for the Feast of St Francis. One afternoon Vera and Winifred walked for an hour up the steep, stony road to the small monastery of the Carceri. They stood on the arched stone bridge where St Francis had blessed the birds, and in the monastery itself descended to the underground passage that emerged in the hillside forest where he had reputedly wrestled with the devil.

They spent their final week in Rome, and on the last leg of their journey made a detour to Roland's grave at Louvencourt, which Edward had visited in 1916. As they drove up a slight hill in bright October sunshine, the well-ordered cemetery which he had so vividly described conveyed to Vera no more than the tranquil impression of 'a number of flower beds planted at intervals in the smooth wide lawn.'

Standing beside Roland's carefully tended grave with its little garden of late-flowering marigolds, Vera found her pent-up emotion stifled by the prosaic incongruity of his final resting place, and later that night, in their Paris hotel, 'I picked a quarrel with Winifred over some futile trifle, and went to bed in a fury of tears.'

They arrived back in London in mid-October, and after a night with the Brittains at Oakwood Court, Winifred returned to Yorkshire. Alice Holtby had acquired 'a whole load of new stories which had to be discharged before we could get anything else done', and the family were all in bed before she had the opportunity to begin a seven-page letter to 'My dear little heart'. 'It has been a wonderful time, dearest', she told Vera. 'But you know the best thing of all was to find out from day to day how dear you are . . . Thank you, thank you, thank you, for being so completely satisfactory you most sweet woman.'

Shortly after their return, Vera developed an acute attack of jaundice and a distended gall bladder. The Brittains made the most of their illnesses, and, as patients who made frequent calls on his services, they had established friendly relations with Dr Hughes, who lived in a first-floor flat at Oakwood Court. Letters passed almost daily between Kensington and Cottingham, with Vera protesting at Dr Hughes's tyrannical regime of bed, slops and beef tea 'when I am hankering in theory after sardines on toast and kidney and bacon'. From Yorkshire Winifred sent rosebuds, books and a nightdress she had made herself, and begged to be allowed to come and look after her. It was too much for her mother, Vera agreed, running up and down to her sickroom and doing the washing-up, 'with Louie [the maid] a fool, and father quite useless', but it was a suggestion that Mrs Brittain did not appreciate. 'Add to the work, add to the cooking,' she huffed. 'I suppose as soon as I recover she will be ill,' Vera wrote to Winifred resentfully. The following day, running true to form, Mr Brittain decided he had a chill and took to his bed, but, with a prod from Mrs Brittain, the resourceful Dr Hughes convinced him it was only muscular rheumatism and got him up again.

Winifred had started to write her novel of Yorkshire farm life called *Anderby Wold* at the end of August, and worked at it throughout November. It gave her, she said, unbelievable joy and pain. There were days when she found herself stuck and unable to write at all, and then 'I have a real rush and write a whole chapter at a sitting, and the next day it all comes out and I have to start all over again'.

At Oakwood Court Vera was bursting with ideas for her Oxford novel about life in a women's college, but she found it difficult writing in bed with a temperamental fountain pen, and she also became acutely conscious of the pitfalls of writing so directly from her own experience. Was she sufficiently objective, she asked herself, was her characterization of Virginia, her feminist heroine, too intense and serious, and would her readers recognize and despise Virginia as being 'my ideal for myself?' 'I envy you with *Anderby Wold*,' she wrote to Winifred, 'serenely detached from your own personality.'

'You won't trust yourself at all', she added in a burst of generosity. 'You get lost in your own tremendous vision. You're *big* – like the Wolds and your Viking ancestors and their wide sea spaces. Don't you realize I feel petty & parochial & conventional beside you, a little vexed worrying gnat bragging impotently about unimportant things. I wonder how soon you'll find me too small to satisfy you?'

After ten days, Dr Hughes allowed Vera to get up and sit by her bedroom fire, and relaxed the slops and beef-tea diet for one of eggs 'eaten plain without bread and butter but with heaps of pepper', blancmange with strawberry jam, and peppermint creams. She had done her hair, she told Winifred, which had become 'lank and straight and in need of the tongs', and she had finished the first chapter of her novel. But again she was overwhelmed with uncertainty and a lack of confidence. Was it good enough to justify her sticking to 'that one talent', or was it simply sloppy and sentimental? 'Above all I'm afraid it may lack humour – knowing how often I lack humour', and she recalled with remorse her hysterical behaviour in their Paris hotel on the way back to England. 'If I have those ridiculous outbursts in future,' she urged Winifred, 'make me see they're entirely the result of lacking a sense of humour; that will soon stop me.'

At the end of November the Brittain and Holtby parents went with them to the Oxford degree ceremony, and after it was over Winifred returned with Vera to Oakwood Court. On 7 December they had promised to help at a Somerville fund-raising bazaar being held in Lady Norman's elegant house in Westminster.

The novelist, Rose Macaulay, who had gone down from Somerville in 1903, had offered to take charge of the bookstall, and with some trepidation Vera had agreed to help her. 'That terrifying woman,' she wrote dramatically to Winifred, 'but what an opportunity . . . [I'm] terrified that she will see me for the egotistical little poseuse I have been so often.' While in bed Vera had read Rose Macaulay's *Dangerous Ages*, and also her sharply critical review in *Time and Tide* of Beverley Nichols's portrayal of undergraduate life in his recently published novel *Patchwork*. Vera had known Beverley Nichols at Oxford and had found him insufferably pretentious, and she was both amused and a little apprehensive that in her review Rose Macaulay had put him down as 'a vain and conceited young man'. In person, though, Rose Macaulay proved far less intimidating than Vera had anticipated, and listened sympathetically as Vera told her of her problems in writing 'Daphne', and of her constant temptation to scrap it.

Arthur and Edith Brittain had long since accepted that, after three years at Oxford and her time nursing abroad, it would be impossible for Vera to return to live contentedly at home. By December Vera was itching to get away from Oakwood Court, and in the weeks before Christmas, Winifred searched Bloomsbury for accommodation within reasonable walking distance of the British Museum Reading Room that she and Vera might share in the New Year. At one point their plans had included Roland's younger sister, Clare, who was a student at the Slade, but while they were in Italy she had found a studio of her own, and they had reverted to their original idea of a flat for two. Board and lodgings in the Bloomsbury neighbourhood, however, were 'almost impossible to acquire'. One estate agent tried to tempt Winifred with 'an eight guineas mansion', another sent her on an abortive visit to one 'dirty, horrid address' in Lamb's Conduit Street. Close to despair, she remembered a friendly landlady she had encountered on an earlier flat-hunting expedition, living near the British Museum, and eventually tracked her down. She still had no rooms available but recommended a ground-floor studio flat at 52 Doughty Street. It was 'a beautiful little flatlette', and Winifred took it immediately.

Shortly afterwards, Vera returned with Winifred to Yorkshire, and was at once involved in the feverish rush of the Holtby Christmas preparations. One afternoon they drove to Hull where a high tide had created havoc by sweeping over the quayside and flooding several of the busy dockside streets, and in Cottingham there was intense excitement when the local hunt killed a fox in the dining-room of a nearby sanatorium for discharged soldiers. In the evenings Winifred read Vera the early chapters of *Anderby Wold*.

Back in London, Vera went with her mother on 22 December to inspect their new flat. '. . . If it weren't for my perpetual dread of mice & beetles I couldn't wish for anything better anywhere', she told Winifred. Five days after Christmas, the day after Vera's twenty-eighth birthday, they moved into Doughty Street. Their London adventure had begun.

II

The flat at 52 Doughty Street lay at the back of a house that had been converted into bedsits which were chiefly inhabited by London University students. It was, Winifred admitted, 'a queer little place', and some of Vera's well-to-do relatives who called, enquired incredulously how she could tolerate such discomfort. Built as an artist's studio, it had skylight windows, and consisted of two cubicle-sized bedrooms, a small sitting-room and tiny kitchen, with dark-brown wood partitions and cream-coloured walls. The rent of £2. 12s a week included electric light and hot water, and 'a nice blue-eyed housekeeper' who brought them their breakfast on a tray. They lunched in one of the numerous restaurants in Theobald's Road, which ranged from the stewed eels and tripe shop on the corner to Tibbald's, an up-market establishment with damask tablecloths and the curiosity value of an earl's great-niece at the cash desk. Tea and supper they prepared themselves, but having little interest in either food or cooking, their supper menus consisted mainly of omelettes, Welsh rarebit, chops and salads. An unwelcome visitor was their landlady's lean, yellow-eyed cat which sat on the partition between the sitting-room and the kitchen, spat at them when they approached, and once pillaged the cold chicken which Mrs Brittain had provided for their supper.

It was a world apart from the Brittains' flat at Oakwood Court with its four bedrooms, dressing-room, sitting-room, dining-room, two kitchens, pantry, bathroom, lavatory, and live-in maid, but for Vera and Winifred it was freedom and independence, uninhibited by parental protocol and expectations. The break from their respective families, though, was neither as final nor as complete as Vera sometimes liked to suggest in her later accounts of their Doughty Street days, and if Winifred went up to Yorkshire to see her family then Vera, terrified of being left alone, invariably returned to Oakwood Court to stay with her parents. Financially, too, both women remained dependent on the allowances that they received from their fathers, which in Vera's case amounted to a little over £200 a year.

Nevertheless, the domestic arrangement at Doughty Street was consciously designed to support Vera and Winifred's disciplined work and intimate companionship, free from the interference of the Brittains and the Holtbys. They offered each other practical and emotional support, sharing ideas and criticizing each other's writing – even analysing each other's dreams ('Winifred, why do your dreams nearly always have something in them about sex, of an unpleasant nature', Vera asked a couple of months before they moved into Doughty Street. 'A sort of sex obsession that seems to creep into your dreams & sometimes into your writings worries me a little . . .').

Yet the pattern of Vera's dependence on Winifred that had been established in the early days of their friendship at Somerville persisted, and in that sense the Brittain–Holtby 'working partnership' was never to be a partnership of equals. Vera remained the emotional debtor in the relationship, acutely aware, as she had been from the beginning, that Winifred offered her more support than she was ever able to return, and openly acknowledging to her that she was guilty of exploiting Winifred's 'sensitiveness & sympathy'. Although Vera had by now recovered from the hallucinations which had plagued her at Oxford, she was still subject to 'apprehensiveness' and a type of depression which, as she explained to Winifred, '. . . always takes the form of feeling I've never done anything worth doing & never been anything worth being . . .'. She was always to suffer from a lack of self-confidence, but never more so than in the early Twenties when she was driven by an overwhelming need to succeed as a writer. Only to Winifred did she feel able to expose the full extent of her burning ambition, and only from Winifred could she be certain of sympathetic understanding in return. 'I don't want to reveal to anyone else the unreasonable ambition', she told her, 'which is arrogantly dissatisfied with anything less than the stars.'

Vera's fluctuating emotions and unpredictable temper demanded from Winifred, and generally received, what Vera herself once termed 'an excess of patience'. Among her papers Vera left a pencilled note, written towards the end of her life, describing a quarrel which she had had with Winifred 'one day after we left College'. No one else was present, and from external evidence it seems fairly certain that it took place in early 1922 when they were first living at Doughty Street. It vividly illuminates not only Vera's volatile temperament, but also her honesty in acknowledging her own flaws and failings.

'WH and I had a quarrel', she wrote, 'or rather I quarrelled with her. I always began it. You may have guessed that I am aggressive by nature . . .'.

> In my angry exasperation I threw a shoe at her. She hardly attempted to defend herself. It struck her on the forehead turning her face pale and making tears start to her eyes. She said nothing. She did not move. She only looked at me – not even reproachfully but sadly. In an instant my rage died within me. She had turned it against myself. I felt the biggest fool and more ashamed of myself than I had ever done in my life.
>
> I don't remember how the incident ended. I only know that I can see her still, kneeling on the floor with her pale face and wet eyes, looking at me . . . no service I have ever tried to render her, no work for her books, or for her memory, or for anyone who depended on her love and charity, can ever make me even with her for that moment. She won an undisputed and permanent victory.

After any such row with Winifred, Vera was always filled with remorse. '. . . I wonder how it is that I can ever be horrid to you', she wrote on one occasion. '. . . I hate the person who hurts you more than you do.'

What is so extraordinary is that Winifred, often in the face of strong provocation, continued to exhibit such patience and forbearance. She admired Vera's fighting spirit and clarity of thought, and valued her approval 'beyond pearls'; but at times she could look upon Vera as a recalcitrant child, and treat her as such. Her friend's diminutive, childlike appearance aroused strongly protective feelings in her, and hand-in-hand with this protectiveness went an almost religious conviction of the necessity of helping others less fortunate than herself. Vera was her 'Very Small, Very Dear Love', her 'most sweet little heart'. 'There's such a little of you', she once teased, ' I sometimes fear that in a high wind, an extra gust will waft you right beyond our reach.'

A letter of August 1923 to Jean McWilliam, her friend from her Huchenneville days in the WAAC, shows how insightful Winifred could be in understanding the influences that had moulded Vera's character. Vera, she explained,

> is a person whom life has battered, and who has been given by circumstance and heredity such a temperament that every blow and every snub, even every casual coldness makes a wound and a scar, where many people would hardly know that they had been touched. The War has left her with a real sickness of apprehension . . . but never for a moment does she give way, nor lose her sweetness, nor her tenderness for suffering, nor an imagination which is

constantly trying to devise ways for protecting other people from the sorrow that she has known.

Until they achieved a foothold as writers and freelance journalists, Vera and Winifred had decided that part-time teaching was the most congenial means of augmenting their private incomes. Through Truman and Knightley's educational agency, Vera was engaged for one morning a week to teach history at a fashionable South Kensington girls' school, while both Vera and Winifred secured part-time appointments at St Monica's from Vera's aunt, Florence Bervon.

St Monica's was still a thriving boarding school, sardonically categorized by Winifred as one of 'the most select academies for the daughters of gentlefolk'. Louise Heath-Jones enlivened the curriculum with a wide range of outside lecturers, and paid them the generous fee of two and a half guineas a lecture. John Marriott, now a Conservative MP, whose extension lectures in Buxton had encouraged Vera to try for Oxford, was one of these visiting lecturers, and came to St Monica's two or three times a term to talk on European history. Vera had been invited to give a weekly lecture on international relations on her return from Italy and France in the autumn of 1921. These had been interrupted by her illness, but she felt 'quite bucked up and keen about the next one' after Florence Bervon called at Oakwood Court during her convalescence and told Edith Brittain that she had given 'a splendid lecture', and that several pupils from other schools were being invited to the next one. Winifred, too, was asked to give a course at St Monica's the following term, and chose six diverse medieval personalities, ranging from St Francis of Assisi and Joanna of Naples to Leonardo da Vinci as her subjects.

For the next two and a half years Vera and Winifred would make weekly visits to St Monica's, with Winifred eventually teaching English when the English mistress fell ill, and Vera giving lessons in political history. Peggy Tignor, one of their former pupils, recalled how from their ground-floor classroom, she and her classmates would hear the brisk click of heels on the paved terrace as Vera and Winifred came round the corner of the verandah, Vera always slightly in front with Winifred at her elbow. Vera's grey-squirrel coat was much admired, and her neat, well-turned-out appearance contrasted sharply with the sober, more serviceable clothes of the resident mistresses.

She seldom smiled, and her grave, serious demeanour intimidated the less confident. 'I'd say about half the class appreciated Vera, but the others found her rather alarming and high-powered', Peggy Tignor recalled. 'It was obvious that Vera had a lot of push and force', another former pupil, Lady Bateman, said. 'I remember I felt quite certain that she would one day be famous. And Winifred too, but she was very amusing and not at all pushy.'

Vera wrote that she had 'no love or gift for teaching as such'. She was, she believed, too anxious to write and too politically involved for her classes to be first-rate. Nonetheless her lessons evidently inspired some of her pupils to follow her example and embark on an independent career. Vera declared that during her own schooldays at St Monica's the ultimate ambition of most of the girls had been to return to impress their schoolfellows with the glory of a grown-up toilette, and to get engaged before everybody else. By the summer term of 1924, however, Winifred was jubilantly reporting that 'a curious change' appeared to be taking place among Vera's pupils. 'Those who are leaving this year nearly all intend to take up some definite work. They are to be actresses, nurses, teachers of history, art or music. One wants to go to college and thence to follow her father as a member of the Canadian Parliament, and so on . . . Before Vera went back there to teach about one a year dragged herself out of the rut of social engagements into an attempt to find work.'

In the winter of 1921 Louise Heath-Jones had suffered a mild nervous breakdown, and although she appeared to recover and returned to St Monica's, her erratic, irrational behaviour persisted. On one alarming occasion she called an impromptu school assembly, and without explanation dismissed all the teachers present. Perhaps obsessed by an anxiety for the chastity of her nubile pupils, she then proceeded to lock all the doors from the outside, leaving the girls imprisoned and frightened.

As her mental condition deteriorated, it became apparent that Miss Heath-Jones could not remain at St Monica's. For the next few years Florence Bervon shouldered most of the responsibility, but no longer young, and with an arthritic hip, she knew that the time was coming for her to relinquish her position as Principal. As her niece and an Oxford graduate, Vera was the obvious choice as her successor, but Vera made it emphatically clear that she had neither the inclination nor the temperament to become a headmistress.

Capable, and popular with staff and students alike, Winifred was the ideal alternative, and in the summer of 1925 Florence Bervon turned to her. But for Winifred the school had by then come to represent an unacceptable social anachronism. In the East End she had seen children herded together, fifty or sixty to a class, 'stunted and thin, and thrown on to an indifferent industrialized world at fourteen', whereas at St Monica's, the girls were 'all so rich and comfortable at home.' 'I have been spending the weekend at St Monica's', she wrote to Vera in July 1925. 'Your aunt was very sweet, a little tired but full of vitality. She besought me again with tears in her eyes to consider the possibility of taking on the school. My dear, how could I explain to her that it is one of my intentions to remove such schools, however admirable, from England altogether? I could only say "impossible", and be very sorry.'

The first six months in Doughty Street were a period of concentrated work and comparative tranquillity. In the morning Vera and Winifred read from ten to one in the British Museum, and most afternoons they went for a walk. They made contact with the League of Nations Union and joined the recently founded feminist organization, the Six Point Group. In the evenings they learned German, wrote articles, and by March 1922 had completed their novels. For advice on where to send her work, Vera turned to Robert Leighton who had acted for some years as a reader for both British and American publishers.

After reading and approving of Vera's novel, now called *The Dark Tide*, Robert Leighton dispatched it to an influential friend with the publishing firm of Putnam, and armed with his introduction she waited hopefully for its acceptance. Its rejection provoked an angry outburst. In thanking Robert Leighton for his help she angrily repudiated Putnam's advice to settle down and acquire more experience before attempting another novel, asked him to return her manuscript, and told him that in future she would herself shoulder full responsibility for her literary efforts.

But her bravado was short-lived. In an exchange of letters with Rose Macaulay, who had just been awarded the Femina Vie Heureuse prize for *Dangerous Ages*, Vera poured out the sorry fate of her own novel. Rose Macaulay offered to read it, invited her to tea, suggested alterations and improvements, and wrote a letter of introduction to J.D. Beresford, the chief reader for her own publishers, Collins, but again *The Dark Tide* returned to Doughty Street. For the next eight months, dogeared and dishevelled, the manuscript, submitted to more than a dozen publishers, shuttled back and forth. 'Have you any use for a recently completed First Novel with an unhappy ending?' Vera asked Macmillan in September 1922, allowing a note of desperation to creep into her voice. They had not. '. . . As I cross the threshold . . .', Vera wrote to Winifred on returning to Doughty Street after spending Christmas with her parents, 'I shall hold my breath because of the bogies of rejected manuscripts.'

To Vera's chagrin Winifred's novel enjoyed a smoother passage. The one stumbling block, Cassell and Methuen informed her, was the tragic ending

– which she was adamant about not changing – but Cassell asked her for the first refusal of her next novel, and she argued animatedly for half an hour with E.V. Lucas of Methuen about pandering to the reading public's insistence on being amused and provided with happy endings. 'Now my idea of a happy ending,' she told him high-mindedly, 'is where circumstances go right and wrong higgledy-piggledy, as they do in life, and at the end the hero or heroine is still undaunted, with plenty of hope and enjoyment of such fine things as are left, and a kind of promise of better luck next time – perhaps.'

In August 1922, Vera and Winifred attended the League of Nations Summer School in Geneva. To Winifred's astonishment and Vera's consternation, awaiting them at Doughty Street on their return was a letter from the publishers John Lane accepting *Anderby Wold* for publication the following spring. 'It had simply never occurred to me,' Vera admitted later, 'that her work could be preferred and published before my own.'

That *Anderby Wold* was to be published while *The Dark Tide* languished, disregarded and unwanted, was a humiliating blow to Vera's pride, and, briefly, it imposed a strain on her friendship with Winifred. As she was older, the published author of *Verses of a VAD*, and had made successful excursions into poetry and journalism at Oxford, Vera had always expected that she would be the frontrunner in their literary endeavours.

At first Vera acted less than generously in failing to congratulate Winifred on her success. By the time she was ready to make amends, Winifred had already left Doughty Street for a short holiday at Cottingham with her family. Back at Oakwood Court, Vera forced herself to come to terms with the fact that *Anderby Wold* was a better book than her own novel, and wrote Winifred a letter of appreciation in which, however, she was unable to withhold her own strong feelings of disappointment:

> My family were quite excited about your book and most delighted ... I couldn't take in the fact on Saturday at all ... It is a kind book as well as a clever one, and has always inspired me with a secret envy. I think I pretended that it bored me because it gave me a despairing sense of my own inability to reach the same level ... Somehow the whole world seems subtly changed by your book getting taken. I suppose it's like what I said in 'Daphne' about crossing the gulf between aspiration and achievement; once people have done it they are never quite the same again. I don't know whether better – certainly not worse – but quite certainly different. Almost I think of you as if you were a stranger; we are not equals any more.

Winifred hastened to revive Vera's confidence:

You must not talk such nonsense, you know. You are perfectly right in saying
we are not equals. We never were and never will be. I have always known how
much keener and clearer and finer your mind is than mine . . .

Refusing to submit herself to further mortifying rejections, Vera
abandoned *The Dark Tide* as a failure, and Winifred became the inevitable
butt for her irascible pessimism. 'I feel quite able to hold my own with WH',
Vera wrote to her belligerently in Yorkshire, 'and to tell the truth, I don't
care a damn if I can't.'

Rose Macaulay had unsuccessfully approached six or seven publishers in
an attempt to stimulate interest in Vera's novel, and she greeted Winifred's
offer to try to place it with scepticism. Undeterred, Winifred took it first to
John Lane, 'and made them interested in it and her', but at the end of
October it was once more back in Doughty Street. 'I've got the MS',
Winifred wrote to Jean McWilliam with some perturbation. 'She doesn't
know yet. It's a horrid thing, for her book's miles away better than mine,
only Yorkshire stories just happen to be in fashion and college ones aren't.'

III

At the end of September 1922, Vera and Winifred moved from their studio
at 52 Doughty Street to a more spacious top-floor flat at number 58 'with
real walls and a real front door', and a woman to do the housework for two
hours each morning.

The small hall led into a sitting-room overlooking Doughty Street, and to
complement the blue and fuchsia covers of the sitting-room chairs they
decorated the oak dresser with Winifred's Delft plates, a blue lustre bowl
filled with dried lavender, and a pottery vase which Vera had brought back
from Malta. They considered it a blessing in disguise that there were a lot of
stairs to climb as they hoped that might deter the importunate visitor and
make them less susceptible to interruptions.

Having completed her first novel Vera was able to devote more attention
to her efforts to establish herself as a freelance journalist. Her first
professional article, as we have seen, had been published in 1919 while she
was an undergraduate at Oxford, but during those first years in London, her
'onslaught upon editorial offices' remained, like Winifred's, 'persistent and
hopeful rather than progressive.' Initially Vera was marginally the more
successful of the two in placing her work, but it would be another four years

before she made the decisive breakthrough. *Time and Tide*, the feminist weekly, was an obvious target for both of them. In early 1923 Winifred attempted an article on Charlotte Brontë, 'but couldn't get it down well enough'; Vera then decided to see if she could do any better, and *Time and Tide* accepted it. Entitled 'The Whole Duty of Women', and drawing comparisons between the ideal of submissive womanhood prevalent in Charlotte Brontë's day and the difficulties still faced by the postwar woman in escaping the tyranny of the domestic round, the article was published on 23 February 1923, and was Vera's first contribution to *Time and Tide*. It was not until the following year when Winifred submitted an unsolicited piece on 'The Human Factor' that *Time and Tide*'s proprietor, Lady Rhondda, realized 'that here was someone who counted and whom I must at once get hold of', and increasingly, as the decade wore on, Winifred's connection with *Time and Tide* would grow stronger as Vera's steadily diminished.

The only child of a South Wales mining magnate, Margaret Haig Mackworth, Viscountess Rhondda, had entered Somerville in 1904, but had been appalled by the privations that then existed in a women's college, and had left after two terms. Influenced by John Stuart Mill's *The Subjection of Women* and Olive Schreiner's *Woman and Labour*, she became a committed suffragette, and after one burst of militancy, during which she set fire to the contents of a pillar box, ended up in the county gaol in Usk on a five-day sentence. In May 1915 while returning with her father from America on the *Lusitania* they were torpedoed off the south coast of Ireland, and the ship went down with the loss of 1,198 lives. Father and daughter survived, but as Virginia Woolf perceived, a deep psychological scar remained. 'I like old [Lady] Rhondda', she wrote to the composer Ethel Smyth, 'but she must have had a fright as a child – nothing else explains her humming and hawing – her indecision, her incapacity . . .'.

When the *New Statesman* was launched by the Webbs in 1913, Lady Rhondda was 'enormously interested'. Five years later she made up her mind to found a weekly review of her own. Her periodical, she decided, would be run by women, and act as a spearhead for the feminist movement, but at the same time it would be sufficiently broad-based and authoritative to attract a wide spectrum of readers. Her purpose would be 'to mould the opinion, not of the large crowd, but of the keystone people, who in their turn would guide the crowd.'

The first issue of *Time and Tide* appeared in 1920, and, as possible subscribers, Vera and Winifred were among the students of the women's colleges to receive introductory copies. Intrigued by this all-women enterprise and sympathetic to its feminist outlook, Vera subsequently took out a postal subscription. For a time Vera and Winifred shared a fascination with Lady Rhondda herself, especially when she obtained a divorce in December 1922 under the most recent change in the British divorce laws.

In addition to launching her weekly review, Lady Rhondda had founded the feminist Six Point Group in 1921 to press 'for the abolition of various inequalities in the laws'. The Six Point Group represented the voice of equal-rights feminism and a younger generation of feminists. As committed 'equality' feminists, Vera and Winifred joined the Group in March 1922. With considerable apprehension in the summer of 1922 they agreed to speak in support of the Criminal Law Amendment Bill – an improvement in the laws governing child assault, included in the Bill, was one of the six points – from a platform lent to the Six Point Group by the London County Council for Promoting Public Morality.

For two untrained speakers, Hyde Park was a nerve-racking baptism. They stood 'on a platform as big as a dinner plate', Winifred reported, and had to contend with the thunderous noise of the Marble Arch traffic, Salvation Army hymns, hecklers and the distracting remarks of passers-by. One evening after speaking in pouring rain Vera developed a temperature and an attack of gastritis. On another occasion Winifred became embroiled in a heated argument with a spirited prostitute and discovered that 'my ideas on morality are drying up . . . I must admit she was the better man of the two.'

In the Twenties, feminism in Britain was undergoing an important period of major ideological shifts. With their motto 'Equality First', the so-called 'old' feminists of the Six Point Group campaigned for six specific objectives founded on social justice for women: pensions for widows, equal rights of guardianship for married parents, reform of the laws dealing with child assault and the position of the unmarried mother, equal pay for teachers, and equal pay and opportunity for men and women in the Civil Service. The 'new' feminists of the National Union of Societies for Equal Citizenship (NUSEC), under their President, Eleanor Rathbone, challenged the traditional feminist preoccupation with political equality, and maintained that sex differentiation would always exist, and that 'in the most important of women's occupations, maternity', women had special needs. Two of their most contentious demands were for family allowances and unrestricted access to information on birth control. The 'old' feminists argued that these reforms 'concern sons and husbands as well as mothers and daughters', to which the 'new' feminists retorted that this was equally true of all the points of the Six Point Group, that organizations of men and women already existed to deal with child assaults and improved legislation for the unmarried mother, and that the Labour Party and many trade unions stood for equal pay and employment.

Vera worked for the Six Point Group throughout the Twenties and early Thirties, and continued to be actively involved well into the Sixties. From 1926 she served on its executive, and was the author of several pamphlets for the Group, including one from 1927 entitled 'Why Feminism Lives' which demanded an answer to 'the fundamental question: "Should a woman be treated as a human being, and if not, why not?" '; and she took a leading role, at the end of the decade, in the campaign to secure the passage of an Equal Rights Treaty at the League of Nations Assembly to counter the League's anti-feminist bias. Essentially, however, she remained a moderate. She was sympathetic to the 'new' feminist stance on birth control and on the need for informed motherhood, and, pragmatic and independent, refused to become involved in any of the disputes which threatened the larger interests of feminism.

On a less serious level, there was a spiky difference of opinion among feminists about the importance of being well dressed. Some women in public and professional life maintained that clothes were an irrelevance, and deplored the time and money wasted on changing fashions and women's magazines, and pointed out that Olive Schreiner herself had decreed that 'an intense love of dress and meretricious external adornment is almost invariably the concomitant and outcome of parasitism.'

Vera did not agree. Both she and Winifred were extremely clothes-conscious, and being attractively and fashionably dressed boosted Vera's confidence. In July 1921 she had described to Winifred, in painstaking detail, what she intended to wear for an interview at the League of Nations Union: 'I am going in my dark blue frock . . . a soft tulle & black straw hat of Mother's with a hanging lace veil & my best buckles on black suede shoes.' She and Winifred deprecated their colleagues who turned up at meetings and conferences in 'dark velour coats with dreary rabbit-skin collars . . . unbecoming hats mostly laden with trimmings which were fashionable five or six years ago . . . [and] with rather untidy hair.' In April 1924 Winifred related to Vera her shock on finding the veteran campaigner, Cicely Hamilton, in the *Time and Tide* office, dressed in a dirty, white, man's shirt. On another occasion Vera and Winifred attended a lecture by Rebecca West on the modern novel at the London School of Economics. She was 'exquisitely funny, brilliant and often wise', but they were almost as impressed by her smoke-grey silk dress, sable coat, and huge hat with drooping plume.

It had been in an issue of *Time and Tide* in the autumn of 1921 that Vera had chanced upon a notice of a new book which, she told Winifred, '. . . I am ordering immediately'. The book was called *The Evolution of World Peace* and consisted of a series of essays by well-known writers – including 'An Apology for a World Utopia' by H.G. Wells – on the theme of 'the various efforts to organize civilization as a unity', dating back to Alexander the Great and coming right up to date with the League of Nations. For Vera it provided nothing short of an inspiration, illuminating and reinforcing her dedication to work for peace. 'My dear – I am so glad', she wrote to Winifred in a mood of optimism, '. . . glad to do anything, however small, to make people care for the peace of the world. It may be Utopian, but it's constructive. It's better than railing at the present state of Europe, or always weeping in darkness for the dead . . .'

The creation of the League of Nations had been the most constructive feature of the Treaty of Versailles which followed Germany's defeat, and its Covenant stipulated that members were to afford each other mutual protection against aggression, and to submit disputes to arbitration. Vera believed in the urgent need to establish international harmony, and that the League's concept of collective security was the best hope of achieving peace where alliances, armed neutralities, and balances of power failed. The League of Nations Union (LNU), founded in October 1918, promoted the work of the League in a variety of ways, including the sponsoring of lectures and study sessions. To a disillusioned, war-weary world it represented a new idealism in international relations, and in the course of the Twenties it became the largest, most influential peace organization in Britain.

It was at Winifred's suggestion that Vera had contacted the LNU, offering her services as a lecturer immediately on finishing at Oxford in July 1921. At first she had little hope of being accepted, telling Winifred that 'It's quite possible I mayn't be sufficiently experienced for them.' When, however, she telephoned the LNU's headquarters at Grosvenor Crescent, her call was answered by Agnes Murray, daughter of Gilbert Murray, Oxford's Regius Professor of Greek and a founder of the LNU. She had been at Somerville in 1914 '& thanks to my first-year reputation . . . remembered me very well!' Agnes Murray arranged an interview for her, but for months afterwards Vera heard nothing further. She was therefore surprised to receive a telephone call early in February 1922 asking her to deputize for an indisposed speaker in the Watford Baptist Hall which had a capacity of two thousand. Dismayed but undaunted, she discovered to her intense relief an undemanding audience of fifteen elderly women waiting for her in the vestry.

The work was often unpaid and sometimes Vera felt exploited, but for the next three years she lectured to meetings all over London, interspersed with excursions by train to the Home Counties, the Midlands, Wiltshire and Kent, and short lecture-tours of four to six meetings in the towns on the Scottish border. Occasionally she spoke at more prestigious engagements, for example addressing an open-air meeting at Beaconsfield with H.A.L. Fisher, the former Minister of Education. Inspired by *The Evolution of World Peace*, she lectured initially on the historical development of the peace ideal, with a detailed exposition of the League's policy of collective security. Later, after attending the annual Geneva assemblies as *Time and Tide*'s correspondent, she extended the scope of her talks to include carefully researched accounts of the League's reconstruction scheme for Austria, the Greek–Italian dispute in which the Italians had bombarded Corfu, and the French occupation of the Ruhr after the Germans had defaulted on their reparation payments. In 1924 in a published Armistice Day address on 'Good Citizenship and the League' she turned her attention to the young, and reminded her audience aged between ten and fourteen that 'the new ideal of citizenship as started by the League is much wider than the old one. Once upon a time we only felt responsible for our own city or at least our own country, now our ideas of service take in the whole world.'

By October 1922 Winifred was reporting to Jean McWilliam that as a speaker Vera was an 'immense success'. 'Everywhere she goes they ask for her again. She has letters from M.P.s and paragraphs in the paper, and all the time she just laughs a little and takes it quite as a matter of course.'

'Why shouldn't you tread also in the path you have marked out for me?' Vera had asked Winifred, and before long Winifred, too, had become almost as active as Vera as an LNU speaker. Each September they visited Geneva together for the annual League assembly.

In the autumn of 1922 one of Vera's LNU engagements took her to Bethnal Green to talk to a small gathering of women at the Liberal Party headquarters. The meeting had been arranged by Percy Harris, the prospective Liberal candidate, and as her chairman he was impressed by her direct, well-prepared address. At that time Vera belonged to no political party. She supported the Liberals 'for the simple reason that I believe in liberty more than in anything', and shortly after the meeting, when the defeat of the Coalition Government precipitated a general election, Percy Harris wrote asking her to be his secretary. Although anxious to obtain practical political experience, her two days a week teaching prevented her from accepting, but she volunteered to give him all the help that she could. At that time, Winifred had only a temporary job coaching a wealthy young woman for her university entrance examination.

She had met Percy Harris, and agreed to become his election secretary in Vera's place.

Despite her other commitments, for several weeks Vera spent her free time in the East End, canvassing for Percy Harris, holding impromptu meetings on street corners and speaking in church halls and poorly lit schools. In November, Percy Harris was elected for south-east Bethnal Green with a comfortable majority, and was to retain his seat for the next twenty-two years. Vera and Winifred again supported him in the 1923 election, but a decided swing to Labour made Vera wonder how much longer it would be worthwhile 'to give lip-service to a party that is not likely to be in power for a generation or longer when everything one wants is in the programme of the Labour party . . .'.

Electioneering in Bethnal Green had been a sobering experience. She had been appalled by the economic depression and hopeless unemployment, and incensed by the poverty, undernourishment and sordid slums. 'At the same time I realised, with a shock of poignant revelation, the kinship between men and women in these wretched homes, and the Tommies whom I had nursed for four calamitous years. The same brave, uncomplaining endurance was there, the same humour, the same rough, compassionate kindness to one another . . .'.

In December 1923 Vera celebrated her thirtieth birthday, and became eligible to vote under the 1918 Franchise Act. The following October, in the third general election in successive years, she became a lifelong Labour supporter, and in 1925 a member of the Labour Party. But as she admitted to Winifred she was interested in the state of the political parties only in the sense that they might further the causes that she cared about most, feminism and peace.

IV

Writing in *Testament of Youth* about the ultimate acceptance of *The Dark Tide*, Vera comments with cryptic ingenuity that 'In the late spring of 1923 my tired and dishevelled novel strayed into the hands of Mr Grant Richards.' It was, in fact, in response to a letter from Winifred that the publisher, Grant Richards, wrote early in December 1922 saying that he would be 'glad to have an opportunity of considering Miss Brittain's manuscript . . .'. Nearly four months later he wrote again asking Winifred to call at his office in St Martin's Street. 'It would be an advantage, no doubt,' he informed her, 'if it could be arranged for Miss Brittain to come with you.'

An innately optimistic man, Grant Richards had established himself as an independent publisher at the end of the nineteenth century, and had survived two early bankruptcies. Vera and Winifred knew of him as the publisher in book form of Marie Leighton's *Convict 99*. Suave and monocled, Grant Richards possessed a reputation for being 'the best dressed publisher in London', but Vera was less impressed and would later describe him to a friend as 'an amiable rascal'.

When they met, Grant Richards expressed his interest in *The Dark Tide* 'on account of certain qualities of freshness and vitality', but told her that it was a risky business publishing a first novel by an unknown author. The chill wind of depression had begun to blow, the price of books was going down, and the bookbinders' strike opposing a reduction in their wages had created further problems. In spite of these difficulties, Grant Richards was prepared to publish Vera's novel, providing that she subsidized the cost of publication by contributing £50 in cash.

This was a substantial sum in 1923, and although Vera later claimed that she paid the contribution out of the fees she had earned from teaching, Grant Richards's account ledgers show that it was Winifred who actually made the payment from her own money. Whether she did so as a loan to Vera or as a gift is a mystery, but undoubtedly she knew better than anyone how important it was to Vera for her novel to be published.

Anderby Wold had been published a few days earlier, at the beginning of April. Although only a promising prototype, as the first of Winifred's six published novels it has a strange affinity with *South Riding*, her last. There is the same clash of feudal tradition and socialist idealism, the same tragic ending of sudden death and unrequited love, the same lyrical evocation of the East Riding countryside she loved. 'After tea she fled the house and went to the gate in the stable yard', she wrote, recalling her adolescence on the Rudston farm. 'Westward before her rose fold upon fold of encircling hills, piled rich and golden beneath a tranquil sky. There was no sound but the crunch, crunch of horses feeding in the pasture.'

Like most first novels, *Anderby Wold* was not financially rewarding: Winifred's first six-month royalty cheque amounted to just £23. Furthermore it attracted a large number of extraordinarily disparate reviews. She wondered that people ever took any notice of them, and came to the conclusion that 'the only thing to do is to decide that nothing really means anything.' But however wildly the reviewers dissented, Winifred had arrived as a young writer of talent and promise. She was interviewed by 'Mrs

Gossip' of the *Daily Express*, but 'did not half use my chance to advertise'; Beatrice Harradan was deeply impressed and assured her that she was putting the novel on the reading list for the Femina Vie Heureuse award; and the following year when Lady Rhondda commissioned articles on education and farming they were publicized with Winifred's name on the *Time and Tide* posters.

In spite of the conflicting reviews, the impact of *Anderby Wold* was a dignified literary event compared to the tumult and criticism that greeted the publication of *The Dark Tide* when it appeared, three months later, on 16 July. 'These unexpected attacks upon my innocent fledgling,' Vera wrote with her writer's predilection for exaggeration, 'reduced me to a condition bordering on nervous breakdown.'

The first broadside was a letter from the *Manchester Guardian*, threatening Vera with libel proceedings. At the end of the chapter describing Daphne Lethbridge, Vera had artlessly written that 'The next day Mrs Lethbridge, with the *Manchester Guardian* on her lap, sat gloating over the paragraph on whose account she had bribed an accommodating reporter with champagne.' With a melodramatic notion of the newspaper sending the police to arrest her, Vera apologized profusely and pleaded that youth and inexperience alone were responsible for an outrageous libel which she had never intended. C.P. Scott himself replied, graciously dismissing the bribery imputation as 'a piece of carelessness', and agreeing to take no further action if a printed slip apologizing for the error was inserted on the appropriate page. When the book was reissued in a cheap edition following the success of *Testament of Youth*, the reference to the *Manchester Guardian* was discreetly amended to the *Manchester Sentinel*.

The reviews of *The Dark Tide* were a significant indication of the reputation for being provocative and controversial which was to attach to Vera for the rest of her life. The first to launch a critical attack was the *Daily Express*, which called the novel 'impossible', and 'an insult to women's colleges'. It followed this a day or two later with a banner headline 'University kisses', and a derisively anti-feminist article containing, Winifred reported, 'the most ridiculous and venomous nonsense'.

In its leading fiction review, the *Times Literary Supplement* re-established *The Dark Tide* as a serious novel, but commented that the women's college setting was 'a strange world to us where much drinking of cocoa goes on.' The reviewer was impressed that 'as the story proceeds the perception of the nature of feminine reactions becomes notably acute.' His conclusion that 'Virginia is an invention we would willingly have seen in more detail, as her keen intelligence and disdainful revolt form an interesting combination' was a welcome antidote to the raillery of the *Daily Express*, especially as Vera admitted that Virginia Dennison was an idealized self-portrait.

Inadvertently the *Times Literary Supplement* put its finger on one aspect of the novel that was to throw Oxford's women's colleges into a ferment of indignation. Pointing out that 'the life of the female undergraduate at Oxford remains something of a mystery long after the veil has been stripped from the activities of her male counterpart', the reviewer remarked with bemused perplexity upon 'this strange world . . . where work is considered with a blind, unlovely intensity, and tears are shed at the tutor's criticism of essays.'

While at Oxford, Vera had assiduously accumulated notes for her novel, and the first ten chapters she later maintained 'did represent with fair accuracy the cloistered lives of women students in 1920, and the relationship between them.' In a curious publicity blurb, however, which stressed the novel's university background, Grant Richards had blandly asserted that he had no information about whether his author had 'drawn any particular college.' 'I fancy not', he wrote tongue in cheek, but Somerville suffered no such illusions.

The women's colleges were outraged by her presentation of their world, and Somerville was beside itself as it identified one fictitious character after another with the living model. It was bad enough for Vera egotistically to portray herself as the rich, brilliant student, small, dark-eyed and pretty, the author of a sensational satire, and 'one of those individuals of whom other people are always aware', but they could not forgive her for her insensitivity in portraying identifiable dons, undergraduates, and other university personalities in unflattering, melodramatic situations.

Especially resented was the presentation of Virginia Dennison's flirtation with Alexis Stephanoff, the witty Polish History tutor, clearly recognizable as thirty-three-year-old Lewis Namier, at the time a Modern History lecturer at Balliol, and Patricia O'Neill, Vera informed one of her correspondents, 'represents what I wish Maude Clarke could have been, but never was.' Daphne Lethbridge, the disorganized, dishevelled daughter of socially pretentious parents, was considered by Somerville to be a personal insult to Winifred. One critic remarked with caustic wit that her marriage to Raymond Sylvester resembled nothing less than 'being run over by a motor-bus'. And wasn't Raymond Sylvester, with his hard brown eyes and beautifully moulded, sensuous lips, none other than C.R.M.F. Cruttwell, the Dean of Hertford College? Miss Lawson-Scott bore an unmistakeable likeness to Emily Penrose, and Somerville's indignant Bursar angrily identified herself with Miss Jenkinson whom 'nobody wanted to marry'.

'I wonder who ever wrote a book who didn't borrow from surroundings familiar to someone or other', Vera had written with some irritation after Hilda Reid had expressed her uncertainty about whether 'one *ought* to write about college'. Throughout her writing career Vera was frequently to appropriate real-life situations and characters for her autobiographical fiction with no apparent thought for the sensibilities of the individuals concerned, but it is nonetheless surprising that in the caricature of Winifred as Daphne Lethbridge in *The Dark Tide* she appears to have been prepared to risk causing offence to her greatest friend. She had, it is true, mentioned to Winifred at an early stage in the novel's composition that the character was not wholly based on her. 'Poor Daphne!' she wrote in November 1921, 'I get more & more cruel to her. The chief consolation is she gets less & less like you.' Furthermore, as the novel progresses, the two main female characters become more representative of the different sides of Vera's own personality, with Daphne exhibiting her insecurity and desire for recognition, and Virginia her 'more autonomous, intellectual, stronger side'. There is, however, no escaping the fact that Daphne, with her golden hair, 'her long legs and large, clumsy hands', and her 'uninspired popularity', is in part a portrait of Winifred, and that in the early chapters Vera was building on her memories of her initial resentment of Winifred and of her anger at her own humiliation at the debate.

Rereading *The Dark Tide* more than forty years later, Vera recognized it as a 'wild little novel, full of undergraduate cleverness, ruthless, even savage', and admitted that she should have been ashamed of her caricature of 'my beloved W.H.'. If Winifred felt hurt or insulted she did not show it, though later she would describe the book to George Catlin as 'crude and immature'. At the time she seems to have lightheartedly dismissed her characterization as Daphne, claiming that she would never be able to portray Vera in a novel with the same success. 'I am too different, my dear, to try to draw anyone just like you', she told Vera, just over a week after the appearance of *The Dark Tide*. 'I should not succeed as well as you succeeded with Daphne . . .'. In fact she would succeed rather well in portraying Vera as Delia Vaughan in her second novel, *The Crowded Street*, which she had already begun to write. Delia, whom Vera later acknowledged to be 'a partial . . . reconstruction of my war-time self', lost her fiancé during the war and dedicates herself to reforming society through the Twentieth Century Reform League.

Other Somervillians were not as forbearing about *The Dark Tide* as Winifred. Cicely Williams disliked the book so intensely that she and a friend burned it page by page in the back yard of her mother's house in

Wallingford. Going into the Cadena Café in the Cornmarket in Oxford a few days later, they met Maude Clarke, and over a cup of coffee they related the story of their back-yard bonfire. 'She didn't say a word', Cicely Williams recalled. 'She simply stood up and shook hands with both of us.'

Maude Clarke's response on receiving a presentation copy of the book from Vera was short and to the point. 'Dear Vera', she wrote that August from her home in Carmoney on the outskirts of Belfast,

> It was very kind of you to think of sending me your book. I cannot honestly say that I see any merit in it as a novel. It also offends against any standards of good taste. I wish I could say anything less and remain
> Yours sincerely
> M.V. Clarke

Vera confided to her friends that she had written *The Dark Tide* partly to open Somerville's eyes to its lack of culture as distinct from education, and she can scarcely have been surprised by what she described as 'the Oxford Authorities' acid disapproval'. Somerville, she said, had vetoed the circulation of the book, and in addition, 'the writing of it has practically placed its author under a ban.'

It is difficult accurately to assess the effect upon Vera of the repercussions that followed the publication of *The Dark Tide*. In her book *On Becoming a Writer* she describes the onset of 'strange daytime hallucinations' and 'a persecution mania', and of how 'I picked up my books and papers and fled from London to an aunt's cottage where I knew my address would remain unknown.'

In her letters to Winifred in Yorkshire she was more preoccupied with her social activities than with her book. She had been invited to lunch, she told her, by an enthusiastic American reader. 'Is this the beginning of "lionization"?' she enquired disarmingly. One tangible result of all the controversy provoked by her novel had been to stimulate interest and boost sales. A fortnight after publication Winifred eagerly anticipated them reaching two thousand so that 'Grant Richards [will] have to pay you that 12 per cent', while Vera reported that in Oxford it had sold 'quite immensely'.

One of the first people to buy a copy in Blackwell's bookshop in Oxford was George Catlin, a twenty-seven-year-old Sheffield University lecturer, who 'felt sufficiently young, adventurous and romantic to send copies of my recently-published exercise in *belles-lettres* to two women: I admired the poetry of one, and the newly published Oxford novel of the other had moved me – a book rather in the spirit of Wells' *Ann Veronica* . . . I got a pleasant letter of acknowledgement from Edna St Vincent Millay, and also one from Vera Brittain.'

SIX

Ave atque Vale

'I do not think I am likely to marry as I am too hard to please & too difficult to understand thoroughly & I would be satisfied with nothing less than a mutually comprehensive loving companionship. I could not endure to be constantly propitiating any man, or to have a large range of subjects on which it was impossible to talk to him.'

Vera Brittain, 7 September 1914

I

Two years' contented and productive life in London with Winifred had persuaded Vera that she was unlikely ever to want to marry. She enjoyed her work, relished her independence, and found that in general the men she had met since the war merely confirmed her belief that the best of the male sex had disappeared from a whole generation.

Clare Leighton's impression of Vera at this time was that she 'felt a sense of being doomed' where men were concerned. 'I think her hardness came from this feeling'. The men she had loved were dead and there was also the memory of her embarrassingly short-lived engagement to Roy Anthony to deter her from any future impulsive involvements. 'I did not wish to live emotionally, any more, for I was still too tired', Vera wrote in *Testament of Youth*, 'I wanted to stand aside from life and write'.

These first years in London, however, were not entirely without incident, and she had lost none of the flirtatiousness with which as a young girl she had teased Maurice Ellinger and Bertram Spafford. In the months following the publication of *The Dark Tide* she was being hotly pursued by Lord Waring with whom she shared an 'exquisite but completely *tête-à-tête* dinner'. He was convinced that she could be an 'immense influence in Parliament', and urged her to start nursing a constituency, hinting that he might put up the necessary finance. 'I must say he behaved like a perfect gentleman', she reported to Winifred, '. . . that he should continue to do so seems too much to hope for.' The MP, Sir Harry Brittain (no relation), another middle-aged admirer, was rather more direct in his approach. At a performance of *Robert E. Lee*, a theatrical extravaganza based on the life of the American General, he squeezed her hand every time the guns went off, which, as Vera told Winifred, 'they do frequently'. More irresponsibly, Vera appears to have done nothing to discourage the attentions of her Aunt Muriel's husband, Leigh Groves, just thirteen years her senior, on her regular visits in the early Twenties to their house, Holehird, near Lake Windermere.

Encounters such as these were little more than romantic diversions. George Catlin, on the other hand, would give an uncomfortable jolt to Vera's complacency about marriage. A distinguished young intellectual, a survivor of the 'War Generation', and a professed feminist, he would eventually be willing to acquiesce in a form of marriage which would attempt to resolve the central conflict of Vera's postwar life: that between the promise of fulfilment and self-respect through a career, and the demands of and desire for husband and children.

When Catlin wrote to her, Vera was nearing thirty, 'a provincial of the provincials, in heart though not in mind', and acutely conscious that she would soon be consigned to the ranks of what, in a callous phraseology of the time, were known as 'superfluous women'. In the last resort her persistent young suitor was bound to prove an irresistible attraction.

II

George Catlin's was the first of several thousand fan letters that Vera was to receive during her lifetime, and accompanying it was a short treatise by him on the seventeenth-century philosopher, Thomas Hobbes. The signature and spidery handwriting seemed vaguely familiar, and she suddenly realized that several weeks before the publication of her novel, back in June, she had received what she considered an impertinent visiting card from the same young man. He had written then that he remembered her from the Somerville debates, and that he believed he had caught sight of her recently in the Radcliffe Camera at Oxford. He had invited her to tea and an afternoon's punting on the Cherwell, but Vera had considered his behaviour to be forward and had torn up the card and thrown it in the wastepaper basket.

From the dust jacket of the monograph she now discovered that George

Edward Gordon Catlin* had been a New College Exhibitioner in Modern History from 1919 to 1920, had won the Chancellor's English Essay Prize in 1920, the Gladstone and the Matthew Arnold Memorial Prizes in 1921, and had been a lecturer at Sheffield University for a year. Impressed by his distinguished academic credentials and flattered by his appreciation of *The Dark Tide*, Vera this time replied, although by now George Catlin was on his way to take up an appointment at Cornell University in New York State.

Soon, though, a regular correspondence developed, and throughout the autumn and winter of 1923 they exchanged views on a wide diversity of subjects: on the state of the novel, on questions relating to the social and economic position of the postwar woman, and on George Catlin's own ongoing research into political theory. Vera admitted later that she kept up her end of 'this strange correspondence' with 'a rage of self-detesting, resentful regularity'; but from the odd autobiographical reference in his letters she was able to work out that had it not been for the war, he and Edward would have been New College contemporaries, and that he, like Roland, was a convert to Catholicism. These coincidences seemed to give this shadowy figure a strange alliance with the past.

By Christmas 1923, Vera was writing to Winifred that she had received 'another long letter from Mr Catlin – intimate and amazingly interesting', but that she felt 'vaguely uneasy and rather miserable.' 'I do hope,' she continued, 'that, after this lovely period of peace, some devastating male is not going to push into my life and upset it again. Just when things look so promising, too. You must exert yourself as a bulwark and protect me from them . . . [but] what after all are a letter from America and a box of cigarettes? And yet I do feel it. Please write and laugh me to scorn . . .'.

Winifred replied that she also hoped that Vera was not going to allow another man to disrupt her life. She was by now only too familiar with Vera's entanglements, and pointed out that although Vera could not help their being difficult, '. . . I cannot help thinking that you can yourself prevent them being devastating . . . Mr Catlin sounds more than a little interesting. Perhaps it is a pity that you have not seen him,' she added, growing impatient with Vera's impetuous romanticism. 'He may be fat and greasy. I sometimes wish that you were!'

In November, Vera and Winifred had moved from Doughty Street to a large unfurnished flat at 117 Wymering Mansions in Wymering Road, a

---

* As his father's names were also George Edward, he was known by his parents as Gordon. He never liked the name, and when his father died in 1936 he reverted to George. Having called him Gordon for twelve years, Vera 'inevitably thought of him by both names'. She said that this was why she always referred to him in her books as 'G.', although when she published *Testament of Youth* in 1933 she knew him only as Gordon and used his initial to protect his anonymity. To avoid confusion we have called him George throughout.

stone's throw from Elgin Avenue, and within easy reach of Paddington Recreation Ground for fresh air and exercise. They had taken the decision to move after the departure of their charwoman. She had left in a flurry of indignation when she discovered what she had taken to be two high-minded young writers, dressing up and going out at five o'clock and often not returning until nearly midnight.

George Catlin wrote to Vera expressing surprise that she should have left the intellectual milieu of Bloomsbury 'for a place in Maida Vale'. She at once took umbrage and enquired sardonically if he was 'over-conscious of its second-rate actresses, its music hall artistes, and members of less reputable professions'. The Maida Vale flat had three bedrooms, and by living in a less expensive district they were able to afford a housekeeper-cook to relieve them of all domestic responsibilities. He might not appreciate this factor, she chided, as he was safe behind 'the sacred right of the male to know nothing of housework'. '. . . Even the vicinity of Eileen Power and Lytton Strachey (whom incidentally I don't know) was not enthralling enough to keep me tied any longer to saucepans and plates and dishes.'

At the beginning of 1924 Vera sent George Catlin a presentation copy of her second novel, *Not Without Honour*. Grant Richards had accepted it 'on much more favourable terms' than her first the previous autumn, and published it in February. Originally entitled *The Prophet*, Richards had pointed out that there was already a book of that name by Kahlil Gibran, and Vera's alternative suggestions of 'The Lost Shepherd', 'The Symbolist' and 'A Martyr's Memorial' were all rejected as too portentous. Eventually, taking her title from St Mark's Gospel, she settled on *Not Without Honour*.

Based on her rebellious adolescence in Buxton, with a fictionalized account of the Reverend Ward's struggles at Fairfield, the book was a ponderous exposé of provincial snobbery and revolt against the middle-class maxim that 'a girl of eighteen ought to get married at the first opportunity'. She admitted that her heroine – yet another self-portrait – was 'a crude little sentimentalist'.

Although George Catlin was later to revise his opinion, his immediate reaction, Vera told Winifred, was '. . . an amazing letter . . . containing a criticism of my book that should raise me to the seventh heaven if it were not rather too agitating . . . I have written – I had to – some kind of an answer . . . all life seems suddenly to be tumbling about my ears'. The reviewer in the *Times Literary Supplement* was less impressed. Unaware that the heroine Christine Merivale's championing of the Higher Criticism and *Robert Elsmere* was autobiographically inspired, he commented that her 'intellectual pretensions' while 'singularly modest . . . seem a little dowdy for 1914'. The reading public had little interest in prewar trivia and the petty occupations of the well-to-do in a fashionable northern resort, and at the end of two years the royalties amounted to less than £18. It was to be the least successful of all Vera's books.

In early April, Vera embarked on a short League of Nations lecture-tour of the small Scottish border towns. She talked mainly about the French occupation of the Ruhr and German reparations, but found it difficult to stimulate an interest in the League as 'most people in these little places don't know the first thing about it, and care less'. At Ayton and Coldringham her audiences averaged no more than fifty.

Stopping at Windermere on her way back to London she visited her father's sister, Aunt Muriel, and her husband, Leigh Groves. In writing to thank Winifred for forwarding her letters, she told her that none of them were interesting 'except Catlin's, which would have entranced you as much as it did me'. The photograph he had enclosed showed him to be anything but fat and greasy. He was 'nice looking, much gayer and less pedantic than his letters sound, dark [a photographic illusion as he was fair], slim, looking on the tall side of middle height . . . clothes neat and well cared for'. George Catlin had requested a photograph of her in return, and in asking Leigh Groves to take some for her, 'I also told him why'. It was obviously provocative, and he responded by 'scenting a romance and dragging from me all the details about Catlin except his name, which I refused to give!'

What Vera had presumably intended to be a frivolous flirtation with her uncle now showed every sign of getting out of hand, and when she returned to London she told Winifred that she was writing to him to deliver 'the knock-out blow'. Before she had posted it, however, she received 'such a very charming letter' that her resolution wavered, and she admitted that her response 'wasn't in the end' intended to be the *coup de grâce*.

Before the summer term began, Vera and Winifred had planned a fortnight's writing holiday in lodgings in Whipsnade. Writing to her in Yorkshire, Vera told Winifred that Leigh Groves would be arriving in London at 4.15 on the day they were leaving, and in making arrangements to delay their departure, she said he wanted her to meet him at Euston and have tea. 'I will do this, I think. I can't attempt to explain these emotional complexes in a letter, but I will try to explain when I see you – in so far as any of these absurdities are capable of explanation.' Presumably, this time she succeeded in delivering the *coup de grâce* to Groves.

With each long letter from George Catlin, Vera's daydreams about him grew. But she was also beset by grave anxieties about this young man whom she had yet to meet but with whom she had been conducting an ardent epistolary courtship. During their time together in London she had relied more and more on Winifred's support, and now, thoroughly disconcerted, she turned to her for reassurance and advice. 'My dear, it seems that one must choose between stagnation and agitation in this world, and for some people the choice is taken out of their hands,' Winifred replied. In response to Vera's dramatic foreboding that her life was about to 'blow up' again with the advent of George Catlin, she tactfully reminded her, 'That all depends upon yourself, I think.'

'As we grow older,' Catlin had suggested, 'we realize – do we not? – that there is less and less value in any passion, more and more in wisdom.' Vera was unconvinced. 'Do we?' she queried, but Winifred pointed out that though the demands of sex are temporal and the demands of idealism eternal, 'both are inevitably part of a woman's life, and neither should be completely ignored'.

In May George informed Vera that he would shortly be returning to England for the summer vacation, and would be staying with his father, a retired clergyman, in Oxford. Could he see her? Vera admitted to an intense curiosity about him and wrote that 'I think on the whole that I will not tell you not to come'.

George Catlin arrived in Plymouth on the SS *Albania* on Tuesday 10 June 1924. He had cabled Vera with details of his arrival and on reaching London made several telephone calls in an effort to contact her, but, panic-stricken at the thought of meeting her persistent suitor at last, Vera deliberately made herself unavailable by arranging an interview with Lady Rhondda and attending a League of Nations Union conference. Baffled and disappointed, George continued to Oxford and telephoned her that evening from his father's lodgings in Charlton Road. Vera accepted his invitation to a performance of *St Joan* on the Friday evening, and asked him to come to tea beforehand. On Saturday they spent the day walking in Kew Gardens and Richmond Park, and on Sunday 15 June he asked her to marry him. His proposal, Vera told him later, intentionally mixing her metaphor, 'overshadowed with light' the fact that it was the sixth anniversary of Edward's death; but in spite of the temptation to believe that the timing was an auspicious omen she had no intention of being stampeded into marriage after an acquaintance of less than forty-eight hours, and refused him.

His whirlwind courtship threw Vera into an acute emotional and physical turmoil. On the Monday she took to her bed while the doctor diagnosed a nervously induced form of colitis. He told her to stay in bed for three days, and prescribed 'nothing to eat and not even much to drink'. The next day, having 'thought about it for many hours', she wrote George Catlin a fourteen-page letter of breathtaking candour.

She realized that he might prefer that she added nothing to what she had said on that Sunday afternoon, but it had been such an emotional situation that 'I am not absolutely certain that I made everything that I meant quite clear to you . . .'. She repeated her suggestion that he either accepted her refusal, or that he gave her 'an indefinite interval' in which to reconsider her decision. 'I could not be guilty of such intolerable cruelty if I were absolutely certain that I could never change my mind.'

George had pointed out to her that those who deliberately refrained from marriage missed 'much of the richness and sweetness of life', but she insisted that this was so only if 'it is a marriage of like minds rather than of desirous bodies, though I do not expect or even wish to eliminate the latter altogether'. She did not believe that her work was best served by 'perpetual virginity', or that it was possible for 'any intensely vital woman . . . to go through life absolutely content to be childless'.

Vera's desire to have children was the decisive factor in her ultimate decision to marry. Since 1918 she had had the desire ('such foolish, fantastic notions some women have'), 'that if ever I am to create physically as well as mentally, I should like to recreate my brother as far as such a thing is possible. Physically he seemed more beautiful to me than anyone I have ever known . . .'. Children, she reminded George, were a joint creation, and 'one can only contemplate sharing them with the best person available in the circumstances (seeing that one cannot raise the dead)'.

She had, she said, the utmost admiration and respect 'for your brilliant, splendid mind'. She had also been moved 'to so unendurable a pity' by what he had told her of his unhappy early life, in which he had been deprived of love and understanding. But 'I must not allow myself to give you all I believe I could give you merely because I am grieved that you have never had it, marriage . . . must have a better and broader basis than this'. And if she had hurt him by her refusal, she had also suffered 'in finding you – as yet – less fine than I had hoped'.

She could not understand how with his brilliant intellect and 'the face and figure of the young Parsifal', he had acquired 'the voice and manner of an Oxford don in a burlesque', and she did not regard this as 'an inessential accident'. 'It seems to me to arise from a deliberate dogmatism, a conscious assumption of complete superiority . . . It is perhaps particularly hard . . . that your liability to patronize others, and to interrupt and disregard their remarks as though nothing they could ever say could possibly be worth saying, should be combined with such an incongruous youthfulness . . . I can only feel that you are a precocious little boy too dreadfully aware of his own cleverness.'

In a week she expected to be quite well again. If it wasn't too painful, 'Would you like me to come down to Oxford for an afternoon on the river?'

To George, Vera's letter was a lifeline of hope, and his immediate response was to send her flowers. 'What *can* I say?' she replied the same evening. '. . . At least you must realize that though I have closed the door I have not turned the key.' An X-ray three days later confirmed that she was medically fit, but she remained on 'famine rations' of no meat, eggs, fruit or cheese, and had been advised to cancel all her engagements. Her father, who was on holiday in Brighton, arranged for her to spend a long weekend at Broadstairs with her mother to recuperate.

In spite of her offer to go to Oxford, she postponed her visit and instead invited George, if he happened to be in London, to any 'meal – or meals – that you like to come for'. Although they were 'freed from the embarrassment of having everything to say', she was still not convinced 'that you really take my work at my own valuation of its importance . . . & that you do not intend to interrupt it'. It was, she explained, only her 'absurd idealism' that had enabled her to survive the catastrophic war years, and she would never compromise her work for women's rights, international harmony, and her ambitions as a novelist. 'That is why . . . I have made a god of my work (& shall always therefore owe it the allegiance due to a god); it is so much less vulnerable than human beings'.

Since the end of the war she had believed that the claims of the mind were incompatible with the claims of the body, and that the satisfaction of one involved the renunciation of the other. But his letters, 'so sincere yet so deceptive', had reawakened the hope that she might after all satisfy both claims 'without losing anything of what is best in either'. Not for anyone, however, could she rekindle the romantic passion of a girl of twenty and, since Roland's death, she had sublimated her emotions with 'repressions, controls, abstentions and inhibitions'. '. . . Let me repeat I do not demand physical demonstrations of affection', she wrote with chilling honesty. 'These, it seems to me, must inevitably anticipate and thereby belittle the ultimate expression which only comes when there is the fullest acceptance on both sides of all that love means. If ever you *do* get my permission for this (& it is only fair to you to go on stressing the doubtfulness of it) it will be after you have created in me something that will enable me to offer you, if not as much as you offer me, at least something that you can accept – something that, if not all that you ask for, is at least more than mere acquiescence.' He had, however, reminded her that she had once felt intensely 'and that I can do so still', and she hoped that with his love and affection she would not always respond with such coldness. She had forgotten that she was still quite young, but 'I cannot help but be slow to believe it possible that, through you, the incredible happiness which I have dreamed of . . . may be coming to me after all'.

'Your dear letter of Thursday – how shall I answer it?' she wrote on 4 July, the day before going to Oxford. 'If only the summer could come and the winter be past! No, it's no use; I cannot write. I will try to answer when I come.'

In *Testament of Youth* she confined herself to a brief, unconvincing account of their courtship, and said with uncharacteristic resignation that when she agreed to go to Oxford, 'I knew then that my resistance was done for'. On 5 July she agreed to marry him. They announced their engagement in *The Times*, and Vera's photograph and a similar notice appeared in the *Daily Express*.

Marie Leighton was one of the first to congratulate her. 'I have just heard that your fiancé is a Roman Catholic and, remembering Roland, I feel quite a heart throb at knowing this,' she wrote from Bishop's Stortford in her extraordinary handwriting which looked as if she had dipped her finger in the inkwell and put it straight to paper. 'It seemed to me that you have needed in your life just that enriching and "strengthening by dilution" that marriage gives,' she continued, unable to resist a barbed dig at Vera's relentless ambition. She ended: 'For, after all, the best intellectual insight must always come from the heart and not from the head. I doubt whether any manifestation of real genius can possibly come from a person who despises human emotions . . . or regards them as a time-wasting hindrance to ambition.'

III

In an autobiography of nearly five hundred pages, George Catlin devotes only two of them to a few sparse details about his mother and father, and his early life up to the spring of 1918 when he was conscripted into the London Rifle Brigade. He had no wish to deny or to forget his painfully unhappy adolescence, but except with his family, it was an aspect of his life about which he preserved a discreet silence.

His father, George Edward Catlin Senior, was born in 1858 of middle-class yeoman ancestry from Bedfordshire. He was, in his son's words, 'a profound believer in Moses and Queen Victoria', but Vera more candidly declared that 'for him life was a conflict between an absolute right and an absolute wrong'. He attended New College, London, as a Nonconformist theology student, but his daunting Old Testament beliefs seriously inhibited his popularity as a Congregational minister. He held several different ministries in various parts of the country, and Christ Church, Llandudno, one of his first, was probably his most successful. In the late 1890s he transferred his allegiance to the Church of England, and after a further short period of theological instruction he was from 1900 to 1905 the Curate of St Thomas's, Stourbridge, in Worcestershire.

His marriage in 1895 to twenty-two-year-old Edith Kate Orton, a tall, fair-haired, blue-eyed girl from the small Warwickshire market town of Atherstone, was on both sides a serious miscalculation. Her father, a carpenter, was dead, and her mother, preoccupied with her clothes and her health, was an exasperating encumbrance. As for many Victorian women with no other alternative, marriage probably represented for her the only escape from an intolerable situation, and too late she discovered that in marrying a dogmatic, domineering Congregational minister fifteen years her senior she had jumped out of the frying pan into the fire. She questioned his authoritarian rule, she answered back, and refused to retract her belief in women's rights. 'It was the sad story of the almost inevitable Greek tragedy', wrote their son. 'Each was right according to their lights, although neither the Mosaic indignation of the one, nor the ingrown refusal to communicate of the other was blameless.'

George was born on 29 July 1896 – and was thus two and a half years Vera's junior – at Island Road, Garston, a Liverpool dockland suburb on the Mersey, where his father was a temporary Congregational incumbent during the Minister's absence on holiday. His memories of his childhood at Stourbridge were happy ones. In old age he recalled nostalgically the tall house with a cook and housemaid in the basement and speaking tubes from floor to floor, the large garden with dahlias, delphiniums, the Canterbury bells, a central mulberry tree, and an inexhaustible supply of apples, pears and plums.

From his parents he inherited a first-class intellect, and, perhaps inevitably, a dogmatic temperament. Until he was twelve he was educated at home, with his father teaching him Latin, scripture, and a smattering of Hebrew, whilst his mother taught him history and supervised his reading. On a holiday in Cornwall he became an addict of Charles Kingsley's historical novels *Westward Ho!* and *Hypatia*, and became convinced 'that philosophy was a beautiful woman'. From 1908 he attended Warwick

School. A born scholar, he collected an array of prizes with seemingly effortless ease, and in 1912, at the age of sixteen, he was awarded a scholarship to St Paul's School, Hammersmith. In 1915 he won an Exhibition in Modern History at New College, Oxford, but as he had by then a Civil Service appointment the Warden and Tutors' Committee agreed to hold this over until after the war.

In 1905, Reverend Catlin had surrendered his living at Stourbridge, under pressure from his churchwardens and parishioners, after five years of altercation and disagreement, and he was reduced to relying on what he could earn as a licensed preacher in the Worcester diocese. At last, in 1912, he was appointed to the living of St Luke's, Kew.

During George's adolescence at Kew his parents' marriage had disintegrated into an intolerable atmosphere of rows, recriminations, and open animosity. Money was not the only source of marital dispute. Mrs Catlin had by now taken her feminist beliefs a step further, and openly displayed her sympathies for the suffragette campaign, in direct opposition to her husband's orders. 'She would not herself have put burning paper in the local letter boxes or set fire to the Kew pagoda', wrote her son, 'but she did not condemn those who did'. With the Reverend Catlin's behaviour becoming increasingly unreasonable, and at times violent, she finally in 1915 decided that she had no choice but to leave her husband and son. Supporting herself on the small private income she had inherited from her mother, she spent the last two years of her life in Ullin Street, Poplar, working for women's suffrage and caring for the poor in the missions of Hoxton and Bromley-by-Bow.

During the war she suffered from progressively debilitating kidney failure, and after an unsuccessful operation, died of uraemia in St Thomas's Hospital on 27 December 1917, aged forty-four. George was with her when she died, but although his father was well aware that his wife could not recover, he refused to be reconciled.

The early months of the war were the most miserable that George ever endured. '. . . A life of such bitterness, such loneliness, such hardship . . .', as Vera commented after he had recounted his story. Alone with his father in the Kew vicarage, and without his mother's contribution to the family finances, they were 'almost bankrupt and very, very bitterly poor'. Reverend Catlin suffered a nervous breakdown, and 'there was a long period of [George] deliberately starving himself in order that his father might have enough to eat . . .'. Reverend Catlin resigned his Curacy in March 1916, and father and son left Kew for lodgings in Douglas Road, Canonbury, but undernourished and desperately seeking to be loyal to both his parents,

George became unwell. On four separate occasions between 1914 and 1918, according to his autobiography, he was rejected by the army as 'totally unfit', and added to his distress at the break-up of his parents' marriage was the ignominy of being unable to fight.

For three years he was engaged as a junior civil servant in the liquor traffic department of the Central Control Board, and on his small salary he was at least able to support both his father and himself, and to pay for the expensive medical treatment his father required. Following the disastrous losses during the German offensive of 1918 he was, as he remarked euphemistically, 'rehabilitated'. He served for a few months with the London Rifle Brigade, but arrived in France just before the Armistice, too late to fight.

He went up to Oxford in April 1919, and on being excused Moderations because of his war service, he undertook a shortened one-year History course, in which he was awarded a distinction. After his brief but brilliant postwar career at New College he naturally hoped for an Oxford fellowship, but was unsuccessful at all three colleges to which he applied. At All Souls he was placed *proxime* for the prize fellowship; at New College he was informed by Warden Spooner that the college already had one Catholic Fellow and was unlikely to elect another; and at Oriel George was too preoccupied with a conversation about the Crusades to notice that the scout was removing the tablecloth. 'First time I have come across a man who did not finish his wine,' remarked the Provost – 'and that', as George later commented, 'was that'.

He felt hard done by, and with some justification. But social ease was one virtue he was never able to cultivate. He was adept at blowing his own trumpet, but often failed to notice that for some his playing went on too long and too noisily. He was a young man in a hurry, desperate to be a credit to his ailing father and to overcome the economic and emotional privations of his youth. In 1921 he accepted a post as lecturer in Medieval and Modern History at Sheffield University. At the end of his first twelve months he obtained a year's leave of absence to take up a fellowship at Cornell. In January 1924 he was appointed to a professorship there.

'He has a complicated mind,' wrote Harry Scott Stokes, one of his New College contemporaries, 'but a very simple nature, whence it follows naturally that he is genuinely devout, though rather at a loss as to where to worship.' It is difficult to overestimate the effect upon George Catlin of having been the only child in a miserably unhappy, divided household. His mother had neglected him and died before he could really get to know her well, and his father, embittered and broken, had become more and more financially and emotionally dependent upon him. When George met Vera he had no home, and his determination to marry her was clearly influenced by a desire for the security and stability he had never known; and in Vera he had found at last a shrine at which to worship. 'On the day that I read *The Dark Tide*,' he told her later, 'I determined that I would win Virginia Dennison, and that if you were Virginia I would win you.' In Vera's uncompromising personality, and especially in her feminism, he found suggestions not only of the fictional Virginia Dennison, but also of his mother, Edith Kate Catlin. Within days of meeting Vera Brittain he was hopelessly infatuated.

Vera was more down-to-earth, and more than a little perturbed at the speed of this precipitate romance. She was unable to resist George, 'the sweet, shy, adoring schoolboy with rumpled hair', but she emphasized that the war had left her emotions paralysed, and for no one could she revive the romanticism of her youth. Nor could she surrender her dedication to feminism or peace; the causes on which she had rebuilt her shattered existence. She wanted 'to solve the problem of how a married woman, without being inordinately rich, can have children and yet maintain her intellectual and spiritual independence as well as having . . . time for the pursuit of her own career'. Love and marriage, she told him, must be subordinate to work. George, more than a little starry-eyed, was utterly compliant.

Mutual admiration, empathy, and 'community of tastes' had drawn them together. She understood 'the dreadful responsibility of being an only child', she wrote to him shortly before their engagement, but there was, she reminded him, 'the worse responsibility of having become one'.

In London following their engagement Vera introduced George to her parents. 'At the risk of a little awkwardness,' she lectured him before taking him to tea at Oakwood Court, 'do not begin by laying them flat (as you so nearly laid me) by the priggish donnishness of those *pince-nez*; they hide all too effectually those amazing blue eyes of yours which will please my mother about as much as they please me, since we have nothing of the kind in our dark-eyed, dark-haired family . . .'.

Her mother had been 'so wise in the idiosyncrasies of my brother's friends', and would put him at his ease in a few minutes. Her father regarded every man who approached her as 'an unprincipled adventurer', but he seems to have been less of an ogre than Vera depicted him, as even before they met he had accepted his future son-in-law 'quite calmly'.

Throughout the summer Vera continued to lecture, write, and attend public meetings. At the end of June *Time and Tide* published anonymously her character sketch of Emily Penrose. 'I'm afraid its origin may be suspected as she inevitably somewhat resembles Miss Lawson Scott in *The Dark Tide*,' she informed George, unabashed at the thought of provoking more controversy. Meanwhile, in Oxford, George spent a considerable part of each day preparing his Cornell lectures, and while visiting him in early August, Vera occupied her time attending both the Liberal and League of Nations Summer Schools. She was especially interested in Gilbert Murray's address to the Liberals on 'The Present Position in Europe', as she and Winifred had arranged to make a three-month tour of Europe to study at first hand the aftermath of the war.

To Winifred, Vera poured out every detail and nuance of her love affair. She had been deeply affected by George's account of his unhappy background with his parents at loggerheads, and by the penury he had endured, caring for his father on his meagre Civil Service salary. '. . . Only a genuine saint could have come through it & remain so good & simple-hearted. Nothing that has happened to me has been comparable to it . . . I think he does not need another's strength so much as another's love . . .'.

She also learned that he had made up his mind in France in 1919 to enter the Dominican Order, but after being demobilized he had decided to go to Oxford. 'Imagine him in that black & white order with his lovable, boyish hair all cut short', Vera prattled on to Winifred. 'I am glad that he is not there – though he has made it quite clear to me that if anything should happen this year to take me from him, either by death, accident, or my own intention to "turn him down", he is going to settle all worldly goods to which he is entitled upon his father & enter the Dominican Order as soon as he can free himself from academic claims.'

From Oakwood Court one Sunday morning he took her to the Dominican church on Haverstock Hill. 'The High Mass is very beautiful. I felt like a child of five, though, having to have my place in the prayer book found for me by George at every turn!' They had already decided to be married as soon as possible after he returned from Cornell the following summer, and while at Haverstock Hill they tentatively arranged with the priest, Father Bede Jarrett, to marry them at St James's, Spanish Place, at the end of June.

To their family and friends George and Vera's engagement seemed to bear all the hallmarks of an idyllic love affair but, beneath the surface, problems of sexual inexperience and maladjustment threatened to undermine an already lopsided relationship. Before he arrived in England, George had confided in discreet and carefully chosen words that he had had no sexual relations with anybody. Vera believed that her own sexual desire had died when Roland was killed, and that it was George's misfortune to have come into her life both too late and too early. By 1924 the sexual spontaneity which would have been normal in her late teens and early twenties had atrophied. For nearly ten years she had been unmoved by any desire for a physical relationship, and had been repelled by the 'passes' made at her by middle-aged men like Lord Waring and Sir Harry Brittain. When, one evening in August 1924, George suggested that they become lovers before their marriage, Vera refused him.

'My reason, based upon my education . . . bade me resist his worship of my body . . . ,' she told Winifred. '. . . he cried out, almost wept, that I made an unclean thing of his instinctive purity, his attempts to free his mind of his body by allowing his body to express itself without shame. After he had gone I wrote him a long explanation of what my resistance was & why my reason approved of it. He has read my letters & has given in to me completely . . .'.

'I am not worthy of you & never shall be,' George had replied. 'I love you as never before, with a new reverence, a new humility, a new humiliation. I tell you frankly that the world will not understand you this way, for you are leaving yourself, as God's saints have always left themselves, without defence . . . Whatever you may have felt, you seem to be still able to hope on, and you hope now as I would wish to hope but cannot . . . I am of the night, sometimes I think I see the second dawn but now I have come to refuse to see it. The dawn is not of this world as yet; only the night is. But then my love for you is not of this world; it is something which raises me above the world.'

George's capitulation threw Vera into a turmoil of doubt. She felt humiliated by his imputation of righteousness which may only have sprung from ignorance and fear. He made her feel

> . . . a little superficial, surburban thing; something that has never really thought & felt, something immature & childish in spirit, mind & body. Sometimes I think it is that I am the opposite of what Harry Scott Stokes called G[eorge]: that I am a person with a very simple mind but a complicated nature . . .
>
> . . . The strangest thing is that, now he has yielded to my resistance . . . my reason approves of it no longer. I feel that my body is only the bread & wine of our love; it is no more the whole sacrament than the bread & wine alone is the whole of the Mass. The body is not the essence of love; the essence lies in that of which it is but the symbol.

As well as Vera's anxiety about the possibility of sexual incompatibility, it was also emotionally difficult to reconcile her love for Roland with what she now felt for George. 'Perhaps the two loves are not two different and antagonistic things, but the later is made the sweeter and fuller because of the earlier,' she wrote to Winifred in an attempt to rationalize her feelings. 'Thus shall she belong to them both at the Resurrection'.

On 10 September George left for Liverpool on the first leg of his return journey to Cornell. Two days later Vera set off with Winifred for Geneva to report for *Time and Tide* on the League of Nations' Protocol on Arbitration.

IV

For Winifred, Vera's engagement had precipitated an acute emotional crisis. She had too much courage openly to admit how much she was affected by the prospect of losing Vera's love and the break-up of their working partnership, and was determined to do and say nothing to distress or influence her. She put a brave face on it after Vera and George were engaged but could not entirely conceal her sense of loss and desolation. Writing to Jean McWilliam to tell her that '. . . I think that my little Vera is going to be married after all', she was superficially cheerful and enthusiastic. George, she said, 'is more charming than I can say', but the heartache remained. '. . . I . . . am very happy, though it means losing Vera's companionship and no one can tell what she has meant to me for these four years. But I covet for her this richer life.' In response to a sympathetic letter from her mother she was more explicit. '. . . She may drop me, but I don't think that she will dupe me . . . As for suffering, dear heart, don't you see that long ago I saw that this was inevitable? It is a thing that one cannot escape from unless one hides from life.'

Most poignantly of all, on the day that Vera agreed to marry George, Winifred had written on the flyleaf of her own copy of *St Joan*, 'Ave atque Vale, July 5th, 1924. W.H.'

After attending the League of Nations Assembly in Geneva, Vera and Winifred set off on a ten-week tour through Germany, Hungary, Austria and Czechoslovakia. They had relied upon books, pamphlets and newspapers for the facts and figures for their political speeches, and they now intended to see for themselves the effect of the blockade, and the postwar miseries and humiliations. In Cologne especially Vera felt German hostility towards the occupying forces, and wrote in her travel diary that 'This country frightens me . . . I see a war in 20 years' time . . .'. A church service in Cologne Cathedral revived memories of nursing German prisoners, seven years before, and confirmed Vera in her feelings of internationalism:

> It was queer to stand in the midst of those Germans, all singing, and think of ten years ago; they made the war seem absurd and unnatural and caused me to feel more of a pacifist [sic] than ever . . . I am glad that what I did was so strictly neutral, even to nursing the Germans . . .

While they were in Basle, Winifred wrote to George that Vera had had one of her slight recurrent chills, a legacy of her time in Malta, and she was keeping her in bed with hot-water bottles and dosing her with brandy. 'Please, will you help me to get this child to bed?' she wrote a week later on their journey through the Saar Valley. Vera had quite recovered, but every day after a long, strenuous programme she insisted on writing to George until well after midnight. 'Please come back soon and marry her,' Winifred entreated, 'or I shall go quite grey-headed and tottering, and have to be wheeled up the aisle of St James's in a bath chair.'

Shortly after returning to London from their European travels at the end of November, Winifred sent George a letter in which she fully explained her feelings:

> I suppose that you guess that when I first knew you wanted to marry Vera and to take her to America, I was about your worst enemy as a lover . . . But when you came and were so completely disarming . . . there was nothing for me to do but make up my mind that only by my losing Vera could she find her greatest richness of life through you . . . my feeling for Vera is based so deeply upon reverence that I could never regard lightly anything that touched her interest . . .

As Winifred was writing Vera returned from the theatre, laughing and happy to find three letters from George which had arrived that day. After she had gone to bed to read them alone in her room, Winifred added a light-hearted but revealing postscript.

> I cannot write of my little and beloved girl without becoming egotistical, for she is more than part of myself. That does not mean, however, that I expect you to be a bigamist, and I assure you that when you return to England you will find that I have effected a quite neat and painless divorce! . . . It will be a decree absolute – unless you ever beat her or in other ways afflict her. No, I believe that there are moods in which she would relish a little beating.

In the long run Winifred's fears of losing Vera were unfounded. In the next few years they would be separated for long periods while George and Vera were in America, and Winifred was on her League of Nations lecture tour of South Africa, but the intensity of their friendship never diminished. Winifred, Vera later wrote, 'was the best friend whom life has given me', and impressed with Winifred's intellect, wit and radiant personality, George accepted her for the time being with good-natured equanimity.

At Cornell George thrived on the academic prestige and social conviviality, and he was exhilarated by the prospect of returning the following year with his English bride. That Christmas, although they were not to be married for another six months, Vera received an embarrassingly trite poem he had written 'To My Adored Wife' –

> Thy bosom is endeared with all hearts
>   Which I by lacking have supposed dead,
> And there reigns love, and all love's loving parts,
>   And all these friends which I thought buried.
> Their images I loved I view in thee,
>   And then (all they) hast the all of me.

In March Vera sent him a copy of *The Harp*, Ethelreda Lewis's recently published novel of life in a small town on the Cape. Writing to congratulate Mrs Lewis, whom she had met through Winifred, Vera told her that she had given her fiancé a copy of her book and that she intended to read the book again the week before her marriage. 'It is such a book for lovers,' she enthused, 'and a book which a man & woman would not dare to read before their marriage unless they were quite sure they were lovers.'

George, however, was not impressed, and informed Vera that he was shocked that she had such a high opinion of the book. He admitted that he had read only the beginning and the end, and to Vera's consternation he dismissed it as trivial and badly written, with overloaded sentences and a multiplication of images.

Beside herself with indignation, Vera retaliated. She rebuked him for his ill-mannered habit of passing hasty judgements upon her friends and relations, and admonished him to exercise the same patience and restraint as she did with his friends. In view of George's ill-starred involvement with Harold Laski,* she concluded significantly that she 'could have given

---

* Harold Laski (1893–1950) was Professor of Political Science at the London School of Economics from 1926 until his death. Sharing the same academic discipline, Laski and George enjoyed a close friendship in the Twenties. Later, when George was unable to obtain an academic appointment in England, he was convinced that this was due to Laski's professional jealousy, and that he was sabotaging his applications behind his back. A better and shrewder judge of character than her husband, Vera disliked and mistrusted Laski from the outset.

you many reasons' why she did not share his enthusiasm for Laski.

Although annoyed by his contemptuous opinion of *The Harp*, she was outraged that in spite of his earlier praise, George should then proceed to criticize her novel *Not Without Honour*, and especially that he should so dictatorially dissect her self-portrait as sentimental and emotional. He was not to imagine that he could 'deliver to me, ready made, the formula' for writing her novels. She was not marrying him to be given a perpetual series of unpaid coachings, and she detested his 'prize pupil' attitude. 'If those are the lines on which our life is to be organized, I prefer that at least an equal share of the coaching should be done by me.' He would no more think of having his lectures ready-made by her than she would consider being 'given' her novels ready-made by him. Was he endeavouring to mould her into an intellectual replica of himself, she demanded. Was she to write what he wanted her to write, to be what he wanted her to be?

> . . . I care for my books much more than I care for you. I have warned you about this over and over again . . . if you cannot keep your hands off my books themselves until they are written, you can go to the devil.
>
> It is the foreshadowed choice that is wrecking me, the choice, which *must* be made if you persist in your present attitude, between my work, which is all my life, and you, whom throughout this year I have loved, and do love, only second to my work.

Vera's behaviour had been partly a result of a crisis of confidence about her writing, and especially the feelings of panic when she thought about the difficulties of combining marriage and a career. She told Ethelreda Lewis that her novels had fallen short of her expectations, and that she had decided that if she waited a little she might be a better writer. Her journalism was only spasmodically successful, and the rejection slips continued to accumulate.

Her apprehensions about going to America were exacerbated by a meeting with the young wife of one of George's Cornell colleagues. She listened with mounting incredulity to her tales about the social obligations of the newly married faculty wife. She reported to George that she had been told that two hundred people would call upon her in the first week. She would be expected to return all the calls within a fortnight, and pestered to join clubs, to hunt, to ride, to participate in winter sports, dance, play bridge, and go to tea parties: a social round which seemed all too reminiscent of her Buxton adolescence.

Two days after dispatching her rampageous letter she wrote again to tell him that all her tenderness for him had returned, and, in an incredible volte-face, that if he resented anything she had said he was to 'put it down to my inadequacy of expression and not my attitude towards you'. The reason for her outburst had been her unallayed anxiety that in marrying him she would put her head into a noose, '. . . the matrimonial noose which strangles the majority of women'.

Reverting to the importance of her writing, she reminded him that in his letters before they met, he had assured her that for both of them their individual work must always be the first consideration. She accepted that he could not return to England without loss of prestige and salary, and that two or three years in America were essential to the advancement of his career.

On the other hand she had come to the conclusion that it might mean disaster to her work to remain abroad for more than a limited time. A year in America was imperative, as without living together for a year they would never properly know one another. It would not in any case be a catastrophic interruption, 'But I am gravely uncertain whether more than a year in America would be anything but sheer loss to me'.

'Here then is my proposal . . .', she wrote. 'Let us – after that necessary year of intimacy – each consider our own interests (not *selfish* interests, but the thousand and one interests involved in our work) as though we were not married . . . Let us then agree that *if* at the end of a year it is still to your interest to remain abroad but mine to come home, that we each abide by our own conditions.'

If necessary, she suggested, George should return to Cornell in September, and she would join him from the end of November until the middle of January. From June to September they would be together in England. She realized that it would mean trampling upon the conventional idea of married life, of always being together, the double bed and one bedroom tradition, 'but I don't think that either of us would mind this.'

She pointed out that she had put these proposals to him before, '. . . but each time you have either disregarded them, or wandered round them, or evaded them by calling them "trivial" . . . You may say, as usual, that such things are best discussed when we meet. Darling, they cannot be postponed . . . when we meet there is only one week until the wedding . . .'.

George could see no reason why Vera could not write as well in America as she could in England, but he reluctantly agreed. For the present the possibility of a semi-detached marriage appeared a far-fetched fantasy, but to impress upon her that he understood and respected her unorthodox proposals he sent her his revised version of the customary marriage vows:

We who have different interests, and serve God in different ways, yet knowing that all interests are poor and worldly compared with that human devotion which is the means whereby we enter into eternal experience, do desire to take each other; not for the incessant cohabitation of the body, but in the unfaltering fidelity of like minds, so long as love lasts, and so long as piety to ancient loyalties and to the sacrament of unrepeatable experience binds us together.

This idealized conception of marriage is a lofty vision that few could hope to fulfil, and until Vera told him twenty years later, George never realized how seriously he had undermined her self-respect

by telling me before we were married that I wasn't the woman you had seen in Oxford and fallen in love with . . . I found it so devastating that I would have put an end to our engagement then and there but for the fact that I couldn't face a third matrimonial catastrophe; the loss of Roland and the foolish mistake over Anthony had already made me feel 'fated' as it was, and I knew too that only by marriage could I escape from such idiotic entanglements as the one with Leigh. But I never could get over the feeling that you had really married me for some ulterior motive than affection; what it was I could never quite be sure, and that added to my feeling of exasperation. Although you were so money-conscious I didn't think it was altogether that; I felt you were more after prestige, though how I could give you any I wasn't quite clear.

The only two idiosyncrasies of an otherwise traditional wedding were Vera and Winifred's dash to Oxford two days earlier to take their MA degrees, and Vera's insistence on keeping her bank account and passport in her own name. Shocked but anxious not to offend, the bank manager rationalized her request by reflecting that it was of course her literary name, but Vera sharply reminded him that it was her name in any case, and only incidentally her writing name.

Obtaining an American visa in her own name demanded a more tenacious struggle. The consulate official in London informed her that it was the first such application that he had dealt with. He prophesied trouble in America, and to Vera's indignation included in her passport a statement saying that her sole purpose in going to the United States was to accompany her husband, and, falsely, that he had paid for her passage.*

* This incident had an amusing sequel. When Shirley was born in 1930 Vera insisted that her name should appear on the birth certificate as 'Vera Brittain' and not as 'Vera Catlin', but the Chelsea Registrar objected. '. . . I am to point out that if the mother's Christian name and maiden name only appear . . . [in] the entry it is liable to give the impression that the mother was not married to the father and that the child was, therefore, illegitimate', he wrote to George. '. . . This might cause some difficulty to the child and affect her interests in the future.' Vera persisted, however, and the Registrar eventually complied with her request.

In every other respect their fashionable wedding at St James's, Spanish Place, on the last Saturday in June 1925 could scarcely have been more conventional. This was partly because her family expected it, Vera explained, and partly, she frankly acknowledged, to satisfy her love of dressing up 'which has filled me at intervals with a wistful longing to exchange for a stage career the pen which destiny seems to have pushed so firmly into my hand'.

She had agreed to a Catholic wedding 'to avoid inconveniencing my husband', and Maurice Richardson recalled more than half a century later that it was 'a very strange affair', with Protestants on one side and Catholics on the other, 'and the guests divided up like sheep and goats'.

Vera confessed the vain, naive pleasure she took in wearing her pink wedding dress and ivory satin gown, with a long tulle veil fastened with a wreath of orange blossom and myrtle. She also wore George's gift of a pearl and gold bracelet. Winifred, her only bridesmaid, gave her a pearl, gold and platinum necklace. Lord Stamford, a New College contemporary of George's, was the best man. The men wore morning coats, top hats and gloves, and although Harry Pearson had been assured that informal clothes were acceptable, he found the fashionable turnout so alarmingly intimidating that he turned back at the church door.

Vera's impression of the service was 'fleeting & dreamlike', and focused principally upon her own unmoved self-possession and George's emotional state which left him 'so speechless that he could scarcely make the responses at all'. Vera was 'white as marble' as she went up the nave on her father's arm, 'but smiling & pink' as her roses, in the sacristy.

Before leaving the reception at the De Vere Hotel she gave Marie Leighton her wedding bouquet of pale pink roses in memory of Roland. Later she and George travelled by private Pullman to Dover where they spent the night at the Lord Warden Hotel before crossing to Ostend on the first stage of their continental honeymoon. 'Saying goodbye to you for even six weeks nearly made me weep. I wanted to take you with us – I *did*, even at that moment,' she wrote to Winifred the next morning.

But first, she continued, 'One or two bits of business. George's, of course, not mine!' – a foretaste of his absent-minded habits which were to send Vera and Winifred on innumerable retrieving errands all over London. Would she send his light-coloured gloves to Vienna, the small plain pen to which he was especially attached to La Grave, and the *Times* report of their wedding to Cornell.

'Darling sweet, I do love you,' Vera ended her letter to Winifred. 'I have my suspicions that, though others are capable of being loved in ways that you are not, the something in you that I love I shall always love best.'

SEVEN

Semi-Detached Marriage

'Human affections mean so much to me, but so does work, and the fulfilment of a dedicated end, and whenever a clash has come – as it has done so often – between intense personal love for individuals and the overwhelming compulsion of some piece of significant work, real suffering and conflict have been involved.'

From a note by Vera Brittain found among her papers after her death

I

After an overcast and chilly crossing to Ostend, they arrived in Vienna to find it raining, no warmer than London, and more like autumn than early summer. 'It seems only yesterday instead of nearly a year since we were here together,' Vera wrote to Winifred the next day.

Vera and George were equally enthusiastic about foreign travel, and their ambitious honeymoon itinerary took them to five countries in less than a month. Neither of them travelled lightly, and with them went a formidable paraphernalia of bags, cases, hat boxes, and the inevitable accumulation of books and papers. In Vienna they were chagrined at having to pay a heavy excess luggage charge, and immediately dispatched George's large and cumbersome leather suitcase to Winifred. It was nearly empty anyway, Vera told her. 'I believe I was guilty of saying, "I told you so".'

In Vienna the interviews with politicians and government officials George had arranged for his research dissolved into hospitable tea parties to welcome the newly married English professor and his bride. Nevertheless, the former capital of the Habsburg Empire was a romantic setting for the first stage of a honeymoon with its magnificent Prater Park, its Gothic cathedral, and its music. Vera especially remembered the happy, relaxed summer evening they dined in a garden restaurant with an orchestra and little table lamps which flickered like fireflies.

As an interesting diversion they decided to travel to Budapest by the river route, but the boat was crowded, hot and uncomfortable, and they reached the Hungarian capital tired and dishevelled. Articulate and politically aware, the Hungarians loquaciously welcomed George's fact-finding interviews, and Vera independently arranged an appointment with the cautiously circumspect British Minister.

She had become accustomed to marriage with remarkable speed, she confessed to Winifred, but she was too old in experience, too critical, and too analytical to be swept off her feet, and she had the impression of it as an interlude, a separate aspect of life. She felt detached with a sense of surprised curiosity, and admitted that it was her fault that she was unable to love as George loved, with abandon and continuity of affection. 'Perhaps in the old days I may have felt something like that about Roland, but that was almost a child's emotion, and anyway it's too long ago to remember clearly and reliably.'

But marriage agreed with her. 'I look prettier than I have ever known myself', and she felt physically fitter than she had done since her school days. George had undergone a complete transformation. He was now more bewitched than devout, she said, 'a sudden descent from the Virgin Mary to the Venusberg', and it was a good job they had gone abroad as otherwise people would be making obscene remarks.

One tranquil summer evening after a late gourmet dinner with a Hungarian financier they drove at 12.30 am to the top of a hill two or three miles beyond the capital. Entranced they stood hand in hand gazing down at Budapest and the Danube far below, a magical vista of mile after mile of twinkling lights. They returned to their hotel at 4.30 am, and tumbled into bed with the sun streaming through the window.

Marriage wasn't a question of being resigned or simply reconciled, she assured Winifred, but a new experience to be welcomed and enjoyed. And yet the impression persisted that it was somehow incomplete, something unconnected with the fundamental business of life, and she had been engrossed in a long soliloquy in an attempt to do as much justice to the disadvantages of being married as to the advantages.

'I am sure beyond doubt that I love you best, and that your companionship is more adequate,' she wrote, like a wilful child to a neglected parent.

But life brought me to a strange pass in which you alone were not enough; yet this by no means implies that *he* alone is enough. He is not. Consequently I need you more than ever, and the ideal life . . . seems to me that in which I come into daily contact with both him and you. You supply everything that he lacks; he supplies what you lack in the formation of me. Because where you tend to spare my strength he makes demands upon it, and demands upon my understanding such as you, being less complex and more completely *en rapport* with me, never need to make.

Insects and dirt were almost pathological preoccupations on Vera's travels. She was convinced that Europe in summer was alive with fleas and bugs, and that for their overnight journey to Ljubljana in northern Yugoslavia they could risk nothing less than to travel by wagon-lit. Stopping briefly for a long weekend they travelled westwards to Trieste, Venice and Vicenza.

In planning their honeymoon Vera had set her heart on 'introducing' her husband to her brother in his grave in the war cemetery at Granczza on the Asiago Plateau. Clutching two battered roses from her wedding bouquet and a bunch of carnations, they were driven up the precipitous and alarming mountain roads with George teasing her for her nervous apprehension.

The following evening on a hill high above Vicenza they discovered the unique Monte Berico war memorial, a large balustraded terrace facing the whole Italian front with arrows pinpointing each distant town, mountain range and battlefield. As dusk fell with the Angelus ringing out from the unseen churches in the Brenta Valley, Vera gazed transfixed as against a grey and crimson sky she watched the Trentino mountains and the long Asiago Plateau fade and disappear in the darkness. She felt nearer to Edward at that moment, she told Winifred, than she had done on the top of the plateau beside his grave. Ill at ease and sensitively aware of Vera's entranced emotional detachment, George 'had become, as he always becomes at the richest and most colourful moments, silent and stiff and conventional'.

Back at the hotel they quarrelled for the first time, over an absurd triviality as to who should wash first 'in that ridiculous double room and George lay on the bed under his mosquito net sulking and silent, and soaking himself in his "pride" '.

Vera loved George, 'the shy, adoring schoolboy', but she was not passionately in love with him as she had been with Roland, and George was a vulnerable lover: younger, naive, infatuated. The quarrel ended, Vera said, as she knew it would, with George abjectly penitent flinging himself down before her with his eyes full of tears.

Sex, she discovered, was less compulsive than she had imagined. Gratifying as it was at the time, she felt no need for constant repetition, and '. . . much as I love my husband, I would not sacrifice one successful article to a night of physical relationship'. Her sexual reluctance provoked periodic attacks of conscience 'because my husband makes such a flight all too easy, asking nothing, but waiting only to be given just what I choose and no more'. Probably one sexual experience 'would go as far as you ever needed', she wrote to Winifred with breathtaking confidence, 'which would make you in this direction an even more unsatisfactory wife than I feel myself to be'.

Winifred replied that this letter had confirmed her view of Vera. The truth lay, she thought, in their strange immunity to magic so that when their nerves, bodies and even their hearts were momentarily enchanted, their eyes remained wide open.

> G[eorge] now has an ecstasy over you. You haven't over him. I think the reason why you and I may always be able to love, to rest in one another, is because neither of us can be, or expects to be, carried away by our experience of love . . . *Les Désenchantées?* Yes. Perhaps.
>
> And then, of course, here I am. And, if even I ever should marry, which is improbable but possible, here I always shall be. And the ideal life will probably be, as you say, when you return to England and we are both here. G[eorge] and I.

Vera received Winifred's letter when they arrived in Verona, and replied immediately. 'Like you, I shall find no full satisfaction this side of the grave . . . such satisfaction as I can find is only to be derived from the gathering and making use of experience.'

Leaving Verona in the early morning they arrived at La Grave after an exhausting ten-hour journey by train, bus and hired car. After their travels through Central Europe they had intended to stay for three weeks at this invigorating mountain resort, which was, Vera reported, emphatically a place in which to walk and eat, live out of a small suitcase, and wear tweeds and riding breeches. To their consternation the Hôtel de la Meije was crowded with English tourists, and the only accommodation available a practically unfurnished double room with no wardrobe or chest of drawers. There was no table at which to write, and the lounge was a hubbub of conversation with the visitors 'all being jolly together'. Having lived out of her boxes for three weeks she could not contemplate three more, and they were returning to London a fortnight earlier than they had originally intended.

'I am aching to see you . . .', she wrote to Winifred. 'Work and you and London call me more urgently than these mountains.' She had so much to say, so much to ask, and so little time before they left for America.

Perhaps for the sake of effect her earlier letters about George had been unjustly sardonic. 'I love him better than when I married him. I never knew a man so patient, uncomplaining, unirritable and adaptable,' and it would be much more helpful if Winifred had a long talk with him now than it would have been before they were married. But there was no danger that she was becoming complacent about her married status, Vera assured her. 'You need not smack me.'

In a postscript she asked anxiously for more news of her Aunt Edith, her father's eldest sister, who, she had learned in a letter from home, had been involved in an accident in Wales.

On arriving home Vera discovered that Aunt Edith's 'accident' had been a euphemistic camouflage, and that she had in fact committed suicide by throwing herself off a mountain near Llandudno. Unhappily married, she suffered like several of the Brittains from periodic spells of melancholia. Vera's father was strangely unaffected by his sister's death and could not bring himself to face the inquest and aftermath of her suicide. Mrs Brittain had rushed off to Llandudno to deal with the practicalities, while her husband remained alone in their London flat.

Winifred was at Wymering Mansions to welcome the honeymoon couple, but a day or two later, feeling inexplicably cross and miserable, she travelled to Yorkshire to help nurse two of her family in bed with mumps. Vera saw her off at King's Cross and returned to the flat perplexed and anxious.

Winifred was nearly always happy and optimistic, and Vera was so perturbed by her uncharacteristic depression that on the way back she provoked an argument 'with a quite benevolent ticket collector', who told her that according to her ticket she ought to have changed at Baker Street and not Paddington.

'What was it really, my most dear?' she asked in a letter she wrote immediately she returned. Was it going home to the mumps? Or Harry Pearson turning up suddenly and then disappearing without a word? Their invasion of the flat, the commotion and the extra work? The shameless way George was in love with her? 'Or was it something so ridiculously impossible as that you feel yourself no longer *the* person to me after having been it almost since you grew up?'

She loved George, she repeated once more, and admitted the wonder and astonishment in finding a love that was warm flesh and blood instead of a few newspaper cuttings, a grave, some faded flowers and a memory. But sex was transitory. 'To fulfil the least of one's ambitions means infinitely more', and a relationship based on sex was not necessarily the best or the most interesting. Winifred was completely wrong, Vera told her, if she imagined that she was less important to her now than she had been before. 'I think I speak the truth when I say that a world with G[eorge] but without you, would be much more lonely than a world without G[eorge] but with you. I mean this as much as I meant it when I once said that if I had been given the choice whether to keep Roland or Edward, I would have kept Edward.'

Winifred replied by return, 'fearfully apologetic' for being bad tempered and for making so much fuss. The reason, she thought, was her anxiety about Harry, and the suspense and physical weariness of a tragicomic nightmare looking for him, taking her from Leicester Square to Peckham and back again to the Air Ministry. She neither respected nor loved him as lovers love. She did not particularly want to see him, and when she did she was quickly bored, but somehow their personalities were strangely linked, and the thought that something might have happened to him had oppressed her beyond words.

It is difficult to believe that Harry's unreliable behaviour was the only reason for her dejection. She was all too familiar with his failure to fulfil commitments, to keep appointments, to telephone. Her love and devotion to Vera ran deeper, their personalities were more inextricably interlocked, and in spite of protestations the thought persists that Vera's marriage had seriously threatened the security and stability which they had built up together since leaving Somerville.

The ultimate experience, Winifred maintained, was in loving and not in being loved. Vera still needed her; she still depended on her. She remained her responsibility, her difficult, petulant child, her 'Very Small, Very Dear Love', her alter ego.

'Do you not realize that I don't care twopence whereabout in the scale of your loves I come,' Winifred reassured her from Yorkshire, 'provided that you love me enough to let me love you, and that you are happy? I love you in a way that part of me has become part of you. When you are troubled, so must I be, whether I like it or not. When you are happy, part of me is happy, whatever else befalls. I who am part of you, can only gain by your gains. This you must and shall believe.'

Vera and George spent the eve of their departure for America with the Brittains at Oakwood Court, and Winifred came round to say goodbye. When she had gone Vera discovered on her dressing table a bottle of expensive perfume. There was no message, no card, no note. The following day when they boarded the SS *Regina* at Liverpool a bouquet of roses awaited her.

'I feel dreadfully as if I had left you in the lurch,' she wrote to Winifred shortly after they arrived at Cornell. 'The thought of it makes me more miserable than I can say.'

II

The Cornell campus is situated on the top of a steep hill and dominated by a brick campanile, with below it a long, thin, ice-cold lake into which run streams through spectacular gorges. Louis MacNeice, who taught poetry there in 1940, had the overwhelming feeling of being back at school. It was, he wrote, infinitely more comfortable '. . . but the basic fact is the same – a closed community', and Vera was to find the claustrophobic life of the university increasingly intolerable.

As a new arrival, an English bride, and novelist, Vera found herself the centre of attention. Though at first flattered she soon became irritated by the profusion of gifts, flowers and invitations, and by the callers who appeared almost before she and George had unpacked. 'During the first week they dropped in one by one, but by the second they were arriving in platoons, and by the third in battalions,' she wrote with a rhetorical flourish. It brought back memories of Buxton's odious affectations, and she bitterly criticized the ritualistic social etiquette and vacuous chitchat. For George's sake she temporarily subdued her irascible resentment, and returned the calls of the families who mattered most in the university hierarchy, but before long she abandoned any pretence at conformity, and every afternoon from 3.30 to 7.00 she worked in the university library uninterruptedly on a book based on her honeymoon experiences.

The faculty wives, the professors' conventional, homemaking spouses, censured her severely for neglecting her domestic responsibilities, and for her unsociable behaviour. While At Homes, parties and endless entertaining admirably suited George's gregarious temperament, Vera, introspective and withdrawn, deplored the kind of life which she described in an unpublished article on 'The Evils of Good Fellowship' as 'lived on the speeding circumference instead of at the quiet centre'.

She 'detested domesticity as the unnecessary and too meekly accepted obstacle to woman's achievement', and in London their housekeeper-cook, Winifred's old nurse, had relieved them of almost all domestic responsibility. The Ithaca apartment had no cooking facilities except an electric grill standing on a marble-topped cupboard, and like many of their university colleagues they ate out. Breakfast invariably consisted of a fried-egg sandwich and coffee at a nearby 'Pop Shop' and they had their lunch and dinner at one of the many local restaurants.

To Vera's frustration domestic help was practically unobtainable and prohibitively expensive. When she found that the Italian student she had engaged to assist her with the cleaning took the best part of half an hour to shake three mats in the garden she decided to do all the work herself. Before his university work occupied all his time, Vera persuaded George, who was completely undomesticated, to give her a hand on most mornings with their two bedrooms, living-room and bathroom-kitchenette by polishing the wooden floors and sweeping the mats, whilst she made the beds, washed the bathroom and dusted. '. . . His feminism is genuine and deep-rooted,' she wrote, pleasantly surprised, to Winifred in mid-October, 'in fact he won't sit down to his work till I am able to, as it only makes him feel restless if he is not sharing the domesticity.' Although she tackled the apartment with 'rapidity and vigour' it was usually at least eleven o'clock before she was able to settle to her writing.

Not Without Honour had done little to enhance her literary reputation, and content for the time being to attempt an alternative to a novel, she had been delighted with George's suggestion that, drawing on her own experiences and her emancipated concept of marriage, she should write a book of honeymoon sketches. After their return to London she had told Winifred that Andrews Dakers had agreed to be her London agent, and that George had written to Dutton, the New York publishers, to ask if they would be interested in 'what we now call *Heracles, or Certain Commandments Reconsidered*', an extraordinarily pompous title, which must surely have made Winifred wonder if Vera had taken leave of her senses.

After they had settled in their apartment on the top floor of a three-storey wooden house on the edge of the campus, writing her honeymoon book became Vera's major occupation. For *Heracles* she now substituted the title 'A Honeymoon in Two Worlds', and later 'Extracts from a Bride's Diary', which even for the 1920s reader must have suggested a book of romantic revelations.

It was her first attempt at writing autobiography. It demanded, she discovered, a completely different technique from fiction, and she was depressed to find herself lapsing into journalistic jargon with cliché-ridden phrases such as 'racial improvement', 'the domestic situation' and 'a limited vocation for marriage'. In spite of her own unorthodox courtship and contentiously feminist view of marriage, she optimistically informed Winifred that she intended her book primarily for the engaged and newly married.

In March 1926 George obtained a five-month leave of absence from Cornell to take up a research appointment on the effects of Prohibition with the Social Science Research Council in New York. Here in their cramped two-room apartment on the eighth floor of a hotel opposite Columbia University Vera revised and retyped her honeymoon manuscript, an arduous labour for a self-taught, two-finger typist. In addition to her book, she agreed to type and give 'a literary polish' to George's recently completed manuscript on *The Science and Method of Politics*. Vera's writing was direct and lucid, but George's abstruse, convoluted style was as much a characteristic of his personality as it was of his books. One of his letters, Vera had told him in 1925, was 'a morass of confusion, wordiness, overloaded sentences and strained metaphors'. The greater part was incomprehensible 'or else it is that I have neither the time nor the patience to dig the principal sentence out of the surrounding forests of subordinate clauses'.

In spite of its undistinguished style, his ambitious and thoughtful work, soon to be published by Knopf, played a major part in establishing his American reputation as a well-regarded pioneer of political science.

Vera was less successful. Her honeymoon manuscript made little impact on either British or American publishers. Her feminist concept of marriage obviously antagonized the Macmillan reader, and he reported that '. . . No one would ever care what happened to this muddle-headed egotist and her invertebrate Professor . . .'. These rejections eventually convinced her 'that my first year in America was just twelve months of wasted time'.

In addition to the failure of her book, all Vera's journalistic efforts in America were unsuccessful. Her articles on the state of Europe, vignettes of life and manners in Hungary, and a dyspeptic denunciation of American small-town and university life were rejected and the reception of her handful of lectures for the League of Nations Non-Partisan Association was equally discouraging. The people couldn't have been more frumpish had they come from small villages in Shropshire or Buckingham, she reported after one meeting, half the audience had not heard of the small countries of Europe, and none of them could pronounce their names. 'Don't be deceived by lectures', she urged Winifred, who early in January had embarked on a six-month LNU lecture-tour of South Africa. 'Lectures are narcotics . . . they give one a sense of being tremendously busy and useful – but all the time they are merely vain repetitions of one another, and form a dreadfully good excuse for not facing the unpleasant, exacting, hard-thinking work of a book well done'.

But if America was oblivious to her talents, she enjoyed a few minor successes in England. From the other side of the Atlantic book-reviewing and topical journalism were out of the question, but until Winifred left for South Africa, Vera sent her several general articles to place. *Time and Tide* accepted as a leader 'America and the Marriage Problem', and an article on 'Married Women's Names', and she was delighted to find herself on the front page of the *Nation*.

Vera had set out for America with pessimistic foreboding, and her lack of success reinforced her eagerness to be back in London. Only a fortnight after arriving in Ithaca, she had confided to Winifred that she had decided to spend the next autumn and winter in London, and three days later she told her that 'unless something unexpected transpires' she did not intend to return to America at all. Accustomed to her impetuosity, Winifred wisely counselled her 'to ride loosely in the circumstances, and to take what comes as it comes'.

Vera believed that George took only a perfunctory interest in her work and endeavours, and that his attitude appeared in marked contrast to the support and understanding she had come to expect from Winifred.

'Did you mention my book to Mr T?' she asked George one day after he had had a discussion with his publisher about *The Science and Method of Politics*.

'Oh, yes. We discussed it for about five minutes.'

'What did he say?'

'Oh – he seemed interested.'

'Yes, but what did he *say*?'

'Well . . . he put cogent questions,' George replied with exasperating evasiveness.

Painfully conscious that his father's dogmatic attitude to marriage had destroyed his parents' relationship and desolated his youth, George had accepted Vera's feminist philosophy of equality, which he later described as 'this strange equal comradeship'. During their engagement he had agreed that if his interests lay in America whilst Vera needed to be in London to pursue her journalistic career, he would accept the inevitability of a semi-detached marriage.

In the early summer of 1926 Vera informed him that she had decided to remain in London the following autumn and winter, and to join him at Cornell for the spring and summer of 1927, but George was not convinced that their temporary separation was really necessary, and he lectured her about her desire for fame. Life alone at Cornell was a daunting prospect for him. There would be speculation, innuendo and gossip as to why after only a year of marriage his wife had chosen to remain in England. Did she really love him, he asked himself. Did Winifred mean more to her than he did?

Writing to the novelist, Margaret Storm Jameson, in 1935, Vera was more explicit. She told her that at the end of their first year together she had 'presented G[eorge] with an ultimatum'; either they made their home in

England or she left him. As a result George had relinquished his full-time appointment at Cornell for a part-time one which kept him in America only four-and-a-half months a year instead of nine, and 'whatever financial responsibilities I have to assume now can never adequately repay him for realizing my situation and making that decision'.

To Winifred she confessed that marriage had been one of the most beautiful experiences of her life. *The Dark Tide* and George, she said, were her two triumphs, and yet no two events ever caused her more upset.

As for G[eorge], I still alternate between being in raptures over his sweetness and intelligence and unselfish patience, and wishing to goodness I had never met him and linked my competent, efficient plans with the adventures of someone else.

He gives delight to a side of me which is biologically beyond you, yet somehow to the rest of me you give more than he; we share more secrets, as it were. He hasn't your love for silly things, and never says 'Tell me some more'. He is a most stimulating companion, yet it never does me as much good to discuss my books with him as with you, for instead of letting me tell him what I want to put and then commenting, he starts off by telling me what he thinks I ought to put! Much of it is good and useful, but it doesn't help me to develop my ideas in the same way.

Leaving George in New York Vera arrived at Southampon on 13 August. Little more than a fortnight later, with a *Time and Tide* commission for two articles, she set off with Winifred for the League of Nations Assembly. It was an auspicious occasion. Germany had applied for membership of the League, and Vera, like many other political observers, believed that it heralded a new dawn in international cooperation. The vote in favour of Germany's admission was unanimous, though the Irish delegate was so agitated that he replied '*Oui*', whilst the Persian representative could only gasp. When the result was announced, Winifred reported, 'we all clapped like lunatics'.

George had only a fortnight in England before returning to Cornell. Vera was still in Geneva when he arrived, and they had barely a week together before he boarded the *Mauretania* and she was waving him goodbye as the ship sailed slowly out of sight down Southampton Water.

This was their first major separation, and the prelude to a long period of adjustment and emotional trauma. The difficulties of combining marriage with her literary ambitions remained for many years the dilemma dominating Vera's life, an insoluble conundrum in which George and Winifred, enmeshed by ties of loyalty and love, were the butts for her fluctuating emotions.

III

In the Twenties and early Thirties journals and periodicals proliferated and freelance journalism flourished. By the autumn of 1926, Vera had a firm foothold on *Time and Tide*, and the acceptance of articles by the *Yorkshire Post* and *Manchester Guardian*, and success in placing articles with the journals *Foreign Affairs* and the *Nation and Athenaeum* soon followed. A major theme of Vera's journalism at this time was the difficulties faced by many women in combining marriage and motherhood with a career, and the absolute right of women to pursue a career on a par with men. 'Work . . . has been the twentieth century's great gift to women,' she wrote in an article for *Time and Tide* in 1927, 'it is dignified work which puts her, as far as the chance of happiness is concerned, upon the same level as men.'

Her journalistic achievements were for Vera a vindication of her decision to remain in England. In mid-October she reported triumphantly to George that she was

> pushing feminism, attacking new papers . . . proving that my career is doing better *after* marriage than it did before . . . fearing nothing, save only such circumstances as sap & devitalise the fountain of this intense energy. To have to 'get tea', make beds, to be called on, return calls, be a 'Faculty Wife', be called 'Mrs Catlin' – God! how I hated it. But I love marriage and adore you. You understand so marvellously. 'What matters is not where you are, but what you are' – no sentence could have expressed more clearly my own idea of what marriage . . . should be . . .

But despite George's outward profession of support for the arrangement, alone at Cornell he was miserable and depressed. His Prohibition research had ended, familiarity had reduced his academic work to a predictable routine, and behind his back there was gossip and conjecture – fanned by Cornell's Professor of History, Wallace Notestein – as to why Vera had remained in England. George missed her desperately. 'My very love for you is a snare,' he wrote to her, 'for when you are absent I can think of nothing else.'

With his Victorian concept of omnipotent husbands and docile wives, George's father regarded his son's semi-detached marriage as an irreverent travesty. Vera's trenchantly feminist articles added fuel to his indignation, and perhaps to preserve the impression of being the sole breadwinner, George informed his father that her journalism had no financial but 'quite ulterior motives'. When she heard, Vera wryly agreed it was probably the best and easiest way to mollify the old man, but pointed out that, except by sponging on Oakwood Court, she would not otherwise be able to live in any sort of comfort, 'to say nothing of crossing the Atlantic twice'.

The primary aim of Vera's journalism was to promote feminism and peace, but she was equally well aware of the value of publicizing herself. *Time and Tide* had taken one of her articles, she told Winifred in 1925, and added ruefully 'but alas, as a leader so I don't propagand [sic] my name'.

Impressed by Winifred's novels and her ability as a journalist, Lady Rhondda had invited her on her return from South Africa in July 1926 to become a director of *Time and Tide*, and Winifred had accepted. Before long Lady Rhondda was depending heavily on her for articles, leaders, reviews, and for her ideas and practical efficiency in the weekly production of the magazine. Lady Rhondda was wealthy, formidable, shy and lonely, and Winifred's company gave her great pleasure. She was, Lady Rhondda wrote, 'almost always happy, full of humour and gaiety, and with a delicious satiric feeling for life and all its oddities that was a sheer joy to listen to'. But she disapproved of Vera. She could neither understand nor accept Winifred's loyalty to her, and she was jealous.

Partly for Winifred's sake, Vera and Lady Rhondda maintained superficially cordial relations. In December 1926, Lady Rhondda gave a luncheon party at Boulestin's for her *Time and Tide* contributors, including Vera, Winifred, Rose Macaulay, E.M. Delafield, Sylvia Townsend Warner, and Lilian Baylis who regaled them with a hilarious account of Dame Nellie Melba's farewell night at the Old Vic when she blatantly manipulated 'spontaneous and overwhelming calls' from the gallery for 'Home, Sweet Home'.

At the end of January 1927, Vera and Winifred were two of the stewards at Kingsway Hall for Lady Rhondda's debate with G.K. Chesterton on 'The Menace of the Leisured Woman', with George Bernard Shaw in the chair. There were no refreshments and no invitations, Vera told George, 'but your friends, since they never answer my letters – about your book or anything else – don't deserve them'.

George accepted in theory their marriage pact of comradeship and equality, and the freedom to pursue their careers unhampered by social conventions. But three thousand miles away, his lonely existence quickly became intolerable. '. . . The world without you is just horrible,' he wrote to

Vera. She had promised to join him at Cornell in the spring, and to return with him to England for the summer vacation. Now, in letter after letter written in the autumn of 1926, he begged, cajoled and admonished her to come at once. 'All my unconscious self continually conspires against my will ... to play on every chord of compunction in you.'

Enjoying her journalistic success and Winifred's companionship, Vera found that George's depressing letters threw her into a turmoil of remorse and resentment. They brought her face to face with the emotional conflict between her loyalty and love for individuals and her ambitions. They had made a pact, she told George, and she had fulfilled her side of the bargain to spend their first year together in America. 'Why is it "massive selfishness" for me to want to do the work I love under the conditions best for it,' she asked, 'and not so for you to want exactly the same thing?'

The quarrel raged throughout November, and Vera realized that in spite of his much-vaunted feminist sympathies George really wanted an intelligent but conventional wife. She was fighting, she told herself, not only for her own interests, but for the freedom of all wives. Male oppression, she protested, sought to own 'not only a woman's person, but her time, her intellect, her whole capacity'. Taking up her pen she reminded him that:

> I did not 'give myself'; I proudly took
> That half of loving which you had to offer.
> Equals we are; as such we shall not brook
> The misinterpretation of the scoffer.
> Meek wifehood is not part of my profession;
> I am your friend, but never your possession.

How comfortable and uncomplicated it would be if she wanted to be nothing but a good wife, she reflected. But she despised wives like Mrs Laski, she said, with her untidy hair and styleless clothes. She had seen her after a lecture, standing a little apart from her husband and Bertrand Russell and his friends, with folded hands and a deprecating smile on her face, 'as if she hadn't *quite* the right to talk to them while he was doing so'.

With their experiment in semi-detached marriage visibly foundering, Vera in desperation suggested a formal separation, 'based not on in-compatibility of temper but on incompatibility of occupation'. Not a judicial separation, nor necessarily a permanent one, but it would regularize the situation and put a stop to the criticism and speculation of their more orthodox relatives and acquaintances.

By December their acrimonious quarrel, and Vera's determination not to join him until the spring, had brought George to the brink of a nervous breakdown. He was, he tormented her, on the verge of a complete 'smash-up'. His letter reduced Vera to a state of panic. She felt herself responsible, and she recalled how his father had suffered a lengthy mental breakdown after his wife had left him. But, while acutely anxious, she could not tell how ill he really was. She was in despair at the prospect of dropping all her commitments and going out to America at once, and it was eventually Winifred who cabled for more information and the doctor's diagnosis.

George's reply arrived late the following night. Aware as he undoubtedly was of the havoc his letter had played with Vera's fragile equilibrium, his resolution to abide by their agreement reasserted itself. Writing to him the next day Vera told him that she felt as if she had been saved from a tremendous catastrophe. 'Had you sent for me urgently I should have come, but it is no use pretending that I should ever have felt the same again, for I shouldn't.t. That is why I am intensely grateful to you for having made, and with apparent success, this effort, this very real effort, to pull through.' Had she thought for a moment that he was a neurotic weakling she would not have married him, 'for to carry a weak man on my back for the rest of my days was no part of my scheme of life'.

She confirmed that she would join him at the beginning of April, and relieved that after all her marriage was not a disastrous mistake she poured out her gratitude. 'Since Edward and Roland died I have wanted nothing to do with any man but thee alone, and I am not likely to love or need thee less, since thou art thine own dear self again. I have been stupid not to realize how ill you were; I have not understood; forgive me, and pardon my bitter letters, for you are the greatest joy of my life.'

Following their reconciliation, Vera's mind turned to the children that they both wanted. She was nearly thirty-three, and pointed out that their family must not be delayed much longer. 'On the same principle that I chose to be married at St James's, and to carry Roland's roses, I should like to produce a baby at Christmas time, and to change a period now always associated with death into one that meant life.' By having a child Vera would also be fulfilling a matter of principle. She had already told George that 'My great object . . . is to prove that work and maternity are not . . . mutually exclusive . . . this is a matter of principle which I care for more . . . than . . . motherhood itself.'

Vera sailed with her mother for America on 28 March. She had hoped that Winifred would go with her, but Winifred was too wise, too circumspect, to be caught up and isolated in a *ménage à trois* in a small, four-roomed apartment on the Cornell campus, while her life in London overflowed with 'tempestuous activity'. She had plunged enthusiastically into *Time and Tide* policy-making and administration, planning new features, contributing leaders, articles and book reviews. Her breakthrough into the world of journalism had also led to requests for articles from half a dozen other newspapers and periodicals, and she agreed to organize and speak at Six Point Group meetings in Hyde Park; and, in addition, whilst Vera and her mother were away, she assumed the responsibility for Mr Brittain's welfare at Oakwood Court.

Why Vera took her mother to America remains a mystery. In-law relationships are notoriously fraught with difficulties. George and Edith Brittain were outwardly civil, but beneath the surface lurked barely concealed feelings of impatience on his part, and antipathy on hers. Perhaps Vera simply wanted congenial company whilst George was lecturing, or her mother's help with the catering which she so much disliked. It may have been that it seemed an excellent opportunity for Mrs Brittain to have a holiday, and a respite from her depressive, demanding husband. Or was it that Vera believed her mother would provide a bulwark against the possibility of a quarrel or emotional discord between herself and George? If this was so then she was disappointed, for Edith Brittain's mere presence seemed to aggravate the tensions between George and Vera. In May Mrs Brittain confided to Winifred that 'Vera is having her ups and downs & is particularly temperamental . . . yesterday a bad one & poor G[eorge] could not do anything right . . . she *will* expect the "mere man" to be what you are & have been to her & that is impossible . . .'.

Before leaving London Vera had asked George to spread the word among his Cornell colleagues that she was too busy for callers, and to make it clear that she would accept only the minimum of invitations. Teeming with ideas she planned a novel centred around her wartime experiences, a factual survey of the prospects of women's employment based on a series of articles she had written for the *Outlook*, and a dramatization of *The Dark Tide*. 'It is just beginning to look, my sweet dear, as if, given time and good health, and no immeasurably bad luck, your wife *might* be a moderately famous woman by the end of next year,' she had written to George. 'And naturally she doesn't want a series of complacent, uncomprehending Ithaca callers to interrupt the process.'

But in less than a week after her arrival she was fractious and disenchanted. Ithaca was the same as ever; sunny, cold, beautiful, and boring, and she had completely lost the enthusiasm which had bubbled over in London.

In going to America the prospect of having a baby was uppermost in

Vera's mind, and less than a month after she arrived she told Winifred she believed she was pregnant. Four days later she reported that she was now in no doubt. Winifred responded with her customary enthusiasm. '. . . What fun . . . it will be next year . . . Really, I'm quite good with babies'.

Vera's pregnancy, despite the early onset of morning sickness which she found 'disconcerting', was a straightforward one, although she was periodically depressed by the thought of the added responsibilities she was about to assume. 'It's queer how it has been my fate to get married, and presumably to have children', she wrote to Winifred, 'when all I really care for deeply is writing . . . and have so little forte for marriage & motherhood. You would have done both so much better . . .'.

Back in England, Arthur Brittain was characteristically inclined to take an even more depressive view of 'Vera's condition'. 'My dear Tiny', he wrote to his wife, '. . . I do not consider that she is sufficiently strong & robust for childbearing, and even if she gets over it, she is likely to have a bad time of it in one way or another, and the game is not worth the candle!' Since Edward's death, he continued mournfully, 'I have no belief in a "special providence" looking after people . . .'.

During Edith Brittain's absence, Margaret Evans, her Welsh maid, had taken over the domestic responsibilities at Oakwood Court, but the brunt of Mr Brittain's melancholia fell upon Winifred. She spent his birthday with him on 6 April, and took with her the present she had bought on Vera's behalf, a Dunhill lighter in a lizard-skin case. She visited him regularly and tried unsuccessfully to persuade him to go to Brighton with a nurse for the sea air and a change of scenery. From her letters Vera quickly realized that Winifred was having 'a dreadful time with father', but Winifred protested that '. . . had it really been unpleasant, shouldn't I have been fortunate to have the chance really to do something quite useful for you for once? . . . I don't know what life means if it does not mean loving, nor love, if it does not mean serving'.

Vera, George and Mrs Brittain returned to London in June, and a major concern that summer was to find more spacious accommodation before the baby arrived. The Maida Vale flat was cramped and sunless, and eventually, with Winifred's help, early in September they rented the first and second floors of 6 Nevern Place, a tall narrow house with bow windows, less than a stone's throw from the busy Earls Court Road. One inducement was a good-sized nursery-cum-bedroom for the baby and live-in nurse. George was provided with a study, while Vera wrote at the dining-room table. Winifred had a bedsit on the first floor. A housekeeper and a maid came in daily. Vera had suggested to Winifred that their living arrangements would not be '. . . at all queer. Half the married couples in this town seem to have a sister living with them, and you are more to me than any sister.'

John Edward Jocelyn Brittain-Catlin was born prematurely on 21 December 1927. The birth was a difficult one, and took place without anaesthetic, and Vera remained in the Chelsea Nursing Home for three weeks. Too physically and mentally exhausted to read or talk much, she amused herself manicuring her nails and making up her face. 'She emerged from the sickroom with vivid cherry-coloured nails and bright lips to match, and the most amazing eyebrows,' Winifred reported. George strongly disapproved of the extraordinary transformation, but Winifred laughed and told him it was only masculine prejudice.

For a hard-headed realist, Vera was strangely superstitious. She believed it more than a coincidence that her son should have been born almost twelve years to the day since Roland had died, and that with his dark hair and brown eyes he should so strongly resemble her beloved brother.

IV

John's difficult birth had been traumatic, and for four months Vera suffered post-natal depression, fatigue and misery. She had wanted children, but was dismayed to find that having a baby had completely disorientated her life. She worried continually about her premature, underweight son, and 'awoke each morning in dread lest I should find that he had died in the night'.

To give her freedom to write involved an increase in the household staff, and brought with it additional distractions and interruptions. Her untrained, happy-go-lucky Irish nursemaid had a natural affinity with babies, but her unhygienic habit of wiping the infant's nose, mouth or chin with whatever garment came to hand filled Vera with consternation. Her pretty young housekeeper enmeshed her with details of 'love-affairs past, present and to come', while her charwoman regaled her with blow-by-blow reports on her own baby's teeth, diet, undergarments and vaccination. Not least among Vera's tribulations were the visits by her mother, father, friends and relatives, who descended without warning to admire the infant or to bring bootees and baby clothes, while the part-time secretary waited impatiently for her to dictate letters or to finish an article. 'Somehow or other I *must* get more freedom from interruption,' she protested to Winifred, 'it is destroying all my work.'

George returned to Cornell at the end of January 1928, and it was Winifred who again came to the rescue. With tact and good humour she soothed Vera's jangled nerves, curbed her outbursts, poured oil on domestic crises, and discussed suggested alterations to her book reviews and articles. She helped to feed the baby, and to give Vera an undisturbed afternoon on the nursemaid's half-day she often set off with him in his pram down the Cromwell Road to Kensington Gardens.

At three months John Edward was still underweight. Grey skies and cold weather brought a heavy snowfall. Early in March Winifred was hastily summoned to Yorkshire. Following the premature birth of a second daughter, her sister Grace lay critically ill with post-natal complications and pneumonia, and died at her home in Bridlington a few days later. To the Holtbys' distress at losing their elder daughter was added their acute anxiety for the welfare of her two infant children, and Winifred remained with her mother and father for several weeks.

Shortly after she returned to London the charwoman came into contact with a smallpox patient, and to Vera's dismay the whole household had to be vaccinated. The inoculation seriously affected John Edward. For several days he was 'awfully ill', Winifred reported, with a temperature of 105 degrees.

By 1928 Winifred was well established as a widely read and nationally known journalist. She was the author of three successful novels, and as a director of *Time and Tide* she got to know many of her well-known contemporaries. 'Many times during the early part of 1928', Vera admitted, 'I was moved by an unworthy envy of Winifred's success, popularity and freedom', but she went on to acknowledge the 'incalculable debt' she owed her friend for her 'stimulating encouragement' during one of the most frustrating periods of her life.

It was almost two years since Winifred had become a director of *Time and Tide*, and as her editor-designate Lady Rhondda depended upon her more and more, both as a colleague and as a friend. On occasions she rebuked her for wasting her time on Vera's baby, especially when Winifred arrived late for a *Time and Tide* board dinner after helping to bath John Edward and put him to bed. The fact that Vera published only a dozen articles in *Time and Tide* between 1927 and 1931 undoubtedly reflects Lady Rhondda's antipathy to her. Book reviews were Winifred's responsibility, and in the same period Vera wrote seventy-five weekly book columns, usually reviewing several books at a time.

Among the novels Vera received to review for *Time and Tide* in the July after John's birth was *The Well of Loneliness*. Under the heading 'Facing

Facts' she wrote of Radclyffe Hall's lesbian story as 'a plea, passionate, yet admirably restrained and never offensive, for the extension of social toleration, compassion and recognition to the biologically abnormal woman, who, because she possesses the tastes and instincts of a man, is too often undeservedly treated as a moral pariah'.

'It may be said at once,' she continued uncompromisingly, 'that *The Well of Loneliness* can only strengthen the belief of all honest and courageous persons that there is no problem which is not better frankly stated than concealed. Persecution and disgusted ostracism have never solved any difficulty in the world . . .'.

They were brave words in the sanctimonious atmosphere of 1928, and in November Vera was one of forty witnesses summoned by the defence counsel, Norman Birkett, when Radclyffe Hall's novel was prosecuted for obscenity. John Galsworthy was among the larger number of well-known writers who declined to jeopardize their reputations by supporting an unpopular cause, but Vera found herself in the distinguished company of E.M. Forster, Desmond MacCarthy, Storm Jameson, Vita Sackville-West, and Leonard and Virginia Woolf.

The Radclyffe Hall novel, Virginia Woolf reported to Roger Fry, was 'so pure, so sweet, so sentimental, that none of us can read it'. The Bow Street magistrate, the 'pathologically boorish' Sir Chartres Biron, entertained no such thoughts. He disallowed as irrelevant the testimony of all the literary experts, and after a week's adjournment pronounced the book an obscene libel.

Almost by chance, Vera's serious and favourable review, and her nomination as a prospective defence witness, were to enhance her opportunities for publicizing her views on the urgent need for social and moral reform.

In December 1927, shortly before John's birth, Vera had completed her handbook on *Women's Work in Modern England*, prefaced with her favourite Olive Schreiner quotation 'We take all labour for our province'. Based on a series of six articles she had written for the *Outlook* on 'Prospects in Women's Employment', the book provided a fully documented survey of opportunities for women in industry, business, the professions, national services and voluntary work. 'It attempts to indicate which vocations . . . offer good prospects to the enterprising and courageous', she wrote in the introduction. It also sought to counteract the tendency of women to drift haphazardly into any form of wage-earning instead of choosing intelligently and making a career of it. 'To a dear pioneer in the great fields of Sociology and Politics – this very small achievement in the same tradition', she wrote on the flyleaf of the copy she gave to George.

The book was published at an especially auspicious moment. A few weeks after its publication, on 2 July 1928, women received equal franchise with men, and consequently *Women's Work in Modern England* received a large number of reviews, many favourable. 'Miss Vera Brittain achieves three important tasks,' opined the *Daily Herald*. 'She brings within the scope of some 220 pages a résumé of the fields open to ambitious women today; she draws attention to the obstructive attitude of the male workers' unions towards women's labour; and she makes a powerful plea for the abolition of sex differentiation in the labour market.' The book established her as a leading writer on women's topics, and brought requests for articles from the *Daily Mirror*, the *Daily Chronicle*, the *Evening News* and the *Westminster Gazette*.

Financially the book was an unexpected catastrophe. Her contract with the small independent publisher, Noel Douglas, provided for a ten per cent royalty payable annually, but before the first payment was due the firm was bankrupt and she received only an insignificant proportion of the £250 the book had earned.

Winifred's third novel, *The Land of Green Ginger*, had been published by Jonathan Cape the previous autumn, and they had negotiated an American edition shortly afterwards. Although not a spectacular bestseller, it added to Winifred's growing reputation as a novelist, and she received what she regarded as a substantial royalty cheque for £30 on the day of publication. 'I *must* write another novel,' Vera wrote to her. 'I feel I have been dreadfully remiss and slack these three years. While you were writing your book I was writing to G[eorge]; I could easily have written a book in the time my letters to him took.'

V

Norah Martin had just completed her training as a Wellgarth children's nurse when Vera engaged her at a salary of £48 a year to look after John Edward. They ate and slept in the nursery on the second floor, and she remembers him as a strong-willed child, but usually amenable. Vera and George made frequent visits to the nursery, but being reassured that she was capable and conscientious they also left her for long periods in sole charge. Vera was not naturally maternal, and appeared vaguely uneasy with babies and young children. 'She had a "special face" for John,' Norah remembered.

In the afternoons Norah often took John Edward to visit his grandparents in Oakwood Court. Mrs Brittain fussed, and 'Mr Brittain was strangely odd. He told John the most terrifying stories about vagrant pedlars who roamed the countryside with knapsacks on their backs full of rats and mice. They were really frightening. I was quite worried, but luckily John didn't seem to understand.'

Norah Martin remembers George Catlin as 'utterly absent-minded'. He lost his umbrella with monotonous regularity until Vera in desperation tied a luggage label on it with his name and address. He appeared completely oblivious to it flapping unceremoniously around his head, and there were frequent telephone calls from all over London to come and collect it. Though serious and academic, there were moments when he relaxed and was less aware of his professional status. 'Winifred, that dress is indecent,' he rebuked her when the three of them were in the nursery before going out. 'It reveals far more than it conceals.' 'Winifred took no notice,' Norah said. 'She could get away with anything.'

By 1929 John Edward was a normal, healthy child, he had a capable nursemaid, and with her life on an even keel Vera's journalistic output reached its peak. She maintained her close association with the *Manchester Guardian*, the *Yorkshire Post*, the *Nation and Athenaeum* and *Time and Tide*, and also contributed to such divergent newspapers as the *Daily Mirror* and *Daily Telegraph*, as well as to the short-lived magazine the *Realist*. George was a founder member of this optimistic, highbrow venture to promote 'Scientific Humanism', but to his discomfiture it failed to attract a viable readership and within a year had disappeared.

Feminism remained Vera's predominant topic. She also extended her scope with articles written principally from the married woman's point of view on 'Midwives and Maternity', 'Wives Who Earn' and 'Future Parents at School'. In 'Celibate Professions' she perceptively anticipated the day when married nurses or teachers with young children 'would be glad to share both hours and salary with another in the same position'. In an article, 'Men Who Write About Women', Vera sharply rebuked the author who suggested that all superfluous women workers who had not yet found a man should be shipped off to the colonies, with the forceful logic that 'Men would complain fast enough if the proposition were put the other way round'.

In September, George accompanied her to the Tenth League of Nations Assembly. Geneva sweltered in an intense heatwave. Vera melted and gasped in the crowded press gallery conscientiously collecting information for a report on 'Child Welfare and the Traffic in Women', while George –

1 Vera's mother, Edith Bervon, with her sisters, in mourning for their father, 1891. Clockwise from left Lillie, Florence, Edith, Belle.

2 LEFT Edith Brittain, Vera's mother, 1890s: 'Mr Brittain liked her to be well turned out'.

3 ABOVE Arthur Brittain, Vera's father, around the time of Vera's birth.

4 RIGHT *Vera and her brother Edward, 'two sweet little mites in white silk frocks', 1900.*

5 BELOW *The Brittain family, with Miss Newby, in Arthur Brittain's new Wolseley 8, at Glen Bank, Macclesfield, March 1905.*

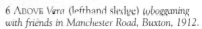

6 ABOVE *Vera* (lefthand sledge) *tobogganing with friends in Manchester Road, Buxton, 1912.*

7 LEFT *Vera enduring a Buxton winter, outside Melrose, c.1912.*

8 BELOW *Vera at St Monica's, aged 16.*

9 ABOVE *Vera in Buxton, c.1911.*

10 BELOW *Edward*, back left, *Roland Leighton*, front left, *Uppingham School OTC camp, summer 1913*

11 ABOVE *Headmaster's garden party, the last Uppingham School Speech Day before the war, July 1914: 'the one perfect summer idyll that I ever experienced'.*

12 BELOW *Somerville College 'billeted' at Oriel, in St Mary Hall Quadrangle, June 1915.* 3rd row: far left *Dorothy Sayers,* 5th from left *Vera.* 2nd row: 10th from left *Emily Penrose,* centre in hat *Hilda Lorimer,* 10th from right *Helen Darbishire ('the Pen', 'the Lorie' and 'the Darb').*

13 *Robert Leighton, Roland's father, who possessed 'the kindest manner in the world'.*

14 *Marie Connor Leighton, Roland's mother: 'a distinguished woman, with a dream, needs a large hat'.*

15 *Roland Leighton: 'At nineteen, Roland looked twenty-four and behaved with the assurance of thirty'.*

16 Victor Richardson, one of Uppingham's
'Three Musketeers'.

17 Geoffrey Thurlow, Edward's 'beloved
friend'.

18 Edward Brittain in 1915.

19 ABOVE LEFT *Vera and Edward in uniform, with their parents, Buxton, 1915.*

20 ABOVE RIGHT *Vera as a VAD, with a nursing sister, Malta, 1917.*

21 LEFT *The original wooden cross on Edward's grave at Granezza, Asiago Plateau, Italy, 1918: 'It's a strange world where the symbols of people count so much more because they're all one has left'.*

'O Wise young man!' she wrote to Winifred – spent most of his time bathing at the Eaux Vives.

She also took advantage of her married status to write about the need for sex education and more enlightened sexual attitudes. Civilization, she believed, was ultimately based upon man's control of his impulses by his will, and in a long letter she joined in the controversy on 'Sexual Gluttony' in the correspondence columns of the *Nation and Athenaeum*. She welcomed the healthy reaction against the puritanical repressions of the nineteenth century, but had the pendulum swung too far, she asked, when it was suggested that the sex impulse 'ought to be satisfied as soon as it exists and merely because it exists'?

'I cannot see that this is ethically any different from saying that as soon as a small boy develops a taste for jam he ought to be allowed immediate and unrestricted access to the jampot,' she wrote.

In February 1929 her intention to embark upon a study of marriage was pre-empted by a request from Kegan Paul to write a book for their 'Today and Tomorrow' publications. This popular half-crown series contained almost fifty pocket-sized volumes, with Bertrand Russell, Robert Graves, J.B.S. Haldane, Dora Russell, C.E.M. Joad and Winifred (on *Eutychus, or The Future of the Pulpit*) among the contributors. Norman Haire, the Australian-born sexologist, had already written on *Hymen, or the Future of Marriage*. Vera decided on a similar theme, but to avoid a clash of titles she produced a ninety-two-page fantasy on *Halcyon, or the Future of Monogamy*.

The book consisted of four imaginary chapters on 'The Institution of Monogamy' from *A History of English Moral Institutions* written in the twenty-first century by Minerva Huxterwin, an Oxford Professor of Moral History, a device which allowed Vera unrestricted scope for her views on sex instruction, birth control, trial marriages, semi-detached marriage, divorce, and married women's careers.

She endeavoured to forecast revolutionary scientific developments, and a radical transformation in moral attitudes in the distant future. She wrote of the perfecting of broadcasting and television between 1925 and 1940, and of air flights in 1985 'from London to New York in under seven hours'. She also described with uncanny accuracy the popularity of the present-day video, and predicted optimistically that 'broadcasting, television and still later the so-called "home-talkies" apparatus would put an end to that widespread domestic boredom which so often in the past could find alleviation only in the excitement of a clandestine love-affair'. She assumed, as a matter of course, the twentieth-century triumph of feminism, with women achieving social and economic equality with men.

231

She prophesied the discovery of the main sex-determining factors in 1955, and a scientific breakthrough in 1973 which led to the production of a Rejuvenating Serum, 'which at the first sign of the menopause restored the sexual activity of women for a further period of fifteen to twenty years'. In a few cases it was found possible to revive the child-bearing capacity in women whose periods had long since ceased. 'One of the most celebrated experiments was that performed upon the first Queen of the re-established Kingdom of Hungary, who by means of three injections . . . was enabled to produce an heir to the throne three days after her sixty-second birthday.'

The central premiss of Vera's final chapter on 'The Triumph of Voluntary Monogamy' was man's ability to exercise voluntary sexual restraint. Monogamy, she insisted, had never been achieved by the rigidity of Victorian law and custom, and 'the ultimately stabilizing effects of the moral revolution of 1930 to 1975 were not immediately evident'. She predicted that towards the end of the twentieth century self-imposed restraint would have already begun to replace promiscuity and sexual licence, and that 'It remained for the generation of 2000 to 2030 to complete this new tendency by the general adoption of that voluntary monogamy which is now so conspicuous a feature of our modern social life.'

The publication of *Halcyon* coincided with the Third Congress of the World League for Sexual Reform, held in London from 8 to 14 September. The speakers at this well-publicized international gathering of almost thirty radical reformers included Norman Haire on sterilization and abortion, C.E.M. Joad on sex and religion, Dora Russell on marriage and freedom, and Naomi Mitchison on the use of contraceptives. Ethel Mannin spoke on 'Sex and the Child', whilst Marie Stopes addressed the Congress on the inflammatory issue of birth control. The last paper was given by Bernard Shaw on 'The Need for Expert Opinion on Sexual Reform'.

Speaking on 'The Failure of Monogamy', Vera put forward six 'sweeping innovations' which she advocated as the essential basis for the establishment of successful monogamous marriages:

The abolition of any form of censorship, and she added – no doubt with *The Well of Loneliness* in mind – 'whatever its literary form'.

The legislation of experimental unions.

Reform of the divorce laws, including divorce by consent.

The liberation of married women from their present property status, with the right to fulfil individual ambition and to achieve economic independence.

Sex instruction from an early age.

Instruction after adolescence 'in the detailed technique of intercourse and birth control'.

As a married woman determined to have both children and a career, she deplored the nineteenth-century hypocrisy which had preached the sanctity of motherhood but regarded contraception as if it were a sort of secret vice. As Winifred was to point out, women were at the mercy of 'time and tide and the rhythm of life's creative current', and unwanted and over-frequent pregnancies imposed a crippling burden of physical and economic catastrophe, while Vera maintained that until birth-control information was openly available, women could never achieve full emancipation and the freedom actively to participate in life. She urged the need for scientific research to improve contraceptive methods, and the public provision of facilities to advise and instruct on their use. It cast an odd reflection on masculine prejudice that whilst the condom was the simplest, cheapest and safest contraception, it was for women that clinics were so urgently required.

In the final chapter of *Halcyon*, Vera had also discussed the imponderable difficulties in achieving complete sexual fidelity. 'While we regard modern matrimony as a relationship of which the beauty is not necessarily spoiled by an occasional and frankly-acknowledged extramarital experience, we recognize that this type of adventure should be indulged in only as the outcome of mutual agreement and full confidence between husband and wife if it is not to destroy the loyal attitude of two individuals towards one another which constitutes true monogamy.' It was a theory which her own experience had already begun to test.

George had returned to Cornell after Christmas 1928. He was finding his five months of enforced celibacy each year an increasingly painful penance. In March 1929, Vera received a letter from him which all too starkly brought home the perils and pitfalls of the form of marriage which she had so ardently espoused. George told her that he was sexually infatuated with a young Russian woman, and asked her for her feelings and reactions should he succumb to the temptation of an extramarital affair.

'You ask me to be as frank about your Russian as you are with me,' Vera replied. 'Well, then, I suppose I must be – but I don't want to be, because it means saying things that I don't a bit want to say and you won't at all like to hear. But there it is – complete frankness means *all* one's reactions, and if you must have them, you must.'

Confronted with her own enlightened arguments she confessed that 'The trouble is that so many of one's emotions refuse to be regimented by one's rational beliefs.' Nothing, she told George, was more abominable than the possessiveness characterized by her aunt, Muriel Groves. She didn't want him to feel that physically he belonged to her, but only to himself.

But in my secret heart I hope that of your own will, you will not take advantage of your freedom – not because I compel you but because – these things can't be rationalized but let me quote your own words – 'it goes against the grain not to keep a certain physical relationship as distinctive to husband and wife'.

I can't imagine being emotionally indifferent to your being promiscuous unless I ceased to care for you . . . I can imagine myself ceasing to care for you quite soon; in fact I can't imagine anything that would more quickly make me feel our relationship smirched and spoiled. I *don't* think it would make me leave you – this would far more likely be caused by your worrying me about money, which drives me nearly mad with exasperation, since one of the few real advantages I have in this world is the certainty of financial security, and since you share this advantage in full I can't think why you don't make yourself do so psychologically and stop regarding my possessions as somehow 'not existing'.

Vera admitted that because of the male preoccupation and dependence upon sex, she had always felt

that men, compared with women, are rather poor things. I don't think you such a poor thing as most; I shouldn't have married you if I had . . . And yet, and yet, if I am frank I think I should admit that I have never expected *quite* the same standard of loyalty and honour and consideration from you as I should take for granted from Winifred.

How much of this whole business – which didn't interest you in the first two years of our marriage, i.e. before I had any children – is due to the fact that a wife and mother of five years' standing is rather stale from repetition, that I am two years your senior . . . that I am something of a martinet and possessed of financial security that makes me damned independent? You love me, yes, of course you do; I am a pleasant habit, even an admirable habit, but am I not just a little dull?

She accepted that there was a conflict between her emotional theories and her own feelings, 'in your own words, that I'm not nearly as generous as I say I am!' If he decided to go ahead and have a sexual relationship 'with your Russian or anyone else, you have the consolation of knowing that you are acting entirely in accordance with the dictates of my reason. And if my emotional inclinations should recede from you a little in consequence – well that is the price one often pays for being rational'.

Several weeks later, when George informed her that he had decided after all not to go ahead with his affair, Vera's relief was palpable. The thing, she told him, which she had feared most was that:

> something might smirch or spoil or render less dignified . . . our relationship, not only in our own eyes but in the eyes of the world. Our work – at any rate . . . my work – depends largely for its success, not only upon the fact that we are ideally happy together, but that we are known to be so. If it seems arrogant to say that the success of our marriage matters to the world, to society, to politics, to feminism, I can only reply that it is the kind of arrogance that one ought to encourage in one's self. Today . . . one happily married wife and mother is worth more to feminism . . . than a dozen gifted and eloquent spinsters . . . T[hat] our experiment in 'semi-detachment' should succeed . . . this I think of the supremest importance . . .

Although George did not pursue his Russian woman, the episode marked the beginning of a significant change in his relationship with Vera. For almost four years Vera's literary ambitions had dictated the terms and circumstances of their married life; but despite George's acceptance in theory of an equal partnership, he had come to resent the long separations and Vera's need to be with Winifred. Increasingly, for much of the next decade, an element of estrangement would sour their marriage as George pursued his own interests and, discreetly, began to have affairs with other women.

This rift in their relationship would be aggravated by Vera's intense absorption in writing her autobiography. Ever since the end of the war she had been attempting unsuccessfully to fictionalize her wartime experiences. By 1929 she had come to the conclusion that whatever the emotional cost, the only course left to her was 'to tell my own fairly typical story as truthfully as I could against the larger background . . .'.

235

EIGHT

Farewell to the War Generation

'How to preserve the memory of our suffering in such a way that our successors may understand it and refrain from the temptations offered by glamour and glory – that is the problem which we, the war generation, have still to solve before the darkness covers us.'

Vera Brittain, *Manchester Guardian*, 11 November 1930

'. . . my brutal, poignant, insistent memories which were too direct for fiction, yet had to be got rid of if I was to go on living.'

Vera Brittain to Elizabeth Nicholas, 16 October 1961

I

On Armistice Day 1921 Vera had written to Winifred, 'I have just been listening to the guns going off for the Two Minutes' silence . . . Today I cannot go out and stand at the Cenotaph or pay homage to the Unknown Warriors or anything . . . I don't require two minutes' silence to think of the dead. They're with me always; it's like putting two minutes aside in which to breathe.'

The war remained the central devastating experience of Vera's life, the full trauma of which nothing could eradicate. Winifred's friendship, marriage and the birth of a child, had slowly restored her emotional security, replacing the sense of loneliness and isolation which she had felt so strongly on returning to Oxford in 1919; but she recognized that ultimately only her writing could provide any decisive coming to terms with her war experience.

In the closing months of the war Vera had completed a novel entitled 'The Pawn of Fate'. The first part of this book is set in a French military hospital at 'Echy', clearly based on 24 General at Étaples. The selfless heroine – another idealized self-portrait – is a VAD called Veronica Beresford, while the eccentric sister of No. 6 ward is an early attempt at portraying Faith Moulson under the name she was later to bear in *Testament of Youth*, Hope Milroy. Although the passages describing Veronica's nursing in a German ward are strikingly similar in some instances to those that later found their way into *Testament of Youth*, the war remains largely incidental to the romantic melodrama which is the novel's main concern. After Hope Milroy has been raped by Basil Raynor, a hospital surgeon, the action moves to a Cornish cottage where Hope, under Veronica's protection, gives birth to Raynor's child, a baby girl. Raynor reappears briefly to claim Hope and the child, but is repudiated by her. The book ends with Hope committing suicide, leaving her daughter to be brought up by Veronica.

In September 1918 Vera asked Robert Leighton to read her manuscript. While he praised it as 'a vivid and accurate account of the life of a VAD in France . . .', and thought that it merited publication, he was also of the opinion that her 'argument against the "system" seemed to me to be quite too emphatic and strong for the occasion'. Stung by his criticism, Vera replied that the hospital scenes were in fact based firmly on experience, which, as a professional publishers' reader, alarmed Robert Leighton even more. 'My caution to you was wholly for your own sake, given in the innocent belief that all doctors in our casualty stations are gentlemen and all sisters and nurses of saintly purity . . . But now your letter opens my eyes to the fact that your "fiction" is much more true than I had suspected. I regret very much to discover, for example, that you had a prototype for Basil Raynor.'

On the reasonable assumption that the real Basil Raynor was still alive, Robert Leighton warned Vera of the danger of a libel action. Even if she published the book anonymously, the depiction of the German ward 'would limit the search for the offender', and make her own identification as the author all too easy. 'Candidly, I want you to publish this book', he concluded. 'The hospital chapters are far too important and informative to be put away in your desk for years.' And yet, he did not see how she could eliminate 'the very human story of Sister Milroy' without damaging the structure of the book as a whole.

Disappointed, Vera put 'The Pawn of Fate' to one side, and in both *The Dark Tide* and *Not Without Honour* made a deliberate attempt to write away from her war experiences. In 1922, however, not long after the completion of her first published novel, she submitted typed selections from the journal which she had kept between 1913 and 1917 for a publisher's competition which offered a prize for a personal diary or autobiography. She entitled her selections 'Chronicle of Youth', explaining that she hoped her record would remind readers of the utter fruitlessness of war, since 'memory is short, and in the after time even those who have suffered most are apt to forget the extent of the despair which wasted so much youthful vitality and darkened the sunshine of the sweet years.' Although the diary was not chosen, the seed of an idea for a fictionalized account of her memories of the war, based on personal records, had been planted in her mind. However, the distinct lack of interest in the war on the part of the British reading public – the 'dance and forget' atmosphere of postwar reaction – made publication of war books difficult. Writing to Vera on 19 December 1923, Grant Richards was obviously responding to a request from her for advice about the market for a war novel she was planning:

> I think it all depends on the strength of the book. Certainly *some* of the prejudice against books of the war has evaporated. I do not think I can safely say more than that . . . If I were in your place and had a novel distinctly clamouring for birth I should let it be born.

The following year Vera briefly experimented with a new version of 'The Pawn of Fate' under the title of 'Folly's Vineyard'. But any serious attempt to bring such a book to birth was frustrated by her marriage, her move to America, and by her determination to establish herself as a journalist, and it is not until 1926 that we hear of further concrete proposals for a war novel. On 28 February of that year she wrote to Winifred in some excitement of an idea for a novel to be called 'The Incidental Adam'. '. . . I can write it very quickly', she told her somewhat optimistically, 'without having to look up anything except my letters and diaries.' She envisaged the book's main theme as that of youth betrayed into cynical disillusionment, set against 'a particular background of time and place.' Once again, though, other projects and a hurried move to New York intervened, and in May she was still 'aching, at long last, to write about the war, all the grieving and the struggle and the loss.'

Any attempt to unravel the evolution of 'The Incidental Adam' into *Testament of Youth* is complicated by the large number of incomplete and discarded drafts, and by the lack of firm dating. Fundamentally, though, there exist various notes from the mid to late Twenties for a long book, beginning before the war and ending after it, which has many titles and arrangements, but substantially the same plot. Plans for this book gradually shift from the fictional towards the openly autobiographical. In the notes for two novels under the general title of 'The War Generation', the clear autobiographical intent is indicated by Vera's note to herself to 'Refer to all friends – except Edward – by their initials.' Another fictional reworking of her war material is 'Youth's Calvary' which once again centres on Vera's surrogate, Virginia Dennison. Related to this are a group of incomplete drafts that appear to be connected to one evolving novel based on the war experiences of Vera and Edward ('Ruth' and 'Gabriel'), with such titles as 'The Great Explanation', 'The Kingdom of Endurance', and 'The Sorrowful Islands' (namely, England and Malta). The overriding impression is of Vera casting about discontentedly for the form best suited to her war book.

By the time she was ready to concentrate on writing it, the literary climate had been transformed. In the decade since the Armistice, writers had sought a period of detachment and emotional distance in which to make their considered responses to their memories of the war. But now the 'great bull market for trench memoirs' had opened: 1928 saw the publication of Edmund Blunden's autobiography, *Undertones of War*, and of Siegfried Sassoon's skilfully fictionalized *Memoirs of a Fox-Hunting Man*, and their success guaranteed war books a popularity even more emphatic than the preceding indifference shown them. In the following year, the spate of war books had already reached its numerical peak: twenty-nine were published that year, including the English translation of Erich Maria Remarque's *Im Westen nichts Neues* as *All Quiet on the Western Front*, which sold 250,000 copies in its first year, Robert Graves's *Goodbye to All That*, and Richard Aldington's *Death of a Hero*.

Vera made a close study of the war memoirs of Blunden, Graves and Sassoon. 'I am reading "Undertones of War"', she wrote at Christmas 1928; 'grave, dignified but perfectly simple and straightforward; why shouldn't I write one like that?' Early in the New Year she went with Winifred to see R.C. Sherriff's trench drama *Journey's End*, the theatrical hit of the season. She reviewed Aldington's bitter *Death of a Hero* for *Time and Tide*, and found it to be 'a devastating indictment of pre-war civilization, with its ignorance, its idiocies and its values even falser than those of today', values which Vera pointed out had vainly sent hundreds of thousands of young men to their deaths.

In the flood of war literature by men, however, Vera found little acknowledgement of the role of women in the war, and what reference was made was all too often belittling and insulting. Either women did not appear at all, or they were portrayed as passive, sentimentalized creatures, 'giving their husbands and sons and weeping unavailing tears, or worse still, as time-servers, parasites or prostitutes.' She was thinking in particular of the characterization of the wife, mother and mistress in Aldington's novel, but also of Sassoon's poems, 'Their Frailty' and 'Glory of Women', with their theme of the selfishness of women's love in wartime.

What Vera chiefly objected to was the lack of emphasis on women's active role in the war. Not only did their achievements remain largely unacknowledged in the books that were being published, but also to a great extent women were unrepresented in the painting and sculpture that the war had inspired. In 'Their Name Liveth: Forgetting the Women's War-Work', an article published for Armistice Day 1929, Vera observed that the Cavell Memorial by St Martin-in-the-Fields and the Edinburgh War Memorial (which has a window dedicated to women doctors, nurses and the auxiliary corps) were almost alone in the commemoration of women at war. Echoing the words of Olive Schreiner, Vera concluded somewhat bitterly that:

> In the Great War, which they then believed to be waged for freedom, the women of this country knew how to bear an active part; they accepted gladly the strain and the burden and the small rewards, though many of them were throwing off parasitism for the first time. But for the most part they did not die ... They worked, but they also went on living and suffering and remembering; and immortality – as so many of the disabled and unemployed have since had reason to realize – is the reward only of a life laid down.

Of course, Vera made no 'puerile claim' to the equality of women's suffering and service in wartime with that of men; but she did argue that 'any picture of the War years is incomplete which omits those aspects that mainly concern women . . .', and claimed furthermore that a woman who worked with the armies could provide 'a wider and more truthful picture of the war as a whole' than the soldier whose knowledge was inevitably 'confined to a small corner of the front.'

Vera's attack on the male domination of war literature tended to overlook the large number of books by women about their war experiences which had been published both during the war and in the years since. She had warm words of commendation for Mary Lee's 1929 novel, *It's a Great War*, written from an American standpoint; and she would later read 'with deep interest and sympathy', Irene Rathbone's novel, *We That Were Young* (1932), based on Rathbone's own experiences of nursing as a VAD at the 1st London General in Camberwell, which conveyed, as no other book had done to date, the full horror of nursing the mutilated and wounded. Surprisingly, she appears to have had nothing to say about *Not So Quiet . . . Stepdaughters of War* (1930) by 'Helen Zenna Smith' (the pseudonym of Evadne Price), a novel about women as ambulance drivers in France, which sold thousands of copies in Europe and America, and which in France was awarded the Prix Séverigné as the 'novel most calculated to promote international peace'.

Vera continued to maintain that there had been no books by women dealing with the war in a comprehensive way. 'The woman is still silent', she wrote in 1931, 'who by presenting the war in its true perspective in her own life, will illuminate its meaning afresh for her generation.' By the time she wrote those words, she had determined that she would be that woman.

In the war book which Vera finally began to plan in November 1929, there was a conscious attempt to fuse together elements of the strictly documentary with a compelling personal narrative: as she admitted in later years, 'I wanted to make my story as truthful as history, but as readable as fiction'. As long ago as 1921, in her first vacation after leaving Oxford, Vera had mused upon the relationship between historical and fictional writing in a letter to Winifred. 'How is one to reconcile the two ideals?' she had asked. 'Are they compatible or not? Can both of them be true at once, and each at different times matter more than the other?' She had always felt uncomfortable with the novel form, and all her mature novels suffer from a too literal transposition of real-life models into thinly disguised fictional characters. An autobiography, or as she always preferred to call it, an autobiographical study of the years 1900 to 1925, would enable her to provide a literary memorial to Roland, Edward, Victor and Geoffrey. It would also illustrate one of the strongest abiding beliefs that the war had left her with, 'the influence of worldwide events and movements upon the personal destinies of men and women'. The story of her early life was originally called 'Chronicle of Youth' until her reading of Robert Bridges' epic poem, *The Testament of Beauty*, inspired her to settle, in August 1931, on the title *Testament of Youth* for the book which she intended would speak for a whole generation of women.

II

All her life the issue of whether women could combine marriage and motherhood with real success in art or a profession was a major concern of Vera's writing. Working on *Testament of Youth*, she found herself providing a test-case for all her own theories. Years later, with one eye on her experience at that time, she would advocate the creation of a 'co-operative home atmosphere' to allow a woman to proceed with her creative work without the household crumbling around her. Fathers, she wrote, could be trained in 'ordinary human efficiency', while 'a minor reorganization of domestic service . . . would save the creative woman from being perpetually at the mercy of the "Fifth Column" below stairs'.

Testament of Youth took more than three years to write, instead of the two Vera had originally envisaged, its progress constantly impeded by 'the perpetual buzz of maids and children'. She sometimes comforted herself with the notion that the frustrations and boredom of married women's domestic work might actually enhance their literary work, and contribute to its vitality. 'I used to rush to my desk with joy,' she told one correspondent years later, 'because even though so much I had to tell was sad, the chronicling of it was a glorious relief from domesticity.'

At the beginning of December 1929, after only three weeks' work on her book, Vera discovered she was pregnant again. She and George had wanted a second child for some time but Vera had been unable to conceive. Faced now with an unexpected interruption, she was at first frustrated and resentful. Soon, however, she adopted a more optimistic attitude, and wrote to Winifred, who was in Yorkshire dealing with a family illness, that 'the end of July won't be such a bad time. There will be nothing doing in the world at large for two months and the infant will have three months of warmish weather before it.' The prospect of a new addition to the family made necessary a move from the cramped and not altogether salubrious conditions of Nevern Place. The first chapter of her book was laid aside, as Vera, George and Winifred set about reviewing houses in Chelsea and Kensington.

Between them they inspected seventy-six properties before settling on 19 Glebe Place, off the King's Road in Chelsea. Chelsea still retained something of its original village charm. In the early 1920s it had been overrun by artists and actors, adding a strong Bohemian air to its more respectable literary traditions. Number 19 was a reasonably large, if architecturally undistinguished, late-Victorian terraced house. Two features of the property were particularly appealing: the spacious top-floor attic, converted into a library, provided a haven for the family's increasing number of books, while in the narrow, west-facing garden Vera was to find a pleasant sun-trap in which to sit and write on summer afternoons.

In April 1930 the family moved into their new home. A larger house required extra domestic staff, and the Catlins were to be especially fortunate in the couple who would give unstinting and loyal service for the next forty years. Amy Francis was employed as maidservant in September, and after her marriage to Charles Burnett in 1934 he joined the household as butler and general handyman, and she was promoted to cook-housekeeper. Nurse Rogers and, later, Fräulein Bleichenbach took charge of the children. From 1933 Rosemary Moore came daily to do secretarial work for both Vera and Winifred. The household in Glebe Place would always represent for Vera the nearest thing to complete happiness that she had ever known.

The months before the baby's birth were occupied with a frenzy of cleaning and decorating, while Winifred also raced to complete her fourth novel, *Poor Caroline*. At four o'clock on the morning of 27 July, Shirley Vivian, named 'after Charlotte Brontë's "gallant little cavalier"', was delivered with the aid of quinine in a comparatively painless birth, closely observed by Winifred, who insisted on being present in case, she said, she ever needed to describe childbirth in a novel.

Relieved at the uncomplicated birth, Vera saw her daughter's flaxen hair for the first time as she sat up in bed to eat a poached egg. Her two children, she thought, 'might have come from families at the opposite ends of the earth'. In looks Shirley was her father's child. Describing her in June 1931 to George, who had seen little of his baby daughter since her birth, Vera wrote:

> . . . I think you will fall in love straight away with your little daughter – who is so entirely yours in every way, blue eyes, wavy fair hair, little pointed face, deeply cleft lips like yours – and I hope she will make up to you for such a tiresome and disappointing wife.

Shirley was a strong and healthy baby who managed in her first month to put on six ounces in one week, despite the intense heatwave which hit London in mid-August, when temperatures soared to 95 degrees. Vera spent several weeks recuperating in bed. By the end of August she was writing to Winifred, who was holidaying with Lady Rhondda in the south of France, that she was enjoying her prolonged bout of domesticity, though she wished that she could 'eliminate the constant wish to work, forget I had ever been ambitious, and cease chasing work-periods which don't materialize because other claims eat into them'.

Vera's literary output in the year following Shirley's birth was considerably reduced. George's absences at Cornell for four-and-a-half months of every year and Winifred's chaotic routine as a director of *Time and Tide* left most of the responsibility for running the household in Vera's hands. Two increasingly energetic and exhausting children, despite the services of a resident nurse, were a considerable drain on Vera's own energy and time. On some days, two hours in the evening, after the children had been bathed and put to bed, was the most she could spare for her writing. Even then, her journalism, her 'bright articles' as she called them, had always to take precedence over work on the book as they were the sole source of her earnings. Vera's financial contributions to the household had become essential as the high cost of running Glebe Place with its large staff put a severe strain on George's limited income. One proposal which George put forward to reduce their cost of living was either that Vera should be more 'careless and slovenly and slipshod' in her household responsibilities, or that she herself should assume some responsibility for the housework. This idea was received with indignation by Arthur Brittain and the matter soon erupted into an acrimonious dispute between father and son-in-law. 'I wish him to understand that you have by inheritance a position to maintain,' Mr Brittain told Vera, 'and I am not going to have you doing domestic servants' work to please him or anyone else.' The upshot of the row was that in July 1932 Mr Brittain made Vera an annuity of £500 which freed her from the slavish necessity to write articles, and enabled her to concentrate on *Testament of Youth*.

She could, however, use much of the time that she was tied to the house by the children in the first half of 1931, in collecting and organizing her primary material. Her diary provided an almost uninterrupted record of the first three years of war, while 'a great search at Oakwood Court – a hauling of boxes & ransacking of cupboards' produced her own and Edward's letters from the front, which Edith Brittain had carefully preserved. Both sides of the correspondence between Vera and Roland survived almost completely intact in Vera's possession, as Vera's letters to Roland had been periodically returned to her for safekeeping during his lifetime. She was determined to quote freely from these personal letters, convinced that they would bring back as nothing else could the essence of the period and the characters of her major protagonists.

In August Vera and George rented a furnished cottage in Ashville, Rustington, for the children's summer holiday. During a fortnight, however, there were only three days of fine weather, and Vera found herself cleaning the house from top to bottom to make it habitable. Following the Rustington disaster, Winifred generously offered to look after John and Shirley while Vera and George took a proper holiday at St Raphaël in the south of France. Mediterranean weather that summer was equally disappointing, though the rain cleared for their visit to Arles. Situated on the banks of the Rhône and surrounded by beautiful country, this Roman town utterly bewitched Vera.

But the holiday was cut short by a telegram from Winifred which summoned George back to London. In a typical piece of vagueness, he had forgotten to tell Vera that shortly before leaving for St Raphaël, he had put his name down as a possible parliamentary candidate for the Labour Party. The Brentford and Chiswick constituency party were now interested in interviewing him for selection, as a by-election looked imminent owing to the probable bankruptcy of the sitting member. He had for some time nurtured an ambition to enter the world of practical politics, though Vera was distinctly pessimistic about his chances. She was annoyed by George's decision to dash back to London. 'A fine gesture of availability,' she called it, 'which will, I imagine, be worth what it cost him – the price of a new dress-suit . . .'. Two days after his return, however, George was selected. Disgruntled but feeling obliged to offer him support, Vera too returned from St Raphaël, despite Winifred's exhortations that she should stay to enjoy the rest of the holiday alone.

In the event, George found himself fighting a general election. Ramsay MacDonald and his minority Labour Government felt forced to go to the country for a renewal of their mandate when in September Britain came off the Gold Standard. Vera had written fifty pages of *Testament of Youth* while in France, but for the next two months her time was given up to practical support for George. Much of the organization of his campaign fell to her, arranging public meetings and persuading people to speak on George's behalf. Autumn evenings were spent canvassing in and around Brentford and Chiswick High Street. On the platform George's academic background was all too evident. He lectured his audience in high-flown discourses on the virtues of constitutional democracy, rarely facing the central issue of the election which he described as 'the People versus the Bankers and their party'. Vera was the better speaker, always ready with a telling phrase or swift riposte.

The result was, in any case, a foregone conclusion. At the declaration of the poll on 27 October, the Conservative candidate, a wealthy mine-owner, was announced the winner. Throughout the country Labour suffered humiliating defeats, with all members of the former Cabinet except one losing their seats.

Winifred had combined electioneering for George (at one point she had taken over from Vera who had lost her voice) with active support for Charles Roden Buxton in the West Riding and Monica Whately in Hertfordshire. When she collapsed, three days after the election, it was naturally assumed that her illness was no more than a reaction to overwork and exhaustion. She convalesced at Clare Leighton's cottage in Monks Risborough for a week before returning to Chelsea. But on 23 November, she once again collapsed, complaining as before of sickness and a violent headache. This time the doctor prescribed a stay in a nursing home in Courtfield Gardens in Kensington for a series of protracted tests, which would do nothing more than establish Winifred's abnormally high blood-pressure.

For the time being Winifred's illness appeared to be no more than a temporary breakdown, although she spent more than a month at Courtfield Gardens. In Glebe Place meanwhile, Vera struggled to cope with Winifred's voluminous correspondence and to correct the proofs of her articles and stories, quarrelling with Mrs Holtby and Lady Rhondda when their presence at Winifred's bedside threatened the period of peace which seemed essential for her full recovery.

At the same time, Vera's agent, David Higham, was pressing for the delivery of *Testament of Youth*, concerned that the peak of interest in war books was long since past. 'It is boiling in my mind and I shall become hysterical if I am prevented from getting down to it very much longer', she had told Winifred. But as 1931 came to a close the prospects for completion of *Testament of Youth* looked far from rosy.

III

Vera began 1932 with feelings of loneliness and isolation which intensified as the year wore on. Winifred was well enough to move to a convalescent home in Sidmouth early in January, before returning to the cottage in Monks Risborough; George left for Cornell as usual at the end of the month. Then at the beginning of February John fell ill with chickenpox, which soon passed to Vera, though Shirley escaped infection. It was two weeks before she was well enough to take up her writing again, and before that she had to supervise the fumigation of the house and the taking of Lysol baths. 'Dismal and wretched', she depicted her monotonous routine in a letter to Winifred: 'Here it is so strange – writing always about the past in a present that has become a kind of vacuum, without friends, without incidents, without conversation. I seem to have the children all day on and off.'

Lack of incident did mean, however, that for the first time her writing could proceed without serious interruption. Undisturbed, her powers of concentration were intense. She would work three hours in the morning, three in the afternoon, reading and organizing material for the next day in the evening after the children had gone to bed. Her narrative had reached May 1917 and her return from Malta, and she was researching the chapter on her service in France. 'If Harry is with you,' she wrote to Winifred with one pressing enquiry, 'could you please ask him if he remembers what month of what year the Étaples mutiny was? . . . Obviously it is not the kind of thing that would be in the war histories . . . and of course I couldn't mention it at the time in my letters home.' Vera's description of the 'Battle of Eetapps' in *Testament of Youth* would be only the second account of the mutiny to appear in book form (the earlier one by Lady Angela Forbes, who ran a canteen at the base, had appeared in 1922).

Vera's main conceptual problem was one of objectivity: '. . . the great difficulty is to make enough of an autobiography *objective* to give sufficient variety to the prolonged subjectiveness.' To achieve a balance she consulted the *Annual Registers* in the British Museum and Chelsea Public Library for a blow-by-blow historical account of the war's progress and researched at the British Red Cross Society and in the Women's Work Collection at the Imperial War Museum (then still situated in Kensington). The *Observer*'s reports of the Italian campaign were also useful; and among other memoirs of the war she found Sassoon's particularly influential.

She badly missed Winifred's company, the stimulus she always gave to Vera's writing, and the constructive criticisms she made of her work. In her diary Vera spoke of lonely weeks of writing: at times it seemed like a throwback to the misery and isolation of the war. She had described her 'anti-solitude complex' in a letter to Winifred the previous year: 'When I am alone I always remember all the times that I was lonely during and after the War – in Malta, after Roland was dead . . . ; in Oxford, after everyone else was dead and before I met you.'

Vera's situation, with Winifred's convalescence looking more protracted and George away until June, served to emphasize her lack of any other close friend to confide in or turn to. On a sudden impulse, at the beginning of April, she wrote to Phyllis Bentley, a woman she barely knew, who was just beginning to enjoy a runaway critical and commercial success with her novel *Inheritance*, inviting her to stay at 19 Glebe Place when she came to London.

Winifred had recommended *Inheritance* to Vera: 'It is *magnificent*. Strong, human, abounding in vital characters, passionate, rich, *really* something worth praising'. Vera agreed: 'it reminded me of *Clayhanger* and also *The Mill on the Floss* and stood the comparison extremely well.' Winifred, back in Courtfield Gardens undergoing yet more tests, painted a depressing picture of Phyllis's home life in Halifax, put upon by a demanding mother and bullying brother. Phyllis's 'grey life', Winifred and Vera agreed, needed and deserved 'compensation by success', but even Winifred was somewhat taken aback by Vera's invitation to Phyllis, and Phyllis herself admitted to some puzzlement.

However, she accepted the invitation and arrived in London on 6 May, for a visit timed to coincide with a meeting with her publisher, Victor Gollancz, and various speaking and literary engagements.

The eventual breakdown of Vera's attempt to establish an intimate friendship with Phyllis Bentley reveals all the barely concealed frustrations and pressures behind the writing of *Testament of Youth*; it also says something about Vera's difficulty in sustaining close relationships, Winifred aside, with other women. Her relationships with Phyllis and later with Margaret Storm Jameson both ended with considerable acrimony to the extent that neither woman could bring herself to discuss Vera in later years. (As Phyllis confided to one correspondent about her relations with Vera after 1933, 'we always behaved well to each other in public, but on my side at least I no longer felt friendship but dread'.)

In her autobiography, published thirty years later, Phyllis recognized the part that the 'severe private tensions' in Vera's life at the time had played in the failure of their friendship. Vera was writing her book 'through every kind of harassment and interruption', while Phyllis admitted that she herself was suffering from a crushing inferiority complex. Despite the success of *Inheritance* – which sold three editions alone before publication – she lacked confidence. In London in May 1932 she was still, on her own admission, 'thoroughly provincial', and felt a deep sense of sexual inadequacy and lack of personal fulfilment.

Born into a mill-owning family in Halifax, West Yorkshire, in 1894, Phyllis had taken a degree at Cheltenham Ladies' College in 1914. She had surmounted her family's intense opposition to her earning her own living, and worked in three West Riding libraries in the 1920s, classifying and cataloguing. By 1923 she had also published four books. Her elder brother, Norman, resented his sister's refusal to be content to stay at home with their mother, and as Phyllis recalled, he regarded her as 'clumsy, gawky, ill-kempt and ill-mannered, and . . . never hesitated to tell me so'.

Her confidence in her powers as a writer, however, had never deserted her, despite a period in the Twenties when she was unable to find a publisher for her work. In 1930 Victor Gollancz published her novel *Trio*, signalling the beginning of a long and mutually profitable association. Phyllis had long been fascinated by the history of the West Riding and this provided the inspiration for her next and widely praised novel, *Inheritance*, a saga of the textile industry in the area, following the fortunes of one family from 1812 to 1931. Her fellow Yorkshireman, J.B. Priestley, opened his review of the book with the words, 'A Promise has been fulfilled'.

Two days after Phyllis's arrival at Glebe Place, Vera gave a party for her.

Among the guests were Ellen Wilkinson, a regular contributor to *Time and Tide*, David Higham, the *Manchester Guardian* journalist Violet Scott-James, and the writer Naomi Mitchison whom Phyllis had been particularly keen to meet. To Vera's surprise Phyllis appeared elegantly dressed in black and silver. In a tone of breathtaking condescension, the fashion-conscious hostess noted in her diary:

> After the oranges and greens of the previous days, and Winifred's remarks about her clothes being terribly provincial and all hung about with beads and things, it was a pleasant surprise; also her face seemed better looking as on Saturday I hinted gently how becoming her horn-rimmed spectacles were, and she thereafter abandoned the pince-nez and stopped looking like a school-mistress. She looked animated too and happily expectant, like a pleased child.

Phyllis, in awe of Vera's social poise, was quite willing to be patronized socially by her more worldly hostess, while Vera enjoyed the vicarious pleasure of Phyllis's reception by London's literary world. At a Gollancz 'At Home' later in the week, to Vera's unconcealed envy, Phyllis was lionized by Priestley and Rose Macaulay. With the glowing pride of a patron for her protégée, Vera was gratified to see Phyllis's increasing confidence and assurance in the face of such attention. Returning home to Halifax at the end of the week, Phyllis expressed her heartfelt appreciation of all Vera's efforts on her behalf. Vera had, she told her, transformed her whole outlook on life.

It was during Phyllis's second visit to Glebe Place for a longer stay on 22 May that the underlying tensions began to show. The results of Winifred's tests still proved inconclusive and she had at last been pronounced fit enough to return to Chelsea. In Winifred's bedroom the three women talked late into the night. Phyllis confessed her admiration for Winifred and Vera's conversation, for Vera's 'gift of life' and her prettiness, while Vera talked about *Testament of Youth* and explained that true fulfilment for her would only come with the publication of a great book.

On Sunday 29 May, however, Vera recorded the first note of discord in her diary.

> Dispute over lunch about respective merit of critical and creative qualities in literature ... and the relation of both to inspiration and sincerity. For some reason or other it developed into a furious argument and ended in a row, with Phyllis and I both losing our tempers. I told her that she put *everything* in her novels and called that creative, and she said in retaliation (though she hasn't

read anything of mine except articles) that my over-critical non-creativeness was the great difference between her and myself. This struck hard because I'd been struggling all morning with a particularly vile part of Chapter IX [' "This Loneliest Hour" '], and I suddenly felt so near to tears I had to get up and pretend to play with John. I said loudly to Winifred on the stairs that P. was 'damned superior' and then P. came to my bedroom and tried to apologize for being horrid about my book, but I wouldn't have it and took John off to Oakwood Court . . .

Later that day they were reconciled, but Phyllis had touched upon a sensitive nerve – Vera's fear that she was nothing more than a competent journalist who lacked a more creative and imaginative faculty.

At the root of Vera and Phyllis's incompatibility was the fact that, much as Vera might patronize Phyllis socially, it was Phyllis, secure in her literary success, who represented the kind of recognition that Vera was still struggling to achieve. Nor was Phyllis willing to accord Vera equal status as a writer. As George acutely observed, Vera treated Phyllis like a country cousin and Phyllis retaliated by treating Vera as a negligible writer. Phyllis might feel in awe of Vera's Oxford degree, envious of her social poise, and of her husband and children, but on one point she was convinced of her superiority: 'I thought I knew how to write novels and fiction-reviews better than anyone in Glebe Place.'

The desire for friendship, though, was mutual. Vera was 'the first really attractive and desired person' to offer Phyllis friendship, while Phyllis was the only person who could understand and sympathize with the extent of disruption to Vera's writing brought about by day-to-day domestic tribulations. As she told Vera, she had finished the deathbed scene in her novel *Carr* in the lavatory, as it was the only place in the house in which she could escape from the incessant chatter about the joint for dinner. For her part, Vera encouraged Phyllis to be more outgoing in company, to put the loneliness of her childhood behind her, and 'make gestures of seeking' towards someone.

There were problems of conflicting personalities to overcome. Vera was possessive and demanding and in constant need of reassurance. Phyllis's blunt Yorkshire manner – 'that mixture of stiff shyness and determined downrightness', as Vera described it – did not mix well with Vera's self-absorption and her tendency to take every criticism as a personal slight. On both sides the relationship had something of the intensity and obsessiveness of an adolescent crush. As Phyllis wrote to Vera after she left London on 9 July:

I can't understand why you should still think me reserved to you. At the beginning of our acquaintance, yes; life had taught me that reticence and surface solidity was my safest way, especially with an alarmingly clever, brilliant, witty person like yourself. But now it seems that I have turned my whole heart inside out for you to see, and touch healingly. Perhaps not the last tiny bit; nobody will ever see that . . . I think about you almost hourly. I know all your frocks by heart . . . You have entered into my heart (said she, being sentimental and not caring two hoots) and show every sign of remaining there, despite a few quarrels which I feel we may sometimes explode into . . .

IV

The news that two publishers, Gollancz and Jarrold, were pressing to see the completed chapters of *Testament of Youth* temporarily lifted Vera's spirits. Phyllis had told Victor Gollancz about *Testament of Youth* before leaving London – 'and as she is his best-seller of the moment she has a good deal of weight . . .' – and he had written to Vera asking to read it. But, much as Vera wanted Gollancz to publish her book, she was unwilling to submit an incomplete manuscript, though she promised him that he would be the first to see it when it was finished.

She was reading early chapters to Winifred who found them moving and well written, despite Vera's dissatisfaction – 'I had imagined it so much better than it is'. She took Parts I and II with her to revise when she, Winifred and the children went to Sidmouth for their summer holiday on 26 July. Apart from a few showery days the weather was better than it had been at Rustington the year before, and the children were able to spend hours playing on the beach. Shirley was a dynamo of energy and difficult to control. Vera was at a loss to explain what she called her 'adventurous rashness', and could only suppose that Shirley had inherited her 'terrifying traits' from George's mother. Shirley celebrated her second birthday while on holiday by biting a piece out of a glass she had been given to drink from; she scaled the walls of her cot and tumbled to the floor, and was continually sick in public places much to her mother's consternation and embarrassment. George, who had returned from America a month earlier, came down to Sidmouth for a few days, bringing with him the additional encumbrance of the cantankerous Reverend Catlin.

Returning to London to the hottest weather for twenty-one years, Vera was in despair about her book. Her depression was compounded by a letter from Phyllis, enclosing a copy of a new novel, *The Lost Generation* by Ruth Holland. This, Phyllis feared, anticipated Vera's theme in *Testament of Youth*. With considerable trepidation, Vera read the novel, only to be relieved to find that similarities to her own book were incidental. Although the chief character of *The Lost Generation* had lost a lover and a husband in the war, the book was 'quite without the current-events-of-25-years background that is so far the chief characteristic of mine'.

Nevertheless, *The Lost Generation* did bring home to Vera the fact that if *Testament of Youth* were not completed soon, another woman might publish a memoir of her war experience that would deprive *Testament of Youth* of much of its impact and originality. But it was not easy to hurry the book when, as she told Winifred, she was 'bored with it, and have lost heart'. She felt that with the three postwar chapters still to go, the book was already overlong, while Naomi Mitchison's comment, in a review of *The Lost Generation*, that writers should not look back to the war any longer, was even more discouraging.

It was Winifred, as usual, who gave her the reassurance to continue. From Cottingham, she wrote:

> What can I say to make you believe in your book as I believe in it? When I read those early chapters . . . I felt 'This is *it*'. This is the thing she has been waiting to do. This is the justification of those long years of waiting.
>
> That you are bored, I'm not in the least surprised. This looking up, verifying and copying would always bore a creative artist. Personally, I'm not in the least afraid of other people's books being like yours. What other woman writing has *both* your experience *and* your political training? But I do want you for *your* sake to get it finished soon, so as not to be bored and depressed by it any longer.

John and Shirley were sent to stay at a nursery boarding school in Burford in the Cotswolds, as Vera grappled with the mountain of material for the final section of the book. She was cheered by the typist's wish to type *Testament of Youth* quickly as she was finding the story so enthralling, and wanted to know what happened next. Vera finished chapter X on 22 September; at last the end of the book seemed in sight.

An obstacle soon presented itself, however, which necessitated rewriting and revision of the war chapters.

Rather late in the day, Vera had discovered that the right to publish letters written to her by Roland, Victor and Geoffrey belonged to the dead men's families. She had already preserved the anonymity of Victor and Geoffrey by putting them in the book without mentioning their surnames. She had now also to paraphrase many of the letters which she had used, rather than quote from them directly.

She had read *But It Still Goes On*, Robert Graves's postscript to *Goodbye to All That*, in which he related how he had spent a year repudiating libel actions arising from his autobiography. Vera was beset by terrible visions of a similar fate – of 'fury from the Brittains, from Buxton, from Oxford, from St Thomas's, from all dons, from all nurses, and so *ad infinitum*.'

Her greatest worry was the Leightons who, she gathered, disapproved of both her political views and her lifestyle. They had moved out to Bishop's Stortford in Hertfordshire and Vera had seen little of them since her marriage. Clare advised writing a flattering letter to her parents, asking for permission to quote some of Roland's poetry; the letters, she told Vera, she would never get permission to use. 'Spent most of Thursday composing the letter,' wrote Vera in her diary on 10 November, 'but don't really expect to get the permission. Anyhow shall have to rewrite large sections; the whole thing has made me feel like hell.'

To her considerable surprise she received an unexpectedly accommodating letter from Marie Leighton giving permission to quote from the poems (she would later relent and allow her to use Roland's letters too). This seemed an all the more remarkable turnabout on Mrs Leighton's part, given the unspoken rivalry that had once existed between Vera and Mrs Leighton about Roland's poetry, but as Clare explained, her mother's benevolent attitude towards *Testament of Youth* arose from her belief that the time for war books was long since past and 'that nobody wanted to read that sort of stuff nowadays . . .'. In any case, Mrs Leighton confided to Clare, it was common knowledge in literary circles that *Testament of Youth*'s publication was being financed by Lady Rhondda! 'I think I'd better lie low & write nothing more about the book to the old Leightons till it's actually out', Vera told Winifred.

Vera had agreed to give a lecture on 'Why Current Events Matter to Us' to the Luncheon Club in Halifax at the end of November, which allowed her to make a long-awaited visit to Phyllis at her home. The strain of rewriting, however, had begun to tell on Vera, and after a five-hour train journey she arrived in Halifax on 29 November feeling tired and ill. The next day she stayed in bed until eleven, and although unable to eat any lunch she gave a confident, effective lecture and received 'a tremendous ovation'. The following morning Phyllis took her on a strenuous cross-country walk across the moors to Haworth Parsonage. Vera was already alarmed about 'all the awful legal bother over *T of Y*', and Phyllis, a Brontë authority, did nothing to allay her anxieties by regaling her with stories about the threatened libel actions with which Mrs Gaskell had been confronted after the publication of her *Life* of Charlotte. Vera was by now close to collapse. She was sick and unable to eat, and thought for a time that she might be pregnant. After a day in bed she decided, much to Phyllis's disappointment, to cut short her visit, and returned to London.

When she reached Glebe Place her doctor diagnosed acute gastritis and colo-cystitis. The emotional and physical demands of *Testament of Youth* were exacting their punishment, and Vera thought her illness 'may be a sort of alternative to a nervous breakdown'. For a week she remained in bed, 'very queer at first; floating on a cloud, quite light-headed at times . . .'.

In this delirious state she wrote two 'very rude & reckless' letters to Phyllis, which are embargoed with the rest of the Bentley papers until 2002. It is, therefore, only possible to speculate on what they contain, but it seems likely that, ill and overwrought, Vera dwelt with obsessive resentment on what she regarded as Phyllis's patronizing attitude towards her as a writer. Phyllis was deeply distressed. She retaliated by replying that the letters were too wild for her to understand, and asked Vera not to write again until she was better. Vera apologized, admitted that she was in the wrong, and cursed what she called 'one of my idiotic flare-ups'. With Winifred the inevitable go-between, the two women continued an erratic correspondence. At Christmas they exchanged presents, and it would be another three months before their friendship finally foundered.

On Boxing Day Vera resumed her work on the final chapter of *Testament of Youth*. She had recovered from her gastric attack, but the row with Phyllis had left her feeling miserable and depressed. She railed against George for going off to dinner with Ethel Mannin, leaving her to cope with the domestic chaos at Glebe Place, where the nurse was ill, and the maids up in arms about their time off.

Despite their troubled personal relations, Phyllis played a major part in finding *Testament of Youth* its American publisher. At the end of January 1933, she invited Winifred to Claridge's to meet Harold Latham of Macmillan, who had accepted Winifred's *Mandoa, Mandoa!* for publication in the United States, and who had also been responsible for the American edition of *Inheritance*. Latham intimated that he would be interested in reading Vera's book, and between them Winifred and Phyllis persuaded Vera to show him the nine chapters which she had revised. In his memoirs, Latham remembered how 'a tiny woman with shining eyes and an immense amount of vitality came to see me one day at Brown's Hotel' bringing with her a 'clean, beautifully typed manuscript'. Within a week Latham had accepted *Testament of Youth* for publication by Macmillan in the United States.

Vera felt a pang of guilt for not having let Victor Gollancz see the manuscript first, as she had promised him. On hearing that it had been accepted by Macmillan he immediately asked to see it. Meanwhile, she was writing the last twenty pages. Just before midnight on 16 February she wrote the final sentence of *Testament of Youth*. There was no one to share her sense of elation and relief. George was at Cornell, and Winifred had returned to Cottingham to her dying father's bedside. In a state of considerable anxiety while nursing John and Shirley through whooping cough, Vera awaited Gollancz's verdict.

On the morning of 21 February, she awoke certain that a letter from Gollancz lay on the hall table. Nevertheless, despite her pent-up feelings, she made herself get dressed first, 'for the sake of discipline'. Downstairs she read:

Dear Miss Brittain,

I have read *Testament of Youth* with the greatest admiration. It is a book of great beauty, and even greater courage, and I shall be very proud to publish it. In places, I confess, it moved me intolerably . . .

v

As Victor Gollancz informed Daphne du Maurier, 'the essence of publishing is to "take the tide"'. He had already taken the tide of war books with the publication in 1928 of R.C. Sherriff's play, *Journey's End*, which had enjoyed prodigious sales, but he correctly surmised that much of the appeal of *Testament of Youth* would derive from its relevance to the increasingly tense political situation in Europe in 1933.

Victor Gollancz Ltd had been formed at the end of 1927 and after only five years was already a commanding presence on the publishing scene. This was due in part to Gollancz's acute business sense and to what he called his *mana* (his power to influence people), but also to his intense and lavish advertising style. His announcements of forthcoming books in literary pages were bolder and bigger than those of any other publishing house, while Gollancz book-jackets, designed by Stanley Morison with large black lettering on yellow, were startling attention-grabbers. Although by 1933 Gollancz numbered among his authors the distinguished names of Daphne du Maurier, Elizabeth Bowen and Dorothy Sayers, the slant of his list, three years before he founded the Left Book Club, was already moving towards books on politics, economics and sociology. To Vera, Gollancz had long seemed the most appropriate publisher for *Testament of Youth*; no other publisher, she felt, would be as sympathetic to the political and social ideas outlined in the postwar section of the book.

By the end of the first week of March, at the expense of both meals and sleep, Vera had completed the revision of the last three chapters and had sent them to Gollancz. She had hardly any time to relax before she had to rush off to Oxford to take care of a responsibility she particularly resented, her father-in-law. The Reverend Catlin, who had grown increasingly difficult, was now incapable of living in lodgings in Oxford and needed the full-time care and attention which only a nursing home could provide. Not only had Vera to fund his stay in a home, she had also to find one which catered for his expensive tastes. Having spent a day travelling up and down the Banbury Road in Oxford, interviewing doctors, matrons and nurses, she settled Reverend Catlin in a home which appeared to be to his liking. Less than a week later, however, the old man was voicing his extreme antipathy to the home and its inmates, and demanding to be moved. The onset of another domestic crisis was too much for Vera. She collapsed once again from nervous exhaustion, and it was left to Mrs Brittain to go to Oxford to placate him.

As her strength returned, Vera could derive pleasure from the compliment paid *Testament of Youth* by Gollancz's lawyer, Harold Rubinstein, who had been reading the book for libel. He wrote of the book's nobility, 'particularly in your treatment of the "Resurrection" – that produced a kind of katharsis I recall from my discovery of the *Odyssey*.' Alterations to *Testament of Youth* mainly took the form of substituting more moderate adjectives for the harsh ones Vera had used to describe St Thomas's and other hospitals in which she had served. With her usual pessimistic outlook, even at this late stage she feared that fate would intervene in some way to prevent the book from being published. But when objections did arise, they came from the most unexpected quarter, and from two people from whom Vera might have expected more understanding.

Before returning to Cornell, George had written Vera a moving letter of appreciation. *Testament of Youth*, he wrote, was 'Powerful, significant, important'. He continued:

for me it is oppressive also – to it I am an outsider, intruding shamefaced, feeling very unworthy, painfully unworthy to the verge of tears. After all Roland is entitled to you; all that is beautiful in love is between him and you. All this I foresaw must come from the book, and I have been right – perhaps shunned it – yet I am glad – for your book is death unless it leads on to that courageous determination that is life . . .

He had told Winifred, however, that she was a 'god-damn fool' to have agreed to her own portrayal in the book.

In April, Vera took John and Shirley to Worthing for the Easter holiday, and it was here that she received an 'almost extinguishing blow'. From America George had returned the copy she had sent him of the last chapter, ' "Another Stranger" '. He had scored out whole pages, and had scrawled in the margins 'intolerable', 'horrible', 'pretty terrible . . .'. In a frenzy of misery and despair she wrote immediately to Dorothy Horsman, the Gollancz Publications Manager, asking her to return the chapter to her before printing, and in a six-page letter to Winifred poured out her feelings of defeat and desolation:

> I suppose I am seeing everything out of proportion . . . But something in me seems to have broken – some element of faith and hope & confidence that I had, at least in some measure, achieved in my book what I had set out to do for my generation. It is bitterness itself that this book – which I meant to be a lamentation of David over my generation's dead and a brave Odyssey of its survivors – should appear, to [the person] most dear to me, to be nothing but a source of wounding and exasperation . . . Is a piece of work that I thought noble and universal – & in which I tried to use the personal only to illustrate the general thesis – really only self-advertising and mean? . . .
>
> Sometimes now I feel near to a sort of breaking point of desperation as if I were doomed to cause trouble to myself & others however much I want to be courageous and constructive . . . I really think I should have committed suicide long ago if I hadn't got you with your unfailing faith and understanding.

The next day she received a letter from George and was somewhat mollified to read that he thought the chapter 'on the whole good', but she did not appreciate his comment that 'the book does not drop off at the end'. 'I wonder why he thought it would', she asked Winifred.

George believed that his appearance in Vera's autobiography would hold him up to ridicule from both his academic and political colleagues, and that the exposure of his personal life would, as he put it, make 'my critics rejoice and my friends writhe'. He was already, so he believed, the victim of misunderstanding which prevented him either from receiving due recognition from an English university, or from being taken seriously by the Labour Party. Convinced that publicity from *Testament of Youth* would have a disastrous effect upon his career, he asked Vera to remove all references to his politics, religion, profession, friends, academic achievements and family background. 'In other words', Vera told Winifred, 'to make him, in comparison with Roland & even with Victor, a complete cipher, & supply the reader with no reason whatever why I should decide to marry him'.

Inevitably it was Winifred who now stepped in to heal the rift between Vera and George, and in an extraordinarily direct letter from Cottingham, where she was helping to settle her father's estate, she attempted to put Vera's point of view.

First she suggested that the picture of George in *Testament of Youth* might actually do him some good in countering his reputation for being inhuman and pompous.

> Certain things have been written about you ... that you were a clergyman's son, a feminist, a philosopher; that you were in the army; that you wrote brilliant and moving letters; that you showed extraordinary generosity towards the living and the dead. Is this intolerable? Is this ridiculous?

She explained how *Testament of Youth* formed an integral part of Vera's life:

> You see, to her this is no ordinary book, no task to be executed well or ill. It represents her whole life and purpose, and she had hoped that, especially to you, it would reveal the intention of her life, the meaning of her activities, and compensate for periods in which she has been difficult and self-absorbed.

Replying to George's claim that he had already subordinated his interests in the marriage 'for long and no little', Winifred, the closest observer of their marriage, delivered her Parthian shot:

> ... but surely all marriages, as all friendships, involve mutual sacrifice in payment for their mutual gain. If you have altered your way of life, so has Vera. The sparse literary product of the past seven years has not entirely been unrelated to housekeeping, children and your interests. She has corrected your proofs and typed your articles; she has done a million chores of varying kinds; she has taken complete responsibility for your children. Surely this is a fair *quid pro quo* for your six months in (or out of) America?

It is difficult not to feel some sympathy for George's position, though wrapped up as usual in his own plans he failed to gauge the effect that his demands would have upon Vera's already fragile state of mind. He knew that for her the story of their courtship and engagement was the essential symbolic ending for her book, and that for no one would she have agreed to omit it completely. However, with both publishers pressurizing her for the finished manuscript, she could not contemplate 'a prolonged wrangle for weeks across the Atlantic', and so spent 'a miserable two days' removing the most obvious identifying detail, and also abbreviating his name to 'G'. She consoled herself that '. . . to spoil 20 pp is not to spoil the whole book, & I daresay to someone who doesn't know what was there before they aren't as spoilt as much as they seem to me'. After taking the revised chapter to a local typing agency she caught a bus to High Salvington 'and walked on the Downs for 2 solid hours till I'd walked off a good deal of my misery and fury'.

But George could never forget what he called 'that intolerable piece of publicity', and forty-five years later when *Testament of Youth* was being republished, he insisted that what little anonymity he had been granted should be preserved. He delivered a furious onslaught on Gollancz, demanding that a note be appended to the original contract to the effect that 'the publisher undertakes that the name of Sir George Catlin shall not appear in any preface, introduction, or any other matter . . .'.

Second only to George's lack of understanding about *Testament of Youth* were Phyllis's comments. Perhaps they cut even deeper, for only to Winifred had Vera confided more about her struggles with the book and her hopes for it.

Gollancz had asked Phyllis, as one of his foremost authors, to write the description for the dust-jacket. He was astounded by the result. 'But she simply hasn't seen the book! She doesn't even seem to have been moved by it!' he told Vera. To Vera it was clear that what she called Phyllis's 'rigidly censorious attitude towards all that I am and do' had seeped into her notice of the book, making it sound 'like the grudging recommendation by a League of Nations Chairman of an inept amateur speaker for whom he was trying to do his best'. In a letter which followed, Phyllis confessed to Vera – and one wonders with what deliberation she set out to antagonize her – that while she had enjoyed the early parts of the book, the provincial background and the battle to get to Oxford, she had not found the war sections as moving as she had expected.

'But how well you write my child', Phyllis continued before going on to discuss John and Shirley's recovery from whooping cough, and what *she* had been doing on the day the Germans shelled Scarborough.

Phyllis's belittlement of her book brought all Vera's stored-up resentment towards her flooding to the surface and, in six closely typed pages, she vented her sense of Phyllis's disloyalty. 'Are you in the habit', she asked, 'of writing to people and saying "I'm so sorry, but your account of your brother's death ... didn't move me at all?" '

> For you are a colossal egoist, Phyllis; the fact may be excused and even justified by the further fact that you are also a magnificent novelist, but it does seem to me at least possible that you have charity and compassion and understanding only for the creatures that you yourself invent.

Vera ended her letter with a reminder of what their friendship might have been, and with an unpleasant gibe at Phyllis's unmarried and childless state:

> I didn't think it would all end like this, did you? It does seem sad that the two of us, comparatively enlightened, comparatively civilized, have not been able to make a better thing of friendship than this. I meant it to be the beginning of so many things for you ... I wanted my household with its freedom, and its warmth and its gaiety – yes, and its problems too – to become a second home where you would always be welcome; for I know that however celebrated a person may be ... the later years of life especially are apt to be lonely for someone who hasn't a household and family of their own.

And with a sense of dramatic finality Vera signed the letter 'Goodbye'. It would be some years before either Vera or Phyllis could overcome their sense of mutual resentment and bear to be in the same room as each other. 'We decided in 1933', Phyllis admitted later, 'that it would be wisest for us to stand at a little distance . . .'.

In place of Phyllis's jacket description, Gollancz asked Winifred to write a notice, to be published anonymously. She spoke of the book's universal quality, and concluded that 'When the final verdict upon our age is passed, this testament of stricken but unbroken youth must be accepted as evidence of its temper'.

'What supreme piece of good fortune gave me, I wonder, the miracle of your friendship', wrote Vera to Winifred on reading this. Winifred's acute understanding of the book's theme served to remind Vera once more of the extraordinary empathy that existed between them and of the irreplaceable nature of Winifred's friendship.

In the aftermath of the dust-jacket debacle, Vera received two letters from Phyllis containing 'vaguely alarming allegations' of what she had written in *Testament of Youth* about people Phyllis knew, which 'jarred on some sore places in my mind and turned my sympathies in directions where they were not intended to go'. At the same time Phyllis wrote to Winifred feverishly protesting that Vera's portrait of her was a gross misrepresentation, but Winifred, with her imperturbable temperament and loyalty to Vera, was unruffled. 'I feel so flattered by the portrait of a noble, self-effacing, thoughtful & unselfish Winifred . . .', she replied, 'that I can't find any connection between the creature and myself at all . . . So do calm down your boiling blood, my lamb'.

George, hypersensitive by now, warned Vera that the Holtbys would object to her references to Winifred in the postwar chapter, 'Survivors Not Wanted', and that they might also adversely prejudice Winifred's friends and colleagues. Vera conceded that Phyllis and George were probably right, and asked Gollancz to return also chapter X so she could 'tone down' her account of their first meeting at Mr Cruttwell's, and remove Winifred's actual speech at the stormy Somerville debate. '. . . We understand each other so well & each knows so exactly how the other *really* feels', she wrote to Winifred, 'that a situation seems to us piquant and amusing . . . that to someone else might seem very different. It really would be worse than death to me if people thought . . . that I was making use of this book to be slyly spiteful towards you, my dearest of dear companions'.

After labouring so long, Vera desperately needed her book to be a major success. She had relied on support and approbation from George and Phyllis, and their unexpected criticism had sapped her confidence and left her suffering 'from a kind of persecution mania'. 'You I can count on, I know', she told Winifred before proceeding to list once more some of the sources from which she anticipated attack and criticism. 'My relations will hate it . . . and none of father's family will speak to me again (not that that is any loss!)'. Somerville would loathe it, the nursing profession detest it, and her St Monica contemporaries '– particularly Stella & Cora – will be furious'. George's friends would disapprove, there would be outrage in Buxton ('I don't particularly mind this'), and 'The Leightons are certain to object to something I have said or done about Roland, & the Thurlows & Richardsons will hate Geoffrey and Victor being in the book at all'. 'Somehow or other I *must* be with you while I'm correcting the proofs', she implored Winifred. '[I] shall need your judgment on a hundred matters of taste & caution'.

To those who shared her own personal losses of the war, Vera sent pre-publication copies and anxiously awaited their reactions. She had already attempted to explain the purpose of *Testament of Youth* to her parents, still after fifteen years locked into a world of mourning for Edward, but with limited success. From Cecilia Thurlow, Geoffrey's older sister, came a warm and affectionate letter reminding Vera of their meeting at the Fishmongers' Hall years before, and praising the portrait of her brother as 'very accurate' and 'very moving'. As for the Leightons, Clare promised to see that her mother 'takes it all right, if there's any need at all to guide her emotionally through it'. Clare herself burst into violent crying on first reading the book, much to the astonishment of Noel Brailsford, the distinguished socialist writer and journalist with whom she lived. 'Noel threatens to hide the book until I'm steadier', she told Vera.

In the remaining weeks before publication, for the first time in more than three years, Vera felt able to relax. Despite the sense of loss she felt now that her friendship with Phyllis had been irreparably breached, she was buoyed by the praise she had received from those who had already read *Testament of Youth*. This had given her a new-found confidence that in the future 'there'll always be publishers (and therefore presumably a public) for what I want to write'.

On 23 July, Vera took a holiday in Hardelot-Plage, eight miles from the scene of her wartime service at Étaples, which she had felt it inadvisable to revisit while writing lest it play tricks on her memory. Her party originally comprised George, Winifred and Violet Scott-James, but after a week she and Winifred were left to continue the holiday together. They explored the countryside around Hardelot before moving to the Somme country, where they visited the battlefields, and once again the cemetery at Louvencourt where Roland was buried. At Étaples itself, Vera stood on the humped, ragwort-covered earth which was all that remained to mark the site of the huts of 24 General. Across the fields Vera recognized where the German ward had once stood, and found it oddly disconcerting that it should now be so quiet and still 'when I remembered it so full of hurry and anxiety, apprehension and pain'.

Back in London on 15 August, Vera's mounting excitement in the days before publication was palpable, as Gollancz's advertisements for the book started to appear. On 28 August, resplendent in bright mustard yellow, *Testament of Youth* was published.

'Never did I imagine that *Testament* would inspire such great praise at such great length, or provoke – in smaller doses – so much abuse', Vera wrote in her diary after a week of reviews. Compton Mackenzie, Pamela Hinkson, John Brophy, and Cecil Roberts, among others, had been unstinting in their praise. Storm Jameson, reviewing *Testament of Youth* in the *Sunday Times*, wrote:

> Its mere pressure on mind and senses makes it unforgettable. The cumulative effect of these pages, on a contemporary, is indescribably troubling and exalting. To later generations . . . it must convey the weight and

the nervous and spiritual excitement of an experience which, though it only struck them a glancing blow, intimately concerns them.

The reviewer in the *Times Literary Supplement* noted with approval:

> In the important things of the story – tragic, noble, and in the end not without consolation – there is, in spite (or perhaps because) of its unshrinking frankness, no failure of taste, no irreverence or theatricality in the lifting of the veil from past sorrows.

Naturally, it was the few adverse reviews that distressed Vera far more than the favourable ones had encouraged her. James Agate in the *Daily Express* was particularly vicious. 'A book for blue stockings by one of them', he wrote. 'Marred by a great fault – the inability to be content with the tragic and to refrain from fussing about it . . . The reader is affected as at the sight of a woman crying in the street.'

But the most sustained attack on *Testament of Youth* came from Margaret R.B. Shaw in the *New English Weekly*. Under a punning title, 'Vera – Sed Non Veritas', she criticized 'the tale of an "Unsophisticated Young Thing from Buxton" ' for having more of literature than life about it.

> Miss Brittain seems to have taken particular pains to demonstrate to her readers that the peculiar temperament with which nature endowed her has acted on each and every occasion of her life as a barrier between herself and the rest of her fellows, forcing her to see the common experiences that all her generation passed through, before and after and during the War, as one who stands in isolation (and – as she would have it – in *superior* isolation). In Buxton, genteel and frivolous town, she has a serious mind; in Oxford, city austere and academic, she has a pretty taste in dress; as a VAD during the War, she is vexed by association with thick-ankled and rough-handed colleagues . . . in Oxford, once more, when the War is over, she censures her fellow-students because they do not appear to recognize that she stands amongst them as one who has had a 'first-hand' experience of something that they have only read about.

If she needed comfort, however, Vera had only to turn to the welter of appreciation flooding in from critics and public alike. She was especially pleased to receive a letter from the irascible Irish writer, St John Ervine, a friend of Winifred's, whom they had visited in Sidmouth in the summer of 1932. It was all the more welcome as he admitted that *Testament of Youth* had engendered growing respect in him for its author and had reversed the previously low opinion he had had of her. He had thought Vera 'a mediocre crank', partly because of her insistence on calling herself Miss Brittain instead of Mrs Catlin ('fancy fussing about *that* when the world is in the mess it is!'). Although he dismissed the early pages as 'old stuff' and thought the last part nothing more than ephemeral politics (a view with which some modern readers might find sympathy), he nevertheless delivered a resounding paean of praise to the rest:

> It is a great feat to write about the War which played such havoc with your personal life and your youth without squealing in a neurotic rage. Very few men have performed it. Even Blunden does not quite pull it off . . . You have courage and determination and a remarkable power of endurance . . . Your sense of humour is not, I should say, your strong point – you couldn't Miss Brittain yourself if it were – but your sense of justice makes up for its lack . . . You moved me to tears with many finely-told chapters of your story . . . The futility of the War becomes clearer and clearer as your tale of young men dying unfolds itself, and I share King-Hall's feeling that here is a superb account of what the War did to our generation. I like your book enormously, and I hope it will be widely read.

VI

Testament of Youth was widely read: the sales on the day of publication exceeded the total of 3,000 copies which Vera's previous five books had sold. Within a week the first impression of 5,000 copies had been exhausted and by the middle of September, 15,000 copies had been purchased. It enjoyed similar success in America in October, where on its day of publication alone 11,000 copies were bought. In twelve impressions in England, up to the outbreak of the Second World War, it would sell 120,000 copies.

Everywhere Vera went, she noted with pride, *Testament of Youth* was being talked about with intense interest. She would have been particularly gratified to learn that it had kept Virginia Woolf out of bed until she finished it, and that she thought it 'a very good book of its sort'. 'I am reading with extreme greed a book by Vera Brittain,' she recorded in her diary on 2 September:

> Not that I much like her. A stringy metallic mind, with I suppose, the sort of taste I should dislike in real life. But her story, told in detail, without reserve, of the war, and how she lost lover and brother, and dabbled her hands in entrails, and was forever seeing the dead, and eating scraps, and sitting five on one WC, runs rapidly, vividly across my eyes.

Every post brought letters of gratitude from women who saw their own experiences reflected in Vera's story. There were also letters from both men and women describing how *Testament of Youth* had hardened their own condemnation of war, and from those, too young to have played any direct part in the conflict, who found in Vera's book the clearest and most eloquent explanation of what their parents' generation had endured.

Inevitably, some doubted the book's veracity. One American reviewer went so far as to describe *Testament of Youth* as 'a novel masquerading as an autobiography'. To correspondents who questioned its authenticity Vera offered sight of the personal documents on which it was based, stating that apart from one conversation between some British soldiers about ghosts at the front which she had not personally recorded, every fact, date, letter and quotation had been carefully verified. Despite her protestations, however, she was secretly flattered that the book read well enough to be mistaken for fiction. She was well aware of the importance of taking advantage of the inbuilt suspense of her story, instructing Macmillan not to give away the cumulative effect of her four personal tragedies in the advance publicity for the book in America.

To the novelist P.D. James, writing in 1978, *Testament of Youth* seemed to be one of those books 'which help both form and define the mood of its time'. Robert Graves and Alan Hodge in their domestic history of the Thirties, *The Long Week-end*, accounted for *Testament of Youth*'s appeal in terms of public concern about the international situation in 1933. Vera herself, always her own books' best publicist, had contributed an article on 'Peace Through Books' to the *New Clarion*, three months before the publication of *Testament of Youth*. In it she reminded readers that not since 1918 had the world been 'so urgently confronted with the desperate choice between life or death, peace or war . . .'.

The first four months of 1933 presented good reason for the greatest cause for concern about the likelihood of European war since the Russo-Polish conflict of 1920. Hitler had become Chancellor of Germany in January; in February the Japanese had renewed their attack on Manchuria; there had been disarmament difficulties in Geneva, economic difficulties in the United States, and in April the British Government had imposed a short-lived trade embargo against Russia. 'Remember 1914' was emblazoned across posters in London at the time of the Manchurian crisis, and comparisons between 1914 and 1933 soon became endemic in the press. The result of the 'King and Country' debate at the Oxford Union in February, where the motion 'That this House will in no circumstances fight for its King and Country' was carried by 275 votes to 153, was interpreted by many at the time as a backward-looking protest against the unscrupulous exploitation of the generation of 1914, who had been carried away by the patriotism and jingoism of their elders.

No wonder then that *Testament of Youth* – one of the aims of which was to 'show why the particular generation caught up in the War was so easily exploited' – enjoyed such success. Ironically the domestic harassments which had hampered Vera's writing and which at one time had appeared likely to deprive *Testament of Youth* of the advantage of peak interest in war books, had contrived its publication at precisely the time when its ideas matched the public mood. War disillusionment had been followed by disillusionment with the chances of peace, and had given birth to a second phase of war literature.

The overwhelming attraction of 'heroism in the abstract' which sends the four young men in her life to the front, is perceptively analysed in 'Tawny Island', the single most potent chapter of the book. Serving in Malta after Roland's death, she is conscious of the origins of the naive idealism of the generation of 1914:

It is, I think, this glamour, this magic, this incomparable keying up of the spirit in a time of mortal conflict, which constitute the pacifist's real problem ... The causes of war are always falsely represented; its honour is dishonest and its glory meretricious, but the challenge to spiritual endurance, the intense sharpening of all the senses, the vitalising consciousness of common peril for a common end, remain to allure those boys and girls who have just reached the age when love and friendship and adventure call more persistently than at any later time.

Her friends had died for 'meretricious gods, believing them to be the true one, and serving them honourably and bravely'. Only she had lived on into a different world, where the compromises and failures of postwar international politics had led her to reflect on what might be saved from the seemingly vain sacrifice of the 'first-rate, courageous men' of her generation:

Perhaps, after all, the best that we who were left could do was to refuse to forget, and to teach our successors what we remembered in the hope that they, when their own day came, would have more power to change the world than this bankrupt, shattered generation.

For at least one modern critic, *Testament of Youth* has earned itself a lasting place in the literature of the First World War as a 'classic example of

English lost generation literature'. Stated in its most basic form, the so-called 'myth of the lost generation' holds that the best men, the noblest, strongest and most cultivated, were killed in the war, and that the impoverishment of their generation contributed to the decline of Britain and the drift into another war.

Testament of Youth is certainly one of the strongest literary proponents of this idea – Vera wrote that '. . . the finest flowers of English manhood had been plucked from a whole generation', and that this had led to 'failure and calamity in every department of human life'. The emotive appeal of the argument has ensured that it has never quite been overthrown, despite an impressive array of statistics to counter its central contention. Robert Wohl has argued that the survival of this myth of a missing élite was strongest in England, and among English intellectuals, because of the feeling that an older generation (whom Vera referred to as 'the worshippers of precedent, privilege and property') had played a dirty trick on the younger. This belief encouraged a cult of the dead which accounted for the disappointments of the present.

Amid all the praise for *Testament of Youth*, there were murmurs of criticism of the book as 'self-advertisement', 'family scrap-album intimacy', or 'muddled egoism' which would mount in a worrying crescendo over the next seven years as *Thrice a Stranger*, *Testament of Friendship* and *England's Hour* appeared. The eminent social scientist, Barbara Wootton, who had herself lost a brother and a husband in the war, later voiced one facet of these reservations in her own autobiography:

> My troubles were, of course, in no way unusual. What happened to me happened also, in one form or another, to thousands of my contemporaries; and that fact served at least to hold in check any temptation I might otherwise have had to dramatize my tragic situation. Indeed what infuriated many of us, when Vera Brittain published her *Testament of Youth*, was the impression she conveyed that she alone of the nurses with whom she worked had to endure the anxiety of knowing that her beloved was at the front.

For the present, though, Vera could afford to ignore such criticism. Of the 1,300 letters which she received following *Testament of Youth*'s publication, the great majority were in its favour. Through *Testament of Youth*, as she confessed to Winifred, she had at last found some measure of peace and reconciliation with the war. In later years she would look back on the revolutionary effect that the book had had on her own life after 1933, when her new reading public demanded her presence on platforms and committees as a 'minor prophetess of peace'. She would also realize, in retrospect, that the publicity and success which surrounded the publication of *Testament of Youth* had made it difficult, perhaps impossible, for her to write anything of comparable effect again. *Testament of Youth* was the high water mark of her literary career. But Vera was grateful enough to have written one book that lived, and which she had little doubt would one day have similar appeal to a new generation of readers. Ten years before her death, she wrote that '. . . some day in the distant future when the First War has really passed into history and all of us who remember it are gone, it may well be that a new type of interest in it will arise . . .'.

NINE

'My Happiness is a House Built on Shifting Sands'

'How deeply I am troubled by the thought of how much I owe all the people I love.'
Vera Brittain's inscription on the flyleaf of a copy of E.M. Forster's *Aspects of the Novel* (1927) given to her by Winifred Holtby

I

Vera's life had been dominated by her longing for literary success and at last, with the publication of *Testament of Youth*, she was able to savour fame to the full. She thrived on the publicity, and with her name stamped on her suitcase, she welcomed the recognition of complete strangers as she travelled around the country.

One unexpected consequence of this success was her warm reception at Somerville, in marked contrast to the cold shoulder of disapproval she had felt there since the days of *The Dark Tide*. In the autumn of 1933 when Vera was in Oxford to take part in a debate, she was invited to stay with the Principal, the English tutor from 1915, Helen Darbishire, asked to dine as a guest on High Table (an invitation she much regretted having to turn down owing to a prior engagement), and generally complimented on *Testament of Youth* by members of Somerville's Senior Common Room. This reinstatement by her former college made Vera feel 'strangely thrilled to the verge of tears'.

But of all the praise and attention Vera attracted from *Testament of Youth*, none was more eagerly awaited than the approval of her peers. She had been especially nervous of the reception the book would meet from the 'Inner Circle', the group of women writers – Rebecca West, Rose Macaulay, E.M. Delafield, and Cicely Hamilton among them – associated with *Time and Tide*. Her fears at first appeared to be unfounded. Just having her book accepted by Gollancz, she noted, seemed to make an extraordinary difference to the way she was normally treated. At a party of Rebecca West's in February 1933, Vera reported to Winifred in amazement, the hostess was unusually friendly and 'actually put her arm round my waist when introducing me to someone'. Even Rose Macaulay, who customarily preserved her distance, embarrassed by Vera's undisguised admiration, sauntered up and said, 'I hear you've written a very good autobiography'.

Rebecca West gave *Testament of Youth* a generous review in the *Daily Telegraph*, but Rose Macaulay, after reading the proofs, became decidedly frostier in her attitude to Vera. Having an intense dislike of personal autobiography, she was appalled to discover the tributes Vera had paid in *Testament of Youth* to her kindness in attempting to find a publisher for *The Dark Tide* back in the early Twenties. 'Coldly angry', she summoned Vera to lunch at Marshall and Snelgrove's and reduced her to tears after scolding her for half an hour. She humiliated her again at a Foyle's Literary Luncheon shortly after the book's publication when, in Vera's earshot, she retorted to George in a loud voice that autobiographies were 'always vulgar'. After that she would always cut Vera, or haughtily look over her head and pretend not to see her at any public gatherings they both attended. This became particularly nerve-racking for Vera in the late Thirties when both women were Sponsors of the Peace Pledge Union. 'I can still remorsefully experience the cold shiver that ran down my spine,' she wrote after Rose Macaulay's death, 'when Rose's tall, donnish figure suddenly reared itself up from some public gathering, dominant and menacing like an unfolding python.'*

Such incidents did nothing to boost Vera's limited supply of confidence. Nor did the publication of a bestseller lessen her social diffidence. Gilbert Murray, the eminent classicist and League of Nations campaigner, wrote perceptively to Vera after reading *Testament of Youth*, 'I think you have a very remarkable power of self-revelation in writing – though the book suggests in ordinary daily life you find it difficult'. In her reply Vera admitted that an autobiography had enabled her to explain to friends and acquaintances many things about her past she might otherwise have been unable to tell them. *Testament of Youth* must certainly have reassured Naomi Mitchison, who had been dismayed at Vera's acute distress on learning that Naomi's

---

*Fate played a cruel trick on Rose Macaulay. In 1961 there was a minor controversy over the posthumous publication of her letters to the Anglican priest Father Hamilton Johnson (*Letters to a Friend*) which revealed that the centre of her life for more than twenty years had been an intimate relationship with Gerald O'Donovan, a married man who had previously been a Catholic priest. George, Vera reported, was feeling 'maliciously triumphant' at the thought of Rose Macaulay writhing in her grave at such disclosures. But Vera, while admitting that she could feel no affection for 'someone who habitually sat in judgement on other people', nevertheless thought it 'monstrous that her letters should be published against her express wishes . . .'.

husband, Dick, had been involved in the fighting on the Asiago Plateau in 1918. A chance remark like this could trigger off an emotional response from Vera which was bewildering to those who witnessed it. 'The accumulated grief of the years has swept over me for so long,' she had told Phyllis Bentley, 'that I merely make myself ridiculous to people who have long forgotten what I somehow can't manage to forget.'

Vera's social awkwardness was at its worst in the ritual round of '6 to 8' cocktail parties, the select literary and political soirées which she loathed, but which she attended for George's sake. Shy and nervous and still looking deceptively youthful, she would stand in a corner, hidden from view, in a state of self-absorption that bordered on the trancelike. It was as if 'some inner spring of joy had been dried up', as one observer put it. She rarely indulged in small talk and could be icily direct and quietly forthright in putting across her point of view. She was acutely aware that she sometimes lacked a sense of humour. Occasionally she would say something inadvertently amusing at one of her lectures, and return home totally mystified as to why the audience had been convulsed with laughter. For some this earnestness made Vera distinctly hard going. David Higham, her agent, sought light relief by nicknaming *Testament of Youth* 'Testicles of Youth' ('though it was by no means all balls'). 'Such frivolous nicknames', he remembered, 'relieve tedium, of which in dealing with Vera I'd had plenty.'

The great and the famous, Vera confessed, made her feel 'genteel' and 'provincial'. Her sense of unease at meeting H.G. Wells, one of the heroes of her childhood, for the first time was only quelled by the combined effects of some *crêpes de volaille*, dry Moselle, and Wells's own geniality. One of the consequences of her new celebrity, however, which Vera most prized was an invitation in May 1934 from 'Mrs Sidney Webb' to visit her at Passfield Corner. Beatrice Webb thought *Testament of Youth* 'a wonderful story', and in her diary she has left us an impression of Vera at forty, still glowing with success, and about to embark on her first lecture tour of the United States:

> Vera is a charmer, a competent writer and, it is said, a brilliant lecturer. F.W. Galton was swept away by her Fabian lecture ['The Anti-Feminist Reaction in Europe', delivered on 8 March 1934]. Her lips and nails delicate crimson, cheeks slightly and skilfully rouged . . . She will succeed in life; her subjects – feminism and pacifism – are a trifle stale, but among women they still have a vogue. Her recent autobiography sold well. Next autumn she goes off on a lecturing tour in the USA, where she will carry all before her.

In the late Twenties and early Thirties when she was occupied in running the household and looking after the children in the intervals from her work, Vera had sometimes looked with envy upon Winifred's expanding group of 'friends of varying degrees of celebrity', contrasting them with her own smaller circle. True, they shared many acquaintances from their Oxford years and early days in London, and large-scale entertaining at Glebe Place enabled Winifred to introduce Vera to many of her social and professional contacts. Among these was Arthur ('Jon') Creech Jones, one of Winifred's associates through the Friends of Africa movement, with whom Vera would establish her own friendly relations for more than thirty years up to his death in 1964. Josiah Wedgwood, the quixotic MP for Vera's birthplace, Newcastle-under-Lyme, was another friend whom she came to know through Winifred's work for Africans.

But Vera's intimate circle, the friends she could see regularly on an informal basis, remained relatively small, and only Winifred was consistently able to penetrate her aura of reserve and vunerability. Winifred's effect on Vera was always marked: many commented on how much calmer and more restrained Vera became in her company. Basking in the sunshine of Winifred's affection, to employ an image which Vera herself used to describe this transformation, she shed much of her diffidence and even acquired an engaging, if limited, sense of fun.

To observers of their friendship the two women seemed like devoted sisters and it is clear that from the early days Vera regarded their relationshp in this light. Winifred was a surrogate sibling with whom she could enjoy an intimacy similar to the kind she had once shared with Edward. From Ithaca in 1925 she had written to Winifred, shortly to set sail for South Africa, asking her to 'never doubt how much you are to me, and that no one in the world can ever take your place. The only person who could possibly have meant the same to me would have been a sister whom I loved as I loved Edward.'

Winifred gave elegiac expression to this special relationship in the poem 'Symphony Concert' which she wrote in the autumn of 1931, and sent to Vera in St Raphaël. She had gone to a Beethoven Promenade Concert given by the Hungarian violinist, Jelly d'Aranyi. Part of the programme was the concerto which had been one of Edward's favourites, and which he had often performed. Listening to this music Winifred's eyes filled with tears as she was overwhelmed by an identification of herself as Edward's 'deputy', coupled with an awareness of how limited her appreciation of the music was compared with what his would have been.

By the early 1930s, and especially after the appearance of *Testament of Youth* with its description of their early years together, Vera and Winifred sometimes found themselves closely linked and, on one memorable occasion, entangled in the public imagination. Hugh Walpole, still smarting from Vera's unfavourable review of his *Farthing Hall*, referred mockingly to 'Miss Brittain and Miss Holtby' as the 'Miss Buss and Miss Beale of contemporary letters'; Winifred recounted to Vera with amusement the story of her setting-off in her car from a school in Barton after having given a speech there in the summer of 1934, pursued by a posse of governors and masters shouting, 'Come back and bring Vera with you!'; but pride of place in Winifred's collection of favourite stories went to an episode at a League of Nations rally later that year when the unfortunate chairman, Lady Steel-Maitland, introduced her as 'Miss Vera Holtby' to loud laughter and applause from the audience.

Rumours of a lesbian relationship between Vera and Winifred circulated from their Doughty Street days. Fuelled no doubt by the postwar vogue for deviant literature, which encompassed not only *The Well of Loneliness*, but also novels like M.J. Farrell's cruelly witty *Devoted Ladies* of 1934, the rumours were soon transformed into myth. Even Vera's marriage did nothing to stem the tide of gossip, and there was some fairly prurient speculation about a *ménage à trois* at 19 Glebe Place. 'No my heart, you must not fall in love with my husband', Vera had once teased Winifred after such a suggestion had been made by Hilda Reid, 'for such an attractive *à trois* arrangement can be manoeuvred if you promise you won't and he is just as keen about it as I am!'

Winifred characteristically treated the whole notion as a joke. With her sardonic sense of humour she would remark 'Look she's got my hair', as she cradled the flaxen-haired baby Shirley in her arms. Vera was less amused and would ask in somewhat naive amazement how anyone could take her for a lesbian after reading *Testament of Youth* 'with its story of passionate love for young men'. She was, for instance, exasperated by the attitude of Monica Whately who could never quite bring herself to believe that her relationship with Winifred was not homosexual.

In September 1929 at the League of Nations Assembly in Geneva Vera and Monica Whately had become embroiled in 'a tremendous & vehement argument which never seems to come to an end ... about feminism and homosexuality'. At one point Monica Whately asserted that men were 'such oppressors & such sources of evil', that if she had a daughter she would deliberately urge her to enter into a lesbian relationship rather than seek marriage. Seething with indignation Vera retorted that 'if this is the logical outcome of feminism, feminists such as she will end by wrecking their own movement.' 'Last evening she roused me to such a pitch of fury', she wrote to Winifred, 'that I told her she was a dangerous & utterly wrong-headed fanatic, & banged the door of the Pension Coupier on her.'

Despite briefly refuting the lesbian imputations in *Testament of Friendship*, her biography of Winifred, Vera was horrified to discover in the years following its publication in 1940 that her friendship with Winifred had given what she called 'a tribe of unconscious spinster homosexuals of all ages' cause to regard her as a substitute for all the lost loves of their lives. 'I don't mind the young ones so much,' she confided to Shirley in 1964 in connection with one particularly over-attentive spinster in Shirley's constituency, '– a "crush" on an author seems fairly normal in one's twenties, but I must say that the older ones just plain revolt me.'

'I am wholly a heterosexual person without an atom of homosexuality in my make-up', Vera declared, and there is nothing in the surviving evidence to suggest that her feelings for Winifred were ever of an erotic nature. Towards the end of her life she felt a growing need to set the record straight about her relationship with Winifred for posterity. In a barely legible pencilled note, written during her final illness, Vera scribbled, 'I loved Winifred, but I was not in love with her.'

The question of Winifred's sexuality is more problematic. 'Certainly if W. was ever subconsciously in love with me', Vera told George in 1936, 'she never displayed it by word or action, but I don't think she was . . .'. Sybil Morrison, a colleague of Vera's later at the Peace Pledge Union, and a self-proclaimed lesbian, took the opposite view. She was convinced that Winifred was in love with Vera, though she added that Winifred may not have known herself where her own instincts lay (looking back on coming to terms with her own lesbianism, Sybil Morrison once commented, 'But we were all very innocent in those days. It took several years to realize it myself'); on the other hand, several people who knew Winifred well, like Phyllis Bentley, Hilda Reid and Amy Burnett, always strongly denied that she had been even latently lesbian.

Their denials were based in part on the assumption that for much of her life Winifred had been in love with the feckless Harry Pearson. Harry, 'a War-casualty of the spirit', as Vera liked to refer to him, had drifted after the war, finding it difficult to settle down or discover any sense of purpose. For six years he had served as an aircraftman on the north-west frontier of India (where he shared a regimental dormitory with T.E. Lawrence). In July 1932 he returned to England and quickly re-established his friendship with Winifred. She managed to place an article by him in the *Manchester*

Guardian, though he showed as little sense of commitment towards her as before. He would turn up unannounced at the cottage in Withernsea, East Yorkshire, where Winifred was staying in the spring of 1934, and then just as suddenly depart, not to be heard of again for weeks. Winifred was unruffled by this behaviour, happy in his company, but not expecting, and perhaps not wishing for, anything more. She was occasionally depressed by her inability 'to rouse him from the lethargy of hopelessness', but for the most part she valued his friendship. 'The sexual philosophers would say our relationship was wrong and unnatural', she wrote to Vera after one of Harry's visits. 'At the moment it is all I want, and seems to be all he wants.'

For Vera though, Winifred's relationship with Harry provided the decisive evidence she needed in *Testament of Friendship* to disprove the lesbian allegations. Justifying his inclusion in the biography as 'Bill' (the name Winifred had given his fictional counterpart in *Mandoa, Mandoa!*), Vera explained to Harry that 'I could not omit you and write a truthful account of her ... Nor was I prepared to leave the ill-natured gossip about her in certain London circles unrefuted by the one thing that could refute it.'

It seems fair to say, however, that in *Testament of Friendship* Vera was guilty of forcing the ill-defined relationship of Winifred and Harry into a rigidly conventional mould to dampen speculation which she felt was detrimental to Winifred's memory. Lady Rhondda, for instance, saw Vera's interpretation of Winifred's relationship with Harry as representing a major point of disagreement. In her review of *Testament of Friendship* in *Time and Tide*, she wrote that she could not believe that Harry had ever counted for as much, or as continuously, in Winifred's life as Vera would have liked to believe.

What is more certain is that Winifred combined a diffident attitude towards sex with a sexual philosophy which expressed a healthy disrespect for the conventional view of a 'normal' sexual relationship. She took too much mental and bodily exercise, she once said, 'for the physical to have much pull over me', and it seems likely that her sexual drive was in any case largely sublimated by her creative passion. In 1925 she had written that she was to a great extent immune from suffering, 'the result of an independent income combined with a personality completely devoid of sexual attraction.' Consequently she always experienced difficulty writing the love scenes in her novels: 'I have a warm, half-humorous affection for them ... but I can't get excited!' This impression is reinforced by the number of obstacles Winifred throws in the paths of her heroines when they are on the verge of making love. In *Anderby Wold* when Mary Robson kisses David Rossitur in the corner of a field, her husband inconveniently passes by the hedge; in *The*

Crowded Street, Muriel Hammond is engaged in her first and last embrace with Godfrey Neale when her mother calls for her, and out of pure habit Muriel rushes off to see what she wants; and in Winifred's most memorable love scene in *South Riding*, Robert Carne has an attack of angina just as Sarah Burton is about to make love to him.

One unpublished letter of Winifred's contains the hint of a suggestion that if erotic feelings did underlie her constant devotion to Vera, the control that Winifred exercised over her emotions prevented them from ever coming to the surface. In the summer of 1928, shortly after the publication of *The Well of Loneliness*, Winifred wrote to Vera that 'Radclyffe Hall has taught me a lot. She's all fearfully wrong, I feel. To love other women deeply is not pathological. To be unable to control one's passions is . . .'.

Whatever the precise nature of Winifred's feelings, she was certainly not oblivious to Vera's faults. She could laugh at Vera's 'rampageous' outspokenness, but she evidently expressed reservations when she felt it had gone too far. She wrote letters to Phyllis Bentley in 1932, mildly critical of Vera's behaviour towards her, while Phyllis claimed that Winifred drew upon the irrational, hysterical element in Vera's personality to create the character of Carne's difficult child, Midge, in *South Riding*.

There was much disparagement of Vera among Winifred's other friends, who were mystified and amazed at the extent of Winifred's devotion to Vera. They were at a loss to explain the strength of a relationship which appeared, at least on the surface, to be so one-sided, with Winifred doing all the 'giving', subservient to Vera's every demand. Any protests, however, fell on stony ground. Stella Benson, who described Vera as Winifred's 'blood-sucking friend', was egged on by Lady Rhondda and Clare Leighton in the summer of 1932 to express her misgivings about Vera's hold over Winifred, to Winifred's face. But as she recorded in her diary, all she could deduce from Winifred's sorrowful reaction to such antipathy against Vera was that 'she likes having her blood sucked'. St John Ervine was pithier. He advised Winifred to divorce Vera, 'citing Catlin as co-respondent'.

To the end of her life Vera was unable to understand the reasons for the bitterness of some of Winifred's friends towards her. Several of them felt strongly enough not to bother to acknowledge the complimentary copies of *Testament of Friendship* which she sent them after its publication. Yet she had never tried to prevent Winifred being friends with other people. Jealousy of people's affections, she felt, was one vice she did not possess (jealousy of their work was another matter).

The accusations of exploitation of Winifred levelled at Vera became more pronounced after Winifred's death. It was in an attempt to deal with these that Vera wrote in her Epilogue to *Testament of Friendship* of Winifred's 'conscience-smitten compassion' which led so many who knew her to take advantage of her good nature. Winifred once said that her life was like a clear stream which reflected other people's lives, and reading through her correspondence after her death, Vera was astonished by the extent of the services undertaken for others as if they were part of life's normal routine – finding lodgings for people, interviewing publishers on behalf of others, reading innumerable speeches and manuscripts. '. . . Everybody's exploitation of her grew by what it fed on', explained Vera to Rebecca West, while George in more cynical mood attributed Winifred's desire to help others to doubts about their efficiency to complete the task themselves, as much as to a spirit of pure generosity.

'I was as bad – perhaps worse – than anybody, with my children, books, anxieties and the rest', confessed Vera in a letter to Sarah Gertrude Millin in 1939, though in the same letter she made scarcely veiled references to the two women she regarded as the other main offenders, Winifred's mother and Lady Rhondda. With neither did Vera enjoy good relations, though the pretence of keeping up an amiable front to their faces established in Winifred's lifetime, continued after her death. Alice Holtby's no-nonsense, down-to-earth approach ('You mustn't forget she was a schoolmarm to begin with,' observed St John Ervine) could not have been further removed from Vera's brand of emotionalism. Nor did Mrs Holtby have any time for what she considered Vera's literary affectations. She believed that the satire and 'lewdness' which she found so distressing in some of Winifred's articles and short stories, and later in *South Riding*, could only have emanated from the literary circles in which Winifred had moved in London, and in this Vera was guilty by association.

For her part, Vera was appalled by the time-consuming demands that this dominant matriarch made on her daughter. Acknowledging the intellectual limitations of her home circle, Winifred had once complained that at Cottingham ' "art" is something as unimportant and incomprehensible as the algebraical implications of the Koran.' Art definitely took second place to the social duties incumbent on Alderman Alice Holtby's only surviving daughter. Even in the final stages of her illness when she was struggling to complete *South Riding*, Winifred was expected to return home to shoulder some of the burden in minor domestic crises or to visit sick relatives round the neighbourhood. Winifred accepted these duties with her usual equanimity; it was Vera who felt the injustice.

The other larger-than-life figure in Winifred's life was Lady Rhondda. Only an unnatural display of decorum by Vera prevented open war breaking out between herself and Lady Rhondda. She had quietly accepted the snub delivered by Lady Rhondda when it was made clear that her association with *Time and Tide* was over, though it was a source of private humiliation for her. For Winifred's sake over the years she made tentative steps at reconciliation, for instance writing to congratulate Lady Rhondda on the publication of her autobiography, *This Was My World*, in 1933. Winifred had hopes that 'she too some day will learn to understand you', but in reality it was mere wishful thinking. Lady Rhondda could only resent Vera when her company or her demands distracted Winifred from undivided concentration on *Time and Tide*, while Vera would increasingly come to regard Lady Rhondda after Winifred's death as Winifred's 'evil genius', who 'used her time, health and energy, and gave little worth having in return for all she took'. Equally Vera failed to appreciate fully the value of the platform which *Time and Tide* provided for the dissemination of Winifred's ideas and beliefs.

What neither Vera, Mrs Holtby nor Lady Rhondda could come to terms with, though, in all their tugging of Winifred in different directions, was the true seriousness of Winifred's illness. Initially Mrs Holtby attributed Winifred's first collapse in the autumn of 1931 to 'psychological causes'. Winifred's sickness and headaches, she was sure, were the result of her 'unwholesome' lifestyle. The hectic pace of London literary life was fundamentally unsuited to someone brought up in the country on a farm. Lady Rhondda, on the other hand, believed Winifred's breakdown was nothing more than a case of bromide poisoning, and at the end of 1932, to Vera's dismay, she assumed Winifred was sufficiently recovered to take over the running of *Time and Tide* while she toured Greece, Palestine and Egypt.

Mrs Holtby's and Lady Rhondda's optimistic view of Winifred's health, encouraged by Winifred's own seeming disregard for it, did not radically alter until her swift deterioration in July 1935. For Vera, though, intimations that Winifred's illness might ultimately prove fatal, began slowly to dawn on her in the year before Winifred's death, though she was periodically unable to face up to their full implications. Winifred's renal sclerosis, a hardening of the kidney tissue then commonly known as Bright's disease, had been finally diagnosed by the German-Austrian arterial specialist, Edgar Obermer, in April 1932. He told Winifred then that if her disease continued at its present rate she might only live another two years. However, the treatment he prescribed (for which he made only a minimal charge of £10 a year as he found her case so interesting), combined with Winifred's extraordinary zest for life and her refusal to be defeated by her illness, meant that after two years the progress of the sclerosis appeared to have been temporarily arrested. Winifred herself came to believe she was a 'freak case'. She had defeated the medical prognostications and might continue to do so. She knew that she could not expect to live to a great age like her mother, but her will to live and buoyant optimism when all her symptoms indicated that she should have been dead, gave her the time to plan and to write.

On the rare occasions when Vera did confront the gravity of Winifred's situation, she revealed just how lost she was when the familiar pattern of her dependence on Winifred was reversed, and she was called upon to provide Winifred with the kind of comfort and support that she had always been able to count on from her. As she told George when Winifred was first referred to Obermer:

> I am so miserable that I keep on wanting to turn for comfort to – whom but Winifred herself! For twelve years she has always been there to turn to when anything troubled me, and I feel so lost when suddenly the one thing happens about which I can't seek comfort but must try to give it, while knowing so well how hollow all my suggested alleviations and compensations must sound, and how easily she must see through them . . .

To Vera, Winifred was deliberately vague or evasive about her health. She was well aware of the burden which the strain of worry would place on Vera should she discover the whole truth. Occasionally the mask of reticence would slip, as when Winifred suddenly declared to Vera 'I'm doomed and damned' while they were sitting in the courtyard of the Blue Cockatoo in Chelsea in the spring of 1935. Other chance occurrences must have led Vera to fear the worst. A doctor, making a routine check of Winifred's blood-pressure during her attack of mumps at Christmas 1934, remarked to Vera afterwards, 'the disease kills in the end, you know'.

But Winifred's continuing, tireless exuberance right up to just before her death, made it easier for Vera to put her fears to the back of her mind. Winifred's high blood-pressure with its accompanying sensation of extraordinary physical exhilaration actually stimulated her to even greater frenzied activity than before. 'Oh Margaret, why haven't we seventy lives? One is no use', she complained to Lady Rhondda, while a distant Holtby relative remembered her, sitting opposite him in a railway carriage on one of her visits home in the last year of her life, with her papers scattered across the seats and cascading to the floor, using every minute of the time that was left to her.

One much commented upon aspect of the set-up at 19 Glebe Place was the apparent ease with which George fitted into the domestic equation of wife, husband, and wife's best friend. Ethel Smyth, writing to Vera after Winifred's death, was full of praise for the way Vera had worked Winifred 'so wonderfully into the tapestry of your life'; but she reserved a special note of appreciation for George's acceptance of the arrangement. 'Your husband,' she wrote, '. . . must be a very exceptional man.'

Although the disagreement over the final chapter of *Testament of Youth* was a rare instance of Winifred siding openly with Vera against George, Winifred and George's relationship was not without other tensions. 'Perhaps I do Winifred an injustice . . .', George wrote to Vera in 1937. 'The absence of sexual interest which seemed to me almost oppressive may not have seemed a characteristic to other people . . . It may be that an agreement to ignore all warmer emotion was a necessary condition of being in the same house and the impression I received was the impression I caused. She was often willing to receive a more emotional response from me and noted its absence in so many words ("Sometimes I think you don't like me") and was hurt by it. But God knows what would have been the consequences of any other line???'

It was certainly a severe affront to George's pride to find himself placed a poor fourth in Vera's priorities after the children, Winifred, and her work when he returned home to Chelsea from Cornell each June. Occasionally his sense of resentment at Vera's closeness to Winifred would boil over, and he would express himself with acid candour on the subject. 'In the thirties you were jealous of Winifred,' Vera wrote in 1952, reminding him of one such incident, 'you once called my devotion to her the final immorality towards yourself.' Winifred cannot have been unaware of George's feelings and they may have provided one reason for her decision to move out of Glebe Place and into a flat of her own which she was apparently contemplating at the time of her death.

That Winifred might have begun to feel that the living arrangements at Glebe Place had outlived their practicality, and that she might choose not to continue as a member of the Brittain-Catlin household, appears not to have crossed Vera's mind, or if it had, she refused to admit it to herself after Winifred's death. In *Testament of Friendship*, Vera wrote that Winifred 'had no intention of leaving Glebe Place', but in 1934 had started to rent a 'single-room flat' as an office and peaceful haven for her writing. According to Hilda Reid, however, Winifred 'was not without hope of making a little money out of *South Riding*, and intended to use it to set up house by herself. 'She loved the children, Vera and George, but she did find them very exhausting – there were too many claims on her from too many quarters.'

George's personal jealousy was accompanied by an envy for Vera and Winifred's professional success, and was heightened by his growing disenchantment with his own career. For a man driven by an almost Faustian compulsion for recognition, it was not easy to live with two women who by 1933 were better known than he was.

'With all the publicity for your wife, you must feel like a hat with the rim knocked off' was the unkindly accurate remark of the hostess at a lecture which George gave in Hamilton, Ontario, in 1934. Even his attempts to take advantage of Winifred's journalistic connections, in an effort to make his name more widely known, fell flat. In the late Twenties he had written the occasional leader for the *Yorkshire Post* – the only activity of his of which his father-in-law ever approved – and had since nurtured an ambition to place articles in the more popular press. Winifred did her best, but had to sugar the pill of his rejections with the comment that they were 'the penalty of having a first-class mind ... if you were a vulgar whipper-snapper like Godfrey Winn and wrote "Why I am afraid of Bachelor Girls", I could be of the greatest possible service!' In 1933 Vera had even toyed with the idea of ghosting George's books and articles in an attempt to make his convoluted prose style more lucid and accessible.

What really rankled with George was that while his success was no less real than Vera's, its narrower, academic appeal made it less conspicuous. His first years at Cornell had, after all, been a period of impressive achievement. In 1924 he had been appointed to a professorship at Cornell at the unusually early age of twenty-eight. He had been awarded his doctorate after only a year's residence – an almost unprecedented distinction – and had published his doctoral thesis, *The Science and Method of Politics*, in 1927. This, together with his *Principles of Politics* of 1930, attempted to establish an empirical political science, systematically linking theory with practice in politics, with an analysis of the concept of power as its central theme.

In Britain at this time, political science tended to be treated as a poor relation of political philosophy and was by and large shunned as an academic discipline by the universities. In the American academic world, however, the whole question of how the scientific study of politics should be directed was being debated with lively interest. George's work was received there with appreciative reviews which singled him out as one of the most promising political scientists of his generation.

Yet the Thirties saw no attempt on George's part to consolidate his position as a major authority in his field as his interests were increasingly diverted into the arena of practical politics.* What was the point of stagnating at Cornell, he asked himself, while exciting developments were taking place on the European political scene which he ought to be observing?

Writing and teaching, he was to claim years later in his memoirs, had never been his primary objectives. Instead, he had always felt compelled by an 'ambitious desire to join action with theory'. Life at Cornell, that 'magic, autumnal paradise', as he called it, was pleasant: he was popular with his students and had gained the respect of his colleagues. But the time had come 'to act and not write prefaces to action'. In 1927 George had arranged to teach only one semester a year at Cornell, leaving him free to spend half the year travelling in Europe acquainting himself with the political *status quo*, and allowing him to take his first tentative steps in British politics. For eight years, until he finally turned his back on Cornell for good in 1935, he was effectively trying to run a semi-detached career as well as a semi-detached marriage.

Unfortunately his dream of playing an influential role in the Labour Party suffered early setbacks. At first he approached active political life from the perspective of his specific academic interests. Attaching himself to Oswald Mosley's office, he contributed to the so-called Mosley Memorandum on economic depression, one of Mosley's schemes as Chancellor of the Duchy of Lancaster in Ramsay MacDonald's Cabinet. However, his hopes of using this as a stepping-stone to higher things were dashed when Mosley broke with Labour and founded his New Party in February 1930. George was also unlucky, as we have seen, in the timing of his first attempt to enter Parliament in the general election of 1931 which was such a crushing electoral defeat for Labour. Even the *Realist*, the journal of 'scientific humanism' with an editorial board of prominent names from the left-wing establishment, which George was instrumental in founding, foundered after six months in 1929 from a shortage of funds and boardroom intrigue.

Over the years George's failure to secure any foothold in British politics – as a Member of Parliament, or member of Labour's National Executive, or in some long-term advisory capacity – developed from a grievance into an

---

*As a result George's *Science and Method* and *Principles* predated more than they influenced. The sporadic nature of his academic career after 1935 meant that it was not until 1962 that George published his *Systematic Politics*, a mature summing-up of his ideas. In the meantime, in the early 1950s, his work had been 'rediscovered' by the American political scientist David Easton in his *Political System*. This book played an important role in directing political science in the United States, and re-established George's reputation there along the way.

obsession which exacted a high price: the ruining of a potentially first-class academic career. He consistently refused to recognize that his gifts lay in the sphere of academic and not practical politics and as a result failed to make any great impact in either. In his mid-fifties he was still nursing a sense of acute disappointment. 'Not being in the House remains to me a running sore,' he wrote to Vera in 1952, 'I *wish* I could convince myself it is unimportant.' By that time she could only respond with sympathetic resignation: 'Yes, politics is a bitter game . . . How often have I wished you had never been bitten by that deadly bug! You have, I suppose, been caused more misery, anxiety and sleepless nights by lost elections and Party snubs than by any other single factor.'

The only practical solution in the Thirties would have been for George to find a teaching post in a British university which would have allowed him to pursue his political ambitions simultaneously with his academic career. But what few appointments there were in Britain in political science went elsewhere. Increasingly in later years George would attribute this lack of success to the intrigues of Harold Laski, Professor of Political Science at the London School of Economics from 1926. To George's face Laski would offer flattery which George, lacking a certain native shrewdness, was only too eager to lap up (as George confessed to Vera, Laski possessed 'an almost feminine gift for flattery in just the way one wanted to be flattered'); behind his back, Laski would be poisoning the minds of those on appointment boards against him.

But there were other factors at work too. One was George's half-hearted approach to university teaching as he relentlessly pursued his political ambitions; another, quite simply, was George's personality.

Stella Benson, meeting him for the first time in 1928, was appalled by 'Vera Brittain's dreadful young husband': '. . . he is so excessively posed, so full of Bloomsbury affectations and Cultchah through being English on American university staffs . . . He annoyed me dreadfully.' Beatrice Webb was struck similarly in the Twenties by his 'artificiality of manner and modish appearance'. When she met him again in 1934 she felt he had matured, although 'glibness and plausibility, shallowness of thought and feeling remain . . .'.

These were not isolated responses to George. On the contrary, reminiscences of him are marked by repeated references to his arrogance and pomposity. Even Victor Gollancz, who genuinely liked him, had to admit that George took self-importance to a new high. All too often his shameless name-dropping, and liberal lacing of his pronouncements with foreign expressions and gratuitous literary allusions, led people to dismiss him as an insufferable bore, and such personal dislike undoubtedly played its part in hindering his political and academic advancement. George's voice – a sort of affected whinny – was also perceived by some as a hindrance. According to one BBC producer in the early Thirties, he possessed 'an Oxford accent developed to the point of affectation as makes it difficult to preserve one's manners in his company.' St John Ervine, Winifred reported to Vera in 1932, liked George and thought him clever, 'but asked could we do *nothing* about his voice. [He] Says that though he realises now that it is the effect of shyness, it gets in between him & every new contact he ought to make.' On Ervine's recommendation George sought professional advice from Elsa Fogarty, the famous voice coach.

Yet for those who penetrated the veneer of pretension and bravado, there was a very gentle man of keen mind, generous spirit and with a delightfully whimsical sense of humour; a man whose vanity hid the emotional scars and deep-seated insecurity which were a legacy of his painful and troubled childhood.

In a bravely frank and searching self-analysis George once admitted to Victor Gollancz that since his youth he had become 'shut in a kind of carapace of self-consciousness and calculated self-defence, a facade of cultured self-protection, a fence of polite conversation which keeps outsiders out but also oneself shut in.'

It was a double misfortune that George should have had not only a mother who showed him scant affection, and who eventually deserted the family home, but also a wife whose work often seemed to matter more to her than her marriage. It is true that with the birth of children Vera had abandoned any thought she might once have had of leaving him, and by the early Thirties had reconciled herself to an acceptable modus vivendi. 'So glad it is now and not then, when we were both unadjusted psychologically and physically', she recorded in her diary in June 1932. At its best, life with George provided 'a peaceful contented resignation to undisturbing affection', and a stimulating companionship of shared ideals. 'You *do* love him, don't you? He's got all the right values', was Winifred's succinct summary of the situation.

But 'undisturbing affection' was not what George had anticipated, and it was a painful realization that he had failed to make Vera fall in love with him. Sympathizing with his mother's desire for independence, he had paid lip-service to Vera's unorthodox conception of marriage, but the reality of living apart from his wife and children for half the year placed a heavy strain on his collaboration. By the mid-Thirties he had lost the gaucheness of youth. He was a good-looking – and as far as external appearances went – self-assured man of the world (he prided himself on his resemblance to the actor, Leslie Howard), and it was perhaps partly to restore his self-respect that he began a series of affairs with other women. The Russian woman at Cornell in 1929 had been merely the first of what Vera would sardonically refer to as 'George's girl friends', and she once remarked that he justified his escapades to her 'on the grounds that it does his psychology so much good to feel that he is attractive to women'. In 1932 he had reported to her that he had just had an affair with a Dutch girl in New York. The writer, Ethel Mannin, had long exercised a fascination for him, and when shortly after Christmas of that year he took her out to dinner, Vera felt forced to tell him 'that this time I was afraid he'd have to take her back to Wimbledon [where Mannin lived], and that I wouldn't spend the night contemplating the Divorce Court if he didn't return the following morning!' 'I have a feeling', she added, 'that once would be more than enough.' His longest-lasting affair was with Letty Jarrard, an actress whom he met in 1930, and whom Vera believed he would have married had he still been single.

By the time George met Letty Jarrard, Vera had reached the conclusion that what he really wanted was 'an intelligent wife but a conventional one'. She confided to Shirley many years later that she had never been 'a really satisfactory wife', and that she had come to accept George's philandering with growing equanimity. In spite of his academic and personal commitments, George maintained friendly relations with his 'girl friends', but he found his extramarital affairs an unsatisfactory substitute for 'a very stable family life which is what I seem never fated to get'. His parents' bitter quarrels had engendered a horror of direct confrontation, and he knew in any case that neither argument nor emotional pressure would persuade Vera to abandon her independent life. He outwardly suppressed his resentment, but his disappointment and unhappiness may to some extent have influenced his decision to embark upon a political career. He took less interest in Vera's work, and she believed that his political pursuits added a further element of strain to an already precarious marriage. 'Had I known he would do this, I don't say I wouldn't have married him . . . But I should have hesitated more.'

IV

Both Vera and Gollancz made a 'big killing' from *Testament of Youth*. Gollancz had negotiated a reduced royalty rate with Vera, enabling him to market the book at a lower price which pushed up sales. Already by the spring of 1934, Vera calculated, she had earned £1,580 in royalties. Hollywood beckoned lucratively too. One producer offered Vera $10,000 for the film rights, but she worried about how Hollywood might sentimentalize or distort the story. 'Of course a dignified, woman's Cavalcade film *could* be made of it, but would it, by America?' Elisabeth Bergner, the 'exquisitely *spiritual*' Polish-born actress, was one suggestion to play Vera. 'She has your high forehead & delicate profile . . .', wrote Winifred. 'Her red hair could easily be darkened.' Vera was more perturbed about Winifred's portrayal. '. . . You yourself might be personified by Tallulah Bankhead or someone worse!!?' While she temporized, the offer was withdrawn.

Money remained a headache and one that was chiefly Vera's. The household at Glebe Place was more dependent than ever on her earnings. When the symptoms of Winifred's illness were at their worst Vera would not allow her to pay her one-third share of the housekeeping. Winifred was badly off at the best of times, saving every penny she could for 'her Africans' ('Think of me if you make any money on a horse,' she used to joke with friends). Nor was it any good looking to George to make up the shortfall. His income was still meagre, a reflection of his erratic career, and he could always be relied upon to fritter away what little he did earn with carefree extravagance before turning to Vera for money. Since 1927 she had never received more than £100 a year from him. Vera happily paid for his trips abroad, looking upon it as some compensation to him for his disappointment in her as a wife; she gave him £590 of the first royalties from *Testament of Youth*, some of which he used to finance his visit to Leipzig as British delegate to the Reichstag Trial Defence Committee; she was prepared, in the event of a general election, to pay for his expenses as a prospective Labour candidate. Less resignedly, she continued to provide for his father's upkeep in an expensive Oxford nursing home at the cost of £300 a year.

There were also charities and causes pressing for donations. 'One of the minor trials of my existence recently,' Vera wrote to Winifred as she weighed up the competing claims of the Women's Peace Crusade and the new Council for Civil Liberties, 'has been confident appeals for money from practically every organization with which I have ever been associated and a great many that I haven't.' She bemoaned the fact that people like Hilda Reid and Mrs Leighton went about giving a vastly inflated impression of how much she had earned. Her aunts Belle and Florence, for instance, were firmly convinced that she was a millionaire. She ended up giving away a significant proportion of the royalties.

'If I don't earn money all the time we aren't even reasonably well off,' Vera complained to Margaret Storm Jameson in what was to become an increasingly familiar refrain over the next twenty years. Gollancz was offering good terms for her next book, a novel, which would be a major source of income once the royalties from *Testament of Youth* had been exhausted. Capitalizing on her new celebrity status, Vera also planned a three-month lecture-tour of the United States. On 18 December 1933 she signed a contract with her American agents, Colston Leigh, which guaranteed her forty-five per cent of all proceeds from lectures and radio broadcasts. Such was Vera's appeal that within a few months of her signing Colston Leigh had negotiated $3,000 worth of business.

The germ of the idea for her novel dated back to 1923 when she had made notes for two books based on the fortunes of a prosperous Staffordshire family, the Alleyndenes – a thinly disguised portrait of the Brittains – through three generations from the late nineteenth century to 1930. 'I shall take Father's generation just as they are,' she had told Winifred with her usual candid view of her family's shortcomings, 'shrewd, lazy, stupid, quarrelsome, unloving.' Only in the third generation would she depart dramatically from fact with the story of Ruth Alleyndene who goes to Westminster as Member of Parliament for her old home town 'to make up to it for the selfishness of past Alleyndenes'. Returning to the idea of an Alleyndene saga after *Testament of Youth*, Vera amalgamated it with another projected novel based on the life of the mother-in-law she had never known, Edith Kate Catlin. Mrs Catlin's refusal to compromise her feminist sympathies in deference to her husband had made her something of a heroine in Vera's eyes (though she severely criticized her for her abandonment of her young son). Her struggle provided the central theme for this long, sprawling epic, the story of the changing institution of marriage set against the history of the Women's Movement. Synopses of the early part of *Honourable Estate* were to travel with Vera to America in the autumn of 1934.

Vera greeted the prospect of her American tour with a distinct lack of enthusiasm. Colston Leigh anticipated 'one of the most successful tours ever booked for a European writer', but by the end of March 1934 when Vera completed her seventy-fourth speaking engagement in Britain since *Testament of Youth*'s publication she felt as though she never wanted to lecture again. She had delivered one of her final lectures of the season with a temperature of 101 degrees and a nurse close at hand, since the mere suggestion that she might cancel provoked 'a perfect tornado of distress' from the organizer. At the beginning of April she fell ill with a bad attack of flu, but went ahead regardless with arrangements for a much-needed holiday in Portofino near Genoa. George, on another protracted sabbatical from Cornell, was attending the Sociological School in Rome and agreed to meet her in Santa Margherita in Florence and travel on with her from there. Leaving John and Shirley once more at the school in Burford, Vera set off for Italy on 11 April.

The fortnight's holiday restored her health and lifted her spirits. Immortalized by Elizabeth von Arnim in her 1922 novel *The Enchanted April*, Portofino had become a fashionable resort among writers, an Italian Riviera for the literary set. Vita Sackville-West had sung its praises, Evelyn Waugh would take his second wife there for their honeymoon, and it was Rebecca West who recommended to Vera the small hotel overlooking the harbour where she and George stayed. Vera read and walked amid olive groves and cypresses, admiring the breathtaking landscape of the Ligurian Alps and the luxuriant displays of wild flowers in full bloom. 'The air is delirious with scent and I can't believe I have ever addressed a meeting,' she wrote to Winifred.

A markedly more relaxed Vera returned with George to London on 25 April only to find that a family tragedy had been narrowly averted in their absence. In recent months Mr Brittain had been making vague suicide threats. While Vera was in Italy, Edith Brittain had woken one night to discover that he had left the bedroom, and she had discovered him in the kitchen with his head in the gas oven. According to Dr Hughes, had she been four minutes later her husband would have been dead.

Years of acute depression had destroyed Arthur Brittain's health. His pocket diaries, with their precise details of his palpitation attacks, the weather, and the number of dividends he cashed each day at the bank, are a sad record of how limited and purposeless his life had become. For some time he had been receiving treatment for heart trouble, but the more recent diagnosis from his doctors suggested that he might be in the early stages of cancer. He was a frail and 'shrunken' old man of seventy, subject to strange moods and delusions. Mentally and physically he appeared to be declining fast and his condition placed Vera's tour arrangements in jeopardy. Could she forgive herself, she wondered, if anything should happen to her father while she was away? Should she delay her tour, or cancel it altogether and pay the heavy compensation that would be due to Colston Leigh? Edith Brittain, threatening to take to her bed with the usual ragbag of psychosomatic symptoms, was quite clear about where Vera's loyalties should lie.

'Of course it's a nuisance for you to have old parents', she moaned before going on to insist that it was Vera's duty to stay at home and care for her ailing parents. This emotional blackmail had a familiar ring to it. It had worked before, bringing Vera home from France in 1918 and keeping her at her parents' beck and call on countless occasions since. This time, however, darker forebodings about leaving the children for three months (admittedly in the capable hands of their German governess. Fräulein Bleichenbach) gave Vera additional reason for reconsidering her trip. Her war experiences still cast long shadows and her instinct now was always to expect the worst. She could not, for instance, watch the children being driven away in a car without imagining them drowned at the bottom of a river, sharing the fate of Isadora Duncan's son and daughter.

Predictably it was Winifred who brought common sense to bear and helped Vera to come to a decision. She was staying in Withernsea, trying hard to be a recluse and labouring over her latest novel (eventually published as *South Riding*), which she had intended to be a satirical comedy, but which kept threatening to turn into a depressing tragedy. She was adamant that Vera should go. It was an opportunity, she wrote to her, to spread the message of peace and contribute to political understanding with the United States which might never be repeated, and she had simply to disregard all the vague disasters which might befall the invalids and dependants in her life. As for John and Shirley, 'the dear, silly children', now six and nearly four, she would be delighted to look after them. She doted on them and they were devoted to her. Vera was a good storyteller and enjoyed reading the children the fairy-tales of Andrew Lang which had enchanted her as a child, but she stayed aloof from the children's playtime. Winifred, by contrast, revelled in the rough and tumble of their games and fantasies. 'When Winifred was in charge,' Shirley recalled, 'my brother and I would pile up tons of cushions, and sit on top pretending to be maharajahs, or dress up in old bonnets and bowlers as fashionable Victorians.' Winifred alone could get obedience from the irrepressible Shirley, sometimes with more than a hint of collusion in the child's naughtiness. But John was her favourite. 'John Edward,' she wrote to Jean McWilliam at this time, '. . . is a radiant joy to me. He is so beautiful and intelligent.'

Winifred's assurance put Vera's mind at rest. 'I used to disregard people with anguish,' she wrote to Winifred on 8 May, 'and that is so nervously expensive that I'm trying to learn to disregard them with equanimity. I could never disregard the children with equanimity, but can leave them to you feeling you will treat them as your own.' Confident that Winifred would refuse any money for herself for looking after John and Shirley, Vera promised ten per cent of any profits from her tour to the cause closest to

Winifred's heart, Ballinger and the South African Industrial and Commercial Workers' Union.

Late spring that year had a depressing aura about it. Mr Brittain was in and out of assorted nursing homes while Mrs Brittain fretted about being left alone without Vera's help; at Oxford the Reverend Catlin entered the throes of his protracted final illness; and from Bishop's Stortford at the beginning of May came the news of Robert Leighton's death, severing an important link with the past. 'It reminded me so much of going to the cottage at Keymer the morning we heard Roland was killed', Vera wrote to Winifred after attending the funeral, 'with Mrs Leighton looking hardly any different – the same rouged cheeks, the same tangle of unbrushed tow-coloured hair, the same general appearance of being half-dressed in clothes that should have gone to the laundry six months ago . . .'. Mrs Leighton fussed about Vera's thinness and told risqué stories over the coffin in her determination to camouflage her feelings. It was to be Vera's last meeting with Roland's mother. Marie Leighton died in January 1940. Her last years were spent living alone with Ossie, her Alsatian 'and closest friend'.

Vera escaped from family problems in early July when she took John and Shirley to Devon for a holiday. At last she was able to give the preparations for her tour serious consideration. From her standard repertoire of lectures she selected six: 'A Personal Confession of Faith' (on why she wrote *Testament of Youth*); 'Youth Morals Today and Yesterday'; 'The University Novel and its Place in Literature'; 'Marriage and the Modern State'; 'Journalism as a Woman's Job'; and 'How War Affects Women'.

Even at this late stage, though, the question of whether she would ever get to America still hung in the balance. In the last week of August she received a heart-rending scrawled note from her father, now in a nursing home in Harrow, which filled her with apprehension:

My dear Jack

I thought you ought to take an early opportunity of seeing me, because there may come a chance [*sic*] when you cannot see me again.

I am afraid that I am getting pains in my head, which I do not like, and the folks here will not let me see you if they develop.

Your affectionate

Father

My brain is distinctly worse.

On 2 September, less than two weeks before Vera was to sail on the *Berengaria*, Mr Brittain's condition suddenly deteriorated sharply and the specialist feared that kidney trouble had supervened on all his other difficulties. 'I am going ahead with my preparations,' Vera wrote to Winifred the next day, 'with the mental reservation that . . . they may all have to be abandoned.'

However, by the time Vera went to see her father, now in the Collingham Gardens Clinic, on the eve of her departure he seemed better, though he insisted that he would never see her again and presented her with a silver bookmark (inscribed with the words 'To dear Jack. Her Father's parting gift, with all love and affection'), a bunch of roses and a brooch in the shape of a bee for Shirley. 'This effort on my behalf and the affectionate greeting on the bookmark made me feel very mournful,' she wrote in her diary. It crossed her mind that he had attempted suicide on the last occasion she was out of the country. Could she prevent a further attempt by staying now? That evening her resolution to go to America almost broke when she went up to say good-night to the children. Years later she would give expression to the mixture of guilt, helplessness and anxiety she felt that night when she wrote, 'Why was a professional job, regarded as meritorious when performed by a man, so often made by circumstances to appear selfish and callous when done by a woman?'

On the morning of 15 September, Vera and George, who was returning to Cornell, travelled to Waterloo on the first leg of their journey. There to see them off were Mrs Brittain and the children, Miss Moore, the Burnetts, John Brophy, the novelist, who had become an avid admirer of both Vera's and Winifred's writing, and Winifred who was also accompanying them to Southampton. Neither of the children seemed particularly perturbed by the prospect of their parents' departure, though Shirley demanded assurance from Winifred that 'Auntie isn't going to America too'.

At Southampton, photographers and reporters jostled them for a sight of the film producer Robert Flaherty who, with his production company, the Man of Aran, was returning to Hollywood to make a new film. Vera, smartly dressed in a black coat with a grey fox collar and a new black Tyrolean hat, answered journalists' questions and had her photograph taken, though she realized that authors 'are birdseed when film personalities are travelling'.

Just after midday, the *Berengaria* sailed. Vera stood on deck with George, waving a red handkerchief at the gradually receding figure of Winifred on the quayside, conspicuous by the tiny mirror which she used to catch the reflection of the sun.

Her tour would turn out to be memorable for the most unexpected of reasons.

TEN

American Interlude

'I often feel that people like myself drift from place to place addressing large audiences but never really getting in touch with many individuals.'

Vera Brittain to Mrs Venice Edmonston, 7 April 1934

'I've been told that my book makes some people weep, but I care more that it should make them think . . .'.

Vera Brittain, 'Youth and War', December 1934

I

The six-day voyage was unexpectedly pleasant. Gales and a rough sea confined Vera to her cabin on the second day, but by the evening of the third the weather was calmer and she and George were able to stroll on deck and dance at a carnival dinner. 'For the first time in any ship on any sea I have enjoyed a voyage', she wrote in an early letter home, remembering the misery of her stormy first Atlantic crossing. Her cabin was palatial, the meals excellent, and many of the other passengers interesting and distinguished. In the ship's gymnasium she found herself exercising next to a portly Margaret Wintringham, Britain's second woman MP. George was delighted to discover that Lord Lothian and Victor Cazalet MP were on board and engaged them in long conversations into the early hours, while Harold Nicolson regaled Vera with stories of his and Vita Sackville-West's mishaps as lecturers in America. She was impressed with the affectionate way he spoke of Vita and reported to Winifred that, contrary to her expectations, he was not at all snooty, but 'straightforward . . . easy to talk to and very anxious to be helpful about my tour'.

Vera was up on deck early on the morning of 21 September after only a few hours' sleep to watch the outline of New York slowly emerge from the vanishing mist. Disembarking from the *Berengaria* in sweltering heat, she and George were met by George Brett, the youthful-looking President of the Macmillan Company, Vera's American publisher, and his wife Isabel.

She had met them fleetingly the previous summer when they had been on a brief visit to London. It was a short drive to the Bretts' apartment which adjoined the imposing Macmillan offices at the corner of Fifth Avenue and West 12th Street. On the way they passed Macmillan's main display window, filled in Vera's honour with the scarlet-jacketed ninth edition of *Testament of Youth* which had come off the presses only that morning.

It was soon down to work for Vera after she had been reintroduced to the company's Vice-President, Harold Latham, who had accepted *Testament of Youth* in London the previous year. An enormous pile of letters from enthusiastic readers awaited her, and despite the heat and her general fatigue she managed to dictate twelve replies before lunch. Would she be willing to meet and talk about active service in France, asked an ex-WAAC living in New York. Would she write a 200-word answer to the question, 'How can we Prevent a New War?' requested the editor of *Scholastic*, the National High School Weekly. In reply to the latter she returned to a well-tried theme of her anti-war speeches and writing. 'The ignorance of the war generation accounted for its easy exploitation', she wrote, going on to recommend that young Americans maintain their awareness of current affairs through travel abroad, by reading books 'dealing with war from every aspect', and by forming 'Youth group study circles . . . in which some international question is discussed'.

After lunch George Brett's car crawled through the Fifth Avenue traffic to take Vera to an appointment with her lecture-manager, Colston Leigh. Leigh, 'shrewd as a ferret and tough as a Brooklyn boy', had booked Vera for thirty-four lectures in twenty-five towns and was proposing to add another six to her itinerary – which worked out at a backbreaking average of four a week with only three days' rest. While Brett and Leigh wrangled over terms Vera was concluding, as she wrote to Winifred later, 'that the real point was not whether I should break down, but simply *when*'. As her first engagement, a Macmillan reception, was not until 29 September, and her tour did not begin until 5 October, the Bretts had invited Vera and George to spend a long weekend with them at their country 'shack', two hours' drive from New York in Fairfield, Connecticut.

Back at her hotel that evening after a visit to the theatre which she had been far too exhausted to appreciate, Vera found a cable from Winifred reassuring her that the children and Mr Brittain were all well. 'I've got a terrific job in front of me,' she replied, reviewing the punishing schedule that lay ahead, 'but think I can get through it if only all goes well at home.' 'Do take care of yourself,' she added. 'You look after everybody and no one really looks after you.'

'Being published by Macmillan is like having a knighthood conferred on you', the novelist Louis Golding remarked to Phyllis Bentley when Macmillan accepted *Inheritance* for American publication. Within days of arriving in the States, Vera was warmly commending the company's 'efficiency, kindness and exquisite courtesy', all of which appeared in striking contrast to the rather more peremptory treatment which she was used to from Gollancz.

At the Bretts' 'shack', a long bungalow surrounded by extensive woodland, Vera was fêted as a guest of honour at lunch, tea and dinner parties attended by members of the Brett family and local worthies. George had left the day after their arrival for the beginning of his semester at Cornell, and Vera occupied her time in tackling her mountainous correspondence and taking long and energetic walks with her host across woodland swamps and fields overgrown with thickets of briar. For these strenuous expeditions, she discarded her fashionable city clothes in favour of a white shirt and pair of linen shorts. In this uncharacteristic garb she looked at least fifteen years younger.

The Bretts were the first family of American publishing. For three generations they had run Macmillan, making it the largest, richest and most powerful of all American publishing houses, a position it was able to maintain until well into the Forties when it was finally overtaken by Doubleday. The prime architect of this success was George Platt Brett Senior, who had arrived in New York from London at the age of eleven in 1869 with his father, an experienced bookseller, who had been sent by Macmillan of London to set up an agency for their books. On the death of Alexander Macmillan in 1896, the English firm became a limited concern and the American branch was incorporated as the Macmillan Company of New York, a separate entity publishing its own books, with George Brett as its President.

The annual turnover, which had been about $50,000 in 1896, would climb by 1943 to close to $10 million. Their almost exclusive monopoly of the market for textbooks was the cornerstone of the company's financial success, but by the 1930s Macmillan's list – which included the names of John Masefield, H.G. Wells and Walter Lippmann – was also the most prestigious and distinguished of any American publishing house. The symbol of Macmillan affluence was the $800,000 eight-storey office building at the junction of Fifth Avenue and West 12th Street, so vast (it contained nearly an acre and a half of book storage space) that George

Brett Junior once seriously considered putting his stock boys on roller skates.

Brett Senior was a man of iron will and determination. Respected and feared by associates and rivals alike, he exercised a tight, even authoritarian, control over the company he had founded. No author's contract, however minor, passed without his personal scrutiny, and although he stepped down as President in September 1931 to be succeeded by his son, George Platt Brett Junior, he continued to dominate Macmillan right up to his death at the age of seventy-eight in 1936.

Born in 1893, Brett Junior had been brought up to regard Macmillan as his birthright. He refused to go to college and entered the firm at nineteen as a stock clerk. His first job was pulling nails from packing cases and he spent a year working as a salesman at Doubleday before returning to Macmillan to sell books in New York, Brooklyn, Newark and Chicago. Enthusiastically patriotic, he enlisted within weeks of America entering the war in 1917, serving with distinction on the Mexican border and later in the Argonne.

He became General Manager of Macmillan in 1928. As President of the company for more than a quarter of a century, he possessed all his father's shrewd business acumen, successfully piloting Macmillan through the depression; what he perhaps lacked was his father and grandfather's intuitive love of books and genuine respect for authors, and he often referred to the company he had inherited as the 'department store of publishing'.

In this shortcoming, however, he was more than compensated for by his Vice-President, Harold Strong Latham. Latham had graduated from Columbia in 1911 and had entered Macmillan through the advertising department. A sympathetic and friendly man (though capable of living up to his middle name in disagreements with the Bretts), he was a popular editor with writers, having himself written plays and stories for boys in the Twenties. In 1929 he had begun making annual trips to Europe, scouting for new talent. It was on one of these that he discovered *Testament of Youth*. But his greatest coup would come in 1935, when on a trip to Atlanta, Georgia, he secured the rights to Margaret Mitchell's *Gone with the Wind*.

A passageway connected George Brett's office to the executive apartment next door ('just 125 feet from desk to bed', he used to joke). Here Brett lived with Isabel, his wife since 1917, and their two sons, George Platt III and Bruce. He was ruddy-faced, quick-speaking, nearly six feet tall, with dark brown hair and startling blue eyes. Debonair, while at the same time retaining the discipline and bearing of his military training – he was a Major in the Reserve Corps in the late Twenties and was promoted to Lieutenant Colonel in the New York National Guard during the Second World War – he bore more than a passing resemblance in middle age to General Douglas MacArthur. He was unusual for his time in that he observed a rigorous routine of exercise and training. The eleven-year-old Shirley Catlin, staying with the Bretts in Connecticut during her evacuation to America in the Second World War, was shocked to see him swimming in the back garden pool in no more than a jockstrap. 'A very masculine man', a touch bullying in his contempt for those weaker than himself, he was an inveterate womanizer. Isabel Brett, slim and chic, relished her position as consort of a powerful and wealthy publisher, and turned a blind eye to her husband's indiscretions. Rumour had it that Brett was not averse to a swift affair with an attractive authoress on Macmillan's list if he felt it would sweeten her relations with the company and help to keep her happy.

At Fairfield Vera was finding Brett to be the most hospitable, attentive and, as she admitted in her diary, attractive of hosts. He reassured her about the length of her tour; flattered her by saying that she ought to be able to serialize her next book for as much as $10,000; and on her last day in Connecticut he presented her with a copy of her own *Poems of the War and After*, in part a reprint of *Verses of a VAD*, which he had recently published and which was already in its second edition. That evening under a full moon they drove out to Brett's yacht on Long Island Sound. When the motor of the cutter failed they remained in the harbour watching the lights visible from Long Island, eighteen miles away.

Back in New York Vera was guest of honour at a Macmillan reception. Officially she shared this position with the Scottish novelist and humorist A.G. Macdonell, and Sean O'Casey whose play *Within the Gates* was about to open in New York. But as Macdonell's boat was late and he arrived two hours after the reception had begun, and O'Casey excused himself halfway through to attend a rehearsal, Vera was left to bear the brunt of the occasion, standing for hours, shaking hands with two hundred and fifty people as 'fashionable New York, literary, social, academic' passed before her eyes. In a letter to his wife O'Casey ungallantly described this 'tattered, worn & fragile figure – though she wore an elaborate orchid in her breast', sucking in the flattery.

After the reception, a party of guests 'put on the smartest hats we had' and went on to dinner and dancing at a fashionable New York restaurant. Discussing Phyllis Bentley's damp-squib of a lecture-tour which had preceded Vera's that summer, Brett told Vera that the first time he had danced with Phyllis, 'she trembled like a jellyfish & held him at arm's length'. This determined Vera to offer a sophisticated contrast. 'So I said', she continued maliciously to Winifred, ' "Well I can't dance, but I won't hold you at arm's length" – which was perhaps a provocative request for about the closest dance compatible with decency; anyway I got it!'

The next few days before she travelled to Wheeling, West Virginia, for her first lecture were a scramble of interviews, and visits to photographers, agents and a film producer. One whole day was set aside for a succession of newspaper correspondents – including the fearsome Lillian T. Genn of the *Florida Times-Union* – to grill Vera on subjects ranging from her view of the New Deal to the desirability of legalizing trial marriages. Between interviews Brett took her to lunch and then to admire the view from the top of the Empire State Building. Archie Macdonell also acted as an escort. In America to collect material for the American sequel to his successful satire on British manners and customs, *England, Their England*, he had initially seemed slightly embarrassed in Vera's presence. This was partly due, she felt, to the emotional letters he had written her when *Testament of Youth* appeared, confessing his love for Agnes Elizabeth Murray, Gilbert Murray's daughter and her Somerville contemporary, whose early death she had alluded to in her autobiography. But, as Vera told Winifred, 'no embarrassment could live long in George Brett's presence', and on her final evening in New York Macdonell took her dancing at the Waldorf-Astoria. Brett's evident pleasure in Vera's company had not gone unnoticed by Macdonell. 'I believe he takes you where there *are* swamps', he joked with her, 'so that he can carry you over them.'

On 4 October, Vera left 'the comforting protection of Macmillan hospitality', boarding a sleeper for the twelve-hour overnight journey to West Virginia.

E.M. Delafield's wry account of an English writer on an American lecture tour, *The Provincial Lady in America*, first published the year before in *Punch*, had given Vera some impression of the ordeal she would have to face on her nine-week tour of eighteen states. She had been warned that she would find American audiences much more critical and exacting than those at home; but more of a shock was the extent to which she found her energy sapped by the ceaseless whirlwind of a schedule which propelled her from city to city with barely a moment to herself. Dismounting from her sleeper at her lecture venue she would immediately be taken on a guided tour of the city, attend a formal lunch, meet journalists for an afternoon of interviews, rush to dress for dinner, deliver her lecture, before returning to the Pullman to travel on to her next destination. In a way it was like the war, she told Winifred, 'One's utmost is continually being required of one – and yet all the time there is a sort of stimulus, a queer excitement and anticipation, that carries one through.'

Most of her lectures that autumn took place in the Middle West which she had disparaged in a letter to her mother back in 1925 as 'not very cultured, very "moral", very narrow and bigoted'. Her first lecture at a women's club in Wheeling, a large manufacturing town, did nothing to sway her from this view and its tepid reception hardly augured well for the rest of the tour. She had been booked to talk about *Testament of Youth* and yet few of the audience appeared to have read the book, and most seemed more interested in the dress and hat she was wearing than in anything she actually said. The same lecture elicited a more favourable response at her next stop, the town of Akron, Ohio, famous for its aircraft, rubber and Quaker Oats. Here she was warmly applauded by an audience of eight hundred before she hurried to catch the midnight train to Chicago.

'I *do* get a thrill out of going to these new cities each day or so', she wrote to Winifred as she travelled across miles of yellow prairie from a writers' and critics' reception in Chicago to a series of engagements in Cedar Rapids and Des Moines, Iowa. Only news of the assassinations at Marseilles on 10 October of King Alexander of Yugoslavia and Louis Barthou, the French Foreign Minister, which seemed 'hideously reminiscent' of Sarajevo in 1914, cast a pall briefly over her travels. If civil war were to break out in Yugoslavia between the Croats and Slovenes on one side and the Serbians on the other, then Italy might intervene, drawing France and other powers into a general conflict. From London on the day of the assassinations, Winifred wrote to Vera, sharing these fears.

> I heard the news as I was going to take the chair at a Woman's Mass Meeting of Protest against the Sedition Bill at Whitfield's Tabernacle. When I came in, sick at heart and apprehensive, I found the loudspeaker braying dance music in my room and as I entered a crooner was wailing: 'Oh, don't let it happen again'. It was the unspoken cry of a thousand listeners that night, I imagine.

The moment of crisis passed, but Vera was left in no doubt by her hosts at Cedar Rapids that what they cared about most was that the United States should avoid becoming involved again in the complications of Europe.

One of the things that struck Vera forcibly as she moved around the country was the number of men of her own age there seemed to be compared with England. 'I suppose other English generations have been like America in this respect,' she wrote home. 'She lost so few.' Nonetheless

America's war dead were commemorated with magnificent memorials like the Memorial Coliseum at Cedar Rapids, dominating 'like a titanic toy the compact bridge over the Cedar River'.

By the middle of the second week of October, when her programme included six lectures and five night journeys as she moved from north to south Iowa, Vera was beginning to wonder whether she would have sufficient stamina to complete her tour. The atrocious state of Iowa's railways added to the strain. At Des Moines the train's late arrival left her with only ten minutes to rush, dishevelled and angry, to lecture to six hundred librarians on 'Should Autobiographies be Forbidden?' On a fifteen-hour trip to Mason City she travelled in uncomfortably burning temperatures in a one-car 'local' with no buffet. Adding to her discomfort, a typical Middle Western dust storm blew up, filling her carriage with so much black grit that hours later on the lecture platform she was still removing it from her eyes, nose, mouth and hair. Following her from engagement to engagement was the gathering snowball of correspondence which the day's packed programme forced her to answer at night, depriving her of much-needed sleep. Winifred's regular letters, filled with tales of the children's antics, provided vital solace.

After a trip to St Louis and three days in Terre Haute, Indiana, Vera moved on to the Twin Cities of St Paul and Minneapolis, in Minnesota. The state had a strong tradition of liberalism and pacifism dating back to its support for President Wilson's 1916 campaign, and when *Testament of Youth* was published its citizens were among its earliest and most enthusiastic readers. In New York before her tour began Vera had received a letter from a Mrs Woodard Colby, inviting her to stay with her in St Paul when she visited Minneapolis. Disregarding the advice of her publisher and manager, that she should stay only in hotels, Vera had accepted the invitation, dimly remembering having met Mrs Colby at a party in London. 'You have made me quite the happiest woman in America', Mrs Colby wrote to Vera, assuring her that '... there will be no visiting, no social obligations, my whole pleasure will be derived from having so rare and dear a person under my roof'. Early on the morning of 22 October, Vera arrived in St Paul for a four-day visit.

Her hostess, she discovered, was 'a charming, young, frail-looking doctor's wife who writes poetry and is a great worker for peace'. Five years younger than Vera, Ruth Gage Colby had been devoted to feminism and peace since her late teens. As a student at the University of Minnesota, she had joined suffragettes in a mass demonstration, and in the early Twenties she had become a member of the recently formed League of Women Voters.

She too had suffered personal tragedy in the war. Hours after the Armistice, in the late afternoon of 11 November 1918, one of her closest friends, serving with the 103rd Infantry, had been killed in a German artillery attack which wiped out the whole company. After the war she joined the Women's International League for Peace and Freedom, the organization which was to have a deep and lasting influence on her life. In 1934 and 1935 she was chairman of the state WILPF. In 1919 she had married Dr Woodard Colby, a specialist in pediatrics, and had one son, Gage, born in 1923.

Vera and Ruth Colby were both small, dark and strong-minded, and fluent public speakers (Ruth Colby had studied voice in Vienna). They shared a dedication to the same causes and spent much of the time between Vera's engagements in rapt conversation. 'I just loved Vera from the time I first met her,' Ruth Colby recalled years later. 'I don't know what it is between two people. You just click.' Their four days together laid the foundations of a lifelong friendship, and while Ruth Colby's adulation of Vera precluded any real intimacy between them, they established a bond of trust which would enable Vera to send John and Shirley to her as evacuees in 1940.

Vera gave three speeches in Minnesota, promoting peace work and careers for women, advocating limited armament for self-defence and emphasizing the dangers that Germany and Japan presented to the world. The culmination of her visit was a lecture on 'How War Affects Women', delivered to an audience of five thousand at a grand assembly of the University Convocation. It was broadcast throughout Minnesota and received with standing ovations. 'Twenty years ago,' she enthused to Winifred, 'it would have seemed like a wild fantasy. I pictured myself then as writing, but never as the centre of cheering, wildly excited crowds.' Later she learned that as a result of her lecture the students had organized a demonstration against war.

In a state of exaltation Vera travelled to Cleveland, Ohio, on 26 October for her last lecture in the Middle West for nearly a month. The high point of engagements in Massachusetts and Ontario were three days in Toronto at the end of October where Vera dined with the Governor of Ontario, the Hon. Dr Herbert Bruce, and lectured to an overflowing auditorium of distinguished guests. The Toronto newspapers were fulsome in Vera's praise. The *Daily Star* reporter succumbed completely to her charms and concluded that 'the testatrix is greater than the "Testament".'

Vera returned to New York on 6 November. After all the exertions of the past five weeks she was pleased to see George, who joined her from Cornell for the Armistice weekend. Together they delivered 'a message from

England' at the Women's Overseas Service League dinner on Armistice Eve. She derived even greater pleasure from the opportunity to spend more time with George Brett. With the Bretts, George and Vera attended the Victory Ball at the Waldorf, Vera wearing her service medals and a flame-coloured taffeta gown which, she told Winifred, 'the Bretts like best of all my evening clothes'.

Seated in the Bretts' box in the huge ballroom they gazed down at the trooping of the colours taking place beneath them. '... Banners and pennons of all kinds', she wrote, describing the scene to Winifred:

> Stars and Stripes, the American Legion, Daughters of the American Revolution, War of Independence ... It was all very colourful and magnificent, and a series of National Anthems were sung while everyone stood to attention. In my mind all the time two distinct points were hammering: (i) this is what the peace movement is up against; (ii) this has nothing *whatever* to do with modern war as it is waged today.

Like the other ex servicemen at the ball Brett wore his full-dress uniform of navy blue adorned with gold braid, and a pale-blue-lined navy cloak, which transformed him from a practical New York businessman into a figure of 'Gilbert and Sullivan fantasy'. But it was as more than a figure of fantasy that Brett was assuming importance in Vera's mind. The initial spark of interest in him which she had felt at Fairfield had developed into an 'inconvenient, unexpected and mainly ... physical attraction'. She talked with him that evening about his memories of the war – 'how wildly patriotic he was when America went into the War, how eagerly he learned bayonet fighting ... and then the mixture of disgust and sheer insanity which seized him when he was faced with the real thing'.

Late that evening in a letter to Winifred she confessed that Brett

> continues to disturb me profoundly. I don't approve of any of his social, economic or political *ideas*; he is superficial in the way that Americans often are, not because they have no *capacity* for thought, but because they never in fact *do* think... I want to contradict him furiously about all his statements and values ... Yet I find him physically attractive to an infuriating degree; I find myself counting the hours each day till I see him again; when I dance with him (he dances divinely and he ... says I do, because physically we 'fit' admirably as dancers & I get his rhythm in no time), I get a thrill that is more than upsetting.

'*Vive l'amour et vive la bagatelle*', replied Winifred. 'Only don't take it too seriously and hurt yourself too much.'

The next day Vera watched Brett marching in the Fifth Avenue Armistice Day parade before attending a service of Remembrance in St Thomas's, New York's largest Protestant church. After seeing the Bretts off to Connecticut for the Armistice holiday, she and George dined in sombre mood in Radio City, the atmosphere only lightened by the arrival at the next table, halfway through dinner, of Vera's Oxford contemporary, Beverley Nichols, 'plump, pink, chubby, with two rather seedy-looking male companions'.

George returned to Cornell the next day, while Vera remained in New York to complete a series of local lectures. The Bretts were still away, and on a cold, windy night she found their apartment silently oppressive, '. . . and I slept uncomfortably, dreaming about George Brett'. Her restless night 'wasn't altogether a waste', as next morning, on an impulse, she decided to use Brett as the prototype for her heroine's soldier lover in her new novel. '. . . This way I shall be able to utilize, instead of having to fight against the overwhelming impulse to think about him all the time when I am not working . . . Well, thank God for books'.

On the evening Brett returned from Connecticut they sat up talking until one o'clock as Vera poured out her difficulties with *Honourable Estate*. ' "The genius of authorship that made *Testament of Youth* is *in* you" ', Brett gushed. ' ". . . What matters now is that you should live this next book in the same way . . .".' In her next letter to Winifred, Vera related how she had made him an extraordinarily direct proposition:

I had another bad night going over what he'd said and wondering how on earth to get in the American scene and background into my portrait of the young American lover of Ruth Alleyndene. Yesterday morning when he was going over the final part of my itinerary with me I suddenly decided to take a chance of getting my material from the . . . best possible source, and said: '. . . I don't know many Americans at all intimately. What would you feel if you found a portrait of yourself in my book? How would you like to be reincarnated as the young American lover of my heroine, during the War, and to die in the last advance?'

He looked at me in such a queer way – almost as if he were too overwhelmed to speak – half-smiling . . . and then burst out: 'Do whatever you darn well like with me, Vera. I don't give a damn so long as the book is the book *you* want to write . . .'.

Rushing about the office he quickly amassed a collection of photographs, maps, official war histories, and his own military souvenirs. Vera realized that Brett was now aware of her attraction to him; his excited readiness to help, she believed, was his way of 'telling me what *he* feels about myself'.

On 17 November Vera prepared to leave New York once more to start the second half of her tour of the Middle West. '. . . Though the spirit is entirely willing, the flesh is a little reluctant . . .', she admitted to Winifred. On the eve of her departure she dined early with the Bretts at their apartment before being driven by Brett to Pennsylvania Station to catch the 9.50 night train to Greensboro, North Carolina.

In the reasonable privacy of her compartment on the sleeper, in what she would later describe as 'a hazardous but stimulating incident', Vera and Brett came together in some kind of passionate encounter. 'If there had been a chance of doing it on the train, I would have', Vera told Winifred in a letter home at the end of the month. '. . . The sudden mutual abandonment of our defenses is still all but unbearable in its results.' For, by the time she reached Richmond, Virginia, two days later, she had come to the 'bitter sweet shock of the first realization' that she had fallen hopelessly in love.

III

Vera's tour continued its inexorable progress into late November, including lectures in Grand Rapids and Detroit and return visits to Pittsburgh and Cleveland. But her heart was no longer in it. She was disconsolate, lonely and frustrated. She had always been relatively successful in insulating her work from the intrusions of her personal life, but now all she seemed able to think about was Brett.

The intensity of her feelings surprised her. Having married a man for whom she felt affection, but for whom she had never felt anything remotely resembling passion, she had not expected to experience this kind of infatuation in middle age. Not that she suffered any illusions about Brett. She distrusted his innate conservatism and disliked his fundamentally militaristic outlook. She told Winifred that he was a man 'one would adore to spend a weekend with', but 'hate to spend one's life with'. She must also have thought twice about his motives in becoming involved with her. He was the clearest example she knew of the iron hand in a velvet glove, and from his reputation in the publishing world as a fairly ruthless operator, she was certain that he would have no mercy on her as an author if she let him down. For the time being he had every reason to be pleased with her: her tour was attracting enormous public attention and *Testament of Youth* was still selling a thousand copies a month in America. But she had to show him that she could maintain that level of success with her next book, *Honourable Estate*. This novel would be something she could do for Brett 'in which he will be at least as interested as I am'; it would also provide 'a vehicle for describing vicariously this absurd and forlornly hopeless passionate obsession'.

Isabel Brett, when Vera saw her again at the end of the month, appeared to suspect nothing. As for George, Vera had decided not to tell him anything about Brett for the present, 'not in the least because I want to deceive him or think he wouldn't understand', she wrote to Winifred, but because it might prove a source of embarrassment in his own business relations with Macmillan. While in New York Vera had persuaded Brett and Harold Latham to give George a contract for his next two books. He was delighted with this, believing the contract to have been won entirely on the merits of his work. It would cause no end of trouble and soured relations were he to discover what had occurred the last night in New York, and get it into his head that Vera had paid for the contract by offering herself physically to Brett!

She and George had arranged to spend Thanksgiving together in Washington, but exhausted by a particularly taxing lecture in Cleveland and depressed by the lack of contact with Brett, with whom she could only correspond on business matters, she was gloomy about his imminent arrival. From her hotel on 28 November she wrote to Winifred that 'this evening George will arrive here – full of his plans which, God forgive me, I don't want to hear about at all!' In fact the three days they were together were very pleasant, though less of a holiday than Vera had intended. A cable from Brett informed her that the League of Nations' Association had arranged for her to give a national broadcast on 'Youth and War' on 13 December, the day before she sailed. As Thanksgiving was Vera's last free period, much of her time had to be spent in the preparation of a two-thousand-word speech.

It was a great honour, she informed Winifred, as national broadcasts were normally reserved for people like 'Presidents and Prime Ministers and Bernard Shaw'.

> I do feel it, of course, but I can't help even more regarding it as something which will prevent my having tea with George Brett that last afternoon before I sail! How odd it is to write so hard for fame and to long for it – and then get it and find it an intolerable nuisance because one has fallen hopelessly in love!

The last two weeks of her tour took her from Cincinnati through Minnesota in a blinding blizzard, to Chicago, Kansas City, and finally back to New

York on 10 December. 'I am so weary of lecturing and packing and being polite,' she wrote to Brett from Chicago on 4 December, 'that I hardly know how to bear these last few days in the wilderness!' She was longing to see John and Shirley again – 'I've almost forgotten their dear faces and voices' – and to talk to Winifred whom she thanked in a letter written a week before she left America for her 'everlasting patience with me in my incessant adventures'. She wanted, though, to have her mind put at rest that Winifred had not been 'annoyed or upset or disgusted by the complete frankness' with which she had written about her relationship with Brett.*

The climax of these last days in America was Vera's broadcast from Radio City. In it she reiterated a theme which she had included in so many of the forty-odd lectures she had given over the past few months.

> If the courage which my contemporaries once gave to the War can be used by our successors on behalf of Peace, the martyrdom of man may still lead at last to his redemption. If modern youth has realized, as I believe it has, that to live for one's country is a finer type of patriotism than to die for it, then the youth of my generation will not, after all, have laid down the best of its life in vain.

The evening of the broadcast she returned to the Bretts' apartment to pack and say her farewells. She must have reflected on what the past three months had given her: a sense of achievement at having survived such a strenuous assault course of a tour, a handful of new friends and many new correspondents, and a totally different perspective on the country she had turned her back on seven years earlier. All these paled into insignificance, though, beside her aching, impractical passion for George Brett.

At midnight on 14 December she sailed for England on the *Majestic*.

---

* Winifred later succeeded in making some creative capital from Vera's relationship with Brett. In chapter 6 of Book VI of *South Riding*, the description of Carne and Sarah Burton dancing in the ballroom of a Manchester hotel – 'I know nothing of his mind, nothing, nothing, nothing. But I know what his body is going to do before he does it' – clearly has its origins in Vera's account of her evening with Brett at the Waldorf.

ELEVEN

1935: 'The Worst, Cruellest, Saddest Year Since the War'

'You're a bit hard, by the way, on Vera Brittain. That's pardonable for Vera invites one's hardness and censure. I was one of the worst of her enemies, but I feel a lot more lenient to her now. She has had a trying life, and may be forgiven for some of her bitter egoism, especially now that she has shed a great deal of it, because she was really devoted to Winifred and did things for her that scarcely anybody knew needed to be done.'

St John Ervine to Annie Swan, 15 February 1940

'It is a great tribute to you that she chose you, among so many who loved and wanted her for her chief friend . . .'

Sarah Gertrude Millin to Vera Brittain, 15 May 1940

I

After all the excitement of her months in America, Vera's return home on 21 December brought her sharply back down to earth. George had remained at Cornell, and after a brief reunion Winifred travelled to Cottingham to spend Christmas with her family. Even Vera's joy at being reunited with John and Shirley was muted by finding them both ill with mumps and confined to bed for the whole of Christmas.

Instead it was Mrs Brittain's demands which overshadowed the festivities. An improvement in Mr Brittain's health and general spirits had led his doctors to suggest that a move from Oakwood Court with all its unhappy associations might prove beneficial. Fired with enthusiasm for the idea, Mrs Brittain had parked her husband in the Collingham Gardens clinic, let the flat, and installed herself in a Kensington hotel where she languished in a red velvet tea gown and complained relentlessly about the food and service. Insistent that Vera accompany her on house-hunting expeditions as 'a nice little recreation', she spent long afternoons with her daughter traipsing around London viewing properties, each one larger and more impractical for an elderly couple than the last. 'I seem to have been drowned in a warm bath of domesticity ever since I arrived home', Vera wrote in her first letter of the New Year to George.

There was another invalid for Vera to nurse when Winifred returned to Glebe Place at the beginning of January and promptly succumbed to a particularly painful attack of mumps. While convalescing she continued to work steadily on the half-finished *South Riding*, moving to lodgings at Clifton Terrace in Hornsea on the East Yorkshire coast in the middle of February to concentrate on her novel. But unlike the period of refreshing solitude at Withernsea the previous spring, she was not free from interruption. She felt duty-bound to visit ill and dying relatives, and against a background of mounting international tension, with the debate over rearmament becoming increasingly heated, was unable to refuse the invitations to speak which pursued her from London. 'Things are getting rather formidable . . .', she had explained to Vera in mid-November, 'all issues, pacifist, feminist and . . . libertarian . . . seem to be crystallizing just now'. Since the summer she had ignored her friends' concern for her health and had resumed a hectic programme of lecturing. She had appeared on public platforms across the country in support of the League of Nations' Peace Ballot, and in the wake of the encouraging reception that greeted her short study, *Women and a Changing Civilisation*, published in the autumn of 1934, had addressed a number of women's organizations. With an undisguised thrill at her own daring, she had also infiltrated several of the British Union of Fascists' meetings, 'investigating' for the National Council of Civil Liberties, and distributing anti-Fascist pamphlets for the Union of Democratic Control.

From Hornsea she wrote to Vera of her guilt that 'all the time the news in the paper is so disturbing that I feel I ought not to be sitting here comfortably writing a novel . . .'. The menacing sound of bombers from the nearby aerodrome, dropping depth-charges into the North Sea, disturbed her concentration and reinforced her fears for the future. 'A war may be coming, but I find it difficult to finish my book among sounds that make me imagine it has started already.'

Despite her prolonged burst of activity, however, the results of recent blood tests provided the most encouraging news about her health that she had received since 1932. All the indications were that the progress of the disease had been halted. On 18 February Vera wrote to her expressing her delight and relief:

It sounds queer & almost unbelievable that you could actually have *improved*

307

in spite of all the work you do – almost perhaps as though you were still young enough for part of the lost tissue to be re-endowed with life. You are such a pathological eccentricity anyway, that almost anything seems possible. This is quite the best news I have had for ages – I don't, deliberately, worry you about your health . . . but I think about it constantly. Not only on your account, but for the most selfish possible reasons . . .

The real point is what you can do with your *own* work if you only have time. You *must* have time – and if only you take reasonable care of yourself, there seems to be now no reason why you shouldn't have. It's marvellous to be as you are after such a complete smash-up only three years ago.

Obermer's optimistic report on Winifred's condition was the one glimmer of light in an otherwise dark and depressing beginning to 1935 for Vera. The miles of ocean between herself and Brett had only increased her 'constant and intolerable desire' for his 'physical presence'. Before leaving America Vera had admitted to Winifred that she was 'torn between the reluctance to make any more demands on you, and the feeling that never before have I needed you so badly'. Now with immediate worries about Winifred seemingly removed, Vera's daily letters to her dwell on the painfully unresolved dilemma of her relationship with Brett.

In a matter of weeks, she told Winifred, Brett had shattered her naive illusion that fame could confer happiness for a lifetime, an illusion she believed she had always suffered from, 'except during the brief period when I was in love with Roland & he was alive'. The only letters she had received from Brett since her return dealt with matters as impersonal and mundane as her income tax. This struck her as absurd and 'too disturbing,' but she had convinced herself that he did so for reasons of discretion. She tried hard to be sensible. For her own peace of mind she realized that 'except for one or two brief intimations of my existence', she had to try to forget about Brett until the summer when she would see him on his annual visit to London. In the meantime she would immerse herself in *Honourable Estate* which she had promised to Gollancz for the spring of 1936. Not only did her family's finances for the following year entirely depend on it, but she also hoped that the process of writing it might be cathartic. She remained unreconciled to three things in her life – the failure of her friendship with Phyllis Bentley, what she had recently learned from Colonel Hudson about Edward's last days in Italy, and her relationship with Brett – and she intended to use *Honourable Estate* to come to terms with them. Into the second half of the novel, as she had planned with Brett, she now introduced the character of an American corporal, the improbably named Eugene C. Meury. Meury was to be a portrait of Brett in the war, twenty years earlier.

'Not so difficult this,' she wrote to Winifred, 'as psychologically he is still 25 . . .'.

Winifred as usual lent a sympathetic ear to Vera's problems. To stave off depression she suggested that Vera take a short working holiday with her in Hornsea. Tempting as this invitation was, Vera felt obliged to be at home when George returned from Cornell at the end of February, especially as he was proposing to spend April as the *Yorkshire Post*'s correspondent in Moscow, reporting on Anthony Eden's visit there. After all, she admitted grudgingly to Winifred, George had 'some rights as a husband'.

As was his habit, George heralded his imminent arrival by dispatching long lists of instructions to Vera as soon as his ship docked at Southampton, leading her to fear that she was about to be submerged under another tidal wave of domesticity which would make work on her novel difficult. However, George turned out to be 'very reasonable about everything', agreeing that the kind of interruptions which had impeded the progress of *Testament of Youth* could not be allowed to prevent *Honourable Estate* from meeting its deadline, and generously lending Vera his mother's diaries as background material for the first part of her novel. Mrs Catlin had kept a journal from the age of thirteen right up to her death at forty-four, and Vera soon found herself swept along by the diaries' 'passion, turbulence and introspection'.

On 11 March Vera embarked on a week of lectures in Chester, Blackpool, Liverpool, Bradford and Huddersfield. It was more than eighteen months since *Testament of Youth*'s publication had launched her series of national lectures and she felt thoroughly jaded by the 'continuous racket'. But she struggled through her by now well-rehearsed talks and spent the long-awaited weekend with Winifred in Hornsea en route to London. In the cramped conditions of Winifred's sitting-room at her lodgings the two women worked long hours on their novels, but returning to Chelsea, Vera collapsed into bed, suffering from exhaustion and acute nausea. After a couple of days of feeling 'out of sorts with no satisfactory explanation' she began to suspect that she was in the early stages of a pregnancy. It was too early for the doctor to say for certain that she was expecting a baby, and in any case a recurrence of her gastric complaint brought on by the work and tension of the past months seemed the more likely diagnosis, but Vera's inability to throw off her symptoms left her too weak to work and full of pessimism about the future.

The fact that she had arrived home just in time to see George depart for Moscow on 23 March added to her depression. 'It was like seeing him vanish into the *Ewigkeit* for 2 months', she wrote despondently to Winifred. With no definite forwarding address for the whole of his two months' absence she felt more than a little desolate, and also resentful that his trip, which had been extended to include a stay in the Caucasus and a return passage via Constantinople and Athens, was as usual being made largely at her expense. She ached in every part of her body and felt overcome with tiredness. She hadn't written anything worthwhile and was being badgered by her mother to help unpack and hang pictures at her parents' new house at 37 Edwardes Square, off Kensington High Street.

Vera's letters to Winifred in the final week of March strike a rare note of despair and, even more uncharacteristically, of indecision. 'You have so much more courage than I have to detach yourself from the circumstances of your life', Vera wrote to her on 23 March. 'You have the ability to concentrate when everything is going badly – even when your own health is going wrong. I alas! haven't.' For a while she toyed with the idea of entering a rest home for professional women, then decided that they sounded 'rather grim and full of discipline', and instead pinned her hopes for a full return to health on an Easter weekend with Winifred at Tenby, on the south coast of Pembrokeshire.

By 27 March she was feeling slightly better: a determined diet of glucose and Bisodol appeared to have done her some good. Nevertheless she had come to some worrying conclusions about her health. If she was not pregnant, she told Winifred, then 'it may be that at long last the war years are taking their toll of my physique'. Exercising her flair for the dramatic, she continued:

> I always rather wondered why they [the war years] didn't have more effect on [my] nerves and glands than they did not because of their hard work, but because of their long strain & sorrow, and their series of shock after shock. It may be that my American experience by reviving the passions and emotions of that time somehow stirred up its latent effects.

The extent to which her love for Brett lay at the root of her illness becomes clearer still, later in the letter:

> I only know that the past three months' anguish of grief and unavailing desire has been comparable to nothing I have ever felt since the war years themselves. I am afraid of June – afraid that when we meet the mutual insanity of last autumn will carry us away again, with the same repetition for me of passion and subsequent pain. And yet to run away from it would be worse . . . it would leave behind a still unreconciled situation . . .

In the grip of her passion for Brett there was no fantasy too far-fetched for her to contemplate. On the one hand, she hoped that she wasn't pregnant as she wanted no more children by George; on the other, she wanted to be able to have children for a few more years. Not, she assured Winifred, that she thought she could ever have Brett's 'without wrecking the basis upon which all that matters most to me of my professional life now rests . . . But just in case . . .'.

Vera's candour must have shocked even Winifred. All Winifred could do was to counsel patience and offer the small comfort that 'passion can become friendship. I don't say without heartache – yes, and a *physical* ache.' Her advice was based on recent painful experience. That spring Harry Pearson had once more been in evidence, appearing at Winifred's lodgings without a word of warning, spending days at a time with her and then, tantalizingly, leaving with no indication of when he would return. 'I can't pretend I don't owe him far more than he owes me', she confided sadly to Vera. 'I love every tone of his voice, every movement of his hands. And I wouldn't *not* love him for anything. But it is . . . a humiliating and ridiculous situation for a woman of my age, intelligence and interests.'

When Vera saw the doctor a few days later he confirmed that there was no question of a baby, though it might still be possible for her to conceive in the future. 'In view of what I both hope and fear from this summer this may be a comfort', she told Winifred. In the first week of April she felt stronger 'for no ascertainable reason', and at Tenby at the end of the month the combined effect of Winifred's company and the fact that she was beginning to make significant headway with *Honourable Estate* contributed to her feeling healthier than she had done all year.

She was relieved too to hear from George in Moscow after a long silence. He had been enjoying the lavish hospitality of the Soviet Government, though the chief purpose of Eden's visit, the negotiation of an Anglo-Russian treaty with Stalin, had failed. His letter caused her to reflect on how much she would miss 'that sympathetic understanding, that sympathetic perception of *nuances* and shadows . . .' were she married to someone like Brett. 'Why is there this strange divorce between one's mind and one's flesh', she asked Winifred, '– why does one's flesh refuse to respond where one's mind loves and admires, yet is kindled to flame by someone without tenderness and compassion?' George's main piece of news must have struck her ambivalently. He had decided, he told her, to resign his professorship at Cornell with immediate effect and return to England to concentrate on active politics. There would be a general election that year or the next and he intended to devote all his time and energy to winning a seat in the Commons.

Vera had always supported George's political ambitions. Ironically, though, his decision came at a time when she had begun seriously to consider joining him in the States and settling there with the children. It was not only the fact that her reputation in America meant that she could now do so without professional disadvantage. There was also the inevitable pull of Brett's presence there.

If she received news of George's plans with any tinge of disappointment, she gave him no inkling of it, lunching with him at the Ivy to celebrate his return on 25 May. Within a month George had been selected to fight the marginal constituency of Sunderland for Labour at the next election.

II

At the beginning of the first week of May, after their holiday in Tenby, Winifred had returned with Vera to Chelsea. Her period of creative isolation was over as *South Riding* was almost complete. Only the last chapter, which was to be set against the background of the forthcoming Silver Jubilee celebrations of George V and Queen Mary, remained to be written.

London, festooned with flags and flowers of red, white and blue, seemed to Vera to be like 'one vast patriotic shriek'. On Jubilee Day itself, 6 May, she, Winifred and the children watched from a window of the Midland Bank in Queen Victoria Street as the royal procession passed by at a swift trot on its return from the service of thanksgiving at St Paul's. A week later Winifred gave what was to be the final public speech of her career. Fittingly, it was at the Jubilee dinner of the Women's Freedom League where, as a representative of the younger generation of feminists, Winifred paid tribute to what the older campaigners had achieved for women in the twenty-five years of the King's reign. With this engagement over she could turn her full attention once more to her novel, writing the Jubilee scenes and revising the early chapters at her new office in the King's Road, where she often worked into the early hours and sometimes stayed overnight.

Vera was 'perpetually troubled' at the prospect of seeing Brett again now that June was getting 'so horribly near'. She was at Paddington with George and Winifred on 6 June to meet Brett and his wife from the boat-train, and throughout their month-long stay her diary excitedly chronicles her continuing infatuation. As Vera's guests the Bretts attended one literary occasion after another: the presentation of the Femina Vie Heureuse prize to Elizabeth Jenkins by E.M. Forster, a Foyle's Luncheon in memory of T.E. Lawrence, and a *Time and Tide* cocktail party where, Vera noted without surprise, the staff all fell for Brett. At a party held at the Savoy in the Bretts' honour, Vera, wearing blue and mauve chiffon to match the mauve orchids that Brett had sent her beforehand, danced three times with Brett, a distinction he did not bestow on any of the other women present. He was keen to read *Honourable Estate*. 'I hardly feel I can wait to read it . . . How long have I to wait?' he asked her. The next afternoon she spent half an hour alone with him, discussing the American dialogue for the novel. 'When that which is perfect is come, that which is in part shall be done away', was Vera's solemn commemoration of the afternoon in her diary, revealing her inflated expectations.

Just how inflated those expectations were must have become distressingly apparent to Vera in the course of Brett's stay. Her description of herself in her diary a few days after the Savoy party as being '. . . full of grief' suggests that if she had been hoping for some acknowledgement from Brett that her feelings for him were reciprocated, none had been forthcoming. Indeed, it appears that the subject of their future relationship was not even broached. Whatever had prompted Brett's part in the 'mutual insanity' of the autumn, he clearly had no intention of repeating it, or of carrying it any further. Yet Vera continued to hope against hope. 'It may have meant a great deal, or absolutely nothing, but I felt snubbed & miserable', Vera wrote after Brett had told her that he couldn't spare another half hour to talk about her book. Her uncertainty persisted as she and Brett said their goodbyes at Waterloo on 4 July:

> Just as the train left he shook hands, said 'I'll be writing you', and looked hard at me from the window as it began to move – but his expression really told me nothing, so I am left (as in the War) with a doubt which may never be resolved.

She might have been able to cope with outright rejection; lingering doubt was harder to bear. '. . . Slowly to bed', she wrote that evening, 'wondering whether it was an end or not'.

It would be a year before Vera saw Brett again. In the meantime she derived what consolation she could from the writing of her novel. Even more perhaps than she had envisaged, *Honourable Estate* would serve as an emotional release and a vehicle for her frustrated love for Brett. Eighty pages at the novel's core dramatically describe the affair in wartime France between an American soldier, Eugene Meury, and an English VAD, Ruth Alleyndene. Both feel at first unable to consummate their strong mutual attraction. Meury has a fiancée back home, while Ruth is inhibited by the conventions of her late-Victorian upbringing. But the night before Meury returns to the front, to his death in action, as it turns out, they make love.

The writing is mawkish and embarrassingly coy, the heroine insufferably noble and self-sacrificing. Meury, with his 'intent, eager profile', 'luminous eyes', and lack of intellectual pretension ('I'm no sort of a highbrow . . . I got through school without flunking, but polo and baseball and skiing were more in my line'), is Brett with the barest minimum of disguise. When Ruth, in asking Meury to be her lover, assures him that 'We shall have created something between us . . . a relationship, a belonging to each other – and nothing that happens afterwards will ever be able to take it quite away', it is not difficult to perceive Vera's attempt at a fictional resolution of her own real-life romantic impasse.

Vera sent Meury to his death, but Brett was back in London in the summer of 1936, as charming and beguiling as ever. Vera passed more 'gorgeous' and 'adorable' evenings dancing and talking with him. On the strength of the Ruth–Meury chapter he told her, with no apparent irony, that she was a 'superb novelist', and that 'the seduction scene was such first-class literature that he would go to court about it if necessary'. Underlying Vera's diary entries for his visit is a calm, resigned acceptance of the fact that despite his continuing attraction for her, friendship is the most that he can offer in return. This time when he left Vera wrote, 'It will be a year, I suppose, before I see him – but I recollect Olive Schreiner's words "Sometimes such a sudden gladness seizes me when I remember that somewhere you are living and working".' Unrequited love, the quotation seems to suggest, is preferable to renunciation of that love.

Brett remained a loyal friend to Vera. 'If we never see each other again', she wrote to him in 1940 during the Blitz, when government restrictions prevented her from travelling to the States to visit John and Shirley, 'I know that you will do your best for my children and my books'. He proved himself on both counts. He was a conscientious guardian of the children's welfare during their evacuation, and her staunch defender at Macmillan after 1944 when her pacifist activities had seriously eroded the sales of her books in America. His letters to her in the Forties, while 'brisk and executive' like those of Meury, his fictional counterpart, do exhibit genuine concern for her safety in the worst of the bombing, and overall give an impression of affectionate regard tempered with respect.

But for Vera, Brett was more than just a friend, and for over a decade he would continue to hold a peculiarly powerful sway over her affections. He had brought into her life, she wrote in 1940, 'a glow and glamour that I never knew existed before'. He appears as 'X' in her letters to Margaret Storm Jameson during the Second World War. 'X' is the man she longs for, with whom she corresponds regularly, but can see only rarely. After staying with the Bretts on her lecture tour of America in 1940 she confides to Storm Jameson that '. . . I always look specially well physically for a few weeks after I have been spending time with X'. In other ways his effect on her is oddly sustaining. Her resolve to stay in England in the first year of the war is strengthened by thoughts of him:

> . . . Even when I am suffering most from X's inaccessibility, some instinct deep down tells me that the feeling he has for me is strengthened, not weakened, by the fact that I am English, and difficult to see, and (from the American point of view) in permanent possible danger. Even when I most want him, I know that if I am to keep my self-respect I must stay here – and therefore make sure of him.

More poignantly, on reading *Europe to Let* by Storm Jameson, she is moved to tears by what she sees as the resemblance of two characters to Brett and herself:

> Oddly enough when I read the story of her and Stelik, I thought, 'Really this is just like X and me' – all the meetings at odd times in strange places, hurried encounters snatched from the midst of work. There was one sentence which brought tears to my eyes as I read it – 'They had as much private life as she had – a day, a week, an hour, perhaps not so much as an hour, and not more than a dozen times a year'. (A dozen times a year – if I only had that, instead of perhaps not even one, in how many years to come!)

There is more than a hint here of self-delusion on a grand scale, and yet it is not so very surprising to find Vera writing of her one-sided infatuation as if it were an illicit affair. Her prolonged separations from Brett allowed her to idealize their relationship in the way that she had once idealized Roland, especially during their long months apart when he was out in France in the trenches. Essentially romantic by temperament, Vera had effectively banished romance from her life in youth, only to be caught unawares by a great passion in middle age.

Bitter disappointment, however, was inevitable when the illusion met head-on with the reality. Amy Burnett recalled an incident on one of Brett's visits to England in the early Fifties when Vera was living at Whitehall Court. Vera had spent all morning getting ready, and waited, immaculately dressed and made-up, nervously anticipating his arrival. When Brett appeared, carrying an elaborate bouquet of flowers for her, he explained that he could stay for no more than five minute as his wife was downstairs waiting in a taxi. Later, after Brett had gone, Amy found Vera in a state of considerable distress, sobbing in her bedroom. Once again, a reunion with Brett had failed to live up to Vera's expectations.

It may have been this episode which provoked from Vera the more critical and detached estimate of Brett's character in a letter to Shirley in 1952:

> George Brett is . . . charming, generous, inconstant, and basically insincere. I must be about the only woman with whom he has remained close friends for 18 years but I don't delude myself that this is not partly good business – it would never have lasted so long if I had not been a Macmillan author!

It was very much, as she had once admitted to Storm Jameson, 'a queer, emotional mix-up'.

III

It must have been all too apparent by the summer of 1935 that Winifred's health had taken a turn for the worse. Vera continued to maintain an attitude of 'self-deceiving optimism' towards Winifred's condition. 'I did not really want to know how ill she was', she would later write in *Testament of Friendship*, 'because I could not picture life without her'. But others among Winifred friends and colleagues were more realistic.

William Ballinger, visiting Winifred at her King's Road flat to discuss African affairs at the end of July, was sufficiently perturbed by her haggard and drawn appearance to express his anxiety and urge her to rest. While he was with her she collapsed on to a divan, feeling sick and faint, though she assured him that it was no more than a mild attack of dizziness. Winifred Cummings, who typed *South Riding*, was convinced that Winifred was in pain when she went to Glebe Place to collect the manuscript from her. After forty years Mrs Cummings retained a clear impression of the ashen-faced woman who came in from the garden to greet her. Winifred's ghostly pallor, she recalled, was accentuated by the bright red lipstick she was wearing, and she appeared to be short of breath. Even Mrs Cummings's young son, Brian, who accompanied her, noticed how ill Winifred was, and remarked to his mother afterwards 'how different Miss Holtby looked *close to*'.

Other worrying signs of Winifred's deterioration were more difficult for

Vera to ignore. It was clear that the pain-relieving drug, Padutin, on which Winifred now habitually depended, was beginning to fail her. In their last days at Tenby, Vera had watched aghast as Winifred suffered an acute attack of headache and sickness. In the final week of July when Winifred was attending the Malvern Festival with Lady Rhondda, she experienced a similar attack, only this time more painful. She managed to conceal her illness from Lady Rhondda, appearing on the balcony of her hotel to be photographed with Shaw on his seventy-ninth birthday, and sitting up half the night to review his new play, *The Simpleton of the Unexpected Isles*, for *Time and Tide*. But in her letters to Vera she admitted that she had 'felt rotten the first three days', and that despite the beauty of the countryside she 'simply could not walk about much'.

While Winifred was at Malvern, Vera had been spending a couple of days with George in North Staffordshire, collecting descriptive material for *Honourable Estate*. Visiting towns and villages associated with her paternal ancestors, she reflected with some sadness on the decline of her family's standing in the area. Ash Hall in Bucknall, Stoke-on-Trent, once the ancestral residence of the Meighs, had been turned into a golf hotel; The Cloughs, her father's boyhood home, was in the hands of the housebreakers and was already a ruin; and the Meigh family vault in Bucknall churchyard had long since been allowed to fall into decay. 'It all represents the death of a tradition', she recorded, 'and though I have probably done more than any member of the family to fight & destroy that tradition the evidence of its departure fills me with regret and sadness'.

Vera and George returned to London by way of Buxton. Vera had not visited her childhood home since her parents' abrupt departure twenty years before, yet the 'complacent little health resort' seemed hardly to have changed at all. In the Public Garden, near where she had once walked with Roland, she located the town's War Memorial. Inscribed on its bronze plaques were the names of many of the young men with whom she had once danced and played tennis. Edward's name was there too, although the local council had omitted to record his Military Cross (an oversight that would not be rectified for another fifty years).

They arrived back in Chelsea on 27 July, in time for Shirley's fifth birthday. Half an hour after their return Arthur Brittain telephoned, anxious to have a firsthand report of the changes that had taken place in his native Staffordshire. He had not felt well enough to visit Glebe Place for several months, but Vera reminded him that it was his granddaughter's birthday and promised him a detailed account of their trip, and to her surprise he agreed to make the short journey from Edwardes Square to Chelsea.

While Shirley played with the tricycle her grandparents had given her, George presented his father-in-law with a stone which he had brought back from the ruins of The Cloughs. Vera had been concerned that he might be depressed by this relic of his childhood, but he seemed undisturbed. The next afternoon Vera took the children for their Sunday visit to Edwardes Square. Although Mr Brittain said that he was in too much pain to accompany Mrs Brittain and the children into the square garden, he was more cheerful and animated than he had been of late, and sat chatting to Vera about France where she was taking the children for their first holiday abroad in three days' time.

On 31 July Vera, the children and Fräulein, their governess, crossed the Channel for their holiday at Wimereux. Edith de Coundouroff and her sixteen-year-old daughter, Margaret, went with them and also stayed at the Grand Hôtel des Anglais et des Bains. George planned to spend most of August in Sunderland, familiarizing himself with the constituency, but he was to join his family for ten days at the beginning of the month. Winifred was to come out later still when she had finished her book.

The weather was fine and for two days Vera wrote her novel in pleasant sunshine in the hotel garden. On 3 August she and the rest of the party were just sitting down to lunch when John suddenly called out, 'Look, there's Auntie!' and Vera turned to see Winifred's gaunt figure in a tweed coat, standing in the hotel lobby.

> As she wasn't coming till next Saturday and it was G[eorge] I was expecting I knew at once something dreadful had occurred & that she had come to tell me. I went out to her at once & said 'Something's wrong'. She said 'Yes' – I said 'Is it G[eorge]?' . . . but she answered 'No, it's your Father' and told me that Father was missing, having disappeared from Edwardes Square sometime during the night of Aug. 1st–2nd . . .

Vera's mother had found his room empty when she went to call him early on the morning of 2 August. The cook had discovered the front door open, prompting Edith Brittain to remember that she had heard a loud noise in the middle of the night, which she now realized had been the sound of the iron bolt dropping against the side of the door. Arthur Brittain had disappeared without a coat, and with thirty shillings in his pocket. After more than a day's intensive police search, he had not been found, and it was feared that there was little hope of his being still alive. To spare Vera the shock of an abrupt telegram Winifred, weak as she was, had come to fetch her home by the evening boat.

'I felt sure Father was in the river', Vera wrote later. He had often talked of throwing himself off Hammersmith Bridge, and on one occasion had got as far as going down there, returning only because he said that there were too many people present to throw himself in.

The strain of the journey had brought on another of Winifred's attacks. She lay on the bed as Vera packed, looking so ill that Vera feared that she might not be strong enough to travel. But she urgently needed to return to London to obtain a new supply of Padutin injections, and after eating something she seemed better. Entrusting the children to the care of Fräulein and the de Coundouroffs, Vera and Winifred left by taxi for Boulogne.

It was past midnight when they arrived back at Victoria to be met by George. Winifred returned alone to Glebe Place while Vera went directly to Edwardes Square to be with her mother. Despite the circulation of a description to police stations throughout London and as far afield as Brighton, where it was thought he might have gone to visit his old holiday haunts, there was still no news of Mr Brittain. Sitting on her bed, unable to sleep, the first full shock of her father's disappearance overcame Vera and she wept at the idea of his frail figure, inadequately clothed and unnoticed, going out into the night.

Early on the morning of 5 August, two days later, a ferryman spotted a body floating in the river near Railshead Ferry at Isleworth. When recovered from the water the body was revealed to be in a severe state of decomposition, but at the mortuary George was able to identify it as that of his father-in-law. There were no marks of violence on the corpse which showed signs consistent with drowning, but he described the face afterwards to Vera, as looking 'black and red and swollen like the bruised face of a prize-fighter'. The inquest on 7 August was sympathetic and dignified, but given Arthur Brittain's history of depression and his previous attempt at taking his own life, the conclusion was inescapable. The coroner returned a verdict of 'suicide whilst temporarily of unsound mind'.

The manner of her father's death naturally made Vera's grief all the more overwhelming. The grim condition of the body seemed strangely at odds with the fastidious and elegant man she remembered. Her mind kept running on all the unanswered questions. How had he reached the river so late at night? No taxi driver had come forward to offer an explanation. Where had he drowned himself, at Hammersmith or further upstream at Richmond, where the river is narrower? The absence of a suicide note begged the question of what had finally driven him to take such action. Her overriding emotion was one of guilt. 'Love never yet cured melancholia any more than it cured any other disease', Winifred wrote, reassuring Vera that she should not blame herself for her father's death. '... I rarely knew a daughter give so much care and attention.'

Vera did not feel that there was any stigma attached to her father's suicide, and spoke quite openly about it to friends who wrote with their condolences. 'After all it was only the logical consequence of his illness and the state of the law which prevents people who wish to die from doing so easily.' Her father's life, she recognized, had really ended with Edward's, seventeen years earlier. 'The loss is irreparable', he had written then, and so it had proved. Edward's death, combined with his own retirement from the paper mill at the age of just fifty-one, far too early for a man of his vitality, had left him rudderless.

In accordance with his wishes, they buried him at Richmond, where he had spent happier times walking along the towpath or in the park. A sundial was chosen to mark his grave, and eventually an inscription in memory of Edward would be added, with the words *Dona Nobis Pacem*.

IV

More misfortune followed closely on this tragedy. Arthur Brittain's funeral was scarcely over when George fell dangerously ill with an obscure form of glandular poisoning, most likely the result of an infection he had picked up in Moscow. Running a high temperature and at risk from total septicaemia, he needed constant nursing. Vera opened up Glebe Place, sent her mother to stay with her sisters for three weeks and, with the aid of the Burnetts, gradually nursed him back to health.

Accompanied by Hilda Reid, Winifred meanwhile had faithfully returned to France to relieve Vera of her anxiety for the children. John and Shirley were taking an altogether sanguine view of their grandfather's death. 'I called the children aside to tell them about their Grandpa,' Edith de Coundouroff reported to Vera, '– and really it was amazing the way they reacted. John was silent a moment and then said, "Oh! as long as it isn't Grannie it doesn't matter – and when we go to see her we can make as much noise as we like." ... Then Shirley said, "Oh! well – I expect I shall be getting a new grandpa soon then, or perhaps Daddy will have to be Grandpa too until Grannie gets another one." ' When she was not revising *South Riding*, Winifred played on the beach at Wimereux with the children, and spent the evenings in the small café on the seafront, sipping *cassis-siphon*, and charming new acquaintances from the hotel. Photographs show her looking strained, her face white and lined with fatigue, although she insisted in letters home to Vera that her enforced idleness and the fine weather were doing her good. The accident of illness had given time to her novel. When she put away its final pages, she was able to relax, confident that after a long apprenticeship she had at last produced a piece of work worthy of her talents.

At Chelsea Vera had no time to devote to *Honourable Estate* as George's temperature, which had at one point reached a high of 102 degrees, consistently hovered around the 100-degree mark. He looked 'dreadfully ill', she reported to Winifred on 19 August and, to add to his discomfort in a stuffy and airless London, was unable to sit out in a chair. His chief worry was the possible repercussions of his illness upon his Sunderland campaign, as he was now prevented from exploring the constituency for at least another month. 'I see myself doing G.'s Sunderland campaign yet!' Vera exclaimed while preparing to deal with the avalanche of political correspondence which had descended on them. The shock of her father's death combined with her concern for George's recovery had taken its toll on her nerves rather than her physical strength. Apart from her legs, which felt like lead, she did not feel exhausted. But visiting the empty house in Edwardes Square on her mother's instructions, 'to make sure that this, that and the other is all right', she was alarmed by what she imagined to be her father's voice asking, 'Is that you Jack?' 'I'm sure that the last thing his normal self would want would be to frighten and upset me,' she told Winifred, before making her next visit there. All the same, she was disturbed by this evidence of the power of her nervous fears which, as always, she attributed to bad heredity. Winifred wrote comfortingly that 'It's not strange or neurotic at all to think you hear your father's voice. One does. I used to hear Father in his room at Bainesse. I think we all have our fears of "tics" and madness to fight.'

By the third week of August George's temperature had at last stabilized, and he felt well enough to start issuing constituency directives from his bed. Winifred had offered to keep the children out in France for another week. She was enjoying her longest break since her collapse in 1931. 'Ochre-brown all over,' she described herself. 'Brains gone to wool. But more physical energy than I have had for months.' She did indeed look tanned and relaxed when Vera met her and the children at Victoria on 28 August. But almost immediately a family matter intervened which required her attention. Peter Tolmie, her sister Grace's widower, had without warning suddenly remarried, leaving Mrs Holtby fearful for her grandchildren's future welfare. Winifred rushed up to Yorkshire for the weekend to discuss the marriage and give her mother support. She returned to London visibly weakened by the effort. While walking back through Hyde Park with Vera a few days later, after a meeting with their agent, Nancy Pearn, she was scarcely able to stand properly, and was too overcome with exhaustion to speak. After spending a day in bed she consulted Dr Obermer, who thought that she might be suffering from an overdose of arsenic in one of her injections, and advised her to rest for a few days.

For ever afterwards, Vera would blame herself for not having been more alive to the seriousness of Winifred's condition. 'My perceptions were dulled by fatigue,' she remembered remorsefully in 1939, 'and I didn't realize that her last attack of illness – similar to so many of hers that I had seen – was just sufficiently different from the others to be the end. So I did not do half for her that I could and should have done if I had known. I shall never forget this; or forgive myself.' However, more to the point, one suspects, was her consistent refusal to face the unthinkable, that Winifred might be dying. There were more than enough other problems to preoccupy her. From Guildford had come the news that her aunt and former headmistress, Florence Bervon, now seventy-one, had been rushed into hospital on 5 September with suspected appendicitis, and operated on immediately. Vera visited her in Chichester and found her making a good recovery given her age (she survived until the following year). But it was another blow for the recently bereaved Mrs Brittain, and placed more heavy emotional demands on Vera. As if this was not enough, George was proving a difficult convalescent and there seemed little chance of taking the holiday they had planned in Monte Carlo. Her novel remained at a standstill, and there were signs that the shocks and strains of that summer were beginning to affect her. Writing to Brett on 9 September to propitiate him for the anticipated delay in the delivery of the manuscript, she explained that her letter had been written with Winifred's help, 'as during the last few days I have begun in the most strange way to lose my memory ... and I have become almost incapable of doing any business at all. I feel as if the month of August has added ten years to my life.'

In her bedroom at Glebe Place, an attic room up a narrow flight of stairs, Winifred's courageous resolve to put a brave face on her illness was finally giving way to the violent pounding in her head and constant feeling of acute nausea. Like Lily Sawdon in *South Riding*, she was facing a future where the drugs she was prescribed – those 'merciful, beautiful, incomparable gifts' – could no longer be relied upon to relieve her suffering. On the night of 9 September her pain was so intense that Vera brought her down to sleep in her bed while she slept nearby in Shirley's room. The next morning Winifred was no better and, after helping her to inject herself with a dose of Impletol, Vera telephoned for Dr Obermer.

There was now no escaping the seriousness of Winifred's condition, though Vera's behaviour continued to suggest a reluctance to confront the worst. Rather than receive Obermer's diagnosis in person, she sent George to meet him in his consulting rooms. There George learned what Winifred had known since April 1932 when Halls Dally, a kidney specialist, had diagnosed renal sclerosis and, faced with a direct question from Winifred, had admitted that she might only have another two years to live. 'Your kidneys have definitely lost over half of their functioning cells, which have been replaced by fibrous tissues', Obermer had told her six months later when she had asked his advice about consulting a Paris doctor who had a reputation for semi-miraculous cures for high blood-pressure. '. . . Unfortunately there is no means and never will be any means, of restoring destroyed kidney cells . . . What has to be done in your case, is to . . . attempt to prevent the sclerotic or fibrous process from proceeding any further.' Now, three years on, Winifred had confounded her doctors' original predictions, and the only prognosis that Obermer could provide was that this latest attack 'might mean anything or nothing'. That afternoon he arranged for Winifred to be admitted to a nursing home for a week of intensive treatment. Vera accompanied her in a taxi to the Elizabeth Fulcher Home in Devonshire Street. A dignified figure in a black cloak, Winifred summoned up the strength to walk to the front door and ring the bell.

Vera's own composure began to falter. At a meeting with Gollancz and dinner with Storm Jameson the next day, she appeared to alternate between numbed disbelief and a state of approaching hysteria. A pitiful sight awaited her on her daily visits to the nursing home. Deprived of sleep and unable to take food or liquid, Winifred moved restlessly about her bed, screwing up her eyes against the pain in her head. Her arms and other parts of her body were covered in bruises and sores where successive injections had failed to have any effect. The question arose of whether to send for Mrs Holtby. Obermer initially resisted the idea, arguing that her mother's presence might alarm Winifred and give her the impression that her illness was critical. In such a baffling case, he said, there was no knowing what part psychological factors had played and might continue to play. At all costs he wanted to avoid undermining her energy and optimism. Within the week, however, it became plain that the news of her daughter's collapse could not be kept indefinitely from Mrs Holtby. Brisk and businesslike as ever, she arrived with Edith de Coundouroff on the morning of 17 September, saw

Obermer who kept the more serious details of Winifred's condition from her, visited Winifred, pronounced everything satisfactory, and returned to Cottingham by the evening train.

In the interests of maintaining their pretence of outward calm, Vera was persuaded to take George for his long-postponed convalescent holiday. She had serious misgivings about leaving Winifred, particularly after finding her swollen-eyed from crying and depressed by her lack of sleep and inability to keep down any food. In the circumstances Monte Carlo was out of the question; instead they decided on a short stay in Brighton. The news on their first day there, 21 September, was cheering. Winifred had had a good night, and a lunchtime telegram from Edith de Coundouroff reported that she seemed much better.

A telephone call the following evening was the first intimation that there had been any change. Vera went to bed 'with the heavy sense of being back in the War again with doom at hand'. It had been at Brighton, almost twenty years before, that she had received the news of Roland's death. On the morning of 23 September, she was awoken by a call from her mother to say that a grave report had come from the nursing home that Winifred was much weaker. Shortly afterwards Edith de Coundouroff rang with the news that her condition had suddenly become acute and that she had telegraphed for Mrs Holtby.

Vera rushed back to London with George, uncertain as to whether she would find Winifred alive or able to recognize her. Arriving at her bedside, she found her semi-conscious,

> her face just slightly puffy & with the yellowish pallor I had seen in so many uremia & nephritis cases during the War. Edith & I went outside and talked for a few minutes; she said the doctors had realized that some 'Factor X' had caused the unexpected change & now knew they must give her up. I told her Winifred had said last week that she wished Harry Pearson would come up & see her, & suggested that we telegraph him: 'Winifred critically ill; still recognizes people; has asked for you; come if you wish.' . . . Edith went out to send the telegram & I spoke to Winifred very gently: 'Sweetie-heart – it's Vera.' She smiled & put out her hand a little and said: 'But I thought . . . Brighton . . .' I explained that Shirley had a cold (which was indeed the case) & that I had come back to see she had the doctor . . . Winifred murmured weakly: 'She would.'

Mrs Holtby meanwhile was holding court in the sitting-room of the nursing home, receiving a continuous procession of Winifred's friends and colleagues, including Lady Rhondda, Violet Scott-James, Hilda Reid,

Edith Smeterlin, and Clare Leighton. Almost sixty years later the way in which she busied herself, delegating responsibility for funeral arrangements, newspaper notices, and obituaries, while upstairs Winifred still kept a tenacious hold on life, may look unfeeling. But in mitigation it should be remembered that Mrs Holtby, a born organizer, had always taken charge in any crisis.

At one point Vera, at Winifred's request, gave Mrs Holtby a copy of *South Riding*'s introduction, in which she had dedicated the book to her mother. In her 'Prefatory Letter to Alderman Mrs Holtby', Winifred had attempted to absolve her mother of any complicity in the portrayal of characters or incidents in the novel, explaining that, while *South Riding* was a story of local government and concerned the workings of a Yorkshire county council, it had neither been taken from her mother's experience (Alice Holtby had first been elected to the council in 1923) nor drawn from material known to her. She ended by placing on record 'the proud delight which it has meant to me to be the daughter of Alice Holtby'.

Sadly Alice Holtby utterly failed to appreciate the 'intense beauty and pathos' of the introduction. As Vera remarked angrily later, she 'only saw the possible effect of it on her own position' on the East Riding County Council. It was an augury of unpleasantness to come.

Harry Pearson, 'blue-eyed, bronzed & handsome like an Army Major', arrived at the nursing home on 24 September in response to the telegram. Winifred was 'in rapture' because he had come, and on two nights running he volunteered to sit up with her. In subsequent conversations with Vera, Winifred dwelt on her past relationship with him, and wondered whether he had really loved her. 'She wondered, too, if he would be willing to marry her. I said: "Does that matter? Couldn't you be happy together . . . without bothering about an actual ceremony?" She replied: "I feel I *want* to be married somehow – I want some sort of security now." ' Hearing this, Vera made a positive resolve: that Winifred should have the one thing she needed to make her life complete and that Harry must be persuaded to play his part before it was too late.

Fourteen years earlier, after Harry had suddenly departed for South America without a word, Vera had written to Winifred: 'I always feel certain that you & he will come together in the end. You may not marry, but you'll come together mentally.' Now she set out to fulfil her own prophecy, motivated by the sincere belief that an understanding with Harry would bring Winifred final happiness. 'Vera liked a tidy end,' recalled Hilda Reid, 'and a conventionally romantic one.' But was this what Winifred really wanted? Or rather, is it what she would have wished for had she been in good health? She had always prized her status as an independent woman, arguing that the 'spinster may have work which delights her, personal intimacies which comfort her, power which satisfies her.' And she knew, no one better, just how unlikely it was that Harry would ever settle down. She understood too that he could never feel passionately towards her: five months before, their one sexual encounter had been disastrous. It might be argued that her faculties had been impaired by drugs and that she was incapable of expressing herself rationally; except that, as Vera's diary account, an extraordinarily moving threnody, makes clear, she remained lucid throughout, and powerful medication was only administered at the end. Alternatively, it is perhaps more likely that Winifred knew all along that she was dying and was prepared to acquiesce in any arrangement that would make her mother – who had known Harry for most of his life and liked him – and Vera happy.

It was 'a mockery' getting Harry to propose, Edith de Coundouroff's daughter, Margaret, remembered. Everything was carefully stage-managed by Vera. George was sent to persuade Harry to tell Winifred that he had always loved her and wanted to marry her when she was better. Vera sat in the café across the street to watch as Harry approached the nursing home with a large bunch of scabious. Elsewhere Lady Rhondda engaged Mrs Holtby in conversation to keep her out of the way. Harry emerged from Winifred's room, sweating profusely, and declaring 'that he never wanted to go through anything like that again'. Edith de Coundouroff 'had to take him off and buy him a stiff drink'. It is difficult to believe that Winifred did not see through this charade. Vera waited expectantly at home. A telephone message from Winifred said simply, 'Yes, all through', meaning Vera thought that Harry had loved her all through. '. . . I'd been counting on seeing her conscious . . . & hearing about Harry from her own lips,' Vera wrote afterwards. But by then it was too late. Obermer had already sedated Winifred with morphia.

For the end now was not far off. In the last days she had seemed to rally to an extraordinary degree. Obermer said that 'he'd never before seen so much vitality displayed by anyone he'd given up'. A blood test on 27 September, which showed that the amount of urea in her blood had increased by three times since her last test, indicated that she ought to have been dead already. 'She really is quite heartbreakingly sweet and considerate as an invalid,' Vera wrote to Rebecca West that day, 'and though she can now no longer see, she recognizes people by their voices and makes the appropriate remarks to them with the utmost lucidity and humour.' On the afternoon of 28 September, she received her last injection of morphia and drifted into unconsciousness.

Mrs Holtby had decreed that if Winifred died in the night, no one was to be called until seven o'clock the following morning; there was nothing anyone could do, she said, and they would only be in the nurses' way. Privately Vera had no intention of allowing Winifred to die alone. She arranged to be contacted if there was any change during the night. At half-past four in the morning she and George were summoned to the nursing home by the night sister. Winifred was breathing very shallowly, her lips slightly parted, her hair brushed back from her forehead. Vera sat by her, sometimes holding her hand, sometimes her wrist with her fingers. Just after six, her pulse became barely perceptible and she seemed to be breathing only from her throat. 'It was strange, incredible, after all the years of our friendship & all that we had shared together, to feel her life flickering out under my hand.' At twenty-five minutes past six, after one final, lingering sigh, she was dead.

'Whatever I may do, remember that I love you dearly,' Winifred had told Vera in one of their final conversations, a few days before she died.

'I'm intensely grateful to you – you're the person who's made me . . . You've got a mind like steel . . . It's the most honest mind I've ever known and the most lucid. Often when I've been all tangled up & haven't known how to get through you've said to me "But this is the end . . . this is how to get out." ' . . . She spoke of the happiness it had given her to have Harry with her during the night, & then said: 'Don't think I mean I love him more than you . . . I love you quite differently.'
One day she mentioned the debate at Oxford and I said: 'But just think – if the debate hadn't happened I should never have come to you afterwards – and think what I should have missed.' 'And what *I* should have missed,' she added.

Word of Winifred's death spread quickly through London on 29 September, through the radio news bulletins and in the later editions of the newspapers.* Even the cheap press carried a misleading sob story of Miss Winifred Holtby, given two years to live, who ran a deliberate race against time to complete her book. Tributes soon started to flow into the office of *Time and Tide*.

---

*Rumours also abounded. More than a week after Winifred's death, Virginia Woolf passed on to Ethel Smyth the details of one story she had heard. 'I'm told . . . that what killed poor Winifred was first an African germ, which they thought was cured; then Vera B's father jumped into the Thames and drowned himself; Vera and W spent several days searching for the body; found it; Vera broke down thereupon; Winifred was sent to look after the children; suddenly the germ revived; she was too exhausted to struggle, and so died; but this comes only second hand.'

Winifred Holtby passed through life like a flame. She had ability in abundance; but her ability was the more valuable because, throughout her life, it was consistently devoted to noble ends. I never knew in her one mean thought; I never found in her any spirit save that concerned eagerly and vividly for others.

Winifred's heart went out most of all to Africa; for in that continent, she felt, humanity had suffered the most grievous wrong.

In Winifred Holtby literature has lost a notable writer; her intimates a selfless friend and an inspiring comrade; the cause of world peace a leader as well as a servant.

Winifred's memorial service was held at St Martin-in-the-Fields on 1 October, the day before her burial at Rudston. At the end of the service the congregation waited for Vera to leave the church immediately following the Holtby family, as a mark of respect and a tribute to her friendship with Winifred.

'For sixteen years we had lived, with rare intervals, under the same roof,' Vera wrote to Sarah Gertrude Millin ten days later. 'No one has ever been mentally and spiritually nearer to me, nor ever now, I imagine, will be again.'

v

Mrs Holtby's reaction to the 'Prefatory Letter', and her tendency to resent her daughter's significance as a writer, would strengthen Vera's resolve to do her utmost to preserve and enhance Winifred's reputation in the years immediately following her death. Driving back from Rudston after the funeral, she found an unexpected ally in Lady Rhondda, who was keen for Vera to write Winifred's biography, and willing to attempt to persuade Alice Holtby that she should do so. In the first week of October, Vera was harried, 'and driven nearly mad', by publishers competing to commission a book about Winifred from her. 'They all want little, cheap, hurried books of the topical kind', she complained, 'mere acts of piety'. She already had in mind a larger, more considered work which would set Winifred against her contemporary background, ranging 'from Yorkshire to Central Europe and S. Africa and back to London', and including 'Imperialism, peace, feminism, women's education, London journalism . . .'. Lady Rhondda was strongly of the opinion that the book ought to be written quickly in order that Winifred should not be forgotten. '. . . But as I have enough material of hers to bring out a book at intervals of six months for the next two years', Vera countered, '. . . her name will be kept before the public'. She actually felt no more inclined to embark on an immediate biography than she had felt like writing *Testament of Youth* in the first years after the war. Her priority, in any case, was to see Winifred's final novel into print.

Under the terms of her will, dated 16 July 1932, Winifred appointed her mother as executor, and Vera as her literary executor 'with full authority to publish any of my hitherto unpublished manuscripts and to draw profits from the same to recompense for her trouble at the rate of 75 per cent up to £10,000 and 10 per cent after that'. The surplus from the literary estate was to be placed in a fund for scholarships at Somerville; if the sum exceeded £3,000, an eventuality Winifred scarcely anticipated, a Dorothy McCalman scholarship was to be endowed (in memory of the friend who had received financial assistance from Winifred to enter Somerville as a mature student), to be offered to women who had already been earning their living for three years or more, who might require extra tuition before coming up to Somerville.

The relationship between executor and literary executor was to prove an uneasy one. Although Mrs Holtby conceded to Vera the powers to publish any of Winifred's literary remains as she saw fit, she emphasized from the outset her moral, if not her legal right, to be consulted. She was soon requesting that Vera edit a selection of Winifred's journalism as a fitting literary memorial, rather than publishing the local government novel, which she believed held potential embarrassment for her. Mrs Holtby had not read her daughter's final work, but the 'Prefatory Letter' had given her sufficient cause to fear it. As she explained to Vera, in the stream-of-consciousness style so characteristic of her letters, 'my trouble is that being so closely connected with much that she said she had made use of I cannot feel the same detachment as you and others do – I know – none better – that she would not hurt me – but her puckish mischief or humour, or satire must find expression – as you say "literature must be served"! . . .'.

It was an unenviable task to act against the wishes of an old woman of seventy-seven, mourning the loss of the third member of her family in seven years (Grace had died in 1928, David Holtby in 1933). 'My position is that of the frog in the pond and you literary-minded people are the boys on the bank', she wrote somewhat pathetically in one final attempt to sway Vera. But as Vera understood the dilemma, to bow to Mrs Holtby's demands would be to do Winifred an even greater injustice. She therefore pursued her deeply felt duty to Winifred's memory with an almost ruthless determination.

She spent a week at Fowey in Cornwall in the middle of October, reading and correcting Winifred's typescript. Despite bearing clear marks of the novel's hurried composition, and indications that there had been no time for revision – several minor characters, for instance, were given one name in the first half and another in the second – it was obvious to Vera at once that this was Winifred's most profound achievement and her lasting contribution to literature. She found herself wondering at the book's power, 'so full of wisdom, compassion and understanding, so rich with pity for human frailty and admiration of human courage. She has never written anything finer than these lovely country scenes of birth & death, seed-time & harvest . . .'. Rejecting 'Take What You Want' as too trivial a title for so major a book, she opted for Winifred's alternative and called the novel *South Riding*.

Returning to London, Vera's pressing concern was to deliver *South Riding* to Collins, Winifred's publisher, before Mrs Holtby asked to read it. She hurriedly composed a short introduction, 'Ave atque Vale' (published as the epitaph), which dwelt on the relationship between the suffering and endurance of Winifred's last months and the intuitive awareness of death which pervades her final novel. Then, enlisting the legal expertise of Harold Rubinstein, the book was 'negotiated' through probate. By 28 October, just four weeks after Winifred's death, *South Riding* was in the hands of Collins.

After this piece of mild subterfuge, and with the certain knowledge that nothing would now stand in the way of *South Riding*'s publication, Vera attempted to reassure an increasingly worried Mrs Holtby. On 10 December she wrote to her:

> Honestly and sincerely, and trying to see the story from your point of view, not mine, I do not think there is anything in it that will distress you. Collins say it is a classic, one of the greatest novels they have dealt with in all their experience . . . It is a beautiful saga of the human side of local government, appropriately produced just when the typical expression of the English spirit has reached its centenary year. [1935 marked the centenary of the 1835 Municipal Corporations Act which began the democratization of local government.]

Try as she might, though, Vera seemed only to aggravate the situation. She inadvertently omitted to send Mrs Holtby a copy of her introduction, leaving her to read of it in the *Yorkshire Post*. Writing to demand a copy, Mrs Holtby, adopting a more hectoring tone, felt forced to remind Vera that while she had been given 'all literary power . . . I may ask for certain courtesies . . .'. Reading the preface, however, did nothing to ease her feelings, nor did it put a stop to the constant stream of chiding letters from

Cottingham which were landing on Vera's desk. 'I hate this reference to her illness,' she complained. 'Oh! why is it necessary "in the cause of literature" to harrow one so . . . need there be any further reference to her illness until Time has made it easier?'

At the end of January 1936, The Book Society announced that *South Riding* had been chosen as their Book of the Month for March. The bitter irony that Winifred should not have lived to see this accolade, when she had felt in her lifetime that none of her novels had really succeeded, was not lost on Vera. She dutifully relayed the news to Mrs Holtby, thinking it might allay some of the suspicions she had about the book. Mrs Holtby, however, was having none of it. Beset by the begging letters which were flooding into Cottingham, a result of the misleading impression of affluence created by the granting of probate on Winifred's will, she was in no mood to deal with any further salvo from the literary world. '. . . Don't ask me to be a rejoicing "proud" mother,' she warned Vera, 'I shall kick the next [person] who tells me – I am – or ought to be . . .'. 'Those who have heard parts of S.R., or have read it,' she added with a clear sense of her betrayal at Vera's hands, 'tell me I shall be hurt as I knew I should . . .'. She was already beginning to have serious misgivings about the approval she had recently given Vera for her projected biography of Winifred, and had begun to plan an edition of Winifred's letters to Jean McWilliam over which she would exercise exclusive control.

South Riding was published on 2 March 1936 to widespread acclamation. 'A great book . . . the most public-spirited novel of her generation a book you can walk about in,' trumpeted *The Times*. After three weeks it had sold 25,000 copies, and the following year was awarded the James Tait Black Memorial Prize for the best novel of 1936. Vera sold the film rights for £3,000 to Victor Saville, representing Alexander Korda, who in 1938 produced the film version starring Ralph Richardson, Edna Best, Marie Lohr and Ann Todd. It was one of the most popular British films of the decade, finding favour with audiences and critics alike. '. . . A scrupulously authentic picture of English life for the first time on any screen', opined the reviewer in the *Daily Mirror*, '. . . I dare to say that it ranks higher than any film ever made here and will do for a long time to come.'

The book's reception failed to appease Mrs Holtby, who promptly resigned from the East Riding County Council when *South Riding* appeared, her worst fears confirmed. 'It is such a travesty on any C.C. [County Council] & on E.R. [East Riding] in particular', she wrote to Hilda Reid in one of a series of letters increasingly critical of Vera, '72 people without officials feel it to be so . . . I could not have sat among them again.'

Not only did she consider the novel libellous, but she also regretted the explicitness of the love scenes ('we do not perform "acts of nature" in public & some things should be left to the imagination') and the story's tragic conclusion. She was not alone in this. Annie Burnett-Smith,* a friend of Mrs Holtby's, concurred in finding *South Riding* detrimental to Winifred's memory:

> I am certain that if Winifred had been normal, and had got the time, she would have modified parts of it. It is full of pain even to savagery – it just rent my heart and there is no hope in it. She was so lovely in life; she bore perpetually the crosses of others and this seems to voice her own suffering and revolt. I should not like my child to write such a book . . .

The only aspect of the interest surrounding *South Riding* which pleased Mrs Holtby was the making of Victor Saville's film version, since this omitted 'all the sordid parts (Lily Sawdon etc.)' and gave the story a happy ending, with Robert Carne, the conservative squire, marrying the head-mistress, Sarah Burton, on the death of his wife. Mrs Holtby thoroughly enjoyed being fêted by the film-makers. She was charmed by the attentions of Victor Saville's screenwriter, Ian Dalrymple, who travelled specially to Harrogate to consult her on local details, while the actress playing Lydia Holly gave her an autographed picture of herself signed 'with sincere thanks'. 'But I did not send you to Denham [the film studio]!' exclaimed Mrs Holtby. 'But if there had been no Mrs Holtby there would have been no Winifred, no *South Riding* and no Denham for me', replied the actress. 'I felt humbled to the dust,' Mrs Holtby confessed to Hilda Reid, adding that it made all her suffering in Gethsemane in the past two years seem worthwhile. She could not help thinking, though, that the book would have been better, and no less successful, had it been more like the film.

Three further posthumous publications of Winifred's work followed *South Riding*, and in the case of two of these Vera was content to let Mrs Holtby have her say. Winifred's letters to Jean McWilliam, *Letters to a Friend*, appeared in April 1937. *Pavements at Anderby*, a selection of Winifred's short stories, followed in the autumn. Although nominally edited by Vera and Hilda Reid, Mrs Holtby closely supervised the selection, issuing strict instructions about which stories were to be excluded because

---

*Annie Burnett-Smith (*nom de plume*, Annie Swan) had suggested the epitaph for Winifred's gravestone, taken from her own book, *We Travel Home*:

> 'God give me work till my life shall end
> And life till my work is done.'

of their unflattering references to people still living in Cottingham and Hull ('far too true and too thinly veiled', she explained to Hilda Reid). Regrettably, this editorial policy meant that many of Winifred's livelier and wittier stories were not included, and the book was criticized by some as unrepresentative.

Finally, Winifred's play about dictatorship, partly inspired by Oswald Mosley's career and called 'Hope of Thousands', which she had begun to submit to producers shortly before her death, was published by Jonathan Cape, in a revised version by the playwright Norman Ginsbury, as *Take Back Your Freedom*, in 1939. The producer Tyrone Guthrie was enthusiastic, while Vera's preface to the published edition stressed the timeliness of its message in Fascist-dominated Europe. But by the time *Take Back Your Freedom* was premiered in 1940, attention was focused on the real threat of Nazi domination outside the theatre, and reviewers were generally dismissive. 'Obvious flop', was Vera's brief comment in her diary, 'Glad W. not here to see this.'

Vera's determination had ensured publication of Winifred's remaining manuscripts. The more difficult task of writing her biography, provisionally entitled 'Brief Odyssey' and later 'A Woman in Her Time', now lay ahead of her and she began work on this in early 1937. She hoped that a life of Winifred, together with a commentary on her writing, would introduce her books to a yet wider circle of readers. She was also keen to dispel the notion which had surfaced in some reviews of *South Riding* and *Letters to a Friend* that, through her concern for accurate, documentary portrayals of social problems in her novels, Winifred had sacrificed her right to be called a 'true artist'.

Most of all, a biography of Winifred would be Vera's way of repaying her own debt to her. If it could 'suggest even a dim reflection of the glowing, radiant, generous golden creature whom we have lost', she told Sarah Gertrude Millin, 'it will be the best way of returning all that she did for me . . .'.

The degree of hostility to the project in various circles was considerable. St John Ervine feared that Vera would make the book another version of her own autobiography (and in one telling slip of the pen Vera did refer to it as 'my autobiography of Winifred'). Mrs Holtby, who had originally sanctioned the biography in the first months after Winfred's death, was a good deal less happy that Vera should write it after their battles over *South Riding*. 'Vera *is* going to let you see what she writes . . . ?' she enquired anxiously of Hilda Reid. 'Oh! that you were doing it if it is to be done. But I still strongly feel it will be an anticlimax.' She added that she would probably be too senile to care by the time the book appeared. Ironically, she died on 31 July 1939, the very day that Vera completed the manuscript, without having read a word of it.

Vera spent more than two years planning the biography and collecting material for it. She could only hope to use a small proportion of the mountain of Winifred's papers at Glebe Place. The press cuttings of articles in about thirty journals and newspapers could be numbered in their thousands, testimony to Winifred's extraordinary versatility and productiveness. For her involvement in South African affairs alone, there were twenty bulging files and a drawer full of pamphlets and letters. Winifred's, however, lent to Vera by a number of her regular correspondents, were often a frustrating source of information. True to her nature, these letters tended to be concerned almost exclusively with the interests of the people she was writing to; only in letters to friends abroad like Stella Benson and Sarah Gertrude Millin were Winifred's feelings about her own life and work expressed.

An additional problem was the dearth of material for her early years. Mrs Holtby had never been a great hoarder, and only some scraps of letters (often with the first or last pages missing) survived, together with a few school reports, a book of early poems and a couple of school magazines. Vera was forced to reconstruct her picture of Winifred's childhood from vague recollections of what Winifred herself had told her, and by building on incidents and remarks in her novels and articles which were clearly autobiographically inspired.

Reading through Winifred's files in the course of her research, Vera expected to find the occasional unflattering reference to herself in letters addressed to Winifred from some of her correspondents. But she was angered by one 'positively abusive' and 'libellous' letter of St John Ervine's, written to Winifred seven months before her death, in which he attacked Vera for her 'incurable egotism and her overwhelming belief that anything that happens to her is somehow more definitely and keenly felt than anything experienced by any other person'. Unable to let his views go unchallenged, and upset by the insidious way in which he had tried to turn Winifred against her, Vera wrote him a remarkable seven-page letter of self-justification which provides evidence of how Vera perceived Winifred's need for her.

. . . If your letter had been written to me I should have been hurt but not really resentful. What I can't get over is the fact that you wrote it to Winifred. If you heard of a man who wrote to another man and disparaged the friend with whom he had lived in close comradeship . . . I think you would be the first to say what a mean and cruel thing it was to write such a letter. But when you are writing to a woman of another woman, your standards with regard to the decent respect that is due to friendship break down . . . The possible effect of your animadversions upon our friendship didn't seem important to you, because you and Lady Rhondda and Mrs Holtby and God knows who else have always regarded me as a selfish neurotic egoist who battened on Winifred's good nature and exploited her generosity. It doesn't seem to have occurred to any of you that in friendship as in everything else Winifred was no fool, and that just possibly she did get something out of me which to her represented an adequate return for all the immense and immeasurable services that she did me.

There are two things about Winifred's friendship for me that you . . . have never understood. The first is that, although we didn't exactly grow up together, we grew mature together, and that is the next best thing . . . We came to understand each other so intuitively that each knew the other's moods, desires and intentions without words being necessary. We were completely at ease with each other as two loving sisters are at ease. When she was with me . . . she didn't have to play any part, keep up any appearances, conceal any feelings. She could, so to speak, completely unbutton her personality.

The second thing is that, consciously for the last four years of her life and unconsciously, I think, for a good deal longer than that, Winifred was a very sick and at last a dying person . . . Now when you are in pain, the only person whose society is tolerable for long intervals of time is the person with whom you can be completely unbuttoned . . . When she was sick I held the basin and emptied it. She didn't mind me because she was used to me, but she would have hated anyone else doing it . . .

. . . She turned to me when her best friends exhausted her. She loved them dearly; it is probable that she respected them . . . more than she ever respected me; but I gave her rest and relief when she was at the end of her tether. After all, you don't worry much whether the person who holds the basin for you to be sick into is your intellectual inferior . . . I *was* her intellectual inferior, of course. You were right in saying that she had more creative power in her little finger than I had in my whole body . . . I know, too, that her powers had not reached their zenith, and that if she had lived another twenty years she would have stood over our age like a colossus. But I don't think those qualitative calculations ever entered into her relationship with me . . . She realized that beneath all my egotism lay a perfectly just and balanced appraisement of comparative human values, and that though I frankly enjoyed and deliberately sought the adulation that is always given to the apotheosis of the commonplace, I wasn't deceived by it in the very least . . .

. . . I do not want you to go on thinking that Winifred – so generous, so gallant, but so clear-headed in her judgements – was a self-deceived and exploited fool in friendship or in anything else.

It was an extraordinary outburst which brought a chastened reply from St John Ervine, asking Vera for her forgiveness. There was some consolation for her in his assurance that Winifred had 'nearly raised the roof off my head' when he had criticized Vera.

Like all biographers writing about the recently deceased, Vera faced the major worry of how to deal with friends and acquaintances of the subject who were still living. She considered a biography worthless unless it attempted to be truthful, yet in her treatment of Harry Pearson and Lady Rhondda she felt bound by a degree of reticence. Harry's identity, as we have seen, was disguised by the name 'Bill' in Vera's overly romantic account of his relationship with Winifred. Initially Vera was concerned that she had written too harshly of him, but Phyllis Bentley after reading an advance copy was able to reassure her that 'you have treated him with great fairness, discretion and even affection, and I think he can have no right to complain or feel injured'.

In the case of Lady Rhondda Vera had some old scores to settle, that she had left an ailing Winifred to bear the brunt of responsibility for *Time and Tide* while she toured the Middle East, for one. But she was unwilling to be outright in her condemnation, wishing to avoid anything which could, as she told Phyllis Bentley, 'justify the accusation of jealous prejudice that Lady Rhondda and her friends will launch at me if they get the slightest chance'. Instead, the accusation of exploitation was there by implication – for instance in the Epilogue where Winifred is described as having been exploited by 'senior people' – rather than more directly.

'How difficult perspective and detachment are when you have loved a person very much,' wrote Vera. She considered excluding herself completely from the biography until dissuaded by George who pointed out that the book would be the weaker without an attempt to describe what Winifred's friendship had meant to her. Recalling Cicero's *De Amicitia*, he suggested the title *Testament of Friendship*. With this title in mind, and inspired by a rereading of Mrs Gaskell's life of her Yorkshire-born friend, Charlotte Brontë, Vera made the nobility of women's friendship one of the book's central themes, and the subject of its most memorable passage:

From the days of Homer the friendships of men have enjoyed glory and acclamation, but the friendships of women, in spite of Ruth and Naomi, have usually been not merely unsung, but mocked, belittled and falsely interpreted. I hope that Winifred's story may do something to destroy these tarnished interpretations, and show its readers that loyalty and affection between women is a noble relationship which, far from impoverishing, actually enhances the love of a girl for her lover, of a wife for her husband, of a mother for her children.

Once she had completed her research, the writing of the book took just four months. It was the one thing she had to complete, she wrote in her diary as Hitler marched into Prague, before the world exploded. Unusually for her, once the book was finished, she exercised great care over its production and appearance, even down to choosing the colour for the binding closest to Winifred's favourite blue. *Testament of Friendship* appeared, with a colour reproduction of Howard Lewis's lively, glowing portrait of Winifred as its frontispiece, on 2 January 1940. Because Vera had by now quarrelled with Gollancz the book was published by Macmillan in both Britain and the United States.

As Vera had expected, the main spur of the adverse reviews of the book was directed against her own presence in it. The *Times* critic noted that 'Miss Brittain's book suffers somewhat from her intimacy with its subject; many episodes of purely personal interest to the author find their place in it, as well as occasionally shrill remarks on extraneous subjects', while the *Times Literary Supplement* similarly criticized its 'mass of irrelevant detail'.

There was some justice in these comments. Vera had striven hard to efface herself from the book, and does not appear at all in ten out of the book's twenty-three chapters. Inevitably, however, her own preoccupations are allowed to seep through, sometimes with a ringing stridency. The most telling instance of this is the extended diatribe against war, interpolated in the account of Vera and Winifred's visit to the Thiepval memorial to the Missing of the Somme in the summer of 1933, where Winifred is almost lost from view in the heat of Vera's analysis. The darkening menace of Hitler had left its imprint on the writing of *Testament of Friendship*.

The question of Vera's detachment was picked up by Richard Crossman in a probing review in the *New Statesman*. Crossman, then Deputy Editor of the journal, was a friend of George's and had occasionally stayed overnight at Glebe Place. Vera was hurt by a sense of his disloyalty, but even more incensed by his suggestion that she had failed to write a biography, and had instead erected a memorial to her own love for Winifred.

Crossman began by praising Vera's remarkable power of self-revelation, 'in spite of the clotted, adjectival redundancy of her style'. But it was precisely this gift of expression, he continued, which prevented Vera from being an effective biographer.

Someone less violently distressed by Miss Holtby's death might have given us a more solid, objective portrait of the many-sided, brilliant woman who was equally at home in politics, literature . . . and the farms of Yorkshire. The very depth of her feeling made this impossible for Miss Brittain; and as a result, it is not Miss Holtby who is the centre of this study, but Miss Brittain herself. We see her friend solely through Miss Brittain's eyes, and it is a sign of the friend's strength of personality that, in spite of this treatment, the reader gets an impression, through the mist of tears, of a real vital character.

Vera's picture of Winifred, constantly torn between her social and artistic conscience until the two were united in *South Riding*, was pounced upon by Crossman. Winifred could never have been a 'pure artist', he wrote, for it is precisely the social content of her writing which gives it its enduring value. If she had written for eternity, as he put it, she would not have progressed beyond her rather sentimental poetry. Vera's interpretation, he surmised, arose from her unconscious attribution to Winifred of her own ambitions and problems. The dichotomy between the pull of duty towards public activities and the desire to lock oneself up in an ivory tower to create literary masterpieces, was a product of Vera's outlook, and not Winifred's.

Whatever the criticisms, *Testament of Friendship* sailed up the bestseller lists in both Britain and America, introducing Winifred's work to thousands of new readers to whom *South Riding* had previously been no more than the vague recollection of a pleasant film.

Some of Winifred's friends were appreciative too. Phyllis Bentley, in marked contrast to her reaction to *Testament of Youth*, offered Vera her 'cordial congratulations on this deeply moving work' ('I always regard you . . . as one of my severest critics . . . for . . . reasons which I need not specify,' Vera responded uneasily); St John Ervine had to admit that 'the book is far better than anyone imagined it would be . . . Winifred shines through it like a warm glow'; even Lady Rhondda managed to subdue her hostility to the extent of writing in *Time and Tide* that any disagreement she had with Vera's portrait of Winifred arose from the fact that 'no two people ever see a third from quite the same angle'.

As for Harry Pearson, by now back in the Air Force on wartime service, his response to the news that he had been sent an advance copy of *Testament of Friendship* was a deliciously mordant letter to Vera, gently mocking her for having assumed the role of judge of his relationship with Winifred:

Dear V.,
>They know, thou knowest, he knows, she knows –
>Reach me my ration of repose,
>Draw me my dreams & let me doze,
>More Bellocose than bellicose;
>And God who guards our liberty and livers
>Forgive us our gifts as we forgive our givers.
>Thanks for letter – expect book will be back at camp when I get back – & anyway its English will read as lovely as you look.
>But it seems you have played God – so I think you should play Good Angel & send me Three Ways of Thought in Ancient China and/or The Apes of Man by way of penance!!
>Ever heard of the dumb blonde who thought the Yankee Clipper [the light aircraft on which Vera was booked to fly to America in 1940] was an American Rabbi?
>A dios
>H.*

Testament of Friendship was Vera's most effective public tribute to Winifred, but it was by no means the last. She was a prime mover, along with Margaret Ballinger, Arthur Creech Jones and other Friends of Africa, in the foundation in December 1940 of a Winifred Holtby Memorial Library in the Western Native Township of Johannesburg.

By 1965 Vera had saved £3,000 to establish a Winifred Holtby Memorial Prize for the Royal Society of Literature. This is awarded annually for the best regional novel by an author of British or Irish nationality under thirty-seven (Winifred's age when she died), and past winners have included Jane Gardam, Kazuo Ishiguro, and Graham Swift. As Vera explained to Shirley, 'I have dedicated myself to keeping her memory alive as the most I can do to compensate for her short life, knowing from the quality of *South Riding* how much she could have done for literature if she had had as much time as myself'.

From a more personal standpoint, however, Vera's determination to keep Winifred's memory alive sprang from her need to assuage a strong sense of guilt. For despite her indignant protests to St John Ervine, there can be no doubt that Vera was only too conscious of the fact that she had often failed to

---

*After the Second World War, Harry Pearson once more drifted aimlessly from job to job. In 1958, Robert Pitman, a *Sunday Express* journalist, reported that Winifred Holtby's old boyfriend was working as a commissionaire at the Victoria Palace Theatre. Over a drink, Pitman chatted with Harry about books, religion and, of course, Winifred. 'When I first knew her she was a very gay sort of person, full of humour', Harry confided to him. '. . . But then she got among such intense serious-minded people. Too serious-minded for me.' Asked by Pitman whether he had ever married, Harry replied, 'No, never – thank the Lord'. Harry Pearson died in London in 1976.

return Winifred's gift of friendship in kind. She had exploited her generosity, and at the end of Winifred's life, when for the first time Winifred's need was overwhelmingly greater than her own, she had been unable to provide the support that she required in her final illness until it was already too late. While rereading Winifred's letters for the biography, Vera had suddenly felt overcome with remorse, and had hurriedly composed a contrite confession for posterity:

> There are no words for the sense of remorse and frustration with which these letters fill me – remorse for my own egotism and selfishness, frustration because I can never now get her back to atone for them and to tell her that I now understand and appreciate everything, including the utter rarity and irreplaceableness of what I have lost.

TWELVE

The Combative Pacifist

> 'As an uncompromising pacifist, I hold war to be a crime against humanity, whoever fights it, and against whomever it is fought. I believe in liberty, democracy, free thought and free speech. I detest Fascism and all that it stands for, but I do not believe that we shall destroy it by fighting it.'

> Vera Brittain in 'Authors Take Sides on the Spanish War',
> *Left Review*, December 1937

I

With Winifred's death Vera marked the end of a personal era. 'Winifred in dying took with her that second life that she initiated for me just after the War,' Vera wrote in her diary; 'can I make a third? Can I, once more, begin again?'

Letters of condolence continued to flow in for months after Winifred's death. One sentence from the normally reticent Brett – 'It hurts to think of the years she has missed' – stood out and seemed to go straight to the heart of the matter. Everyone else thought of their personal bereavement, 'or Mrs Holtby's, or mine, or Lady Rhondda's'; only Brett appeared to share Vera's grief for Winifred's own loss of opportunities and all that she might have done with them.

Inevitably, though, Vera's own sense of loss, and the bleak prospect of a world devoid of Winifred's stabilizing presence, kept breaking through. 'It is difficult to know how to go on living without her', she told Labour Party activist Winifred Horrabin, 'and especially I have the feeling that whatever I write will be poor and pointless because the person whose judgement I most trusted and admired will never read it again.'

Disbelief at the abrupt end to their friendship was quickly succeeded by an acute bitterness which left her railing at the 'cruel stupidity of fate'. Unable to sleep, she lay awake at night, watching a long procession of all those closest to her who had vanished from her life in the past twenty years, asking herself how she could possibly regard her world with confidence or optimism 'after such a devastating tale of personal loss'. For a time work offered the only solace, and an article written barely a month after Winifred's death carried echoes of 1918 in its insistence that it was work rather than her husband, children or friends which was 'the main business of a woman's life.'

> Friends may fail and loves may vanish; the tide of time will carry away the older generation to oblivion and the younger beyond our control, but work is available so long as life lasts and will prove in the end to be the one interest that has never let us down.

Rather than bringing her closer to George, Winifred's death proved only a cause of further estrangement. On holiday at Fowey in early October they quarrelled as George, uncharacteristically ill-tempered and restless after his illness, grew resentful of Vera's silent contemplation of her dead friend. He had been 'cold & mean & unsympathetic', she told him later, nagging her when all she desired was a 'warm, silent, almost purely physical comfort . . .'. A member of the audience at a Fabian meeting in Hampstead shortly afterwards, at which George gave an impromptu address about Winifred, thought that he overdid his grief and recalled him 'practically wringing his hands'. A more honest reflection of his feelings is probably to be found in a 1937 letter to Vera where he revealed more than a hint of animosity towards Winifred's memory: 'You preferred her to me . . . It humiliated me and ate me up. That's why of course I could not read *South Riding* and probably never shall be able to do so . . . The point is, not sex but preference is what matters.'

Honourable Estate was again put to one side as Vera grappled with *South Riding* and the intricacies of Winifred's literary estate. Severe eyestrain, brought on by shock and overwork, constantly impeded her progress. The short spell in Cornwall had provided little respite and plans for a long-delayed recuperative cruise to Palestine were suddenly swept aside in mid-October by a warning from Ellen Wilkinson, who advised George not to leave the country as a general election was about to be called. The news was just what was needed to galvanize Vera out of her brooding introspection and into action. While George travelled up to Sunderland after the dissolution of Parliament on 24 October to begin a three-week campaign, she placed articles on his behalf, organized publicity in the press, and set about finding speakers for him. Sir John Simon was speaking for George's opponent and Vera persuaded Sir Charles Trevelyan, who had written

22 ABOVE LEFT *Winifred Holtby in her graduation gown, 1921.*

23 ABOVE RIGHT *The photograph of himself at Cornell that George Catlin sent to Vera in April 1924: 'nice looking, much gayer and less pedantic than his letters sound'.*

24 LEFT *Vera's engagement photograph, 1924.*

25 *The wedding of Vera and George Catlin, St James's Spanish Place, June 1925. In the background,* left to right, *Reverend Catlin, Edith Brittain, Winifred Holtby.*

26 *Winifred Holtby, John, Vera and, right, Phyllis Bentley at 19 Glebe Place, 1932.*

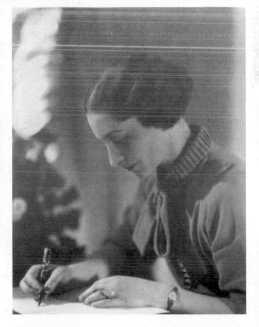

27 ABOVE *George P. Brett, Jr, President of the Macmillan Company, Vera's New York publisher, 1940s.*

28 RIGHT *Vera as bestselling author, on her first American lecture tour, 1934.*

29 ABOVE *Winifred with her mother, Alderman Alice Holtby, the indomitable matriarch of Cottingham, 1934.*

30 BELOW *Winifred, 2nd from left, on the beach at Wimereux the month before she died, with Edith de Coundouroff, centre, Hilda Reid, 2nd from right, and Shirley, centre foreground, August 1935.*

31 ABOVE *Vera speaking at the
Dorchester Peace Rally, 20 June 1936
Behind her on the platform, George
Lansbury, Laurence Housman,
Florence Hardy.*

32 LEFT *Left to right, George
Lansbury, Dick Sheppard, Donald
Soper, Vera, at the Dorchester Peace
Rally.*

33 TOP *John and Shirley at Allum Green Cottage in the New Forest, 1939.*

34 ABOVE *George in Leslie Howard guise, 1940s.*

35 RIGHT *US journalist Dorothy Thompson informs British readers of American outrage at Vera's protest against saturation bombing, 1944.*

THE VOICE OF AMERICA

British Woman Pacifist Rouses U.S. Fury

by DOROTHY THOMPSON

Specially written for "The Sunday Chronicle"

THE chief subjects under discussion in America this week have been : The pacifist appeal not to bomb German cities, made by an Englishwoman, Vera Brittain, and backed up by 28 pacifists, all but one a clergyman ; soldiers' votes ; and the execution of America's No. 1 gangster, Louis (Lepke) Buchhalter.

The article by Vera Brittain appeared here in "Fellowship," the official organ of "The Fellowship of Reconciliation," a long-standing, pre-war organisation largely supported by Protestant clergymen.

Her article entitled "Massacre By Bombing," was accompanied by an appeal against saturation bombing of European cities, enemy and occupied, signed by twenty-seven prominent Protestant clergymen and Oswald Garrison Villard, who has always been a consistent pacifist.

There have been two types of reactions — those of professional editorial writers, columnists and radio commentators, and that of the public itself.

Harsh Letters
From the Public

WE can say generally, of both types of reaction, that the repercussion was enormous; everybody talked about it, and 98 per cent. rejected it.

I take the figure of 98 per cent. from the mail of "New York Times," which has the heaviest reader-contributions of any paper in the country.

Actually, the letters from the public at large were much harsher and more furious than the comments of professional publicists. The latter showed a humane understanding of the issue.

The line taken by almost all of them was that serial warfare is of exceptional cruelty, but that it is unavoidable since the instrument was thrust upon us, and because it is demonstrably the chief instrument of victory or defeat, and that since the success of the alternative — land operations — depends upon the preparatory destruction of the German war machine, it attacks from the air, it is the only way by which we can minimise the casualties of our troops.

VERA BRITTAIN
"She appeals against saturation bombing of European cities."

relatively an unknown name. So they fear Mr. Roosevelt will profit from this fact — or they will be driven to nominate Mr. Willkie.

The public is more generous minded than the politicians. It is overwhelmingly in favour of a simple ballot that will make it possible for every soldier to register his wishes, and it is to be hoped the public will win.

It may seem odd that in a time of great military and diplomatic operations, the state of an American gangster should be front-page news for several days. But Lepke Buchhalter, who was executed a week ago, was a special type of gangster — the type who made crime into big business.

"Lepke" — the affectionate abbreviation for his forename Louis — was, in his way, an intellectual of crime.

Although Lepke was already a criminal in prohibition days, he kept strictly aloof from beer and spirits bootlegging rackets, believing that dealing in materials illegal per se was a stupid game. Instead of that he specialised — like Hitler — in exploiting social tensions and disturbances, and became a settler by violence of problems for both labour unions and manufacturers, taking therefrom his rakeoff.

He was not afraid of murder. It has been estimated that he was directly responsible for sixty to eighty deaths — but there is no evidence that he ever directly soiled his own hands with blood. And in every crime he committed he implicated people who afterwards were forced to back him up, at the risk of their lives.

He Had His Own
'Army' and 'Courts'

HE set up what was really the equivalent of a little criminal State, of which he was dictator.

He had a private army of gunmen. He had his own courts, in which sentence of death was passed on "traitors." He protected labour unions and manufacturers and taxed them for it.

East Side, where he confined operations. He even boasted that he had brought "peace" to lower East Side, by ending a warfare between rival gangs.

He broke all of them — merged the survivors in his organisation.

The State had every kind of evidence against Lepke except murder, which would send him to the electric chair.

But his accomplices were not clever as he. And finally, after years of his unchallenged reign, they began to turn State's evidence to save their own skins.

Lepke finally was forced by his own colleagues to "unconditional surrender," and he gave himself up in August, 1939. But then fought for four years to save his head, and even while he was in prison — on minor charges — followers feared him.

Finally, he went to the Chair when one of his victims, slated for extermination, was shot, but not die. He pinned the charge of murder on Lepke, and a court — criminal and unrepentant master-mind was snuffed out King-Sing prison.

He did not, however, periodically. Two accomplice executed with him, showed more nerve than he. Apparently he lived to the very last minute the State could "not do that to me."

Dorothy Thompson's U.S.

36 ABOVE *Vera in her writing shelter in the garden at Allum Green Cottage, 1949.*

37 BELOW *Family scene at John's wedding, 1951.* From left, *Vera, Amy Burnett, George, Shirley.*
2nd from right, *Ruth Gage Colby.* Back right, *Charles Burnett.*

38 LEFT Left to right, *John, his wife Jennifer and children Timothy and Daniel, with Vera, Bernard Williams, Shirley and their daughter Rebecca, 1965.*

39 BELOW *Vera with Shirley, 'my brilliant and beloved', Whitehall Court, early 1960s.*

admiringly of *Testament of Youth*, to act as 'a doughty antagonist'. She was feeling remorseful about her behaviour at Fowey and wanted to do all she could to see George elected. She had been aware for some time that he would be far happier as an MP than 'gradually ossifying as an American Professor'.

Arriving in Sunderland on 3 November Vera threw herself into canvassing and public speaking. In ten days she made thirty-three speeches, and although at first George was concerned that she might come across as too ladylike, it was evident before long that she was winning supporters over to him. Harry Pearson, who had been brought in as George's agent, remembered in old age her 'great sense of presence on a platform', and thought that she would have stood a better chance than George of winning the seat. George himself showed improvement as a speaker, but still had a tendency to be nervous, was frequently inaudible and lacked constructive ideas, a telling defect in an area hard hit by the depression. There was also a lack of accord between him and his Labour colleague (Sunderland was a two-member constituency), Leah Manning. While George was a moderate who draped the table at public meetings with the Union Jack, Manning was well to the left of the Labour Party leadership. Both suffered from well-orchestrated smear campaigns: Manning at the hands of the local Conservative newspaper which made much of her past Communist associations, and George from a scarcely credible story that Catlin, in reality an old Bedfordshire name, was of Polish-Jewish origin.

However, the crucial factor in Labour losing the Sunderland seats was a shrewd piece of political manoeuvring on the part of their opponents. A Conservative–Liberal pact, which ensured that George and Manning faced two candidates running on the National Government ticket rather than two sitting Conservative members, put paid to victory. Late into the night of 14 November George and Vera listened to the results as they came over the hotel wireless. It was the final catastrophe of 1935. '. . . Your life lately has been as though you were wearing through some sort of curse', wrote Clare Leighton in words that rang all too true. They had lost a large sum of money – *Vera's* money – in return for nothing more than 'some rather bitter political experience'. It was left to Alice Holtby to add insult to injury with a remark which possibly crept a little too close to the truth. Allowing that George's 'integrity would indeed be valuable in the House', she added elliptically that he 'never was meant for Labour . . . the woman in the street . . . he need not waste his time.'

The necessity of earning money from *Honourable Estate* had acquired a new and critical urgency. On New Year's Day 1936 Vera travelled down to

Sidmouth, taking her mother with her, for a concentrated period of writing. Her spirits, though, were flagging and the novel itself was showing signs of having been too long in the works. The presence of Edith Brittain in her room while she worked, knitting, stitching and sighing 'all day just under my nose', was an added irritant, and the proofs of *South Riding* which had just arrived made her wish that her own novel was even half as good. ' "Honourable Estate" doesn't get on', she complained wearily to Margaret Storm Jameson.

> I've written 350 pages manuscript but it's only a third of it. Never, never, if I'd known when I began it a year ago, what last year was to be, would I have started a book of such dimensions. To try to get the whole of the women's movement in all its aspects – political, professional, social, moral, economic – within the covers of one novel is to court defeat. I wouldn't mind a failure if it were only a glorious one, but the burden of life weighs me down and I can't even progress.

Back at Glebe Place her pace of writing quickened and by the end of the month she had completed half the book. But the mounting tension of international events after Hitler reoccupied the Rhineland in the first week of March, constantly obtruded on her work, and when the *Sunday Chronicle* (which had serialized *Testament of Youth*) offered to commission three articles from her on German reactions to the occupation, she leaped at the opportunity to observe the Nazi regime at first hand. Accompanied by George she left for a three-week trip on 25 March. They visited five German cities, Berlin, Cologne, Aachen, Frankfurt, and Heidelberg. In the first of these they witnessed Goering stirring the crowd to a terrifying emotional pitch, while in Cologne, unrecognizable from the war-torn city Vera had last visited with Winifred in 1924, they watched as Hitler delivered a speech, beating his breast 'like a penitent in an agony of religious fervour'. Conscious of being watched and supervised all the time that they were in Germany, they crossed with some relief into France at the beginning of April so that Vera could collect material for the war section of her novel. In the marketplace at Verdun they unexpectedly encountered sixteen hundred men and women who had come on a 'Pilgrimage of Peace', organized by La Ligue des Anciens Combattants Pacifistes, to visit the French–American battlefields in the surrounding countryside, and to affirm their 'Oath for Peace' at a service in the restored cathedral.

Vera was in England again for only ten days before setting off once more for the Continent, this time to Holland and a short lecture tour for the Anglo-Netherlands Association. On her return to Chelsea she drastically curtailed her speaking engagements and started a race to meet her publishers' deadline. In the final week of June, when she still had 45,000 words to go, Gollancz and Brett announced *Honourable Estate* for simultaneous autumn publication in Britain and the United States. '... I've promised to be a heroine and *try* to finish at the end of July so that they can', she told Eric Gillett, an old acquaintance from prewar Buxton days, who had acted with her in *Raffles* and was now himself a writer and drama columnist. Freed from interruptions at her mother's house in Edwardes Square, she worked 'at high speed', frequently writing eight hours a day. She finished the first draft in the third week of July and finally laid down her pen on 2 August. But she was in a mood of flat dejection as she corrected the typescript on the beach at Sandown on the Isle of Wight where she was holidaying with the children. She was upset to learn that Brett had shown the Eugene Meury–Ruth Alleyndene section to his wife ('it was intended for your eyes only', Vera admonished him); and was moved to anger by the Macmillan reader's criticism of the first half of the novel as 'extremely interesting', but also overlong and too solemn. 'Last year', she reminded Brett tersely, had been 'hardly conducive to the development of one's sense of humour.' Nonetheless she knew that the book badly lacked vitality and was expecting a critical backlash from reviewers to whom she presented an obvious target after the success of *Testament of Youth*. Not even these forebodings, though, could seriously mar an idyllic stay in Capri with George for three weeks that September when at last 'the cycle of work and sorrow' was broken.

Honourable Estate. A Novel of Transition finally appeared on 2 November 1936 ('Tomorrow! Vera Brittain breaks a three years' silence' had been Gollancz's portentous announcement in the previous day's *Sunday Times*). Large claims in recent years have been made for this, Vera's most ambitious novel, chiefly by feminist critics eager to champion the book's broad historical coverage of women's issues from the late-Victorian era through to 1930. In her foreword Vera explained that '*Honourable Estate* purports to show how the women's revolution – one of the greatest in all history – united with the struggle for other democratic ideals and the cataclysm of the War to alter the private destinies of individuals'; and in her analysis of the three marriages which provide the novel with its narrative thread, she sets out to explore developing attitudes to women in the decades before and after the attainment of the vote. In the book's first section, the restrictive type of Victorian wifehood in which 'the Jehovah-like' husband dictated the wife's every thought and action is represented by Janet Rutherston who, while possessing strong feminist sympathies, is unhappily confined in an oppressive marriage by a domineering clergyman husband some eighteen years her senior. Janet and her husband quarrel bitterly about her open support for the suffragettes and her refusal to conform to the narrow, conventional life of a country curate's wife. Eventually she escapes, leaving behind her young son, only to die broken and exhausted in an East End slum settlement a few years later. The marriage of Jessie and Stephen Alleyndene is less openly hostile than that of the Rutherstons though Jessie, like Janet, is only permitted to find self-fulfilment through her home and family, and realizes too late in life that she has never properly explored her own potential.

It is left to Ruth Alleyndene and Denis Rutherston in the next generation to learn from their parents' mistakes and to seek in their own marriage to establish a union of equal partnership in which Ruth can bring up twins – with, of course, the full-time assistance of a young lady from the 'Wellgarth Nursery Training School' – while pursuing a political career. In the final chapter Ruth is elected as MP for her Staffordshire home borough of Witnall, becoming one of the first women to enter Parliament after the passing of the 1928 Equal Franchise Act. *Honourable Estate* ends on a note of enlightenment and reconciliation with the past, and with a sense of the common identity of women through the ages. But there is also a grim warning of the gathering of 'dark forces'. The rise of Fascism in Europe has revived hostility to feminism, a fact which, as Vera acknowledges in her introduction, 'makes it the more important to contemplate that which was gained during the four decades which ended in 1930.'

Vera's attention both to detail, and to the integration into the story of aspects of the 'women's revolution', had been assiduous. Her notebooks are packed with information for background material: customs, clothes and expressions of the 1890s for the opening chapters, notes from books and interviews about the history of the Potteries for the Staffordshire sections, even copies of eyewitness accounts of the Russian famine on the Eastern Front, obtained from Archie Macdonell who had worked on a Quaker mission there, for Ruth Alleyndene and Denis Rutherston's meeting after the war. In the course of well over six hundred pages, no major feminist issue is allowed to go unaddressed: politics, education, economics, sex, and family life are all brought into play, giving the novel at times an awkward textbook quality. Vera had taken a defensive stand in her foreword by arguing that fiction was doomed as an organic art if it limited the novelist's legitimate concerns to personal relationships and showed itself incapable of dealing with large social and political movements. Yet all too often in *Honourable Estate* the tracing of the course of actual history is accomplished at the expense of the development of the characters who appear much of the time to exist merely as mouthpieces for the novelist's personal philosophies – and rather talkative ones at that. As Mary Cadogan and Patricia Craig noted in 1978 in their survey of the fiction of the two world wars, 'The author's admirable convictions get in the way of artistic necessity.'*

Most of the characters had been taken directly from life and yet no spark of invention breathes vitality into them on the page. Despite Vera's opening denial that the novel was autobiographical, she had kept to her original plan of using the book to reconcile herself to various unresolved episodes in her life which were a source of continuing pain. 'So often one can put the real truth about people in novels . . .', she told Sarah Gertrude Millin at this time, and in *Honourable Estate* her affair with Brett, Edward's homosexuality, and the unhappy demise of her friendship with Phyllis Bentley are all treated as creative fodder for her *roman à clef*.

Predictably, Phyllis Bentley fares worst. In the guise of Gertrude Ellison Campbell, a successful playwright tied to her home by the demands of an invalid brother, she is presented as an example of the desiccated spinster. Gertrude Campbell survives into old age to become 'The Grand Old Maid of English Drama', but her friendship with Janet Rutherston founders early on because of Gertrude's selfish jealousy of Janet's political interests.

George was by now resigned to finding himself portrayed in his wife's books, and while Ruth Alleyndene is a representation of Vera's best self, Denis Rutherston is essentially an idealized version of a more compliant George. Nothing, however, had prepared him for Vera's wholesale appropriation of his parents' stormy relationship, as recounted in Edith Catlin's diaries, to create Thomas and Janet Rutherston. With endearing naivety he had given Vera the journals to read so that she could develop a feel for the period. What in fact she had done was to use them to present a thinly disguised account of the breakdown of the Catlins' marriage. To George, who suffered from acute sensitivity about his unhappy adolescence, and who had always maintained a public silence on the subject, this must have amounted to a betrayal of confidence. Compounding the hurt was the vicious caricature of his father, the Reverend Catlin, as the irascible parson Thomas Rutherston. By an unfortunate coincidence of events, the death of Mr Catlin, after more than three years in a nursing home, had preceded the publication of the novel by barely a

---

*While criticizing Vera for her 'cumbersome' narrative, Cadogan and Craig compliment her on a rare bon mot. When Denis Rutherston proposes marriage to Ruth Alleyndene, she feels obliged to tell him that she isn't a virgin. ' "I was asking you to be my wife", Denis replies, "I'm not exclusively interested in one part of your anatomy." '

fortnight. George had remained deeply attached to his father (the description of his death and funeral is the only point in George's autobiography at which he lays himself emotionally bare) and the unkind portrait in *Honourable Estate* merely added another dimension to his grief.

In her dedication, 'To G. with love, and in memory of E.K.C. [Edith Kate Catlin] who worked for a day that she never saw', Vera tacitly acknowledged her debt. The relevance of the story to her main theme had simply been too great for her to resist, and as before, she was not going to allow family sensitivities to interfere with her self-allotted task of relating the individual's experience to the impersonal forces of history. Their battle over *Testament of Youth*'s final chapter had taught George that little was to be gained from direct confrontation, and he therefore made no protest. But after Vera's death he consistently opposed any plans to republish *Honourable Estate*. Of all Vera's books, he remembered in 1970, it was the one he had liked the least. 'It was pretty grossly libellous of my father and although being consulted by Rubinstein I raised no objections, I think I ought to have been more firm. Identification is all too easy.'

Far from showing the hostility Vera had expected, the reviews of *Honourable Estate* were restrained to the point of indifference. She was encouraged by a pre-publication notice in the *Manchester Guardian*, calling it 'a fine, a very fine novel'; but the critical consensus concurred with the Macmillan reader in finding the book worthy but dull. There was 'passionate sincerity' in the writing, but also an 'intense seriousness' which some had difficulty in stomaching. 'It must be admitted that on occasion Miss Brittain is more emotional than expressive', wrote Alfred Kazin in the *New York Times Book Review*, in a notice that was typical of the American reception. 'There is a heavy-handedness about her touch that quite frequently betrays her without conveying anything.' On the whole Vera felt damned with faint praise. Compared to the rapture which had greeted *Testament of Youth* the reception did indeed seem disappointingly lukewarm.

Sales too, though initially brisk on both sides of the Atlantic, failed to match the performance of the novel's famous predecessor. In Britain, where one of the effects of the Abdication Crisis was to send the book market plummeting at Christmas 1936, *Honourable Estate* sold 25,000 copies, a mere sixth of *Testament of Youth*'s total before the outbreak of the Second World War. (The novel would continue to be ill-fated: a cheap reprint was destroyed by the Luftwaffe in December 1940 and it has never been reprinted since.) In the United States, Brett understandably regarded the sales figures as a drop in the ocean when set against those for Macmillan's autumn blockbuster, *Gone with the Wind*. His evident disappointment was a source of profound regret to Vera. She had looked to the novel's success as a means of improving both her personal and professional standing with Brett. More than anything else it had been conceived as his book, written in the increasingly forlorn hope 'that it might bring a new sparkle of interest' to his eyes.

Harold Macmillan, a director of the family firm in London, tried to compensate for Brett's lack of enthusiasm by telling Vera that he had read *Honourable Estate* while ill in bed with flu, '& much admired it – espec.[ially] the objective reconstruction of [the] War part.' But Vera made no attempt to disguise her own dissatisfaction with the novel. 'It was written too much in the shadows', she admitted to Sarah Gertrude Millin, '& they lie across it.'

Letters requesting Vera as a public speaker had been arriving at the rate of two or three a day that summer, but in order to complete *Honourable Estate* she had declared 'a close season' on all speaking engagements. She felt 'dreadfully conscience-stricken' whenever she had to refuse a peace meeting and for one large-scale open-air Peace Rally in June she had made an exception. The rally was to take place near Dorchester and would be attended by peace groups from all over the south of England.

As the day grew closer, however, she was experiencing misgivings. Not only was the meeting an interruption she could well do without, but also the weather was proving uncomfortably humid. 'A thunderstorm last night – today a grilling like a Turkish bath', she wrote on 19 June to George, who was back in Heidelberg researching a book. 'Dorchester tomorrow seems a terrible burden.'

At least ten, and possibly as many as fifteen thousand men and women converged in sweltering heat on the Roman amphitheatre at Maumbury, just outside Dorchester, on the afternoon of Saturday 20 June 1936 for what Lord Soper now recalls as 'one of the most remarkable peace rallies I've ever been at.' Whether in the reserved seating in the arena or on the commanding grassy slopes surrounding it, the vast audience, said to be the largest ever assembled to that date for a peace demonstration in Britain, was able to listen to the speeches relayed on powerful loud speakers.

Vera's hostess for the day was Thomas Hardy's widow, Florence, and in between lunch at the Town Hall and the opening of the rally, there was just enough time for Vera to peer, through the pervasive gloom, at Max Gate, the writer's old home.

On the platform, protected by a striped parasol from the glare of the sunlight, sat the chairman, Laurence Housman, a number of local worthies including Florence Hardy, and the four speakers: Vera, the Reverend Donald Soper, already the most renowned preacher in the Methodist ministry, George Lansbury, whose pacifism had led to his enforced resignation from the leadership of the Labour Party the previous autumn, and Canon Dick Sheppard, who had sent a letter to the press in October 1934, calling on all men to sign a pledge renouncing war, thereby providing the impetus for the foundation of the pacifist Peace Pledge Union less than a month before the rally.

The crowd was full of 'fervour and enthusiasm', the atmosphere close to that of an 'evangelical rally', as first Lansbury and then Sheppard spoke. By the time Vera rose to address the audience she had been thoroughly disconcerted by the religious content of the speeches which had preceded hers. The promoters had emphasized the 'non-political and non-sectarian' character of the rally, but distracted by work, she had agreed to speak at Dorchester without realizing that she was being asked to appear on a Christian pacifist platform. Having come prepared with 'her customary little speech in support of collective security', she had suddenly become aware that on such a platform it would strike 'a discordant note'. 'Its basis was political', she was to write years later in *Testament of Experience*, 'but the message of my fellow-speakers sprang from the love of God.'

So instead she substituted a hastily improvised, and 'somewhat ineffective' speech, quoting Bunyan's valiant pilgrim, and recounting the story of her encounter with the Anciens Combattants at Verdun ten weeks earlier, and then sat down, acutely conscious that she had been the biggest disappointment of the afternoon.

'I travelled back to town in a first-class dining-car ... with George Lansbury, Dick Sheppard, and Donald Soper', she told George the next day. 'Most interesting – I heard all about Lansbury's American tour and Dick Sheppard's "Peace Pledge" movement and the Fellowship of Reconciliation. I find myself more and more sympathetic with the complete pacifist outlook.'

Seven months later, at Dick Sheppard's invitation, Vera became a Sponsor of the Peace Pledge Union. It was a far-reaching decision which would alter the whole course of her life.

II

For fifteen years, ever since joining the League of Nations Union (LNU) on coming down from Oxford in the summer of 1921, Vera had pinned her hopes for a lasting peace to 'the brave new banner of collective security' embodied in the articles of the covenant of the League of Nations. Like many other supporters in the early Thirties, she had watched with growing disquiet as successive crises, beginning with Japan's invasion of Manchuria, had demonstrated the League's ineffectiveness as an arbiter in international disputes, and its inability to achieve disarmament and check the rise of military aggression in Germany, Italy and Japan.

Yet although her initial optimism had faded, she had maintained her faith in the ideal represented by the League. In 1934 she, along with George and Winifred, had been among the fifteen British writers invited to contribute to *Challenge to Death*, 'a symposium against war', published with an introduction by Lord Cecil, President of the LNU. Vera's article on 'Peace and the Public Mind' endorsed collective security, which she defined as 'the collective ownership of armaments and the collective enforcement, in the last resort, of sanctions against an aggressor', and tried to defend the League against criticisms which had grown increasingly vocal. Addressing herself to those members of the public who were disappointed not to find a heaven on earth created at Geneva, Vera argued that the fault lay not with the peace machinery itself, but with the 'cynical determination' of the statesmen who had used the League 'as a camouflage behind which to return to the disastrous intrigues of the old diplomacy.'

Nothing, she believed, pointed more clearly to the dire consequences of the loss of a generation than that the world should be dependent for its future security upon a set of ageing and fallible politicians at Geneva – 'men whose mental processes were already becoming fossilised before the war'. Reflecting this distrust of the older generation, her work for the LNU in the first half of the decade had to a large extent centred on appeals to youth groups. She argued that the peace movement's most urgent requirement was to find a spirit of adventure which would both ensure a constant supply of young recruits and work as a counter-attraction to the fatal glamour of war. 'Why Not A Real Peace Crusade?' she asked in a 1934 article which advocated 'a real uniformed peace crusade . . . on the largest possible scale.' Action 'of the most spectacular kind' might include the use of banners and sky-writing to advertise slogans, demonstrations whenever rumours of war threatened to destroy peace, and celebrations when a measure of disarmament was passed. Only in this way would the peace movement lose its identification 'with perpetual pamphlets and the dreary droning of tired voices in somnolent lecture halls.'

Writing and speaking for the LNU did not, however, represent the sum of Vera's peace activism at this time. She had long felt that the staff at the Union's headquarters in Grosvenor Crescent undervalued her services, and although her increased public exposure after the publication of *Testament of Youth* prompted them to court her as a prominent voice and, for instance, to appoint her a Vice-President of the Youth Movement in early 1935, she was often critical of what she considered their uninspiring organization. This fact, together with the difficult position the LNU found itself in once the League's policy on collective security had begun to falter, encouraged her from the early Thirties to increase her involvement with other organizations working for peace.

These were many and diverse, and Vera's prominence after 1933 led to her affiliation, sometimes grudgingly, with numerous others. Chief among those to which her commitment went deepest were the National Peace Council, a supervisory body set up to coordinate different sections of the peace movement (dismissed by George as 'a kind of eunuch organization' because it was prevented from dealing with anything which smacked of controversy), the Union of Democratic Control, and the Women's International League for Peace and Freedom. It was for these last two that she was most active, serving as a council member of the UDC from 1927, and as a Vice-President of the WILPF.

The UDC, originally established by neutralists in 1914 to work for a negotiated peace, was turned into an anti-Fascist research and propaganda body by Dorothy Woodman in the early Thirties. Vera admired Woodman's boisterous, no-nonsense courage, and lent her support to one of the UDC's main objectives, an attack on the private manufacture of arms. MPs and other individuals of public standing had been approached to buy shares in Armstrong Vickers or one of the other armament firms which would allow them to ask awkward questions at shareholders' meetings, exposing the sometimes dubious means by which companies sold arms to foreign governments. 'I have a little money on deposit for my children's education', Vera wrote to Dorothy Woodman in May 1934. 'Would it be of any help if I were to invest, say, £100 of this in one of the large armament firms where you have at present no observer?' She would have to invent a bogus name and 'in order to keep a clear conscience' would donate any profits she made to the UDC for its propaganda, but she was convinced 'that exposures of this kind are one of the most valuable aspects of peace work today.'

For so long as a genuine programme of collective security appeared an attainable goal, the wide spectrum of opinion within the peace movement, encompassing internationalists like Vera and pacifists of a collaborative orientation, was able to find common cause. 'The great thing now is to prevent another war, whatever slight differences the peace-loving people have among themselves', were Vera's somewhat evasive words in a letter to one of her younger readers in the summer of 1935, in which she added that 'I myself have not entirely made up my mind to which group I belong . . .'. Within a matter of months these 'slight differences' had emerged as a major rift which it was no longer possible to ignore. The international crisis of 1936 – the final subjugation of Abyssinia by Mussolini's forces, Hitler's remilitarization of the Rhineland, and the outbreak of civil war in Spain – exposed once and for all the fatal impotence of the League and caused a dramatic polarization in the peace movement. The 'wide moral division between the supporters of collective security and exponents of revolutionary pacifism had always existed but had not been emphasised', Vera wrote later. 'But with the threat of a second world war, the gulf had become clear. Individuals who believed that war was wrong in all circumstances could no longer join with those who were prepared to fight in the last resort.'

As Vera had watched Winifred's life ebbing away in the last days of September 1935, she had been only too aware from the newspaper placards outside the nursing home announcing the mobilization of Abyssinia, that their shared hopes for a peace based on a new international order were also fading. The British Government's failure to enforce sanctions against Italy deprived the League of what little authority it still possessed; and the LNU's subsequent decision to support rearmament as part of a credible collective security policy effectively removed everything that had previously distinguished it from conventional defence measures. The choice was now clear cut: collective security, a 'compromise with militarism', meant war, only pacifism could ensure peace.

Martin Ceadel, the historian of British pacifism, has described the upheaval in the peace movement which followed the Abyssinian crisis, the 'two-way' traffic towards and away from pacifism in the course of which some former pacifists were jolted into the realization that they must arm against Fascism, while others, inspired by a Christian or humanitarian faith, renounced their links with internationalism and espoused pacifism. It was against this background of realignment that the Sheppard Peace Movement, as the Peace Pledge Union was originally called, was born.

Hugh Richard Lawrie Sheppard – or 'Dick' as he was almost universally known – had become a household name in the Twenties when, as Vicar of St Martin-in-the-Fields, his Sunday evening broadcasts had made him famous as the 'Radio Parson' and his services had attracted record congregations to St Martin's. It had been in recognition of this, and of his work in making the church crypt a centre for the homeless and destitute, that he had been made a Companion of Honour in 1926. Despite being an outspoken critic of established religion – 'what . . . does duty nowadays, through the Churches, as Christianity, is a caricature of what Christ intended', he had written in *The Impatience of a Parson* – he had gained preferment as Dean of Canterbury, and latterly as a Canon of St Paul's.

Although Sheppard had professed an uncompromising pacifism as early as 1927, he had continued to be assailed by doubts which, together with his chronic asthma, had prevented him from taking a definite stand on the issue. However, in October 1934, spurred on by the urgency of the international situation and by the violent displays of British Fascists at Olympia which he had witnessed earlier that year, he sent a letter to the press, making 'A Peace Appeal to Men'. The peace movement, he wrote, had 'Up to now . . . received its main support from women, but it seems high time . . . that men should throw their weight into the scales against war.' All those men who felt as he did were asked to send him a postcard with the words: 'We renounce war and never again directly or indirectly will we support or sanction another.'

Within two days 2,500 cards had arrived; after a few weeks their number had climbed to 50,000 (the pledge was not extended to women until July 1936). Simultaneously stunned and delighted at the response, Sheppard continued to procrastinate about consolidating this support into a coherent and official body. Only in July 1935 did he follow up his original letter by inviting its signatories to a rally at the Albert Hall, attended by an audience of 7,000. By then the momentum of the Peace Appeal was too great to stop. On 22 May 1936 the Peace Pledge Union (PPU) was officially launched.

Among its initial Sponsors were Storm Jameson, Arthur Ponsonby, George Lansbury, Donald Soper, and Charles Raven, and they were soon joined by an array of intellectual, political, and literary luminaries, including Rose Macaulay, Bertrand Russell, Siegfried Sassoon, Ellen Wilkinson, and Aldous Huxley. Overseeing them all, and providing an essential focus in the absence, as yet, of any firm policy line, was the charismatic and messianic Sheppard. To George it seemed that there was more than a touch of the actor in Sheppard's make-up, while Huxley briefly sketched him into *Eyeless in Gaza* as Purchas, the pacifist parson with the 'muscular-jocular Christian manner'. His combination of warmth, intuitive sympathy, and lack of intellectual pretension was an important factor in attracting to the PPU support which was both overtly Christian and of a more secular and political nature. 'He had a genius for drawing people out by his intense sympathy with their difficulties, and also, I think, by the fearlessness of his own faith', wrote Laurence Housman, a close friend and colleague, after Sheppard's death.

Overburdened with work and weighed down by the accumulation of problems which followed Winifred's death, Vera appears scarcely to have noticed the sequence of events leading up to the foundation of the PPU. However, shortly before her visit to Germany in the spring of 1936, she had moved perceptibly closer to pacifism by confronting the central painful dilemma that so many would-be pacifists had found themselves locked into at this time – of whether in the last resort she would be prepared to sanction the use of force against Fascism. 'I fear War more than Fascism', she had concluded in her diary; 'anyhow I am sure that you can't use Satan to cast out Satan; that Fascism which sprang from colossal injustice will only grow stronger if that injustice is rammed home . . .'.

Three months later the Dorchester Rally clarified her thinking still further and she wrote to George, outlining the reasons for her growing attraction to 'the complete pacifist outlook':

a) Because what the pacifists prophesied from the beginning about the unworkableness of sanctions is exactly what has happened; b) Because once you admit the possibility of war at all, 'a righteous reason for it' – call it security, League of Nations, defending the world against wicked Germany, wicked Italy or wicked Japan – will *always* be found; c) Because scientific inventions have made warfare . . . of a barbarity incompatible with a civilized world . . . d) Because I don't think the over-running and temporary occupation of any country by a foreign power (in view of the size and economic strength of the British Empire it *could* be only temporary) would be such a blow to civilization in general as another European War; e) Because I think that a few people . . . are needed to hold up before humanity the, as yet, but not always, unattainable ideal.

She omitted to mention one other significant factor which was drawing her closer to pacifism: Sheppard himself. The impact on Vera of his open friendliness on the return journey to Waterloo after the rally had been instantaneous. In his rolled-up shirt-sleeves and with his engaging air of informality, she was to recall, he had resembled nothing so much as a slightly tipsy cricketer returning home after the afternoon's match. In the lighthearted atmosphere she relaxed and talked openly of her interest in pacifism. It may have been at this point that Sheppard first broached the possibility of her becoming a Sponsor of the PPU.

If this was so, nothing conclusive resulted from their conversation, for in an exchange of letters later that week she neatly sidestepped any direct reference to the PPU while he simply struck a note of courtesy by telling her 'how really delighted' he had been to meet her at long last. 'I should so much have liked on Saturday to have thanked you for your Testimony', he wrote, 'but I felt that everybody was doing that and you would only be bored with another bouquet.'

Less than a fortnight later she was writing to him again with the explanation she felt she owed him 'after our conversation in the train the other day.' Her own views, she admitted, had for a long time been tending 'towards the complete pacifist position maintained by your organisation', but the task of completing *Honourable Estate* left her with 'neither the leisure nor the freedom of mentality' to tackle a subject as 'complex and important as the current peace position'. To offer him public support now, she explained, would mean not only rethinking her whole position, but also relinquishing her connections with those other peace organizations which might prove incompatible with membership of the PPU. 'Frankly I have not yet decided exactly where I stand', she wrote in a final paragraph,

and before I commit myself to any further undertakings . . . I should greatly welcome the opportunity of talking the whole thing over with you if you could possibly spare the time for someone who might not even then fully support you . . . Would you perhaps be able to spare a few minutes some time in August or September when my book will be finished?

The excuse provided by her book was genuine enough and she sounds as if she badly wanted Sheppard to convince her. But George had in the meantime been urging caution. In response to her letter enthusing about Dorchester, he had swiftly announced that he could never become a pacifist – for fear that such a step might 'wipe myself out as an effective politician' – and had then proceeded to outline the case against the PPU. While he did not doubt that pacifism was a noble end, as a means of preventing war it was impractical. Peace, he maintained, could only be achieved by opposing the dictators with the combined strength of the democracies. 'I will not stop to inquire whether pacifism as an *absolute* principle is sound', he told her. 'In measurable time you will not convert to it the majority of this great nation and therefore . . . it will not, as a public fact, avert war.'

For the present she found it difficult not to agree. Several months earlier she had noted that Christianity, though 'apparently unattainable', was 'the only commonsense left and the only condition of survival'. But she interpreted Christian pacifism, as espoused by Sheppard and his followers, as a state of mind, offering a 'revolutionary principle' ultimately rooted in Christ's teaching in the Sermon on the Mount, rather than a constructive policy which could provide an alternative to war. Impressed as she had been by the strength of the Christian witness of her fellow-speakers at

Dorchester, she was not yet ready to surrender all hope in political expedients.

Nevertheless, throughout that autumn Vera's thoughts on the subject remained in a state of turmoil. With her novel out of her hands, and having talked with Sheppard in late August, she decided on a new strategy, designed principally to test her allegiance to the League of Nations. By accepting several outstanding invitations to address LNU meetings, she hoped to discover whether she could continue to uphold the position of collective security which she had been endeavouring to maintain.

This brief tour at the beginning of September turned out to be the most disconcerting that she had ever experienced. Wherever she spoke she was heckled by members of local PPU groups, and the more she fended off their questions, the more deeply she found herself in agreement with their case against the League of Nations: 'It had become a mere French-dominated instrument for continuing the unjust *status quo*, set up at Versailles, of which Hitler was the appalling consequence.'

She had demonstrated to her own satisfaction that she could no longer support a League which showed every sign of political and moral bankruptcy, yet still she stopped short of embracing pacifism. 'I need hardly say that Canon Sheppard's organization is working for the objective that I personally wish to see', she told Captain Philip Mumford of the PPU at the end of October, '. . . and yet I cannot see how the pacifist position can ever be widely accepted as a policy until after some experiment in genuine collective security has succeeded the current phase of reactionary nationalism.'

Mumford, a PPU Sponsor and one of Sheppard's most devoted lieutenants, took up the invitation implicit in Vera's letter to argue the case for pacifism with her. On 5 January 1937 Mumford came for tea at Glebe Place, and by the time he left later that afternoon Vera had taken the decision that had come to seem inevitable: she had agreed to join the Peace Pledge Union and to address meetings for them. But although she found Mumford 'decent, agreeable and clear-headed', she confessed in her diary that it was Bertrand Russell's recently published *Which Way to Peace?*, rather than anything in Mumford's conversation, which had finally won her over.

In fact it seems that Russell's book did not so much convert her to pacifism as confirm her in her own way of thinking. Russell's main conclusion that 'modern war is practically certain to have worse consequences than even the most unjust peace' – principally because he was convinced that any future conflict would result in the total destruction of

Europe – bore a striking similarity to the arguments Vera had advanced to George in the wake of the Dorchester rally; and as Alan Ryan has suggested, *Which Way to Peace?* is too obsessed with strategic logic, and 'too little tempered by common sense' to persuade anyone but the already convinced. In the event, Russell himself was to repudiate the book publicly in the immediate aftermath of the outbreak of the Second World War.

Prominently featured in the PPU's New Year campaign for 1937, Vera attended her first public meeting, chaired by Sheppard, at the Central Hall in Bristol on 13 January where she shared the platform with three Sponsors, Mumford, Canon Stuart Morris, and Siegfried Sassoon. Sassoon, Vera reported, 'seemed an epitome of the war generation at its gentlest and most pathetic.' While he read from his poetry, she sat 'with reddening nose, mopping my eyes . . .'.

Bristol was followed by Sheffield on the 18th where Vera was joined by Sheppard and Charles Raven, and although she cried off a further meeting at Hull on the 23rd, she wrote to Sheppard soon afterwards, formally announcing her decision to sign the pledge. Sheppard 'shouted with joy' when he read her letter, and wrote thanking her 'quite immensely for all that you have done for us' and 'if I may say it, for what your name means to the cause.'

He asked if she would be prepared now to become a Sponsor of the PPU. 'I know my colleagues would love to have you, but please don't think I want to rush you.' Vera responded at once, requesting that her name be put forward.

She had searched long and hard for the confidence to make this decision, believing that it was a step which, once taken, would be difficult for her to retrace; and she had finally reached the conclusion that in a world of heavily armed nations and self-interested governments, collective security 'can lead us nowhere but the edge of the abyss.' Pacifism, she freely admitted, was not without its risks, but at the very least the PPU advocated 'practical and effective methods of resistance to war itself without recourse to arms.'

Hitherto Vera had understood the case for pacifism in terms that were largely political, and as the threat of war grew ever more insistent a pragmatic outlook would continue to predominate. But already signs of a developing religious perspective were discernible. In a letter written that January she had commented that the PPU

stands for such an utterly different conception of international relationships from anything we have had before that it seems strange and unthinkable to many people. It is, in effect, asking people to accept Christianity as a way of life when they have hitherto given it only lipservice and gone on as before.

Vera had little time for organized religion; she was not even sure that she believed in God, and many readers of *Testament of Youth* had remarked upon her 'professed agnosticism'. She strongly believed, however, that the faith by which an individual lives is very different from any theological expression that he or she is able to give it. She had always regarded herself as a religious person,

> for it seems to me that the essence of religion is not so much a blind faith in a known or unknown god as the extent to which one's work is disinterested and one is moved by a desire to contribute to 'that long age which we shall not see', rather than to one's own petty profit here and now.

'I am not a pacifist for reasons of Christianity . . .', Vera stated in one of the first articles she wrote after joining the PPU; but she was coming increasingly to believe that the basic Christian doctrine, 'Whatsoever ye would that men should do to you, do ye even so to them', was the soundest rule for human conduct, whether between nations or individuals.

She recognized, and sometimes appreciated, the paradox that someone so naturally provocative and combative as herself – 'that warlike champion of peace' as the chairman of a public meeting once referred to her – should ever be a pacifist. And she would attribute whatever success she achieved in conquering that 'inherited temperament' to her connection with pacifism, 'since working with them opened my eyes to the fact that it wasn't much use working for a Christian spirit in politics if one didn't at least try to achieve it at home.'

'Good for you and grand for us', Sheppard wrote, welcoming Vera to the PPU on 29 January. Three days later the PPU minutes record that 'A proposal to make Miss Vera Brittain a sponsor was unanimously accepted'; and on 8 March Vera attended her first Sponsors' meeting at the PPU's offices at 96 Regent Street.

III

Among the Sponsors present at Vera's first PPU meeting was a fragile-looking woman with delicate features and honey-blonde hair. This was Margaret Storm Jameson who, 'Since the death of Miss Winifred Holtby', as Vera informed Colston Leigh in the spring of 1936, '. . . is the greatest friend I have.'

359

It was Storm Jameson who had made the first overtures of friendship to Vera, almost a decade earlier, in the summer of 1927. She had written to her and they had found common cause in the difficulties of combining marriage, motherhood and a career, a subject which Storm Jameson, with a young child of her own, was exploring at the time in a series of articles for the *Evening Standard*. She had visited Nevern Place while Vera was heavily pregnant with John. 'I was immensely impressed at your coming to see me', Vera wrote some years later, remembering how surprised she had been by Storm's youthful appearance, 'for I had assumed – or perhaps my forlorn ambitions had hoped – that you must be much older than myself because you were so much better known.'

The two women had remained on friendly terms throughout the early Thirties, and Storm had been one of *Testament of Youth*'s earliest and staunchest supporters, contributing a glowing review of the book to the *Sunday Times*. With Winifred's death their intimacy deepened. On the day that Winifred died, George had to rush to Brighton for the colonial debate at the Labour Party conference, leaving Vera to be comforted by Storm and her husband, Guy Chapman, and to spend the night at their St John's Wood flat; and it was to Storm that Vera clung, shivering, as Winifred's coffin was carried through St Martin's at her memorial service.

This image of clinging dependence is not entirely inappropriate for their relationship as it developed in the years just before the Second World War. Bereft of Winifred's support and guidance, Vera was to turn increasingly to Storm Jameson, seeking to mould her as a substitute friend and confidante. She signalled her intention early on by appointing Storm as her literary executor in place of Winifred, and by 1939 could write that she felt the same kind of confidence in her as she had once done with Winifred. However, proud and strongly individualistic – 'I would not be beholden' was her chosen epitaph – Storm was to remain wary of Vera's emotional demands.

Herbert Gray, a Presbyterian Sponsor of the PPU, once remarked to Vera of Storm Jameson that he had seen few faces on which suffering was so clearly written; and in many ways Margaret Storm Jameson – to Vera she was always 'my dearest' or 'my darling Margaret' – had experienced a life as marked by personal sorrow as Vera's. Her younger brother, a pilot in the Flying Corps, was shot down and killed over France in 1917. In her early twenties she made a disastrous first marriage, and was plagued by guilt when she went out to work and neglected her young son, Bill. Nor was she to have an untroubled middle age: her younger and favourite sister, Dorothy, would be tragically killed in an air raid in 1942. Moreover, unlike Vera, her life was never cushioned by anything remotely resembling financial security. Money, or more specifically her own extravagance and disregard for personal wealth, was a constant worry. 'I give it away or spend it . . . with reckless indifference', she admitted. 'I shall die on straw.'

Born in January 1891 at Whitby on the East Yorkshire coast, Storm Jameson was the oldest of four children. Her father was a merchant seaman, often away from home, and it was her mother who exercised the dominant influence on her early life. Zealous for her children's future, Hannah Jameson instilled ambition and discipline into them with the aid of frequent thrashings. Storm won one of the North Riding's county scholarships, and was the first woman to read English at Leeds University, receiving a first-class degree. Afterwards, with a research fellowship at King's College, London, she studied modern European drama.

Following her marriage in 1913 to Charles Douglas Clarke, and the birth of her son, Bill, she started writing novels as the easiest way of earning money with a young child at home, and as an escape from the domesticity she detested. Her first 'gloriously bad' novel appeared in 1919, and throughout the Twenties and Thirties she produced, on average, a book every other year. Even so, her income still lagged far behind her expenditure and, by the early Twenties, she had begun to make forays into London literary life as a talent scout for the American publisher, Alfred Knopf. One of the English novels for which she expressed 'profound admiration' in 1923 was *The Dark Tide*.

When Vera met her, Storm Jameson was divorced from her first husband and had recently married Guy Chapman, whose fine war memoir, *A Passionate Prodigality*, had been published eight months before *Testament of Youth*. Chapman was a mature student at the London School of Economics, and the larger share of supporting both him and Bill was falling heavily on Storm Jameson's shoulders. She bore the brunt of it because of her devotion to Chapman, but the ceaseless churning out of novels was having a serious effect both on the overall quality of her writing and on her health. Between 1933 and 1936 she suffered two breakdowns. Storm habitually fell into a pattern of denigrating her own work and Vera was not the only friend over the years to wonder at her apparent willingness to eclipse herself for Chapman's sake.

Vera responded with well-timed generosity whenever Storm was ill or unable to work, offering her money and sending her delicacies from Fortnum and Mason's, or small packages of cheese and honey from Devon to 'add a little variety to your tedious housekeeping'. Once when Storm was broke, Vera tried to use her influence with Colston Leigh to get her a lecture contract in the United States, and later when she quarrelled with her

American publishers, it was Vera who persuaded Brett to sign her for the Macmillan list. Nor was Storm slow to express her gratitude. In February 1937 Vera proudly announced to George that a note had just arrived from Storm which ended with the words, 'you are the best friend any one ever had and I thank God for you.'

Yet while Storm could go some way towards filling the gap in Vera's life left by Winifred, giving her the reassurance she needed and listening patiently to her problems, it is also clear that she tended to shy away from Vera's claims on her intimacy and could be resentful of what she saw as her proprietary interest in her life. 'You have always made me feel a little embittered', Vera told her several years later, 'because I took for granted that you wanted nothing from anyone ... but reticence, and, where personal emotions were concerned, a vigilant self-restraint.' Vera had to tread carefully when offering Storm advice on the basis of her own marital arrangements. 'The last thing I want is to be, even indirectly, a dividing line between you and anyone else', Vera assured her before counselling her nonetheless that no one is ever justified in sacrificing their work to the interests of another person.

But there was also unquestionably an element of self-interest in Vera's attitude to Storm's independence. She too wanted Storm's attention, and when denied her company was liable to reveal a streak of possessive jealousy. In May 1936 Vera wrote to her that

> ... It does seem to me that when you always treat the demands of your relatives upon you ... as a kind of Medes & Persians before which your own work, your friends, your interests, have inevitably to give way, that you are doing them a disservice as well as yourself & society.

As writers Vera and Storm Jameson did more than merely support each other's work: they shared a common outlook. Vera's assertion that she had 'very little use for the pure stylist who remains untouched by the problems of his age' was one with which Storm heartily concurred. *No Time Like the Present* (1932), her semi-autobiographical essay – which, as she generously told Vera, she hoped would serve as a kind of John the Baptist crying in the wilderness to announce the coming of *Testament of Youth* – was conceived as a memoir of the war generation, but, before she was halfway through writing it, had expanded to include a violent diatribe against the irrational forces driving humanity towards war.

Inevitably Storm had been drawn into active politics, sitting on the mushrooming anti-war and anti-Fascist committees like so many other writers of left-wing sympathies. Together with Philip Noel Baker, she had been responsible for recruiting Vera and other well-known contributors in defence of collective security and against war for the polemical volume, *Challenge to Death*. She had also been one of the founder Sponsors of the PPU. 'I was interested to see in the *Herald* yesterday that you had decided to support Dick Sheppard's Peace Pledge Union, as it is a position towards which I feel I am moving myself', Vera had written to her in July 1936.

Yet in her heart of hearts Storm was never wholly convinced that absolute pacifism was the answer. In 1936 she had challenged herself: 'If I believe that concentration camps, the torture of Jews and political opponents are less vile than war, I must say so plainly, not pretend that the price is something less.' It was to become increasingly difficult for her to assert this point of view, especially after 1938 when she became President of the English section of PEN and witnessed at first hand the effects of Nazi persecution while rescuing and assisting writers from countries under German domination.

Her loathing of the Nazi creed was in fact as deep as her loathing of war and she never managed to achieve a single mind on the issue after 1933. One result of this ambivalence was that she tended to adjust her feelings according to the person she happened to be with. Vera sometimes sensed the 'dubious' quality of Storm's pacifism; but it was only after the actual outbreak of war that tensions arising from their differences would begin to erect a barrier between them. Long before that, Storm's active involvement in PPU affairs had dwindled to practically nothing.

Vera had hoped, like Storm Jameson, to contain her activities on the PPU's behalf, and Sheppard had initially promised her that she would not be called upon more than once a month. She quickly realized, however, what an understatement this was, and that she was in effect 'at the mercy of the exploiting, insatiable pacifist movement, forever demanding time, money, talents, strength.' On a bitterly cold day at the end of February 1937, Vera ('a recent notable addition to the Sponsors' reported *Peace News*) attended an outdoor rally at Hyde Park, her first such occasion since joining the PPU. She hated open-air meetings, she complained to George beforehand, and, with all the confidence of someone with nearly fifteen years' experience behind her of Speakers' Corner and other similar venues, feared that Dick's 'literary and aesthetic followers aren't tough enough for Hyde Park. You have to be an incurable egotist, complete with lipstick and a permanent wave, for that.'

She had a point. Amidst flurries of hail and snow and a gale-force wind, some of the 'crocks' who had bravely turned out had a struggle competing with the elements to be heard. Balanced precariously on a cart, Vera spoke while the wind thumped her back and sleet lashed her front, worrying all the time that she had developed 'a red nose and a dead-white face'. 'It was very nice of you to say that you thought my speech effective and also that I didn't look too bad!' she wrote afterwards to fellow PPU activist Sybil Morrison. Despite the weather an audience of between two and three hundred had assembled, most of whom seemed to be in support of the PPU's protest against the Government's rearmament plans. Referring to 'Rearmament Insanity', Vera speculated on the immediate results of another war, evoking a horrific picture of London burning, with gas in the streets and 'panic stricken hordes'. When she spoke of being unable to understand why the women of Britain 'do not rise in protest against the fate that is awaiting their children', her words were greeted with loud shouts of 'hear, hear' from the crowd. The next day Sheppard wrote to tell her that she had been 'a sportsman' and pronounced her speech 'simply A.1.'

Over the next decade, and indeed until her final illness, thirty years later, Vera was to appear on countless platforms expounding her pacifism. She often resented the time taken away from her writing, sometimes she managed to resist the way in which causes and organizations threatened to monopolize her life; but more often than not 'the inconvenient protest of conscience' made her steel herself to go ahead and deliver her message, at outdoor meetings or in the more formal atmosphere of the lecture hall, to friendly and hostile audiences alike.

Although she knew full well that she could be an effective speaker, she considered public speaking 'a trifling & unsatisfying thing to be good at'. Her style of speech, even at larger-scale, rowdier occasions, was far removed from that of a rabble-rouser. On the contrary, it was the lucid and logical presentation of her argument which seized the attention of her audience. She chose her words carefully and always looked well-dressed, remembered one rank-and-file member of the PPU, who felt nonetheless that she lacked 'the common touch' and was divorced from the concerns of the man or woman in the street. While this may have been true, it does not appear to have affected her drawing power. Sybil Morrison recalled the distinctly audible groan from a crowd of about a thousand people at a peace meeting at Kendal in 1938 when the chairman announced that Vera was unable at the last minute to be present.

Her 'possibly instinctive clothes sense' and her immaculately groomed appearance – the result of at least one weekly facial and hair appointment – were important confidence-boosters on these occasions, as well as serving a more serious underlying purpose. 'If I always appeared in ultra respectable clothes at these gatherings', Vera wrote towards the end of her life, 'this was not intended as a criticism of the other participators, but was due to the belief I have always held that minorities who bear witness to unpopular convictions should appear as though they bore their witness from choice, and not because their circumstances deprived them of alternative opportunities.'

She admitted that 'the obstinate remnants of my Buxton upbringing' made it difficult for her to acclimatize herself to the sartorial habits of some of her fellow-workers. Middle-aged women in particular, in their drooping skirts, were singled out for disapproval; and later, at Sixties protests and sit-ins, she was to find it hard to overcome her initial suspicion of young men with beards and duffle-coats.

When, as was frequently the case, she was inundated by invitations to speak from all manner of pacifist as well as feminist organizations, Vera would forcefully remind those responsible that she considered herself a writer first and foremost. 'My life is not my own', she exclaimed in her diary after one post brought no less than six requests, ' – and everyone all over the country is doing their best to prevent me being the writer which alone makes me of value to their cause!' The PPU was especially guilty in this respect, and Vera was outraged in August 1937 when John Barclay, the PPU's National Group Organizer, had 'the impertinence' to suggest 'that it was selfish and disloyal of me to spend so much time on writing when I could be speaking!' Dorothy Plowman, wife of one of the PPU's most popular Sponsors and its one-time General Secretary, Max Plowman, earned herself this stinging rebuke from Vera when she too broached the subject in February 1938:

If . . . I am of no use to the P.P.U. unless I can be continually available for meetings, my only course will be to send in my resignation as Sponsor. I am not primarily a speaker but a writer, and I do not again intend to sacrifice writing to speaking to the extent that I have done in the past two or three years.

The effect of Vera's political activism upon her literary output can be seen most clearly in the declining number of articles and reviews she was producing. It has been calculated that while she published, on average, over forty pieces a year between 1930 and 1934 (after reaching a peak of a hundred pieces in 1929), her output suddenly fell in 1935 to eighteen, its lowest for ten years, and only once during the rest of her career did it rise above twenty. There were, of course, other reasons for this decline: the continuing impact of the slump upon the demand for freelance journalism, for one, and the difficulties Vera was increasingly to face as a pacifist in getting articles as widely commissioned as before. It was also undoubtedly true that having established a name for herself as a bestselling author, Vera preferred to devote her time to the writing of books.

Where her books were concerned, the effect of her political involvement was more insidious, depriving her of the freedom in which to contemplate new ideas and develop her range as a writer. On completing *Testament of Youth*, Vera had announced to Phyllis Bentley that she had 'coherent plans in my head for no less than four books to cover the next five years . . .'. One of these was a sequel to *Testament of Youth*, provisionally entitled 'Black Decade', covering the years 1926 to 1936. Looking ahead into the more distant future, she hoped that this would form one of a number of volumes of autobiography under the general title of 'Panorama', which would eventually include her 'Mature Impressions' and a 'Testament of Age'. Another promising idea, favoured by Gollancz and later Harold Macmillan, was for a novel, 'Behold, This Dawn!', based on the life of Mary Wollstonecraft and set against the backdrop of the tumultuous years of the French Revolution.

'Behold, This Dawn!' never progressed beyond the planning stage, while 'Black Decade' had to wait another twenty years before materializing in a different form as part of *Testament of Experience*. Both were delayed in the short term by Winifred's death, and the two or three years of preparation and research that went into writing her biography. Vera, though, had no doubt that without 'the perpetual requests to be a speaker, sponsor, Chairman [or] Vice-President' she would have managed to be at least twice as productive as a writer in the same period.

She would discover that it was not only demands on her time which prevented her from writing the kind of books she had set her heart on. In the early Forties she entered into negotiations to write a biography of George Lansbury, and subsequently one of Amy Johnson, only to experience, in different ways, obstruction from their families. Lansbury, the former Labour leader and an uncompromising pacifist, who died in 1940, had obvious appeal as a subject for Vera. 'There is no book that I should better like to do', she told Lovat Dickson, her editor at Macmillan, in June 1940. 'It would . . . be a magnificent saga of both the Labour & Peace movements . . .'. However, a month later it had become clear to Vera that '. . . Quite obviously the Lansbury family doesn't want me to do it . . .'. Later it transpired that the Lansbury family's reluctance to appoint Vera as biographer derived from their fear that a book by her would not only concentrate too narrowly on the peace movement, but might also contain too much of her own autobiography.

Vera's failure to write a life of Amy Johnson, the celebrated aviator, who flew solo to Australia, and perished in mysterious circumstances over the Thames Estuary in 1941 while flying for the Air Transport Auxiliary, was more regrettable. The major themes of Johnson's story – 'youth, adventure, the development of civilian flying, a woman's conquest of man-made obstacles in a singularly difficult profession' – would have presented Vera with a welcome challenge. But although Johnson's parents were anxious that someone of Vera's literary standing should write about Amy, her younger sister, Betty, who had first claim on the subject, was determined to produce a book of her own and, after a time, nothing more came of the idea.

While Vera perceived her work for peace as posing a threat to her writing, she regarded her feminism and pacifism as closely interrelated. A consistent strand of argument in her articles and lectures from 1934 onwards was directed against what she termed the 'terrible, inert mass of lethargic womanhood', who needed to be roused from their collective apathy and domestic myopia in order to start exercising some influence on behalf of peace. The 'infinite capacity of most women for resignation', she wrote in an article on 'Women and Disarmament,', was 'a menace to the civilisation which their united efforts could save.'

It was no good a woman becoming obsessed by the domestic routine, worrying about keeping her house clean and her children tidy, when 'the ideal nursery and its inhabitants upon which so much of her time has been spent may be annihilated by enemy bombs within two or three years.' If, as Vera believed, feminism proclaimed the equality of women with men, then feminism also gave women the responsibility to think about world affairs, and take an active part in politics.

The chief shortcoming of Vera's case for the awakening of women's political consciousness, as with so much of her feminist writing, is that it is concerned, almost exclusively, with the experience of middle-class women. But that aside, in the years ahead Vera was often to emphasize the complementary nature of feminism and pacifism. A true pacifist society, she believed, would be one in which aggression and the use of force would be removed from every sphere of human life. In 1941 she would link together her twin goals of feminism and pacifism by recognizing that

> . . . the struggle against war, which is the final and most vicious expression of force, is fundamentally inseparable from feminism, socialism, slave emancipation and the liberation of subject races.

IV

References to her children often featured in Vera's lectures and speeches for the Peace Pledge Union. So much of her work for peace was inspired by the wish to save John and Shirley from 'the shadow of death' which had been cast over her own generation. She did not want 'all that is left of my son ten years hence' to be a few letters; and she sometimes reflected that had she faced the choice of having children after, instead of before, 1931, 'when the world outlook became so black', she would not voluntarily have given birth to another human being.

In the spring of 1937 John was nine years old while Shirley was approaching her seventh birthday. Before her marriage Vera had dreamed of producing a son who would be a re-creation of Edward, and in John's dark eyes and strongly marked arched eyebrows, she fancied she saw a close physical resemblance to her brother. She also believed that, as with Edward in her youth, an instinctive sympathy existed between John and herself. Although not a demonstrative child, John possessed 'a sensitive responsiveness' to other people's moods and would happily sit reading with Vera in an armchair by the fire, expressing his affection by gently stroking her sleeve.

Vera was always especially protective towards John. He had been a sickly baby and for a time, when he was about five or six, had been made to wear an uncomfortable leg-brace to strengthen his knee joints. He was a bright boy, near the top of his form at Gibbs', the day school in Sloane Street which he attended from the beginning of 1936, but both his parents had recognized at an early stage that he was of a quieter and more artistic disposition than his younger sister, and that his talents inclined him towards painting and drawing rather than more solidly academic pursuits. 'Dear love', Vera wrote of him in her diary, '– neither excessively "intellectual", nor disgustingly ambitious, what a comfort he will be in a family which has hitched all its waggons to inaccessible stars!'

The fact that it was John who from babyhood had inspired Winifred's deepest affection, above all the other children she had known, was something else which marked him out as special in his mother's eyes. Within the family, John's grief for Winifred was second only to Vera's. He had received the news of her death with 'half-concealed' heartbreak which made him silent and miserable for weeks afterwards; and even several years later, while he remembered Winifred vividly, he was unable to speak of her.

More than usually full of forebodings as she embarked on her second American lecture-tour in the autumn of 1937, Vera wrote a letter to John, to be given to him only in the event of her death, in which she spoke of the depth of her feelings for him:

> I think you are the mainspring of my existence, in so far as anyone can be the mainspring of someone creative and ambitious. This does not mean that I do not love your father, and Shirley, perhaps equally with you . . . But there is always somebody for whom, and by whom, one chiefly feels that one lives, even though at the same time one may be passionately absorbed by someone else. Edward was such a mainspring to me once; and at a later stage Winifred Holtby (though there was never any hint of a homosexual relationship between us. If you hear that rumour, do not believe it; it has no foundation in fact, and never had.)

Shirley, or Poppy (her father's name for her), exuded confidence and was of an altogether tougher and more fearless character than her older brother. From an early age her delight in human company had been equalled by a passion for animals, and when only three she used to run into the road to stroke the legs of horses, much to her mother's alarm. At two-and-a-half she had been well in advance of other children of her age at the Open Air Nursery in Glebe Place, but although it was a source of secret feminist pride to Vera that her daughter showed every sign of being the cleverer of her two children, she nonetheless felt for John.

Shirley's attainments at school were not matched by high standards of behaviour at home. Her manners were frequently 'riotous' and her natural boisterousness made her difficult to control. Try as she might, Vera could discover nothing of herself in Shirley. She was wholly her father's child, Vera decided, and had inherited from the Reverend Catlin not only his tendency to critical intolerance, but also the feeling that she was in some way entitled to have things go right for her. Paradoxically it was Shirley rather than John, with her demands for her mother's undivided attention, who caused Vera to suffer pangs of guilt about being a working mother. Shirley's school report from 1934 suggests that the effect on her of having two parents in pursuit of independent careers had not gone unnoticed. It remarks, somewhat reproachfully, that 'Her affectionate nature has been tried this term by the absence of her parents.'

The overriding principle of John and Shirley's upbringing was that they should be treated alike and afforded the same opportunities. Vera wanted to ensure that, in marked contrast to her own girlhood, there would be no double standard, and that Shirley would start on more or less the same level as a boy of her age with comparable gifts. A strong opponent of 'our unnatural system of separate education' for boys and girls, which she believed was the root cause of anti-feminism, Vera was also determined that her children would be taught on progressive, coeducational lines for as long as possible.

'Talks continuously' a teacher wrote of Shirley when she was three; and there can be little doubt that exposure to the constant flow of conversation and exchange of ideas at Glebe Place had an entirely beneficial influence in making both brother and sister articulate and well-informed individuals. Brushed and tidied, and dressed in their best clothes, they were sometimes allowed to wait on their parents' guests. On one occasion they handed out lemonade to George Lansbury, and on another, in January 1936, sat through tea with Pandit Nehru whom George, at the start of his long interest in Indian affairs, had invited to Glebe Place to meet members of the Labour Party sympathetic to the cause of Indian Independence.*

On 3 May 1937 the family left 19 Glebe Place, their home for seven years, and moved to 2 Cheyne Walk, a narrow, six-storey Georgian house at the east end of the long Chelsea terrace which numbered George Eliot, Mrs Gaskell, Dante Gabriel Rossetti, and Swinburne among its former inhabitants. The weight of Glebe Place's associations with Winifred had become too oppressive for Vera, and George in particular welcomed the move to the larger house, with its well-proportioned rooms, as an opportunity to entertain on a large scale. Number 2 had been refronted in 1879, but its interior retained several period features, including banisters on the lower floors with finely carved fruit and flowers. The balcony of its first-floor drawing-room looked south across the Thames towards Battersea Park.

Amy and Charles Burnett, the young couple who ran the household, moved with them to Cheyne Walk. Now in her mid-twenties, Amy had graduated from maidservant to cook and housekeeper, and was in her third year of marriage to Charles Burnett, the kindly and humorous north-countryman who acted as butler and general handyman. A forthright and intelligent young woman, Amy had aspired to a scholarship to grammar school as a way out of her poverty-stricken beginnings, only to have her ambition denied because her father, a coalman, could not afford the school uniform (Amy had been devoted to Winifred and the character of Lydia

---

*Nehru had been sent *Testament of Youth* while he was in prison. In June 1936 he informed his daughter, Indira, that 'I wrote to you once about Vera Brittain's *Testament of Youth*. I have been reading bits of it here to try to get my mind off politics . . . Shall I send it to you?'

Another member of a famous political dynasty, Winston Churchill's youngest child, Mary (now Lady Soames), was also reading *Testament of Youth* at about this time. She was given the book by a Quaker mistress at school and remembers that it affected her deeply and led to the one and only occasion when she questioned her father's vision of combating Hitler's tyranny.

Holly in *South Riding* is partly based on her). Inevitably there were sometimes ructions when Vera thought that Amy was getting a little too 'uppish', but Vera, who found the bare thought of housework or cooking stultifying, grew to depend on her more and more as the years went by, and also came to look upon her as a friend. For Shirley especially, the Burnetts were like part of the family. Amy's younger siblings, Renee, Lily, Sheila, and Ronnie, the only boy, all 'came, went, and came again' below stairs at Glebe Place and Cheyne Walk. But Amy – 'Aunt Amy' as she became known – and Charlie, later with their own children, Marian and Peter, remained, 'the other pole of our household'. Above stairs, Rosemary Moore continued as part-time secretary with a 'metallic efficiency' which even Vera found daunting; and for a short period in 1937, Suzanne Piaget, a young Swiss woman, daughter of the famous educationalist, was engaged to teach John and Shirley some basic French and German, though without, it must be admitted, any dazzling success.

The Burnetts were Catholics and took Shirley with them to church every Sunday, an early introduction to Roman Catholicism which influenced her later conversion at eighteen. Neither John nor Shirley had been baptized. 'If they wish when they are adult, to become members of a Church which combines lip-service to Christ with the championship of rearmament', their mother wrote in 1939, referring to the Anglican Church, 'that will be their own affair. But I shall not commit them to it in their childhood.'

Perhaps most significantly, the Burnetts reinforced Shirley's socialist beliefs while they were still in embryo. As a pupil at Mrs Spencer's school in Brechin Place in South Kensington, in the summer of 1938, Shirley suddenly announced to her mother, 'I'd like to go where there aren't so many rich children.' Although intended for St Paul's Girls' School, Shirley spent a brief period in the late Thirties at the local elementary school in Christchurch Street. As the only middle-class child at the school, Shirley came in for some rough treatment and adopted a Cockney accent to avoid 'getting my head bashed into the tarmac'. She also returned home by the basement entrance and played in the kitchen, never making it clear to her friends from humbler backgrounds that Amy was not her mother.

The family's lifestyle at Cheyne Walk verged on the ascetic. Neither Vera nor George paid much attention to food, preferring to eat out on special occasions at restaurants like the Café Royal, providing Shirley with added reason for creeping down to the basement where the meals prepared by Amy were often more appetizing than those served upstairs. Vera's study was right at the top of the house, up several flights of stairs, and 'calling her to lunch', Shirley remembered, 'was an expedition in itself'. Both children learned early that their mother's strict daily routine of working in her study, seven hours a day, was sacrosanct. When they were off school, Vera might take them for an afternoon walk in the Embankment Gardens and most evenings she would put them to bed. Another family ritual, never missed when Vera was in London, was Sunday afternoon tea with Edith Brittain at Edwardes Square. Approaching seventy and conveniently deaf when it suited her, Mrs Brittain liked nothing better than to dwell on the shortcomings of her son-in-law as a husband and breadwinner, and consequently George rarely joined Vera and the children on their visits.

For three weeks at the beginning of 1937 George had been in Spain, investigating the needs of the population in the war-torn areas of Valencia, Madrid, and Barcelona on behalf of the National Joint Committee for Spanish Relief. Like most left-wing intellectuals at this early stage in the conflict, George regarded the Spanish Civil War as a power clash of liberal democracy and military nationalism, and accepted Republican Spain 'as a genuine symbol of persecuted democracy'. He had gone to Spain, however, not to unite with the Loyalist cause, but with the wholly admirable intention of reporting objectively on the issue of humanitarian aid. Walking through heavily bombarded cities, spilling over with refugees desperate for food and medical supplies, George had realized that there was a compelling case for the setting-up of a mission, comparable to the International Red Cross, for the relief of victims, 'irrespective of party but in accordance with need.'

He returned to Britain, driven by enthusiasm for the idea, but despite George's best efforts the scheme 'foundered on the rock of Spanish obstructionism'. He was wasting his time and personal money, he was told by the Ambassador in London: the Spanish Government was interested in international intervention for relief only insofar as they could present it as a propaganda coup. Otherwise the Government objected to outside interference.

George was keenly disappointed. For a time it had looked as if he might have been able to make a more solid contribution, for once, to international affairs – to translate his ideas into action. Instead, he was thrown back again on to his old irregular pattern of employment, accepting a journalistic assignment or giving the occasional lecture series, while he waited impatiently for the next general election which he hoped, third time lucky, would put him into Parliament.

Vera was sympathetic despite the financial burden which continued to be hers alone. 'Every scrap of success I ever get is made bitter by the fact that he has so little', she wrote two years later when a Cambridge Chair in political science, for which George had been considered, went elsewhere. But her suggestions for remedying the situation were not always realistic or welcome. In November 1936, a couple of months before his Spanish trip, she had offered George a divorce. Believing that he still partly attributed his lack of success, 'his sense of being thwarted', to her failure to be a conventional wife, she told him that she 'would take myself off – without bitterness or anything but the desire to see you succeed which I seem unable to help you do with my presence.' His reply was sharp and to the point. Of course he did not want her to 'take yourself off'.

On 18 September 1937 Vera sailed for New York from Southampton on board the *Georgic*. This time her voyage was an unpleasant mixture of homesickness and seasickness, and for several days she hardly ventured outside her cabin. She was haunted by the memory of Shirley's tearstained face, after she had fallen and bruised herself while saying goodbye to her mother at Waterloo. And she must also have been full of trepidation at the prospect of seeing Brett again for the first time in more than two years. With this reunion in mind as she sighted the lights of Staten Island, she wrote home to George:

> For all my domineering ways & imperious attempts to reconcile the domestic & professional obligations which it is so hard to reconcile, & for all the irritation & shortness of temper to which this leads, you never do doubt that you are the centre of my life, do you darling, or that I am often speechless with gratitude for the way in which you understand things and in which (whatever superficial protests you sometimes make) you identify yourself with my desires & hopes & aspirations. Whatever emotional experiments I may have made, or may make, they are only surface adventures, never to be confused with my fundamental love & loyalty towards you.

But there was to be no repetition of the emotional experiments which had accompanied her 1934 tour. '... What matters most to me over here continues to give me long periods of depression', Vera confided to Storm Jameson from a tour stop in Illinois at the end of November, 'and just one or two occasions which make up for everything.' Brett looked older and thinner, and was consumed by the business responsibilities which had passed to him on the death of his father the previous year. The day after her arrival in New York they breakfasted together, and later that afternoon he drove her out to the house in Fairfield for a few days' stay; but otherwise there were precious few opportunities to be alone with him before her programme of lectures began.

There was time enough, though, to discuss her next book, a quick and, it was hoped, money-spinning project which would help Vera to bridge the gap financially until *Testament of Friendship* was finished. 'Three Americas' (the title was later altered to *Thrice a Stranger*) would follow the course of Vera's three trips to the United States and Canada, and describe 'the comparative impact of America on a European in 1925 – prosperity; 1934 – depression; 1937 – normality'. It would have to be at least 60,000 words in length (the end result was double that), Brett told her, and would need to be written in three months so as to catch the topical market. Together with the tour, the book 'might make anything from $2000 to $5000', she informed George back in England. '. . . It would pay for your next election. *Time* is all that I want.'

Her forty-lecture tour differed from its predecessor only in respect of the two weeks she spent in the South-West and Deep South. Her first lecture on 5 October at Bryn Mawr was, she conceded, 'heavy and dull', but she soon got back into her stride, and by the time she reached the familiar territory of the Middle West in the second and third weeks of October she was performing to large and appreciative audiences. Wherever she travelled the chief topic of interest seemed to be the Abdication crisis of ten months earlier. Even in the midst of the swamplands of Louisiana, she believed that it was her 'illusory' resemblance to Wallis Simpson – she was 'the spit and image of Wally' several of her listeners told her, on the basis of little more than that Vera was also small and dark and parted her hair in the middle – which boosted attendances at her lectures.

On long train journeys and overnight in hotels, she kept rest to a minimum and spent much of her time writing a seemingly interminable series of letters home. George, she had learned shortly after her arrival in New York, was in a state of high contentment as he had just begun work on a new book, *The History of Political Philosophers*, which had almost immediately been accepted for publication in the States. 'Go to & *finish your book* before everything', Vera warned him, concerned that he would be easily sidetracked on to other issues.

As so often, a prolonged separation encouraged Vera to dwell on the state of their marriage in her letters to George. 'Perhaps you ought to have had an auxiliary wife', she chided him after he had let slip some remark about being pursued by 'designing females'; 'perhaps you still ought to; if so it is better to say so before it is too late, and let me remove myself from your path.'

Nonetheless she was frustrated by his unwillingness to engage on the subject, and begged him to make his letters 'lucid & as little *allusive* as possible'. His reply gave her rather more than she had bargained for. 'What you said in the same letter of your jealousy about Winifred', she wrote back to him, 'upset me so much that I can't attempt to answer it in any detail. Why do you *have* to write me all these terrible, cruel letters while I am on tour . . . I *never* had any sort of sex feeling towards her.'

On 9 November Vera's itinerary took her back to New York after the first leg of her tour. Awaiting her was a packet of letters from home, and opening one from George she found that it contained the news, already ten days old, of Dick Sheppard's death. He had been discovered, slumped over his desk in his study at Amen Court with a half-finished letter in front of him, on the early morning of 31 October. No intimation of his death had reached Vera in New Orleans where the newspapers carried practically no English news.

Vera was devastated. 'It was as though the bottom had dropped out of the world . . .', she wrote immediately to George. 'All day I have wanted to go away and weep . . .' She recollected how, just seven weeks earlier, she had gone down to her cabin on the *Georgic*, 'feeling rather forlorn' after leaving her family, and had found a cable from Sheppard sending her love and best wishes for a successful tour ('Really, his capacity for remembering other people's affairs is an aspect of his genius', she had commented at the time). Her last communication with Sheppard had been from St Louis on 24 October when she had cabled to congratulate him on winning the Rectorship of Glasgow University. He had 'romped home' against Churchill and J.B.S. Haldane, in a victory that was seen as marking a tremendous advance for the pacifist cause. 'Bless you. Come back soon', had been his reply, though by the time Vera read these words a fortnight later in Nashville, Tennessee, he was already dead.

The unhappy state of Sheppard's personal life compounded the tragedy of his sudden end. In the last months of his life he had suffered some distressing publicity when his wife, Alison, who had long found it difficult to live with a man popularly conceived of as a saint, left him for Archie Macdonell, who had been Vera's companion in New York in 1934. 'Damn Archie Macdonell', Vera wrote, expressing a widely held opinion, '– an insensitive bounder, I suspect, to all feelings but his own.'

A little later, after the first shock of the news had subsided, Vera wrote again to George, in a crisis of confidence about the future of the PPU:

> I can't visualize my own public work in England without Sheppard. After so many years with the negative or warlike 'peace' societies, to find that lovely group which stood for all I wanted, and then to lose it. I know [Max] Plowman says it will go on, but he was its source, its inspiration . . .

The power of that inspiration was very much in evidence in London in the first week of November as thousands of men and women filed past

375

Sheppard's coffin, while it lay in state in St Martin's, to pay their final respects. A couple of days later, George watched the funeral procession as it solemnly made its way along the Embankment to St Paul's: '. . . Police holding the traffic down to the Embankment, people standing hatless, the police on point duty saluting – most touching of all, Thames barges and tugs and the men coming up on board and taking off their hats.' This spontaneous display had left him with something very serious to think about, George told Vera, and for an instant he flirted with the idea of joining the PPU ('Life without ideals is sordid . . . One seeks vision'). Reading his description of the funeral while in New York, and appropriately enough at the end of Armistice week, Vera was struck by the extraordinary way in which Sheppard's simple idea had managed to achieve such universal recognition: 'When the spirit of man at its noblest and best, does shine through, unimpeded by worldly interests . . . it appears to have a more compelling influence upon other men than anything else in the world.'

The second half of the tour proceeded smoothly, disturbed only by the news towards the end of November, while Vera was staying in Massachusetts with the novelist Mary Ellen Chase, that Shirley had been seriously ill with flu which had threatened at one point to develop into pneumonia. She was well on the way to recovery by the time George cabled, but in a spiral of panic Vera rushed off a note, instructing him to 'Be sure that Poppy is warm enough clad, & that people know when she gets her feet wet. She is an uncomplaining & philosophical little girl – *much* too clever to take any risks with.'

The climax of Vera's visit, an invitation to lunch with Eleanor Roosevelt at the White House, took place on 14 December, nine days before Vera sailed for England on the *Aquitania*. She found Mrs Roosevelt impressive, like an English Duchess, but also rather alarming. She had not expected to meet President Roosevelt as she had been told that he was working on an emergency dispatch to Japan about the sinking of the American gunboat the *Panay*; but after lunch she was conducted to his study where he received her with 'genial informality', and questioned her closely about her experience of Middle-Western isolationism.

In these weeks Vera's thoughts often turned to how the PPU was organizing itself without Sheppard, and how she might serve it in the future. George suggested that she write Sheppard's life; but she demurred. 'His real story is at St Martin's and Canterbury. . .', she explained. 'He will come into my books in so far as he influenced the peace movement and touched my own life.'

Later, though, she came to regret that she had been out of the country when Sheppard's official biographer was appointed, and that the commission had gone to Ellis Roberts, 'a nice fellow', as George said, 'but with more priestly decorum than prophetic fire.' Vera, too, thought it unlikely that Roberts would make 'an emotional, histrionic, humorous, idealistic character like Dick come alive'; and when Roberts's book appeared in 1942 it was indeed found wanting because of the emphasis it placed on Sheppard's unhappiness at the expense of his extrovert charm.

Instead of a biography, Vera used Sheppard as the model for the hero of her final novel, *Born 1925* (1948), in which she attempts to solve the conundrum of what Sheppard would have done had he lived to see the catastrophe of another war fall upon the world. Through the character of Robert Carbury, the pacifist vicar of a fashionable West End church, who continues to lead the peace movement undeterred in the darkest days of the Second World War, Vera effectively answered those critics of Sheppard who had questioned whether his commitment to pacifism would have remained steadfast.

As she sailed home from New York in December 1937, Vera's expression of her own unwavering commitment to pacifism was to be found in that month's special issue of the *Left Review*, 'Authors Take Sides on the Spanish War'. A questionnaire, sponsored by, among others, Nancy Cunard, W.H. Auden, and Stephen Spender, had been sent to 149 writers throughout the British Isles, asking them to express their views about the situation in Spain. The questions were framed in such a way as to make it clear that anyone who did not support Republican Spain's war against Franco would be considered a supporter of Fascism. The 127 writers who replied on the Republic's side included three Sponsors of the PPU, Aldous Huxley, Rose Macaulay and Storm Jameson, all of whom, in so doing, avoided confronting the possible conflict between their pacifism and their professed anti-Fascism.

Vera, though, who saw the whole question of Spain as a testing-ground for the pacifist, did not evade the issue. She might detest Fascism, but she felt under a moral obligation to declare herself an uncompromising pacifist, thereby earning herself a 'begrudging' classification as 'Neutral?' from the editors of the pamphlet.

Three weeks before leaving the United States, Vera sent a message to the Peace Pledge Union through its new Chairman, Stuart Morris, who had so often deputized for Sheppard in the past. Her words were offered as a tribute to Sheppard himself, and also as a ringing declaration of her renewed confidence in the PPU's future:

Our movement will go on, of course, – not only as a tribute to him, but for the larger reason . . . that it is an expression of those spiritual forces of this world which will ultimately overcome the entrenched powers of self-interest and materialism. His spirit will be among us on our platforms, even though he, alas, can no longer be with us.

V

Vera arrived back in London in early January 1938 to find the Peace Pledge Union in a state of disarray and torn by internal dissension. As she had anticipated, Sheppard's death had deprived the PPU of the charismatic leadership which alone had managed to unite the widely differing conceptions of pacifism contained within it. Canon Morris had been appointed Chairman, with Soper as his deputy, while George Lansbury filled the new office of President; but no amount of reorganization and argument about a formal constitution could disguise the developing rift in the PPU between those pacifists still set on prevention of war as their primary object, and a growing number – always a minority in the movement but well represented among the Sponsors – who were beginning to see pacifism as apolitical or, in the broadest sense of the word, religious. 'I do see coming very soon a split between the religious minded and the political minded Sponsors', Vera wrote to Morris in March, 'as to which type of objective is the most important for the PPU at the present moment . . . willing martyrdom on behalf of Peace . . . [or] influence on the side of negotiation.'

Vera respected the quietists for their calm insistence on bearing witness to a personal faith, but still numbered herself among the more politically minded of the Sponsors. Consequently she believed that all avenues of negotiation with the dictators should be explored, and that where there were genuine grievances stemming from the injustices of the Treaty of Versailles, the validity of the claims should be acknowledged and treated fairly. Although she was not blind to the fact that Germany was the immediate cause of the present tension, she regarded Hitler as the inevitable product – 'the historical retribution' – for all the blunders of statesmanship of the past twenty years.

This standpoint became official PPU policy on 8 March when Lansbury rose in the Commons to announce a new manifesto based on 'economic appeasement and reconciliation'. Its similarities to the policy of appeasement soon to be adopted by the Chamberlain Government was to prove a source of embarrassment to pacifists who vigorously denied, however, that their idealistic plans for a new world order had anything to do with the 'mere bargaining or bartering of the politicians.'

In the circumstances Vera felt that she ought to offer the PPU 'all the services possible' the moment that she returned from America – 'and yet I know I can't do much for a bit.' She was exhausted from the 'crushing effect' of her tour, but had to pick up work immediately on *Testament of Friendship*, which she was now attempting to write in tandem with *Thrice a Stranger*. Throughout the first six months of 1938 she worked intensively on both books, sitting up night after night into the small hours, and sometimes retiring to bed in a state which she described as little short of delirious stupor.

There were days, though, when news of political events made concentration impossible, and she would abandon her study to wander restlessly along the Chelsea Embankment where the power station across the river was rehearsing its air-raid siren. On 12 March Hitler sent his armies into Austria and the international situation, which had been precarious for so long, suddenly became inflamed.

Vera's first thoughts were for John and Shirley. '. . . The time may not be far ahead when I shall have to decide to bring the children over to your side of the Atlantic', she wrote to Brett the day after the Anschluss. In Dallas the previous autumn she had discussed the possibility of sending Shirley, in a few years' time, to the local school which Vera had much admired, run by a Miss Hockaday. Originally she had considered the idea simply as a means both of providing a useful break in her education, and of combating 'the hoydenish dowdiness' of the English schoolgirl with 'a measure of young America's chic maturity'; but now she was forced to revise her plans in light of the question, which was to worry her intermittently for the next two years, of whether to evacuate the children overseas in the event of war.

George reasoned insistently that, should war break out, the children would be safest in American schools, cared for by friends like the Bretts and the Colbys. He emphasized that neither he, as an opponent of Fascism, nor Vera as a pacifist could hope to survive a Nazi invasion of Britain, and that the children would be almost certain to share their parents' fate. But Vera was deeply ambivalent about sending John and Shirley away. She believed that as a pacifist she was morally obliged to remain in Britain to maintain her point of view, and she was by no means certain that the children's best interests would be served by separating them from their parents.

They debated the issue back and forth in letters, and argued heatedly over the subject while on holiday in Biarritz in August. No difference of opinion that she could remember had ever divided them so sharply. However, by the first weeks of September, with the fate of Czechoslovakia hanging in the balance and the country once more on a war footing, George won Vera's agreement that they should go to the States until the crisis had resolved itself one way or the other. On 22 September Vera was a member of a PPU delegation to 10 Downing Street and the Foreign Office to deliver a statement of their 'conviction that nothing can justify a resort to war'. Two days later she sailed for New York with George and the children. 'I am off to the U.S. tonight on S.S. *Paris*', she wrote to Norman Ginsbury, the playwright who was revising Winifred's play *Take Back Your Freedom* for publication. 'As I warned you, I am taking my young children to friends over there till this trouble is past – as I pray it soon will be, & that we shall be back in a few weeks.'

While they were in mid-Atlantic the situation dramatically altered. On 28 September Chamberlain made the sensational announcement that he had been called to Munich for a meeting with Hitler and Mussolini to settle the Czech crisis. Returning to Britain on the 30th, the Prime Minister announced triumphantly that he had secured Hitler's signature to a note expressing the desire 'of our two peoples never to go to war with one another again'. The actual terms of the agreement decreed the cession of the Sudetenland and its occupation by German troops. The British Government had acquiesced in the dismemberment of Czechoslovakia, but an 'uneasy truce' had been called, and war had been postponed.

These new developments called a halt to immediate plans for the children. '. . . I shall bring them back by the first boat we can get on as soon as our re-entry permits are in hand', Vera informed Storm Jameson from the small hotel opposite Columbia University where they were staying. By 26 October, a little over a month following their departure, the family was back in Cheyne Walk.

Munich, Vera told pacifists in an article written shortly after her return, was 'an inglorious peace, purchased at the expense of a small power whose sacrifices left her greater neighbours free to make none.' However, for those who shared her belief that any kind of peace was preferable to any variety of modern war, it was an inescapable conclusion that Chamberlain had made the best possible decision at the given moment. By choosing the lesser evil of a bargain with Hitler he had averted a European war which, she argued, would have resulted in two immediate and disastrous consequences: the annihilation of Czechoslovakia, and – here she spoke with special foresight – 'a massacre of the Jews on a scale to which the past and present Jewish persecutions, bitter as they are, bear no comparison.'

The task of the pacifist in the wake of Munich, as Vera saw it, was to transform that 'uneasy truce' into a permanent peace by arguing the case for economic appeasement and for a world conference in which political, economic and territorial grievances could be sorted out. The Munich crisis had seen a surge in the PPU's recruitment, and until disillusionment set in, five months later, with Hitler's seizure of Prague, Vera believed that a real will to peace existed throughout Britain, together with an openness to the idea that conciliation and not punitive action might be the only longterm answer.

For some, though, the price exacted by Hitler had been too great to be morally acceptable. In Storm Jameson's case Munich marked a personal turning-point in finally forcing her to renounce her pacifism. At some point after November 1938 – when exactly is unclear as her own and the PPU's dates do not tally – she resigned as a Sponsor of the PPU, citing the PPU's 'pro-Nazi attitude over Czechoslovakia' as her reason. She appears not to have informed Vera of her decision; nor does she seem to have been open with her at this time about her changing attitude to pacifism. To withhold such information from a close friend is surprising, perhaps even shocking, until one remembers Storm's remark that she always adjusted her feelings about war according to the person she happened to be with. 'My refuge from all quarrels and scenes', she was to tell Vera after their full differences had emerged, 'has always been never to tell anyone what I'm thinking or feeling.'

The twentieth anniversary of Armistice week had Vera 'literally running from one peace meeting to another to deliver speeches'. She also spoke at a meeting in Richmond to protest against the treatment of the Jews in Germany, 'not only because of my own grief and horror', but also because she hoped to encourage the Government to allow more refugees to enter the country. She was intent on finding a more constructive role for pacifists to counter those in the peace movement who wished merely to indulge in 'anti campaigns' in order to satisfy an 'exhibitionist desire for martyrdom'. She had no time, she wrote in January 1939, 'for the present PPU line of hysterical campaigns to oppose A.R.P [Air Raid Precautions], oppose conscription, or whatever new cause for opposition arises.' If war came, the country would inevitably get conscription, and no amount of protest from peace groups would prevent it. All that opposition would achieve would be the early suppression of the pacifist movement at precisely the moment when it was most needed to 'maintain a measure of sanity and work for an early peace.'

War again looked imminent when Hitler committed a further act of aggression by invading Prague on 15 March. Vera hurriedly made arrangements to keep the children out of London and redoubled her efforts to rescue a Czech-Jewish dentist from Nazi-controlled Prague. George was in Washington delivering a course of lectures and she felt depressed at being cut off from him at a time of such intense anxiety. She was 'so *tired*', she told Storm Jameson, of feeling frightened on the children's behalf. 'If it were not for them, I should not feel frightened at all, except for the moments of physical fear that we all go through. I should simply move my desk from the attic to the basement, and let the bombs come.'

The news was still grave, five days later, when she went to Chelsea Town Hall to attend a Left Book Club meeting at which Victor Gollancz was speaking. As Stafford Cripps, the other speaker for the evening, arrived late, Gollancz had the platform for three-quarters of an hour. Vera was horrified by the 'hysterical' tone of his speech. 'Never since the recruiting meetings of 1914', she wrote the next day, 'have I listened to such a passionate and deliberate working up of hatred against not merely Fascism but Germany as I heard from him . . .'. Much of what he had to say sounded 'exactly like attempts made during the Great War to cause detestation of a whole nation on account of atrocities committed by a few.' What appalled her even more was the speed with which the audience was roused. 'There is an excellent case against Fascism but this hate-mongering does not strengthen it.'

She spent most of the following day wondering whether she should continue to publish with Gollancz, but concluded that political differences were not a reason for severing a business relationship. When, however, correspondence relating to the meeting began to appear in the *New Statesman*, she wrote to give her own account of Gollancz's speech, commenting that 'The passionate conversion of sincere, benevolent and intelligent persons to a war policy under new names but old disguises is already a grave feature of this as of all preceding international crises.' Gollancz issued a swift rebuttal, disputing Vera's report, and accusing her of serious distortion.

I have the greatest possible respect for pacifists – and would not even presume to criticise those few . . . of them who left hurriedly for America last September when War seemed to threaten, instead of remaining here either to help the suffering or to testify to their beliefs. Many of us, indeed, who loathe war more than anything in this world often wish that we were *able* to be pacifists. But why bring disrepute, as Miss Brittain does, on the whole pacifist case by distorting the words of those who detest war every bit as much as she does – but happen to think that not pacifism, but collective security, is the only thing that can prevent it.

She thought his sneer about their American trip 'caddish' and irrelevant, and decided that 'since V.G. has descended to a somewhat crude level of personal attack . . .', she would have seriously to consider looking for another publisher. There was clearly some 'fundamental incompatibility' which it was impossible to bridge.

The British branch of Macmillan had been interested in poaching Vera from Gollancz since 1937 when Harold Macmillan had first written to her about contracting her books. Although their London agent Lovat Dickson's monthly report to Harold Macmillan in November 1938 had noted that 'Vera Brittain's sales must show a steady decline since the publication of *Testament of Youth*', he had advised 'a continuance of our present policy of sympathetic interest'. *Thrice a Stranger* had not broken the downward trend of Vera's sales when it appeared during the Munich crisis in September 1938, but *Testament of Friendship*, a more compelling title than Vera's humdrum narrative of her American travels, looked fit to arrest that decline. As soon as Lovat Dickson got wind of the breach with Gollancz, he stepped in with a generous contract for Winifred's biography and an option on Vera's next two books.

Gollancz 'would rather lose an author than apologise to one', Vera told Harold Macmillan. But she was genuinely saddened that their relationship had come to this untimely end, and that Gollancz would no longer be exercising his extraordinary talents in the interests of her future books. She instructed Macmillan to make it known in the publishing world that she had left Gollancz because of a political dispute and not because of any business shortcomings. Apart from the fact that she had hardly ever seen him, he had contributed immeasurably to her success. They would be reconciled in time, but it would be almost twenty years before Gollancz published another major book by Vera.

The family's rapid trip to America at the time of Munich, Vera wrote to George at the beginning of March, had confirmed in her 'more vehemently than ever' the desire 'to remain a European, war or no war, and to have the children remain European too'. Nonetheless she realized that London was no longer a fit place for children. War might not be an immediate prospect, but most commentators were now estimating that it might be only a matter of four or five months away.

John was safely out of harm's way. He had settled quite happily at The

Downs, a Quaker school at Colwall near Malvern. Plans for Shirley's future schooling, though, had still to be finalized. Vera's concern for her was heightened when Shirley started to have nightmares about air raids, dreaming of 'headless bodies' falling into the nursery where she was sleeping. Vera was much relieved, therefore, when at the end of April Shirley began the summer term at Oldfeld, a progressive school at Swanage in Dorset which Shirley had inspected and approved earlier that spring. With 'Complete sang-froid and no tears' she joined the school train and was immediately captivated by a wire-haired terrier belonging to the mistress in charge of the party.

Vera had often dreamed of finding a country retreat, but had been discouraged by George's dislike of the country and his desire to be always in the thick of things in town. However, the pressure on her to find a base outside London for the children had made Vera take up the search for a suitable property with a new seriousness. In mid-April she looked over what had once been a gamekeeper's cottage in a small hamlet called Allum Green, one-and-a-half miles outside Lyndhurst in the New Forest. Allum Green Cottage was right on the edge of the forest, 'with 20 miles of unspoiled country at its front door & a tiny but sufficient cottage garden at the back.' It badly required decoration, but was quite spacious, with seven small rooms, a kitchen, scullery, bathroom, and lavatory.

She fell in love with the cottage at once and purchased it at the end of May with the remainder of her savings from *Testament of Youth* (and the cottage remains in Vera's family to this day). The Burnetts came from Chelsea to decorate while Vera sat in a small wooden shelter in the tangle of a garden, working on the final draft of *Testament of Friendship*.

After she had delivered the typescript to Harold Macmillan in early August she spent most of her time with the children at Allum Green, playing with them in the forest, or busying herself with odd jobs around the cottage. George came down for most weekends. It was a lovely late summer and the natural beauty of the forest made the gathering crisis seem all the more malevolent and incongruous.

When war was declared on Sunday 3 September, George was up in Rochdale for a selection meeting, leaving Vera behind at Allum Green in the company of the children and the Burnetts. Grouped around the wireless set in the small upstairs study at 11.15 that morning, they listened to Chamberlain's trembling voice as he announced the expiry of the British Government's ultimatum to Germany. Sitting between the children, Vera realized the failure of all her hopes for peace over the past twenty years and suddenly found herself in tears. While Charlie Burnett slipped discreetly out of the room to find her a handkerchief, Shirley hugged her mother and all but licked her face 'like a puppy'.

Walking out into the forest after the broadcast, Vera attempted to come to terms with the enormity of the catastrophe. Returning to her study later that afternoon she gathered her thoughts and found comfort in writing an article addressed to pacifists throughout Britain. Their first and foremost task, she told them, was to hasten the coming of peace, 'and to set our faces against all that delays it – the surging tide of hatred, the rising flood of mendacity. Let us look carefully for the truth, and when we have found it, let us tell it lucidly and without provocation.'

It would be a painful and arduous struggle, but for the next six years she would dedicate herself to doing exactly that.

THIRTEEN

Humiliation with Honour

'Someday I suppose it may be known to posterity whether the books I
have written & shall write, and the peace testimony that I have made as
one of a *very* few voices crying in a very dark wilderness, will have been
worth all this personal sacrifice, yours, the children's, even my own.'

Vera Brittain to George Catlin, 8 October 1942

I

Brilliant weather and an unnatural peacefulness descended on Allum
Green in the first weeks of September. The huge barrage balloons creeping
around the coast from Southampton and the constellation of searchlights
which swept the sky at night were the only persistent reminders that the
country was once again at war. It was so quiet, Vera had written to George
from the cottage on the evening of Chamberlain's broadcast, that it seemed
unbelievable that they were on the brink of chaos. Against this background
of deceptive calm she lost no time in making plans to adapt her work for
peace to the circumstances of war.

In many ways the immediate task she set herself was to prove the most
influential. Throughout that troubled summer the volume of unsolicited
mail which Vera normally received from unknown correspondents, seeking
advice or offering their own comments on the current situation, had swelled
to unmanageable proportions. It had reached the point where she could no
longer reply personally to each letter without abandoning all her other work.
The outbreak of war crystallized in her mind the idea of a regular printed
broadsheet or circular letter, available by subscription and addressed to all
those peace-lovers who were eager to see an end to the hostilities. Writing to
Storm Jameson two days after the declaration of war, Vera enlarged upon
her scheme, explaining that she would like

a) To write a weekly letter . . . to keep the peace movement together and
maintain its purpose unshaken throughout the War. b) To help organize and

386

work in a Pacifist Service Corps . . . I think that the maintenance of the spirit of reason and compassion till the time comes for actually discussing peace terms is of the first importance . . . Probably it is arrogant to suppose that I could have any affect [*sic*] on the course of history, but I'd like to try.

By 12 September the letter had received the endorsement of both the PPU Council and the Fellowship of Reconciliation, and Vera had drafted and typed a specimen of the introductory number. After John and Shirley returned to school in the last week of September she was able to spend more time in London, organizing the production of the letter with the help of a band of volunteers. Until Vera was able to find a more permanent office, a makeshift arrangement in the bathroom of Dick Sheppard House, the PPU's newly acquired headquarters in Endsleigh Street, with a board across the bath, had to suffice.

The introductory issue of 'Vera Brittain's Personal Letter to Peace-Lovers' (later simply, 'Letter to Peace-Lovers') was officially published on 4 October 1939. It was not a newsletter, she stressed, for her main purpose was not to give information, nor was her object to criticize the Government and its military machine, as there were already other organizations which had undertaken that task. 'What I do want is to consider and discuss with you the ideas, principles and problems which have concerned genuine peace-lovers for the past twenty years.' Vera had not been mistaken about the nature of the demand. The immediate response to the introductory letter, sent out to a chosen few and advertised in a couple of small-circulation magazines, was 'a shoal of enquiries'.

At the outset Vera certainly did not envisage producing the Letter uninterrupted for the duration of the war and beyond (the postwar series continued until the end of 1946). But 'Once started, it never seemed possible to stop.' As she wrote to Storm Jameson, herself an early subscriber, on 12 October, 'It does seem to meet more of a need than I ever expected.' Although initially published every week, this proved impractical after the first year and thereafter the Letter appeared fortnightly. The original subscription of 2s 6d for six months (raised towards the end of the war to 3s) barely covered the cost of printing, postage, and the salaries of the secretarial staff, and only donations from generous subscribers and contributions from Vera's own pocket kept the enterprise afloat.

Within two months the Letter had over a thousand subscribers and this figure continued to grow, with only paper rationing and the small subscription – designed to make the Letter available to even the poorest reader – finally fixing the maximum circulation at two thousand. A Cabinet memorandum of May 1940 would single out the Letter as one of the most successful of all anti-war publications.

The nucleus of support came from members of peace organizations, but readers also included men and women in the Forces, and there were correspondents from twenty-five countries. Among the Letter's better-known subscribers were Sybil Thorndike (who had recently become a Sponsor of the PPU) and Arthur Creech Jones, the future Colonial Secretary whom Vera had come to know through Winifred, and who was inclined to be sympathetic towards pacifists, having himself spent almost three years in prison as a conscientious objector during the First World War.

It was a remarkable achievement and one that owed a good deal to the administrative flair of Winifred Eden-Green, 'an attractive girl' in her mid-twenties, who, when Vera met her in September 1939, had been recently dismissed from the BBC because of her marriage. Until the birth of her son in April 1944, Mrs Eden-Green assumed almost total responsibility for the considerable effort of organization that lay behind the Letter. Her ingenuity surmounted many of the difficulties that arose in the printing and distribution. She was assisted by several other voluntary workers, including Derek Edwards and Irene Mills (who later took over the running of the Letter). Even Vera's mother, who had, it seems, signed the peace pledge largely because of her admiration for Dick Sheppard ('his influence has been behind me ever since Winifred's funeral'), occasionally helped with the dispatch of the Letter, and worked the old hand-operated Addressograph machine.

The 'Letter to Peace-Lovers' met a wartime need 'for fellowship, advice, elucidations, and suggestions'; and in so doing, it sometimes helped to mitigate the loneliness of a minority, and perhaps to strengthen the resolve of those holding unpopular opinions. From Vera it demanded nothing less than an up-to-the-minute analysis of international events and the pacifist's relation to them. The rushed and hazardous conditions in which many of the letters were composed – in shelters during air raids on some occasions – had an entirely beneficial effect on her writing. Whereas much of her more considered prose appears laboured, the Letter put to good use her extraordinary ability to convey complex ideas with clarity and showed off her 'punchy style' to good advantage. Taken together as a series, the letters display the principles which were to sustain Vera's unwavering adherence to her pacifist beliefs throughout the Second World War.

The most fundamental of these was her insistence that pacifists in wartime could not altogether escape the demands that citizenship laid upon them. They had an obligation to the community in which they lived, and although their protest against war meant that they could play no part in any activity which furthered the purposes of 'the war machine', they had no right, Vera believed, to remain resolutely passive while the world was in such a state of turmoil.

She possessed little sympathy, therefore, for the views of the more intransigent absolutists in the movement who refused any form of alternative service which the state demanded of them, and whose rejection of any complicity in the war effort meant that they were prepared even to go to the lengths of refusing firewatching duty when it was made compulsory for men in 1940. 'I would rather soil my hands than remain so self-righteously pure', was Vera's forthright response to this attitude, which she regarded as an unhealthy form of sectarianism. She argued instead that it was the responsibility of the pacifist both to maintain contact with humanitarian supporters of 'legitimate' war (like Bishop Bell of Chichester) and, at every opportunity which presented itself, to relieve the suffering of war's victims: of the children, refugees, and civilian casualties, and also of the prisoners of war and the wounded on both sides of combat.

The central tenet of her pacifism was the maintenance of civilized values in wartime. She understood how swiftly the 'spiritual havoc' wrought by war would result in the 'demoralising eclipse of the noblest human values', and she wanted to do all she could to save those values from being submerged in a tide of hatred and fear.

She knew only too well, from the history of the preceding twenty years, how important the preservation of a rational and civilized outlook would be in hastening the end of the conflict and in laying the foundations of a just and lasting peace. In the unsettling nine-month period of Phoney War, Vera would join with other members of the PPU in a 'Stop-the-War' campaign which advocated early peace by negotiation as 'better for our own country than the bitter war required to "smash Hitlerism" '; and after the German military breakthrough in the spring of 1940, when the possibility of a negotiated peace receded, she would continue to write and speak against the propaganda of those like Sir Robert Vansittart and his followers, whose pursuit of an organized policy of calculated revenge against the entire German nation would, she feared, be the upshot of any future peace settlement. The influence of the pacifist as a perpetual evangelist for peace would provide the vital counterbalance to this kind of propaganda, and would ensure that there would be no repetition of the 'vindictiveness' which had wrecked the Treaty of Versailles.

While contemplating her 'Letter to Peace-Lovers', Vera had also been considering the implications of a request from the Ministry of Information, asking her as a 'valuable' author to refrain from any other form of national service until she received their instructions. She had no intention of 'leasing her mental integrity' to the Government for the duration, and on 10 September replied rejecting any notion that she should act as a propagandist:

> I shall be happy to co-operate with the Ministry of Information in any way which does not conflict with my beliefs as a pacifist. Though I could not undertake any form of military propaganda, I would gladly assist in the study, discussion and exposition of peace aims, preliminary peace terms, and peace negotiations.

In spite of this unequivocal statement Vera soon found herself faced with another dilemma. The previous autumn she had been contracted for a third lecture-tour of North America, booked to start in January 1940. Getting wind of this, the Ministry of Information joined with Colston Leigh, Vera's agent, in putting pressure on her to anticipate her tour and go out to the States immediately to lecture. They had strong reasons for wishing her to do so. Americans wanted British lecturers, but were also deeply suspicious of unfamiliar visitors from Britain who might be war propagandists in disguise (there was a widespread belief, encouraged by isolationists, that cunning British atrocity stories in 1917 had lured the United States into the First World War). A lecturer like Vera, with her longstanding American connections and, more critically, her pacifism, was viewed as being above suspicion, and was therefore in a position to maintain friendly Anglo-American relations while reporting back to Britain on the reactions to the war which she had encountered.

Colston Leigh was sending 'colossal cables', urging Vera to agree to an immediate tour. 'It is the first time I ever knew my pacifism to have any commercial advantages!' she commented wryly. But she could not face leaving the children behind when it was still too early to tell how the war would develop, especially as George would also be spending most of the next six months in America raising support for an Anglo-American project of his own.

So she decided to stick to her original plan of going out in January. There was an important job to be done in America 'but I don't think it will be less important in the spring than it is now . . .'. As a future precaution, though, she appointed as the children's guardians Storm Jameson and Henry Andrews, Rebecca West's husband, who was a friend of George's from his Oxford days and who had been at Uppingham with Edward and Roland.

She was at pains to stress to people like Phyllis Bentley that she would not be lecturing in America under the auspices of the Ministry of Information: 'As an individual lecturer under a private manager I am free to express my own views as fully as I wish.' The Government was not offering her money, but was merely facilitating her arrangements for leaving the country. Vera had re-established cordial relations with Phyllis since Winifred's death – Phyllis had been surprisingly cooperative while she was writing *Testament of Friendship* – though animosity could sometimes flare up, as of old. 'Of course I shall not underestimate the nightmare of Hitler's regime for so many', Vera exclaimed in one letter to her that September. 'I am not a Fascist, my dear Phyllis!'

As the date of her tour drew closer, she was suffering renewed anxiety at the prospect of leaving the children in a dangerous country while she went to a safe one, even though war operations remained virtually at a standstill. Their schools had agreed to look after them in the event of emergency, until she returned from America, but was it fair to entrust overall responsibility for them to their elderly grandmother, who had already announced, in a burst of pessimism, that the blitzkrieg would probably start as soon as Vera left England? Memories of her voyage to Malta in 1916 also revived Vera's fears of travelling by sea in mine-infested waters, and she was relieved when Colston Leigh reserved her a seat on the Clipper, the transatlantic passenger air service, which flew twice-weekly from Lisbon to New York. She finally resolved her doubts by reasoning with herself that the children would not benefit from having a mother who made fear an excuse for shirking her job.

Vera had arranged to fly to Paris on 5 January, where she would connect with the night train to Lisbon. On New Year's Day 1940 she attended a luncheon party at the Carleton Hotel, given in her honour by Harold Macmillan, to celebrate the publication of *Testament of Friendship*. Friends of Vera's and Winifred's were present – Lady Rhondda, Arthur Creech Jones, Storm Jameson, Phyllis Bentley, Ellen Wilkinson, and Archie Macdonell among them – as well as prominent literary critics such as Desmond MacCarthy. Worry about her impending departure had at least the advantage of lessening Vera's concern about the reception of her book, and she felt flattered by Macmillan's treatment of her. 'No English publisher', she wrote to Harold Macmillan the next day with an obvious sideswipe at Gollancz, 'has ever paid me such a compliment before . . .'.

Her journey was more tortuous and subject to delay than she could have imagined. Bad storms delaying the Clipper had caused a large accumulation of passengers at Lisbon, which made it impossible to predict the exact date of Vera's flight. Altering her arrangements so that she could travel to New York on the *Vulcania*, an Italian ship which fortunately called at Lisbon on the very day that she had been due to leave by the Clipper, she was further beset by the cancellation of her Paris plane owing to poor visibility. Cursing this newfangled mode of transport, she transferred to the cross-Channel night steamer which offered the last chance of reaching Lisbon in time. After travelling by wagon-lit through France to the Spanish frontier, where she was arrested and briefly detained by the police at Irun for bringing pesetas into the country, she finally boarded the *Vulcania* on 10 January. A week later she arrived in snowbound New York where she was met by George. She had already missed five of her lectures, and would be leaving for Louisville, Kentucky, the next morning.

Meanwhile in Britain, unknown to Vera, her movements were being closely monitored.

On 2 January – the day after she had been a guest at the luncheon for *Testament of Friendship* – Lady Rhondda had paid a call on Charles Peake, the Head of the News Department of the Foreign Office and Chief Advisor to the Ministry of Information, at his office in Whitehall. As Peake reported in a Foreign Office minute:

Lady Rhondda came to see me today. She recalled that some weeks ago a meeting of the Peace Pledge Union took place presided over by Dame Sybil Thorndike and addressed by Miss Vera Brittain. It had been the intention at the close of the meeting to march to Buckingham Palace but this the police had declined to allow.

Now Miss Vera Brittain is leaving for the United States this week, Lady Rhondda thought, carrying with her the resolution of the Peace Pledge Union meeting according to which the women of England were determined on peace and appealed to Mrs Roosevelt whom Miss Brittain was to see, to do her utmost to bring about a cessation of war by means of negotiation with Germany.

Miss Vera Brittain is a determined pacifist and it is for consideration whether we ought to stop her going. She is also a crank, and a self-opinionated one at that, but she must be well-known in the United States by reason of a remarkable book entitled 'Testament of Youth' which she wrote some years ago and which I suppose must have had a large circulation in the United States.

To stop her journey now may draw undesirable attention to what is in itself an unimportant body but it may be well to telegraph to Lord Lothian [the British Ambassador in Washington] letting him know how little representative of British women Miss Brittain really is.

Lady Rhondda's motives in drawing the Foreign Office's attention to the purposes of Vera's visit may only be surmised. Undoubtedly concern for the war effort played its part – she had angrily denounced what she referred to as the betrayal at Munich – but the opportunity to thwart Vera's plans may also have been seized upon with personal relish. Lady Rhondda had always seemed to resent Vera's dominant role in Winifred's life, while Vera had just published a book in which she had included oblique references to Lady Rhondda's exploitation of Winifred. But whatever the reason, Lady Rhondda's intervention marked the beginning of a long episode which was to have bitter repercussions for Vera for the rest of the war.

The Foreign Office mandarins followed Peake's line. The Ministry of Information had obviously been mistaken in allowing Vera to go to the United States (Frank Darvall of the Ministry of Information's American Division denied, most improbably, that he had been aware of Vera's connection with the PPU), but decided not to refuse her an exit permit. Vera, ran one assessment, 'is of the kind that thrives on opposition and counter-blast will merely call forth counter-blast and give her more publicity than before.' Nevertheless a coded telegram was sent to Lord Lothian asking him to report back on her activities.

In fact, Vera confounded her critics less than a fortnight after her arrival in the States by sending a letter to the Ministry of Information, as she had promised she would, detailing the views of her lecture audiences in the Middle West towards Britain especially 'with respect to such issues as the war debt and British censorship of US mails.' The Foreign Office expressed surprise: 'Miss Brittain is quite sensible in this letter – may she remain so!'.

Reports from Washington at the end of her tour would echo this view. Lord Lothian concluded that Vera had 'not done any real harm by what she has said or done . . .'; and the British Library of Information in New York also sent back a 'substantially favourable' report to Whitehall. There, for the time being, the matter appeared to rest.

In Colston Leigh's opinion, it was the most successful of her three tours. For Vera, however, it was by far and away the most gruelling. The 'intolerable difficulties' attached to being a British lecturer 'here at the present time' – the fruitless task of trying to satisfy both the isolationists and interventionists in her audiences, for instance – had added immeasurably to the normal strains of a lecture-tour, and had made her ill. 'I have had two breakdowns on this tour', she wrote to Harold Macmillan at the beginning of April, '. . . three different American doctors have urged me to knock off work for two or three months when I get home . . .'. Shortly after reuniting with George in Los Angeles at the beginning of February she had gone down with a severe attack of flu, which left her feeling shaky and unable to appreciate a dinner with Bertrand Russell and an evening in Hollywood with Upton Sinclair and Charlie Chaplin. A month later she had collapsed again while lecturing at Washington State College in Pullman.

Moreover, she attributed her general fatigue and sense of depression to the fact that, at forty-six, she was entering the menopause. This 'change of life', she told George, was 'best faced up to with as much philosophy as one can muster.' There could be no escaping the conclusion that in the future she would need to adopt a quieter, more restrained lifestyle. Clearly, she continued to George, the natural processes of the climacteric made a nonsense of the arguments for monogamy that she had once espoused, given that a man was potent for at least fifteen years longer than a woman.

News from Britain contributed to her disquiet. Attacks in several newspapers on the PPU had marked the beginnings of a hostile campaign in the press against pacifists. Furthermore, there had been a question in the House of Commons about Vera's activities in the States. Sir Henry Page Croft was Conservative MP for Bournemouth, and Allum Green was therefore part of his constituency. He was a notorious right-winger, a member of Churchill's inner circle and a future Under-Secretary for War. On 21 February Croft had asked Sir John Reith as Minister of Information whether Vera was employed by the Ministry of Information, and whether she was in America performing duties on their behalf. Reith had answered 'blandly' – with no hint of his ministry's earlier encouragement to Vera to fulfil her lecture contract – that she had no connection whatever with his department.

II

With deep relief and overwhelming tiredness, Vera finished the final lecture of her tour at the end of March and secured a berth for George and herself on the first liner that was sailing for Europe. This happened to be the *Vulcania* again which departed from New York on 6 April.

It was a 'nightmare of a voyage' which began with a terrifying storm, and continued to be rough until they were within a few hours of Lisbon. In the midst of it came the news of Hitler's lightning invasion of Scandinavia. It did indeed appear that they were returning home just in time.

Vera was full of apprehension and tried to forget her worries by losing herself in a good book. The ship's library offered nothing more absorbing than 'saccharine literature' so she settled down to read an advance copy which Storm Jameson had sent her of her new novel. *Europe to Let* consists of four novellas, portraits of Cologne, Vienna, Prague and Budapest which foreshadow, 'from different angles', Europe's eventual domination by Nazism. Storm had begun the book in the autumn of 1938, in the middle of the Czech crisis, and the longest and most powerful of the stories, 'The Hour of Prague', reflects her disgust and shame at the treatment meted out to the Czechs at Munich.

It was in the Prague story that Vera, as she later told Storm, found 'a portrait that I took to be myself as a fake, a charlatan, a worker with bogus values, and in *your* eyes – you of all people, the most honest and uncompromising person I know.'

Vera was overwrought and tired. She had been reading some uncomplimentary reviews of *Testament of Friendship*, which, in attacking her for self-advertisement, had undermined her belief in her own sincerity. Given her fragile state of mind, it is no wonder that she overreacted to the superficial resemblances between herself and Olga Stehlík, one of the least sympathetic characters in Storm Jameson's book.

Olga Stehlík, née Johnson, is an Englishwoman who writes novels under her own name and lectures in America on subjects she is said to know nothing about. She is a member of a Peace League and objects to people speaking unkindly about the Germans because ' "It's foolish and very wrong to revive war hatreds".' She complains that her husband doesn't read her books and that ' "it doesn't trouble him if the conditions of our life make it very hard for me to work".' She has published four volumes of her own letters, and her secretary has a green slip which she sticks on every letter she sends out, 'Please do not destroy'. It is a cruel picture of a capricious woman.

Going over and over these points of resemblance in her mind drove Vera 'to the point of lunacy'. She talked them over with George, who agreed that there was some substance to her belief – 'the woman having double-jointed hands and asking her friends to keep her letters were the two points of solid fact that impressed him most' – but warned her not to mention the subject to Storm Jameson until she was rested, and then only to touch on it 'lightly and amusedly'.

Driven by an obsession, however, Vera unwisely disregarded George's advice, and within days of returning to England had written to Storm, asking to see her. They snatched a hurried meeting at Paddington Station where Storm was on her way to Mortimer, the small village outside Reading where she had taken a house. Blurting out her accusations, Vera behaved 'idiotically and hysterically', and felt stunned when Storm 'thoroughly' lost her temper with her. 'I am just as capable as any other novelist of using, consciously or unconsciously, the traits of friends and acquaintances in the make up of a fictional character', Storm wrote of the incident many years later, 'but in this case my innocence was so complete that I was reduced to stammering protests.' If she had had anyone in mind when portraying Olga Stehlík, she maintained, it had been E.M. Delafield.

Full of contrition, Vera wrote to Storm from the cottage the next day. 'I don't know what to say to you and yet I feel I must go on writing, for fear that by any post may come from you something irrevocable which will silence me and make me realise that you have no use for me any more.'

> What on earth possessed me to talk to you about a quite minor matter (even if it had been correct) on which I felt myself injured, instead of the hundred and one things I had to thank you for, I cannot imagine. You have given your time and thought to the children, dealt with mother who is so difficult, written me at length, cabled me, followed up the question in the House, even procured me the Hansard which contained it, and instead of expressing my indescribable gratitude as best I could . . . I had to maunder away about the fancied resemblance to myself of one of the less agreeable characters in your finely written and remarkable book. Really, I can't ask you to forgive me. At times I find myself so detestable that I can't forgive myself . . .

Two letters from Storm arrived by the following afternoon's post. They were conciliatory but also guarded in tone. She did not trust people easily, she admitted, and clearly did not succeed in intimacy. Although hurt by the suggestion that she was unsafe to trust, Vera responded with open relief. She had found it difficult to believe that all Storm's kindness could suddenly be transformed into 'cold hard unforgiving anger like Phyllis Bentley's'. Recalling the occasion when she had treated Phyllis 'abominably' while suffering from acute gastritis, Vera confessed that

> If there is one thing I ought to know about myself, it is that illness and fatigue invariably destroy my discretion and judgement, and I ought to keep away from my friends at such times. My way of being sorry for myself is to go for them! Winifred, being the saint she was and knowing me better than anyone ever has, never held it against me; she understood that a sudden apparent mistrust of her did not mean that I had really ceased to believe in her, but merely that I was physically over-wrought.

'Have you forgiven me properly?' she asked at the close of her letter. Storm had, but she would be even more circumspect in her dealings with Vera in the future. At the end of April, Vera reflected sadly that because she had 'behaved like a fool', Storm had chosen to go away to Devon with Irene Rathbone instead of taking the holiday with her that they had so often talked about.

Within a fortnight of John and Shirley's return to school after the Easter holidays came the news that everyone had been dreading for so long. On 10 May, while Churchill was in the throes of forming his National Government, the Nazi invasion of Belgium and Holland began. In five days Holland was overrun, and in ten the French line was broken. A week later the British Expeditionary Force started its withdrawal from Dunkirk. 'Since I dictated this a few days ago', Vera wrote in a hurried postscript to a letter to Sarah Gertrude Millin in South Africa on 15 May, 'the world has blown up and half Europe is, or will be, in flames. We know our turn is next, and not one of us knows how long we shall be here ... Pray for us, dear Sarah.'

The burden of being a member of an unpopular minority was now at its heaviest. Scaremongering in the press against fifth columnists – an amorphous group, defined by one newspaper as 'Fascists, Communists, peace fanatics and alien refugees in league with Berlin and Moscow' – reached a hysterical pitch as it became increasingly likely that Hitler would attempt an invasion of Britain. The *Sunday Dispatch* went so far as to allege that the PPU constituted an 'underground political force' which endangered 'the very life of the nation'.

Determined to counter these attacks, to demonstrate a love of her country and to show that she had no interest in anything so purely negative as obstruction of the Government's war effort, Vera volunteered her nursing experience and offered assistance in setting up a government-sponsored scheme to evacuate British children to the United States and the Dominions. She also attempted to correct, wherever she could, a common misrepresentation of the views of pacifists like herself which tried to insinuate that they were opposed to war against Hitler rather than to war itself.

To a great extent, though, she remained impressed by the degree of official toleration shown towards members of the pacifist minority at this stage of the war. Pacifist citizens, she had written back in February, were straws which showed the direction of the wind. 'So long as we are allowed that traditional liberty which permits us to express our opinions and meet to discuss them, the rest of the country may feel assured that freedom here is still a living reality.' For Vera, the outcome of the so-called Poster Trial at

Bow Street Police Court, in the first week of June, upheld her faith in this freedom. Six defendants from the PPU, including Stuart Morris, John Barclay and Alex Wood, were prosecuted under defence regulations for the publication and display of the poster, 'War will cease when men refuse to fight. What are YOU going to do about it?' In fact the poster was from two-year-old stock and Stuart Morris immediately agreed to withdraw it; but Vera was so inspired by the tolerant attitude of the magistrate and the Attorney-General in merely ordering the defendants to be bound over that she offered to pay the £30 costs.

Dick Sheppard had once predicted that if war came, roughly fifty per cent of those who had signed the pledge would change their minds. With the threat of invasion his prophecy began to come true. In May the PPU's membership suffered its first net loss with a total of 627 resignations, including those of two Sponsors, Bertrand Russell and Philip Mumford. Before long other leading names were recanting their pacifism: among them Rose Macaulay (who had ceased to be a Sponsor in 1938), A.A. Milne, Maude Royden, Ellen Wilkinson, and Cyril Joad, who had proposed the winning motion at the Oxford 'King and Country' debate in 1933.

With the exception of Joad, whom she suspected of having 'cleverly furthered' his own interests 'in the process of recantation' by selling his services to the Ministry of Information, Vera refused to condemn her former colleagues for their decision. She felt that she could understand the agony of self-questioning which they had gone through to reach it. It was not a path, however, that she could follow. As she later told Denis Hayes, the author of a study of conscientious objection, she was unlikely to renounce her own pacifism because it 'was rooted in first-hand experience of war'. She was coming painfully to the conclusion that even a victory for Hitler could not be a worse blow to humanity than war itself.

This was the extreme choice that faced pacifists as the Germans made their military breakthrough in the spring of 1940: was any peace really preferable to war? As John Barclay saw it, in his regular *Peace News* column, 'Unless we have really faced up to possibility of military defeat we cannot claim to have examined the faith called pacifism.'

The prospect of a negotiated peace, Vera admitted to the readers of her Letter on 23 May, was in the present circumstances remote. Pacifism was, for the time being, a lost cause. 'It has no hope of triumphing, and little of increasing its power.' And yet, she continued, 'perhaps the lost causes are the only ones worth fighting for.' She was closer now to the apolitical pacifists and had allied herself to the quietists in the PPU by joining their think-tank, the Forethought Committee, whose main object was to give guidance on a pacifist way of living. Furthermore, her sense of the religious underpinning of her own pacifism was growing stronger all the time. 'I went to the P.P.U. Council yesterday', she wrote to Storm Jameson on 18 May, 'and nothing could have been saner than the attitude that most people (led by Ponsonby, Donald Soper, & John Middleton Murry) are now taking. Since the war can't be stopped, all propaganda of a government-opposing kind is being abandoned, and their object is to become a sort of religious fellowship, a nucleus of sanity, to help prepare people for what is coming.'

Vera had insisted to George that the children should remain with her until their actual safety was threatened. But though that moment seemed to have arrived, the wrench of being parted from them was still too unbearable to contemplate. At Cheyne Walk she pondered their future as she removed the pictures from the walls, filled the bath with water, and made arrangements to safeguard other possessions in anticipation of air raids. 'Attempted invasion of these islands now almost certain', she noted in her diary at the end of May. 'Feel sick at heart when I think of John & Shirley, & can only pray that the tide of war will roll over their heads without harming them.'

Once again, as at the time of Munich, Vera and George wearied themselves in debate on the subject. Eventually he prevailed on her to send the children to America with the argument that since their own work during the war was as likely to be on the other side of the Atlantic as in Britain, it was better to have John and Shirley over there than to repeat the 'intolerable situation' of that past winter 'when we were there and they were here'.

Their decision was confirmed by the arrival of a cable from Ruth and Woodard Colby, whom Vera had visited in Minnesota on her recent tour, asking her to send John and Shirley to them for the summer. 'We should have been guilty of criminal negligence', Vera later admitted to Jim and Mannie Putnam, friends from the Macmillan Company in New York, 'if we did not try to use on their behalf our fifteen years' close contact with the United States.'

Still unresolved, though, was the question of whether the children should go alone or be accompanied by their mother, and this was to be by far the most agonizing choice Vera had to make. She knew from past experience that her self-respect would suffer should she turn her back on Britain in its hour of greatest danger; and she believed too that to run away when the country faced bombardment and possibly invasion might have a detrimental effect on the morale of the readers who had come to know her through her books and the Peace Letter.

Arrangements, therefore, were made for John and Shirley to travel alone.

'It was the most terrible decision I have ever made . . .', Vera wrote to Storm Jameson. Right up to the day of their departure, Storm badgered Vera to change her mind and go with them. Duty to the children, she argued, outweighed duty to a cause. 'The cause of peace will not die of your going to the States.' Understandably sensitive to any implied criticism of her performance as a mother, Vera responded defensively:

> The point is that, strange as it seems to me and must seem to you, there are literally hundreds of people (subscribers to my letter, P.P.U. people, etc.) who now look to me to help them to maintain their own courage. I get letters from them every day. Would I be justified, even for the children, in saying to them: 'Well, goodbye. I'm going to quit with my family, and you and your troubles don't interest me any more. You can sink or swim; I don't care.'

She had been 'literally overwhelmed' with offers of hospitality for the children and the difficulty was to sort them out tactfully. She cabled Brett, asking him for a guarantee to show immigration officials (so that the children would not become public charges), and was touched by his generosity in not only guaranteeing the children's maintenance, but also in offering them a home indefinitely. They would therefore go immediately to the Colbys in St Paul, Minnesota, but travel east to stay with the Bretts in Connecticut in the school holidays. Whatever Vera's own anguish it was clear to her that the children were 'obviously going to have a gorgeous time'. And some of her sadness was obviated by the hope that the invasion scare would soon pass and that she would be able to visit them at frequent intervals.

On 24 June John and Shirley came up to London from their schools, 'full of zest and excitement, and *thrilled* at the thought of going off on their own.' Two days later George and Vera went with them to Liverpool on a boat-train 'filled with agonised parents who had all spent a week in the throes of the same indecision.' Hundreds of children, of all ages, from a few weeks to fifteen years, were leaving with friends, nannies or stewardesses, on board the *Duchess of Atholl*. After a two hours' wait for the immigration officials on the dock, the noise of crying from tired babies began to sound 'like the parrot-house at the Zoo.'

As the only children with re-entry permits to the United States, John and Shirley were accorded special treatment. A high-ranking official of the line took them through immigration himself and ushered them on to the ship. Vera and George's last sight of them was of 'two small upright creatures trotting cheerfully and confidently away, almost without looking back.'

And then, they reached the entrance to the gangway. The tarpaulin flapped behind them, and they were gone.

III

In the aftermath of the First World War, Vera had vowed that she would never again offer hostages to fate. And yet now, twenty years later, she watched as her two young children embarked on a perilous journey across the Atlantic. 'If they are torpedoed I don't intend to go on with my life', she told Storm Jameson as she commenced the anxious days of waiting for news of them. After little more than a week of 'nightmare-ridden darkness', she received a cable on 4 July, informing her that John and Shirley had reached Montreal and had started on the two-day train journey to the Colbys in St Paul, Minnesota. As the first English evacuees to the area, their arrival there would be greeted by a wave of publicity and an intensive debate in the local press about the case for American isolationism.

Out of gratitude for their safety Vera worked several hours daily for the Children's Overseas Reception Board (CORB), a government emigration scheme set up to hasten the largescale evacuation of British children to the Dominions. Headed by Geoffrey Shakespeare, Under-Secretary for the Dominions and a distant cousin of Vera's on her father's side, CORB was run from the offices of Thomas Cook in Berkeley Street. Vera was a member of an advisory panel led by the MP, Thelma Cazalet, with the primary responsibility of interviewing would-be escorts to accompany the 200,000 children already registered for evacuation. By early August they were working at 'full blast', seeing a total of 15,000 applicants in order to find just 'five hundred dependable men and women'. Only about 2,500 of these 'seavacuees', as they were known, had been sent abroad when, at the end of September, the sinking of the *City of Benares*, with the loss of seventy children and five escorts, forced the Government abruptly to abandon the scheme.

What time Vera had over from her duties at CORB and running the Peace Letter was devoted to researching a new book. Escapism was impossible in wartime, she told Lovat Dickson, and she wanted to write something relevant to the times. *England's Hour*, the short book she began working on that July, was originally intended as 'a wartime variety' of J.B. Priestley's famous *English Journey*, a collection of impressions, gathered from around the country, of England at war. But no sooner had she signed a contract with Macmillan than she was forced to revise her plans. The difficulties of wartime travel made her projected long journeys to the remoter corners of the country unfeasible, while more damaging to the main object of the book was the Ministry of Information's 'point-blank' refusal to give her permission to visit any defence areas or factories. She could still write the book without their permission, but it would be much less effective. 'I can also, of course, just go to the areas and try to get in', she declared. '. . . I merely stand more chance of being shot without an official pass.'

Harold Macmillan, Vera reported, was so incensed by her official treatment that he was prepared to make personal representations on her behalf to Sir John Anderson, the Home Secretary, and to the War Office, requesting that they grant her a permit. As a member of the Cabinet his intervention would obviously carry weight, but Vera had no great hopes that 'even he can do much good'. For by now her suspicions were mounting that certain government departments were directing some kind of 'behind-the-scenes drive' against her.

The first intimation came at the end of July when she made a routine application for an exit permit to the United States. George had been contracted for a series of lectures that autumn at Kansas City University and to his request for an immediate permit Vera added a provisional one of her own. While she had no plans to visit America again before *England's Hour* was finished, Colston Leigh was encouraging her to think about another lecture-tour which she might combine with a visit to the children later that year. Merely as a formality, she visited the American section of the Ministry of Information, confident that they would be as accommodating as they had been the previous autumn about arranging a permit for her.

Instead Vera was confronted by 'an extremely embarrassed' Frank Darvall who informed her, 'off the record', that the next time she applied for an exit permit to go to America she was unlikely to be given one. This meant in effect that she would be unable to visit the United States again for the duration of the war. The only explanation Darvall would give, 'after much beating about the bush', was that she was a member of the PPU and that the question asked about her in the House of Commons by Sir Henry Page Croft had been a source of embarrassment to the Ministry.

The shock of this unexpected blow left Vera reeling. She found it difficult to conceive of the Government actually imposing such a ban, but could not ignore the calamitous set of consequences that would ensue if it did. All her lecturing contacts would 'go to the wind' and she would lose a sizeable proportion of her income, she would 'get right out of touch' with Brett; and, much the most terrifying prospect of all, she might be separated from John and Shirley 'for indefinite years'.

She tried not to give in to a rising mood of panic. 'Of course I shall fight for my permit', she wrote with brisk determination to Storm Jameson. To clarify matters, she was making a formal application through Darvall for an exit permit to lecture in America in November. Storm suggested using the influence of PEN on her behalf; but Vera was aware of the need to avoid drawing public attention to her case for the time being. George sailed for the States at the end of August and she wanted nothing to interfere with his smooth departure. If all else failed, her only way of getting out to America – there was a nice irony here – might well be as a university wife. Under passport regulations wives were automatically allowed to join husbands working abroad though, as Darvall pointed out, being so well known in her own right, Vera could find even this option closed to her.

She was preoccupied by a bitter sense of injustice. '. . . If I had wished to work against this country', she wrote to Storm Jameson,

> or to avoid working for it, I could easily, as a resident alien, have remained in America when I was over there, and with considerable profit to myself have joined the group of British authors living in safety and comfort in Hollywood. Because I deliberately chose to come back, to identify myself with this country in its time of adversity, to submit myself to perils which I might have avoided, and to volunteer for various humanitarian jobs . . . I am to be penalised by being refused permission to return to America, and being forbidden the necessary facilities for my literary work here. So much for British justice after a year of war.

One thing puzzled Vera. It seemed odd that Storm should receive 'such utterly different treatment' from the Ministry of Information when she too was a PPU Sponsor and, so far as Vera was aware, held much the same views on peace and war as her own. She mentioned it to her in passing and received an immediate admission from Storm that she had resigned as a Sponsor at the time of the Czech crisis. Vera was surprised: *Peace News*, after all, was continuing to print Storm's name in the list of Sponsors every week, and Vera herself had 'in perfect good faith' referred to her as a Sponsor to many people. She took the news calmly, however. The root of their differences, Vera concluded after they had discussed the matter, was that unlike Storm she had never believed that Nazism 'could be effectively beaten *by force*, since it is on force that it thrives.'

In the skies above south-east England the Luftwaffe was intensifying its attack, and on 15 August the German raiders penetrated the London area for the first time, dropping their bombs on Croydon. In the weeks that followed, the London sirens rarely fell silent, and at Cheyne Walk the household soon became accustomed to taking cover in the front half of the coal cellar which served as their air-raid shelter. On 24 August Vera, George and Charlie Burnett watched from the Embankment as the huge glow of a City fire lit the sky like a flaming sunset. Four days later, while Vera was in the bathroom, a delayed-action bomb whistled past the window and fell on a nearby block of flats.

Her blood chilled each time she heard a plane overhead, and yet when George expressed his reluctance to leave her to face the bombs alone while he went to the United States, she placed no pressure on him to stay. He had a job to do and she had no alternative but to remain to do hers. But as she saw him off at Euston, in the middle of an air raid, on 30 August, her resolve faltered and she was filled with a sense of quiet desperation. A huge slice of her life had suddenly disappeared now both George and the children were out of the country. After another night at Cheyne Walk, lying awake listening to the sound of persistent gunfire, she arranged to join her mother at Edwardes Square.

Edith Brittain was relieved to have her company as the blitzkrieg on London steadily worsened. On the evening of 7 September, Vera had just entered the first-floor drawing-room with her mother when a terrific crash shook the house. The blast from the bomb, which had fallen and exploded on a house in an adjoining crescent, was so powerful that, as they turned to rush downstairs, the two women were practically blown into the basement. Vera's face was lightly scorched and both she and her mother were badly shaken. The following night's raid was more prolonged: ten hours of continuous bombing while Vera lay in the shelter face downwards with a pillow over her head.

'Half-dead', they took refuge at her Aunt Lillie's house in Woking where Vera at last got a good night's sleep. She was still suffering violently from the after-effects of shock, but, in spite of tearful pleas from her mother, made immediate plans to return to London. Safe areas could be no part of her scheme of living. She needed to bear witness to all the destruction and to record her observations for *England's Hour*. In her absence a delayed-action bomb had fallen behind the Cheyne Walk house. The bomb exploded ten days later, causing only minor damage, but in the meantime Vera had already decided to close the house until 'normal days' returned. Amy Burnett and her new baby were safe in lodgings in Woking, and Charlie had remained in Chelsea, overseeing the evacuation of 2 Cheyne Walk, while he waited for his call-up papers for the RAF.

Vera moved temporarily into a service flat, near the BBC in Portland Place, at 2 Devonshire Street. Since this was in the same area as a major target, bombs fell incessantly and yet she seemed almost to relish the opportunity to test the limits of her courage. 'If I dropped my book every time I heard the heavy hiccuping drone of Jerry overhead or the crash of bombs in the distance', she wrote to Brett, 'you never would get that manuscript which I am trying so hard to give you . . .'. 'Nowadays', she continued with studied indifference, 'I only make for the shelter when the bombs are actually dropping quite close, or there is a fight going on overhead.'

In fact, despite the bravado, she was close to breaking point. She was 'intolerably lonely'. She had had nothing but interrupted sleep for nearly a month and her powers of concentration had so far disappeared that she could not even follow an ordinary conversation properly. When Storm Jameson came up to London on 17 September she saw at once the state Vera was in and insisted that she return with her to Berkshire, where she could at least spend nights in the country until her book was finished.

Heathfield, the large Victorian house which Storm and Guy Chapman shared with Storm's youngest sister, Dorothy Pateman, was in the village of Mortimer, just outside Reading. With its kitchen garden and orchard it provided a haven of comfort and companionship, if not of peace. 'It isn't safe', Vera explained to Brett, 'for nowhere is that within 100 miles of London, but by day there is an illusion of peace, and though the nights are rather grim there is not the same continuous noise as in London.'

The only sour note to the arrangement lay in Vera's relations with Dorothy after she returned at the end of October from seeing her children safely to America. Quick-tempered and sharp-tongued, 'pitiless in her dislikes' and contemptuous of her older sister's 'softness' with people, Dorothy saw no reason to treat Vera with any special sensitivity. When Vera found her 'small north room' too cold to work in, she was banished to the attic and asked to pay £3 a week in rent. There were petty squabbles, too, about provisions, which Storm was placed in the awkward position of having to referee.

For ten weeks Vera divided her time between Mortimer and London. It was a punishing existence. On frequent visits to London in the second half of September, she trailed through the streets, often ankle-deep in glass, to face more 'polite stone-walling' from the passport office about her exit permit. She also regularly checked that her own and her mother's house were still standing. 37 Edwardes Square suffered severe bomb damage at the beginning of October when all its doors and windows were blown out.

Fortunately Edith Brittain had remained at her sister's in Woking and left shortly afterwards for an extended stay in a hotel at Dawlish in Devon.

In spite of the unsettled life she was leading, Vera was at last making substantial progress with *England's Hour*. She spent one weekend in Oxford, 'now a general sort of dump for evacuees', and got 'some marvellous material' for two chapters; and she made a long and tedious expedition to the Potteries in order to get a picture of the industrial Midlands in wartime, which she hoped would provide a contrast to the numerous London chapters.

From Kansas City George criticized her for her 'reckless irresponsibility' in staying in London during the blitz. Nevertheless his letters troubled her in one respect, 'namely, that you don't seem . . . to have realised even half of the HELL that some of us have been through . . .'. Only gradually did it become apparent that Vera's letters to him had been heavily censored, and that consequently he had no knowledge either of the time-bomb at Cheyne Walk, or of Vera's narrow escape while staying with her mother.

George had visited the children in Minnesota, but mentioned them in only two of his letters before they vanished from his correspondence completely. 'He is far too preoccupied with what he is doing even to remember their existence or my burning desire for news of them', Vera complained. Although often delayed, and sometimes lost in the erratic North Atlantic airmail service, Ruth Gage Colby's long and informative letters, in which she conscientiously provided a detailed report of the children's development and their progress at school, were always eagerly awaited.

It was clear that both children were enjoying themselves enormously. Even John's normal diffidence had disappeared, and he seemed to be making the most of his new situation. There was obviously something in American life and the American climate which increased his confidence and made him give of his best ('He is like his mother in this!' Vera commented to Brett). As for Shirley – 'or Robin as she prefers to be called "lest people be reminded of Shirley Temple" ' – she was absolutely in her element. 'Shirley is going to be a person who can do almost anything she wants to do', Ruth Colby predicted.

> She is so bright and warm hearted and so determined to be a boy in this Man's World that I find her tremendously interesting, lovable and amusing. Sometimes in our intimate conversations, however, she displays astonishing evidence of staunch feminism. 'A woman would never do such a thing' she will exclaim over some masculine folly. And again [,] 'We women can do some things – lots of things – better than men, can't we, Rue?'

At Summit School later that autumn, Ruth Colby reported, Shirley 'is already getting what she wants and going where she wants'. She was planning a party and a bobsleigh ride for her classmates which she 'secretly regards . . . as a political affair because she is "running for President of her Class for the Second Semester".' Shirley's popularity occasionally gave Vera cause for concern that the Colbys might be favouring one child above the other, but Ruth Colby hastened to reassure her that this was not the case. 'I do love [Shirley] very dearly, but it is John who has quite won my heart and allegiance.'

It was also John who, at twelve-and-a-half, undoubtedly felt the separation from his mother more acutely than did his younger sister. He seemed happy at the St Paul Academy, although he was regarded there as something of a loner, but missed home and worried about his mother more perhaps than he was able to admit. In late August Ruth Colby had written:

> The war does bother him, Vera, he wouldn't be your child if it didn't. There isn't a day we don't warn him to discount the headlines. We don't bring EXTRAS into the house, we don't listen to the radio until late at night when they are in bed and asleep . . . We don't talk war at the table, but almost every afternoon at tea time John and Shirley ask me questions which I try to answer with as much wisdom as my understanding of the situation provides . . . I can't shut out the war completely. Hiding things too much would lead to apprehension on his part and distrust.

'I never allow myself to forget for a minute that I shall one day have to give them back', Ruth Colby wrote of the children to Brett; and these were words that Vera herself badly needed to hear. For the longer she was separated from John and Shirley the more her fears grew, not only that they would forget her, but also that when they did return to Britain, 'their own sad and impoverished land', the process of readjustment would be difficult and painful, and they would identify her with 'sadness and poverty', and the Colbys 'with all that has brought them happiness'.

She dreamed of being reunited with the children in America in time for Christmas. But on 25 September, after weeks of delay, she finally learned that her exit permit to the United States had been refused. The passport office supplied no explanation and would only state that the decision had not rested with them but had been taken elsewhere.

Throughout the course of the next few months Vera lobbied intensively to appeal her case, writing letters to influential MPs like Pethick-Lawrence, who saw the Home Secretary, Herbert Morrison, on her behalf, and to Morrison himself and Harold Nicolson, among members of the

Government. Creech Jones remained her one staunch ally and an invaluable parliamentary contact. His investigations revealed that the real opponent of her going to the United States was Osbert Peake, Parliamentary Under-Secretary of State at the Home Office, who objected to Vera's opinions and her membership of the PPU, though he always strenuously denied this, even to Creech Jones. 'I have a hunch', Vera was later to write of Peake, 'that he thinks of me as quite a different person from the one that I am – a sort of wild revolutionary who is out to make trouble!' Before the end of 1940 she made two further applications for an exit permit. Both were rejected.

There was never any question in Vera's mind of trimming her opinions to suit her personal interests, though early the following year she would briefly consider leaving the PPU in a last-ditch attempt to encourage the Home Office to reverse its decision. But it was a plan born out of desperation and one that she quickly realized would have little or no effect.

The enforced separation from the children, with no prospect of bringing them home for the foreseeable future, was a source of profound sorrow and nagging pain. After more than two years apart from them she would describe the blow as one from which 'I have never recovered and . . . never shall'. That first autumn at Mortimer her distress was sometimes overwhelming. 'Only this afternoon, walking through a country lane', she wrote to George on 19 October, '. . . I suddenly came to myself to find I was sobbing like a baby from sheer loneliness and unavailing grief . . . At times, having lost the children, I feel I *can't* go on.' Inevitably it was also George at whom, in her deepest troughs of depression, she lashed out:

> You write so glibly about the advantages of a little persecution, the grand success I am sure to have with my book . . . and leave out entirely the other side of the picture – the awful misery of having lost the children till God knows when, which makes me almost incapable of writing at all.

She came close to losing George forever that December when the *Western Prince*, the ship on which he was returning to England, was torpedoed and sunk in mid-Atlantic. George and the other survivors were on the sea in open boats for nine hours before they were rescued by the crew of a small freighter. For two days Vera waited in anxious suspense, with no certain news of his survival. Bereft of his customary elegance, he was at first unrecognizable when she met him at Euston on 18 December. He had a black eye, no hat, and wore his suit and overcoat over his pyjamas.

The *Western Prince* had at least served one valuable purpose, Vera wrote later: it had taught her just how fond of him she really was, 'which you usually don't learn about people till they're dead and it's too late.'

They spent Christmas crammed into the tiny cottage in Carbis Bay in Cornwall which Edith Brittain now shared with her sister, Belle. Still suffering from shattered nerves after that summer's bomb blast, Mrs Brittain watched over everyone's movements 'with the vigilance of a policeman'. It had been a terrible year of ordeals and disappointments, Vera reflected, and writing to Storm Jameson at the end of December, she expressed her gratitude to Storm for providing her with a temporary home at Heathfield. 'For what my life and work are worth . . . you have saved them, and you alone.'

IV

England's Hour was published on 11 February 1941. Vera had completed the book in early November after a drive around the bombed districts of London with Storm, surveying 'The Ruins of Troy'. She had never achieved anything quite equal to it, writing 70,000 words in three months – 'and *such* months too!' she exclaimed to Sybil Morrison. 'I still don't know how I did it, since the first half was all written in London.'

The book was dedicated to Storm, who politely predicted great success for it, though Vera thought that it was sure to have a bad press since 'some reviewers will dislike its pacifist outlook and others will ignore it because of its slightness.' Even so she was unprepared for the barrage of abuse to which the book was subjected.

She concluded that the reviews were less an example of literary criticism 'than a method of telling me how much certain reviewers dislike my opinions and me.' She was accused of sentimentality and egotism, and of having exaggerated the chaos and destruction caused by the air raids. Lorna Lewis objected to 'this attitude of the tragic sightseer', while the poet and novelist, Stevie Smith, wrote that 'A stranger reading Miss Brittain's observations of England's civilian population under fire might get the impression that not one stone was left standing upon another . . . it is unfortunate that never once does she catch the authentic voice of England, as little hysterical as the growl of her guns.'

In *Time and Tide* Vera's plea for forgiveness and a rejection of vindictiveness was attacked by E.M. Delafield:

The individuality of the book lies in the point of view of the author, and here I find myself – as I imagine that many others will – in profound disagreement with her. It is a point of view that is neither virile nor constructive, and one that tends . . . to lower English *morale* at a time when it should be, and thank God *is*, high. It is in fact, the antithesis of nearly everything that the Prime Minister stands for and brilliantly puts across in his wireless speeches.

Vera made no claims for literary merit on behalf of *England's Hour*. In a candid moment she later admitted that she ought to have had the strength of mind to scrap the book when the Ministry of Information denied her access to the defence areas instead of continuing with it as 'a kind of feeble autobiography'.

Nevertheless she was stunned by the ferocity of the attacks and in some cases suspicious of critics' motives. She identified Rose Macaulay as the correspondent on the *Time and Tide* letters page who signed herself 'Ambulance Driver', and who contradicted her by saying that no particular damage was noticeable in the East End (several readers leaped to Vera's defence and wrote to thank her for having the courage to describe exactly what she had seen). As for Graham Greene, who had castigated *England's Hour* in the *Spectator*, it seemed 'rather specially sinister' that he had been the official in the Ministry of Information who had failed to get her permission to visit the coastal defence areas. 'Could he, do you think, have been ordered by the M of I to try to discredit me for being a pacifist? Vera enquired of Lovat Dickson.

The reception of the book in the United States, where it appeared as *Britain's Hour*, could hardly have provided a greater contrast. She had not had such a press in America since *Testament of Youth*: over one hundred laudatory reviews and a position halfway up the *New York Herald Tribune's* non-fiction bestseller list. Brett, she reported, was 'frightfully keen' about it, and she treasured a letter from Oswald Garrison Villard, the former editor of the *New York Nation* and a Great War pacifist, who told her that the book 'brought tears to my eyes more than once', and that he was 'as sure as . . . I am alive that yours is the finest spirit of England.'

On George's return in December, he and Vera had searched for another temporary London flat. An incendiary bomb had burned a large hole in the roof of 2 Cheyne Walk at the end of October making it necessary to put all the furniture into store, while Allum Green Cottage, which, without the children, stood empty much of the time, had been let to a Southampton family who had been bombed out of their own home. In January 1941 George and Vera moved into 43 Athenaeum Court in Piccadilly, over-looking Green Park.

Vera had been making regular financial contributions to the work of the

Kingsley Hall Settlement at Bromley-by-Bow in the East End, which offered shelter to families from London's poorest areas who had been bombed out of their homes. Responding to their 1940 Christmas Appeal, Vera had told Dorothy Hogg, one of the workers at the settlement, that she still hoped 'someday to help you in a more active fashion than by writing cheques'; and on cold winter nights in January and February, she could be found handing out soup and mugs of cocoa to women and children in trench shelters which were flooded to a depth of two or three inches and dripping water from the ceiling. Less frequently she joined the Friends' Ambulance Unit in a shelter under Leadenhall Street and worked on a mobile canteen in Bermondsey, serving shelters in the blackout.

But the bulk of what she called her 'war work' in the first quarter of that year took the form of a number of visits to stay with PPU groups in bombed cities around England. Once again, she was moved by 'an inner compulsion' to find out for herself the truth of the suffering caused by war so that one day she might record it. In the first week of February she travelled to Coventry, which she described as by far the worst-damaged place she had yet seen. It was as if 'one stood in Piccadilly Circus & saw everything between one's self & Trafalgar Square laid in ruins.' From Coventry she moved on to Birmingham, and then in the ensuing weeks to Manchester, Hull and Plymouth. She made two visits to Plymouth, the second at the end of March after a two-day blitz had completely devastated the city. 'Except for the quarter mile of Bow', she reported on her return to London, 'I have seen nothing grimmer than Plymouth. I went by car from St Ives, and as we drove back towards the Sound, it startled me as much as the sudden realisation of spring after the great German offensive of 1918, to see a bank of daffodils in full bloom, brilliantly gay, after all that ruin.'

She was much impressed by the courage and positive outlook of the ordinary PPU members she met in these bombed cities; but what struck her most was their sense of fellowship as a minority united in adversity. Her own feelings of isolation, intensified by the recent spate of attacks, may have influenced her to approach Max Plowman in late February about playing some part in the pacifist community centre that he was attempting to establish at The Oaks at Langham near Colchester. '. . . It seems to me quite insane', he responded warmly, 'that you should suffer such circumstances as would make you feel stranded & lonely when there is such a terrific need for pacifists to get together constructively.' On 3 April Vera went to Langham for the first time, and the following week arrived for a longer stay over Easter.

The Adelphi Centre at Langham was essentially an attempt at putting into practice the ideal of community living, 'a possible society of peace', as one of its leading advocates, John Middleton Murry, put it. In more down-to-earth fashion, Vera described Langham as 'a bit like living in a monastery, very simple and lacking in heating.' The Centre consisted of a large house, The Oaks, where the community provided shelter for twenty or so elderly evacuees from the East End, and a cooperative farm on which a group of young conscientious objectors worked about seventy acres on a subsistence basis.

Vera found the Centre 'intensely interesting' and thought pacifism far more alive there than on PPU committees. In the course of several more visits that summer, she worked with Plowman and Murry on a comprehensive scheme for extending the educational work of Langham, and wrote for the *Adelphi* magazine. 'I know that a writer's job needs seclusion', Plowman had told her (and as the author of *A Subaltern on the Somme* he was no mean writer himself), '& so tends to sort ill with community & its insistent multifarious duties.' But to her own surprise, Vera entered fully into the social life of the community and undertook her fair share of household responsibilities as well, resolutely rolling up her sleeves to do the washing-up after a meal.

Time was running out for the Adelphi Centre, however. On 3 June, Max Plowman died of pneumonia after a short illness. He was a great man, Vera wrote in a short tribute in the Peace Letter, 'who not only forgave those who trespassed against him, but was seldom even conscious that he had anything to forgive.' Although it has been said that he was 'organizationally incompetent to a degree', Plowman had inspired the community at Langham by the example of his personal integrity, and without him much of the enthusiasm for the experiment was lacking. In 1942 when the Centre was commandeered by the Air Ministry for an aerodrome, Murry moved on to a new cooperative farm at Thelnetham in Norfolk.

Vera continued to stay at Langham after Plowman's death, though the 'latent antagonism' that existed between herself and Murry made these visits less pleasurable than before. The root of this antagonism lay in what Vera called Murry's 'D.H. Lawrence inspired attitude towards women'. At Langham, she commented scathingly, his view of the relative position of the sexes was of 'a masculine *Herrenvolk* with an auxiliary chorus of women.' Murry apparently regarded Vera as the only serious potential challenger to his editorship of *Peace News* (a post he had held since July 1940); and he certainly tended to play down the significance of any articles or reviews she contributed to the paper. Later, they would clash over Murry's obstructive editorial policies, which she believed were deliberately designed to deny publicity to the PPU's food relief campaign which she chaired, and of which Murry was a leading opponent.

A new series of air raids, fiercer than those of the autumn, had struck London in mid-April. Crouching in the basement shelter of Athenaeum Court, or trying to sleep under her writing table in the flat, Vera listened to the bombs dropping with a new attitude of detachment and resignation. It helped, of course, that George was now with her, but during the heaviest raids she found herself accepting quite philosophically that they might not live to see morning.

These raids together with George's experience on the *Western Prince* had alarmed Vera into preparations for remaking her will lest the children should suddenly be left without cither parents or American guardians. Both the Bretts and the Colbys were already shouldering a heavy financial burden – Brett, for instance, had defrayed the entire cost of John's school fees – as the maximum contribution under Treasury rules which British parents were allowed to make to their children's maintenance amounted to no more than £10-worth of clothing per child a year. As well as making generous financial provision, Brett had also agreed to act as the children's guardian in America. In the event of George and herself being 'bombed or torpedoed out of existence', it had been decided that John and Shirley should remain in the United States and be raised as American citizens.

While considering the changes to her will – and in her lifelong preoccupation with that particular testament she showed herself very typically a Brittain – Vera confirmed Storm Jameson as her literary executor and as one of the children's English guardians, and wrote to tell her that she had left her a legacy for her trouble. Storm's reply was adamant. She would do her best as executor, and would do anything she could for the 'adorable' children, but she was determined not to benefit from Vera's or any other friend's will. 'Besides I haven't the slightest intention of surviving you. Why should I? I feel in my bones that you'll live to be very old, very respected, fairly serene.'

Storm's refusal to be a beneficiary of Vera's will may well have been due in part to other tensions in their relationship that spring. Vera and Dorothy Pateman, Storm's sister, had finally fallen out. Vera accused Dorothy of behaving like a heavyhanded landlady for ordering her to remove her remaining belongings from Heathfield when she had nowhere else to store them. Storm admitted that it was 'a sort of dishonour to me' that 'your things are being chased out of a house which is nominally half mine'; but inevitably her loyalties were divided.

More damaging to the future of their friendship was Storm's attempt to explain the reasons for her desertion of pacifism in a short booklet for PEN, entitled *The End of This War*. Although no more than twelve thousand words long, *The End of This War* took her three long and painful months to write. Often exhausted and existing on a diet of milk and potatoes, Storm came close to breakdown as she struggled to put her case into words. She knew that war bred as much evil as it destroyed, 'perhaps more'; and yet, as she wrote later,

> ... to accept, as genuine pacifists do, anything rather than war, total disrespect for freedom, the systematic crushing or deformation of the spirit, is to accept a death as final as the death of the body. Even in hell, one could not give up fighting for freedom of mind.

By the end of March 1941 Storm had completed her first draft. But, as her correspondence with Vera shows, her new openness about pacifism was leading to their increasing estrangement. '... I think it was probably wrong of me to let pass opinions or statements of yours about the war which struck me and strike me as wish-fulfilment and worse', Storm admitted to her on 5 May.

> The result of my weakness is that you now suspect me of a much too radical change of mind ... Anyhow I'm going to put a new page in my pamphlet, and deal, with all the frankness I can raise, with a thing you wrote to me about the war. Only you will know who wrote it.

'Please don't let us quarrel – either about my Will or your opinions!' Vera begged her. She accepted the need for her to be frank and was happy for Storm to use her letter if it served the purposes of her argument, though she pointed out that something she had written months or even weeks ago did not necessarily represent her current thinking on the subject. However, she could not let Storm's remarks about wish-fulfilment pass without further comment. Why should wish-fulfilment be such a deadly sin?

> I don't suppose that the band of Galilee fishermen who propagated the Gospel ever seriously believed that they were going to make much headway against the enthroned militarism of the Roman Empire, but they left behind them a creed which survived the Roman Empire, and which the decent minority of mankind have struggled to follow ever since. No pacifist seriously believes that his faith and his fellowship is going to defeat Hitler now; he merely believes that by keeping it alive he will help people to keep their heads amid the present tide of violent propaganda, and thus perhaps help to avoid another and even worse era of Hitlers in the future.

Storm's response revealed the depth of the chasm that was opening between them. 'Despair', she wrote, 'the realisation that good is not stronger than evil, seems to me the truth for now', and she could not help but look upon pacifism as a refuge from that despair. To 'sneak back into pacifism' would for her – and she emphasized that this was a personal standpoint – be 'lying and cowardice'. From where she was standing pacifism looked like 'mental dishonesty' and, she continued, she was not even sure 'that it isn't, from *any* angle, mental dishonesty!'

Her mention of cowardice touched Vera on the raw, and she was infuriated by the slightest suggestion that the position she had adopted was mentally dishonest. Without telling Storm, she acted on a sudden impulse and removed her as literary executor and guardian from her will. She did not want someone who disagreed with her on so many vital points to be responsible for either her children or her books.

In the autumn of 1940 Vera had been invited to attend the All-India Women's Conference at Mysore that December. Her invitation had arrived just at the time when she was being refused a permit to travel to America, and her plans to visit India also fell victim to government obstruction. In June 1941 the invitation was renewed for that year's conference, reviving the whole question of Vera's exit permit and her right to leave the country.

This time, however, Vera's known sympathy for Indian Independence led to her case being taken up by the influential Women's Liaison Group, whose members included the feminist and internationalist, Margery Corbett Ashley. Although these women did not share her views about the war, Vera convinced them that if she was allowed to go to India she would not embarrass the Government and would act as a 'reconciler' in Indian affairs. With Mrs Corbett Ashley's support, Vera was permitted an interview with the Secretary of State for India, Leo Amery, on 16 July.

Amery was the first member of the Government who had been prepared to see her. Despite having taken a large dose of sal volatile that morning, Vera felt close to tears throughout their meeting, 'owing to the ignominious position into which my views on war are constantly placing me.' Amery listened sympathetically, and she thought him 'very decent'; but he was unable to grant her request. He did not doubt her honesty or her sincerity, but if the Government let her go to India, the Congress Party would almost certainly make propaganda capital out of her pacifism. For Vera his refusal was a double disappointment: the six-week journey to India would have taken her via America, allowing her the opportunity to visit John and Shirley.

At the beginning of August Vera went down to Carbis Bay where she was 'under promise' to stay with her mother and aunt for a fortnight. She had not heard from Storm since their last exchange back in May, and she felt guilty for not having consulted her about the alterations to her will. Nevertheless the 'tactless and abrupt' letter she finally wrote to her from Cornwall dealt only in half-truths: she had removed her from her will, Vera explained, because she had refused to accept a legacy for the heavy obligations she was undertaking. The full force of Storm's reply struck her like 'a blow in the face':

> You have, you know, behaved very shabbily to me in the matter of your literary executorship and the guardianship of the children [Storm wrote to Vera on 19 August]. I did not ask you for either of these privileged tasks, but I accepted them willingly and seriously . . . You now wait 'a long time' before casually telling me you don't need me . . . It would be dishonest of me to pretend that this makes no difference to our friendship. It closes it, in effect.

Vera was shamed into admitting that she had behaved shabbily, but, she went on, when it came to shabbiness of treatment, Storm too was a competitor for having quoted her letter in her booklet 'in order to prove the stupidity of pacifists'. The final paragraph of her letter, however, sounded a note of conciliation: 'I don't want you to acknowledge any fault if you are not fully convinced of it, but I do freely acknowledge mine and hope you will forgive me.'

Storm's reply from London, where she was organizing PEN's international congress, expressed quiet exasperation, but offered a 'bridge back to a calm friendship' which Vera seized on with relief: 'Anything that promises calm – a calm friendship – in a world where one's nerves get constantly rasped . . .'. Yes, she continued, returning to the subject of their recent disagreement, she fully agreed with Storm that pacifists were mentally dishonest if they believed a victory for Hitler would be a worse blow for humanity than war itself; but *she* herself was not mentally dishonest 'because I *don't* think Hitler's victory would be worse for humanity in the long run . . . than recurrent war.'

For two months there was an uneasy truce between them. They did not meet and exchanged only the occasional letter. But fundamental differences continued to push them further apart. In order to get to America and see the children, Storm strongly advised Vera to plead her case in person with Herbert Morrison, the Home Secretary, and to give up 'even the mild forms of public life' and to promise not to lecture. She could then live in America 'with the utmost simplicity, and if necessary in obscurity' while she wrote to support herself and the children. 'What in effect she suggests', Vera wrote incredulously to George, 'is that for the sake of peace and comfort we sacrifice principle to expediency.'

At the beginning of October Vera and George moved from Piccadilly to a modern flat at 67 Richmond Hill Court at Richmond in Surrey. They intended to stay only three months, but ended up remaining there until April 1943. George was starting work on his autobiography – a book he would be writing on and off for the next thirty years – and wanted to recapture memories of his childhood in Kew. At first Vera only reluctantly accepted the 'isolation' of Richmond. Before long, though, she had come to appreciate its wonderful views and rural setting, and on warm days liked nothing better than to sit out in the Terrace Gardens overlooking the river, while writing the latest issue of her Peace Letter.

The arrival at Richmond Hill Court of a copy of the published version of *The End of This War*, in the first week of November, effectively delivered the terminal blow to Vera and Storm's friendship. '. . . Your style is as economical and incisive as ever', Vera told her. 'I am only sorry that this beautiful instrument could not have been used for a survey more dispassionate, less emotional, and more comprehensive.'

The use Storm had made of the paragraph from Vera's letter – 'a letter from a well-known pacifist' as Storm had described it – was 'most unfair, as I knew it would be'. The passage which dealt, not with anything directly relating to pacifism, but with the position of France and the possibility of averting its fall as a democracy through the creation of pockets of democracy by 'compromises of the Munich type', was dismissed as 'wishful thinking of the blindest and most childish.' And yet, Vera countered, by taking what she had written out of context, Storm had contrived to give a false impression that the basis of Vera's pacifism was ' "appeasement" due to funk, whereas it is mainly religious.'

Vera had read with 'sad amusement' what Storm had written about British writers like Auden and Isherwood, who had stayed in America at the outbreak of war – sad, because while she heartily agreed with her that by so doing they had demonstrated 'that they were not worth saving', she could not help but recollect how often Storm had urged her to imitate their behaviour: 'This gives me the true measure of what you think of me – a person only fit to be told to run away and seek a hide-out in America!'

Their correspondence grew more acrimonious. 'These slanging matches really are unworthy of us', Vera wrote after Storm had rubbed salt into 'this unhealed and unhealable wound' by saying that Vera should never have allowed John and Shirley to go to America alone. The atmosphere between them of mistrust and dislike was by now so intense that to Vera there seemed to be only one solution:

> At the moment I think you are as incapable of being just to me as I probably am of being just to you. You have so evident a contempt for everything I am, think, and do – the way I work, the company I keep, the decisions I make. And who shall say that you are not right? . . .
>
> . . . I don't want to lose your friendship because my experience tells me that it is the war, and nothing else, which has come between [us], and that if we are both here when it is over, we shall wonder how ever such a tiny rift looked like such a wide chasm.
>
> So I don't propose to see you just yet. Not, indeed, so long as the risk of another quarrel is there. Don't answer this letter. But if, a month hence, you feel that you would like to see me again, just ring me up and say so.

There would be no telephone call, however. And despite a conciliatory gesture from Vera, early in 1942, the rift remained permanent.

v

The end of her friendship with Storm Jameson left Vera with a deep sense of personal failure and humiliation. It had made her see herself 'in a very clear – and not at all attractive – light', and she was ashamed of the depths of hatred that she felt towards Storm for a time.

She turned to George and was grateful for the support and understanding she received from him. 'Personal differences of this kind', he remarked, were 'usually a 50-50 affair'; and it was true that there had been misunderstandings on both sides, aggravated by suspicion and hypersensitivity on Vera's part, and by secretiveness on Storm's.

Perhaps only Ruth Gage Colby, on the other side of the Atlantic, appreciated just how isolated Vera now felt without a really intimate friend to turn to. 'I realize how Winifred would have sustained you in your stand for peace', she had written to Vera early in 1941, '. . . and how with her still here in the world you would neither have felt so alone in your belief nor missed the children so terribly.'*

---

*It is, of course, open to question whether, had she lived, Winifred would have shared Vera's pacifism during the Second World War. Vera thought, on balance, that Winifred's 'horror of immunity' would have made it difficult for her, although she was certain that she would never have been in any sense a 'war propagandist'.

Ruth Colby's letters that summer had let Vera know that the children would be spending the holidays apart. While John, engrossed in his painting, had chosen to remain at St Paul, Shirley had travelled east to stay with the Bretts in Connecticut. Shirley – 'a complete tomboy wishing to be called Charlie' – was 'a perfect peach', Brett reported to Vera, enclosing some snapshots of her. These were the first proper photographs that Vera had seen of either of the children since their departure, and the sight of Shirley, still blonde, but thinner and much taller, made her realize, with a stab of pain, the extent to which she missed both the children growing up. She bemoaned her separation from them as 'a disintegrating anguish' which only worsened with time.

While the official restriction on Vera's movements, which prevented her from visiting the children, was undoubtedly the most serious repercussion of her adherence to pacifism, there were other indications of the distrust and disapproval which she faced because of her opinions. People she had known for years publicly snubbed, or even insulted her. And despite the fact that her postbag still contained an overwhelmingly greater proportion of letters written in friendship rather than abuse, she was well aware of the hostility she sometimes aroused. In December 1940 Phyllis Bentley mentioned to her that she had recently engaged in a long argument about free speech with a Huddersfield woman who had written to the Home Office protesting about Vera's right to speak in public.

'It does seem to me that the suppression of potentially influential individuals who hold unpopular opinions . . . goes further in this war than in the last . . . though it is done very quietly', Vera commented in 1942, referring to the system of 'private warnings, private threats and private controls' which she believed to exist. She was convinced that she was kept under surveillance and that her mail was intercepted and read. In the latter part of the war, after the family had returned to Cheyne Walk, she would often ask visiting friends to post letters for her outside the Chelsea district to foil any such attempts. The survival in the Foreign Office files of a copy of one intercepted letter *to* Vera from the United States shows that her fears were not without foundation. Dated 4 December 1944, the letter is signed by Dorothy Detzer of the Women's International League for Peace and Freedom, and criticizes the terms of unconditional surrender which were then being offered to the German people.

At the beginning of 1942 Vera was briefly alarmed that the Peace Letter was under investigation and might be suppressed. One day in early February a police officer arrived at Winifred Eden-Green's flat in Blackheath – tactfully parking his car round the corner – and started making enquiries about her PPU activities, 'and said he understood I sent out a large number of letters every fortnight.' Mrs Eden-Green assured him that the Letter was an independent publication which had no direct connection with the PPU, and the officer seemed quite satisfied. 'I don't think anything will come of it . . .', Winifred Eden-Green wrote to Vera, 'but I didn't quite like all the other seemingly irrelevant questions. I told him I thought it savoured of Nazi methods . . .'. Nothing more was heard of the matter.

In areas like broadcasting, where, for instance, even an innocent passing reference to the PPU had to be censored from one wartime broadcast, Vera did not share the fate of her fellow PPU Sponsors, Charles Raven and Donald Soper, who were banned from speaking on the BBC expressly because of their pacifism. Instead she was rejected for a 'Britain Speaks' broadcast to the United States in August 1940 on the grounds that she was felt to be an inadequate speaker! (Vera had first broadcast on the BBC in 1937 on a programme called 'Scrapbook 1912', in which her impeccably elocuted vowels provided an amusing contrast with Dame Ethel Smyth's rougher and throatier delivery, and a massed choir of contralto voices singing Smyth's suffragette hymn, 'The March of the Women'.) 'Although, obviously, her name is known in the States', runs a BBC internal memo,

> she has a very weak, ineffective voice at the microphone. I don't think she would strike at all the right note at the moment. Whenever I have heard her talk, she always sounded rather sad and complaining!

George believed that he was suffering by association from official disapproval of Vera's pacifism, and to the end of his life would claim that her pacifism had done him 'immense damage' in the Forties. He had been having a frustrating war. 'He has . . . found nothing of real value to do here', reported one Foreign Office official whom George had been attempting to interest in a scheme for an Anglo-American Institute of Cultural Relations in July 1942. 'He has done a certain amount of lecturing to the Forces, and he has been associated with the British American Commonwealth Association but he has been able to obtain no really effective or official work.'

Vera was initially sympathetic to George's complaints that the cold wind of government suspicion was beginning to blow on him, especially after both their names were crossed off the guest list for an official party for Wendell Willkie, the Republican candidate in the 1940 presidential election, to whom George had briefly acted as foreign affairs adviser. But she soon lost patience with him whenever he tried to lay all the blame for his setbacks on her. In August 1941 she had written bluntly to tell him that it was his habit of 'holding and dominating' conversations which was 'the *sole* and *only* reason for any failure' of which he felt conscious. 'This association with myself', she concluded, 'this connection with a set of now unpopular principles ... may add to other things, but is not *the* explanation ...'. Her conclusion was borne out by information which Storm Jameson obtained, on Vera's behalf, through her government contacts in PEN. She picked up 'a good deal of largely inarticulate dislike' of George, based on the idea of him 'as a person who wants to break in'.

The suspicion and obloquy which Vera experienced as a pacifist during the Second World War – the frustration of her attempts to travel, the misrepresentation of her opinions and, perhaps above all, the undermining of her prestige as a writer – were severe blows to her self-confidence and pride. She never claimed that these blows were comparable to the suffering of those who faced imprisonment or worse; but as so often in her life and in her writing, the 'egotism' of her personal experience gave her a special insight into – and a special compassion for – the suffering of other victims of war.

In her Peace Letter for 20 November 1941 and again, fifteen years later, in *Testament of Experience*, Vera recounted how she had struggled to overcome self-pity and her feelings of bitterness at her separation from the children, and how she had suddenly become aware that her grief and 'humiliation' were part of a healing spiritual experience which brought her close to the heart of a new religious conviction.

One day in the autumn of 1940, she had been walking in the countryside around Mortimer, considering ways in which she could get her own back on the officials who were blocking her visit to the States, when 'an inconvenient second self addressed me firmly':

'Don't you realise that this is a spiritual experience? For the past few years you have had far more honour and appreciation than you deserve. Now you know what it is to be humiliated; and this gives you a new kinship with those to whom you have hitherto felt superior – prisoners, refugees, the unemployed, the down-and-outs, and all the despised and rejected of men.'

'Humiliation' was a common word in Vera's vocabulary, derived perhaps from her familiarity since childhood with Bunyan's *Pilgrim's Progress*, and often used by her to denote embarrassment or shame. In this passage it signifies, more than anything else, her loss of respectability, an attack on her sense of dignity and standing in the world. Winifred's premature death had taught Vera something about the fickle nature of fame, but she had been unprepared for the loss of her ability to command widespread respect, which had been one much-prized consequence of the worldly success she had enjoyed since 1933. 'I am afraid I have come to the conclusion, though I have long resisted it', she wrote in December 1941, 'that to work effectively on behalf of oppressed humanity you have to give up all hope of remaining respectable. Like Christ himself you have to put yourself among felons and just endure as best you can the calumnious and malicious assertions that are made about you.'

In her work on behalf of 'oppressed humanity' – chiefly the campaigns for food relief and against saturation bombing which she took up with enormous energy and commitment from 1942 onwards – Vera would demonstrate a new fearlessness in the extent to which she was prepared to forgo that hard-won position as a 'respectable' insider. In *Humiliation with Honour* – her 'small book of ideas of the "What I believe" order' – she gave expression to her pacifist philosophy and revealed the wider implications of her own wartime 'humiliation':

> Once we can achieve the imaginative realisation that the sufferings of many are greater than ours, we can find ourselves possessed with a desire to relieve them which causes our own sense of injury to be set aside and forgotten.

Humiliation with Honour had its origins in the 'Minority book' Vera had been planning since at least the end of 1940 when she completed *England's Hour*. In January 1942, with the aid of back numbers of *Peace News* and more than seventy editions of her own Peace Letter, she began her research, and two months later started writing the book as a short series of essays. But her progress was slow and painful, and by the end of May she had decided that the book was lifeless and read like a tract, and that a more invigorating approach was needed to revive it. A sudden inspiration gave her the idea of writing it in the form of letters to John who, she learned from Ruth Colby, had of late been questioning and critical of his mother's attitude towards the war. She was neither surprised nor upset by this, accepting it as an inevitable part of the behaviour of an intelligent adolescent, and seeing it also as a reflection of her own critical teenage self. 'I need hardly say that I do not expect you . . . to endorse any beliefs that I hold just because they are mine', she told him in the Prologue. '. . . What matters most at your age is that you should think for yourself.' In *Humiliation with Honour* she was presenting him with the arguments which would allow him to do so. Laurence Housman told her that she had paid John a compliment by treating him as an openminded rational person, and wondered how he would react. In fact John was not to read the book until long after his mother's death.

The epistolary form was one that she was well used to by now, and her writing swept along with a new impetus. She completed the first draft in July and her final revisions at the beginning of August. Macmillan were reluctant to publish *Humiliation with Honour* because of its pacifist outlook ('they said they would if I "insisted" '), but Vera preferred a smaller firm who were more enthusiastic about the book. Andrew Dakers ran a small company in Hertfordshire, dedicated to publishing books which furthered the causes of peace and international relations. He had published George's disquisition on Federal Union, *One Anglo-American Nation*, the previous year, and considered *Humiliation with Honour* the best statement of pacifism for non-pacifists that he had yet come across.

With a starkly effective cover design by Arthur Wragg, showing a shackled figure bathed in light against a black background, *Humiliation with Honour* appeared on 28 October 1942. To Vera's own and Dakers' astonishment the book quickly went into three editions, selling ten thousand copies within three months.

VI

In one sense *Humiliation with Honour* may be defined as a response to *The End of This War*. Whereas Storm Jameson had argued that only the evil of war could destroy the greater evil of Nazism, Vera questioned the nature of a victory, achieved through the abandonment of Christian and humanitarian values, which would effectively reduce Britain and her allies to the level of unrestricted cruelty against which they had professed to be fighting.

Vera dedicated the book to the 'Victims of Power', and among their number included prisoners and refugees, the transgressors against the state of two world wars, the bereaved, and the young who were paying with their lives for the mistakes of their elders.

The spiritual inspiration behind *Humiliation with Honour* is evident throughout. The basis of Vera's pacifism was now avowedly Christian. Her agnosticism, she wrote, had not wholly disappeared by 1939, but with each year of the Second World War she perceived, ever more clearly, the downward spiritual trend which had made the conflict inevitable, and she had come to believe in the existence of God 'as the fundamental fact of man's life here on earth.' Sheer disobedience to His laws, she was convinced, had been solely responsible for the 'apocalyptic crises' of her time.

'The pacifist tries to live in accordance with the standards of a society which has not yet come', Vera wrote in December 1941, eleven days after the Japanese attacked Pearl Harbor, in what she believed to be the best definition of pacifism she had yet evolved. '. . . He must point ceaselessly to the ideals of a nobler community even though he knows it is far away and that he is unlikely ever to see it.'

FOURTEEN

One Voice

'. . . I am not responsible for the cruel deeds done by the Nazis in the name of the Germans, and much as I deplore them I cannot prevent them. But so long as the breath is in me I shall protest against abominations done by my government in the name of the British, of whom I am one. The mercilessness of others does not release us from the obligation to control ourselves.'

Vera Brittain, 'Letter to Peace-Lovers', No. 111, 17 June 1943

'Vera Brittain, Journalistin, 19 Glebe Palace [*sic*], London.'

Sonderfahndungsliste GB, 1939–40

I

Vera's tireless dedication to working for food relief for the starving populations of Nazi-occupied Europe, and to opposing the Allies' policy of the saturation bombing of German cities, was to consume the greater part of her energies in the latter half of the Second World War. She regarded her involvement in these campaigns as a practical expression of her belief in the pacifist's duty to mitigate the worst excesses of total war, and as part of the larger struggle to preserve Christian and humanitarian values at a time when they were coming under the greatest threat. She took it upon herself to appeal 'to the conscience of Great Britain', and in so doing she was prepared to be an outspoken critic of government policies, forgoing all notions of 'respectability' in order to proclaim 'the sacredness of human life'.

For the PPU's Food Relief Campaign, of which she was Chairman from March 1943, and as a founder member of the Bombing Restriction Committee, Vera worked with non-pacifist, humanitarian supporters of 'legitimate war' like Bishop Bell of Chichester and Professor Stanley Jevons. On both campaigns she fought a defensive rearguard action against absolutists in the peace movement who argued that, by singling out one or two of war's atrocities, she was 'humanizing war', rendering it more tolerable and therefore more likely to be prolonged. Her response to these pacifists, and to those on the PPU Council, like Murry and Sybil Morrison, who felt that such protests were inconsistent with the 'pure' pacifist position, was always reasoned and pragmatic: the 'humanization' of war should be looked upon as a preliminary, not as an alternative, to its eventual abolition. It was the difference between an evolutionary and a revolutionary approach. While, historically, the more spectacular renunciations of war had never succeeded, less ambitious attempts at limiting war's worst evils had sometimes proved remarkably effective.

Vera had made her first protest against Britain's economic blockade of Germany within months of the outbreak of war. 'It's war on babies' had been the banner headline of her article in the *Daily Herald* for 15 November 1939. Her revulsion at the suffering being visited on pregnant women, mothers and children was heightened by her recollections of the social deprivation and misery caused by the Allied blockade during the First World War which she had witnessed on her visit to Germany with Winifred in 1924.

By the autumn of 1941 the situation had worsened considerably, but it was Britain's fallen European allies rather than the Germans who were now experiencing the most devastating effects of the blockade. From June 1940 the blockade had been extended beyond Germany and her allies to include all of occupied and neutral Europe. Those members of the population of these countries who did not starve to death were often left with their health impaired and with a lowered resistance to disease. Allied Greece and Belgium suffered most acutely. In December 1941, nearly two hundred Greek men, women and children were said to be dying of starvation each day; while a report in America's *Life* magazine just before Christmas of that year warned that lack of food with the necessary nutritive value could result in two million young Belgians with stunted physique and mental degeneration.

Campaigners for food relief did not demand the abandonment of the blockade or even that it be relaxed to any great degree. They simply hoped to persuade the Government to allow small quantities of food to pass through the blockade to those suffering most severely from the shortage of adequate food. These minimal supplies, even if they were commandeered by the Germans, would do imperceptible damage to the war effort. But the official line was unbending: the blockade was an essential weapon in modern warfare, and any relaxation of it would benefit the enemy.

At the beginning of 1942 Vera felt that the time had come for a 'strong and sustained' effort to overcome the Government's intransigence, and on

24 January she appeared on a PPU platform at London's Aeolian Hall to publicize the plight of the Belgians and Greeks. 'I am not a defeatist', she told the audience.

> I want to see our victory in this war, but victory for me *does not mean acquiring the power* to push another people into the outer darkness of desperation, which gave birth to the ugly militarism in Germany and Japan, that is now our Nemesis. It means the triumph of those *spiritual qualities* to which many individuals in this country are as sadly indifferent as those whom we call our enemies – truth, justice, brotherhood and compassion.

She had expected the audience to be indifferent or even hostile, and was surprised at the end of the meeting when they turned out to be solidly behind her. This success in rousing public opinion, together with the massive response to the PPU's 'harrowing' news bulletin, *Famine*, which sold fifty thousand copies in under three months, spurred Vera on to greater involvement in the campaign. Until late 1944 when food supplies began once more to flow freely into liberated Europe, she did not spare herself in the punishing round of speaking engagements and meetings she undertook in support of food relief. She travelled around the country to small gatherings in village halls, arranged by local relief groups, and in July 1942 attended a mass demonstration in Trafalgar Square, where she spoke, without the aid of a microphone, from a dizzying height on top of one of the plinths. She also devoted no less than thirteen issues of her Peace Letter between January 1942 and December 1944 to the subject of food relief, and pushed through a proposal at a PPU Council in October 1943 for a Famine Relief Fast after she herself had tried a forty-eight-hour fast and experienced no ill effects.

Within the PPU, Vera and Roy Walker, the youthful secretary of the Food Relief Campaign and its driving force, encountered studied opposition from Middleton Murry to the PPU's involvement in the campaign. Murry considered it 'to be [an] unwise use of the small forces of pacifism to concentrate them on a campaign which has no hope of success' and took every opportunity he could to obstruct it, from sneering remarks about the 'middle-class mentality' behind the proposed fast, to denying publicity to food relief in the columns of *Peace News*. Vera and Murry tended to clash at PPU meetings on any number of subjects and, after one such altercation in February 1943, Vera commented with exasperation in her diary that if Murry would only depart, the PPU might regain some of the spiritual power that it had lost with the death of Dick Sheppard.

The Food Relief Campaign also experienced a lack of cooperation from the other body dedicated to advocating relief measures, the Famine Relief Committee. The FRC had been set up in early 1942 at the instigation of the PPU leadership to coordinate discussion of relief, but as it was intended to maintain contact with the Government, it had been kept deliberately non-pacifist in character. George Bell, the Bishop of Chichester, headed a committee, made up of 'bishops, headmasters and impeccable social workers', who saw their primary function in terms of keeping in 'friendly touch' with the Government and seeing 'what could be done through representation from time to time'. In a stance which ran directly counter to the PPU's strategy of bringing pressure to bear on the Government, the FRC did not consider that public agitation for food relief was either 'necessary or advisable'.

Yet while the FRC's freedom from pacifist associations gained it access to government contacts, its quietist tactics achieved nothing of substance. It was left to Vera to alert the public in October 1942 to the conditions of mounting hunger in Greece by urging the readers of her Peace Letter to write letters of protest to MPs and members of the Government. Within a week of her appeal, officials at the Ministry of Economic Warfare were reporting the arrival of a flood of letters demanding that supplies of milk and other foodstuffs should be allowed to pass through the blockade to Greece. In the minds of civil servants at the ministry there was no doubt that these letters had a common source of inspiration in 'one of Miss Brittain's latest outbursts'.

Increasingly Vera came to understand her role in the campaign for food relief as that of 'a kind of spearhead', making way for the more 'discreet' – and more respectable – Famine Relief Committee to follow. But at times she felt a strong sense of frustration, too, at the FRC's unwillingness to present a common front with pacifists which might have been strong enough successfully to challenge government policy.

The absence of that common front was all too evident when it came to the publication and reception in February 1943 of Vera's personal plea for food relief, '*One of These Little Ones . . .*'. In January, barely a month before the Archbishop of Canterbury, William Temple, was due to address both Houses of Parliament on relief for Greece and Belgium, Vera suddenly resolved to write a pamphlet on the subject, which she hoped might reach 'a large non-pacifist public of novel-readers'. Andrew Dakers agreed immediately to publish an edition of fifty thousand copies, supported by the royalties from *Humiliation with Honour*, and Vera hurriedly assembled her research and started to write. It was the tightest deadline she had ever worked to. She completed '*One of These Little Ones . . .*' just over two days later, having written and typed out ten thousand words.

Vera sent a draft of the pamphlet to Edith Pye, the secretary of the Famine Relief Committee, requesting the committee's backing. But although the FRC was willing to distribute it to their groups and assist in its sale, the pamphlet's tone was thought to be 'a little too anti-Government for the Famine Relief Committee to put its name to it.' The pamphlet's mild criticism of the Government was also the reason given by the Archbishop of Canterbury for his refusal to allow its publication to be associated with his address. This confirmed Vera's worst feelings about the Established Church, and she privately denounced its 'dreadful willingness' to let the Government 'get away with anti-Christian evil without ecclesiastical protest!'

However, once again, Vera succeeded in rallying support for food relief when the more respectable approach faltered. While the Archbishop's speech to Parliament on 17 February was almost completely overshadowed by the debate on the Beveridge Report, '*One of These Little Ones . . .*', published the same day, sold over thirty thousand copies. Despite their differences, Vera donated half the royalties to the Famine Relief Committee.

The PPU marked the end of its Food Relief Campaign, nearly two and a half years later, with a farewell concert, on 20 July 1945, at the Guildhall School of Music. Benjamin Britten and Peter Pears were among the performers, and Michael Tippett and Vera were the main speakers. It is true that the campaign achieved only limited concessions for food relief, and never seriously challenged government policy.* Yet, as the historian Aleksandra Bennett has recently observed, through her work for food relief, Vera made 'a signal contribution' to keeping moral protest alive in wartime Britain 'by reminding the nation of the threat to the very fabric of Western civilization posed by total war.'

Vera's protest against saturation bombing (sometimes known as 'area', 'mass', or 'obliteration' bombing) was also directed against the killing of civilians in enemy and enemy-occupied countries, and challenged the premiss that targeting areas of civilian population would break German morale and thereby shorten the war. Half a century later, arguments about the morality of the Allied bombing of German cities – and about whether it achieved anything of military value – continue unabated.

---

* Under Vera's chairmanship, the Food Relief Campaign had persuaded the Government, at the beginning of 1944, to extend Greek relief by a thousand tons of food a month. 'It was not much', Vera conceded, '. . . but the small concession enabled a number of young Greeks to survive the war.'

The Bombing Restriction Committee, which was to play such an important part in organizing opposition to the Government's bombing policy, grew out of the Committee for the Abolition of Night Bombing which had been established by the Quaker, Corder Catchpool, in the summer of 1941. On 17 April 1941, *The Times* had published a letter from the Bishop of Chichester in which he asked 'if Europe is civilized at all, what can excuse the bombing of towns by night and the terrorizing of non-combatants', and urged that Britain and Germany should reach an agreement to refrain from night-bombing.

Catchpool had taken the lead by inviting Vera, Stuart Morris, T.C. Foley, the economist Stanley Jevons, and several others to serve on a committee whose first act was the circulation of a petition requesting that the Government announce its intention to discontinue night-bombing from a given date, reserving the right to resume the practice if the German Government did not follow suit. The petition forms bore the names of three bishops, including the Bishop of Chichester, six MPs, and both pacifist and non-pacifist signatories. But while German raids on British cities persisted, it was difficult to win significant support for the measure, and the number of signatures obtained amounted to just over fifteen thousand.

In April 1942, however, following the appointment of Sir Arthur Harris to the control of Bomber Command, the committee reconstituted itself as the Bombing Restriction Committee and increased its activities fourfold. For with Harris's appointment as Air Officer Commander-in-Chief came a change in RAF policy, from 'precision' bombing of military or industrial targets to 'area' bombing in which large forces dropped high explosives and thousands of incendiary bombs to set whole cities alight. Harris did not initiate this policy – in fact it originated in a Whitehall directive a week before his arrival at Bomber Command – but it was his ruthless determination which saw it through to the end. His broadcast to Germany on 28 July 1942 can have left no one in any doubt of this:

> We are bombing Germany, city by city, and ever more terribly, in order to make it impossible for you to go on with the war. That is our object. We shall pursue it remorselessly . . . Obviously we prefer to hit factories, shipyards and railways. It damages Hitler's war machine most. But those people who work in these plants live close to them. Therefore, we hit your houses and you.

In just four months he had been as good as his word. The old north-German Hanse town of Lübeck had been the first to suffer ('more like a fire-lighter than a human habitation' according to Harris), followed by raids on Rostock and the first thousand-bomber raid, at the end of May, on Cologne, in which a neutral report estimated the number of people killed in one night as twenty thousand.

Vera remembered, long afterwards, 'the passionate and all but unbearable indignation' which the bombing offensive inspired in her. 'Has any nation the right to make its young men the instruments of such a policy?' she asked in one of her Peace Letters.

There is no need to wait for the end of the war before we consider exactly what we are doing as a nation, and decide whether we desire the government which we elected to continue to carry out, through its Bomber Command, a policy of murder and massacre in the name of the British people.

The burden of the work for the Bombing Restriction Committee fell most heavily on the shoulders of four of its members: the Chairman, Stanley Jevons, Corder Catchpool, Tom Foley, and Vera herself. Much of it was concerned with research into the origins of bombing and the relevance of international law, suggestions for 'sanctuary areas' supervised by the International Red Cross, and the collection of statistics which were used by the Bishop of Chichester, to devastating effect, in his attacks on bombing policy in the House of Lords. In contrast to the rather more cautious stance he had taken on food relief, Bishop Bell was a savage critic of the indiscriminate bombing of Germany, and his outspokenness on the issue is widely thought to have been a major reason for his failure to become Archbishop of Canterbury in 1944, in succession to William Temple.

The primary objective of the Bombing Restriction Committee was to inform the public in the face of government ministers' lies and prevarication about the true nature of the bombing offensive. Posters were printed and displayed, leaflets and books prepared, and questions asked in Parliament through the MPs Reginald Sorensen, Richard Stokes, and Rhys Davies.

The committee was run from Corder Catchpool's home on Parliament Hill in Hampstead. Corder was a gentle, kindly man of sixty who had served in the Friends' Ambulance Unit during the First World War until the introduction of conscription made him take his stand as a conscientious objector, for which he was imprisoned with hard labour for over two years. Between the wars, he and his wife Gwen had lived in Germany, dedicating themselves to humanitarian work in the furtherance of a spirit of reconciliation.

Vera grew to be '*very* fond' of him, and depended heavily on his moral support when she came to write her protest against mass bombing, *Seed of Chaos*. 'I never told you the "inwardness" of my wartime relation to Corder', Vera wrote to George after Corder's death in 1952 in a climbing accident in Switzerland, 'except to mention mildly, when you accused me of having no friends, that I *was* rather fond of the Catchpools.'

> For when we were working together on the Bombing Restriction Committee I fell in love with Corder – not in any physical sense of the word; one would as soon think of having sexual relations with one of the twelve Apostles! – but rather as a nun might fall in love with a Father Confessor, or, let us say, a woman organist with a peculiarly inspired and sympathetic priest. I don't think that that shy and humble man ever realised what I felt about him, but he did, I think, have a real and affectionate regard for me, and invariably turned up to support me at any meeting which for some reason was particularly difficult or worrying.

Unhappily, after the war, the mild (and unsuccessful) pursuit of Shirley by Corder's son, Neave – 'the affair Neave' as Vera liked to call it – seemed to cast a faint shadow of embarrassment over their friendship, and they never regained their former familiarity.

However, in early 1942, Corder Catchpool's influence on Vera caused her briefly to consider becoming a Quaker. In April of that year she stayed with the Catchpools in Hampstead, and sat up half the night discussing with Corder the possibility of her joining the Society of Friends. Vera was attracted to Quakerism by its 'collective social conscience' and, above all, by its uncompromising attitude to war; but at the same time she was repelled by the absence of mysticism and its lack of reverence for beauty. She also considered herself in many ways unsuited to the Quaker way of life. She was too egotistical, too combative, and her tastes – chiefly, her love of clothes and dancing – too frivolous for membership of the Quaker community. Furthermore, she doubted whether the Society of Friends was 'quite the right home' for a writer. 'The unkind, of course, call us egoists, which is doubtless true', she wrote, 'but it is probably a necessary qualification for solitary creative work.'

She realized that she had disappointed Corder Catchpool when she decided not to join the Quakers, but he never reproached her for it. She would remain a 'denominational hybrid', a 'Quaker-inclined Anglican married to a Catholic'.

II

Vera's efforts on behalf of the starving children of Europe had given her a new perspective from which to view her separation from John and Shirley, and one from which she could take some consolation. 'Believe me, I know what it means to suffer as a mother', she wrote in '*One of These Little Ones* . . .', '. . . But even while I grieve I realise that I have to thank God for sparing me the far worse agony suffered by millions of mothers on the continent of Europe.'

However, ever since the prospect of invasion had ended, she and George had been faced with the new dilemma of whether to submit the children to another dangerous journey, or remain parted from them for perhaps a further prolonged period. As they approached the second anniversary of their departure in June 1942, Vera's hopes of seeing them again before the end of the year had risen when she managed to register them for a return journey on the Clipper travelling via Ireland that autumn. But immediately George had dampened her enthusiasm by arguing that the uncertain situation in North Africa meant that they should postpone their return a while longer. They compromised by agreeing that they could begin to plan on the basis of bringing both John and Shirley home in the spring of 1943. At the very least this left Vera feeling that finally '*something* is in train.'

Increasingly, as 1942 wore on, Vera's concern for the children centred on John. From Ruth Colby's letters she learned that he was becoming more recalcitrant and difficult to handle, partly, Vera suspected, because Shirley was so obviously the favourite at St Paul. His school work had deteriorated and, to his parents' alarm, he had been moved from the St Paul Academy to a smaller school which catered for his special interest in art, but gave him no tuition in the more rounded curriculum which he would need for his future education in England. The fact that John seemed to have grown away from his American surroundings added to Vera's anxiety to have him home again as soon as possible. She was convinced that if he had to remain in the United States indefinitely, it might well be worse for him than if he were forced to run the risks of a second wartime journey across the Atlantic.

She suffered continually from 'inward agitation' over John's situation and blamed herself for having allowed him to be sent to America in the first place. 'Poor John', she wrote while in the depths of a depression about him at the beginning of 1943, ' – pushed perilously across the Atlantic, horribly mismanaged, & now to be pushed perilously back.' The Clipper service had its usual long waiting-list, so in March Vera booked two single passages on the Portuguese ships which regularly made the crossing from New York to

Lisbon, from where a connecting plane service flew to Britain. John would come first, in June, closely followed, it was hoped, by Shirley a month later.

With provisional dates set for the children's return, the time had come to reopen 2 Cheyne Walk which had been lying empty since September 1940. Charlie Burnett was with his squadron in North Africa, but Amy and her baby daughter, Marian, would be returning as part of the household. On 27 April Vera left Richmond Hill Court, driving back in the removal van with Amy to a Chelsea that was more bomb-damaged than she remembered. Bomb wreckage – including the blackened ruins of what had once been Chelsea Old Church – surrounded Cheyne Walk, but number 2 itself stood largely intact. Inside, dust and fallen plaster covered everything, and the lack of carpets and furniture gave the main rooms a rather shabby appearance. But after a fortnight of cleaning, with Amy working 'like a Trojan', the house began to look more like its normal self.

The first large gathering held at 2 Cheyne Walk was a party on 5 June to celebrate the hundredth issue of the 'Letter to Peace-Lovers' (somewhat belatedly as it had been published in January). Two hundred people 'scrummed in', as Corder Catchpool put it, bringing with them contributions from their ration allowance: small quantities of tea, milk, and a variety of cakes and sandwiches. Before tea there was a short conference on the purpose of the Letter, with suggestions invited from readers about methods of making it better known. To many of those present Vera had become a beacon of inspiration, often through the personal letters she wrote to them, providing support and offering advice. 'I first started corresponding with V.B. as a conscientious objector at the time of my tribunal around 1940–41', remembered Hugh Maw in 1983 in a reminiscence that is typical, 'and I went to any meetings I could where she was speaking. I was especially thankful for and inspired by her *Humiliation with Honour* and her regular encouragement, particularly at Easter and Christmas, to keep the faith and one's courage up.'

Throughout June, Vera waited expectantly for news of John. At the beginning of the month the shooting-down between Lisbon and England of a passenger plane carrying the actor Leslie Howard, had made everyone understandably apprehensive at the last minute about whether John should be travelling at all. 'You will realise, I am sure, what a bad headache we have had over the recent disaster to the transport plane . . .', Vera wrote on 15 June to Susan Lowndes-Marques, who had kindly agreed to meet John off the ship at Lisbon. 'Had our son been very happy where he is we would probably have left him alone, but only within the last few days, we have had a letter stating how extremely anxious he is to get back.'

On 3 July they received a cable from the Colbys, informing them that John was on his way, and just over a fortnight later, on the 18th, his plane from Lisbon safely touched down in Bristol.

Shortly before his death in 1987, John recalled that as his train approached Paddington, where he was being met by his parents, he experienced 'feelings of malaise if not mild claustrophobia' when he observed 'the row upon row of suburban houses', which were such a striking contrast to the wide-open spaces of the Middle West he had recently left behind. Vera was disconcerted too. The boy of twelve who had left Liverpool in 1940 had been replaced by a young man she hardly recognized, five inches taller than her and speaking in a voice which betrayed unmistakeable American intonations. And these, as John later admitted, 'were only the outward signs' of the changes for which she had been unprepared.

Shirley's journey home was much more protracted and adventurous. She boarded the *Serpo Pinto* in Philadelphia in early September, but halfway across the Atlantic the ship was caught in a cyclone for five days which drove it off course as far south as Madeira. Not until 22 September did word finally reach London that the ship had docked in Lisbon. Here Shirley faced more delays. The Allied offensive in Italy had led to all the large air transports being sent to the Mediterranean. There was already an accumulation of two hundred children waiting to fly to England from the previous Lisbon boat, and the additional 170 from the *Serpo Pinto* meant that it might be a matter of weeks before Shirley returned home.

'It is a great comfort to us to know that you are, so to speak, keeping your eye on Shirley . . .', Vera wrote to the cooperative Madame Lowndes-Marques. 'I envy her her chance to see Lisbon, which must be lively at this time of year.' Just how lively her daughter was finding Lisbon, Vera could hardly have guessed, for without supervision and accompanied by her friend, Rosemary Roughton, thirteen-year-old Shirley spent much of her time in riotous pursuits, scaling the roof of her hotel and consuming large quantities of Madeira over dinner.

For weeks Vera had not dared to leave the house for more than two or three hours in case Shirley should arrive home, but on 17 October she had no alternative but to attend a speaking engagement in Nottingham. Returning to Cheyne Walk later that evening, she was called into the drawing-room by George. There, to her joy, behind the curtains, she found 'a tiny fair-haired creature in red jumper & plaid skirt'. In a particularly telling passage in *Testament of Experience*, Vera related how she had clasped her tightly 'in a surge of emotion which I never allowed myself to show again . . .'.

435

They spent a happy family Christmas, their first together since 1938. Edith Brittain, who had returned to live in London, joined them, and was delighted to be reunited with her grandchildren, having feared at one time that she might never see them again, though she could not resist commenting on the sharp deterioration in their manners and general behaviour since they had been in America.

It would take time to get to know John and Shirley again. Quite quickly their lives resumed some semblance of normality, with John being sent away to Harrow and Shirley attending St Paul's Girls' School. It would be many years, though, before Vera could altogether lose her regret at having been deprived of three vital years in her children's development.

III

In November 1943, shortly after Shirley's return, Vera began work on her 'final appeal' against saturation bombing. By the end of that year Bomber Command had carried out a further series of intensive raids on German cities, including Düsseldorf, Hamburg, Nuremberg, and Berlin. Hamburg – 'the City without Nazis' as it was sometimes known because of its large Jewish population – 'surpassed them all in horror'. On the night of 27–8 July alone, several square miles of the residential and commercial heart of the city were engulfed in a firestorm which burned for several hours at a temperature of 1,000 degrees centigrade. More than forty thousand people were killed. There were charred adult corpses in the streets which had shrunk to the size of children. And worse was to come. 'Our plans are to bomb, burn and ruthlessly destroy ... the people responsible for creating this war', the Minister of Information, Brendan Bracken, informed a Quebec press conference only days after the bombing of Hamburg.

Vera felt compelled to protest. She was disgusted by the exultant tone which accompanied the reporting of the bombing in some sections of the press, and resolved to stir the 'uneasy' consciences of the British people by making them face the truth of what was being done in their name. Putting to one side *Account Rendered*, a novel that she had been working on, she started to write a pamphlet for publication by the Bombing Restriction Committee. The weight of research materials collected by the committee, however, would eventually turn the planned pamphlet into a book of over a hundred pages. Taking her title from a couplet in Book IV of Pope's

Dunciad ('Then rose the seed of Chaos, and of Night, / To blot out order and extinguish light'), she called the book *Seed of Chaos. What Mass Bombing Really Means.*

Seed of Chaos is, to a very large degree, a work of cool exposition in which Vera's arguments are buttressed by an extensive array of eyewitness reports and statistical information. At the outset, she hammers home three central contentions.

> ... *first*, that there is no *certainty* that ... a shortening of the war will result; and that nothing less than an absolute certainty entitles even the most ardent of the War's supporters to use these dreadful expedients ...

> *Secondly*, when the word 'shorten' is used, it generally implies the limiting or reduction of the total amount of human suffering and destruction ... In fact, the mass bombing of great centres of population means *a speed up of human slaughter, misery and material destruction superimposed on that of the military fighting fronts.*

> *Thirdly*, the 'experiment' has demonstrated, so far, that mass bombing does not induce revolt or break morale. The victims are stunned, exhausted, apathetic, absorbed in the immediate tasks of finding food and shelter. But when they recover, who can doubt that there will be, among the majority at any rate, the desire for revenge and a hardening process, even if, for a time it may be subdued by fear?[*]

One chapter dealt with the history of the bombing offensive, including the change of tactics from 'precision' to obliteration bombing, while another took a sample of ten German towns and cities and asked what had actually occurred when 1,500 tons of bombs were dropped on them. The section on Arthur Harris himself, in which Vera wrote that he should one day be arraigned as a war criminal, was considered libellous and had to be toned down on the advice of Corder Catchpool's solicitor.

Subsequent chapters covered the response to bombing policy in Parliament and attempted, in so far as it was possible, to gauge public opinion on the subject. At the end of the book, Vera made one final plea for a return to the standards of international law established by Grotius, over three hundred years earlier, in reaction to the cruelties of the Thirty Years' War.

---

[*] In February 1943 Corder Catchpool had written to Vera to tell her that he had recently received information from a German Quaker which suggested that the resilience and fortitude of the German people was being strengthened by suffering, and that the collapse of civilian morale was therefore unlikely.

Revising her first draft on late January evenings, she was repeatedly disturbed by the noise of bombers overhead, preparing for the latest of their fifteen massive raids on Berlin. On 9 February Bishop Bell of Chichester rose in the House of Lords to make his most sustained condemnation to date of the strategy of area bombing. As Frank Field has put it, 'he not only undermined every argument the Government put forward in favour of the policy, but exposed every half-truth that had been uttered in its defence.' Furthermore, he showed up the logical inconsistency in the Government's defence on the one hand of its policy of area bombing, and its demands, on the other, for an unconditional surrender from the Germans. As Bell pointed out, if area bombing was in fact aimed at destroying German morale, then only the offer of a negotiated peace could drive a wedge between the Nazi regime and the German people.

These arguments went unheeded, and the Air Ministry, led by Sir Archibald Sinclair, the Secretary of State, continued to adhere to its line that military targets alone were being hit. Rose Macaulay observed 'a lamentable lapse in the moral outlook of the British people', and summed up what she saw as the prevailing mood of the nation in a letter to her sister:

> I wonder what it is about any plea for greater humanity or civilized care in war that makes so many people see red. I have heard the most passionate references to 'those old bishops' in shops; one woman said it was lovely to think of the way we 'gave Berlin a doing' on Tuesday night; and she'd like to 'throw old Chichester on the top of the bonfire'. It is nonsense of Lord Latham [leader of London County Council] to say 'there is no gloating or exultation' among the English; he can't listen much . . .

Vera was shortly to experience a taste of that kind of outrage for herself, though unexpectedly it would emanate from across the Atlantic.

Seed of Chaos was still six weeks away from publication when, on 10 March, Vera learned from her press-cuttings that a so-called 'article' of hers on saturation bombing, appearing in the February 1944 edition of *Fellowship* (the magazine of the Fellowship of Reconciliation in the States), had caused 'a real furore' in the United States, provoking three-and-a-half columns of abuse against her in the *New York Times*.

In fact, the article was none other than the first draft of *Seed of Chaos* which Felix Greene, a supporter of the Bombing Restriction Committee, had offered to take with him to New York, just before Christmas, to deliver to the Fellowship of Reconciliation. The typescript had been retained for a while by the censor, and when it had finally reached the FoR, there had been no time to consult Vera before publishing it as a supplement to

Fellowship, under the more emotive title of *Massacre by Bombing*. John Nevin Sayre, a secretary of the FoR, had contributed an 'American Postscript', but what had really grabbed attention was a preface signed by twenty-eight leading American clergy and writers commending what Vera had written, and declaring that 'Christian people should be moved to examine themselves concerning their participation in this carnival of death, even though they be thousands of miles away.'

Vera admitted to Brett that she felt 'rather as if I had turned on a tap expecting the usual thin trickle, and found I had released Niagara instead'; while Oswald Garrison Villard commented that in his entire journalistic career he had never seen 'a more remarkable phenomenon' than the way in which Vera's protest had seized the headlines. Describing this phenomenon in 1968, an American historian, James Martin, wrote that 'Attacks on Miss Brittain occurred from coast to coast by the hundreds in every imaginable medium of communication; the printed condemnations alone would have filled a number of volumes.'

Newsweek, in an article on the 'Revolt Against Bombs', reported that the reaction to *Massacre by Bombing* was immediate and one-sided, and the *New York Times*, which had the largest number of reader-contributions in the country, estimated in a front-page story that ninety-eight per cent of its letters from the public were against Vera's article. Particularly extreme were attacks from members of the clergy who supported area bombing. The editor of the *Christian Herald* accused Vera and her allies of giving comfort to the enemy, while the rector of a Polish National Catholic church in Connecticut was among the fiercest and most belligerent of critics. 'There is no other way', he thundered, 'but to attack these beasts in their lairs – that is the German cities – where they plan further mass murders of innocent people.'

There was some support for Vera's position, as was to be expected, in the journals of liberal Catholicism and Protestantism, *Commonweal* and the *Christian Century*. The latter's editorial concluded by saying that 'The question which Miss Brittain's pamphlet [*Massacre by Bombing* was by now circulating in a twenty-cent reprint] raises in the mind of every thoughtful reader is as to whether victory won in this fashion is worth having.' But the two strongest voices of liberalism in the country, the *New Republic* and the *Nation*, advocated area bombing based on reasons of military necessity, with the *Nation* at one point even denying that such bombing was taking place.

'British Woman Pacifist Rouses U.S. Fury', Dorothy Thompson, the well-known American journalist, informed British readers in her 'Voice of America' column for the *Sunday Chronicle*. Far from 'awakening squeamishness', Thompson reported, 'Miss Brittain's article ... has actually released a more furious defence of air warfare than any single political action to date.' Thompson, who had made Vera feel uncharacteristically tonguetied in her defence of pacifism on meeting her in 1937, was herself a signatory of Freedom House, the propaganda body which had announced its support of 'all available means' to defeat the enemy.

The only attack which Vera thought it necessary to respond to was a 'Rebuttal to the Protest Against Bombing' by William Shirer, which appeared in the *New York Herald Tribune* on 12 March. Shirer was already something of a celebrity, and his major pieces of journalism tended to be treated as news events. Three years earlier, he had published his bestselling *Berlin Diary*, a close-up view of Hitler and the Nazi regime, based on the diary he had kept as a journalist in Berlin in the late Thirties. Shirer accused Vera of reproducing Nazi propaganda in her accounts of the Allied bombings, and suggested that Dr Goebbels 'would hardly have written it differently.'

'It is much what one would expect from Shirer', Vera wrote to George,

– not only saying that we are Nazi dupes, but virtually suggesting in so many words that we are actually Nazi agents! Its methods of attack are also what one would expect – e.g. it suggests that all my sources of information are German or Nazi-inspired sources, & omits to mention that most of these sources were British newspaper correspondents & British papers – to say nothing of repatriated prisoners of war!

By the final week of April, the controversy had filtered through to the White House from where President Roosevelt delivered 'a stinging rebuke' to the twenty-eight who had signed the preface. As the *New York Herald Tribune* reported on 26 April, Stephen Early, the President's secretary, had sent a letter to *Fellowship*, stating that while the President was 'disturbed and horrified' by the 'destruction of life' in the war, the easiest way to prevent many more civilians being killed was to compel the Germans and Japanese to change their philosophy. For as long as that philosophy lasted 'we shall have more deaths, more destruction and more wars.'

But *Massacre by Bombing* had clearly disturbed the Roosevelt administration. Undersecretary of War Patterson denounced the protestors, accusing them of giving encouragement to the enemy; and in June, shortly after D-Day, Secretary of War Lovett, during a visit to air force leaders in England, warned United States Air Force General Spaatz of the serious repercussions that would ensue in Congress should indiscriminate bombing be announced as American air force policy. Even Mrs Roosevelt played a part in the denunciations. At the end of May, she was reported as having branded Vera's arguments against 'the Bitter-Enders' in Britain and America, who advocated Germany's unconditional surrender, as 'all sentimental nonsense'.

In Britain, meanwhile, the appearance of *Seed of Chaos* on 19 April attracted scant attention in the press. (Remarking on the contrast between the British and American responses, Vera wrote that it was the Americans' immunity from bombing which was largely responsible for the complacent manner in which so many of them had publicly demanded substantial retaliation against the German people.) The *Times Literary Supplement* gave the book a cursory review and correctly predicted that her 'rebellion' would not gain many recruits in Britain. Only from George Orwell in *Tribune* was Vera faced with anything resembling a sustained attack, in two pieces in which he pronounced the arguments she had advanced about 'limiting' or 'humanising' war as 'sheer humbug'. Orwell, Vera responded in a letter to *Tribune*, 'seems to assume that if pacifists do not succeed in preventing a war, they must throw up the sponge and acquiesce in any excesses which war-makers choose to initiate.' Orwell would undergo something of a change of heart after visiting Germany as a war correspondent, in the wake of the advancing Allies, in the spring of 1945. 'To walk through the ruined cities of Germany', he wrote in the *Observer*, 'is to feel an actual doubt about the continuity of civilization.'

The abusive letters that Vera received from the United States and Canada, as well as Britain, had grown to alarming proportions (and on one occasion, an envelope containing dog faeces was pushed through the door of 2 Cheyne Walk). But they gave her few qualms. After all she had never shied away from unpopularity. 'Regarding the furore in America about my article on bombing', she told one correspondent,

> it is oddly enough a satisfaction rather than otherwise. When you are putting forward unpopular views, the thing that really creates despair is to be ignored; when people take notice, abuse you & defend themselves, you know you have got under their skin & uncovered a bad conscience!

She was, however, increasingly concerned – and with good cause, as it turned out – about the possible effects of the controversy on her reading public in America. 'And you had such a large and enthusiastic American public', wrote a reader from Florida, who had been 'upset' by the strength of Shirer's invective which she had seen reported in her local press.

Seed of Chaos also inspired praise from some unlikely quarters. Basil Liddell Hart, one of the most distinguished prewar thinkers on military affairs and defence strategy, had consistently opposed the bombing offensive on the grounds that terrorizing the enemy's population into demanding peace from their leader made no sense when viewed against the background of the Allied doctrine of unconditional surrender. In July, he wrote to Vera, after reading *Seed of Chaos*, to express his 'profound respect for your courage in upholding the claims for human decency in a time when war fever is raging . . . Since you are likely to have abundant evidence of the resentment you create, you may like to have some evidence of the respect you inspire.'

'For better, for worse, it looks as though the bombing controversy has become part of my literary history', Vera told Brett in May 1944. And yet Vera's contribution to the protest against saturation bombing has sometimes been overlooked by those engaged in the often bitter debate centring on the morality of the RAF's bombing offensive. History has tended to vindicate her position, and the moral courage and clearsightedness with which she took her stand is still deserving of recognition and respect. At the end of *Seed of Chaos*, she had been able to look ahead and prophesy, 'with complete confidence',

> that the callous cruelty which has caused us to destroy innocent human life in Europe's most crowded cities, and the vandalism which has obliterated historic treasures in some of her loveliest, WILL APPEAR TO FUTURE CIVILISATION AS AN EXTREME FORM OF CRIMINAL LUNACY WITH WHICH OUR POLITICAL AND MILITARY LEADERS DELIBERATELY ALLOWED THEMSELVES TO BECOME AFFLICTED.

IV

In the first months of 1944 the bombing of London had reached a new pitch of violence in what was to become known as 'the little blitz'. For a second time air raids broke up the household at Cheyne Walk. On the children's return from America, Vera had given notice to the tenants of Allum Green Cottage, and in March she reopened it as a home for Amy Burnett, who had become 'more & more upset' by the raids, and for her little girl, and sister Sheila. John, too, stayed there in his school holidays, while Shirley, who had been removed from St Paul's when the bombing was at its height and sent to school in Bournemouth, came over at weekends. Not until September 1945, when Charlie Burnett was demobilized from the RAF, would the household once again be united under one roof at 2 Cheyne Walk.

Vera divided her time between the cottage and a one-room flat in Sloane Avenue Mansions which she and George had taken. The night before they moved in, a bomb fell just opposite the flats, and they arrived to find all three hundred windows in the block broken, the front door off, and their own flat on the top floor filled with broken glass and crockery. '. . . At that point', Vera wrote to a friend, 'after the anxiety about John, Shirley, Amy and Marian, I sat down in the debris & wept, & said I never wanted to see a broken window again!' Allum Green also displayed the depredations of wartime. The large house next door to the cottage was now no more than a bomb-scarred ruin, while the cottage itself looked dilapidated and the garden was badly overgrown. The district was in the midst of the preparations for the second front, and frequent sirens and 'other warlike noises', like the rumbling of tanks on the Bournemouth to Southampton road, filled the forest. Nonetheless, as Shirley remarked, it was 'a heavenly paradise' compared to London where, from June, there were new terrors in store for its inhabitants with the coming of the first flying bomb. 'I agree with you about [the] "V2" ', Vera wrote to Sarah Gertrude Millin, after Hitler's latest weapon had hit London in the autumn of 1944. 'Most people prefer them to the flying bombs because you can't hear them coming or take any precaution, and when you hear the noise you know you aren't dead!'

In January 1943, George had conceived the idea of an anthology of acts of kindness and compassion between enemies in wartime. It was to be a compilation from contemporary newspapers, books and journals, under such headings as 'Respect for the Enemy' and 'Helping the Wounded', which he and Vera planned to work on together. Vera had immediately suggested the title *Above All Nations*, taken from Goethe's maxim, 'Above all nations is humanity', which she had seen carved as an inscription on a building on the campus at Cornell, and had encouraged George to write to Victor Gollancz with a proposal. Her own relations with Gollancz had been on a firmer footing since May 1942 when they had met on cordial terms, and shaken hands, for the first time in three years, at a conference on Vansittartism.

Gollancz had welcomed the idea of *Above All Nations*, which he saw as another opportunity to press home opposition to Vansittart's Germano-phobic message, and over the course of the next year Vera and George had selected material for it. But he had been dissatisfied with their first draft, submitted in the spring of 1944, and had urged them to concentrate more on compassionate action in the present war, and less on general instances of mercy. Mildly irritated, Vera had resumed work on the anthology, only to have it rejected again, six months later, as too long, not specific enough, and too pacifist-inclined.

Gollancz proposed that one of his 'associates', Sheila Hodges, a young director of the firm, should be brought in to work on the book, and Vera readily agreed. She had spent more than enough time and money on *Above All Nations*, and now that George seemed to have absolved himself of responsibility for it, she did not want to have to struggle on alone.

By January 1945 she was reporting to George that the revised manuscript was 'much better than I hoped or thought possible.' Sheila Hodges had shortened and simplified it, but most of the 'really good stories' had been retained, 'and a certain amount of admirable material' had been added. Her only slight apprehension was that Gollancz himself had decided to write a long introduction, 'thereby virtually converting it into *his* book', though she conceded that 'there is no doubt that his words will reach far further than ... mine under present circumstances.' She was also encouraged by the thought that, having played such 'a prominent part' in the enterprise, Gollancz would work hard to sell it. 'From the financial angle', she told George, this might mean 'timely' royalties of as much as £500, to be shared between them. She was certain that 'V.G.' would not be content with sales of less than fifty thousand copies.

Vera's estimate of the sales proved accurate – two months before publication, orders for the book already amounted to forty-five thousand – but her concern about the introduction was misplaced. In a foreword of less than three pages, Gollancz dealt sensitively with the main theme, and concluded that while it was well known that he and Vera differed in their attitudes to the problem of war, a faith 'deeper than this division' united them:

> the faith which answers with a calm and sure affirmative the ancient question 'Are we not all' – Germans and Englishmen, Gentiles and Jews – 'Are we not all children of one Father? Has not one God created us?'

Above All Nations, as John Betjeman remarked in a review for the *Daily Herald*, was 'a bravely inopportune book'. Published on 23 April, it appeared just ten days after the shocking truth of the atrocities of the concentration camps had been revealed to the world by the liberation of Belsen and Buchenwald. The message of *Above All Nations* was quickly submerged by the tide of public loathing of the entire German nation which was sweeping Britain, though as Betjeman pointed out, the book was a record 'of hundreds of instances where Germans acted, for a moment, as humans instead of as Germans, where they obeyed their consciences instead of their State.'

Vera shared the overpowering horror of millions at the revelations of the camps. But like Gollancz in his 'remarkable & timely' pamphlet, *What Buchenwald Really Means*, she chose to dwell on the significant number of German Gentiles among the starving survivors of the camps. These men and women, she insisted, were proof positive that thousands of ordinary Germans had been persecuted for protesting against the Nazi regime, and she dismissed all idea of the collective punishment of the German nation. Instead, she pointed an accusing finger at those in Britain who had possessed some knowledge of Hitler's Final Solution, but by whose complacency and failure to assist Jewish refugees while it was still possible, European Jewry had effectively been condemned to mass extermination.

Confronted by irrefutable evidence of the heinous nature of the Nazis' crimes, some pacifists felt forced into the painfully frank admission that pacifism was faced with a situation with which it was unable to cope. 'The conventional pacifist conception of a reasonable or generous peace is irrelevant to this reality', Murry had commented in *Peace News* before he surrendered to his doubts and discarded his pacifism. Vera's pacifist faith, however, remained unshaken. Unlike Murry, who had been sceptical about the first reports of the Holocaust when they reached Britain in 1943, Vera had experienced few illusions about the true plight of the Jews, and had often drawn attention to the extent of their suffering in her Peace Letter. She had argued consistently, though, that the war was not being fought to save European Jewry, and that the intensification of Nazi persecution of the Jews in enemy-occupied countries had only been possible because of the prolongation of the war.

On 8 May 1945, V-E Day, Vera joined the crowds in Parliament Square to listen to Churchill's voice proclaiming the end of hostilities in Europe. Then, walking alone up Whitehall, as on that first Armistice Day, over a quarter of a century earlier, she was suddenly filled with the certainty of God's existence. This assurance, she was to write later, had come 'neither from deep grief nor from resounding success', but from the humiliation that she, as a pacifist, had experienced throughout more than five years of war.

The weight of that humiliation was lifted, four months later, when the discovery of the Gestapo's *Sonderfahndungsliste GB*, or 'Black Book', revealed that the names of both Vera and George were included on the list of 2,820 British subjects and European exiles who would have been arrested or 'taken into protective custody' in the event of a successful invasion. This list, published in British newspapers in mid-September, gave Vera 'a remarkable experience of catharsis'. It placed her 'once & for all, above the further possibility of suspicion', and yet left her with the knowledge of 'what being a "suspect", & humiliated' meant. Furthermore, it showed that the Nazis had understood, far more clearly than the British Government who had attempted to identify pacifists with Fascists and pro-Nazis, that the faith by which the Christian pacifist lived 'was a power inimical to, because precisely the opposite of, their own doctrines.'

Vera had ended the First World War doubting the existence of a divine architect in human affairs; at the close of the second great conflict in her lifetime she possessed an absolute conviction of his existence. And,

> *Because* God exists, we shall survive only by living, as nations and as individuals, in accordance with values and standards of conduct that are precisely the opposite of those to which, especially during the past thirty years, human society has subscribed.
>
> In that belief my halting voice has spoken, and, so long as life remains to me, will continue to speak.

FIFTEEN

'But the Prestige Goes to Hell'

'. . . the deep fatigue of those whose impersonal hopes do not march with history.'

Winifred Holtby, *South Riding* (1936)

I

The end of the war, first in Europe and then in Japan, found Vera dispirited and exhausted. Five years of fatless rations, constant anxiety, 'adverse criticism and partial ostracism' for a view of the war which 'I only wish I could *honestly* have changed', had led to inertia and a deepening sense of her own inferiority.

She was badly underweight and suffering, like much of the population, from a vitamin deficiency. At the end of 1944 she had celebrated her fifty-first birthday, but she looked older and the reduction of her face 'virtually to its bony contours' contributed to feelings of low self-esteem. Freely confessing her vanity, she had worried that peace, 'with its relative freedom from tension', would come too late ever to restore her 'worn, haggard and anxious face . . .'.

In the autumn of 1944 Vera had visited The Coombs at Coleford in the Forest of Dean, a nature-cure home recommended by the Quaker, Stephen Hobhouse, for a fortnight's rest. The following June she went back for a more intensive course of treatment, and found that the relaxed atmosphere, and 'the complete unquestioning acceptance of all I was and tried to be', helped to revitalize her.

She returned to London, and to the general election of July 1945 which unexpectedly produced a landslide victory for Labour. It was the first general election since that of 1924 in which Vera had played no part and, in a fateful miscalculation, the first since 1931 in which George had decided not to seek election. 'No my husband is not standing this time . . .', Vera had written to a friend in June. 'We think that the Conservatives will get in by a small majority & hence soon be defeated . . .'. Although there would be some talk of his standing for North Hendon in 1950 ('You are well out of that lethargic place', Vera told him when he failed to win the nomination), and for Govan in 1951, this effectively marked the permanent frustration of his hopes of entering the Commons. As Florence Wedgwood (widow of Josiah Wedgwood for whose former seat of Newcastle-under-Lyme George continued to hanker) remarked, the problem was that Professor Catlin was too 'high class' to represent 'unintellectuals'.

In a new series of thirty-two 'Letters to Peace-Lovers' to the end of 1946, Vera kept her readers informed of the situation in postwar Europe. As in the aftermath of the First World War, she was to spend much of the two years following the declaration of peace travelling around Europe, witnessing the conditions of starvation and destruction for herself. 'In Europe we are confronted with a scene of havoc and anguish', she wrote, 'such as the most hideous devastations in all history have never equalled.' A tour of Sweden, Denmark and Norway in late September and October 1945 was preceded by a trip to Holland with five other writers, including Marjorie Bowen and Henrietta Leslie, sponsored by the 'Help Holland Council', 'to describe to the British public "the dire straits" of the Dutch people.'

Four months after the war in Europe ended, Victor Gollancz had launched a 'Save Europe Now' appeal for the millions of homeless refugees in Germany, Austria and Hungary. The public's response was overwhelming: ten thousand postcards offering support flowed in, and throughout the winter of 1945–6 Vera spoke at numerous meetings to raise money. At one Hampstead meeting alone, at which Gollancz was also present, contributions reached £1,200. In May 1946 Vera embarked on an eight-week fund-raising lecture tour of the United States arranged by the American Friends Service Committee. She gave nearly forty lectures and nineteen radio broadcasts, and at just one lecture in Berkeley, California, raised $800 for European relief. On Vera's brief lecture stop in Canada, one journalist described her acidulously as 'a thin dark woman who looked as if she could do with some of the rations which she was so anxious to give away.'

Despite the success of the tour in raising money and drawing American attention to Europe's plight, it had by now become clear that Vera's protest against saturation bombing had badly affected her popularity as a writer in the United States. The American publication of Vera's novel, *Account Rendered*, in November 1944 (preceding British publication by almost a year) had marked the beginning of this downward trend. The bombing controversy, nine months earlier, undoubtedly accounted for many of the novel's 'bitter' and 'narky' reviews, and led consequently to negligible royalties. The postwar sales of Vera's books in America slumped to between two and five thousand per title (when they had previously been almost five times that figure), and a significant proportion of her income disappeared. Since *Testament of Youth* she had relied on literary earnings of approximately £2,500 a year. By 1949 they were less than half that amount, and in 1951 they had dropped to £700. 'American readers know that something serious is wrong with me – I'm a Communist or something. So they no longer read my books.' During her 1946 tour, Oswald Garrison Villard told her that the best thing he knew about George Brett was that he had not kicked her off the Macmillan list.

The decline in her American readership was just one aspect of the changing circumstances of Vera's public life and professional career as a writer, which she would struggle painfully to come to terms with in the years immediately following the end of the Second World War. While she retained a faithful nucleus of British readers, she would find herself increasingly out of step with the literary fashions of the postwar era; and in her peacetime involvement with pacifist organizations she would recognize the paradox, ably expressed by Sybil Morrison in her history of the PPU, that a pacifist finds it easier to wage peace when others are waging war. 'I caught the mood of the thirties exactly', Vera remarked almost wistfully, 'but it only lasted for six years.'

II

Vera had twice been asked to be Chairman of the Peace Pledge Union, and had twice refused. She had too many professional and personal commitments, she said, and believed that as a writer she could make a far greater contribution through the dissemination of ideas and the pacifist philosophy. But when George Davies retired at the end of 1948 the pressure intensified, and, 'not wishing to be "a cause of stumbling" ', she reluctantly agreed to succeed him. It was a difficult and depressing time for the PPU. Support had receded dramatically since the heady days of Dick Sheppard and George Lansbury in the Thirties. The end of the war, Sybil Morrison remembered, had 'left everyone exhausted and flat; a focal point had been removed and the sense of urgency had departed.' The recorded membership had reached its peak in April 1940 with 136,000, and in 1945 there were still 98,414 pledges in the PPU's 'live' membership file. But the National Council elections at the end of the war had presented a different picture. Across the country the PPU was only able to muster 4,000 voters. By the time of the Annual General Meeting in 1947 only 16,000 active members remained, and membership continued steadily to decline.

In her inaugural address in April 1949 Vera told her audience that 'As your Chairman I am concerned less today with the international crisis than with the crisis in the PPU.' She asked members to consider the addition of a constructive pledge to the original promise to renounce war. They might pledge themselves 'to try and live, "both publicly and privately a life which shall make me an instrument of peace." ' 'I know I do not live it myself, being an aggressive person in individual and social relationships,' she acknowledged, but she wholeheartedly believed that the maintenance of high personal standards was the chief answer to their problem of falling membership.

An inevitable consequence of the lack of support was a serious shortage of money, and before leaving for India in December 1949 to attend The World Pacifist Meeting Vera embarked on a series of fund-raising lectures for the PPU. Apart from Kendal, Wednesbury and Wellingborough, every town on 'My Seaside Tour' was on the coast or an estuary – Bournemouth, Weymouth, Plymouth, Bristol, Colwyn Bay, Liverpool, Glasgow, Edinburgh and Hull. She paid her own expenses, and takings exceeded her expectations: at three functions in Bristol she raised almost £50. 'Can't make out how I seem to have the faculty of picking it up . . . An inherited Brittain knack, I suppose – but just a useful knack, not a quality of any moral importance.' She was also pleasantly surprised at one meeting by the remark of a 'very frank young pacifist' who complimented her on her appearance, saying that he had 'thought they were going to hear "an old stick" – much to the annoyance of the Chairwoman, who was one.'

Before she had left London, her own publishers, Macmillan, had published *The Meaning of Treason*, Rebecca West's book, based on her acclaimed firsthand reports of the trials of William Joyce (the notorious 'Lord Haw-Haw'), John Amery, and Norman Baillie-Stewart. Vera dismissed the book as 'turgid and superficial', and in places almost incoherent, but admitted that 'Rebecca has involved me in the devil of a situation by her ignorant & abusive references to the P.P.U. . . .'. The most potentially libellous of these described the PPU as 'that ambiguous organization which in the name of peace was performing many actions certain to benefit Hitler.'

A solicitor from 'a much respected City firm' recommended that the PPU deal with the matter through the courts to clear its name 'from this kind of implication' once and for all. Vera agreed, but envisaged the nightmare scenario of having personally to appear in the witness box '*contra* Macmillan & Rebecca! I suppose I must go even to this length if truth demands it, but oh, God!'

Later, though, she had second thoughts, and wrote to George that

> After thinking over the Rebecca West matter for much of the night I have decided that however good our legal case may turn out to be, I will not stand for any court action by the PPU. I hope to think that this is not due to any nice considerations of my own professional interests. But I don't think that a group which has renounced war should ever go in for legal warfare. We shouldn't preach reconciliation and forgiveness on platforms, and then take action against those who have injured us.

The decision as to what action the PPU should take rested ultimately with its Council, but Vera was well aware that any court action would inevitably lead to the disinterment of the wartime case of Stuart Morris, the PPU's General Secretary, who had been sentenced to nine months' imprisonment in 1943 under the Official Secrets Act.

The almost complete silence surrounding his trial at the time had effectively stifled any mention of the offence committed, and the public – and undoubtedly Rebecca West – had been left with the impression that the PPU had been involved in dealings with the enemy. In fact, with information obtained from an India Office messenger, Stuart Morris had been compiling a damaging dossier on the Government's policy in India. The PPU was repeatedly warned that anyone who divulged that the charge involved India would also be liable to arrest.

The case had caused a serious rift in the PPU ranks. Dominated by Murry, and obsessed with Stuart Morris's 'moral turpitude', the Council had voted overwhelmingly that he should be removed from his post, with Vera in a minority of three. 'The Council of that day were an incredible set of fools and poltroons', she declared.

Stuart Morris, Vera wrote, was 'an attractive but weak & emotional man who likes to find himself in dramatic situations'; but she did not think that he should have been let down as he was by the PPU during his imprisonment. Murry had 'repudiated' him in *Peace News*, and it was Vera who, on Morris's release from prison, had provided him with financial assistance, in return for his help with the research for *Above All Nations*.

Vera was certain that if the PPU was driven to taking legal action, the Stuart Morris case would be brought forward to justify Rebecca West's allegations. She wrote to Stuart Morris that in order to vindicate the PPU she was prepared to testify that he had been collecting information about India. 'I am absolutely clear here that it would be morally right to act illegally', she informed George. 'I doubt if a government which has itself abandoned the policy which Stuart was investigating would do more than bring a formal charge, but if it did mean a period of imprisonment I would willingly accept it in such a cause.'

The PPU agreed as a first step that the General Secretary should request Macmillan either to alter or withdraw the allegation, and to point out that Vera had been as much on the Nazi blacklist as Rebecca West herself. After a lengthy correspondence, Macmillan agreed to delete the offending passage from all future editions of *The Meaning of Treason*, and there the matter ended.

Rebecca West was unrepentant and refused to make any personal apology or approach to the PPU. Outwardly at least, her social relations with Vera and George survived, although privately she later dubbed Vera 'a trumpeting ass'. Vera, too, had her reservations about Rebecca, and much preferred Henry Andrews, her husband. 'Rebecca's present values and methods are the exact opposite of what I ever want to adopt', she remarked in 1949. 'Once she was a passionate feminist, Fabian Socialist and rebel; now . . . she is a cautious and self-seeking Conservative.'

Vera's concern about having insufficient time to devote to being Chairman of the PPU was soon justified. She was often unable to attend the fortnightly meetings, and felt that increasingly she had become 'a figure-head Chairman', overshadowed by Stuart Morris, whose reinstatement as General Secretary she had vigorously supported.

As a nationally known writer and among the most prominent of the PPU's supporters, Vera found herself under heavy pressure to attend meetings, committees, and other PPU activities. '. . . I do recognise that I have been edged into *organised* pacifism and exploited by it to an extent that I never intended', she told George. '. . . The process has become cumulative till it tends to threaten my characteristic contribution, as a *writer* . . . through lack of time I have had practically to drop the whole field of articles and book reviews.'

In August 1950 she resigned the chairmanship of the PPU to take effect from the spring of 1951. She could no longer go on trying to ride two horses at once, she told Stuart Morris. The attempt to do so had degenerated into her being both an unconscientious writer and an inadequate chairman. '. . . I have done my share for organised pacifism', she wrote to George, '& should spend the remainder of my life on more permanent things (the same principles but differently approached.)' In the future she would make her main contribution to the pacifist cause through *Peace News*. First published in June 1936, *Peace News* had achieved a weekly circulation of between eighteen and twenty thousand copies during the war, the only period in which the paper ever made a profit. After the war the paper found itself hampered by Murry's editorship as he became increasingly unsympathetic to mainstream pacifism, and its circulation dropped dramatically. From the mid-Fifties, under the editorship of Hugh Brock, the fortunes of *Peace News* improved, and as Chairman of the board of the paper from the late Fifties, Vera would find herself in profound agreement with Brock's radical pacifism. She would later write regular articles supporting the Campaign for Nuclear Disarmament, colonial freedom, and the anti-apartheid struggle which led to *Peace News* being banned in South Africa. In 1950 and 1951 she contributed several articles about the World Pacifist Conference in India, which she had attended, drawing attention to the relevance of Gandhian ideas – especially satyagraha units, trained in non-violent intervention – to Western pacifists.

Vera's support for the Indian demand for independence was in many ways an extension of her awareness of the social and political oppression of the South African blacks, which Winifred had sought to publicize and alleviate after her visit in 1926. This was coupled with an intense, reverential admiration for Mahatma Gandhi, whose political tactics of civil disobedience and passive resistance had exposed an uneasy British conscience, and a bankrupt imperialistic policy increasingly dependent on physical force.

For several years Vera had hoped to visit India. Twice during the war, in 1940 and 1941, she had been invited to attend the All-India Women's Conference in Mysore, but had been frustrated by the refusal of the Whitehall authorities to provide the necessary exit visa. After the war she received an even more compelling invitation to a select pacifist conference to discuss with Gandhi his ideas and techniques of peace-making, and 'the creation of peace through spiritual power'.

In August 1947 Indian independence became a reality. Six months later Gandhi was dead, assassinated by a Hindu fanatic as he made his way to evening prayer. Gandhi's death brought inevitable postponement and delay, until eventually a reconstituted World Pacifist Meeting was arranged for December 1949. 'I can hardly believe that in five weeks I shall be *en route* to India – more scared of the prospect of snakes & spiders than of air travel, climate or politics,' Vera wrote in late October.

The Conference Centre at Santiniketan, 'The Abode of Peace', had been the 'ashram' or retreat of the poet Rabindranath Tagore, and it was here at supper soon after her arrival that she met A.C. Barrington, the New Zealand delegate, who remained a loyal friend for the rest of her life. Physically and temperamentally Vera and 'Barry' were opposites, with totally different lifestyles. Twelve years younger, married with three children, over six feet tall, and powerfully built, Barry was one of the pillars of the Riverside Community, a non-personal-profit farming enterprise at Lower Moutere in the South Island. A great admirer of Vera's books and pacifism, he could hardly believe that she was to be his almost constant companion on what he described as 'their scurry through India'.

Always stay at the best hotels and always travel by air, George had urged her before she left, but having survived the rough and ready experience of living in camp, washing on doorsteps, primitive lavatories, and filthy railway carriages, she was glad, she told Barry, that she hadn't taken his advice. She had learned that she was much tougher than her husband supposed, but 'I think it is more than probable that if it had not been for you I should never have got through the past eight weeks . . .'.

The better he knew her the more Barry respected and admired her adaptability, and her driving sense of purpose. 'I may be complex and temperamental, & my husband is always saying I am inhuman', she said, but Barry sensitively perceived that beneath the worldly façade she was 'devout, sober-minded, almost, if not quite, a Puritan in many ways'.

As her self-appointed factotum he carried her bags and bed roll, found railway carriages, conjured up hot-water bottles, lifted her bodily up steep steps and on to walls to obtain a better view, argued endlessly, chided her for being stubborn, and playfully teased her. 'What do you expect me to wear with a thin silk dress?' she demanded when he scolded her for wearing open-work sandals as they stumbled across rough stubble. 'Brogues?'

'The light of my life went out – or at least dimmed a bit – when you went away,' he wrote to her the day after she left on the voyage home. 'As for seeing that you didn't fall out of railway carriages and all that, wouldn't I have done that for anybody anyway? To do it for the great VB was a peculiar pleasure.'

Before leaving for India she had agreed with Macmillan to publish a book about her travels. She later signed a contract that paid her a ten-per-cent royalty on the first five thousand copies. In the summer of 1950 she spent several weeks at the New Forest cottage struggling to finish *Search After Sunrise*. As a topical book about India after independence, it had to appear as quickly as possible, but she was interrupted by a steady influx of visitors. Ruth Gage Colby, with her interior decorator's eye, distracted and exasperated her by insisting on washing dirty curtains, replacing broken lampshades, and buying new covers on a fraught and unsatisfactory shopping expedition to Southampton. 'The chapters I wrote when Ruth was here were so bad I couldn't believe I had written them, they had to be completely redone.'

Before her book appeared in November 1951, Reginald Reynolds, one of the five British delegates, had already published his account of the conference, while Ethel Mannin's *Jungle Journey* was being advertised in a pre-publication blurb as 'the first book to come out of the new India and Pakistan'. She wouldn't read it, Vera told George. Ethel Mannin had an obsession for litigation, and had once threatened to take Margaret Storm Jameson to court for libel, simply because Storm had given the heroine in one of her novels honey-coloured hair similar to Ethel's own. 'Some accidental likeness of theme might be used against me . . . I'm sure it [*Jungle Journey*] won't be in the least like mine – she'll spend all her time being brave on elephants.'

Even before publication Vera had accepted that *Search After Sunrise* was unlikely to sell more than four thousand copies. 'Few people are interested in India except the Indians', she wrote to George despondently, and either forgot or was unaware that in Labour circles Nehru was a cult figure of considerable significance. Macmillan, she believed, were of the same opinion, and their £250 advance was 'a shrewd guess at the amount it will make'.

As the predominant theme, her account of the World Pacifist Meeting mingled uneasily with colourful impressions of India and Indian life, autobiographical anecdotes, and pen portraits of Manilal Gandhi, Nehru, and the Begum Liaquat Ali Khan, the wife of Pakistan's Prime Minister. In a discreetly toned-down account of the interview with her in Karachi, Vera diplomatically omitted any criticism of the Begum's tough, wilful attitude towards India, of her openly expressed hatred of Nehru, or her allegation that he was having an affair with Lady Mountbatten.

The Conference had owed much to the inspiration and organization of Horace Alexander, a leading English Quaker. In a *Peace News* review he dismissed *Search After Sunrise* as 'a blur', and criticized Vera for her failure to form 'rich friendships' with her fellow delegates from all over the world. 'No, it was not her hard work at the press table (a job she did magnificently) that cut her off from this; but, presumably, something in herself'.

'But I would not be downed, and sent him a Christmas card wishing him good luck on his American tour,' she wrote to Barry.

III

Between 1945 and 1951, Vera published five books – two novels, a historical biography, the Indian travelogue, and a practical manual, *On Becoming a Writer*. This was intended 'to save the gifted beginner some of the disappointments which arise from inexperience', and combined sound, practical advice on 'First Essentials', 'Markets', and 'How to Submit a Manuscript', with autobiographical anecdotes. She also wrote a forty-page booklet, *The Story of St Martin's*, at the request of its Vicar, the Reverend L.M. Charles-Edwards, the future Bishop of Worcester, which was published to coincide with the Festival of Britain in 1951. St Martin-in-the-Fields had emotive associations for her with Dick Sheppard, and she dedicated her booklet to his memory and to 'his predecessors and successors'. She and her mother regularly attended services there, and from the late Forties, Vera served for several years on the church council.

Back in the spring of 1940 Vera had signed contracts with Macmillan, in both London and New York, for 'her next long novel'. *Account Rendered*, originally called 'Day of Judgement', was concerned not with the roots of war, but with its indirect effects, and was based on the story of Leonard Lockhart, a doctor employed by Boots in Nottingham. Lockhart had written to Vera in 1937 after reading *Testament of Youth*, and she later met him at one of her lectures. Since being shell-shocked in France in 1918 he had suffered from periodic loss of memory, and in 1939, when another war looked inevitable, he had inexplicably killed his wife before attempting to take his own life in some kind of suicide pact.

From her own bitter experience, Vera empathized with Lockhart's postwar neuroses. She was impressed by his obvious sincerity, and offered to give evidence in his defence at his trial in November 1939. She was not called, and sat in the public gallery taking copious notes. Backed by expert neurological testimony, Lockhart's counsel successfully argued that he had killed his wife while suffering from amnesia. The jury returned a verdict of 'Guilty but insane', and later, on several occasions, Vera visited Lockhart in Broadmoor.

The idea of exploring in a novel 'the psychology of a highly sensitive mind forced to confront the barbarism of war' by using the Lockhart story appealed enormously to Vera, and while Lockhart was still in Broadmoor she won his agreement to the idea of 'Day of Judgement'. In the autumn of 1942, she retreated to a small hotel in Somerset to begin writing the novel, and was excited to find it 'all bubbling & surging out of my mind.' Lockhart was unexpectedly freed in 1942. In April the following year Vera had already dispatched a typescript of her novel to Macmillan in New York when Lockhart read the book and told her that he could not agree to its publication. 'I saw her a day or two later', Sybil Morrison remembered. 'She was completely shattered. She was quite sure the book would have been a big success. I told her that the best thing to do was to put it away and forget about it, and to immerse herself in something entirely different. I never imagined that anyone would have the stamina to slog through a complete re-write.'

Vera was undaunted. With the help of Dennis Gray Stoll, the writer and broadcaster, she transformed her central character, Francis Halkin, into a musician, removed all identifiable detail, gave the novel a Staffordshire background, invented new peripheral characters and incidents – while reintroducing Ruth Alleyndene from *Honourable Estate* as Halkin's sympathetic MP – and obtained legal clearance from Harold Rubinstein. While the American publication of *Account Rendered* was a crushing failure, the entire British edition of fifty thousand copies, in the autumn of 1945, was sold out before publication.

But the vicissitudes continued. The novel was too indirect a medium for Vera's intense temperament, and lacking Winifred's rich, humorous imagination, the murder story appeared of less concern to her than the antiwar propaganda. As one American critic had put it in a particularly savage review, *Account Rendered* marked 'the final collapse of the artist and the emergence from the novelist's ashes of the unapologetic propagandist.' As a final irony, under the Inland Revenue regulations then current, half of the considerable royalties from the British publication disappeared in tax.

The Christian pacifist message was stronger still in *Born 1925*, the last of Vera's five novels, published in 1948, and the one that she regarded as the most important. *Testament of Youth*, *Testament of Friendship*, and 'the novel about Dick Sheppard', *Born 1925*, were the only books that Vera had felt both inspired and compelled to write. To Dick Sheppard she owed her conversion to pacifism and her return to her own personal Christian faith. The idea for *Born 1925* had come to her when she spent a fortnight at Allum Green Cottage with John and Shirley in the summer of 1944. Again linking the two world wars, the novel focuses on the relationship between Adrian Carbury and his father, Robert. Robert Carbury is awarded the Victoria Cross in 1915, but afterwards enters the Church, convinced that killing can never be justified. In the Second World War he leads the peace movement as the pacifist Vicar of St Saviour's, easily recognizable as St Martin's.

To establish his own individuality, John liked to taunt his mother that he never read her books, but he was convinced that Adrian in *Born 1925* was a portrait of him. 'It is and it isn't', she replied, while admitting that 'in one or two cases when you annoyed me . . . I did deliberately use the incident in the story because I wanted to get it off my mind.' Adrian's younger sister, Josephine, she said, 'is more like Shirley than the Adrian of the story is like you.'

Testament of Youth had ended with the year 1925. By choosing the same year for Adrian's birth, Vera was able to have him called up for active service, and in the latter part of the book she drew upon the experiences of Paul Berry, a young bomb-disposal soldier she had befriended in London. He talked to her about his early life and adolescence, his growing awareness of the inevitability of war, and described in detail actual incidents from his army life. For authentic background they visited his wartime billets in Chiswick and Balham. '. . . I want to get your conscious reactions to the age you were born into . . .', she told him.

> Since my boy is only 20 when the story ends, I am especially interested in reactions between the ages of 16 & 20 if you can remember these. You were, I think, 19 when the War broke out. How did you feel then . . . Resentful? Resigned? Excited? . . . I can never get John's real reactions – or only a few, & probably none of his deepest ones . . .

She intended to give Paul Berry a cut of her royalties when the book was published, and on the day of publication in 1948 he received a cheque from Macmillan for several hundred pounds. 'It was unbelievable', he said. 'By the same post came a letter from Vera saying that she hadn't had an agent for the book, and that as I had given her more help than any agent could have done, she had asked Macmillan to pay me 20 per cent of the royalties on the British edition.'

Anticipating predominantly critical and derogatory reviews, Vera decided not to read them for at least a year, and told Durrant's Press Cutting Agency not to send them until she asked them to. Commercially the book was a success, once more selling out the edition of fifty thousand. 'More and more I become just a "popular" writer who makes money', she declared. '. . . But the prestige goes to hell.'

She talked to George about her defeated hopes as a writer, and asked despondently, 'What is one to do when the majority of literary critics combine against one?' George, with his sublime belief in cultivating the influential and famous, told her that she was too withdrawn and didn't entertain enough, a suggestion that she sharply repudiated. What the literary pundits most detested, she replied, was her pacifist-religious outlook, 'and if I wrote with the pen of an angel I should never get a line of support from such critics . . . I don't see how any amount of entertaining would alter that. Even supposing one were prepared to do it, they wouldn't come; it would only mean more snubs.'

In the summer of 1946, the literary agent, Spencer Curtis Brown, had suggested to Vera that she should write a biography of John Bunyan for the Rich and Cowan series initiated by H.V. Morton's *In the Steps of the Master*. She was immediately attracted to the idea. 'I hope to finish my novel [*Born 1925*] by the end of this year or the beginning of next,' she wrote to her Swedish friend, Ellin Wägner, 'and then to . . . set to work on a lovely book of biography.'

As a result of the suspicion and opposition that she had experienced as a pacifist, Vera identified closely with Bunyan's simple faith and religious inspiration. She believed that 'the Independents of the seventeenth century are definitely near relatives of the pacifists of today. In each case the chosen judge has been God and the individual conscience, and the antagonist the State . . .'.

In the autumn of 1947 she embarked on an arduous programme of reading and research. She discovered, however, that there were so many traditions and so few positively known facts that 'no sooner do I get down my version of some event than I get a letter from some "expert" giving me a different one.' By October 1948, Vera reported being 'absolutely bogged in Bedford', studying books and documents only available in the Bunyan Library, and visiting, mainly by bus, more than twenty-five towns and villages associated with Bunyan. At Harrowden on a damp autumn afternoon, she plunged unceremoniously through a field of Brussels sprouts in an attempt to locate the site of Bunyan's birthplace.

In the Steps of John Bunyan was published on 29 June 1950. The reviews were few and tepid, and after a month only four thousand copies had been sold. The Korean War 'plus the price (and perhaps the subject) has, I fear killed it', she admitted to George. To add to her disappointment, Ailsa Trickett, her devoted Sheffield fan, delivered a backhanded compliment when she congratulated Vera on 'having written so very readably on such a very dull and tedious subject.'

Of her £500 advance, Vera had spent £300 on photographs, typing, and staying in Bedford. 'What a result for two years' solid work . . . I don't like writing a book on which the publisher loses. In the long run it damages one . . . I have an idea that my "fans" look to me to interpret the contemporary scene and don't like it when I depart from it.'

She accepted reluctantly that 'new generations have new styles, preferences and standards of achievement', and that 'if the very changes which push me on to the sidelines did not occur, mankind would have become static and incapable of progress.' She shuddered, though, when she thought of what 'the NEW STATESMAN plus HORIZON highbrows say about my work when they get together', and she could not avoid feeling hurt when the slights against her books accumulated. She attributed the exclusion of all her books from the Festival of Britain Book Exhibition to the personal animosity of the 'violently anti-pacifist' Maurice Marston of the National Book League; and she was even more dismayed when, in a widely publicized survey the following year, *Testament of Youth* was omitted from the critics' choice of the one hundred most influential books of the past thirty years.

Vera's literary reputation was the cornerstone of her life, and for some years she was unable to accept the fact that she would never be a major writer. 'But I can now be realistic and philosophical', she told George eventually. 'I think that long after I am dead . . . I may achieve some kind of permanent minor reputation based on the *Testament* books . . .'.

Towards the end of her life, she did have an idea for one more novel. After a decade of writing non-fiction, she looked for a more imaginative challenge, and asked Macmillan at the end of 1960 if they would be interested in a short piece of fiction. 'I don't know how much novel reading you now do,' Rache Lovat Dickson replied, trying to be politely discouraging, 'but the tempo, the idiom, and the angle at which novels are written have changed utterly in the past twenty years, and I think it would be difficult to break in successfully now if one's style and approach, so to speak, are cast in the older form.'

Vera was not amused. Macmillan had been her publishers for twenty years, and she was not prepared to accept meekly the insinuation that as a novelist she was old-fashioned and out-of-date. 'Of course I read a good many novels', she replied testily, 'both the new-style variety and the older more classical style, such as one gets from Phyllis Bentley, Storm Jameson, and our senior, Compton Mackenzie, all of which seem to be much read. I intend to write the novel I mentioned to you, though not necessarily as my next book, as the story has haunted me for years.' At her death it remained unwritten.

To Shirley, however, she frankly admitted her limitations. 'How few of us can do exactly what we want even when we are doing the *kind* of thing we prefer. I, for instance, would much rather be a writer of plays and really first-class novels, instead of the biographies and "documentaries" to which such talent as I have seems best suited.'

SIXTEEN

Family Quartet

'... I have come to the conclusion that loneliness and nostalgia are
greater interruptions than anything.'

Vera Brittain to George Catlin, 4 September 1952

I

Vera had always suffered pangs of guilt from knowing how much she had
disappointed her mother by her failure to conform as a young woman to the
conventional pattern of the domesticated daughter. In Vera's youth they had
sometimes clashed over what Edith Brittain regarded as Vera's headstrong
independence, and even in middle age Vera had found it almost intolerable
trying to resist her mother's domination. As if to atone for the distance
between them – 'spiritual not physical' – Vera had always visited her mother
regularly, and whenever she was away had written long letters. '... Don't
ever again suggest that you'll pay me a dutiful Sunday teatime visit as I used
to do Granny', she gently chided Shirley after she had left home. 'A routine
visit conscientiously paid every Sunday with one eye on the clock!'

Yet in spite of their differences in personality and outlook, Vera's love
and loyalty were the mainspring of her mother's life, and in her later years,
especially after her husband had become a semi-invalid, Edith Brittain had
often been supportive of her daughter's career and interests. She had joined
the Peace Pledge Union, and on one occasion in the Thirties had even
'shyly opened' a small appeal meeting for the Six Point Group.

In 1945, when Edith Brittain was in her late seventies and in failing
health, Vera was deeply concerned about how best she could give her
mother the practical and emotional support she needed. George kindly
suggested that she should live with them, but conscious of her mother's
meticulous habits, Vera repudiated this as 'an arrangement to which under
no circumstances of financial stringency will I ever consent. We should be
quarrelling within a week, and without staff within a fortnight ...'. Her
solution was to find her mother a flat close by in Rossetti Mansions in Flood
Street.

Here she visited Edith Brittain daily, but at the same time tactfully refrained from giving her a key to Cheyne Walk, knowing that she would call whenever she took it into her head, interrupting Vera's writing, and antagonizing the Burnetts, of whom she did not approve.

In April 1948, Mrs Brittain suffered a minor cerebral thrombosis, and further attacks left her confused and enfeebled. Vera arranged for twenty-four-hour nursing, but was almost constantly with her, and while her mother dozed she sat beside her bed, replying to letters or correcting the proofs of *Born 1925*. Edith Brittain died on 24 June 1948, five months before her eightieth birthday, and her death affected Vera more than she had thought possible. Vera's overwhelming grief suggests that the conflict between her love for her mother and her need to assert a separate identity remained unresolved to the end.

George was in America with John, and 'To break the post-funeral gloom, for her sake even more than my own', Vera took Shirley and Amy Burnett to the Aldous Huxley play, *The Gioconda Smile*. Afterwards they met Paul Berry, recently demobilized, for a late supper at the Arts Theatre Club. After a week of sleepless nights, Vera was pale and withdrawn; she ate little and only sporadically joined in the conversation. The following day she went alone to the Golders Green Crematorium to scatter her mother's ashes, and 'found myself weeping as I had never wept for Roland or Edward or Winifred.'

'I miss my mother almost unbelievably', she wrote a month later after clearing Mrs Brittain's flat in Flood Street. 'I can't believe that there is not still someone round the corner always longing for me to come, and running to the door the moment my key sounded in the lock.'

With her mother's death Vera, now fifty-four, became the trustee and beneficiary of her father's estate. In his will Arthur Brittain had included a trust for John and Shirley 'continuable at discretion for five years after they reach twenty-one'. Vera just 'loathed' being regarded as 'a "rich" woman' and 'an object of plunder for dependents of all kinds . . .', even if most of her money '*is* all going down the drain and benefiting me personally in no way at all . . .'. The sharp decline in her literary earnings had precipitated a financial crisis, and she was soon dismayed to find that it took all the trust income to pay the rent on 2 Cheyne Walk, the rates, the Burnetts' wages, and the day-to-day living expenses. 'Everything else', she pointed out to George, '[the children's] college fees, travel, and of course your £200 a year, clothes for myself and the children . . . have to come out of my literary earnings.'

She resented the fact that she was steadily being worn down by the strain of having to work in order to maintain a house of which she did not really approve. 'The belief that I *can't* relax', she told George, 'is everyone's illusion but mine.' She did not intend to give up the Cheyne Walk house while the children were still at college, but she proposed that eventually they should move to a modest flat where they would need only the minimum of domestic help. Just when this would take place was a matter for discussion, but she suggested that they should start to look for a suitable service flat.

George was unhappy with this proposal. He was deeply attached to the Georgian house, which in his mind he had always equated with the realization of his political hopes. But the irony of the situation was that he was unable to keep the house without her earnings. Beauty, cleanliness, and order, she must have, 'but ostentation I definitely detest – and we have come very close to it.' She was no longer prepared to live expensively and shoulder all the worry, and 'to that conclusion I have definitely come.'

In 1949, a year after Edith Brittain's death, the strains of their semi-detached marriage brought Vera and George to the brink of a separation. She insisted that she would never initiate a divorce unless he asked for one, and pointed out that the Catholic Church would not allow him to divorce her. No sudden row or extramarital affair precipitated the crisis. After twenty-four years of marriage they still spent as much time apart as together, due as much to Vera's commitments as to George's absences abroad and busy social life. She didn't resent the people he spent his time with, and 'you attribute too much anxiety on my part over your girlfriends. I haven't worried about them for years. I honestly don't think jealousy anyhow is one of my vices – I merely sometimes get disgusted with *myself* because other writers do better . . .'.

From the outset the inequality of their love for one another had caused friction and frustration. In 1925 George had been passionately and romantically in love, but the girl he married had 'never quite come to life', and in the Twenties and Thirties she had needed Winifred more than she needed him. He had concealed his hurt, and slowly evolved a self-protective veneer of independence and indifference.

Vera identified romantic enchantment with Roland. By 1921 it had been replaced by her literary ambitions, and her dedication to her work for peace and the continued liberation of women. She had also a strong impulse to get married, and knew that she would never find complete fulfilment without a home, husband and children. The difficulty of combining her career with marriage and motherhood remained the unresolved dilemma, and an underlying cause of their marital unhappiness: '. . . *not for anyone on earth* could I have rekindled the passions of twenty, or abandoned the dedication for a purely personal loyalty. That is the point; for *no one*. You weren't a failure; it was due to no lack in you; in so far as I could love anyone then, I *did* love you.'

She had believed that with openness, trust and affection it was possible to lead independent lives and still remain intimate, and to find her marriage in disarray caused her acute distress. 'Your remark in your study some weeks ago that you really didn't care if I quit the house and went off on my own', she wrote bitterly after one of George's franker outbursts, 'gave me the impression that your only reason for remaining yourself is that I am a convenience who pays for the things you want and otherwise couldn't have'. The marriage had survived many crises, and the threat that in middle age the whole fabric of her life might be torn apart filled her with despair. Relationships, she believed were 'cumulative achievements, to be built up by time and experience and treasured for that very reason'.

The turmoil of their relationship made her critical and short-tempered. In August 1949, she stayed for several weeks at Allum Green. She liked the family to come down one at a time as then she saw more of them individually, and there was less disruption. George preferred an urban life, and described the cottage as 'tolerable only in terms of a large party'. Vera at once took him to task. 'I adore this cottage and should like to live here permanently . . . If you dislike it so much you should never come. You are the only member of the family who doesn't love it. Don't spoil its pleasure for me and the others.' One day when they were all together at the cottage she could stand the interruptions and incessant conversation no longer. Her patience snapped, and beginning with John, she told each of them to take a train and leave the next day. George, conciliatory and good-natured, treated it as a joke and laughed, 'yet the fact remains that it just a bit hurts'.

Vera apologized. She had behaved badly; she had been unkind. In a sad revealing letter that followed George to London she explained that 'I *still* prefer being alone with you . . . It isn't so long since you did like being alone with me . . . What has changed? Am I now so boring? – or is it that a repressed jealousy and resentment has grown with the years? Thinking over this just now I was so preoccupied that I banged the lavatory door on my finger – and found myself weeping hard as I made my bed. I still don't know whether it was from physical or mental pain.'

That winter Vera spent two months in India attending the World Pacifist Meeting. At Suez on the voyage home she received two letters from George telling her he had been in bed for five days with influenza 'in a condition of general feverish misery'. Convinced that he had actual or incipient pneumonia – and perhaps tormented by the memory of their arguments and recriminations – she abandoned the ship and caught the first flight to Heathrow. George had made a quick recovery, and to her genuine relief she arrived to find him waiting for her in the airport lounge. In *Testament of Experience* she would say little about their difficulties and disagreements, but she referred to this incident as giving her new-found hope 'that our life together would go on'.

Although they had common interests in politics, writing and travel, Vera was in many other ways George's opposite. Shy – and he alleged 'unsociable' – she preferred small gatherings of one or two friends, whilst for him, gregarious and extrovert, social engagements were a major part of his life. He was an enthusiastic partygoer, he dined frequently at the Café Royal, the Garrick Club or the Savoy, and took a particular delight in entertaining political and academic colleagues to lunch or dinner at Cheyne Walk.

Harold Latham 'enjoyed many a dinner in the cheery dining room with the dumbwaiter popping up at appropriate moments from the regions below and presenting culinary triumphs from the kitchen'. He remembered:

> After dinner at the Catlins comes an evening of conversation before the open fire in the drawing room. Conversation is not a lost art in this household even if it is, as some maintain, elsewhere. And it is lively conversation, too, with George striding up and down the room, his hands clasped behind him, pausing now and then to warm himself at the fire and making some pronouncement to which Vera will very probably take immediate exception. There were always exchanges between the two; they often did not see eye to eye on some issue. It was refreshing, sometimes exciting, to see these intelligent clashes of opinion . . .

Harold Macmillan took a different view. After dinner one evening at Cheyne Walk, he found the intense discussion in the drawing-room distinctly heavy going and disappeared to the basement to listen instead to a boxing match on the Burnetts' radio.

Vera's first concern outside her immediate family was for her books. She resented the time and effort spent on entertaining George's friends, and was appalled at the idea of cultivating the influential and socially prominent. 'I definitely do *not* think of my social circle . . . as a means of getting on, or a source of "impeccable introductions" . . . I want to have no calculations in relation to the people I regard as my friends. I want to associate with people because I like them, and for no other reason. Deliberately to cultivate people "more important than myself" seems to me just terrible.'

She dismissed as 'just NOT TRUE' George's allegation that she did not like entertaining. What she objected to was entertaining in his way, ostentatiously, or in large groups, 'with some kind of *arrière pensée* . . . Like Winifred, I cannot and will not "calculate".'

At the same time she made it clear that she assumed neither a moral nor a mandatory right to tell him how he ought to lead his life. As his wife she was prepared to cooperate in his entertaining 'up to a point', but asked him not to involve her more than was strictly compatible with social etiquette and good manners.

In cooperating with George's entertaining Vera sometimes found that an affront to her principles was involved. Hugh Gaitskell, then leader of the Labour opposition, gives an account in his diary of a luncheon that George gave for the Mountbattens in the Fifties. Mountbatten did all the talking, saying that the country had to make the choice between being a world power and a land power, and suggesting that the land forces in Europe should be given up, and that the navy was the best base from which to fly atom-bombers. 'Mrs Catlin is a pacifist', Gaitskell noted in his diary, 'and therefore not particularly interested in hearing Mountbatten put forward his views on defence . . .'. As the host, George was cock-a-hoop, but Vera was ill-at-ease. For George's sake she played a low-key role and said little about her pacifist beliefs, but she would almost certainly have agreed with Gaitskell that, 'on the whole, the lunch, was, I thought, rather a ghastly failure.'

In his autobiography George would write that 'my world was not entirely Vera's, although they overlapped.' Indeed, she was convinced that some of his friends actively disliked her. She believed that Dick Crossman, as Assistant Editor of the *New Statesman* from 1938 to 1955, had deliberately continued the journal's policy of belittling her, and of 'almost always reviewing my books badly.'

Their different religious faiths caused few problems. George never tried to persuade her to become a Roman Catholic, and she made no attempt to convert him to her Anglican pacifism, 'which you could not adopt, though I think you respect it in me just as I do Catholicism in you'. When she was in London she regularly attended St Martin-in-the-Fields, but when abroad often went with George to a Catholic Mass and, later, on a brief holiday in Italy in the Sixties they attended an impressive papal audience in St Peter's in Rome.

But the repercussions from her pacifism caused George considerable agitation, which Vera did her best to dispel. In 1952 she received a letter from Doris Lessing asking her to sign a British authors' petition for clemency for the American atomic spies Julius and Ethel Rosenberg. At that time George had an appointment at the University of California as a Visiting Professor, and Vera replied that she deeply regretted being unable to do so because 'any protest I might make to the American Administration would inevitably fall on him and not on me. This would be exceedingly unfair since he is not a pacifist, and though very tolerant, does not share my point of view in many respects'. Writing to George she told him that she hadn't signed the appeal, entirely for his sake. 'This is one of those occasions when integrity becomes very difficult. What is integrity when one can't stand up for one's convictions without asking another person who doesn't believe in them to pay the cost?'

George often pointed out to Vera that as well as reflecting adversely on him, it was highly unintelligent to allow her pacifist activities to absorb so much of her time, and to impair her already declining literary prestige. He urged her to stick to writing, and to keep quiet about her pacifist views 'because they are so inconvenient for both of us'. Vera admitted in her weaker moments she was sorely tempted to do just that, but 'pacifism is to me what Catholicism is to you ... It is my creed, my faith, my real Church, my profound obligation ...'.

In spite of their differences, they finally decided that their unconventional marriage offered more advantages than disadvantages. It gave them the freedom they both wanted, and provided also the security and reassurance of family life, however unorthodox.

In June 1950 they celebrated their silver wedding. George was delighted to have an opportunity for large scale entertaining, and on this occasion Vera was equally pleased to have a party for her friends. They decided to keep the guests separate, with an early evening 'At Home' from five to seven for hers, and a later supper party for his. More than ninety people converged on Cheyne Walk for Vera's 'At Home', and 'to our astonishment we received no less than fifty gifts, almost more than at our original wedding ... It was great fun but [the] next day I had almost lost the use of my legs!'

That Christmas George and Shirley went to Rome for the final festivities of the Holy Year, while Vera and John entertained his Oxford friend and contemporary, Raghavan Iyer, the Indian Rhodes Scholar from Bombay. Vera was herself an Anglican but believed in 'complete religious toleration'. She had explained to John in 1948, 'I wanted to leave you and Shirley free to choose [your religion], and not take the more comfortable but also the more cowardly method of choosing for you ...'. In his youth John had been an Anglican, but at eighteen he became a Catholic. Writing to a friend at Christmas 1950, however, Vera told him that John was 'now a

Protestant; he was never happy in the Catholic Church', but he subsequently re-adopted Catholicism. His religious ambivalence is one indication of the restless temperament which was to cause his mother such distress.

II

Her increasingly unhappy and often painful relationship with John preyed constantly on Vera's mind after his return from America, and was to be a source of sorrow right up to Vera's death more than twenty-five years later.

She recognized that John had inherited many of the Brittains' less attractive characteristics, and thought that it was, after all, her own father, rather than Edward, whom he most closely resembled as he grew older. But she could not believe that heredity alone was responsible for his perverse, materialistic personality. She confided to Shirley that it had been a big mistake to send him to America, 'for I think it knocked the security from his existence and left him rudderless . . . I feel if he had never been far removed from family influences he would never have changed as he did, even in adolescence . . . We behaved unfairly to John but the on-coming war was really responsible; "old sins have long shadows".'

Perhaps reflecting that her First World War experiences had been the cathartic influence in her own life, Vera was now certain that John was the wrong person to have been spared the dangers and hardships of war. She maintained that, safe, comfortable and well-fed, he had thought only of himself, with the result 'that he has neither the insight into, nor pity for, what five years of war have meant . . . The worst thing is his deliberate sadism, deliberately exercised against those who are vulnerable.'

John was well aware of Vera's irreconcilable regret abbout sending him to America. He provocatively declared that he had never felt homesick, and that he had regarded it 'as an adventure to look forward to, rather than the break-up of our family.' People outside the family, however, had no doubt that he had had a difficult time settling down to life in St Paul. Shirley had made friends easily while John, though accepted by the other boys at his school, had been less sociable. He had never much cared for Ruth Colby, whom he found humourless, and he had resented her insistence that he helped with the household chores. He later admitted that he had asserted his independence by being disagreeable and rebellious.

However, if Vera thought that it had been a serious misjudgement to have sent him to America, John was convinced that it had been a worse blunder to have insisted on his returning home in 1943. In America he had possessed freedom from parental pressures; he believed in retrospect that he would have had better opportunities to study art; and he was indignant at being separated from the girl with whom he had fallen in love at a Minnesota Summer School when he was thirteen-and-a-half.

Following his return from America, the relationship between John and his parents had deteriorated rapidly. He had grown up expecting George to be away from home for long periods, and as the permanent presence and family exchequer, Vera was an irresistible target for his adolescent hostility and sarcastic criticism. He resented the hours she spent alone in her study, and was convinced that her books mattered more to her than her family. He deplored her preoccupation with her own prestige and pacifist causes, and 'persistently pin-pricks and chivvies me', she wrote to George.

During the Christmas holiday at Allum Green in January 1945 he was for several days cooperative and equable. He made his bed, brought in logs, and worked in the garden, but suddenly without warning he indulged in a noisy bout of anti-mother criticism. 'The richest people always imagine they are poor', he retorted when Vera protested at some new extravagance, and 'his remark about my "precise and vinegary face" devastated me so much I was incapable of commenting'.

John admitted that he said whatever came into his head, without thinking. 'Well, that is characteristic of all my family, including myself; our motto ought to have been "Set a watch at the door of my lips, O Lord". What matters is not so much that John has inherited this characteristic . . . but that he should *care* enough, as I have cared, about kindness and decency as ends in themselves . . . The trouble is not that I feel resentment against him, for I don't, but that my own sense of inferiority is deepened'.

George was well aware of John's difficult, unpredictable behaviour. Not wishing to become embroiled in family quarrels, he usually took the line of least resistance and stood aside, but on this occasion he promised Vera he would take a strong line. 'Of *course* I didn't want you to slang, scold or thrash poor John', she replied, 'but only to point out to him at some suitable moment how devastating the effects of his tongue can be. I admit that I haven't any right to judge him for making me suffer as I have made others suffer, but the fact that I didn't even begin to try to conquer this tendency for years is really not a good reason for him to take an indefinite licence to indulge it.'

John was fifteen-and-a-half when he returned to England in 1943. At a loose end and without close friends, he decided to look for a temporary job, and Vera arranged with Christina Foyle for him to be employed in the second-hand department of the Charing Cross Road bookshop. Impatient, and quickly bored with the routine and repetition, he relieved the tedium by spending most of his wages on antiquarian biographies and books of poetry. He didn't read them, and remarked in later life that he believed a passion for collecting to be a substitute for a satisfying human relationship.

That autumn he went back to school. The fact that he knew no Latin prevented him from taking the Eton entrance examination, and after various enquiries and several interviews it was decided that he should go to Harrow. On account of the difficult transition from American to English education, he was allowed considerable latitude, and in spite of the school's long tradition for games he was excused both cricket and football. He was also the only boy to be exempted from the Army Cadet Corps. He claimed that this was in deference to his mother's pacifism, but as he strongly disagreed with her beliefs it is more probable that they provided a useful pretext to avoid the military discipline and physical training he disliked.

While at Harrow he decided that he would like to be an architect. George approved, but Vera was disappointed. She believed not only in the lasting value of an academic training, but also that university life provided the fertile soil in which lifelong friendships took root and flourished. She agreed with the headmaster that John should have stayed at school and attempted the New College scholarship examination.

John enrolled in the school of the Architectural Association in the autumn of 1945, and was quickly disillusioned. A large part of the initial training consisted of mathematics and drawings of exacting accuracy, which he found 'excruciating, monotonous and dull', and it was almost a relief when at the end of the first term he received his National Service call-up papers for the RAF.

In January 1946, at just eighteen, he reported to the RAF recruitment centre in Padgate. Always more concerned about him than about George and Shirley, Vera admitted being anxious and depressed, for 'though I know I must want hardship and not only smooth places for him . . . I do wish it wouldn't rain so, and there wasn't a 'flu epidemic'.

For John the main attraction of National Service was the prospect of an overseas posting, and at the end of May he was drafted to a small embarkation unit in Port Said. As the unit clerk he had little to do, and with none of Shirley's friendly rapport with other people he felt lonely and bored. National Service was a waste of time, he wrote to Vera, and asked her to do all she could to obtain a university place to enable him to apply for an early discharge.

Vera had disciplined herself to write her books in the morning, but replied immediately after breakfast, 'because after all you are a priority even over my work'. She felt rather to blame because she should have persuaded him to stay at school and try for a university scholarship. Had he done so he would not have been conscripted, but she had been reluctant to be too emphatic because he would have suspected that her real reason was a pacifist objection, 'though it wasn't; I am not a fanatic'.

She promised to contact the Harrow headmaster, and had asked George to make appointments with the New College Warden and Professor of Philosophy. 'I am sure they will do all they can, but . . . you could hardly expect, and I am sure would not wish, to be put in front of some young man (called up like Paul Berry, just after leaving school) who has spent six years of hell in, say, Burma and at 25 or 26 is exactly where you are today.'

'Your impatience is your worst quality . . . I know precisely how hard it is to conquer, because it is my own worst fault, too . . . So, my dear John, be patient. Be assured that we will both do our best . . .'.

Unhappy and actively disliking the rough-and-ready service life, John decided in the autumn of 1946 to apply for a commission on the assumption that 'this would at least provide some novelty'. The first step was a thorough medical examination. This revealed a tubercular patch on his left lung, and for the next two months he was confined to hospital in Ismalia. He had, he wrote despondently, 'exchanged the golden treasures of my home life for a stone wall', but it was not until she passed through Ismalia on her way to Port Said more than a decade later that Vera realized that this was not a symbolic reference but a literal description.

Upset and anxious, she wrote almost daily and sent regular parcels of books and magazines. His replies were 'thoughtful and often beautiful', but the temptation to criticize her persisted. She explained that her concern about the length of his letters was practical and not sentimental, because she was worried about him writing when he should have been resting. He had also conceived the idea that she regarded his letters as public property, and she convinced him only with difficulty that she never showed them to anyone but George. 'I think I can honestly say that I have never attempted to conceal anything from you in my letters', she wrote, 'except perhaps the extent of my affection . . . you once told me you did not share it, and . . . I don't want to bore you.'

'My problem is that I love him without, as yet, liking him,' she confided to George.

In December, John was transferred to a larger, better-equipped hospital on the Mount of Olives. From here in mid-January 1947 he was repatriated to an RAF convalescent hospital in South Wales. 'We have already been down there and found him very lively, and delighted to be home again and out of Palestine', Vera reported. He looked well, his temperature was normal, and the X-rays showed a marked improvement. 'St Athan, of all back-of-beyond places, is right on the Bristol Channel and the air is wonderful, so the inconvenience to us is nothing.'

When later transferred to George V Sanatorium at Hydestile in Surrey he was already well on the road to recovery. As he was less than an hour by train from Waterloo, Vera visited him regularly. Shirley on one occasion decided to cycle, 'and will therefore make the excuse that she must wear old clothes', Vera warned John. 'I am tired of talking to her about her appearance.'

Although ostensibly studying for his university entrance examination, John spent most of his time writing poetry, and, more ambitiously, an oratorio, which he asked Vera to read. She was impressed, she told him, with the simplicity of his work, and his ability to adapt to the demands and limitations of such an enterprise. Shirley had thought it sentimental, 'but she may be wrong, because she has not experienced enough to know that something which has to get to the public through *two* media – both words and music – must be more obvious and even crude . . .'. The distinction between sentimentality and true emotion was much more a matter of taste and feeling than definition. A word or a phrase which was sentimental in one context was not necessarily so in another, 'nor can one even say that a *cliché* is always out of place'. One has to learn by practice, empirically, and she was very pleasantly surprised by his knowledge and understanding of the difference between sincerity and insincerity.

After his discharge from the sanatorium in the summer of 1947 John had more than a year to fill in before going to Oxford. He returned for a few weeks to the second-hand book department in Foyle's, and later, through George Brett and Harold Latham, Vera arranged for him to acquire practical publishing experience with the Macmillan Company in New York. He was now nearly twenty, and she believed that his difficult adolescent years were at last behind him.

'John and Shirley went up to Oxford last week and both seem quite happy,' she wrote in October 1948. 'John decided in the end to do a new Philosophy and Psychology School, not Literature. Shirley of course is keeping to politics.'

Vera and George had impressed upon John the many advantages of a university education, but, aware of his likely reaction to parental advice, they left him free to make his own decisions. In going to New College he may have felt he had complied with their wishes, but that in applying for Philosophy and Psychology he had asserted his independence and free will.

He was at Cheyne Walk only during the college vacations, but his attitude to Vera remained critical and aggressive. 'His continued adolescent anti-mother complex deeply disturbs me,' she wrote to George in the summer of 1950, 'no patience or gentleness or generosity seems to touch it . . . I am not so much concerned with the effect of his continued sadism on me, as on himself. If it wears me out, as it definitely is doing, well, I have had the best of my life . . . But for him it means that his treatment of me will eventually be transferred to his wife or mistress . . . No good can come out of continual cruelty to a woman for the person who is cruel, let alone to her; in the end it will destroy him . . . I don't expect him to love me – it is clear that he doesn't – but I don't want him to hurt and ruin himself.'

She frequently asked herself where she had failed in John's upbringing, and was particularly anxious when he returned to Oxford after the spring vacation and for more than a fortnight she heard nothing at all. When Edith de Coundouroff called, Vera confided how concerned she was, and, perhaps trying to console her, Edith replied that if she had had a son she hoped he would have been like John. 'Perhaps she would have handled him more wisely than we have, being more "homely" and less easily exasperated,' Vera reflected.

Edith de Coundouroff, a kind, motherly woman, died in 1956, but her daughter, Margaret, remembers that she 'always saw a great deal of good in John, and was very fond of him . . .'. After he returned from America he sometimes dropped in at her Fulham flat to have tea, and after the formality at Cheyne Walk he clearly enjoyed the relaxed atmosphere and light-hearted conversation. At one of his parents' cocktail parties he met Edith de Coundouroff at the door. 'Hello, Aunt Edith. Come in', he greeted her, adding, 'this house is more of a house than ever, and even less of a home'.

Vera admitted that she was not easy to live with. Her preoccupation with cleanliness, tidiness and punctuality – in which, ironically, she had come to resemble her own mother – provoked frequent arguments, and John told her that it was 'too much to expect everyone to attain your own high standards'. She told him she agreed with Rose Macaulay, 'Better a house unkept than a life unlived', but that she found it difficult to put this principle into practice 'because a house wholly unkept would be intolerable to me . . . I don't *want* to be a disciplinarian . . . or glorified housekeeper, demanding standards from people that are mine, not theirs, and yet I hate to see things done badly. Only from Charles [Burnett] do I get perpetual spontaneous co-operation – except sometimes when you are at home . . .'.

Before the end of his first year at Oxford, John had found the lectures, tutorials and essays more demanding than he had expected. The fact that the syllabus of the Psychology/Philosophy School was comparatively new probably created problems for him as it was less tried and tested than those for long-established schools like History and English Literature. In spite of his difficulties John was pleased to be away from home. He had several girlfriends, and Oxford afforded a diverting round of social activities.

Aware that Vera was financially worried because of her reduced royalty income, Mrs Brittain had offered to pay John's college fees, but when she died four months before he went to Oxford the responsibility had reverted to Vera. She also made him a generous allowance to cover the cost of his lodgings, food, clothes, books and general expenses, but, like his father, a free and easy spender, he was frequently short of money.

Vera maintained meticulous household accounts, prepared advance budgets, and constantly exhorted George to follow her example and to pay his bills 'on the nail'. She was careful but generous, and apart from travel and clothes, had no extravagances. She had more interest in propagating her beliefs than in making money, and her future daughter-in-law – who nicknamed her 'The Bush Baby', because of her small stature and large eyes – described her lifestyle as 'fundamentally ascetic'.

She felt deep compassion for the afflicted and less fortunate, and John believed that she spent money on other people that should have been kept in the family. During the war, when Ailsa Trickett, her diminutive Sheffield fan, was in hospital for three months with a serious heart complaint, Vera sent paperbacks, money for flowers, and the whole of her sweet ration, and anonymously paid for her to go to a Quaker guest house to convalesce. She insisted on paying for a holiday for Charles Kett, her accountant, who had been seriously ill with a perforated ulcer; she sent a cheque for £100 to Patricia Battey of the Winifred Holtby Writers' Circle when she heard that her house had been destroyed by fire; and when she and George moved to a flat in Whitehall Court she lent the Burnetts £750 to start a café (which never actually got off the ground): '. . . when I see how other people's domestic "helps" behave I realize they are worth everything'.

Convinced that since Mrs Brittain's death Vera was a rich woman, John's latest form of persecution 'is trying to squeeze money out of me'. She said he had too little to do during the college vacations, and urged him to return to Foyle's, or to find some other temporary job. 'It is really disgraceful that a young man of twenty-two, no longer ill and perfectly able-bodied now, should badger me to pay for his suit and his railway fares instead of maintaining his self-respect by going out and earning. I should say the same if I were a millionaire.'

He had inherited the Brittain attitude that money was about the most important thing in life, 'and he sees people in terms of it. We may not like this, but it is one of those facts that one has simply to accept. You can't change him . . .'. What Vera, perhaps, was unable to contemplate was that John demanded money from her to test the limits of her affection and to punish her for not being available when he wanted her.

She showed remarkable prescience, though, in her prediction that 'as long as I stand between John and what he regards as "his" money, so long as I have any financial control over him, there will never be any peace between us. The older he grows, the more he will keep a hawk's eye on what I do with "his" money . . .'.

John's persistent demands for money caused Vera constant anxiety, but she was more perplexed than worried by his endless stream of girlfriends. She said he had been chasing them ever since he was fourteen, 'and proposing to them from about the age of eighteen . . . some of the many were quite unsuitable, and round about the age of twenty he developed a predilection for hospital nurses which filled me with gloom'.

During his second year at university, John fell in love with Jennifer Manasseh, a first-year undergraduate of twenty-one studying English at Lady Margaret Hall. She was the fourth of five children of wealthy parents, 'but I honestly don't think John knew this as he proposed to her at Oxford before he had seen her comfortable Kensington home'. John impetuously decided to announce their engagement immediately, but Mr Manasseh 'very wisely' stepped in and insisted that he must first find a job. John announced that his real ambition was to be a stockbroker, and Vera was relieved when after several interviews he accepted a job in the Publicity Department of Plant Protection at an annual salary of £475.

She was 'glad beyond words' that John was at last happily engaged, and, as a future daughter-in-law, Jennifer was an immediate success. Vera told her friends that as well as being beautiful and elegant, Jennifer was also amiable, calm, capable and self-possessed, and the ideal counterpart to John's volatile temperament. Jennifer's first impression of Vera was of a very small, tired-looking woman, and after her Campden Hill home, Cheyne Walk seemed gloomy, cold and inexpensively furnished. She felt that George had all the quixotic qualities of Dickens's William Dorrit.

The children of eminent parents have a heavy cross to bear. Vera told John bluntly that his third-class degree was disgraceful, and that he had squandered his chances by virtually abandoning his studies while pursuing Jennifer. She admitted that 'a mediocre degree doesn't matter as much in business as in professions'.

She had no reservations about his marriage. The Manassehs agreed to an Anglican wedding provided a ceremony first took place in a synagogue. In spite of numerous enquiries no synagogue would accept them and they were married at Kensington Register Office on 12 December 1951. Vera lavished gifts on the young couple: securities valued at £1,000, and a house, estimated to be worth £1,200, which George had inherited in Leamington Spa and which she had bought from him, as well as more than thirty household items, many of which had belonged to her mother.

On the eve of John's twenty-fourth birthday Vera and George saw them off on a delayed honeymoon in Paris, and although the wedding had torpedoed all Vera's Christmas plans, 'my feelings were of total and unmitigated relief'.

Her relief, however, was short-lived. Fog disrupted John and Jennifer's air flight to France, and their hastily improvised travel arrangements involved a rough overnight Channel crossing from Southampton to Le Havre. In Paris in cold, wet, winter weather their honeymoon was a strenuous round of sightseeing, galleries and entertainment, and John returned home with a persistent cold. An infection of the right lung developed, and early in February he was admitted to the Brompton Hospital.

Vera was deeply distressed. 'I want to wrap him up and deposit him on some sunny balcony far away.' She visited him almost daily, bewildered by his fluctuating moods of vindictive criticism and almost jaunty cheerfulness. George was in Colombo, and on 6 February she told him that she had that afternoon found John in one of his worst moods, 'ready to turn every trifle into a quarrel and work himself into a passion about nothing . . . I can only think he has some compelling need to turn all his resentment and anxiety over what is admittedly a very hard fate into a weapon against somebody whom he can safely treat as a safety-valve, and I am the only one of whose endurance he can be sure. But it is hard when one is all alone . . . His attitude to me was something as close to hatred as if he had been brought up by parents who loathed each other, or in a bad home, or by a possessive, domineering mother. But none of those things *have* handicapped him; Poppy's lovely charitable character could not have grown from a bad home . . .'.

Taking Amy Burnett with her the following day 'as a precaution', she found him 'as cheerful as he had been savage the day before – glorying in the fact that he had decided to remain in his private room at eleven guineas a week instead of taking the free bed offered him . . .'. The doctors attributed his illness to an obscure physical cause, but Vera wondered whether some psychological factor might not also have played a part, and if he had inherited the Brittain propensity for psychosomatic illness.

For Jennifer she had nothing but praise. She spent every afternoon with John, 'not talking much but just reassuring him by her presence . . . I do admire her for never uttering one word of complaint or self-pity'. Over dinner one evening she discovered that John's money – apart from the capital she had given him to renovate the Leamington Spa house – had all been spent and that Jennifer was proposing to break into her own savings. 'This I forbade', Vera told George, and she at once sent John a cheque for £25 to pay for his hospital room, with a promise of a further payment the following month. The next day she arranged an annuity of £250, and 'if need be I could make another covenant of £150 in the autumn'.

After a six-week course of streptomycin injections, John left hospital at the end of March. Vera helped to finance his convalescence at Worthing, and told George that John would continue to have all the money she could spare. 'You are better able to work than he . . . and can always get a job if you wish.' With characteristic generosity Shirley volunteered that he should have all the family money available; she didn't need it, and could always earn.

Early in September John obtained a job with a light-engineering firm, but was quickly disenchanted with the nine to five routine of office work. After a few weeks he proposed to give in his notice and concentrate on becoming a freelance artist. It was some years since he had taken art seriously and Vera thought that if he was at home all day he would drive both Jennifer and himself crazy. Shirley urged him to consult a job counsellor, and told Vera that she was sure that business bored him, 'but I wonder if a job in buying antiques or old furniture or even in real estate or decorating would? . . . I am certain that John without a definite job will go to pieces, and next time he must take a long time choosing and then really stick to it'.

III

Vera had long recognized that she and Shirley were unalike in temperament, but she believed that Shirley had acquired from her an aptitude for public speaking and a capacity for sustained and concentrated effort. She was, Vera said, 'one of the most gifted natural speakers that I have ever known', having 'addressed us all on political subjects since childhood, and hence being totally free from all nervousness or inhibitions.' Vera thought that Shirley also possessed several other characteristics which were essential prerequisites for the aspiring politician. One was her tendency to categorize everything: '. . . for her black is jet black and white is dead white. There are no greys.' Another was the 'spiritual pride' which made her refuse ever to admit that she was wrong; and from her paternal grand-mother, Edith Kate Catlin, Vera felt sure that Shirley had inherited 'an intense private reserve' which at times amounted to 'a pathological secretiveness . . . totally inconsistent with her open, friendly disposition.'

On returning to England in October 1943, Shirley had gone daily to St Paul's Girls' School in Hammersmith. At the age of thirteen she was an independent, precocious adolescent, and her secretiveness, combined with her 'untidiness, unpunctuality and sheer naughtiness', frequently drove Vera to distraction. When the air raids on London had resumed in February 1944, Vera had been beside herself with anxiety one night when Shirley vanished with Sheila Francis, Amy Burnett's younger sister, to watch a tobacco factory burning on the other side of the Thames. The next day, without a word to anyone, she disappeared again to cycle around Fulham inspecting the bomb damage.

When her school suffered considerable damage during the raids, Shirley spent three months in Cambridge, staying with her friend, Rosemary Roughton, whom she had met on the *Serpo Pinto* on the return voyage from the United States. In the autumn of 1944 she attended Talbot Heath School in Bournemouth. During the general election, the following summer, she went to many political meetings. On one occasion when she asked the Conservative candidate an awkward question, he protested, 'Surely this young lady hasn't got a vote?' 'People don't believe in him and he doesn't believe in himself', she commented sagely after another meeting.

In September 1945 she returned to St Paul's, and Vera admitted that she was constantly baffled about how to modify what she saw as her daughter's shortcomings. After a visit from Ruth Colby in 1946, Vera complained that Shirley had made a point of wearing especially old and dirty clothes, and keeping her hair as untidy as possible. Shirley told her mother that she had been afraid that Ruth would be too demonstrative, but Vera pointed out that Ruth was too practised in self-restraint to be effusive. Shirley 'can look very nice when she chooses', Vera wrote to John. 'I bought her a long royal blue evening frock in which she looks charming – *when* she wears it, about once in three months!'

At St Paul's, Shirley took the School Certificate, Ordinary Level, but left before she was old enough to sit the Advanced Level examination. Like her mother, Shirley had always known what she wanted to do. Politics had captured her interest from an early age, and at the age of five she had told Vera that when she grew up she was going to be a member of the Agricultural Workers' Union. Now her intention was to go to the London School of Economics and she baulked at Vera's suggestion that she sit the Somerville entrance examination. Nevertheless she took the exam and in the autumn of 1947 she was awarded a Somerville History Scholarship. When she went up the following year she changed schools to read Politics, Philosophy and Economics. In the meantime she worked for several months farming in Essex, and during the summer as a chambermaid in a Whitley Bay hotel as she claimed that she knew nothing about life in the north-east of England.

Gregarious, and with multifarious interests and inexhaustible vitality, Shirley's three years at Somerville became a hectic round of extracurricular activities. To her tutors' consternation she was almost immediately immersed in undergraduate politics, and in the Oxford University Dramatic Society – and she fell in love.

Peter Parker, a Lincoln College undergraduate six years her senior, was also a member of OUDS. He spent many weekends with his family in Bedford, and in the autumn of 1948 Vera was also there working on her Bunyan biography. Shirley frequently stayed with her at the De Parys Hotel, an ideal arrangement for seeing both her mother and Peter. George had a poor opinion of Peter Parker. He didn't consider him good enough for his eighteen-year-old daughter and protested, perhaps a little prematurely, that Shirley was in danger of wrecking her political career by drifting into 'careless matrimony'.

Vera empathized with Peter Parker, who had lost two older brothers on active service with the RAF in the war, and on closer acquaintance she liked him 'better and better'. She sent him two photographs of Shirley and in thanking her he mentioned that he and his mother were nursing his terminally ill grandmother. 'When he wrote me he had been sitting up with her all night from 1 a.m. to spare his mother,' she told George. 'A boy who can act *King Lear* before a crowd of adoring undergraduates and then humbly turn to nurse his dying grandmother is admirable, I think . . . My doubt now is that she is worthy of *him* – too immature for a boy who has been, and is going, through such deep waters.'

Shirley believed she had only a one-in-three chance of being selected when she auditioned for the part of Cordelia in the OUDS production of

King Lear, and was delighted to be successful. During the 1950 summer vacation they embarked on an American tour of universities from New York to Ohio, and from Massachusetts to Indiana. Writing from Purdue University, Indiana, she told Vera that they were playing to 'the most incredible crush of hicks and clots who seem to find much of this play very funny . . . One could shake these people until they learned to weep with the world'.

In the Michaelmas term of 1948, the Labour Club had invited Vera to address a small lunch-time meeting. Peter Parker was the Chairman, and Shirley, in her first term at Somerville, 'was the rawest of freshers'. 'I was . . . obviously scared stiff that she would mention me', and as Vera spoke Shirley nervously tore her programme to shreds. Vera believed that Shirley's anxiety betrayed a lack of confidence in her competence as a lecturer, and in view of her experience on both sides of the Atlantic she considered it to be oddly illogical. 'I forgave her because that particular audience was largely composed of her undergraduate friends and if I *had* made a fool of myself it would have been a pity, but I continued to think her apprehensions a little unrealistic'.

Two years later Shirley was herself elected Chairman of the Labour Club. '. . . so that particularly feminist idea of breaking up the run of men since the beginning has come off', she wrote to her mother. 'But, dear me, the work this means. I wonder if and whether I'll ever get a degree'. She was also the Features Editor of the undergraduate magazine *Isis*, and was not alone in her anxiety about her academic prospects. Somerville's Senior Common Room persistently protested that her acting and Labour Club activities seriously jeopardized her academic studies, that her attendance at lectures and tutorials was erratic, and her written work scrappy and late. Finally, Janet Vaughan, the Principal, warned her that unless her tutors reported a marked improvement her scholarship would be withdrawn.

Shirley responded, and to master the complexities of Philosophy she enlisted the help of her friend Bernard Williams, a Balliol Greats Scholar who had come up in 1947, and who graduated with her in 1951. In January 1950 she wrote to Vera, who was in Madras, that she was 'working like crazy', and concluded that 'John and I were discussing last night how . . . really intensely we were missing you. I know when I was coming home, the idea of going into Cheyne Walk without you being there had no appeal at all.'

In October 1950 Vera received a letter from the Somerville Treasurer apologizing for the long delay in sending the bill for Shirley's fees. She explained that as there was a possibility that her scholarship would be withdrawn it had been held back until after the Education Committee had met and discussed the matter, and that 'as her period of probation has now happily been brought to an end we have taken account of the scholar's allowance of £30'. After her finals the following year Vera admitted that Shirley was lucky to have achieved a good second, but agreed with Janet Vaughan that 'she had contributed far more to Oxford life than a high class in Schools'.

Shortly after graduating, Shirley acquired practical political experience as the Labour Agent for Chelsea in the October 1951 general election, and the following January sailed for New York to take up a Smith-Mundt scholarship to study Trades-Unionism at Columbia University. Her relationship with Peter Parker had ended. Her new boyfriend, Roger Bannister, the first man to run a mile in under four minutes, had promised to say goodbye at Waterloo, but his train from Harrow was delayed. He sprinted through pedestrians and traffic and ran along the platform waving as the boat-train gathered speed and disappeared out of sight. Vera and George went with Shirley to Southampton. The next day Vera wrote apologizing for being so tearful, due, she said, as much to Shirley's depression as to her own unhappiness 'at having to face being without her for a year'.

IV

After John and Shirley left Oxford, Vera and George put in hand the sale of the Cadogan Estate lease for Cheyne Walk. They considered numerous properties before deciding on a modest first-floor flat in 4 Whitehall Court with two large south-facing rooms overlooking the Embankment. This large residential complex had its own restaurant and room service, and its proximity to Charing Cross, Trafalgar Square, St Martin's and the Strand was an added inducement. It had once housed authors and other celebrities, including Bernard Shaw and Sir Adrian Boult, 'but was now regarded as a "venue" of the *nouveaux riches* . . .', with the smaller two-room flats providing a pied-à-terre for rich country people. 'I am amused to find that we are definitely among the proletarians in this extensive Whitehall Court set-up', Vera wrote to George. Most of the residents had their own servants besides the 'service', and the maid who cleaned their apartment daily told her that some of the large corner and top-floor flats were 'like museums'. 'However, I am well content . . . 2 Cheyne Walk was all the magnificence *I* ever want, and I am glad to be quit of keeping up appearances on too little money'.

George commented disconsolately that his dream of political achievement was now over. Vera agreed and replied that 'I am afraid Poppy with her dynamically honest disposition will find it a difficult job, and in the end will probably lose out by refusing to compromise'.

She told George that the Upper House rather than the Lower would now be a more realistic objective, 'but how one could set about it . . . I just don't know. Have you any ideas of anything I could do without being regarded as a "pusher" . . . which would indeed be ludicrous, since for my own part I should heartily dislike a title and would never use it.'

Less than ten days after Shirley sailed for America in January 1952, Vera travelled to Tilbury to see George off on a three-and-a-half-month lecture-tour of India, south-east Asia and Australia, and 'the solitary sojourn begins which I have dreaded . . . ever since I first realized that you would all be going off together'.

Preparatory to the Catlins moving to Whitehall Court, the Burnetts had taken a Chelsea council flat, but continued to go to Cheyne Walk daily. Alone at night Vera found 'the dark empty house all round me made me sick with a sense of loneliness and of missing you both'. Single-handed she tackled the fifteen-year accumulation of family possessions and was 'up clearing half the night'. There were 'so many stairs [her study was on the fifth floor], so many dead papers, so many books'.

In February 1952, in deep snow and falling temperatures, she gave three lectures in Sheffield, and stayed briefly in Halifax with Phyllis Bentley, whose house without central heating was cold and cheerless, and she returned to London tired and depressed. A fortnight later she was tempted to cancel long-standing lecture engagements in Bolton, Nottingham and Mansfield. 'They will all expect me to be attractive and stimulating, but I never felt less like inspiring anybody.'

In London she was besieged with commitments: a PPU rally at Central Hall, articles for *Peace News*, an All-India Radio broadcast, and a Six Point Group meeting at Cheyne Walk, and she told George that he was making her life impossible with all the jobs he wanted her to do. She was 'quite worn out' telephoning, answering his letters and searching through files, '. . . and if I were trying to write *Testament of Experience* – as I should be in the autumn – it would drive me crackers. The moral of all this is that you must appoint someone – if necessary a Peter Jones secretary – *all the while* you are in America.'

Early in May she returned home, after visiting John and Jennifer, with a temperature of 102 degrees and a severe attack of flu. She had only partially recovered when she succumbed to an attack of bronchitis, and never forgot 'the horrible solitary nights at 2 Cheyne Walk when I felt so ill and listened for every sound'. She was still convalescing and suffering from a chronic cough when George returned a fortnight later.

The Catlins moved to Whitehall Court on 17 June, and a few days later George left London for a series of Summer School lectures in Kansas City University, following by an eight-month teaching appointment at the University of California. The rediscovery of his early work in political science had produced a number of invitations to lecture. Vera had still not fully recovered, and an X-ray revealed a patch on one lung. Partly to convalesce, but primarily to help tackle a family crisis, she spent three weeks with Aunt Belle at her home in Kingsdown on the outskirts of Deal.

Belle, the youngest and only surviving Bervon sister – Lillie had died in April at the age of eighty – had inherited the investment income from the estate of her sister Florence, as well as taking on Frances, Florence's personal maid from 1915 to 1936. With a limited income she found it increasingly difficult to maintain the upkeep of her large house and garden, and in old age had become demanding and cantankerous. She paid Frances thirty shillings a week as her companion-cook and expected her to be always on call. At the end of her tether, Frances said she was leaving. Vera insisted that Frances must have half-days and regular free time, and when Belle raged about her 'daring to go off', Vera told her firmly that Frances 'was a wonderful woman', underpaid, and entitled to some life of her own. 'Of course Belle made one of the scenes I loathe, stormed, wept, and said she would never sleep, though she was snoring loudly an hour later.' Until Belle died on Christmas Day 1954 Vera regularly sent her money to pay for extra help and, as the residuary beneficiary of the Florence Bervon estate, she made Frances an annuity for life.

At Whitehall Court, Vera was living alone for the first time in her life. The flat was comfortable and reassuring after the echoing emptiness of Cheyne Walk, but the prolonged chaos of moving, a series of minor illnesses, and George's absence had taken a heavy toll of her morale. She felt weighed down with a sense of deadness, and constantly below par. From Kansas George did his best to restore her confidence. 'One fights and fights to recapture the early sense of worthwhileness, to recapture the sense of dedication,' he told her. 'We flog ourselves too hard and the poor brute of a nervous system bucks.'

'What I have always respected, admired and loved in you is your integrity and your honesty. Your misfortunes have been your fortresses . . . Maybe had you been *more* successful I would have had *less* reason to be loyal.'

Vera's physical condition fluctuated with her spirits. In August she felt 'absolutely normal again' and happy to be working, but found it difficult to get back into her routine. An X-ray a month later still showed a slight shadowing of her lung, 'which makes me anything but tough and ebullient'.

Alone, physically debilitated, and facing a nine-month separation she was deeply conscious of how emotionally dependent on George she had become. 'Your suggestion that it might be possible for us to spend half-years *together* in California and alternate half-years in London is perfectly delightful and would suit me down to the ground . . . At any rate I *never* again want so many months all alone . . . I could be happy living on a Campus now, for I am no longer a "little English bride" or an anonymous "Faculty wife" '.

For two or three days she worked 'quite peacefully', and then suddenly melancholia overwhelmed her and 'I have to go out and find people somewhere, anywhere, and waste hours walking round the West End and sitting in tea shops . . .'. 'The Widows' Weekends' were the worst of all. She had a real homesickness for Chelsea, and dreamed nostalgically of going back some day to a small house near the river, facing south, with a garden.

In spite of being physically fragile she worked for long hours on two books. For two or three hours each morning she wrote her short history of women since 1900, and spent the same time later in the day sorting and assembling material for an autobiographical sequel to *Testament of Youth*. Rereading her own and George's letters unleashed a multitude of conflicting memories. It had been 'monstrous' of her, she told George, to remain in London with Winifred in 1926, and that night she 'relived your desolation in returning to Ithaca alone . . . thanked Heaven that parting was long over and that you were with me again . . . and awoke to find the nightmare true, with you even further away and for longer than you were then. Oh, please, never again.'

She was delighted when George sent her three pairs of 'adorable' nylon lace panties, but to her dismay they were far too small. 'I could weep bitter tears for they are so lovely – so *exactly* the type I wanted.' To avoid further disappointment she proposed sending a paper pattern of one of her old pairs, and those he had sent would at least make ideal Christmas presents for her little Sheffield 'fan', Amy Burnett's daughter, Marian, and one of George's women friends who lived in a neighbouring flat. The last suggestion filled George with apprehension, and he casually disclosed that as he was having an affair with the friend in question it would be a tactless indiscretion to give her panties. Vera had suspected nothing. The news 'pushed me down to the depths . . . all the wind went out of my sails and the remaining vestiges of self-assurance out of my system'. She had long since accepted 'that from the standpoint of what the Law Courts call "conjugal rights" I am a very unsatisfactory wife'.

> Although I am not in a position to object, I still do wish that you would not choose your girlfriends from among people I know socially . . . However much I may wish to be civilized and tolerant, and sadly conscious though I am of my own deficiencies, such social contacts inevitably embarrass me and make me feel inferior – a poor mutt of a betrayed wife . . . But to tie yourself up with someone on the very doorstep, whom we had frequent social contact with and whom you knew I didn't like yet insisted that I should see at frequent intervals – I couldn't believe you could possibly love me if you did that . . . And since I am not normally jealous and have certainly been distressed by no one else within recent years, it can only mean that I love you and don't want to lose you – as indeed and indeed I don't.

At the University of California George embarked on an uncommissioned volume of autobiography. He envied Vera for having two contracts, but she told him her 'Woman' book for Andrew Dakers was just a moneymaking chore. 'What I hate is the collection of the horrid facts . . . it really is little better than précis writing, however lively one tries to make it.'

> The woman question is now a bit *vieux jeu* for the cruelty and injustices are past and it is up to women themselves to prove what they can do; the opportunities are there though the weight of custom still operates against women. But it all seems to belong to my early, not my later married days and I never have been interested in just recording history if I can't write it up with something organic that is still a vital issue.

In spite of her lukewarm interest, she worked with characteristic self-discipline to produce a lucid history of the feminist revolution. She combined pen portraits of Mary Wollstonecraft, Olive Schreiner, Mrs Pankhurst and other influential feminists with straightforward accounts of the suffragette crusade, and the campaign for equal pay and opportunities. 'I believed – and still believe – that women have something special to contribute which could bring peace where men have failed.'

She emphasized in the dedication to Shirley, that she had not attempted to be soberly impartial about the emancipation of women. 'I believe it to be more significant and more beneficial than any great constructive change of the past fifty years . . . Your paternal grandmother was a pioneer suffragist; your mother grew up with the eager generation of young feminists who were the first to inherit the freedom won for women by women. You have repaid us both by making a full and early use of your heritage.' She had practically completed the manuscript when Shirley suggested the title *Lady into Woman*. She was right, Vera said, 'to propose a form of words which implies that the democratic movement described in this book has not been concerned exclusively with sex equality'.

Vera had completed the manuscript of *Lady into Woman* on 15 March 1953. Three days later she was on her way to Southampton to meet George on his return from America on the *Queen Mary*, determined that this was to be the end of their semi-detached marriage. 'I would like to feel that we have learned enough wisdom to make a real success of whatever time is left to us . . . Let us share whatever comes – America or elsewhere – no more self-inflicted loneliness, *please*.'

Shirley's absence at Columbia preyed heavily on Vera's morale. She assured her that 'You are everything that I hoped and prayed a daughter of mine would be', but was determined not to burden her with 'quite irrelevant' parental expectations. She told her friends that Shirley was being 'wildly successful' and addressing Trade Union Conferences all over America, and that she would make her way 'by charm, vitality and sheer goodness'. To Shirley herself she admitted that 'Emotionally there are times when I don't know how to go on without you . . . I get the sort of sick pang that I used to have when you were in America during the war – a kind of almost intolerable hunger . . .'.

It was clear that John didn't love her, she wrote to George after a particularly critical outburst, and 'So far as love goes, my only hope lies in Poppy, though I naturally don't ever expect her to put me first, or even second or third. She does seem as she grows up to be developing quite an affection for me, for which I am deeply grateful. One can live without happiness in its usual sense – indeed in this generation one has learnt not to expect it – but one cannot live wholly without affection.'

While in America, Shirley had been nominated by her friend Joe Watson as the prospective Labour candidate for the Essex seaport of Harwich. He was the only other nominee, but made it clear that he intended to withdraw when Shirley returned. George was elated and suggested a variety of ways in which he could promote his daughter's political career. Determined not to exploit parental influence, and perhaps worried that it might prove counterproductive, Shirley told Vera that deeply attached as she was to her father she wanted no help from him. '. . . I am very scared of getting railroaded into politics before I am absolutely ready', she wrote from New York. 'Success comes fairly easily to me, but success means neither happiness nor goodness. The further I go, the more I want to make sure of these latter two. I am frightened of getting beyond my personal relationships too; becoming a figure of envy rather than of affection. I shall fight Harwich hard – but afterwards . . . I want to get away from politics for a year into writing or something attached to one of the arts'. On her return to England Shirley lived briefly at Whitehall Court and accepted a job in the features department of the *Daily Mirror*. Later she transferred to the *Financial Times*.

In the New Year's Honours List in 1954, Sir Stanley Holmes, the Conservative Member for Harwich, was elevated to the House of Lords. At twenty-three Shirley fought her first election in bitterly cold winter weather against an unassailable Tory majority. Vera hated the cold. 'I suffered poignantly with her throughout the campaign', and in a strangely uncharacteristic burst of maternal solicitude she bought her 'woollen vests and pants of the kind neither of us ever normally wore. "Wear now," I urged her, but I doubt whether she ever actually abandoned her scrappy lingerie and short socks.' Early in February, Vera spent two days canvassing in Harwich, and addressed an eve-of-poll meeting. She again supported Shirley in the 1955 general election and although she knew there was little hope in a Tory stronghold, she welcomed the practical political experience Shirley acquired. She would, she prophesied, 'Go up like a rocket'.

Her family was now the focal point of Vera's life. She was delighted at the arrival of her first grandchild, John and Jennifer's son, Daniel Edward, born on 31 August 1953, and Shirley's marriage at St James's, Spanish Place, in July 1955 to Bernard Williams, by now a Fellow of New College, Oxford, was an additional source of happiness. Shirley, her mother reported, 'made an enchanting bride', her 'clear, full-toned voice was so different from the timid squeak perpetrated by most brides married in a large church', while the bridegroom 'in his own very dark Welsh fashion is quite an Adonis.' Characteristically, Shirley spent most of the day before the wedding writing an article for the *Financial Times* on French exports; and at noon on the wedding day itself was busy fixing up her WEA classes for the autumn.

Between 1952 and 1957, Vera was working on the sequel to *Testament of Youth*. The book presented her with many problems. She refused to compromise and wrote fully of her pacifist beliefs and activities, but her relationship with George was more difficult. He told her of his 'bitter hurt' when he discovered that she did not love him as he loved her, and she asked him if he wished he had stayed at Cornell and taken American citizenship.

For if this is the truth and the whole truth, I must face it and, in fairness to you, reveal it, so that all those who wonder why you are not a College

President or a Cabinet Minister may know that the fault was entirely mine, and at last do you justice.

Compensations there may have been – must have been, or we should not have remained together . . . We can consider together what they are, so that I don't exaggerate and try to excuse myself. One is, perhaps, that the idea of equality which experimentally we tried to live up to cannot be attained without costing one partner more than the other. Usually it is the wife who pays it, but in our case it was yourself, for I have at least had what the majority of women desire – husband and children – plus what only a few desire, a measure of national achievement . . .

Testament of Youth had been her memorial to Roland, Edward, Victor and Geoffrey; *Testament of Experience* became her atonement and apologia to George.

SEVENTEEN

The World Widens

'. . . [I] should have proved altogether a more effective person had I not been obliged – and not only in my youth – to spend time and energy in learning to believe in myself and my purposes . . . That you, who have been spared that particular battle, will live to see women ascend to heights of achievement hitherto undreamed of and make your own contribution to the future stage of a great revolution, is the constant and joyful hope of

Your Mother.'

Vera Brittain in the 'Dedication to My Daughter' of *Lady into Woman* (1955)

'. . . the *Radio Times* seems to think my daughter the product of parthenogenesis.'

George Catlin to Donald Hodson, 31 May 1953

I

The postwar decline in her popularity had been a cause of painful readjustment for Vera, but she was confident that *Testament of Experience* would restore her literary standing. She told Sybil Morrison that she intended to contrast 'the pre-war period of glory, when pacifism was fashionable and everyone ran after me', with her 'successive humiliations' in the Second World War. 'Above everything else I want to make my readers see how the position in the Second War rose directly from the events of the First . . .', and she felt certain that her 'Autobiographical Story of the Years 1925–1950' would induce people to read or reread *Testament of Youth*.

In writing about her pacifism she felt that she could express her views without constraint, but the story of her marriage was a two-way proposition. George had dropped the idea of structuring his own autobiography around the story of Faust in favour of a more direct approach. Vera agreed that the use of such symbolism might have appeared 'a little sententious and artificial'.

All the more I feel that you must be honest – we both must ... the truth, though it may be sorrowful, is nothing to be afraid of ... Feeling literary ethics as obligatory as I do, I think I can say that I am *quite* prepared for you to be frank about your own disappointment and my shortcomings of the thirties, provided you are fair ... to the woman of today who loves you with a tender and enduring love ...

Thwarted in his political ambitions, George was acutely sensitive to the idea that some people thoughtlessly or maliciously dismissed him as 'Vera Brittain's husband'. He had raised a storm of protest at being included in the final chapter of *Testament of Youth*, and only Vera's persistence and Winifred's conciliatory tact had overcome his objections. In *Testament of Experience* Vera had intended to write fully and frankly about the tensions and difficulties of their marriage, but after many discussions George persuaded her that their relationship was only of peripheral interest, and that her pacifist odyssey was of far greater significance. The inevitably blurred, disingenuous portrait of their marriage that resulted deprived the sequel to *Testament of Youth* of much vitality and veracity, and made Vera's dedication – 'To G. Beloved Companion of these rich and challenging years "*Confirma hoc, Deus, quod operatus es in nobis*" ["Strengthen this thing, O God, which you have worked in us"]' – seem strangely paradoxical.

In *For God's Sake Go!*, his own autobiography, published two years after Vera's death, George was even more reticent. He seldom mentions Vera, and when he does it is usually as his 'wife', rather than by name. He writes that she 'put her literary standing in jeopardy by her integrity and unwavering stand on pacifist principles', and relates that she offered him a divorce if he felt that her pacifism was inhibiting his political ambitions. But of their forty-five-year relationship, he says practically nothing.

Vera had still to finish *Lady into Woman* for Andrew Dakers when she signed an agreement with Macmillan for *Testament of Experience*. She began work on the new book in 1952, but came increasingly to believe that the expression of her pacifist and socialist convictions might seriously embarrass her rather more conservative publishers. It was probably Harold Macmillan's appointment as Minister of Defence in 1954 which finally decided her to arrange for the cancellation of her contract. Victor Gollancz was the obvious alternative choice. Their relations had steadily improved since they had campaigned together for 'Save Europe Now', and in 1952 Vera had told Shirley that 'Victor ... recently announced to the press that he was now a pacifist, and seems to have been more cordial to me ever since.' In the autumn of 1955, after more than three years' work, Vera submitted to him her typescript of well over a thousand pages.

The vogue for the blockbuster book had passed, and *Testament of Experience* was only reduced to a more practical length with the 'brilliant editorial help' of Sheila Hodges at Gollancz. '[Vera] was marvellous to work with', Sheila Hodges remembered, 'she had absolute grace and we had no disagreements.' Rose Macaulay had for many years been one of the most successful of the Gollancz authors, and Vera consented without protest to the excision of the account of their lunch in Marshall and Snelgrove's when Rose Macaulay had reduced Vera to tears. She also agreed to cut numerous references and anecdotes about Shirley. While impressed by Vera's integrity and generosity, and 'her passionate desire that mankind should move in a better direction', Sheila Hodges also found her lack of humour, impenetrable reserve, and sense of her own importance, insurmountable barriers to a closer understanding. 'I was also very surprised at the way she abnegated herself for George. She bent over backwards to promote his interests.'

Testament of Experience was published in England in June 1957, and in America by Macmillan two months later. With more optimism than conviction Vera hoped that it would repeat the success of her other two *Testaments*, but admitted that 'my imagination pictures rows of critics armed with scathing reviews all determined that I shan't do the hat trick'.

In spite of her forebodings she was encouraged by letters from Diana Collins, the wife of the Canon of St Paul's, and Phyllis Bentley, 'that uncompromising woman who never flatters – and Canon Raven, who also doesn't, writes of "an astonishing achievement" '. A full-page notice in the *Friend* was magnificent, and Sybil Morrison's review was 'very good but I thought a bit too uncritical'. Dennis Gray Stoll disagreed with some estimates of people and events, 'But because of that we are not going to follow the current literary trend and call Miss Brittain's a bad book. On the contrary, we found her story enthralling, and willingly concede to her the respect to which a fine woman, a brave pacifist and a good writer is entitled'. But these people, she noted, 'are all my friends'.

By the time she read Stoll's notice Vera had endured a barrage of fierce criticism. One reviewer satirized her prose as slack and cliché-ridden, 'suggesting at its worst a *mésalliance* between a fatigued leader writer and a compiler of travel brochures'. Nancy Spain, the book critic for the *Daily Express*, went further. She had read *Testament of Youth* as a schoolgirl, and 'Funnily enough I disapproved of Vera Brittain's writing at the age of seventeen almost as much as I do this morning ... For of all the worthy writers whose work has vexed me in the last five years I think Vera Brittain tops my list for lack of charm. *Testament of Experience* is indeed a charmless book. But worse than this, it is also a woeful account of IN-experience'.

The attacks continued, and in August, under a banner headline 'New Testament of Tedium', *Books and Bookmen* 'went all out against, not so much the book, as myself'. N.R. Longmate, the reviewer, declared that 'Miss Brittain has assumed that her not very eventful life is of inexhaustible interest to the reading public. As a result she has continued her literary dance of the seven veils long after the most hopeful customer has put down his opera glasses and gone home.' 'The old familiar formula – titbits of intimate personal information eked out with comment on contemporary events – has this time failed to work its customary magic', he continued. 'The horse and rider are the same but at last they have come a cropper.'

Urged on by George and Shirley, 'I have been prevailed on to do something I have never done before – send a solicitor's letter asking for damages'. Bernard Williams, her son-in-law, particularly objected to the comment that her 'sole contribution to the war effort seems to have been seeking out safe houses and hotels where she could write her books in comfort . . .', and he resented the characterization of her as a coward. 'That was one thing she definitely was not', he said. 'I felt it a grave injustice and helped to draft the initial letter to her solicitor'. Vera did not like litigation, and explained that she had brought the case 'partly to vindicate myself against false, trumped up charges, but also because all literary criticism will take a header into the abyss if critics use their reviews as vehicles for personal hostility.'

Vera was in Montreal when the libel action was due to be heard in the High Court of Justice in January 1958. Announcing an out-of-court settlement of £300 damages, together with £15 costs, and an apology in the next issue of *Books and Bookmen*, her counsel said that Vera 'would distribute one hundred guineas to each of three literary charities [the Royal Society of Literature, the Society of Authors and PEN] and she had no desire for damages for her own benefit'.

The hostile reception of *Testament of Experience* left deep scars. 'I sometimes wonder why one writes books', she wrote to Paul Berry. 'The answer is, I suppose, that overriding compulsion which, as Plato puts it, "lays hold of one by the hair".'

On a personal level, the publication of *Testament of Experience* marked the end of Vera's tenuous forty-year contact with Clare Leighton, by now a much admired and respected woodcut artist who had lived in the United States since 1939. Their relations had never gone beyond superficial friendliness, but in the Thirties Clare had increasingly come to resent what she saw as Vera's appropriation of Winifred, and had made the decision 'to go apart from them.' In *Testament of Experience*, Vera's characteristic desire for frankness and literary effect had overridden a proper consideration for Clare's feelings. In her account of Robert Leighton's funeral in 1934, she had not only described Marie Leighton as looking like 'an elderly chorus girl', but had also suggested that the burial itself resembled nothing better than a pauper's funeral. It was true that the Leightons had gone through hard times since the end of the war, but Clare, who had singlehandedly supported her parents and paid her father's nursing fees from a minuscule teaching salary, was deeply wounded, and cut her links with Vera completely.

Over the course of the next eight years, Vera published a further five books. Apart from the novel she had abandoned after receiving Lovat Dickson's discouraging response, she had no impelling ideas for another book, but by the time *Testament of Experience* was published she had already made considerable progress with a historical survey of *The Women at Oxford* for the publishers George G. Harrap. Subtitled 'A Fragment of History', it 'represented the quintessence of the whole movement for women's emancipation, the contest for equal citizenship of the mind'. It traced the founding of the first two women's colleges in 1879 (Somerville and Lady Margaret Hall), the fight for degrees, and the abolition in 1957 of the restriction on the number of women undergraduates, combined with profiles of some of the outstanding Principals, dons and graduates. *The Women at Oxford* was published in 1960. Vera generously divided the royalties between the five Oxford women's colleges, but believed that sales were badly affected by a scathing review by Marghanita Laski, herself an old Somervillian. '. . . The most sensible behaviour', Laski wrote, 'for any newly emancipated group in any reasonably tolerant community is to keep its mouth shut about the "differentness" that imposed its former inferiority . . . To pinpoint in any field the achievements of the newly emancipated is . . . to express surprise that they are capable of behaving like normal human beings.' She also stigmatized the book as not very well written and occasionally inaccurate. 'But what is the greatest pity of all is that it is so painfully embarrassing to read, in its own way as embarrassing as that standard setter of academic embarrassment, Dorothy Sayers' *Gaudy Night*.' Janet Vaughan, then the Principal of Somerville, had a more favourable opinion. She believed it to be a useful history of the Oxford women's colleges, and a valuable contribution to the literature on women's education.

Vera's biographies of *Pethick-Lawrence* (1963), and Vijaya Lakshmi Pandit, *Envoy Extraordinary* (1965), represented her own interests and preoccupations as much as those of her subjects. Fred Pethick-Lawrence and his first wife, Emmeline, had been her friends for twenty-five years, and as one of the young women of the war generation, she had been in the vanguard of those who had benefited from their hardship and self-sacrifice in the cause of women's suffrage. 'As we have no children of our body', Pethick-Lawrence had written to Vera in 1935 as Winifred was dying, '. . . I always feel that those who fulfill [sic] the vision are children of our spirit.' Absorbed by Pethick-Lawrence's work for the suffrage campaign and Indian independence, it was perhaps inevitable that in a short book of seventy-five thousand words Vera did less than justice to his contribution to British socialism, his eighteen years as a Member of Parliament, and sixteen as a Labour peer in the House of Lords.

Vera admitted that *Envoy Extraordinary* was a stopgap book suggested by George 'while I was waiting for a new inspiration'. Her first contact with Vijaya Lakshmi Pandit, a member of India's politically influential Nehru family, and the first woman President of the United Nations General Assembly, had resulted from an invitation for Vera to attend the All-India Women's Conference in 1941. Their friendly acquaintance developed between 1954 and 1961 when Mrs Pandit was the Indian High Commissioner in Britain, although, engulfed by her diplomatic responsibilities, she appeared to Vera 'vague and inaccessible'. Early in 1963 Vera stayed with her in Bombay for three days, and in the course of several interviews was able to obtain the biographical information she required. She knew that for several years Mrs Pandit had been trying to write her autobiography, but believed that she had shelved it indefinitely. To Vera's chagrin, however, it appeared in India shortly before her own biography was published. A few weeks later she told George that she had received 'not one review except for Ernest [Kay]'s too flattering little notice in *Time and Tide*', and felt sure that the £175 advance 'is all the money I shall see for this book . . . Clearly India is no longer "news" except when it goes to war'.

To commemorate their fiftieth anniversary, the Fellowship of Reconciliation (FoR) decided to publish a history of the organization, which had been founded in Cambridge in 1914, and to include the International Fellowship established five years later. When asked to undertake this commission in 1962 Vera protested that she was a novelist and biographer, and had little interest in institutional history. But the FoR persisted, persuaded and pressurized, until 'I finally gave way out of sheer weariness'.

With an eighty-thousand-word limit, she endeavoured to present a comprehensive history for the FoR, with brief profiles of its leading members. From some countries the information available was sparse, unreliable and difficult to obtain; others flooded her with material. The book had become 'a kind of crazy nightmare', she told Ruth Colby. '... At one period [I] was not only counting the words on each page but the words in every sentence.' Swamped by material and working to the publisher's deadline, she had little time to check the manuscript, and after publication of *The Rebel Passion* – the title was taken from Gilbert Murray's introduction to *The Trojan Women*, 'Pity is a rebel passion' – received a steady stream of letters pointing out misprints, inaccuracies and factual errors. One Lancashire correspondent remonstrated that a well-known pacifist vicar 'appears to conduct a funeral service eight years after his own death'. Finally, in desperation, Vera asked the FoR to insert a note in the next issue of *Reconciliation* requesting readers who wished to correct or criticize to send their letters to the General Secretary.

In the late summer of 1955, George had left London for a temporary teaching engagement in Minnesota. Shortly after he arrived, McGill university, Montreal, offered him a full-time appointment, to commence the following September, and he at once contacted Vera. 'Favour McGill', she cabled, convinced that at nearly sixty he had little hope of an active political career.

George sailed for Montreal at the end of August 1956. Vera still had to complete her revision of *Testament of Experience*, and followed two months later. It was her seventeenth Atlantic crossing, 'the roughest I ever remember'. For seven months of each of the next three years the Catlins lived in Montreal, alternating with five months in London during the university's summer vacation. In Montreal they rented a third-floor furnished flat in the Rockhill Apartments, an enormous residential complex at the foot of the Côte des Neiges.

Vera had come to Montreal as Mrs Catlin, the wife of a McGill professor, and out of deference to George she made no attempt to obtain local lecture engagements, or to publicize *Testament of Experience* when it was published in North America in August 1957. Inevitably her presence there became known and she was prevailed upon to talk to various women's groups and luncheon clubs. 'To earn my keep', she undertook lectures in America to clubs and colleges, and each year arranged short tours for the American Friends' Service Committee. In the spring of 1959 she embarked on a four-week West Coast itinerary and she was also interviewed on television and radio.

Professor James Mallory, who was in charge of the postgraduate programme in the Economics and Political Science Department, knew George well during his three years at McGill. He stressed that in his day George had been a notable political scientist, and that *The Science and*

Method of Politics (1927) had been the first serious attempt to analyse power. George had, however, failed to consolidate his position as a leading authority in the field, and it was on the strength of his early work that McGill had offered him an appointment.

Many of George's students believed that they had derived a great deal of benefit from his lectures and tutorials. Professor Mallory agreed that 'he added a sort of eccentric distinction to our department, which was stimulating in its way even though he devoted most of his energy to the mirage of Atlantic Union. We missed him after he left, still regretting that we had not had him at the height of his powers'.

He knew Vera less well. 'She struck me as basically shy and uncomfortable with people she didn't know'. When the Catlin's were out together at a university function or private party, 'the public attention was focused on Vera. While he bore this well it undoubtedly accounted for the fact that wherever he was he seemed to be striving for attention and wanting to be centre stage'.

Sheila Fowler, the wife of the Head of the Institute of International Affairs at McGill, knew Vera better, and often lunched with her. 'She was a wonderful listener. She wanted to hear what you had to say and never talked about herself or her work. It was obvious that she was the one that mattered, but when she was with George she let him do all the talking and never interrupted. I couldn't understand it. Did she feel that her marriage was a penance or something? But for what? I know people said she had no sense of humour, but that didn't matter. I just liked the woman.'

Before returning permanently to England in June 1959, Vera had wondered how best she could commemorate the twenty-fifth anniversary of Winifred's death the following year. Her letters to Vera were the only unpublished material that remained. Some had been destroyed when a flying bomb had brought down the ceiling of Vera's study at Cheyne Walk in 1944, but they still formed an extensive collection, and among them were the letters that Winifred had written from South Africa in 1926. To present a balanced picture Vera decided to interpolate her own letters with Winifred's, and, in collaboration with Geoffrey Handley-Taylor, a privately printed subscription edition of five hundred copies of the *Selected Letters of Winifred Holtby and Vera Brittain* was published in 1960. Barely a month before, Vera herself had returned from South Africa.

II

At the end of February 1960, Vera was surprised and pleased to receive a letter from Dr Malherbe, the Principal and Vice-Chancellor of the University of Natal. It was, he wrote, their jubilee year, and the celebrations included a National Conference on Education. Sir Vivian Fuchs, Sir Julian Huxley, Laurens van der Post and Sir Edmund Hillary were among the overseas speakers who had agreed to participate, and they anticipated an attendance of at least two thousand people. He asked Vera if she would address the conference in the section dealing with English and literature. He added that he had enjoyed friendly relations with Winifred Holtby when she lectured in South Africa for the League of Nations Union in 1926.

Vera accepted the invitation almost at once. She had never been in the southern hemisphere, but Winifred's compassionate and tireless work for the black population had been part of her consciousness for more than twenty-five years. At the time South Africa was a member of the Commonwealth, and the hope still prevailed that persuasion, pressure and protest might yet influence the reversal of the South African Government's policy of apartheid adopted in 1948. Less than a month later the situation had changed dramatically. At Sharpeville on 21 March, to worldwide horror and anger, sixty-nine Africans were killed by the police at a non-violent anti-pass demonstration. Seventy per cent of the casualties were shown to have been shot in the back as they ran when the police opened fire, thereby nailing the lie that the demonstrators had been attacking the police.

On 16 June, the Catlins left London for South Africa. In sending Vera details of their celebrations, Dr Malherbe had stressed that 'the main purpose I have in organizing this conference is to get people's minds diverted from this extreme obsession which they have with race here in South Africa at the present time, and to concentrate on the wonderful contribution which science, art and literature can make to our youth'. In spite of his reassurance, Vera was only too well aware that Sharpeville, and the South African Government policy of apartheid and segregation, were the crucial, inescapable issues, and that feelings ran too high to stifle comment and criticism. She had been invited to give an address of special interest to women, and as she prepared her lecture on 'The Expanding Horizons of Twentieth Century Women' she thought long and hard about how most effectively to express her abhorrence and opposition to apartheid.

She had been told that when they landed at Cape Town her papers would be meticulously scrutinized. Taking no chances she parcelled and posted home all the letters she had received giving her political information about the South African situation, 'just making a few odd, crazy-looking notes on stray bits of paper. I don't remember having to do that even in the Rhineland of 1936, but then Nazi Germany was not a member of the Commonwealth'.

Media interest in her visit began before they disembarked. In a radio interview on board she emphasized that she did not necessarily believe all she read in the newspapers, and that she had come to South Africa to investigate the situation for herself. They had scarcely booked into the Mount Royal Hotel before she found herself besieged by telephone calls and her four days in Cape Town congested with engagements.

Before leaving England she had agreed to lecture for the National Council of Women on 'Autobiography in Literature', but had promised Dr Malherbe that she would accept no further engagements before the Natal conference. The Metropolitan Hall in Cape Town was packed, extra chairs were brought in, and most of the men had to stand at the back. Jean McWilliam and Gwendolen Newman, Winifred's WAAC friends from 1918, were there to meet her, and she carried on to the platform a colourful posy given to her by the widow of the novelist Francis Brett-Young.

Vera defined autobiography as 'a conscious effort by writers of prose to produce a literary experience', and referring indirectly to *Testament of Youth* and South Africa's racial ferment, she pointed out that 'autobiography with a background of war or revolution belongs to a special category in which its significance depends not only on the skills of the writer, but borrows greatness from the apocalyptic quality of the epoch described'.

To form her own impression of the apartheid situation she questioned, listened and observed. In an interview with Owen McCann, the Roman Catholic Archbishop of Cape Town, he informed her that South Africa belonged to both white and black, the black population depended on the white for employment, and the white on the black for work. Neither apartheid nor the transfer of power to the Bantu was a practical proposition, and he suggested that the way forward was in provincial governments with MPs for the Bantustan territories such as the Transkei, and a federation of black and white communities.

Over tea two days later, a young woman working for the United Party told her that when a consignment of office furniture was delivered by some coloured workers she felt that to tip them might be resented as patronizing, and decided instead to give them a cup of tea. 'Those were our cups,' one of her colleagues rounded on her. 'Now none of us can drink out of them again. We can't drink out of cups used by coloured people.' It was her belief, she said, that colour prejudice was rooted in an irreconcilable physical revulsion, and that it was impervious to rational argument. At the entrance to the renowned Botanical Gardens at Kirstenbosch Vera noticed public lavatories for 'European Ladies', 'European Gentlemen', and 'Non-European Ladies'. 'Presumably the Non-European Gentlemen have to go to the back', she commented sardonically.

The day before leaving for Durban was crowded with engagements. In a free half-hour after breakfast Vera had just started to repack and was startled to be told that Sarah Gertrude Millin, the South African writer, was in the hotel lounge and wanted to see her at once. Vera and Winifred had met Sarah Millin in London in 1923, and they were among her first friends in England. Winifred met her again in Johannesburg in 1926, and the tripartite friendship revolved principally around books, publishers and literature. 'When I speak of Winifred's goldenness I mean her spirit,' Sarah wrote to Vera after reading *Testament of Friendship*. '. . . I loved her goodness and vitality . . . She had . . . a superb generosity, and what she most generously gave was herself.'

During the Second World War Vera's and Sarah Gertrude Millin's sharply differing beliefs had created serious disagreement. Sarah was fiercely anti-Nazi. Being Jewish she especially resented Vera's pacifism, and convinced herself that this was tantamount to condoning the Nazis' persecution of the Jews, and the horrific barbarity of the concentration camps and gas chambers.

With extraordinary inconsistency however, Sarah, was completely unable to transpose her wartime concern for the oppressed and persecuted Jews to the black and coloured population of her native land. She insisted that apartheid remained the vital policy, and segregation the essential element for peaceful coexistence. '. . . I have pain over the pro-Nazism of our present government,' she wrote, 'but I will not be dominated by a continent of cruel, diseased savages.' To her intense indignation Vera had conspicuously aligned herself with the anti-apartheid movement.

Sarah deplored the fact that Vera had come to South Africa to attend the Natal University Education Conference, and 'began to scold me in the usual fashion for being so much engaged and daring to pack my things instead of talking to her'. Fortunately Vera's car and chauffeur soon arrived 'and we were able to get away from Sarah's bullying'.

Wishing to see as much as possible of the beautiful South African countryside, Vera and George chose to travel to Durban on the four-day 'garden bus'. They left Cape Town on a bright, chilly morning. Swathes of mist still hung over the low-lying ground, and the isolated native reserve between Table Mountain and the main road, sited on monotonous coarse shrub-covered flats, appeared to Vera 'more like an unenclosed concentration camp'.

Port Elizabeth was known as 'The Friendly City', but Vera was not impressed. It was 'exactly like St Anne's or Blackpool'. As they left the next morning they passed the huge shanty town of Port Elizabeth's native reserve, New Brighton. The local power station dominated the landscape, and the usual scrubby wasteland divided the township from the main road. 'Are names like Brighton and Windermere chosen for the hideous areas allocated to the Africans as a kind of mental camouflage?' she asked herself.

Vera had been deeply moved by the compassionate sincerity of Alan Paton's novel *Cry, the Beloved Country*. As the bus climbed from Umzimkulu on the road to the Zulu village of Ixopo, she saw before her the huge, bowl-shaped valley where, in Paton's words, 'These hills are grass-covered and rolling, and they are lovely beyond any singing of it'. From the bus window she identified the little mission village and the church from which Stephen Kumalo set out to look for his son, and the tiny railway line by which he travelled on the first part of his journey to Johannesburg. In her mind's eye she imagined his return to watch brokenhearted the sunrise on the morning of his son's execution, and she reflected on 'the contrast between beauty and tragedy in this sad country'.

III

Vera had not expected a controversial inaugural ceremony for the official opening of the university conference at City Hall in Durban. However, sitting on the platform she listened with growing mortification to the opening address by the Governor-General, the Hon. C.R. Swart. Ignoring the conference brief to concentrate on the educational potential of art, science and literature he harangued his audience with a political tirade, extolling the Government's policies and deploring that they were so widely misunderstood and misinterpreted. Many of the audience did not agree, and laughter, loud coughing, and at times ironic clapping, drowned many of his remarks. '. . . By making a political speech himself and describing his government's achievements as "magnificent and fantastic" – his actual words – [he] in effect gave *carte blanche* to the visitors to be political, too,' Vera wrote in her diary.

Of all the overseas speakers, Sir Julian Huxley, the former Director-General of UNESCO, was the most courageously outspoken. He had seen the shanty towns, the small cement boxes, the squalid mud-and-tin townships, the hopeless poverty. He deplored the low-paid work and desperate efforts of the non-whites to obtain adequate education. His lecture on 'Man's New Vision of Himself' was an explicit condemnation of the apartheid policy of 'the racially bigoted Boers'.

'In the first place, the policy of the South African Government is a racist one', he told his audience to wild applause. 'Racism is based on the same belief that inspired Hitler – the belief in the inherent superiority of some races, and the inherent and permanent inferiority of others. I said "belief"; I should have said superstition, for our modern knowledge shows that it is not true.'

'We (the overseas speakers) by now were all realizing that we were part of the University of Natal's Resistance Movement,' Vera reported.

Each day the *Natal Mercury* carried a full-page personality profile of one of the star speakers. On the morning of her City Hall lecture Vera was featured under the banner headline 'The Women of South Africa Demanded Her'. She had been interviewed by their chief reporter, Dennis Henshaw, who, to her astonishment, reminded her that in 1934 when he was a boy of twelve she had presented him with a Speech Day prize at the Bemrose School in Derby. She was, he told her, the first woman to be guest of honour. He remembers Vera as handsome, dark-haired and a very precise speaker. 'One would not dare to misquote her! Charming, but I would say a formidable opponent . . . a remarkable woman.' She had insisted on being photographed alone, and George explained that 'It's just that she's rather tiny and appears so much shorter than I if we are photographed together.'

Wearing a black dress with a large white collar, she spoke from a prepared text, and the capacity audience of two thousand was larger than any she had addressed since the days of her American tours. She began by referring to Harold Macmillan's Cape Town speech about 'the wind of change' blowing through Africa, and told her audience:

> this 'wind of change' is nothing new. It has been blowing throughout the twentieth century, not only for subject races, but for subject classes and the subject sex. Everywhere, second-class citizens of all kinds have been in revolt, and it is surely the function of an expanding civilization to draw as many as possible into the first-class, whatever their origin, race, nation or sex, so that the rich and colourful possibilities of humanity may be fully realized, unhampered by restrictions due to prejudice and tradition.
>
> Freedom and equality have proved, like peace, to be indivisible. You cannot free one category of human beings without contributing to the

liberation of all the others, and hence it always seems to me that women who have now attained at least a large measure of freedom should be on the side of everybody who is still in subjection.

Her hour-long lecture was punctuated by spontaneous applause. 'I had a splendid reception when I finished,' she wrote, and she was delighted that at sixty-six 'I had not lost the power to handle a large crowd'.

The Chairman for Vera's City Hall lecture was the seventy-nine-year-old Mrs Eleanor Russell, a former Mayor of Maritzburg, and the President of the South African Association of University Women. She had stirred up a storm of protest when she discovered that only male celebrities and no outstanding woman speaker had been invited to address the Durban conference, and she told Vera that it was due to her intervention that Dr Malherbe had sent her a belated invitation. The following morning at nine o'clock Mrs Russell called to drive them to Pietermaritzburg for a luncheon engagement sponsored by three women's organizations. Vera spoke without notes on 'Women's Responsibilities', and later, at her request. Mrs Russell drove them to see 'her' African village of Sobantu. It had been in existence since 1928, but it was only during her mayoralty in the 1940s that it had been developed and modernized with communal water taps and a hot baths system. The village consisted of small red-brick houses of three or four rooms with tiny gardens, and the school, which had only twenty-seven pupils in 1930, now had 1,750.

The village on the outskirts of Maritzburg was a direct violation of the government policy of remote native townships. They officially proscribed it as 'unsuitable' for Africans and ordered their removal, but Mrs Russell had thwarted them by insisting that another twenty years were needed for the occupants to repay in rent the City Council's original capital outlay. 'She is quite clearly at the very centre of the South African White Resistance Movement,' Vera wrote in her diary.

Vera's first concern when she arrived in Johannesburg was to visit the Winifred Holtby Memorial Library in the Western native township. It was, she discovered, an unpretentious, pleasant red-brick building surrounded by a dusty square of ground and some eucalyptus trees, and consisted of two good-sized book-lined rooms with dark wooden floors, a small office, and a Board Room, which, when not required by the Library Advisory Committee or the local Workers' Educational Association, was used as an overflow for the crowded Reading Room. On the wall was a framed memorial inscription to Winifred. When she returned home Vera sent a portrait of Winifred, which she inscribed 'A Friend of Africans'.

On 28 July the Catlins left for Pretoria, where Vera had a morning engagement at the Luncheon Club. Her talk to over four hundred European and African women was an almost unheard-of event as the two groups scarcely ever met. It was preceded by the usual mid-morning tea and sandwiches, and when she spoke without notes on 'Lady into Woman', 'I was now too tired to care what I said or did'. Nadine Gordimer was there as well as Mrs Swart, the Governor-General's wife, and Lady Maud, the wife of the United Kingdom High Commissioner.

In Pretoria Vera had two priorities. It was comparatively easy to attend the notorious treason trial, but to visit Chief Albert Luthuli in Pretoria prison appeared to present insuperable difficulties. As the President-General of the African National Congress, he was the most prominent of 156 people arrested for high treason in December 1956. In 1958 and 1959, 126 of the accused had been either acquitted or the charges withdrawn. Over lunch Mr Johnson, the Deputy British High Commissioner, congratulated Vera on her talk to the Pretoria Luncheon Club, but, she said, 'I was more interested in the possibility of seeing Chief Luthuli'. Nobody was allowed to see him, Mr Johnson told her, a visit was out of the question, and he was sorry he couldn't help them. Vera was not to be deflected so easily, and after talking to George 'we decided to tackle the matter ourselves'. From their hotel they made numerous telephone calls. They emphasized their distinguished status as a writer and academic, and after they had been transferred from one official to another the security police eventually agreed to see them.

The interview was less intimidating than they had expected. They were at first 'extensively catechized', and then 'they questioned us closely about the Swaziland Multiracial Conference and brandished the paper with an account of it in our faces. When we said we had nothing to do with it, and had been to an Educational Conference in Durban their opposition collapsed', and they were given permission to see Luthuli that afternoon.

Vera had neither met nor corresponded with Luthuli. Her visit was an explicit expression of goodwill and her anti-apartheid convictions. During their ten-minute interview they sat facing one another across a table in the presence of the young security officer they had seen in the morning. In her diary she described Luthuli as 'a mild-looking, smiling Negro of Gandhian gentleness whose face lighted up the moment I mentioned Muriel Lester', a mutual friend and staunch pacifist. She talked of their visits to India and Gandhi, and asked about his health. 'Luthuli was very cheerful and did *not* look ill,' she wrote to Shirley. 'He said he had had treatment for his high blood pressure in the prison hospital, and it was much better. He added, actually laughing, "There's nothing wrong except this detention, and that can't be helped".' The United States Ambassador had been the only one to see Luthuli, and he told Vera 'he thought him a good inoffensive old man. "The government should let him out and make him a minister".' At the end of August Luthuli's six-month sentence for burning his passbook was suspended because of his health, and he was acquitted on 102 charges of inciting others to do the same. In July 1967, he was killed by a train when crossing a railway line near his small farm at Stanger.

The European and press galleries were empty when Vera and George attended the treason trial being held in a converted synagogue. Three red-robed judges presided, and the accused sat together at the back of the court. In April they had cancelled the mandate of their counsel, and Duma Nokwe and Nelson Mandela, the African National Congress hero and a qualified lawyer, had taken charge of their defence. In the dock were two women, forty-nine-year-old Lilian Ngoyi, Vice-President of the Federation of South African Women, and Helen Joseph, the Secretary of a Transvaal Medical Aid Society. Political consciousness came to her not through reading books, she said, but through years of daily contact with misery, poverty and racial oppression.

It was dark and pouring with rain when the Catlins arrived in Bloemfontein on their way back to Durban. It was a brief overnight stop, and Vera's first concern was to arrange appointments with the Anglican and Catholic bishops, a visit to the Women's Memorial, and to confirm the details of her evening lecture to a hastily improvised meeting organized by the National Council of Women and the Business and Professional Women's Club.

Before leaving England Vera had sought information from Dr Ambrose Reeves, the Anglican Bishop of Johannesburg, who was then living in London. 'Don't go to Bloemfontein,' he urged her. 'It's an Afrikaans centre, and you won't be welcome there.' Believing that national animosities are seldom directed against individuals she decided to regard his advice as a challenge rather than a warning, and she especially wanted to see the celebrated Women's Memorial commemorating the 26,370 mothers and children who had died during the Boer War in the British concentration camps. She also intended to visit the grave of Emily Hobhouse, the English Quaker, who had cared for the victims. Her guide and companion was Gladys Steyn, the daughter of Jan Steyn, the last President of the Orange Free State, one of the two Boer Republics which fought against Britain in South Africa. At the base of the memorial stood the bronze figure of two women, one holding a dying child, and alongside was a small grave with the simple Afrikaans inscription 'Hier rus Emily Hobhouse, 27 October 1926'.

At a farewell buffet supper in Durban to meet a group of African and Indian lawyers, psychologists and educationalists, Vera was delighted to find Alan Paton among the guests. Her impression was of 'a shortish, very lined, red-faced and rather peppery-looking man who reminded me of Guy Chapman, except that Guy is pale. In manner he was very friendly and not irascible at all.' Vera told him how much she admired *Cry, the Beloved Country*, of stopping for tea at Umzimkulu, and of seeing Stephen Kumalo's little mission village from the bus window. As she and George were entering the Gulf of Aden on the voyage home, she read in the ship's news bulletin that Alan Paton had won the American Freedom Award for his fight against apartheid. She met him again in London at the end of September at the home of Canon John Collins to discuss a Christian Aid appeal for the treason trial victims. They talked also about the intolerable racial regime in South Africa, 'and at the end of the evening we more or less came to the conclusion that though none of us wanted to see war or disastrous revolution, there didn't seem to be any positive solution so long as the Afrikaan government of today lasted'.

On 5 October, the white electorate, by a slender majority, voted in favour of the conversion of the Union of South Africa into a Republic. On Union Day, 31 May 1961, South Africa became a Republic and withdrew from the Commonwealth. Shortly afterwards Vera attended an anti-apartheid rally in Trafalgar Square to protest against 'the campaign of mass repression now being conducted against the people of South Africa'. With more than two thousand demonstrators, she turned to face South Africa House in silent defiance as Fenner Brockway posted on the gates a resolution that 'this meeting of British people expresses its fullest support for the three-day strike against the apartheid Republic, and feels the time has now come for the British Government to exert official sanctions against South Africa'.

IV

Before Vera sailed for South Africa serious dissension had arisen between *Peace News* and the Peace Pledge Union. Disagreements had surfaced in the early 1950s with some PPU members protesting that *Peace News* 'put too much emphasis on matters not wholly pacifist', and the climax had come with the paper's all-out support for the Campaign for Nuclear Disarmament. The pacifist idealists believed that it was illogical and futile to remove the threat of nuclear destruction 'while leaving warfare by "conventional" weapons as it was before'. Vera had a more pragmatic approach. 'Nuclear disarmament may be an illogical cause,' she wrote, 'but it is a half-open door to world peace. Those pacifists who do not push against this door after hammering on locked gates for two decades may well be losing an opportunity which will never recur.'

Vera had been in Canada when CND was launched, early in 1958, at an informal gathering at the home of Canon Collins in Amen Court. This had been followed by a mass meeting in February of that year at Central Hall in Westminster where the speakers had included Bertrand Russell (as president of the campaign), Canon Collins, J.B. Priestley, Michael Foot, and A.J.P. Taylor. In principle Vera supported both CND, and later, after interminable wrangles between Bertrand Russell and Canon Collins, the breakaway Committee of 100.

George objected even more strongly to Vera's 'Ban the Bomb' activities than he had to her outspoken pacifism. At sixty-four he had set his sights on a peerage, and Vera tried to avoid any publicity which might compromise either his or Shirley's political prospects. When, in October 1960, Bertrand Russell invited her to become a member of the Committee of 100, she declined 'as this would inevitably mean that other members of my family . . . would be penalised for opinions they do not share'. Nevertheless she made generous financial contributions to both the Committee of 100 and CND, and played a more prominent part in Canon Collins's less controversial organization, Christian Action.

However, the clash between her convictions and family loyalties continued to try her. 'I want to see you *very* much', she wrote to Shirley in September 1961,

and darling lovely Rebecca [Shirley's four-month-old daughter] with her private language and bells on her toys. But not next Sunday . . . in case I feel compelled to take part in the Committee of 100 demonstration. It is a horrid decision to take because G. is so vehemently opposed to anything of the kind (you may remember he begged me not to join the Committee of 100 a year ago after the Press had prematurely announced that I was supporting it). Yet my convictions . . . run in that direction – I have so often advocated non-violent direct action in my articles and ought to practise what I preach.

I don't know yet what I shall do. Not being one of the ringleaders [ie the 100] I am hardly likely to get imprisoned, but might be fined. In practice it may well be impossible to get near either of the Squares! So I must just wait and see what happens, and hope to feel braver than I ever do!

In the event Vera did attend the mammoth occupation of Trafalgar Square and the surrounding area. Harry Mister, the former distribution manager of *Peace News*, remembered her arriving 'indignantly and a little out of breath' because she had been unable to find the centre of this vast demonstration, 'and so had sat down on her own in the middle of Whitehall, only to be politely refused arrest by an avuncular police officer.'

Bertrand Russell approached Vera again a year later, asking her to sponsor a national appeal for financial support. This time Vera felt forced to be a little more categorical in the face of his persistence. 'I enclose a donation towards the Committee's expenses', she replied,

> but I fear I cannot sign an advertisement asking for funds because this would immediately involve my husband, who neither endorses civil disobedience nor supports any part of the C.N.D. organisation. For twenty-five years he has been seriously penalised by my pacifist affiliations, and it would be wrong and unfair further to impose on his tolerance . . . This means that such help as I can give to the C.N.D. or the Committee of 100 must be confined to occasional money gifts, to the membership of inconspicuous committees and above all to my work as Chairman of the Board of *Peace News* . . .

Influenced by the example of Gandhi's Civil Disobedience Campaign in India, Vera fully agreed with the commitment of *Peace News* to non-violent direct action. She wrote many articles on the subject, and also contributed a pamphlet on 'The Meaning of Aldermaston' to the PPU series on 'Disarmament, Nuclear Weapons and the Cold War'.

> The meaning of Aldermaston will have been imperfectly understood if those who marched, watched, or followed the whole astonishing episode only at a distance . . . do not begin to recognise the power of non-violence in both political and human life, and to consider what further spiritual mountains this power gives us the strength to ascend.

Vera was in her late sixties at the height of the nuclear disarmament campaign, and felt able to undertake only a few strenuous overnight journeys to speak at public meetings. In 1962 the Midhurst, West Sussex, CND had hoped to obtain Canon Collins for a well-publicized meeting. 'If you don't succeed,' Vera wrote, 'I wonder if I would be of any use as a substitute?' As a member of the Christian CND Committee, she emphasized in her Midhurst talk that 'all nuclear weapons were in direct opposition to the Gospel teaching on the value of individual life', and dwelt on 'The Implications of Nuclear Weapons to Religious Leaders'. The meeting attracted an audience of nearly two hundred. She was 'amazed', she wrote the next day, 'that such a small and, one would have expected, reactionary place should have produced one of the most inspiring meetings that I remember in recent years'.

As the *Peace News* Chairman, she spent much time during the CND years on the difficult negotiations between the paper and the Peace Pledge Union. She believed that *Peace News* should be free to serve the whole pacifist movement and not a particular organization, and gave Hugh Brock, the Editor, unstinting support. In December 1959, Hugh Brock had been sentenced to two months' imprisonment for inciting members of the public to break into and enter a ballistic missile base at Harrington. Vera visited him in Brixton prison, and invited his wife and two young children to a Christmas party at Whitehall Court. Eileen Brock didn't know Vera very well, and felt diffident and apprehensive. 'Don't be worried', her husband reassured her. 'She is, I'm sure, much more anxious and concerned about doing the right thing than you or Jeremy or Carolyn will be – in fact I don't know anyone who makes me feel more that *I* have to try not to make her nervous.'

At the Peace Pledge Union AGM in Birmingham at the end of April 1961, it was agreed that *Peace News* should become an independent newspaper. Four years later Vera decided that at seventy-one the time had come to relinquish the chairmanship. It had been suggested that Vanessa Redgrave might succeed her, and over tea at Whitehall Court Vera's impression was of 'a charming, unspoilt girl . . . and doubtless very good-looking, but like most young actresses today seemed bent on looking as ugly as possible with large coloured glasses and long ropes of flaxen hair. Wore a beautiful short coat however, in a lovely shade of red'.

v

The late 1950s had been a dispiriting period of 'literary and political setbacks', with the attacks on *Testament of Experience* followed in 1959 by Shirley's third election defeat. Harwich had been a Conservative stronghold, but Vera had been confident that Shirley would succeed in the marginal constituency of Southampton Test. To her disappointment the anticipated swing to Labour failed to materialize and the Macmillan Government was returned to office with an increased majority.

When she called to see Shirley a few days later she found her sitting disconsolately on her bedroom floor amidst a profusion of clothes and papers, the aftermath of the election turmoil. 'She was too much the "gallant little cavalier" of Charlotte Brontë's *Shirley*' for Vera to underestimate her courage by feeling sorry for her. After this defeat Shirley considered giving up politics altogether. Bernard reminded her that 'backroom boys' were often more influential than back-bench MPs, but Vera did not agree. Shirley had already contested three elections at an age when most aspiring MPs had not fought even one, and Vera felt sure that she would eventually be successful. Early the following year Shirley succeeded Bill Rodgers and became the first woman General Secretary of the Fabian Society. The *Guardian* pronounced her the most important woman in the Fabian movement since Beatrice Webb. 'But, small and delicately blonde, she bears no resemblance to her formidable predecessor.' Vera was aware that it was not the parliamentary life for which Shirley had hoped, but pointed out that it was a prestigious appointment, which offered a wide range of valuable political experience.

Shirley's selection as the Labour candidate for Hitchin in the 1964 election, however, involved Vera 'in some difficult moral problems'. On many political issues they were in deep agreement, but Shirley was not a pacifist and 'well aware that G felt that his own career had been hampered by the expression of principles on which we differed, I did not propose that this should happen in another generation'. Before this election was called, Vera had agreed to support the pacifist Fellowship Party, and to speak for their candidates. Shortly after the campaign began she was asked to take the chair at a meeting in nearby Hendon in support of the Reverend Patrick Figgis. Deeply concerned that her appearance on a Fellowship Party platform might provoke allegations by Shirley's opponents that she was also a pacifist 'I decided that my principles did not compel me to take this drastic step and – feeling nonetheless a Judas – I told Patrick that on this occasion I could not support him'. She believed that she could best help Shirley 'by keeping out of the way', and her only visit to the constituency was to attend an all-women's meeting in Stevenage addressed by Harold Wilson. She had contemplated going to Hitchin on polling day but thought better of it, and went instead to Oxford for the presentation of an honorary degree to Mrs Pandit by Harold Macmillan.

That night at the Reform Club, Vera was 'almost too tense to take in the results'. Richard Dimbleby announced shortly after midnight, 'Here's a

Labour gain from Hitchin', as Shirley's 'charming face, so young and attractive', lit up the television screen. The day after she had taken her seat in the House of Commons, Shirley was embarrassed to read an interview with Vera in the *Daily Mail* in which under the heading, 'Could she be Britain's first woman Premier?', Vera had commented that 'I'd like to live long enough to see her get a top ministerial post. She would make a first-rate Chancellor of the Exchequer . . . I wouldn't say she couldn't become Prime Minister.'

Shirley made her mark in her first Parliament as a very able Parliamentary Private Secretary in the Ministry of Health. She also succeeded Roy Jenkins as Chairman of the Labour Committee for Europe. After being re-elected in 1966 she was appointed Parliamentary Secretary to Roy Gunter the Minister of Labour, which for Vera represented 'the apotheosis (or almost) of all I have hoped and sought for Shirley for thirty years . . .'. At the Ministry of Labour Shirley was immediately involved with the implementation of equal pay for women, and concluded her first ministerial speech, 'We will achieve this. We will achieve it with humanity, we will achieve it with sympathy, we will achieve it without high unemployment. But achieve it we shall.'

Her words took Vera back 'to the many women I had loved and admired who in their own way, against seemingly impossible odds, had struggled for this end – Olive Schreiner, Eleanor Rathbone, Elizabeth Abbott, Winifred Holtby, Virginia Woolf, Ethel Smyth, Emmeline Pethick-Lawrence – and now Shirley was standing in the place they had created for her, and uttering words that they had dreamed that someday, perhaps, a woman endowed with a measure of political power would be able to speak'.

When the children were young it had been John, whom she had envisaged as the embodiment of Edward, on whom Vera had concentrated her affection, but now it was Shirley, 'my brilliant and beloved', who illuminated her life. She acknowledged that both temperamentally and intellectually they were quite different, and 'Like you', she wrote to Ruth Colby a year later, 'I wish that Shirley were more revolutionary in her politics. But really she never has been! She takes after George – discreet, sage, judicial, an ideal Minister, and much admired for this. But if she doesn't espouse pacifist and revolutionary policies, she sets a marvellous example to all women for the courage and initiative she shows at such a relatively early age . . .'.

Sometimes thoughtlessly, but sometimes, Vera suspected, with an element of malice, people asked her whether she was envious of her daughter's success. At a Somerville Gaudy in the late Sixties, Shirley (who was not present) was referred to so often in the public speeches that Mary Ogilvie, Vera's college contemporary and a former Principal of St Anne's, leaned over to Vera and said, 'After all, they do climb on our shoulders'. '. . . I think she perhaps felt that you were putting my nose out of joint', wrote Vera afterwards, relating the incident to Shirley, 'but I have never, never felt like that, and never could'. Towards the end of her life Vera wrote of her hopes for her daughter's future: 'She will go, and was intended to go, much farther than I was, but how far I shall probably not survive long enough to know. I think she will be one of those who will help to achieve the heights that I believe humanity can reach if it is permitted to survive'.

In later years Vera revelled in family life and took a deep interest in her grandchildren. Shirley's daughter, Rebecca Clare, had been born in May 1961, and John and Jennifer's second son, Timothy, little more than a month later. Their third son, William, was born in May 1966. For her adored eldest grandson Daniel's eighth birthday in August 1961, Vera wrote and illustrated a twelve-page booklet entitled 'The Adventures of Daniel'. When he wanted a conjuring set she interrupted her work to make a special expedition to Regent Street. For Rebecca who was coming to tea she set off in pouring rain to buy the toy that she had demanded.

In the autumn of 1965 Vera accepted immediately when Shirley telephoned unexpectedly before breakfast one morning to ask if she would like to go with her to see John, Jennifer and the children, who were staying at Kingsgate in Kent. 'I couldn't write you yesterday as I was out all day', she told George, 'such a lovely day with the darling family. Sometimes it thrills me to think how you and I, both in fact "only" children, have managed to bring four charming adults and three lovely children into our lives. That is something to thank God for.' Rebecca and Timothy played very happily in the courtyard all day, and to Vera's consternation, Shirley climbed a high tree in order to rescue Daniel's kite. 'I was scared because the tree looked dead; I kept reminding her that the Government would fall if she broke her neck . . . !'

Vera's delight in her grandchildren was overshadowed by her unhappy, and, at times, agonizing relations with John. He had never accepted what he regarded impatiently as a dead-end office job, and in 1955 – probably helped by Vera – he bought a large house in Kensington. He intended to convert it into flats, but without experience or practical ability he soon decided to sell it and buy another. In spite of this setback, but full of confidence, he nevertheless embarked upon a freelance career as a property entrepreneur.

Vera lent him money to finance his enterprises, and in 1958 he had asked her to arrange for the Brittain Trust to guarantee his personal account. She had pointed out that this was not legally possible, but John had persisted, pressuring her to dissolve the trust and divide the capital. Believing it was 'only fair that money intended by father for the family should be divided between them without waiting for me to die', she had agreed. With the help of her accountant, Charles Kett, she had succeeded in realizing the capital in the trust. She had given John a £30,000 quarter-share, and had retained a half-share for herself and George. John had at once launched out on various ambitious ventures. He formed several companies, over which he had complete control, and invested on the Stock Exchange in the hope of making a quick profit. When in need of money he persuaded Vera to invest more than £21,000 in his business, which, she told Shirley, she felt she had an obligation to do as 'he has been so much less gifted and less lucky than you'.

With her investment income drastically reduced she was now compelled to realize capital each year. In 1965 when she told John she was financially unable to purchase 'a house which you wish to get rid of but I don't want to buy . . . you proceeded to abuse first your father and then me over the telephone, as though we were a couple of juvenile delinquents . . . Never at any time have you shown any gratitude or appreciation of what I have tried to do to help you, to my own disadvantage and increasing financial insecurity. Instead you merely persecute me if I don't do exactly what you want in order to get some more of the family property into your hands, though my own share is steadily diminishing . . . I can no longer endure my final years being tormented by financial persecution instead of dedicated to my own work. I have some projects which I want to carry out before I depart hence, but instead of furthering these, you bully me mercilessly until I am half crazy with totally unnecessary anxiety.'

Endeavouring to restore her mother's morale, Shirley told her that she was sure that in his heart John really loved her. 'I hope this is true,' Vera replied, 'since it is better for John to love people than to hate them, even when he is angry with them. And for all his naughtiness and unkindness, I could never stop loving him.'

John and Jennifer's separation in the summer of 1966 caused her deep distress. After ten years of tension she decided that 'it was not only useless but unfair to try and persuade [Jennifer] to stay with John as I did when Daniel was three . . . it is clear that her marriage to John has meant fifteen years of straight purgatory ever since John unfairly persuaded her to cut her time at [Lady Margaret Hall]'. The breakdown of John's marriage preyed constantly on Vera's mind. She found it 'quite heartbreaking' to think of her three forlorn and bewildered grandsons, and insisted on paying Jennifer's half-share of Daniel's school fees. By his second marriage to Elaine Drakeford, John had two more children, Larissa and Alexander, who was born after Vera's death. In contrast with his treatment of his mother, and remoteness from his and Jennifer's sons after their divorce, John was steadily devoted to his younger children; his love for them remained strong in their memories after his death.

While writing *Testament of Youth* Vera's imagination had been captured by a fairy story from Andrew Lang's *Pink Fairy Book* which she was reading to John and Shirley. Catherine, the only daughter of a rich merchant, 'was sitting in her own room when suddenly the door flew open, and in came a tall and beautiful woman, holding in her hands a little wheel. "Catherine," she said, going up to the girl, "which would you rather have – a happy youth or a happy old age?" ' In spite of John's financial harassment, in Vera's later years she at last found peace and comfort in George's affectionate companionship. She wanted to be with him. When he was out she listened impatiently for his return. He persuaded her not to drive herself so remorselessly, to go to bed before midnight, and to give up arduous journeys to those meetings where 'they only want you to make a crowd'. When they went out these days she took his arm.

In the autumn of 1965 George was in America on a short money-making lecture-tour. 'I write as always on the day you leave in the hope of catching you at an early address in case you are feeling homesick', Vera wrote; '. . . when you leave me, it is your pipes curled up in their little bowls that get me down – so redolent of yourself and yet such poor substitutes'. 'How I miss you! If only my feelings of love for people were less intense, I should have so much less pain to suffer!'

Early in October she travelled to Hull to present her correspondence with Winifred and the manuscript of *Testament of Friendship* to the Central Library. 'It was sad giving Winifred's letters away . . . [but] what was the good of keeping them hidden in my dressing-table for a few more years at most?' After a civic luncheon at the Guildhall she spoke for half an hour from a few rough notes, but she spent 'three weeks on and off' preparing a provocatively feminist lecture on 'Women Pacemakers' for the Literary Circle of the National Liberal Club a week later. She was too conscientious, George told her, and ridiculous to think the talk important. 'I still think that my priorities were right', she replied; '. . . the Nat. Lib. lecture was given to an audience of very intelligent and potentially critical people (mostly retired MPs and Civil Servants – about sixty of them) who had inherited a long history of contempt for women, and took for granted that I should be inaudible! . . . I was only the fourth woman ever invited to address this literary circle, the others being Mrs Pandit, Barbara Wootton and Veronica Wedgwood. To have succeeded merely leaves a pleasant and capable impression on the record, but to be the kind of "flop" they quite expected would have been terrible; it would have got round to Poppy and Heaven knows who else.'

Vera remained true to her feminist principles to the end of her life. In 1966 Muriel Box, the film director and writer, launched her publishing company Femina Books and invited Vera to become a director. In a series on 'women on trial' Muriel Box embarked upon an account of the birth control campaign and persecution of Marie Stopes, and Vera agreed to contribute a book on Radclyffe Hall and the obscenity ban imposed upon her lesbian novel, *The Well of Loneliness*.

Now in her seventy-third year Vera was also assembling material for a third and final volume of autobiography which she was intending to call 'The Citadel of Time', or 'Testament of Faith'. In refusing an invitation to a European Peace Forum in the summer of 1966 she explained that she had been 'endeavouring to begin this book without success for the best part of a year, and only within the last two months have I perceived what method to adopt'.

It was raining when she set off just after six o'clock on 2 November 1966 to give a talk at St Martin-in-the-Fields. Crossing Northumberland Avenue she tripped over some builders' debris piled up in the gutter, and fell headlong on both arms.

EIGHTEEN

'*A Prayer for the Close of Life*'

'Lord, teach me to accept my coming end, and grant that it may not be a burden to others. Let me not grieve because I must say farewell to Thy beautiful world, but rather thank Thee with humble gratitude for the rich experience, the stimulus of work, the discipline of sorrow, and the love and kindness of those dear to me, that my share of time has brought me.

And in Thy mercy grant them the joy of achievement, and a world at peace in which to live and serve Thee.

Amen.'

Vera Brittain, November 1963

Vera was helped to her feet by 'a kind young man', and assuring him that she was all right, cautiously made her way to St Martin's. She found the church with difficulty, perturbed that her reactions were no longer automatic. During her talk to a small audience of parishioners, about past vicars of St Martin's, her arm became increasingly painful, and aware of a sudden weakness, she finished sitting down.

She arrived home by taxi shortly before George returned. After he had bandaged her arm and a finger on her right hand, she went straight to bed. An X-ray at Westminster Hospital the next morning revealed a fractured left arm and a broken finger. Shortly afterwards she suffered an acute nosebleed which, alone and handicapped with one arm in plaster, she had difficulty in staunching. A recurrence a few days later convinced her that the consequences of her accident were more serious than she had first thought. Her sense of unease was increased by 'the strange experience of being totally unable to fit the tops of bottles on to the containers made for them. I tried them one after the other but never got them all to coincide.'

Vera knew that Victor Gollancz had had a stroke, and in December she received a message saying that he would like to see her. In the late Thirties their personal relations had been severely strained by their differing attitudes to the approaching war, but they had come together again in 1945 for the publication of *Above All Nations* and to support the 'Save Europe

Now' campaign, and Vera had later very favourably reviewed Gollancz's *Timothy* autobiographies. When she and George visited him a week before Christmas 1966, they found him sitting in a chair, still capable of talking and understanding. When they left he said ' "Goodbye Vera" rather conventionally. I said, "Oh no, Victor not goodbye, only Au Revoir – I'm coming to see you again" '. He only repeated firmly 'Goodbye Vera'. Realizing that it was his final farewell, she replied, ' "All right, Victor, Goodbye. But I'm going to kiss you good-night." ' The next day she wrote telling him how much he had meant to her. 'My dear Vera', he replied in tremulous capitals, 'I can only say "Thank you very much". This is the first note I have written, my dear Vera . . .'. She was deeply conscious that Gollancz's enterprise and flair had been a vital factor in the success of *Testament of Youth*. When he died at the beginning of February, 'I felt as though a pillar of the temple of my life had fallen.'

Vera and Victor Gollancz were almost the same age, and she took his death as an intimation of her own end. 'Darling Shirley', she wrote a month later, 'I am clearly approaching the end of my journey; it may be a matter of weeks or months but not much longer I think. G. regards this idea as fantasy and "self-hypnotism", but I don't think it is; I believe that a rational person knows when their end is coming . . . I *would* have liked to write two more books . . . I am grateful to Providence because you are here to continue so much of what I started, and because you are what you are.'

Vera had always faced adversity with courage, but her sudden physical and mental decline was a catastrophic torment. In spite of intensive physiotherapy her weakness persisted, and she resigned herself to the fact that 'my leaden legs will never improve except marginally.' Her memory and concentration faltered, and though 'longing to get back to writing' she decided for the time being that it was best not to try. A week's convalescence at St Leonards-on-Sea in February was 'boring in the extreme', the wind made it impossible for her to stand up, and George, deeply anxious, persuaded her to take a holiday in the sun and warmth of the Mediterranean.

She had gone to Malta in her 'first incarnation', a young, inexperienced VAD, and returned fifty years later, 'relatively famous but elderly & fragile'. The flowers, the vivid sunsets, and 'the gaily painted *dhaisas* [small Maltese fishing boats] still bobbing on the water', were just as she remembered them. 'Lovely St George's Bay', on the other hand, was an unrecognizable conglomeration of hotels, villas and new roads, but 'I am pretty sure I identified our old night quarters at the far end of the compound with the series of rocks below the building on which I sat for about 4 hours in April

1917 with the telegram in my hand saying that Geoffrey had been killed, & decided to go home & marry Victor.'

Despite her impaired concentration, she continued to write throughout 1967. For George Panichas of the University of Maryland she wrote an essay for a volume commemorating the fiftieth anniversary of the Armistice, and was the only woman among the contributors. The *Guardian* published a moving article on her casualty department experiences, she contributed an appreciation of Gandhi to an Indian anthology, and for Allan Chappelow, who had received early encouragement from Vera's own *On Becoming a Writer*, she wrote an introduction for his book, *Shaw – 'The Chucker-Out'*. She also agreed with some amusement to write a preliminary obituary for the *Guardian* of Barbara Castle, seventeen years her junior, and at the time Minister of Transport in the Wilson Government. '... Rely on your daughter to give you due warning if she suddenly begins to look moribund', was the editor's advice to Vera.

But her *Radclyffe Hall. A Case of Obscenity?* contract filled her with despair. As the law stood in 1928, no witnesses could be called to testify to the literary merit of *The Well of Loneliness*, and the Bow Street magistrate, Sir Chartres Biron, had pronounced the book an obscene libel. The limited material relating to the trial led to insurmountable difficulties, and after 'endless boring research in nooks and crannies' Vera's manuscript amounted to less than 22,000 words. In a desperate attempt to complete her twenty-ninth book, she interpolated more than thirty pages of often repetitive 'Contemporary Comment' researched for her at the British Museum. She also negotiated a 5,000-word introduction by C.H. Rolph, highlighting 'the Pecksniffian 1928 attitude to sexual inversion', and the barrister, Richard du Cann, dealt with the legal aspects of obscenity in an appendix. Published in the summer of 1968, Vera's last book was a sad, anticlimactic ending to a writing career which had spanned fifty years, but by then arterio-sclerosis had seriously affected both her perception and her aspirations. 'I really didn't put very much hard work into Radclyffe Hall', she wrote to Paul Berry whom she had appointed as one of her literary executors. 'It didn't interest me enough, and I only hope it's readable.'

Early in September 1967, the Catlins sailed for Montreal on their way to the University of Illinois, where George had a one-semester appointment as a Visiting Professor of Politics. Vera had intended to stay for a fortnight before returning to London to work on the final volume of her autobiography, but less than a week after they arrived '[I] suddenly decided ... that I wouldn't go home on October 2nd/3rd but stay with G. – who wouldn't say he was pleased but appeared to be . . . Felt so happy to think we needn't part after all.'

During her four months in Illinois her health gradually deteriorated, and at the end of October she was distressed to hear the news of the death of her PPU friend and colleague, Stuart Morris. Professor Clarence Berdahl recalled that she had great difficulty in walking, and getting in and out of cars. She led a reclusive life in their campus apartment, and spent much of her time writing to family and friends. The occasional dinner or cocktail party she found dull and exhausting. She struggled to complete a final chapter for *Radclyffe Hall* on 'The American Trial', and made notes for her autobiography. She told George that 'my mind seems as if it is covered in blotting paper.'

As a result of a letter to the press, George received a subpoena to testify in November at the Old Bailey prosecution for obscenity of Hubert Selby's *Last Exit to Brooklyn*. Ironically, his son-in-law, Bernard Williams, was also called, but as a witness for the defence. For some time Vera sat at their apartment window hoping to see George's plane leave, and wondered how she could bear to be without him, 'but I have to . . . so that's that. He is such a perfect husband; he has made himself indispensable to me.'

In December she wrote to Shirley with 'a rather special request'.

> Please write to G a *very* nice letter implying how much you value him . . . He has had a heavy blow this week, as his favourite girlfriend (whom he would certainly have married if he had not been already married to me when he met her in 1930) died a few days ago from cancer. We knew she was dying, but the telegram came from her daughter yesterday. She was about G's age, and a very good-looking retired actress . . . G thought he had said goodbye to her when we came here, but just managed to see her again when he went to London for the *Last Exit* case. I have never in any way resented her relations with G; I know I have never been a really satisfactory wife, and he needed someone else . . . He will miss her very much . . .

'I am just longing to see you', Vera wrote to Amy Burnett who had promised to meet them at Heathrow on their return to London on 2 February. She had never liked flying, but George had arranged a series of interviews, and their journey involved five successive flights via Chicago, Washington, New York and Bermuda. 'I shan't swim in Bermuda', she assured Shirley. 'Even a puddle might be more than I could manage.'

In March George returned to America for a two-month engagement with the University of Michigan. Vera had intended to go with him, but apart from her physical frailty, her mental state had deteriorated too much for her to be away from home for so long. 'My mind varies a good deal but it is usually better early in the day ... fatigue comes on so suddenly.' Spasmodically she sat at her desk, making notes for her book, but her concentration wavered. On occasions as she sat writing or reading she would fall asleep. Most of the letters she received she put aside half-read for Anne Hewitt, her part-time secretary, to deal with, but to those closest to her she wrote a steady flow of short letters or postcards, sometimes sending identical notes by the same post.

In spite of her debility she insisted on attending a meeting at Central Hall on 27 March 1968, to mark the fiftieth anniversary of the granting of suffrage to women over thirty in 1918. Among those invited to speak were the leaders of the three main political parties, Harold Wilson, Edward Heath, and Jeremy Thorpe. Shirley, then Joint Minister of State at the Department of Education and Science, was one of the principal women speakers, who also included Edith Summerskill, Sybil Morrison, Joyce Grenfell, and Margaret Thatcher. A seat on the platform had been reserved for Vera, and as a prominent and influential post–First World War feminist, it was appropriately symbolic that this Golden Jubilee celebration should have been her final public appearance.

Before George left for America, he had been attempting to obtain some mark of official recognition for Vera. He was angry that the women's organizations with which Vera had long associations, especially the Society of Women Journalists of which she was Life President, had done 'exactly nothing' to this end, and had set about canvassing support himself. When Joyce Grenfell wrote to 10 Downing Street to propose the idea she received 'a quite favourable response'; but by then Vera was too ill. As she had always intended, Vera would go to her grave as plain Vera Brittain.

During George's absence Amy slept at Whitehall Court. Shirley visited her mother almost daily, despite the heavy demands on her time, and Sybil Morrison and a few close friends called regularly. By the spring of 1968 Vera had reached the conclusion that her illness was placing too heavy a burden on her own family and she asked Anne Hewitt to obtain details of a suitable nursing home. George had been utterly selfless in his care of her, and she had always maintained that 'if ever the time comes when I am helpless, the last person on earth I would want to give up her life to look after me would be my daughter.' George, however, dismissed the idea of her entering a home at this stage.

Vera's determination to get better alternated with spells of despair. 'I am unlikely ever to be able to work again', she told Sybil Morrison at the end of April. 'My instinct is to shriek and howl aloud, but that wouldn't be any good

. . . I still had a great deal more to say only I can't say it . . . Don't be sorry for me, but tell people where I am and what I am trying to do if they ask.'

A week later she wrote again, with renewed determination. 'I certainly do not intend to give everything up, whatever I may have said in a fit of depression. I am trying very hard to get back to my normal life . . . I more than agree with you that one should try everything rather than give up.'

Her overwhelming desire was to have George home again. She continually forgot the date on which he was due to return, wrote to him constantly, and sent him a sad self-analysis on 'The Loss of a Mind'.

According to those who judged its performance, I have always had a good mind . . . But now this too has gone, vanished with the aspirations of which it was part. When H.G. Wells wrote *Mind at the End of its Tether*, did he think of that mind as a permanent and peculiar possession which was indubitably his, and would never be subject to the mutabilities of chance? I find myself asking the simple question because a mind that is not even sure of its existence is not a permanent possession.

Her doctor would give her no hope of a permanent cure,

though I sought it carefully and with tears. I do not intend to abandon the quest, though I know it must involve both pain and depression. Probably there is no cure and so nobody wants to tell me. I just have to discover this for myself and learn to accept the fact that I am never again to be sure of either the past or the future, and to see adversity in different terms from those of the immediate past.

Vera had told Amy that John only added to her troubles, and Amy was aware that when he called to see his mother while George was out, he bullied her for money. 'When he'd gone Mrs Catlin would be terribly upset. Sometimes I found her sobbing her heart out, and hardly able to speak. I didn't know what to do to comfort her. If Charlie was there he'd give John a piece of his mind. More than once he and John nearly came to blows.' '*Please*', Vera begged John in one of her final letters to him, 'don't let all our years together, which must soon terminate anyhow, end in sorrow.' Eventually George was forced to curtail John's visits.

One afternoon Amy was surprised to find Vera putting on her hat and coat to go out. 'Where're you going, Mrs Catlin?' she asked. 'Would you like me to come with you?' 'Mind your own business', Vera retorted. Taken aback at this uncharacteristic snub, Amy discreetly followed her as she slowly made her way down to the Embankment and stood looking at the river. ' "Oh Amy, I didn't know you'd come with me", she said, as I took her arm. I told her it was time to go home, and I'd make a nice cup of tea. You know, I'm sure that she meant to drown herself just like her father.'

From Michigan George suggested that when he returned in June they should take a holiday in Fiesole, which she had first visited with Winifred in the autumn of 1921. Instead of being the morale-boosting diversion he had intended, however, his letter filled her with anxiety. 'The fact that I once made all our travel plans does not mean that I can do it now. Even the money aspect of it utterly defeats me . . . I'm just lost and muddled.'

In Fiesole she attempted to get back into a writing routine by recording her impressions of the Monastery of the Villa San Michele, but soon drifted into reminiscing about the First World War instead. Roland, she wrote, 'had always represented to me a kind of vision of our joint future; when that vision died much of the life we had shared together died with it.'

Early in August, BBC Television arranged to film a 'Yesterday's Witness' interview with Vera at Whitehall Court. Although her powers of recollection were by now seriously impaired, it was hoped that she might rally sufficiently to talk about *Testament of Youth* and her nursing experiences in the First World War. Ian Keill, the producer of the programme, remembered how shocked he had been at her condition. She was, he said, 'rather silent for the first quarter-of-an-hour, and after that was unable to remember anything.' In answer to a question about Roland she replied, 'Who is Roland?'

In response to a letter from George in the autumn of 1968, Hugh and Eileen Brock arranged for their daughter, Carolyn, to look after Vera for a month at Whitehall Court. George often left a few papers for Vera to sort, or some other small task. Over lunch they discussed the day's events, but Vera quickly became confused, and unable to find the words that she wanted. Carolyn Brock recalled that George showed immense patience with her sometimes incomprehensible conversation, though in private the strain on him was beginning to show. At times, he wrote, he could break down and cry to see someone of Vera's distinction reduced to her condition.

By 1969 Vera was not only mentally confused but also physically very frail, and unable to walk without assistance. Foreign travel had always been her favourite relaxation, and in February George decided that a holiday in Morocco would perhaps revive her interest and morale. Taking Amy with them, the Catlins arrived in Marrakech late at night, and were dismayed to discover that Vera's wheelchair had been taken on to Agadir. At their hotel the difficulty of getting Vera to her room presented no problem to the young Moroccan receptionist, who without a word picked her up and carried her upstairs. 'She was still protesting when we got there', Amy recalled, 'but I made her laugh and the incident amused her for quite a while.' The wheelchair arrived several days later and Amy was able to take her out in the hotel garden. Vera's greatest enjoyment was to have tea beside the swimming pool. In her room she spent her time writing letters to 'Dear George', not realizing that he was with her.

On their return to England, day and night nurses were engaged, but a year later, on 22 January 1970, when more intensive medical care was required, Vera entered the St George's Nursing Home in St George's Square, Pimlico. '. . . I am just too tired to carry on', George admitted to Anne Hewitt. He, Shirley, the Burnetts, Anne Hewitt, and Paul Berry visited Vera regularly. She seldom spoke and, as if deeply troubled at being a burden to others, invariably turned her head and gazed out of the window. When Paul Berry visited her one afternoon her face at once lit up. As he leant over to kiss her, she smiled, screwing her eyes up as she had always done. 'Oh Paul, I'm so glad you've come. Sit down and tell me everything you're doing', but almost at once confusion again enshrouded her.

In the middle of March she was transferred to a smaller nursing home at 15 Oakwood Road, Wimbledon, and it was here that Vera died, early on the morning of Easter Sunday, 29 March 1970. She was seventy-six years old, and the cause of death was recorded as cerebral vascular disease. George was the last member of Vera's family to see her, on one of his regular visits to the home, the evening before her death. Shirley was in Northumberland with Bernard and Rebecca, taking a much-needed break from her ministerial duties, when the news of her mother's death reached her. She had required a good deal of persuasion to take a holiday, and had gone away only after being assured that no sudden deterioration in Vera's condition was expected.

A private funeral service was held at St Martin-in-the-Fields, followed by cremation at Golders Green. In June, a memorial service at St Martin's was crowded with Vera's family, friends, and representatives from the many organizations with which Vera had been associated. The Bishop of Worcester, the Right Reverend Charles Edwards, read the lesson from St Matthew V, and Sybil Thorndike's reading from *The Pilgrim's Progress* was followed by the John Bunyan hymn, 'Who Would True Valour See', which Vera had chosen for Winifred's memorial service, thirty-five years earlier. On the centenary of Vera's birth, twenty-three years later, Shirley would unveil a plaque to her mother, with the inscription 'Blessed are the Peacemakers', in the Dick Sheppard chapel in the St Martin's crypt.

When Vera died her reputation was at its nadir. 'Indeed', Shirley wrote in

1993, 'she believed that as a writer she had been forgotten, the fading voice of a dying generation.' The obituaries were respectful, but failed to do justice to Vera's true significance as a writer, pacifist and feminist. *The Times* devoted more space to Vera as a novelist than to the 'controversial causes' which she 'vehemently advocated'; while in a column in the *Daily Telegraph*, David Holloway, the paper's Literary Editor, put forward the rather eccentric view that *Testament of Friendship* was 'a much better book' than *Testament of Youth*, and argued that 'Vera Brittain was one of those figures in the literary world whose position stemmed more from the fact that she was known to be a writer than from the importance of anything that she wrote.' Within a decade of Vera's death, however, the process of rediscovery and reassessment of her life and work would begin.

In her will Vera had put on record 'my deep appreciation and gratitude [to George] for his loving companionship during the years of our marriage, for his support in adversity, for the patience and kindness from which I have so often benefited, and for the many happy experiences we have enjoyed together, and I trust that if and whenever he desires to do so he will marry again without being deterred by conventional scruples, and that he will enjoy many years of happiness with my successor . . .'. George was knighted in 1970 for his work for Anglo-American relations, and married Delinda, widow of Lieutenant-Commander Victor Gates, on 16 April 1971. He died on 7 February 1979 aged eighty-two, and was buried beside his father in the Holy Trinity churchyard at Old Milverton in Warwickshire. John survived his father for little more than eight years, dying of a cerebral haemorrhage in 1987, on the anniversary of his mother's death, soon after completing the final draft of a book about his family, entitled *Family Quartet*.

For her daughter, Vera had had a special mission in mind. 'I want someone', she had told Shirley, ' – not necessarily you – to fulfil a request in my will which is to scatter my ashes on Edward's grave on the Asiago Plateau. Edward was as dear to me as you are, which is saying a very great deal, and for nearly fifty years much of my heart has been in that Italian village cemetery.'

There, on that lonely plateau, on a warm September afternoon of fitful sunlight, Shirley, Bernard Williams and Paul Berry fulfilled Vera Brittain's last request.

NOTES

Sources

Four principal manuscript collections have been used:

1 **The Vera Brittain Archive**, housed at McMaster University, Hamilton, Ontario. This vast collection comprises diaries, letters, manuscripts of published and unpublished works, lecture notes, articles, reviews, photographs, and other memorabilia. Aside from the correspondence, it has been catalogued in *McMaster Library Research News*, vol. 4, nos 3, 4 and 5 (1977–9). A checklist of correspondence at McMaster addressed to Vera Brittain is available in the Paul Berry Collection. The papers of Sir George Catlin are also at McMaster.

2 **The Winifred Holtby Archive**, housed at Hull Central Library, Albion Street, Hull. Manuscripts and printed sources, including the correspondence between Vera Brittain and Winifred Holtby from 1920 to 1935. A guide to the collection, *Winifred Holtby 1898–1935* by Jill Crowther, was published by Humberside Leisure Services in 1985.

3 **Paul Berry Collection**, Somerville College, Oxford. Manuscripts, notebooks, lecture notes, contracts, carbon copies of correspondence, and an extensive collection of letters from Vera Brittain to Paul Berry from 1942 to 1969, as well as letters from Sir George Catlin, John Catlin, Shirley Williams, Clare Leighton, Hilda Reid, A.C. Barrington, Sybil Morrison, Amy Burnett, etc.

4 **The Archive of Macmillan Publishers Ltd** in the British Library, London. Series of over 500 autograph and typed letters from Vera Brittain, 1922–60.

Additionally, the following archival sources have also been consulted:

BBC Written Archives, Caversham Park	Vera Brittain and George Catlin files
Bodleian Library, Oxford	Gilbert Murray papers. Vera Brittain notebooks, 1949–50; Vera Brittain, memorandum on Famine Relief, 1943
British Library, London	Northcliffe papers
British Library of Political and Economic Science, London	Women's International League for Peace and Freedom archive

Brynmor Jones Library, University of Hull	National Council for Civil Liberties archive
Fawcett Library, London	Six Point Group collection
Imperial War Museum, London	Women's Work collection
Modern Records Centre, Warwick	Victor Gollancz papers
Oxford University Press, Oxford	Correspondence with Brittains Ltd
Peace Pledge Union, London	Peace Pledge Union archive
Public Archive of Canada, Ottawa	Lovat Dickson papers
Public Record Office, Kew	First World War Battalion diaries; Home Office and Foreign Office records
Somerville College, Oxford	College records, minutes and JCR logbook
University of Illinois	Grant Richards archive
University of the Witwatersrand, Johannesburg	Sarah Gertrude Millin papers
Victor Gollancz Ltd, London	Publishing papers
Winifred Holtby Collection, Bridlington Library, East Yorkshire	Vera Brittain, 'The Mother of Michael's Child'

Family papers in the possession of Shirley Williams, David Leighton, and Miles Hudson.

Abbreviations

The following abbreviations have been used throughout the notes:

BL	Macmillan Publishers Ltd Archive, British Library	PhB	Phyllis Bentley
		RL	Roland Leighton
CF	*Chronicle of Friendship. Vera Brittain's Diary of the Thirties 1932–1939*, edited by Alan Bishop (Gollancz, 1986)	SL	*Selected Letters of Winifred Holtby and Vera Brittain 1920–1935*, edited by Vera Brittain and Geoffrey Handley-Taylor (A. Brown & Sons Ltd, 1960)
CY	*Chronicle of Youth. Vera Brittain's War Diary 1913–1917*, edited by Alan Bishop with Terry Smart (Gollancz, 1981)	SW	Shirley Williams
		TAB	Thomas Arthur Brittain
		TE	*Testament of Experience* (Gollancz, 1957)
EB	Edith Brittain	TF	*Testament of Friendship* (Macmillan, 1940)
EHB	Edward Brittain		
GC	George Catlin	TG	*Testament of a Generation*, edited by Paul Berry and Alan Bishop (Virago, 1985)
GT	Geoffrey Thurlow		
Hull	Winifred Holtby Archive, Hull Central Library		
		TS	*Thrice a Stranger. New Chapters of Autobiography* (Gollancz, 1938)
JC	John Catlin		
LF	Winifred Holtby, *Letters to a Friend*, edited by Alice Holtby and Jean McWilliam (Collins, 1937)		
		TY	*Testament of Youth* (Gollancz, 1933)
McM	Vera Brittain Archive, William Ready Division of Archives and Research Collections, McMaster University Library	VB	Vera Brittain
		VR	Victor Richardson
		WC	*Wartime Chronicle. Vera Brittain's Diary 1939–1945*, edited by Alan Bishop and Y. Aleksandra Bennett (Gollancz, 1989)
MSJ	Margaret Storm Jameson		
PB	Paul Berry		
PBC	Paul Berry Collection, Midhurst, West Sussex	WH	Winifred Holtby

Source Notes

Where only a short title for a book, article or thesis is provided, the full reference may be found in the Bibliography.

ILLUSTRATION ACKNOWLEDGEMENTS

Introduction Courtesy of Somerville College, Oxford. 1, 2, 3, 4, 5, 6, 8, 10, 15, 18, 21, 23, 24, 25, 26, 28, 31, 33, 34, 36 Courtesy of Shirley Williams.

7, 16, 17, 19, 22, 29, 35, 39 from the Paul Berry Collection, Somerville College, Oxford.

9, 20 Courtesy of McMaster University, Hamilton, Ontario.

11 Courtesy of Jonathan Elliman.

12 Courtesy of the Principal and Fellows, Somerville College, Oxford.

13, 14 Courtesy of David Leighton.

30 Courtesy of Hull Central Library, Humberside.

37 Courtesy of Timothy Brittain-Catlin.

38 Courtesy of Lady Catlin.

EPIGRAPH

vi   VB to Emmeline Pethick-Lawrence, 17 November 1933. McM.

CHAPTER 1: 'A BAD HISTORY OF INHERITANCE AND ENVIRONMENT'

11   **'ugly old Staffordshire'**: VB to MSJ, 23 April 1940. McM.

11   **'The old . . . ghosts'**: 'Staffordshire "ghosts" still dominate her novels', *Staffordshire Evening Sentinel*, 26 July 1965.

12   **'A pall of'**: VB, 'Memories of a Staffordshire Londoner', *Gallery* (April–May, 1966).

12   **'a strong vein'**: VB, 'Staffordshire Memories', *Staffordshire Life* (September 1949).

12   **Meigh pew**: We are grateful to Mrs Olwyn Bradbury of St Mary's Church, Bucknall, for providing us with details of Meigh's case as plaintiff in the High Court in February 1885.

12   **'staid Midland yeomen'**: VB, *TS*, 131.

13   **Ivy House Mill**: Much of the information about the Brittain paper mills which follows is derived from Robert Milner's thesis, 'Brittains Limited. Cheddleton and Hanley Paper Mills in the

context of the history of paper making in England'. The Ivy House Paper Mills continue to operate today in Commercial Road, Hanley.

13   **'man of indefatigable . . . noble character'**: Brochure, *Brittains Limited. Fine Paper Specialities* (February 1932), 9. PBC.

14   **Park Fields**: More properly known as Parkfields Cottage, built in 1805 for Sarah, the widow of Josiah Wedgwood.

14   **'the oldest of eleven children'**: In *TY*, 18, VB states that her father had eleven brothers and sisters; in *TE*, 29, she writes that 'Counting three deaths in infancy, they had been eleven all told . . .' Census and birth records, however, show that there were eleven children in all, and that only one died in infancy.

14   **'a three-storied house'**: *TE*, 126. The house is described in John Ward's *Borough of Stoke-on-Trent* (W. Lewis, 1843), 525. The Cloughs was demolished in the mid-Thirties.

14   **'sound wisdom'**: *Brittains Limited*, 9. PBC.

15   **small Oxford Bible**: Sutcliffe, *The Oxford University Press*, 39–40.

15   **'dowdy and stolid'**: VB to WH, 22 April 1933. Hull.

15   **her unwedded cook**: VB tells the story in *Lady into Woman*, 151.

15   **'without money'**: *TY*, 19.

15   **Jewish blood**: e.g. VB to George Brett, 12 November 1940. McM. 'There is *no* Jewish blood in our family.' In notes for a lecture, 'Answers to Correspondents', in May 1938, VB commented 'Have no Jewish blood. Wish I had. Guarantee of children's intelligence.' McM.

15   **scrapbook**: At McM. Further information about the Bervons from 1871 census records for Aberystwyth.

16   **series of concerts**: 'Mr Bervon's Farewell Concert', *The Aberystwyth Observer*, 10 June 1871.

16   **'one of the best voice trainers'**: *Staffordshire Sentinel*, 18 December 1890.

16   **'a graceful'**: *TY*, 20.

16   **'moved heaven . . . comforts'**: *CY*, 34.

16   **'Please don't excite . . . church'**: TAB to EB, 6 April 1891. McM.

17   **their first child**: Revd David Marshall, Vicar of St George's, Newcastle-under-Lyme, kindly permitted us to consult the church registers which show that EB attended a service of churching, after the stillbirth of her son, on 25 May 1892.

17   **29 December 1893**: VB always preferred to draw a discreet veil over her true date of birth. SW remembers that 'There was always quite a mystery about how old my mother was. She kept it terribly dark. She always managed to slip it towards 1894, 5, 6.' As she got older VB became increasingly reticent about her age. In the early Fifties, when approaching 60, she went so far as to alter the year of her birth in her passport from 1893 to 1898.

528

18   'I often picture': A.M. Newby to EB, 22 July 1918. McM.

18   'a hard, undemonstrative': VB, *Honourable Estate*, 273.

18   'my unaltruistic': VB to PB, 16 May 1952. PBC.

19   'looking very ill': VB to SW, 8 August 1960. McM.

19   'insane, suicidal ... mental defective': VB to WH, 22 April 1933. Hull.

20   'attributing monstrous': VB, 'Answers to Correspondents'. McM.

20   one occasion in the Forties: Reported in VB's diary for 26 December 1966. McM.

20   'the melancholy': *CY*, 52.

20   'only too aware': VB to PhB, 29 April 1933. McM.

21   'strange medley': *TY*, 24.

21   an unfinished novel: VB, 'The Great Explanation', ch. 1. MS McM. One of the many precursors of *TY*.

21   'practical capacities ... matter of course': VB, obituary of Florence Bervon, *The Times*, 23 May 1936.

22   'indispensable ... trenches': *TY*.

22   'Fancy him going off': VB, 'Managing the Male – A Vanishing Occupation', TS of article. McM.

22   'Never a Trade Union man': The resistance of Brittains Ltd to union power is illustrated by the concern expressed by Frederick Haigh, the director with special responsibility for the manufacture of Oxford India paper, when trade unionism strengthened its hold at Oxford University Press's Wolvercote mill. 'Trades Unionism [is] no real remedy,' he wrote, 'brings no real help or healing to the workers themselves. On the other hand the real remedy is the hearty and active effort of the Employers, with the willing and loyal co operation of the workers, to bring about better and happier conditions both with regard to work and wages.' Haigh to Joseph Castle, 11 August 1913. Oxford University Press Archive.

23   "Arthur Band Box": Hugh Brittain to SW, 15 November 1979. PBC.

23   'imprint of suave prosperity': VB, *Honourable Estate*, 230.

23   'Yesterday we went to Buxton': VB to EB, 'Sunday 1904'. McM.

23   'incredible energy': VB to GC, 26 June 1924. McM.

24   'a very pretty woman': Elizabeth Rokeby to PB, 19 October 1981. PBC.

24   the promising musician: EHB's file cards on which he kept a record of his sheet music collection are at McM.

25   'adored': *TY*, 27.

25   'We want to go': VB to EB, 27 September 1903. McM.

25   'I saw a mouse': VB to EB, 24 September [probably 1902]. McM.

26   'I cannot remember': VB, 'My Three Rules for Happiness', *Evening Standard*, 31 January 1935.

26   'precisely nine books ... uncomfortable questions': VB, 'Children and Books', *Manchester Guardian*, 26 July 1927.

26   childhood 'novels': MSS McM.

26   'full of misunderstandings ... stories': VB, 'The Road to the Temple (A Fragment of Autobiography)', January 1935. TS McM.

27   "inclined to be fanciful": VB, *Honourable Estate*, 295.

29   'exactly like a cook's': VB, 'The Road to the Temple'. McM.

29   'a very intelligent pupil': Report dated 21 September 1905. McM.

29   'all that was worst': Tozer, *Physical Education at Thring's Uppingham*, 243.

29   'the main object': C.R.W. Nevinson, *Paint and Prejudice*, 8.

30   'a good and desirable boy': 'Term Report of the Progress and Conduct of Brittain', Christmas 1910. McM.

30   'For girls': 11 July 1914, *CY*, 78.

30   'The Ladies': Louise Heath-Jones, the daughter of a Wolverhampton manufacturer, was born in 1869. She was awarded an *aegrotat* in the History Tripos in 1894, and after six years of teaching at a variety of schools, including St Leonard's and Heathfield, established St Monica's at a small house in Tadworth village in Surrey. The larger site at Kingswood was leased to Heath-Jones and Florence Bervon in 1906. St Monica's still stands, only slightly enlarged since VB's schooldays.

30   'bracing, sunny ... of the day': Prospectus for St Monica's. PBC.

31   'its tasteful decorations': *TY*, 75.

31   'Miss H-J said': VB to EB, 16 November 1910. McM.

32   'did not turn out': *CY*, 64.

32   'was far in advance': VB, 'The Road to the Temple'. McM.

32   'To us women': St Monica's School Notes, 1911–12. McM.

32   'a very great amount': VB to RL, 24 May 1914. McM.

32   'We had report today': VB to EB, 16 November 1910. McM.

33   'one of those unhappy': VB, 'The Seeing Eye', *Manchester Guardian*, 29 June 1931.

33   'there was very little': *CY*, 78.

33   romantic friendship: See the examination of the schoolgirl friendships of this period by Vicinus, *Independent Women*, 187–99.

33   ' "Chief Events of the Year" ... too great for words': VB's diary summary for 1910 and daily diary for 1911. McM.

34   'a tale': Incomplete untitled novel, c. 1907. McM.

34   'to become the writer': *TY*, 40.

34   'passionate four-page editorial': VB, 'The Road to the Temple'. McM.

35   'which opened ...': *CF*, 103.

35   'My ... writing': VB, diary summary for Michaelmas Term 1910. McM.

35   'When competition ceases': VB, 'Morris' Idea of Art as a Remedy for Social Evils'. McM.

35   essay on ... *Utopia*: VB, 'The Dream Element in More's Utopia', 3 November 1911.

36   'sounded with a note': VB, 'Olive Schreiner', *Nation and Athenaeum*, 23 October 1926.
36   'born feminist': Gorham, ' "Have We Really Rounded Seraglio Point?" ' 86.
36   'Girls did not mean': VB to Maurice Richardson, 13 February 1958. Copy in PBC.
36   'The name of Mrs Pankhurst . . . witch-burning': VB, *Manchester Guardian*, 20 June 1928, *TG*, 100–2.
36   'an ardent if discreet': *TY*, 42.
36   'supplied the theory': *Manchester Guardian*, 20 June 1928.
37   'independence . . . wider life': VB, daily diary, 8 January 1911. McM.
37   'such places': *TY*, 67.
38   'I am really beginning': 3 January 1913, *CY*, 25.
38   'most thrilling': 17 November 1913, *CY*, 42.
38   'I put on . . . billy-oh': VB, 'Reflective Record', 25 May 1913. McM.
39   'to get seriously': *CY*, 34.
39   'the mean, fault-finding': VB, 'Noisy London a Haven of Peace'. TS PBC.
39   'My picture': VB to Helena Swanwick, 20 July 1933. Copy in Fawcett Library.
39   'cry with relief': VB, 'Reflective Record', 25 January 1913. McM.
40   'very heatedly': 27 May 1914, *CY*, 70.
40   'I may leave': 2 January 1914, *CY*, 51.
40   Her father's: The historian A.J.P. Taylor was a schoolboy living in Buxton (in Manchester Road) in 1914. In old age he recalled that he had known Arthur Brittain 'quite well at one time', but, he added, 'this was not enlightening', A.J.P. Taylor to M. Bostridge, 11 September 1984. For Taylor's own impressions of life in Buxton before the First World War, see his *A Personal History* (Hamish Hamilton, 1983).
40   'He is such': VB to RL, 4 September 1915. McM.
40   'not as sensible . . . to him': 15 November 1913, *CY*, 41.
40   her mother: see the discussion of VB's relationship with EB in Gorham, 'The Friendships of Women'.
40   'She was brought up': *CY*, 58.
40   'we certainly don't': VBC, Reflective Record', 14 June 1913. McM.
41   'conscious all my life': VB to SW, 25 August 1952. McM.
41   'self-appointed elite': MS note. PBC.
41   'bright sane personality': 6 May 1914, *CY*, 63.
41   'power of making': 29 November 1913, *CY*, 46.
41   'Yes I know': VB to EHB, 10 November 1916. McM.
42   'special prerogative': EHB to EB, 5 July 1914. McM.
42   'I have been impressed': VB to RL, 1 September 1915. McM.
43   carrying a small torch: VB to TAB, 10 November 1911. McM.
43   'ardent impersonal dreams': 29 September 1915. VB, 'Reflective Record', MCM.

43   'to disclose': 4 March 1913, *CY*, 30.
43   'murmured something': 8 January 1913, *CY*, 27.
43   'a large, athletic': *TY*, 48.
44   'hard-hearted': 28 June 1914, *CY*, 74.
44   'My Dear Vera': Bertram Spafford to VB, n.d. McM.
44   'immediate . . . reaction': *TY*, 48.
44   'Dear Mr Spafford': VB to Bertram Spafford, 22 September 1913. McM.
45   'Dear Mrs Vera Spafford': EHB to VB, 28 September 1913. McM.
45   'sleepless nights': VB to Arthur Creech Jones, 20 November 1933. McM.
45   'pleb talking to plebs': 15 February 1914, *CY*, 56.
45   'this brilliant man': VB, 'Rereading *Not Without Honour*', MS note. PBC.
46   'hot & shy . . . near me': 14 April 1914, *CY*, 65–6.
46   'careful not to': 'Sir John Marriott', *Dictionary of National Biography*.
46   'Unintellectual Buxton': 22 January 1913, *CY*, 28.
47   'the smallest intellectual': 5 February 1913, *CY*, 29.
47   '. . . The Testament of Youth': Marriott, *Memories of Four Score Years*, 44.
47   'recently erected': VB to RL, 18 October 1914. McM.
47   'gay attire': 27 August 1914, *CY*, 98.
48   'Violent in speech': *TY*, 63. That TAB's objections to VB attending university had always been based upon worries about how it might affect his pocket, rather than on any argument against higher education for women on principle, could perhaps be inferred from the evidence of his will which makes a generous bequest to poor students at Somerville in the event of VB dying without issue.
48   'In a small narrow place': 21 October 1913, *CY*, 40.
48   'The more I think': 25 March 1914, *CY*, 63.
49   'Oxford is heaven': EHB to VB, 7 December 1913. McM.

CHAPTER 2: ROLAND

50   'I know I haven't': Quoted in M. Leighton, *Boy of My Heart*, 43. The original letter from RL to his sister Clare has since come to light. Dated 4 November 1915, it reads, 'I am afraid that I must be a protagonist or nothing: I have not in me that which makes a Bystander.' Original in possession of Leighton family.
51   'My letters': RL to VB, 18 July 1915. McM.
51   '*in loco parentis*': David Leighton to PB, 15 October 1980. PBC.
51   'Our mother': C. Leighton, *Tempestuous Petticoat*, 125.
51   'the kindest manner': WH to Jean McWilliam, 25 July 1921, *LF*, 53.
52   *Treasure Island*: Robert Leighton's part in accepting Stevenson's story for publication is mentioned by Clement Shorter in a brief obituary notice for RL in *The Sphere*, 22 January 1916, and

by J.C. Steuart in *Robert Louis Stevenson: Man and Writer* (Sampson Low, 1924), 319.

52   knew by heart: According to VR. VR to VB, 28 January 1916. McM.

53   'The Serial': British Library Add. MSS 62183/77.

53   'audacious letter': Marie Leighton to Lord Northcliffe, 12 December 1913. British Library Add. MSS 62324/140.

53   'I like him': 29 June 1913, *CY*, 38.

54   'reserved conceit': VB, 'Reflective Record', 10 July 1914. McM.

54   'At nineteen': *TY*, 81

54   'various matters ... very much': 17–18 April 1914, *CY*, 66–7.

55   'Dear Vera': RL to VB, 22 April 1914. McM.

55   'a great book': 3 May 1914, *CY*, 68.

55   'very much': VB to RL, 3 May 1914. McM.

55   'Its power': Bishop, 'With Suffering and Through Time' 88.

55   'the first wholly': Showalter, *A Literature of Their Own*, 199.

55   'Nothing is nicely': VB to RL, 3 May 1914. McM.

56   'then she can't be': M. Leighton, *Boy of My Heart*, 26.

56   'I spend much': 2 July 1914, *CY*, 75.

56   'heartless, retrospective': *TY*, 101.

57   '... My interest': 10 July 1914, *CY*, 77.

57   'fine sight': 11 July 1914, *CY*, 78.

58   'Somehow I have': VB to Maurice Richardson, 13 February 1958. Copy in PBC.

58   'The echo': VB in Panichas (ed.), *Promise of Greatness*, 317–18.

60   'Nothing like it': 5 August 1914, *CY*, 88.

60   'He suddenly'. Ibid.

60   'After dinner': 2 September 1914, *CY*, 101.

61   'his obvious strength': VB, 'Reflective Record', 6 September 1914. McM. Five months later in January 1915, Spafford wrote to Arthur Brittain, accusing him of having deliberately snubbed him in the street because of his failure to enlist, and offering once again his business as the reason for his not having done so. Spafford eventually served as a Captain in the Irish Guards. He survived the war and died in 1957.

61   'Current events': VB, 'Why Current Events Matter to Us', lecture given at the Halifax Luncheon Club, 30 November 1932.

61   'Women are just': VB, 'Women and Disarmament', *Highway*, February 1934.

61   'Kitchener's finger': In Panichas (ed.), *Promise of Greatness*, 316.

62   'It was very hard': VB, 'Reflective Record', 28 August 1914. McM.

62   'fulminating furiously': *TY*, 92.

63   'our destinies': 30 August 1914, *CY*, 101.

63   'with a kind': 1 October 1914, *CY*, 114.

63   'except for': RL to VB, 30 September 1914. McM.

63   'I don't know': VB to RL, 14 October 1914. McM.

64   'It will be strange': RL to VB, 7 October 1914. McM.

64   'I live': 14 October 1914, *CY*, 118.

64   Somerville: Until as late as 1932, when the college's new frontage was being built, Somerville was approached from the Woodstock Road gatehouse along a carriage drive, densely overshadowed by trees, past two dilapidated cottages, with a public house, the Waggon and Horses, situated rather incongruously to the east of the entrance.

65   Joanna Richardson's phrase: *Enid Starkie*, 30.

66   'in spite of': 22 October 1914, *CY*, 119.

66   'He came up': VB to EB, 18 November 1914. McM.

67   'pattern of black': VB to EB, 31 January 1915. McM.

67   'you have to': VB to EB, 28 February 1915. McM.

67   'on the cheap': VB to EB, 18 November 1914. McM.

68   'insufferably': VB, 'Reflective Record', 24 November 1914. McM.

68   'strange how': VB to RL, 15 April 1915. McM.

68   'it took': Farnell, *A Somervillian Looks Back*, 35.

69   'past mistress of scorn': 21 November 1914, *CY*, 126.

69   'From thinking': 1 December 1914, *CY*, 129.

69   'feeling useless': VB to EB, 29 November 1914. McM.

70   'sinfully extravagant': 24 December 1914, *CY*, 133.

70   'In the vestibule': M. Leighton, *Boy of My Heart*, 30.

70   'for intruding': C. Leighton to PB, 7 October 1976. PBC

71   'But when I saw': 31 December 1914, *CY*, 137.

71   'I know you're': ibid., 139.

71   'I am very fond': VR to VB, 28 January 1916. McM.

71   'very, very much': RL to VB, 1 January 1915. McM.

72   'I felt': VB to RL, 4 January 1915. McM.

72   'Taken by surprise': 16 January 1915, *CY*, 148.

73   'sham fights': Mottram's impressions of 'Ronald Aubrey Leighton' are contained in several letters to his mother in February 1915, now in Norfolk Record Office. See also R.H. Mottram, *The Window Seat* (Hutchinson, 1954), for his account of his training at Lowestoft.

73   'I think': RL to VB, 12 March 1915. McM.

73   'seemed I said': 19 March 1915, *CY*, 157–8.

74   'intangibility': VB to RL, 7 June 1915. McM.

74   'I had another': 19 April 1915, *CY*, 179.

74   green army envelopes: All ranks had occasional access to green envelopes, which were used on the understanding that the contents of a letter were of a private or family nature, and could be opened only by the Base Censor.

74   'You know': RL to VB, 14 May 1915. McM.

75   'strong unconquerable': 3 April 1915, *CY*, 171.

75   'Love and Hope': RL to VB, 26 March 1915. McM.

75   'an appropriate': VB to RL, 22 March 1915. McM.

75   battalion diary: 7th Worcesters, Public Record Office, Kew, WO95 2759.

75   'The trenches': RL to VB, 11 April 1915. McM.

75   'These have': RL to VB, 12 April 1915. McM.

76   'I shall be glad': RL to VB, 20 April 1915. McM.

76   'but no one': RL to VB, 12 April 1915. McM.

76   'a most nerve-wracking': RL to VB, 17 May 1915. McM.

76   'crooning whistle ... expert': RL to VB, 13 June 1915. McM.

76   'The ground': RL to VB, 20 April 1915. McM.

77   'lying very still': RL to VB, 9 May 1915. McM.

77   'You would have': RL to VB, 3 June 1915. McM.

77   'I am writing this': RL to VB, 17 May 1915. McM.

77   'It is all': RL to VB, 20 April 1915. McM.

77   'real fighting ... *Lusitania*': RL to VB, 14 May 1915. McM.

78   'I never thought': VB to RL, 17 April 1915. McM.

78   'When all is finished': RL to VB, 20 April 1915. McM.

78   'a queer exultation': 15 April 1915, *CY*, 175. Three days later VB wrote to EHB, 'His letters do thrill me ... I quite envy you; don't you feel you wouldn't miss it for anything! Somehow it seems as if to die out there wouldn't be so very hard as it would anywhere else.' VB to EHB, 18 April 1915. McM.

78   'The terrible things': VB to RL, 25 April 1915. McM.

78   'I am not sure': 25 April 1915 *CY*, 184.

79   'Suffering myself': VB to RL, 25 April 1915. McM.

79   'in every way': Farnell, *A Somervillian Looks Back*, 40.

79   'the Principal's ... is of use': VB to RL, 11 April 1915. McM.

80   'I sit': VB to RL, 25 April 1915. McM.

80   'But for this': VB to Lovat Dickson, 3 March 1954. BL.

80   'all sad': 12 May 1915, *CY*, 195.

80   'too soft': VB to RL, 25 April 1915. McM.

80   limited response: Among those Somervillians absent for war work by Hilary Term 1916 was VB's friend, Norah Hughes, who had become a checker of forage under the War Office. One other undergraduate apart from VB was working as a probationary VAD. Hilda Lorimer, VB's classics tutor, was given leave of absence with effect from Michaelmas Term 1915 for relief work in Serbia. Somerville JCR logbook.

81   an open letter: Dated 8 February 1917 and published in the *Oxford Magazine* for 16 March under the heading 'Robbing the Future'.

81   VAD under contract: Details of VB's VAD service are held on her record cards in the British Red Cross Archives.

81   'Oh! I love': 27 June 1915, *CY*, 215.

82   'shittishness ... Triumvirate': RL to EHB, 27 August 1915. McM.

82   'The earthly': Quoted in *TY*, 174.

82   'And so': RL to VB, 13 June 1915. McM.

82   'the premature air ... a kind of dread': 20 August 1915, *CY*, 235.

83   'with boyish': 21 August 1915, *CY*, 240.

83   'best self': 23 August 1915, *CY*, 261. VB continues, 'Certainly I have, owing to unfortunate heredity, a trace of conventional social instinct ...'

84   'I hadn't realized': 23 August 1915, *CY*, 263.

84   'The worst part': RL to EHB, 27 August 1915. McM.

85   'A thoroughly': Quoted in VB, 'Reflective Record', 1 September 1915. McM.

85   'with a love': M. Leighton to EB, 31 August 1915. McM. EB wrote to RL that '... I do not think it possible that she [VB] could meet another man who would be able to understand her unusual temperament as I know you will in time ...' 29 August 1915. McM.

85   'I thought': VB to RL, 27 August 1915. McM.

85   'his quiet smile': VB to RL, 14 September 1915. McM.

85   'I shall probably': RL to VB, 10 September 1915. McM.

86   'If this word': Quoted in *CY*, 278.

87   'In spite of': VB, 'A Volunteer Nurse on Active Service', *The Trained Nurse and Hospital Review*, November 1934.

87   'butchers' shop': VB to RL, 21 October 1915. McM.

87   'they throw': Ibid.

87   'I am sitting': VB to RL, 18 October 1915. McM.

88   'you have written': RL to VB, 19 September 1915. McM.

88   to block out memories: This is also suggested by a letter written by RL to his mother on 10 December 1915. 'I seem to be very much cut off from everything and everybody just lately. Sometimes I rather exult in it; sometimes I wonder how much of the old Roland is left. I have learnt much; I have gained much; I have grown up suddenly; I have got to know the ways of the world.' Quoted by M. Leighton, *Boy of My Heart*, 15–16.

88   automatisme anesthésiant: Marc Boasson quoted in Eksteins, *Rites of Spring*, 237.

88   André Bridoux's: Ibid., 239.

89   'the Beauty': RL to VB, 2 August 1915. McM.

89   Samuel Hynes: Hynes, *A War Imagined*, 113.

89   'To Monseigneur': VB, *Verses of a VAD*, 18.

90   'a wild man': RL to VB, 7 November 1915. McM.

90   'Do I seem': RL to VB, 17 November 1915. McM.

90   'I literally . . . France': VB to RL, 8 November 1915. McM.

90   'No . . . you haven't': VB to RL, 4 December 1915. McM.

90   'into the seventh': 1 December 1915, *CY*, 291.

90   'Otherwise nothing': RL to VB, 28 November 1915. McM.

90   'to a still colder': RL to VB, 26 November 1915. McM.

91   'My leave': RL to VB, 28 November 1915. McM.

91   'Well, after all': RL to VB, 3 December 1915. McM.

91   'in various stages': RL to VB, 9 December 1915. McM.

92   'After all': VB to RL, 17 December 1915. McM.

92   'Believing that': *TY*, 236.

92   'I went up': Capt. Adshead to VB, 6 February 1916. McM.

93   'Mr Leighton's hit': M. Leighton to VB, 25 February 1916, McM. This letter enclosed a plan, drawn by Robert Leighton, showing how RL was hit in No Man's Land.

93   official report: Battalion Diary, 7th Worcesters, Public Record Office, Kew, WO95 2759.

93   'a very big . . . went out': Capt. Adshead to VB, 6 February 1916. McM.

93   ominous remark: RL to EHB, 27 April 1915. McM.

94   'almost devotional': VB, 'Reflective Record', 3 January 1916. McM.

94   attraction to Catholicism: See 'Reflective Record', 30 April 1914 in which VB mentions receiving a letter from RL arguing that 'the Roman Religion was at least up to date . . .' McM.

94   'This is not': VB to Mrs Gibson, 8 June 1934. McM.

94   'to inspire': *TY*, 337.

95   'What did he mean': *TY*, 253.

95   another gloss: We owe this interpretation to Marion Shaw.

95   'When I get': VB to RL, 29 August 1915. McM.

96   'Next to the loss': VB to St John Ervine, 8 February 1939. Hull.

96   Whether she ever asked: The evidence suggests that she did not do so at the time. On 14 January 1916 VD wrote to EHB, ' "Hédauville" is perhaps the most wonderful of all the poems. And it was his last – it must have been written only about a month before he died. And I wonder if he was prophetic in that – and I wonder quite what he meant. Oh! there are such millions of things I want to ask him – now.' McM.

96   'I doubt': VB to GC, 15 September 1952. McM.

CHAPTER 3: 'I, TOO, TAKE LEAVE OF ALL I EVER HAD'

97   'I, Too, Take Leave': This line from Robert Nichols' 'Farewell' (1915) was often quoted by VB during the war.

97   'like courtiers': 1 January 1916, *CY*, 301.

97   'Poor dear little girl': Stella Sharp to VB, 27 December 1915. McM.

98   arrived at an opportune moment: Hilary Bailey, *Vera Brittain*, 31–3, pointed out certain discrepancies between VB's descriptions in *TY* and *CY* of the return of RL's belongings to his family, and the accounts given by Clare Leighton in *Tempestuous Petticoat* and in her Preface to *CY*. In fact the two versions are not incompatible. Clare Leighton's omission of VB from the scene at the cottage at Keymer may in part be due to failing memory, but is more plausibly attributed to her wish to exclude VB from anything she wrote about RL because of her own bad relations with VB. For further information about Clare Leighton's relationship with VB in later years, see Chapter 17.

98   'This is a book': M. Leighton, *Boy of My Heart*, Foreword.

98   'the reader': *Times Literary Supplement*, 29 June 1916.

98   'How Mrs Leighton': GT to VB, 15 February 1916. McM.

99   'The Mother of Michael's Child': 'Notes for an unwritten novel by Vera Brittain. The Mother of Michael's Child, *c*. 1924. Contained in a notebook belonging to WH. WH Collection, Bridlington Library.

100   'In the utter blackness': 30–1 January 1916, *CY*, 313.

100   'Last time': VB to EB, 1 February 1916. McM.

100   'with their strange': *CY*, 96.

100   'a grey': *TY*, 255.

100   'is the most': VR to VB, 15 February 1916. McM.

101   'I am a very ordinary': VR to VB, 19 January 1916. McM.

101   'Very nice': M. Leighton, *Boy of My Heart*, 22.

101   'You can imagine': VR to VB, 8 February 1916. McM.

101   'in good order': VR to VB, 26 January 1916. McM.

102   'Tah says': VB to EHB, 24 January 1916. McM.

102   'I understand': VR to VB, 17 February 1916. McM.

102   letting her know: VR to VB, 21 February 1916. McM.

102   'very little doing': VB to EB, 1 February 1916. McM.

103   'very taken . . . trustworthy': 10 October 1915, *CY*, 288.

103   'I was quite alarmed': GT to VB, 15 December 1916. McM.

103   'His manner': 2 March 1916, *CY*, 318.

103   'strange': 10 October 1915, *CY*, 288.

103   'conduct and character': *The Chigwellian*, July 1917.

103   'non-militarist': 2 March 1916, *CY*, 318.

103   'Those days': GT to VB, 18 November 1916. McM.

104   'the stiff': GT to VB, 4 July 1916. McM.

104   'any earthly use': GT to VB, 30 December 1916. McM.

104   'I only hope': GT to VB, 3 November 1916. McM.

104   'He spoke': 4–10 June 1916, *CY*, 325.

104   'There seems': *TY*, 274–5.

105   'I was wounded': 4 July 1916, *CY*, 326.

105   the first wave of attack: See Middlebrook on the 11th Sherwood Foresters' part in the attack, *The First Day on the Somme*, 150, 159–60.

105   'He says': 5 July 1916, *CY*, 328.

105   'indignation': Bishop, 'The Battle of the Somme and Vera Brittain', 128.

106   'some of the most representative': VB, 'Youth and War', *New York Herald Tribune*, 11 November 1934.

106   'He is sustained': VR to VB, 11 June 1916. McM.

106   'How we ever': VB to EB, 29 March 1917. McM.

106   the *Britannic* and the *Asturias*: the *Britannic* struck a mine on 21 November 1916 while carrying over 1,000 wounded soldiers; about 50 people were drowned. February 1917 saw the beginning of a period of unrestricted submarine warfare, and the *Asturias* was one of several hospital ships to be torpedoed and sunk. She was hit by a torpedo on 20 March 1917 while steaming with navigation lights burning and the Red Cross sign brilliantly illuminated; 43 were killed and 39 injured.

106   'Discipline is very strict': VB to EB, 27 September 1916. McM.

107   'to manage as best': VB to EB, 3 November 1916. McM.

107   the dress regulations: 'We . . . wear soft low collars and panama hats which you can buy here', VB told her mother; 'no one seems to be very particular about uniform unless you meet the Principal Matron who of course has to be. The difference between the stiffness & starchiness of the Nursing Profession in England & the free & easiness here is quite remarkable. No one minds whether you come into meals in your mess-dress, your blouse & skirt & hat, or your ordinary indoor uniform . . .' VB to EB, 25 October 1916. McM. The salient details of VB's picture of life in Malta are confirmed by Amy Innes-Lillingstone, a former VAD who recorded her memories of her service there for the Imperial War Museum's Women's Work collection.

107   'I am ever so': VB to EB, 3 November 1916. McM.

108   'a feeling': VB to EB, 29 March 1917. McM.

108   'all the unhappy . . . case of Stella': VB to EB, 20 April 1917, McM. After the war Stella Sharp married Herbert Looker who was Conservative MP for Essex S.E. from 1924–9. She lost a son in the RAF during the Second World War, and was awarded the OBE in 1952 for her record of public service. VB had little contact with her in later years.

108   'Fancy it being': VB to EB, 16 December 1916. McM.

108   'when one has looked': VB to EB, 12 October 1916. McM.

108   'bright golden flowers': VB to EB, 16 December 1916. McM.

109   'as I don't believe': VB to EB, 2 February 1917. McM.

109   'the most exquisite . . . think about this': VB to EB, 16 December 1916. McM.

109   'I feel so far away': VB to EB, 12 October 1916. McM.

109   'the sparkle': VB to EB, 16 December 1916. McM.

109   'It is no good': VB to EB, 29 March 1917. McM.

109   Oakwood Court: The Brittains moved from 8 Oakwood Court, W14, to number 30 in April 1917.

109   'than to be prosperous': VB to EB, 10 March 1917. McM.

110   'Glad in a way': GT to VB, 8 October 1916. McM.

110   'The trenches': VR to VB, 31 October 1916. McM.

110   'Vera says': GT to EHB, 5 December 1916. McM.

110   'You seem to think': VR to VB, 6 December 1916. McM.

111   'You say': GT to VB, 28 August 1916. McM.

111   'I remember': GT to VB, 15 February 1917. McM.

111   'No . . . I dislike': GT to EB, 13 August 1916. McM.

111   'life on its way': GT to VB, 21 September 1916. McM.

112   'I often long': GT to EHB, 12 November 1916. McM.

112   'I'm not the slightest': GT to EHB, 8 February 1916. McM.

112   'Don't you often': GT to VB, 25 March 1917. McM.

112   'our next meeting': GT to EHB, 8 February 1917. McM.

112   'ought save': GT to EHB, 5 December 1916. McM.

112   'one picture': Cecilia Thurlow to VB, 24 June 1934. McM.

113   'tragical reading': *TY*, 333.

113   'the spirit': VR to VB, 30 January 1917. McM.

113   'Well, Vera': VR to VB, 24 March 1917. McM.

114   'The longer': VB to EHB, 17 April 1917. McM.

114   'There really doesn't': VB to EB, 20 April 1917. McM.

114   'I am quite broken hearted': VB to EB, 23 April 1917. McM.

114   continued to press forward: For his part in the attack VR was awarded the Military Cross.

115   'This morning': EHB to GT, 22 April 1917. McM.

115   Monchy-le-Preux: For details of the action see Battalion Diary, 10th Sherwood Foresters, Public Record Office, Kew, WO95 2008.

115   'and was soon hit': EHB to VB, 7 May 1917. McM.

115   '& if he wishes it': 1 May 1917, *CY*, 340.

115   Footnote: Tragically, the Thurlow family were to suffer bereavement again a year later when

on 24 April 1918 – almost a year to the day of Geoffrey's death – his older brother, Lieutenant John Kennings Thurlow of the 1/10th Scottish battalion, King's Liverpool Regiment, was killed in action in France.

116 'has always been': VB to EB, 20 April 1917. McM.

116 'accurate, clear & reverent': 18 April 1917, CY, 339.

116 'I don't think': EHB to VB, 7 May 1917. McM.

116 'to offer him': VB to EHB, 6 May 1917. McM.

116 'meandered off': TY, 357.

117 'As for Victor': VB to GC, 26 June 1924. McM.

117 'We started': EHB to VB, 11 June 1917. McM.

117 early morning attack: For further details of the participation of EHB's unit in operations near Lens on 1 July 1917 see comments of the Company Commander, H.G. Wildbore, in a letter to VB dated 25 January 1935 in which he confirms the account of the attack which she had given in TY. VB replied to him on 28 January that 'This ... show does seem to have been complete chaos, and one cannot help wondering ... how much of the War was conducted on these lines.' Imperial War Museum.

118 'small weary part': 18 April 1917, CY, 339.

118 'It was the land': VB, 'Folly's Vineyard', 1924. McM.

118 'The place': VB to EB, 3 August 1917. McM.

118 'like passing through hell': Quoted by Gill and Dallas, 'Mutiny at Étaples Base in 1917', Past and Present. For a map and descriptions of the base in 1917, see also Putkowski, 'Toplis, Étaples & "The Monocled Mutineer" ', Stand To!. For further impressions of nursing at Étaples, see the memoirs of Mrs D. McCann who served as a VAD at 18 General Hospital. Women's Work Collection, Imperial War Museum.

119 '... To have real': VB to EB and TAB, 5 August 1917. McM.

119 'It was with very mixed': VB, 'Inter Arma Caritas. The experiences of a VAD nurse among wounded German prisoners in France', 1918, McM.

119 'Am frantically busy': VB to EB, 5 August 1917. McM.

119 'Every serious': VB, 'Inter Arma Caritas'. McM.

119 'In the ward': VB to EB and TAB, 8 August 1917. McM.

120 'to see a limb': VB, 'Inter Arma Caritas'. McM.

120 none of the antipathy: Kissen in 'Vera Brittain: Writing a Life' draws an interesting contrast between VB's attitude towards nursing Germans, and that of Violetta Thurstan who nursed German soldiers in Belgium. Thurstan comments on the irony of 'putting hundreds of cold compresses on German feet, that they might be ready all the sooner to go out and kill our men.' After the soldiers leave her hospital she feels 'a very joyful free sort of feeling at having got rid of the German patients.' Violetta Thurston, Field Hospital and Flying Column: Being the Journal of an English Nursing Sister in Belgium and France (Putnam, 1915), 158.

120 'You will be surprised': VB to EB, 5 August 1917. McM.

120 'One can only feel': VB, 'Inter Arma Caritas'. McM.

120 'ladies': VB to EB, 25 September 1917. McM.

120 'little after-supper': VB to EB, 23 October 1917. McM.

120 'a little skit': VB to EB, 30 November 1917. McM. The skit was to be a curtain-raiser to a performance of Thackeray's The Rose and the Ring.

120 'though you would probably': VB to EB, 25 September 1917. McM.

121 'brilliant ... profession': VB, 'Inter Arma Caritas'. McM.

121 'She suddenly felt': VB, 'Folly's Vineyard'. McM.

121 'The white forehead': Ibid.

121 'rather shy': VB to EB, 5 September 1917 McM.

121 'through beautiful ... jelly': VB to EB, 9 September 1917. McM.

121 'bewildering rumpus': TY, 380.

121 'to think on ... pacifist': VB, 'What Can We Do in Wartime?', August 1939. Reprinted in WC, 18–21.

122 'first angry': Ibid.

122 'I wish those': VB to EB, 5 December 1917. McM.

122 taking a formal position: We owe this interpretation to Deborah Gorham, 'Vera Brittain and the Great War'.

122 wartime ignorance: As evidence of this lack of awareness, one might point to an entry in Vera's diary, from her second term at Somerville, in which she records Charles Trevelyan's visit to the college to give a talk on 'The Way to Permanent Peace'. Not only did Vera clearly have no inkling who he was or what he represented – he was in fact a founder member of the Union of Democratic Control which was working for a negotiated peace settlement – but, as Claire Tylee has remarked (The Great War and Women's Consciousness, 69), she also appeared rather more intent upon receiving compliments about the dress she was wearing than listening to what he had to say

123 'shouldn't have had a word': VB to Helena Swanwick, 20 July 1933. Copy in Fawcett Library.

123 'You have no idea': TY, 389.

123 'I ought to have been slain': TY, 387.

124 'diminishing hope': TY, 427.

124 'I hear': EHB to VB, 19 February 1918. McM.

124 'and discussing': EHB to VB, 21 October 1916. McM.

124 'The sorrow of parting': TY, 404.

124 as Victor had remarked: VR to VB, 18 November 1916. McM.

125 'There have been wonderful sights': EHB to VB, 'Easter Sunday 1918'. McM.

125 'to be dispatched': *TY*, 411.

126 'a complete general breakdown': *TY* 421. TAB's letter must have been written in March, not April as VB writes in *TY*.

126 'Father appears': VB to EB, 31 March 1918. McM.

126 'a cowardly deserter': *TY*, 424.

126 she thought . . . of returning to Oxford: VB also considered joining the WAAC.

126 'I quite expected': EHB to VB, 24 May 1918. McM.

126 'lurid': *TY*, 447. VB had been writing a novel based on her war experiences since at least the summer of the previous year. See VB to EHB, 4 June 1917, McM, in which she mentions it as 'progressing', but adds that 'Mrs Leighton & I have decided that it cannot be published until sometime after the War as there's too much truth in it about things & people.'

126 'I am so glad': VB to EB, 25 September 1917. McM.

127 'experimental publisher': VB, *On Becoming a Writer*, 177. Harold Monro of the Poetry Bookshop had apparently warned Wilfred Owen, two years earlier, against publishing his work with Erskine Macdonald. According to Dominic Hibberd, Macdonald 'was an unscrupulous publisher of amateur verse, making profits out of his unsuspecting authors'. In 1922 a court case revealed that 'Erskine Macdonald' was an alias for Galloway Kyle, 'who had played a double role throughout the war of helpful critic and demanding publisher'. Dominic Hibberd, *Owen the Poet* (Macmillan, 1986), 63.

127 'ten reams': 'Memorandum of Agreement' between VB and Erskine Macdonald Ltd, 8 June 1918. McM.

127 'I have just written': VB to EB, 3 March 1918. McM.

127 'would do something': VB to EB, 10 March 1918. McM.

127 'What is Erskine Macdonald': EHB to VB, 24 May 1918. McM. VB had often sent poems to EHB for criticism, e.g. EHB to VB, 24 October 1917, McM, 'About the poems – The Last Post is best . . . the German Ward is a good idea and a good picture . . .'

127 'My son': TAB to Mr Bell of Brittains Ltd, 27 June 1918. Brittains Ltd.

127 'My dear, dear Vera': Marie Leighton to VB, 'Sunday morning'. McM.

127 his batman: Private A. Barrett to TAB, 2 July 1918, McM, quoted in *TY*, 439–40.

127 the morning of 15 June: For a detailed account of the battle, see Fryer, *The Men From the Greenwood*, 114–22. See also the Battalion Diary of the 11th Sherwood Foresters, Public Record Office, Kew, WO 95 4240 and the diary of Private Harry Tomlinson of the 11th Sherwood Foresters, Imperial War Museum. Private Tomlinson, who was a battalion runner in the action on the Asiago Plateau, recalled coming to the lodge which constituted the battalion headquarters and seeing EHB laid out, 'head and upper part of body covered. . .' H. Tomlinson to SW, 17 June 1979. PBC.

127 He had been buried: Today EHB lies buried in Plot 1, Row B, Grave 1 at Granezza British Cemetery, situated about 8km to the south of Asiago, in the commune of Lusiana. '. . . I write to inform you that we buried Captain Brittain on the 16th', the chaplain of the 11th Sherwood Foresters wrote to TAB, '. . . No doubt you have heard by now from his brother officers how he died while exposing himself to greater dangers in order to better command his men . . . There was no nicer company to go into than that of his mess. He had a wonderful way of keeping all under his command together.' Revd I.R. Jones to TAB, 25 June 1918. McM.

128 'I tried to': C.E. Hudson, 'Memoirs', chapter 7, 277–8. We are most grateful to Miles Hudson for permitting us to see the typescript of his father's book.

128 'that he knew': *TY*, 442.

129 'To a V.C.': VB, *Poems of the War and After*, 50. The poem was originally published in *Oxford Magazine*, 14 March 1919.

129 drifted out of Vera's life: There are three letters from Hudson to VB at McM, written in November and December 1918, apparently in response to letters from her.

129 'a matter': C.E. Hudson to VB, 30 June 1934, McM. Hudson's letter was apparently prompted by Leslie Halford, who had served under Hudson, and who, unbeknownst to him, had written to VB to tell her that she was 'dead out' in her 'diagnosis' of Hudson's character in *TY*. L. Halford to VB, 21 June 1934. McM.

130 '. . . a stiff young disciplinarian': *TY*, 443. VB had already tempered the strength of her outburst against Hudson at Victor Gollancz's insistence. Dorothy Horsman to VB, 19 May 1933. Victor Gollancz Ltd.

130 'somewhat bitter': C.E. Hudson to VB, 30 June 1934. McM.

130 'It is quite possible': VB to C.E. Hudson, 4 July 1934. McM.

130 'a most disturbing . . . had received': C.E. Hudson, op. cit., 258.

130 'I did not realize that letters': Many of EHB's letters to VB, for instance, are only stamped 'Passed Field Censor', though censorship by the base censors – who could read even the contents of green envelopes – was the prescribed practice. See *Censorship Orders and Regulations* (Army Document S.S. 660), and 'Behind the Lines 8 – "Letters Up" ', *Stand To!: The Journal of the Western Front Association*, 1988.

131 'had he taken': C.E. Hudson, op. cit., 277.

131 Footnote: Jolliffe (ed.), *Raymond Asquith*, 290–3. Hudson's memoirs make it clear that the incident involving Edward was not the only case of homosexuality in the battalion. In February 1917, 'M.W.', a regular soldier and the commanding officer of the battalion agreed to 'go sick' after 'a specific charge of homosexuality' was made against him. 'It seemed he had succumbed to a vice which no battalion would tolerate in their commanding officer, combined as it was with complete loss of nerve . . .' C.E. Hudson, op. cit., 237–8.

131 'some subsequent': VB to C.E. Hudson, 12 July 1934. McM.

132 'shot through': VB, *Honourable Estate*, 371.
132 'After a few weeks ... hero': Ibid., 368–70.
133 His self-containment: 'I know you and your mother have always said that he [EHB] has either nothing in him or else he conceals very well what he has.' VB to RL, 28 March 1915. McM.
133 'women are a great problem': EHB to VB, 4 February 1917. McM.
133 'a most improbable': EHB to VB, 22 December 1917. McM.
133 'which she had never ... much exaggerated': VB to GC, 21 July 1939. McM.
133 Footnote: VB, 'Reflective Record', 25 June 1913. McM. In 'The Education of Vera and Edward Brittain', 29, Gorham appears to suggest that EHB's friendship with RL may have had homosexual undertones. However, while RL was the object of EHB's hero-worship, it is also clear that RL was not one of Maurice Ellinger's circle, and was not implicated in homosexuality at Uppingham. '. . . I never knew him', RL wrote to EHB on learning of Maurice Ellinger's suicide attempt, 'except through you, of course – not intimately, I mean.' RL to EHB, 13 May 1915. McM. For a discussion of the Public School traditions of romantic friendship, see Parker, *The Old Lie*, 105–15.
134 'homoerotic warmth': Fussell, *The Great War and Modern Memory*, 296. VB's last birthday present from EHB in December 1917 was a copy of *Ardours and Endurances*.
134 'leave him': Ibid., 297.
134 Martin Taylor: Taylor, *Lads*, 15–58.
134 the tunic: TAB to VB, 6 October 1934. McM.
134 'such fundamental doubts': VB to WH, 10 November 1934. Hull.
134 'a scientist': VB to PB, 31 March 1967. PBC.
134 'One of Edward's correspondents': VB to PB, 9 May 1967. PBC.
135 'It seems to me': VB to EB, 16 December 1916. McM.
135 'at every turn': VB to C.E. Hudson, 4 July 1934. McM. 'Edward's birthday – would have been 72. Still remembered with love and longing after nearly 50 years.' VB, Diary, 29 November 1967. McM.
135 'ushered unobtrusively': *TY*, 447.
136 the flyleaf of ... *The Muse in Arms*: This is now in the possession of SW.
136 'her well-finished': *Times Literary Supplement*, 19 September 1918. See Fred D. Crawford, *British Poets of the Great War* (Associated University Presses, 1988), 151–3, who calls VB 'the best of the women poets', and argues that 'She demonstrated a much more mature grasp of the struggle than any of the other women poets, and certainly than most of the men.' Nosheen Khan, *Women's Poetry of the First World War* (Harvester, 1988), places VB's poetry in its contemporary context.
136 'I ended the First World War': VB to GC, 15 September 1952. McM.

CHAPTER 4: LAMENT OF THE DEMOBILIZED

137 'I have a "sense" ': VB to PB, 14 August 1944. PBC.
138 'why it had been': *TY*, 471.
138 'brief and laconic': *TY*, 474. Thirty years later, however, VB revised her assessment of Miss Penrose. She recognized that Emily Penrose was 'an outstanding person, both in ability and stature, and one of the greatest heads the women's colleges have known.' She acknowledged that Miss Penrose's acute shyness gave the impression of 'an intimidating woman, alarmingly suggestive of a tiger about to spring', but paid tribute to her deep concern for anyone in trouble or want, 'and not least for the bereaved students of the First World War.' VB, *The Women at Oxford*, 121.
138 'because at College': VB, MS note, PBC. Four years after Hilda Lorimer's death in 1954, as a gesture of affection and respect, VB commissioned the drawing of her by J.A. Grant which hangs today in Somerville.
139 'a fire every evening': VB to EB, 12 October 1919. McM.
139 'Don't worry': VB to EB, 26 October 1919. McM.
139 the depression: 'I am sorry Father is so depressed. I wonder if he will improve at all when I come home.' VB to EB, 18 November 1919. McM.
139 'If I were you': VB to EB, 8 June 1919. McM.
139 'I had to see': VB to GC, 7 December 1926. McM.
139 the 'beard': See Kennard, *Vera Brittain and Winifred Holtby*, 153–4, for this interpretation, and also Susan J. Leonardi, 'Brittain's Beard: Transsexual Panic in *Testament of Youth*', *Literature Interpretation Theory*, vol. 2, 1, 1990, for a different view.
140 'Such a state': Winter, *The Great War and the British People*, 302.
140 'On the first day': Constance Savery to Joanna Richardson, 20 March 1971. Somerville College.
140 Women's Army Auxiliary Corps: WH recalled her experiences in the WAAC in *Time and Tide*, 16 May 1930.
141 'Quite half my life': *TF*, 264.
141 'tall, massive': Kathleen Taylor to PB, 10 October 1983. PBC.
141 'and at the ages ... nauseatingly insincere': WH, 'Mother Knows Best', *Lovat Dickson's Magazine*, December 1934.
143 'a creature': WH, 'Mother Knows Best'.
143 'We did not': *TF*, 92.
143 'perpetually parted': VB, *The Dark Tide*, 34.
143 'colourful': *TF*, 93.
144 'Altogether she gave': VB, *The Dark Tide*, 38.
144 'always very well dressed': Kathleen Taylor to PB, 10 October 1983.
144 'our foolish rivalry': *TF*, 150.
144 'my immensely long': WH, 'Mother Knows Best'.

145 'a wreck of the war': Evelyn Waugh, *A Little Learning* (Chapman & Hall), 182. See Selina Hastings, *Evelyn Waugh. A Biography* (Sinclair-Stevenson, 1994), 85–7, for the best description of Cruttwell at this time. VB seems not to have realized that Cruttwell was a notorious misogynist who referred to women as 'drabs' and 'breast-heavers'. As an undergraduate at Hertford, Evelyn Waugh developed an animus against Cruttwell, and in every novel he wrote up to *Scoop* named his most ignominious minor characters after him. Cruttwell's publications included *A History of the Great War, 1914–1918* (Clarendon Press, 1934). He died insane in 1941.

145 'a lengthy eulogy': VB to EB, 15 December 1919. McM.

145 'She overlooked': Hilda Reid, interview.

146 'to tell her daily': VB, *The Dark Tide*, 46.

146 'a most revolutionary': VB to EB, 2 November 1919. McM.

146 a practised debater: For VB's part in debates at Étaples, see VB to EB and TAB, 9 February 1918. McM: 'The nurses' club . . . has started a debating society . . . I have to second the motion on Monday night; it is about whether women should continue their present unusual occupations after the war or not. I don't know yet which side I have to take.' VB took part in another Oxford debate in November 1919 at Oriel College when the motion wat that 'This House regrets the obsolescence of parental control'. VB spoke against the motion and talked of 'relentless parental tyranny'. Quoted by Richard Perceval Graves, *Richard Hughes* (André Deutsch, 1993), 43.

146 'a kaleidoscope . . . with their heads': VB, *The Dark Tide*, 47–8.

147 'I lay on the cold': *TY*, 490.

147 'substantially correct': *TY*, 488.

147 'You think you can': VB, *The Dark Tide*, 55.

147 'the whole episode': WH to VB, 14 April 1933. Hull.

148 'serene detachment': *TF*, 84.

148 'The Lament of the Demobilised': Reprinted in *TY*, 467. Cicely Williams maintained that the poem was specifically directed at Maude Clarke.

149 'Passionately as I desired': *TF*, 119.

149 'Very fond': VB to EB, 6 February 1920. McM.

149 'patient, eager': *TY*, 500.

150 'she united': Dorothy L. Sayers, MS. Somerville College.

150 'unbalanced excursion': *TY*, 514.

150 'he had had the luck': William Anthony to PB, 12 March 1993. PBC. Robert Maltass Anthony was born on 5 March 1895.

150 'Dear Miss Brittain': Roy M. Anthony to VB, 27 April 1920. McM.

151 'error of judgement': *TY*, 499.

151 'without thanks': Roy M. Anthony to VB, 20 July 1920. McM.

151 'ludicrous little engagement': *TY*, 514. See VB to GC, 7 December 1926. McM, in which VB attributes her impulsive engagement to her '*crise des nerfs*'. William Anthony, Roy's son, writes that 'the funniest thing about it was that Vera . . . [in *TY*], described her fiancé as belonging to a minor college and . . . my father resented her calling St John's a minor college!' After leaving Oxford, Roy Anthony became a civil servant, and also joined Michael Franklin and David Gourlay (later Janet Vaughan's husband) in establishing the Wayfarers' Travel Agency which catered primarily for the individual itineraries of business and professional people. VB and WH used it whenever possible. We are most grateful to Mr Anthony for his reminiscences of his father.

152 'Surely now': VB, 'Reflective Record', 8 October 1914. McM.

152 '"an idea" ': WH, *The Crowded Street*, 270.

152 '"Your life" ': Ibid., 232.

152 'I'm intensely': 26 September 1935, *CF*, 210.

153 'To us the Degree': VB, 'The Point of View of a Woman Student', *Oxford Outlook*, November 1919.

153 '. . . Not by Miss Penrose': VB to EB and TAB, 2 November 1919. McM.

153 'with partisan': *TY*, 505.

154 'no one noticed': VB, *The Women at Oxford*, 156.

155 'perhaps the most important': WH, *A New Voter's Guide to Party Programmes*.

155 'that egotistical': VB to GC, 15 September 1952. McM.

155 'Because I dare': 'The Aspirant', VB, *Poems of the War and After*, 46.

156 'to a social circle': VB to EB, 18 October 1919. McM.

156 'taken a great': VB to EB, 8 November 1919. McM.

157 'I can't think . . . heart's desire': WH to Jean McWilliam, 28 August 1921, *LF*, 55.

157 'by analyzing': WH to GC, 26 January 1925. McM.

158 'to the limit': *TY*, 514.

158 'almost more': WH to Jean McWilliam, 'Easter Term 1920', *LF*, 12.

158 'Oh no . . .': VB, *The Dark Tide*, 53.

158 'that rag-time': *TY*, 515.

158 'I went for my viva': WH to Jean McWilliam, 25 July 1921, *LF*, 53.

159 'Going Down Play': On the tradition of the 'GDP', see Vicinus, *Independent Women*, 144. Details of *The Professor's Love Story* from Somerville College. The programme of the Going Down Play for 1921 is reprinted in *LF*, 42–4.

159 'I have got': *TY*, 513.

159 'out of bedspreads': WH to Jean McWilliam, n.d., *LF*, 47. Jean McWilliam had been up at Somerville before the war.

159 'adventurous, experimental': *TY*, 108.

159 'queer little jumbled': WH to Jean McWilliam, 25 July 1921, *LF*, 53.

160 'The results': VB to EB, 30 July 1921. McM.

160 'I was never': *TY*, 515.

160 'After the Viva': VB to Dorothy Horsman, 20 May 1933. Victor Gollancz Ltd.

160   'longing to get': WH to Jean McWilliam, 25 July 1921, *LF*, 54.
160   'I was greatly': C.R.M.F. Cruttwell, 15 February 1921. McM.
161   'Miss Brittain's': Emily Penrose, 26 March 1921. McM.

CHAPTER 5: 'VERY SMALL, VERY DEAR LOVE'

162   'the most perfect': *TF*, 121. WH described it as the 'one perfect time which nothing can take away . . .' WH to VB, 29 October 1921. Hull.
162   'armed with small': WH, 'Books, Snobs and Travellers', *Time and Tide*, 30 May 1931.
163   'where there is a wonderful . . . stone-covered hillside': WH to Jean McWilliam, 8 September 1921. *LF*, 58–9.
163   'after a climb . . . their loneliness': VB, 'The Asiago Plateau', TS McM.
163   'which rise': WH to Jean McWilliam, 18 September 1921, *LF*, 61.
163   '*Doing* Italy': WH, 'Books, Snobs and Travellers'.
163   'our hair rises': WH, 'Italy in August', *Time and Tide*, 11 May 1928.
164   'a number of flower beds': *TY*, 533.
164   'I picked': Ibid., 534.
164   'a whole load': WH to VB, 29 October 1921. Hull.
164   'when I am hankering': VB to WH, 4 November 1921. Hull.
164   'With Louie': VB to WH, 5 November 1921. Hull.
165   'I have a real rush': WH to Jean McWilliam, 13 November 1921, *LF*, 69.
165   'my ideal': VB to WH, 4 November 1921. Hull.
165   'You won't trust yourself': VD to WH, 'Nov.? [4] Friday anyway' 1921. Hull; *SL*, 16.
165   'eaten plain': VB to WH, 7 November 1921. Hull.
165   'that one talent': VB to WH, 'Nov.? [4] Friday anyway' 1921. Hull; *SL*, 16.
166   'That terrifying woman': VB to WH, 6 November 1921. Hull.
166   'terrified': VB to WH, 4 November 1921. Hull.
166   'almost impossible . . . flatlette': WH to Jean McWilliam, 3 December 1921, *LF*, 73–4.
167   '. . . If it weren't': VB to WH, 23 December 1921. Hull.
167   'a queer little place': WH to Jean McWilliam, 1 January 1922, *LF*, 83.
168   'Winifred, why do': VB to WH, 7 November 1921. Hull.
168   'sensitiveness . . . apprehensiveness': VB to WH, 27 June 1921. Hull.
168   '. . . always takes': VB to WH, 4 November 1921. Hull.
168   'I don't want': VB to WH, 28 October 1921. Hull.
168   'an excess': VB to WH, 22 October 1921. Hull.
168   'one day after . . . permanent victory':

VB, MS note. PBC. VB refers to hitting WH with a shoe in a letter to WH dated 30 April 1922. Hull.
169   '. . . I wonder how': VB to WH, 23 October 1921. Hull.
169   'beyond pearls': WH to VB, 27 August 1926. Hull. 'I value it beyond pearls. It is about the only approval which does not result in a nauseating [*sic*] reaction of disgust.'
169   'Very Small, Very Dear Love': WH first used this form of epistolary address (abbreviated to 'vsvdl') in a letter to VB dated 28 July 1923. Hull. VB later adopted it as her nickname in letters to WH.
169   'There's such a little': WH to VB, 18 August 1921. Hull.
169   'is a person': WH to Jean McWilliam, 28 August 1923, *LF*, 213.
170   John Marriott: John Marriott was knighted in 1924, and served as the Conservative MP for Oxford City from 1917 to 1922, and for York from 1923 to 1929.
170   'quite bucked up': VB to WH, 7 November 1921. Hull.
171   'a curious change': WH to Jean McWilliam, 15 July 1924, *LF*, 264.
172   'I have been spending': WH to VB, 25 July 1925, Hull; *SL*, 46.
172   'Have you': VB to Macmillan Ltd, 1 September 1922. BL. J.D. Beresford of Collins had already offered to accept *The Dark Tide* if VB would rewrite the second half of the novel. See VB to WH, 28 April 1922. Hull.
172   'I shall hold': VB to WH, 25 December 1922. Hull.
173   'Now my idea': WH to Jean McWilliam, 20 June 1922, *LF*, 114.
173   'It had simply': *TY*, 597.
173   'My family': VB to WH, 21 August 1922. Hull.
174   'You must not': WH to VB, 22 August 1922. Hull; *SL*, 20.
174   'I feel quite able': VB to WH, 24 December 1922. Hull.
174   'and made them': WH to Jean McWilliam, 29 October 1922, *LF*, 136.
174   'with real walls': WH to Jean McWilliam, 30 August 1922, *LF*, 122.
174   'onslaught upon editorial': *TY*, 592.
175   'but couldn't get it': WH to Jean McWilliam, 27 February 1923, *LF*, 166.
175   'The Whole Duty of Women': VB, *Time and Tide*, 23 February 1923. *TG*, 120–3.
175   'that here was someone': *TF*, 142.
175   'I like old': Virginia Woolf to Ethel Smyth, 30 March 1933, V. Woolf, *Letters*, vol. 5, 173.
175   'enormously interested': Margaret, Viscountess Rhondda, *This Was My World*, 128. On *Time and Tide* see Dale Spender, *Time and Tide Wait for No Man* (Pandora Press, 1984).
176   'on a platform': WH to Jean McWilliam, 14 June 1922, *LF*, 110.
176   'my ideas': WH to Jean McWilliam, 24 July 1922, *LF*, 121.
176   Six Point Group: On VB's equal rights feminism and her membership of the Six Point

Group, see Gorham, ' "Have We Really Rounded Seraglio Point?" '. See also Pugh, *Women and the Women's Movement in Britain 1914–1959*, 49–50. WH defined 'old' feminism's central concerns in 'Feminism Divided', *Yorkshire Post*, 26 July 1926; *TG*, 47–50. Eva Hubback answered her on behalf of the 'new feminists' in *Time and Tide*, 20 August 1926.

177 **continued to be actively involved:** For instance, VB was active in 1943 in the campaign for an 'Equal Citizenship (Blanket) Bill', the first clause of which demanded 'equal rights for men and women' as 'an established principle of law'. See VB, 'Equal Citizenship and the Blanket Bill', 'Letter to Peace-Lovers', 9 September 1943. Reprinted in *Testament of a Peace Lover*, 159–63.

177 **several pamphlets:** e.g. *A Memorandum showing the connection between the Status of Women and the Relations between Countries and Geneva – the Key to Equality*; both 1929, Six Point Group.

177 **'an intense love':** Schreiner, *Woman and Labour*, 66.

177 **'I am going':** VB to WH, 12 July 1921. Hull.

177 **'dark velour':** WH, 'Fashions and Feminism', *Manchester Guardian*, 16 October 1927.

177 **man's shirt:** VB to WH, 19 April 1924. Hull.

177 **'exquisitely funny':** WH to Jean McWilliam, 12 June 1923, *LF*, 189.

178 **'I am ordering':** VB to WH, 4 November 1921. Hull.

178 **'My dear':** VB to WH, 9 November 1921. Hull.

178 **League of Nations Union:** See Birn, *The League of Nations Union 1918–1945*, and Duncan Wilson, *Gilbert Murray OM 1866–1957* (Oxford: Clarendon Press, 1988), 244–57, 295–311.

178 **'It's quite possible':** VB to WH, 2 July 1921. Hull.

178 **'& thanks':** VB to WH, 12 July 1921. Hull.

179 **'the new ideal':** VB, *Good Citizenship and the League. An Armistice Day address to children between 10 and 14* (Pelican Press, 1924).

179 **'immense success':** WH to Jean McWilliam, 4 October 1922, *LF*, 130.

179 **'Everywhere she goes':** WH to Jean McWilliam, 14 October 1922, *LF*, 134.

179 **'Why shouldn't you':** VB to WH, 5 July 1921. Hull.

180 **'to give lip-service':** VB to GC, 10 February 1924. McM.

180 **'At the same time':** *TY*, 576.

180 **as she admitted to Winifred:** VB to WH, 15 August 1925. Hull. 'As for myself, I want if possible to stand as an L-C-C candidate in 1928; whether as Liberal or Labour I don't much care. It rather depends on the state of parties then. I am not interested in parties, but in feminism & peace . . .' VB considered joining the Independent Labour Party, which supported the idea of a negotiated peace, at the beginning of the Second World War, but out of deference to GC eventually decided against doing so.

180 **'In the late spring':** *TY*, 600.

180 **'glad to have':** Grant Richards to WH, 14 December 1922. Grant Richards Archive, University of Illinois.

180 **'It would be an advantage':** Grant Richards to WH, 9 April 1923. Grant Richards Archive, University of Illinois.

181 **'an amiable rascal':** VB to PB, 21 May 1954, PBC. On Grant Richards, see Richards, *Author Hunting*.

181 **'on account':** VB, 'Preface to the Reprinted Edition of *The Dark Tide*', 1935, 5.

181 **'After tea':** WH, *Anderby Wold*, 103.

181 **'the only thing':** WH *TF*, 102.

182 **'These unexpected attacks':** VB, 'Preface', 7.

182 **'The next day':** VB, *The Dark Tide*, 157. Grant Richards to VB, 24 April 1923. Grant Richards Archive, University of Illinois, writes that the paper will be satisfied with a retraction in the form of correction slip stating that the suggestion has been 'unreservedly withdrawn'.

182 **'impossible':** WH to Jean McWilliam, 19 July 1923, *LF*, 200.

182 **'a strange world':** *Times Literary Supplement*, 12 and 19 July 1923.

183 **'did represent':** VB, 'Preface', 2.

183 **'one of those':** VB, *The Dark Tide*, 31.

183 **'represents what I wish':** VB, MS note. PBC.

183 **'being run over':** H.C. Harwood, *The Outlook*, quoted in VB, 'Preface', 3.

184 **'I wonder who ever wrote':** VB to WH, 16 November 1921. Hull.

184 **'Poor Daphne!':** VB to WH, 5 November 1921. Hull. That VB had kept WH informed of the autobiographical basis of the novel as it related to her is clear from VB to WH, 7 November 1921 (Hull), where VB remarks that one conversation between Daphne and Virginia 'is a gorgeous but somewhat cruel travesty of that conversation we had after one of Mr Cruttwell's coachings, when you said you were up at Oxford to enjoy yourself & didn't mean to take your work too seriously. And I thought you so contemptible for your superficiality & lack of ambition!'

184 **'more autonomous':** This is Jean Kennard's phrase, *Vera Brittain and Winifred Holtby*, 47. Kennard is particularly good on this idea of Daphne as representing two sides of VB's character.

184 **'her long legs':** VB, *The Dark Tide*, 24.

184 **'uninspired popularity':** Ibid., 43.

184 **'wild little novel':** VB, 'Plunge Into the Past. *The Dark Tide*', 1965. MS note. PBC.

184 **'crude and immature':** WH to GC, 16 January 1925. McM.

184 **'I am too different':** WH to VB, 28 July 1923. Hull; *SL*, 25.

184 **'a partial':** *TF*, 160.

185 **'Dear Vera':** M.V. Clarke to VB, 16 August 1923. McM.

185 **'the Oxford Authorities':** VB, *On Becoming a Writer*, 184.

185 **'the writing of it':** VB to GC, 10 February 1924. McM.

185 **'strange daytime':** VB, *On Becoming a Writer*, 184.

185 'Is this the beginning': VB to WH, 25 July 1923. Hull; *SL*, 23.

185 'Grant Richards': WH to VB, 28 July 1923. Hull; *SL*, 24.

185 'quite immensely': VB to GC, 10 February 1924. McM.

185 'felt sufficiently': GC, *For God's Sake Go!*, 128.

CHAPTER 6: AVE ATQUE VALE

187 'felt a sense': C. Leighton to PB, 7 October 1976. PBC.

187 'I did not wish': *TY*, 608.

187 'exquisite but completely ... do frequently': VB to WH, 28 July 1923. Hull; *SL*, 25–6. Samuel, First Baron Waring (1860–1940), a decorative art enthusiast, established the firm Waring & Sons which later joined with Gillow. Sir Harry Brittain (1873–1974) was Unionist MP for Acton from 1918 to 1929. Both men were married at this time. VB seriously considered nursing a constituency as an Independent Liberal, VB to WH, 24 December 1923 (Hull), reveals that she had hopes of standing in Staffordshire.

188 'a provincial of the provincials': VB to GC, 9 March 1924. McM.

188 short treatise: *Thomas Hobbes as Philosopher, Publicist and Man of Letters*, GC's prize-winning Matthew Arnold Memorial Essay at Oxford in 1921, published by Basil Blackwell, 1922. 'I have read with the utmost pleasure your "Dark Tide". Perhaps you would do me the favour of accepting the enclosed. I fear you thought my impromptu card as being (as indeed it was) impertinent. I need scarcely add that there is no necessity to acknowledge this.' GC to VB, 4 August 1923. Original in possession of SW.

189 'a rage': *TY*, 611.

189 'intimate and amazingly interesting': VR to WH, 27 December 1923. Hull; *SL*, 28–9.

189 'I cannot help thinking': WH to VB, 29 December 1923. Hull; *SL*, 30.

189 117 Wymering Mansions: A plaque commemorating VB was unveiled here by SW in September 1994.

190 'for a place ... plates and dishes': VB to GC, 9 March 1924. McM.

190 'on much more': *TY*, 604.

190 'a crude little': VB to GC, 9 March 1924. McM.

190 'an amazing letter': VD to WH, 19 April 1924. Hull; *SL*, 36.

191 'intellectual pretensions': *Times Literary Supplement*, 20 March 1924.

191 the least successful: *The Dark Tide* had earned VB £22 19s. in royalties by the end of 1926.

191 'most people': *TY*, 556.

191 'except Catlin's ... refused to give': VB to WH, 10 April 1924, Hull. *SL*, 33.

191 'the knock-out blow': VB to WH, 21 April 1924. Hull.

191 'I will do this': VB to WH, 23 April 1924. Hull.

192 'My dear': WH to VB, 22 April 1924. Hull; *SL*, 37.

192 'As we grow ... Do we?': VB to WH, 19 April 1924. Hull; *SL*, 36.

192 'both are inevitably': WH to VB, 16 May 1924. Hull.

192 'I think on the whole': *TY*, 615.

192 'overshadowed with light': VB to GC, 20 June 1924. McM.

192 'nothing to eat ... afternoon on the river?': VB to GC, 17 June 1924. McM.

194 'What *can* I say?': VB to GC, 18 June 1924. McM.

194 'meal – or meals': VB to GC, 20 June 1924. McM.

194 'That is why': VB to GC, 2 July 1924. McM.

194 'so sincere ... coming to me after all': VB to GC, 19 June 1924. McM.

195 'Your dear letter': VB to GC, 4 July 1924. McM.

195 'I knew then'. *TY*, 617.

195 'I have just heard': Marie Leighton to VB, 20 July 1924. McM. 'If there has been any shadow of reserve at all between us, it can only have been because we have lately been looking at everything from different view-points ...'

195 'a profound believer': GC, *For God's Sake Go!*, 14.

196 'for him life': *TE*, 102.

196 'It was the sad story': GC, *For God's Sake Go!*, 14.

196 'that philosophy': Ibid.

197 won an Exhibition: See the Minute Book of the Warden and Tutors' Committee at New College for confirmation of GC's Oxford career.

197 Mrs Catlin: See the Parish Magazine of St Luke's, Kew, in Richmond Local History Collection for details of the Catlins' time there. A letter from Edith Catlin to the Church of England newspaper, *The Challenge*, dated 23 August 1916, makes it clear that Edith Catlin was also a fervent advocate of the campaign for the ordination of women, led by Maude Royden.

197 'She would not': GC, *For God's Sake Go!*, 14.

197 George was with her when she died: GC witnessed the death certificate.

197 'A life of such bitterness ... enough to eat': VB to WH, 1 September 1924. Hull.

197 Reverend Catlin resigned: See the Parish Magazine of St Luke's, Kew, April 1916, for Reverend Catlin's farewell letter to his parishioners, dated 22 March 1916.

198 'totally unfit ... rehabilitated': GC, *For God's Sake Go!*, 7–8.

198 'First time': GC, *For God's Sake Go!*, 22.

198 'He has a complicated': *TE*, 21.

199 'On the day': *TY*, 614.

199 'the sweet, shy': VB to WH, 10 April 1924. Hull.

199 'to solve'. *TY*, 653.

199 'the dreadful responsibility': VB to GC, 23 June 1924. McM.

199 'At the risk ... brother's friends': VB to GC, 21 June 1924. McM.

199 'an unprincipled adventurer': VB to GC, 19 June 1924. McM.

199   'quite calmly': VB to GC, 26 June 1924
'5.30 pm.'. McM.

200   'I'm afraid its origin': VB to GC, 20 June
1924. McM.

200   'Only a genuine saint . . . every turn': VB
to WH, 1 September 1924. Hull.

200   George had confided: According to VB in
a letter to WH, 10 April 1924. Hull.

201   'My reason . . . at the Resurrection': VB
to WH, 29 August 1924. Hull.

202   'I think that my little . . .': WH to Jean
McWilliam, 15 July 1924, LF, 263.

202   'She may drop me': TF, 144.

202   'This country': VB, Diary, 'Travels in
Central Europe. September–December 1924', 14
October 1924. McM. Two pieces of journalism by
VB resulted from this trip; 'The Transformation of
Krupps', Nation and Athenaeum, 3 January 1925,
and 'A City of Sorrow and Hate', The Weekly
Westminster, 10 January 1925.

203   'It was queer': VB, Diary, 'Travels', 8
October 1924. McM.

203   'Please will you help': WH to GC, 6
October 1924. McM.

203   'I suppose . . . a little beating': WH to
GC, 9 December 1924. McM.

204   'Thy bosom': GC, Christmas 1924.
Original in possession of SW.

204   'It is such a book': VB to Ethelreda Lewis,
3 March 1925. Copy in PBC.

204   'could have given you . . . only second to
my work': VB to GC, 3 April 1925. McM.

206   'put it down . . . until the wedding': VB
to GC, 5 April 1925. McM.

206   'We who have different': GC. Copy in PBC.

207   'by telling me': VB to GC, 11 January
1945. McM.

207   Vera's insistence on keeping . . . her
own name: For VB's account of obtaining an
American visa, see TS, 24–5. See also VB, 'Married
Women and Surnames', Time and Tide, 15 January
1926, and 'Should a Wife Change Her Name?',
Daily News, 20 April 1929. Later VB would go to
some lengths to register the copyright of her books
in the United States 'as a matter of principle' under
her 'correct legal name of Vera Brittain'. Rubinstein,
Nash & Co. to George Brett, 5 January 1935. McM.

207   Footnote: W. Minch to GC, 3 September
1930. Original in possession of SW.

208   'fleeting & dreamlike': VB to WH, 4 July
1925. Hull.

208   'white as marble': WH to VB, 29 June
1925. Hull.

208   'Saying goodbye': VB to WH, 28 June
1925. Hull.

CHAPTER 7: SEMI-DETACHED MARRIAGE

209   'I believe': VB to WH, 2 July 1925. Hull.

210   'Perhaps in the old days': VB to WH, 4
July 1925. Hull.

210   'I look prettier': VB to WH, 2 July 1925.
Hull.

210   'I am sure': VB to WH, 4 July 1925. Hull.

211   'had become': VB to WH, 17 July 1925.
Hull.

211   '. . . much as I love': VB to WH, 2 July
1925. Hull.

211   'because my husband': VB to WH, 4 July
1925. Hull.

212   'G . . . now has': WH to VB, 7 July 1925.
Hull.

212   'Like you': VB to WH, 17 July 1925. Hull.

212   'I am aching to see you': VB to WH, 20
July 1925. Hull.

213   'with a quite benevolent . . . kept
Edward': VB to WH, 28 July 1925. Hull. The
edited version of this letter in SL, 48–9, contrives to
give the impression that it was Harry Pearson, and
Harry only, who had caused WH's unhappiness.

214   'fearfully apologetic . . . shall believe':
WH to VB, 29 July 1925, Hull. SL, 50.

214   'I feel dreadfully': VB to WH, 8 October
1925. Hull; SL, 63.

215   'but the basic fact': Louis MacNeice, The
Strings Are False: An Unfinished Autobiography (Faber
& Faber, 1965), 24.

215   'During the first week': TS, 41.

215   'The Evils of Good Fellowship': TS at
McM.

215   'detested domesticity': TS, 61.

216   'His feminism': VB to WH, 15 October
1925. Hull.

216   'what we now call': VB to WH, 15 August
1925. Hull.

217   'a morass of confusion': VB to GC, 3
April 1925. McM.

217   'No one would ever care': Reader's report
on 'A Honeymoon in Two Worlds', 1927. BL.

217   'that my first year': TS, 65.

217   'Don't be deceived': VB to WH, 13
January 1926 Hull.

218   'unless something unexpected . . . as it
comes': WH to VB, 21 October 1925. Hull; SL, 61.

218   'Did you mention': TS, 109.

218   'presented G . . .': VB to MSJ, 17 October
1935. McM.

219   'As for G . . .': VB to WH, 29 November
1925. Hull.

220   'Work . . . has been': VB, 'Women's place:
the passing of the married woman's handicaps', Time
and Tide, 25 November 1927. On marriage see, e.g.,
' "Semi-Detached" Marriage', Evening News, 4 May
1928, TG, 130–2.

220   'pushing feminism': VB to GC, 15
October 1926. McM.

220   'My very love': GC to VB, 16 November
1926. McM.

221   'quite ulterior motives': VB to GC, 17
December 1926. McM.

221   'but, alas': VB to WH, 29 November 1925.
Hull.

221   'almost always': Lady Rhondda, Time and
Tide, 21 January 1936.

221   'but your friends': VB to GC, 20
December 1926. McM.

221   'The world without you': GC to VB, 22
September 1926. McM.

222   'Why is it': VB to GC, 7 December 1926,
McM. 'If you give a general impression', she had

written to him the previous day, '... that I am here in London *against* your will, playing, not the part of a cooperator, but the undignified part of a truant wife ... then indeed the value of the whole experiment as one solution of the difficulties of modern marriage, does disappear.' VB to GC, 6 December 1926. McM.

222   'not only a woman's person': VB to GC, 19 December 1926. McM.

222   'I did not "give myself": VB, 'Married Love', *Poems of the War and After*, 80.

222   'as if she hadn't': VB to GC, 7 December 1926. McM.

223   'Had you sent for me': VB to GC, 8 December 1926. McM.

223   'Since Edward ... meant life': VB to GC, 20 December 1926. McM.

223   'My great object': VB to GC, 22 October 1926. McM.

224   'Vera is having': EB to WH, 26 May 1927. Hull.

224   'It is just beginning': VB to GC, 17 December 1926. McM.

225   '... What fun': WH to VB, 14 May 1927. Hull; *SL*, 163.

225   'disconcerting': VB to WH, 5 May 1927. Hull.

225   'It's queer': VB to WH, 19 May 1927. Hull.

225   'My dear Tiny': TAB to EB, 14 May 1927. Hull.

225   '... had it really been': WH to VB, 14 May 1927. Hull; *SL*, 163.

226   'at all queer': VB to WH, 21 May 1927. Hull.

226   'awoke each morning': *TE*, 51. VB attributed JC's survival to the medical advice and guidance she received from the Chelsea Babies Club. As she pointed out in an article for *Time and Tide* ('Welfare for middle-class mothers', 30 March 1930), the middle-class mother was just as much in need of the 'advantages which the poor mother obtains at the public expense', and yet 'is tremendously on the defence against education, feeling that she has nothing to learn'. At the cost of an annual subscription of five guineas a year, the Chelsea Babies Club provided a weekly clinic, classes for expectant mothers, lectures on the health and education of children, and, if necessary, a home visit from the Nurse-Superintendent. VB described the Chelsea Babies Club as 'the first welfare centre for middle-class mothers'.

226   'Somehow or other': VB to WH, 1 July 1928. Hull; *SL*, 169.

227   'Many times': *TF*, 279.

227   'awfully ill': WH to Jean McWilliam, 14 June 1928, *LF*, 453.

228   'a plea': VB, 'Facing Facts', *Time and Tide*, 10 August 1928.

228   'pathologically boorish': VB, *Radclyffe Hall*, 87. Radclyffe Hall wrote to VB to thank her for having attended the trial. Radclyffe Hall to VB, 15 November 1928. McM.

228   'It attempts': VB, *Women's Work in Modern England*, 2.

229   'Miss Vera Brittain': *Daily Herald*, 2 July 1928.

229   'I *must* write': VB to WH, 19 May 1927. Hull; *SL*, 166.

230   'would be glad': VB, 'Celibate Professions. Problem of the Married Woman Worker', *Daily Telegraph*, 27 March 1929.

230   'Men would complain': VB, 'Men Who Write About Women. The Things They Say', *Manchester Guardian*, 4 November 1927.

231   'O Wise young man!': VB to WH, 5 September 1929, Hull; *SL*, 178.

231   'ought to be satisfied': VB, 'Sexual Gluttony', *Nation and Athenaeum*, 18 August 1929.

231   a study of marriage: It was to be entitled 'The Liberation of Marriage'. There are incomplete drafts at McM.

231   'from London': VB, *Halcyon, or the Future of Monogamy*, 60.

231   'broadcasting': Ibid., 55.

232   'which at the first sign'. Ibid., 72–3.

232   'the ultimately stabilizing': Ibid., 79–80.

232   Third Congress: *Proceedings of the Third Congress of the World League for Sexual Reform*, ed. Norman Haire (Kegan Paul, Trench, Trubner & Co., 1930).

232   'sweeping innovations': VB, 'The Failure of Monogamy', Haire, *Proceedings*, 40–4.

233   'While we regard': VB, *Halcyon, or the Future of Monogamy*, 87.

233   'You ask me to be as frank ... for being rational': VB to GC, 28 March 1929. McM.

235   'Something might smirch': VB to GC, 27 April 1929. McM.

235   'to tell my own': *TY*, 12.

CHAPTER 8: FAREWELL TO THE WAR GENERATION

236   'I have just been': VB to WH, 11 November 1921. Hull; *SL*, 18.

236   'The Pawn of Fate': The holograph notebook of 'The Pawn of Fate' is at McM.

236   Faith Moulson: VB had kept in touch with Faith Moulson who had spent most of the Twenties nursing in Poona in India. She returned to England in 1935 and settled in London, in Victoria.

237   'a vivid and accurate' ... as a whole: Robert Leighton to VB, 10 September 1918. McM.

237   'memory is short': VB, 'A Chronicle of Youth', Foreword. TS McM. See Alan Bishop's Introduction to *CY*, 13–14. 1922 is confirmed as the year of the diary extracts by VB's letter to WH of 24 December 1922. Hull.

238   'dance and forget': Herbert Read, 'The Failure of War Books' in *A Coat of Many Colours* (Routledge & Kegan Paul, 1945), 73.

238   'I think it all': Grant Richards to VB, 19 December 1923. Grant Richards Archive, University of Illinois.

238   'Folly's Vineyard': The typescript of this novel is at McM. See VB to WH, 25 December 1923, ' "Folly's Vineyard" will not dawn in my mind; I shall have to talk it out to you first.' Hull.

238   '... I can write': VB to WH, 28 February
1926. Hull; *SL*, 97. 'The Incidental Adam', later
called 'When the Vision Died' (a title derived from
May Wedderburn Cannan's poem of the same
name), and then 'This Was Their War', was to be 'A
woman's development through, roughly, a decade,
shown through her contacts with different men who
are only incidental to what she believes to be her
chief purpose in life.' MS McM. Thus 'The
Incidental Adam's' theme was not intrinsically
connected to the war at all.

238   'aching': VB to WH, 29 May 1926. Hull;
SL, 131.

238   the evolution of ... Testament of Youth:
The complications of the incomplete and discarded
drafts at McM mean that these can be no more than
preliminary conclusions. Alan Bishop will be treating
the subject in more detail in his forthcoming book
on VB as a writer.

238   'The War Generation': See the letter from
Jonathan Cape to VB, 6 December 1929 (Hull),
which refers to a war book by VB of this title.

239   'great bull market': Correlli Barnett, *The
Collapse of British Power* (Eyre Methuen, 1972), 428.
The best discussion of the late Twenties' market for
war books is Martin Ceadel, 'In focus: The War
Books of 1928–30', in *20th Century Britain. Economic,
Social and Cultural Change*, 228–34, ed. Paul Johnson
(Longman, 1994).

239   'I am reading': VB to WH, 26 December
1928. Hull.

239   'a devastating': VB, *Time and Tide*, 4
October 1929.

239   'giving their husbands': VB, *Time and
Tide*, 21 February 1930.

240   'In the Great War': VB, 'Their Name
Liveth: Forgetting the Women's War-Work',
Manchester Guardian, 13 November 1929. *TG*,
205–8.

240   'puerile claim ... concern women': VB,
Nation and Athenaeum, 24 January 1931.

240   'a wider and more truthful': VB, *Time
and Tide*, 17 January 1930. Deborah Gorham, 'Vera
Brittain and the Great War', convincingly argues
that whereas a war memoirist like Blunden is intent
on conveying the incomprehensibility of trench
experience, not least through the deft use of irony,
VB 'has something to offer' that Blunden's
'understated irony' does not: 'a reasoned analysis of
why the war happened, and of how to prevent a
future war.'

240   'to overlook ... books by women': As
Kennard, *Vera Brittain and Winifred Holtby*, 129–30,
points out, VB fails to mention some of the more
famous firsthand accounts of the war by women, e.g.
Enid Bagnold's *A Diary Without Dates* (1918), Olive
Dent's *A V.A.D. in France* (1917), or even E.M.
Delafield's best early novel, *The War-Workers*
(1918), based on her experience as a VAD at the
Exeter Voluntary Aid Hospital. For a comprehensive
bibliography of war books by women published
before the Second World War, see Tylee, *The Great
War and Women's Consciousness*, 263–71.

240   It's a Great War: VB mentions Mary Lee's
novel in an exchange of letters on the subject of

whether women are bored by war books in *Time and
Tide*, 7, 21, 28 February, and 7 March 1930. She
also commends Mary Borden's *The Forbidden Zone*
(1929), but argues that women's interest in war
books will not be aroused 'until a war-book is
published which removes the impression that one
sex only played an active part in the war, and one sex
only experienced its deepest emotions.'

240   'with deep interest': VB to Irene
Rathbone, 7 September 1933. Original letter in
possession of Mrs Patricia Utechin.

241   'The woman is still': VB, *Nation and
Athenaeum*, 24 January 1931. The same point had
been made by WH, 'War Books and Women',
Yorkshire Post, 19 March 1930.

241   'I wanted': In Panichas (ed.) *Promise of
Greatness*, 368.

241   'How is one': VB to WH, 27 June 1921.
Hull; *SL*, 189.

241   'the influence': *TY*, 12.

241   to settle ... on the title: 'I want to call my
book "Testament of Youth" – so much more
interesting than "Chronicle" – unless it strikes
people as too like Bridges.' VB to WH, 23 August
1931. Hull; *SL*, 7.

241   'co-operative home ... below stairs':
VB, *Lady into Woman*, 221.

242   'I used to rush': VB to Cyril Hargreaves, 5
March 1949. McM.

242   'the end of July': VB to WH, 6 December
1929. Hull; *SL*, 179.

243   'might have come': *TE*, 62.

243   'I think you will fall': VB to GC, 12 June
1931. McM.

243   'eliminate the constant wish': VB to WH,
31 August 1930, Hull. *SL*, 181.

244   'careless and slovenly': GC to VB, 11
January 1932. McM.

244   'I wish him to understand': TAB to VB,
21 March 1932. McM.

244   'a great search': VB, 'Origins of
Testament of Youth'. MS McM.

244   Vera's letters to Roland: The only period
for which letters were missing was that between 20
October and 29 November 1914. As RL and VB
were writing to each other at this time, one must
assume that either he wasn't keeping her letters
then, or that he never returned them to VB.

245   'A fine gesture': VB to WH, 13 September
1931. Hull; *SL*, 193.

246   'It is boiling': VB to WH, 24 August 1931.
Hull.

246   'Here it is so strange': VB to WH, 7
March 1932. Hull; *SL*, 206.

247   'If Harry': VB to WH, 14 March 1932.
Hull; *SL*, 209.

247   'the great difficulty': VB to WH, 5 March
1932. Hull; *SL*, 203.

247   'When I am alone': VB to WH, 13
September 1931. Hull; *SL*, 193.

247   'It is *magnificent*': WH to VB, 2 April
1932. Hull; *SL*, 214.

247   'it reminded me': 6 April 1932, *CF*, 35.

247   'grey life': 7 April 1932, *CF*, 35.

248 'we always behaved': PhB to Margaret Waley, 20 May 1974. PBC.

248 'severe private tensions': PhB, *O Dreams, O Destinations*, 178.

249 'After the oranges and greens': 9 May 1932, *CF*, 39.

249 'Dispute over lunch': 29 May 1932, *CF*, 44.

250 'I thought I knew': PhB, *O Dreams, O Destinations*, 163.

250 'that mixture': 91, *CF*, 160.

251 'I can't understand': PhB to VB, 9 July 1932. McM.

251 'and as she is': VB to GC, 10 May 1932. McM.

251 'I had imagined it': 24 July 1932, *CF*, 73.

252 'quite without . . . have lost heart': VB to WH, 26 August 1932. Hull; *SL*, 222.

252 'What can I say': WH to VB, 27 August 1932. Hull; *SL*, 223.

253 'fury from the Brittains': VB to WH, 17 March 1932. Hull; *SL*, 210.

253 'Spent most': 10 November 1932, *CF*, 107.

253 'that nobody wanted . . . actually out': VB to WH, 20 March 1932. Hull.

253 'all the awful . . . flare-ups': 5–17 December 1932, *CF*, 114, 116.

254 'a tiny woman': Latham, *My Life in Publishing*, 155.

255 'for the sake of . . . intolerably': VB to WH, 21 February 1933, Hull; *SL*, 231.

255 'the essence of publishing': Quoted in Hodges, *Gollancz*, 102.

256 'particularly in your': Quoted in VB to PhB, 25 March 1933. McM.

256 'Powerful, significant': *TE*, 91.

257 'almost extinguishing . . . faith and understanding': VB to WH, 10 April 1933. Hull.

257 'I wonder why': VB to WH, 12 April 1933. Hull.

258 'In other words': VB to WH, 10 April 1933. Hull.

258 'Certain things . . . in (or out of) America': WH to GC, 11 April 1933. McM.

259 'a prolonged wrangle . . . fury': VB to WH, 12 April 1933. Hull.

259 'But she simply . . . do his best': VB to PhB, 29 April 1933. McM.

259 'But how well': PhB to VB, 8 April 1933. McM.

259 'Are you in the habit . . . of their own': VD to PhB, 29 April 1933. McM.

260 'We decided': PhB, *O Dreams, O Destinations*, 179.

260 'When the final verdict': WH, *SL*, 248.

260 'What supreme piece': VB to WH, 3 April 1933. Hull; *SL*, 249.

260 'vaguely alarming': VB to WH, 16 April 1933. Hull.

261 'I feel so': WH to PhB, 12 April 1933. Copy at Hull.

261 'We understand': VB to WH, 16 April 1933. Hull.

261 'You I can count on . . . caution': VB to WH, 17 March 1933. Hull.

262 'very accurate': Cecilia Thurlow to VB, 24 June 1933. McM.

262 'takes it all right': Clare Leighton to VB, 13 July 1933. McM.

262 'there'll always be': VB to WH, 17 March 1933. Hull. *SL* 241–42.

262 'when I remembered': 12 August 1933, *CF*, 143.

262 'Never did I imagine': 28 August to 3 September 1933, *CF*, 148. Compton Mackenzie reviewed *TY* in the *Daily Mail*, 31 August 1933, and found it not only 'profoundly moving . . . but also extremely accurate.' Review Scrapbook, McM.

262 'It's mere pressure': MSJ, *Sunday Times*, 3 September 1933.

263 'In the important things': *Times Literary Supplement*, 31 August 1933.

263 'A book for blue': James Agate, *Daily Express*, 31 August 1933.

263 'Miss Brittain': Margaret R.B. Shaw, *The New English Weekly*, 12 October 1933.

263 'a mediocre crank . . . widely read': St John Ervine to VB, 24 July 1933. McM. Stephen King-Hall (1893–1966) was a writer and broadcaster on politics and international affairs.

264 'a very good book . . . across my eyes': Woolf, 2 September 1933, *Diary*, vol. 4, 177. On 15 June 1934 Virginia Woolf wrote to VB, 'May I take this opportunity of saying how much your book, a Testament of Youth, interested me?'. McM.

265 'a novel': *SL*, 264.

265 instructing Macmillan: VB to Miss Hutchinson, 26 July 1933. McM.

265 'which help both form': P.D. James, *Times Literary Supplement*, 5 May 1978.

265 Robert Graves and Alan Hodge: 'The success of the Coles's *Europe Today*, Vera Britain's *Testament of Youth*, Edgar Mowrer's *Germany Puts the Clock Back*, and Vernon Bartlett's *Nazi Germany Explained*, were not signs only of another war . . . they showed, too, that the public were anxious to learn how war situations developed, and how wars might therefore be prevented.' Graves and Hodge, *The Long Week-end*, 294.

265 'so urgently been confronted': VB, 'Peace Through Books', *New Clarion*, 20 May 1933.

265 'King and Country' debate: See Martin Ceadel, 'The "King and Country" Debate, 1933: Student Politics, Pacifism, and the Dictators', *Historical Journal*, 22, 1979.

266 'show why the particular': Manuscript material relating to *TY*. McM.

266 'It is, I think': *TY*, 291–2.

266 'meretricious gods': VB to Helena Swanwick, 20 July 1933. Copy in Fawcett Library.

266 'Perhaps, after all': *TY*, 645–6.

267 'classic example': Wohl, *The Generation of 1914*, 110. The demographic consequences of the depletion of the privileged classes in the First World War are studied in Winter, 'Britain's "Lost Generation" of the First World War'. Winter concludes that while the 'Lost Generation' is not a myth, it became 'a legend' in the inter-war years which, 'though it had a basis in fact took on a life of its own'.

267   'My troubles were': Wootton, *In a World I Never Made*, 51.

267   'minor prophetess . . .': VB, Notes for 'Introduction to War Diaries', *c.* 1939, *CY*, 15.

268   '. . . some day': VB to Hilary Rubinstein, 18 March 1960. Victor Gollancz Ltd.

CHAPTER 9: 'MY HAPPINESS IS A HOUSE BUILT ON SHIFTING SANDS'

269   'strangely thrilled': 2 November 1933, *CF*, 162.

270   'actually put her arm': VB to WH, 24 February 1933. Hull; *SL*, 234.

270   'Coldly angry': VB to Elizabeth Nicholas, 12 October 1961. PBC.

270   'always vulgar': GC, *For God's Sake Go!*, 104.

270   'I can still remorsefully': VB, 'Serial Requiem: Rose Macaulay'. PBC.

270   Footnote: VB to Elizabeth Nicholas, 12 October 1961. PBC.

270   'I think you have': Gilbert Murray to VB, 21 January 1934. Bodleian Library MS Gilbert Murray 66, 132–3. VB replied to Murray, '. . . one of my minor motives in writing it was to explain to friends and acquaintances many things which I should never have been able to tell them otherwise.'

270   Vera's acute distress: Naomi Mitchison to PB, 8 September 1979. The incident is mentioned in *TY*, 523. Dick Mitchison had been a liaison officer with the French on the Italian front.

271   'The accumulated grief': VB to PhB, 29 April 1933. McM.

271   'some inner spring': Derek Savage to PB, 1980. PBC.

271   'though it was by no means': Higham, *A Literary Gent*, 174.

271   'genteel' and 'provincial': VB to WH, 8 May 1934. Hull; *SL*, 280.

271   'a wonderful story': Beatrice Webb to VB, 28 September 1933. McM.

271   'Vera is a charmer': Beatrice Webb, 3 May 1934, *Diary*, vol. 4, 331.

272   'friends of varying': VB to WH, 25 September 1928. Hull.

272   'never doubt how much': VB to WH, 27 December 1925. Hull; *SL*, 74.

272   'Symphony Concert': Reprinted in *TF*, 313.

273   'Miss Buss and Miss Beale': Hugh Walpole, 'Book-Ballyhoo: a conversation', *The Week-end Review*, 18 July 1931.

273   'Come back': WH to VB, 29 July 1934. Hull; *SL*, 291.

273   'Miss Vera Holtby': WH to VB, 4 November 1934. Hull; *SL*, 318.

273   'No my heart': VB to WH, 6 August 1925. Hull.

273   'Look she's got': VB, 'Estimate of Self: Popularity'. MS note, PBC.

273   'a tremendous & vehement': VB to WH, 5 September 1929. Hull.

274   'I don't mind the young ones': VB to SW, 23 September 1964. McM.

274   'I am wholly . . . in love with her': VB, MS note in PBC.

274   'Certainly if W.': VB to GC, 19 May 1936. McM. VB was notably on the defensive, though, when editing the correspondence between herself and WH for their *Selected Letters* in 1960. She paid scrupulous attention to excising many of the professions of love and affection which some of the letters contain. 'VSVDL', standing for 'Very Small Very Dear Love', was the most common form of salutation used by WH in her letters to VB, and VB quickly adopted it as her nickname. Other endearments were stronger: VB was WH's 'lover', 'husband', 'beloved', and in one letter WH writes of kissing VB's 'pretty fingers tip by tip', and of loving her 'small beloved body'.

Shaw, ' "A Noble Relationship" ', 38, has also drawn attention to the fact that VB carefully edited WH's letters from the mid-Twenties to 'smooth away' the stress of WH's writing in the period immediately following VB's marriage. 'It certainly was "a noble relationship",' Shaw concludes, 'but it was also intense, hungry and anxious in ways that Brittain did not want, or could not bring herself, to acknowledge.'

274   Sybil Morrison: Morrison admitted, however, that she had only met WH once. In 1975 Morrison wrote: 'About Vera and Winifred. I didn't mean to say that there was a lesbian relationship between them because, knowing Vera I am sure that there was not. What I am quite sure about is that Winifred was in love with Vera; there are those . . . love letters and there is all that she did and gave of her own life to help in Vera's life.' Sybil Morrison to PB, 29 July 1975. PBC.

274   'But we were': Sybil Morrison interviewed by Jilly Cooper, *Sunday Times*, 6 June 1976.

274   lesbian: In recent years there has been a lively ongoing debate among feminist historians about the nature of women's friendships, and about the use of the word 'lesbian' to describe emotional attachments between women. The relationship of VB and WH has been widely used as a focus for such studies. See, for instance, Jeffreys, *The Spinster and her Enemies*, 123–4, who suggest that VB deliberately repressed the lesbian element in her relationship with WH, or Faderman, *Surpassing the Love of Men*, 310, who argues that VB hid the fact that the relationship was lesbian, out of fear. Both Jeffreys and Faderman base their conclusions on conjecture rather than on actual evidence. Gorham, 'The Friendships of Women', 50–1, surveys the literature on the VB–WH friendship. B.E. Raychaba in an unpublished paper, ' "I Love You Quite Differently": Historical Reflections on the Companionship of Vera Brittain and Winifred Holtby', sees their relationship as following in the tradition of the nineteenth-century 'romantic friendship'. We are grateful to Mr Raychaba for allowing us to see a copy of his paper.

274   'to rouse him': WH to VB, 4 November 1934. Hull; *SL*, 317.

275   'The sexual philosophers': WH to VB, n.d. [1926?] Hull.

275   'I could not omit': VB to Harry Pearson, n.d. [December 1939]. McM.

275   In her review: *Time and Tide*, 6 January 1940.

275   'for the physical': WH?
275   'the result': WH to VB, 23 March 1926. Hull
275   the paths of her heroines: We owe this point to Philip Brooke, 'Winifred Holtby: Her Novels and their Context'.
276   'Radclyffe Hall': WH to VB, 21 August 1928. Hull.
276   to create the character . . . in *South Riding*: PhB to Margaret Waley, 7 July 1976. PBC. PhB claimed that WH had told her this in confidence.
276   'bloodsucking friend': Quoted in Grant, *Stella Benson*. 298.
276   St John Ervine . . . advised Winifred: St John Ervine to WH, 22 February 1935. Hull.
277   'Everybody's exploitation': VB to Rebecca West, 4 January 1940. McM.
277   George in more cynical mood: VB to Sarah Gertrude Millin, 15 May 1940. McM.
277   'I was as bad': VB to Sarah Gertrude Millin, 10 January 1939. Sarah Gertrude Millin Papers, University of the Witwatersrand.
277   'You mustn't forget': St John Ervine to Annie S. Swan, 15 February 1940, *The Letters of Annie S. Swan*, 243.
277   ' "art" is something': *TF*, 233.
278   'she too some day': WH to VB, 7 April 1933. Hull; *SL*, 252.
278   'evil genius': 19 February 1939, *CF*, 338.
279   'I am so miserable': VB to GC, 18 April 1932. McM.
279   'the disease kills': *TF*, 386.
279   'Oh Margaret': 'Some Letters from Winifred Holtby, Arranged by Lady Rhondda', *Time and Tide*, 25 April 1936.
280   'so wonderfully': Ethel Smyth to VB, 31 December 1939. McM.
280   'Perhaps I do Winifred': GC to VB, 18 March 1937. McM.
280   'In the thirties': VB to GC, 15 September 1952. McM.
280   According to Hilda Reid: Hilda Reid to PB, 10 March 1976. PBC.
281   'With all the publicity': GC, *For God's Sake Go!*, 130.
281   'the penalty': WH to GC, 11 April 1933. McM.
281   ghosting George's books: 'Do you think it would be right, or honourable, to act as G's permanent collaborator without having my name on his books & articles? . . . For the sake of having a peaceful marriage I feel I *am* prepared to collaborate secretly . . .' VB to WH, 17 March 1933. Hull.
281   to establish an empirical political science: For a summary of GC's work in this field see Francis D. Wormuth, 'The Political Science of Sir George Catlin', *Fortuna*, 2, 1976.
281   political science . . . a poor relation: As late as 1946 Denis Brogan was telling the audience of his inaugural lecture at Cambridge as the new Professor of Political Science that he doubted 'whether any such academic discipline as political science exists'!
282   The *Realist*: VB contributed an article on 'Monogamy and Censorship' to the December 1929 issue.

283   'Not being in the House': GC to VB, 12 December 1952. McM.
283   'Yes, politics': VB to GC, 17 July 1952. McM.
283   'an almost feminine': GC to VB, 8 November 1952. McM.
283   'Vera Brittain's dreadful': Quoted in Grant, *Stella Benson*, 251.
283   'artificiality': Webb, *Diary*, vol. 4, 331.
283   Even Victor Gollancz: Dudley Edwards, *Victor Gollancz*, 623.
284   'an Oxford accent': BBC Internal Circulating Memo, George Catlin file, 21 September 1934. BBC Written Archives.
284   'but asked could we do': WH to VB, 16 March 1932. Hull.
284   'shut in': GC to Victor Gollancz, 27 February 1956. Modern Records Centre, Warwick.
284   'So glad': 27 June 1932, *CF*, 60.
285   a Dutch girl: VB to WH, 24 February 1932. Hull.
285   'that this time': VB to WH, 26 December 1932. Hull.
285   'a really satisfactory': VB to SW, 9 December 1967. McM.
285   'a very stable': GC to VB, 9 October 1952. McM.
285   'Had I known': VB to JC, 12 June 1947. McM.
285   'big killing': David Higham, *A Literary Gent*, 174.
286   £1,580 in royalties: VB to WH, 19 May 1934. Hull.
286   'Of course a dignified': VB to WH, 22 May 1934. Hull.
286   'She has your high': WH to VB, 25 May 1934. Hull. 'Cathleen Nesbitt would do for the older you . . . What a superb reversion of parts! I'd love to see C. Nesbitt acting you acting C. Nesbitt in the G.D.P.!!'
286   '. . . You yourself': VB to WH, 22 May 1934. Hull.
286   as British delegate: GC went in place of VB who was a member of the Relief Committee for the Victims of German Fascism. See *Dictionary of Labour Biography*, vol. 9, ed. J.M. Bellamy and J. Saville (Macmillan, 1993), 21.
286   'One of the minor': VB to WH, 19 May 1934. Hull; *SL*, 285. VB had been present at the first meeting of the National Council for Civil Liberties, in the crypt of St Martin-in-the-Fields, earlier that year. See K. Martin, *Editor*, 138 3.
287   'If I don't earn': VB to MSJ, 27 September 1937. McM.
287   'I shall take Father's': VB to WH, 27 December 1923, Hull; *SL*, 27–9.
287   'one of the most': W. Colston Leigh to VB, 6 June 1934. McM.
287   'a perfect tornado': VB to WH, 1 April 1934. Hull; *SL*, 270.
288   'The air is': VB to WH, 15 April 1934. Hull; *SL*, 276.
288   four minutes later: For TAB's suicide attempt, see VB to WH, 5 May 1934. Hull.
288   pocket diaries: TAB's diaries for 1931 and 1933. McM. e.g. 5 January 1933, 'Palpitation Attack

9.10 am to 1 pm. 4 hours. Got up afterwards & cashed 2 Dividends at Bank.'

288   'shrunken': VB to WH, 22 April 1933. Hull.

288   'Of course': VB MS note. PBC.

289   'When Winifred': SW, 'My Mother and Her Friend'.

289   'John Edward': WH to Jean McWilliam, 10 April 1934, *LF*, 460.

289   'I used to': VB to WH, 8 May 1934. Hull; *SL*, 281.

290   'It reminded me': VB to WH, 12 May 1934. Hull.

290   'and closest friend': Marie Leighton to VB, 12 October 1938. McM.

290   'My dear Jack': TAB to VB, 23 August 1934. McM. 'The anguish of soul in the complaint', TAB wrote to EB at this time, 'beggars description, & I am terrified out of my life – *and cases don't get better . . .*' n.d. McM.

291   'I am going ahead': VB to WH, 3 September 1934. Hull; *SL*, 292.

291   'This effort': 14 September 1934, *CF*, 167.

291   'Why was a professional': *TE*, 111.

291   'Auntie isn't': 15 September 1934, *CF*, 167.

291   'are birdseed': *TS*, 123.

CHAPTER 10: AMERICAN INTERLUDE

292   'For the first time . . . my tour': VB to WH, 20 September 1934. Hull; *SL*, 295. Harold Nicolson wrote to Vita Sackville-West on the same day, 'We had Professor Catlin and his bright little wife to lunch . . . He is an austere and vain type. She is like a thin robin pecking with bright eyes.' *The Letters of Vita Sackville-West and Harold Nicolson*, ed. Nigel Nicolson (Weidenfeld, 1993), 251–2.

293   'The ignorance': VB to Kenneth M. Gould, 21 September 1934. McM.

293   'shrewd as a ferret': *TE*, 112.

293   'that the real point . . . looks after you': VB to WH, 24 September 1934. Hull; *SL*, 297–8.

294   'efficiency': VB to WH, 26 September 1934. Hull; *SL*, 299.

294   The Bretts: See Tebbel, *A History of Book Publishing in the United States*, and Morgan, *The House of Macmillan*. The Macmillan Company of New York's records are in the Rare Books and Manuscripts Division, New York Public Library.

296   'tattered, worn': Quoted in Garry O'Connor, *Sean O'Casey: A Life* (Hodder & Stoughton, 1988), 102.

296   'put on the smartest . . . got it': VB to WH, 29 September 1934. Hull.

297   'no embarrassment . . . over them': VB to WH, 6 October 1934. Hull.

297   'the comforting': *TS*, 146.

297   'One's utmost': VB to WH, 13 October 1934, Hull; *SL*, 310.

298   'not very cultured': *TS*, 146.

298   'I *do* get a thrill': VB to WH, 10 October 1934. Hull; *SL*, 309.

298   'I heard the news': WH to VB, 10 October 1934. Hull; *SL*, 308.

298   'I suppose other English . . . Cedar River': *TS*, 157.

299   'there will be no visiting': Ruth Gage

Colby to VB, 2 October 1934. McM. VB had been introduced to Mrs Colby at a party given by Maude Royden in London.

299   'a charming, young': VB to WH, 26 October 1934. Hull; *SL*, 314. See Pat Kulisheck, 'Ruth Gage-Colby'. Copy in PBC.

300   'Twenty years ago': VB to WH, 26 October 1934. Hull; *SL*, 314.

301   'the Bretts . . . waged today': VB to WH, 12 November 1934. Hull; *SL*, 322.

301   'Gilbert and Sullivan': *TS*, 215.

301   'inconvenient': VB to WH, 12 November 1934. Hull.

301   'how wildly': *TS*, 216.

301   'continues to disturb': VB to WH, 10 November 1934. Hull.

301   '*Vive l'amour*': WH to VB, 26 November 1934. Hull.

302   'plump, pink . . . for books': VB to WH, 12 November 1934. Hull.

303   ' "The genius" . . . about myself': VB to WH, 15 November 1934 (continuation of 12 November). Hull.

303   'a hazardous': VB to WH 6 December 1934. Hull.

303   'If there had been': VB to WH, 28 November 1934. Hull.

303   'bitter-sweet shock': VB to MSJ, ?. McM.

303   'one would adore': VB to WH, 10 November 1934. Hull.

304   'not in the least . . . hopelessly in love': VB to WH, 28 November 1934. Hull.

305   'I am so weary': VB to George Brett, 4 December 1934. McM.

305   'I've almost forgotten . . . frankness': VB to WH, 6 December 1934. Hull; *SL*, 334.

305   'If the courage': VB, 'Youth and War', 13 December 1934. McM. *TS*, 225.

CHAPTER 11: 1935: 'THE WORST, CRUELLEST, SADDEST YEAR SINCE THE WAR'

306   'a nice little': WH to VB, 23 November 1934. Hull; *SL*, 327.

307   'I seem to have been': *TE*, 118.

307   'Things are getting': WH to VB, 16 November 1934. Hull; *SL*, 324.

307   Women: In *Time and Tide* for 20 October 1934, Cicely Hamilton wrote that *Women* 'is not only a book of first-class thought and first-class writing; it is a book that needed to be written.'

307   'all the time . . . already': WH to VB, 5 March 1935. Hull; *SL*, 335.

307   'It sounds queer': VB to WH, 18 February 1935. Hull; *SL*, 337.

308   'torn between': VB to WH, 6 December 1934. Hull.

308   'except during': VB to WH, 18 February 1935. Hull.

308   'too disturbing . . . existence': VB to WH, 20 February 1935. Hull.

309   'Not so difficult': VB to WH, 12 November 1934. Hull.

309   'very reasonable': VB to WH, 20 February 1935. Hull.

309 'passion, turbulence': VB to WH, 6 March 1935. Hull; *SL*, 340.

309 'continuous racket . . . explanation': VB to WH, 25 March 1935. Hull.

309 'It was like seeing him': VB to WH, 25 March 1935. Hull.

310 'You have so much': VB to WH, 23 March 1935. Hull.

310 'rather grim': VB to WH, 25 March 1935. Hull.

310 'it may be that . . . But just in case': VB to WH, 27 March 1935. Hull.

311 'passion can become . . . and interests': WH to VB, 12 April 1935. Hull.

311 'In view of what': VB to WH, 27 March 1935 ('Later'). Hull.

311 'that sympathetic': VB to WH, 11 April 1935. Hull.

312 'one vast patriotic': 5 May 1935, *CF*, 177.

312 'perpetually troubled': VB to WH, 11 April 1935. Hull.

313 'I hardly feel': 18 June 1935, *CF*, 183.

313 'When that which is perfect': 19 June 1935, *CF*, 183.

313 'full of grief': 22 June 1935, *CF*, 184.

313 'It may have meant': 2 July 1935, *CF*, 187.

313 'Just as the train': 4 July 1935, *CF*, 187.

314 'I'm no sort': VB, *Honourable Estate*, 379.

314 'We shall have created': Ibid., 422.

314 'superb novelist': 11 June 1936, *CF*, 291.

314 'It will be a year': 22 June 1936, *CF*, 291.

314 'I know that you will': VB to George Brett, 15 September, 1940. McM.

314 'a glow and glamour . . . sure of him': VB to MSJ, 23 April 1940. McM.

315 'Oddly enough': VB to MSJ, 22 April 1940. McM.

316 'George Brett is': VB to GW, 23 January 1952. McM.

316 'a queer, emotional': VB to MSJ, 23 April 1940. McM.

316 'self-deceiving': *TF*, 386.

317 photographed with Shaw: The photograph is reproduced in *SL* and *TG*. WH's strain is evident.

317 'felt rotten': WH to VB, 29 July 1935. Hull; *SL*, 349.

317 'It all represents': 25 July 1935, *CF*, 189.

317 'complacent little': 26 July 1935, *CF*, 189.

318 'As she wasn't': 3 August 1935, *CF*, 191.

319 'I felt sure Father': Ibid., 192.

319 a ferryman spotted a body: 'Vera Brittain Bereaved', *County of Middlesex Independent*, 10 August 1935.

319 'black and red': 5 August 1935, *CF*, 194.

319 at Hammersmith or . . . Richmond: Six years later, when VB was living in Richmond, she came to the conclusion that TAB couldn't have drowned himself at Richmond since his body was found at Isleworth, on the other side of Richmond lock, and in August when the river is low. TAB must, therefore, have jumped from Hammersmith Bridge.

319 'Love never yet': WH to VB, 21 August

1935. Hull; *SL*, 361. 'One thing I do feel: that the invalid who went out into the night was not really the same person as the handsome, fastidious, genial and attractive man who was so kind to me when I first visited Oakwood Court.' WH to EB, 6 August 1935. McM.

320 'After all': VB to WH, 7 August 1935. Hull; *SL*, 352.

320 'The loss': TAB to Mr Bell, 27 June 1918. Brittains Ltd.

320 'I called the children': Edith de Coundouroff to VB, n.d. [August 1935]. McM.

320 at Wimereux: See the impressions of WH in France in Hilda Reid, 'Winifred Holtby', *Oxford Magazine*, 14 November 1935.

321 'dreadfully ill': VB to WH, 19 August 1935. Hull. *SL*; 358.

321 'I see myself . . . is all right': VB to WH, 16 August 1935. Hull; *SL*, 356–7.

321 'I'm sure': VB to WH, 20 August 1935. Hull; *SL*, 359.

321 'It's not strange': WH to VB, 21 August 1935. Hull.

321 'Oohre-brown': WH to VB, 24 August 1935. Hull; *SL*, 363.

322 'My perceptions': VB to St John Ervine, 8 February 1939. Hull.

322 'as during the last': VB to George Brett, 9 September 1935. McM.

322 an attic room: 'Perhaps it wasn't an actual attic – but there were the devil of a lot of stairs going up to it.' Hilda Reid to PB, 25 March 1976. PBC.

322 'merciful, beautiful': WH, *South Riding*, 354.

323 'Your kidneys': Edgar Obermer to WH, 22 November 1932. Hull. 'If you want to go on for a long time quietly writing books and doing quiet journalism, you will have to alter the rhythm of your existence: once you have tuned it down to a certain quiet rate and avoid rushing about, travelling, anything hectic, political meetings . . .'

323 'might mean': 10 September 1935, *CF*, 200.

324 'with the heavy sense': 22 September 1935, *CF*, 205.

324 'her face': 23 September 1935, *CF*, 206.

325 'the proud delight . . .': WH, *South Riding*, vi. 'I'm sorry about that dedicating letter – don't worry – she sent it downstairs for me to read and I did so with tears and in such distress I could not grasp or remember it – but I did *not* grasp it was to be published . . .' Alice Holtby to VB, 30 November 1935. McM.

325 'intense beauty': 24 September 1935, *CF*, 208.

325 'blue-eyed': Ibid, 207.

325 'She wondered': 27 September 1935, *CF*, 211.

325 'I always feel': VB to WH, 27 June 1921. Hull; *SL*, 7.

325 'Vera liked a tidy': Hilda Reid to PB, 25 March 1976. PBC.

326 'spinster may have': WH, *Women and a Changing Civilisation*, 131.

326 their one sexual encounter: WH to VB, 16 April 1935. Hull.

326 'Yes, all through': 28 September 1935 *CF*, 215.

326 'he'd never before': 27 September 1935, *CF*, 212.

326 'She really is': VB to Rebecca West, 27 September 1935. McM.

327 'It was strange': 29 September 1935, *CF*, 217–18.

327 'Whatever I may do ... she added': 26 September 1935, *CF*, 210.

327 Footnote: Virginia Woolf to Ethel Smyth, 8 October 1935, Virginia Woolf *Letters*, vol. 5, 431.

328 'Winifred Holtby passed': Harold Laski, *Time and Tide*, 5 October 1935.

328 'Winifred's heart ... as a servant': C.F. Andrews, Maxwell Garnett, *Time and Tide*, 12 October 1935.

328 'For sixteen years': VB to Sarah Gertrude Millin, 11 October 1935. Sarah Gertrude Millin Papers, University of the Witwatersrand.

328 'and driven ... before the public': VB to MSJ, 17 October 1935. McM.

329 'with full authority': WH's will. Hull.

329 'my trouble': Alice Holtby to VB, 11 December 1935. McM.

329 'My position': Alice Holtby to VB, 4 February 1936. McM.

330 'so full of wisdom': 22 October 1935, *CF*, 228.

330 'Honestly and sincerely': VB to Alice Holtby, 10 December 1935. McM.

330 'all literary power ... made it easier': Alice Holtby to VB, 9 December 1935. McM.

331 misleading impression: The value of WH's estate, published in the newspapers, gave a misleading impression of her financial position, since it included all the money that would have eventually come to her under a variety of different settlements, but from which, at the time of her death, WH had received practically no benefit.

331 'Don't ask me': Alice Holtby to VB, 4 February 1936. McM.

331 one of the most popular British films: See Jeffrey Richards, *The Age of the Dream Palace. Cinema and Society in Britain, 1930–1939* (Routledge & Kegan Paul, 1984), 320–2. A 1974 adaptation of *South Riding* by Stan Barstow for Yorkshire Television was less successful.

331 'It is such a travesty': Alice Holtby to Hilda Reid, 11 October 1937. Copy in PBC.

332 'we do not perform': Alice Holtby to Hilda Reid, 25 July 1937. Copy in PBC.

332 'I am certain': Annie Burnett Smith to Mrs Elystan Miles, 3 March 1936, *The Letters of Annie S. Swan*, 177.

332 'all the sordid ... dust': Alice Holtby to Hilda Reid, 11 October 1937. Copy in PBC.

333 'far too true': Alice Holtby to Hilda Reid, 29 September 1937. Copy in PBC.

333 'Obvious flop': 20 August 1940, *WC*, 50.

333 'Brief Odyssey': This was Gollancz's title for the biography. Collins commissioned a biography of WH from Evelyne White, the editor of *The Schoolmistress*, to which WH had contributed a regular column. But *Winifred Holtby as I Knew Her*, published in 1938, had one overwhelming drawback: that Mrs White could claim no more than a cursory acquaintance with the subject of her book.

333 'suggest even a dim': VB to Sarah Gertrude Millin, 10 January 1939. Sarah Gertrude Millin Papers, University of the Witwatersrand.

333 'my autobiography': VB to Nancy Pearn, 5 April 1937. McM.

333 'Vera is going': Alice Holtby to Hilda Reid, 11 October 1937. Copy in PBC.

334 'positively abusive ... or in anything else': VB to St John Ervine, 18 February 1937. Hull. VB did not send the letter until March 1939.

336 'you have treated him': PhB to VB, 14 September 1939. McM.

336 'justify the accusation': VB to PhB, 27 September 1939. McM.

336 'How difficult perspective': VB to Sarah Gertrude Millin, 10 January 1939. Sarah Gertrude Millin Papers, University of the Witwatersrand.

336 'From the days': *TF*, 2.

337 favourite blue: VB to Lovat Dickson, 7 November 1939. BL.

337 'Miss Brittain's Book': *The Times*, 2 January 1940.

337 'mass of irrelevant': *Time Literary Supplement*, 2 January 1940.

337 'in spite of the clotted ... vital character': Richard Crossman, 'A Life Worth Living', *New Statesman and Nation*, 13 January 1940. In defence of VB's interpretation, though, it should be noted that WH herself had written that her political involvement inhibited her development as an artist. See WH, *Virginia Woolf* (Wishart, 1932), 28. A modern critic, Marion Shaw, returns to the question of VB's detachment in *TF*, in a powerful article, ' "A Noble Relationship" ', in which she argues that VB's portrayal of her friendship with WH in *TF* takes on an idealized character, becoming 'the stuff of elegy rather than biography ... "I never feel I've really had a life of my own", Holtby wrote, and after her death she still hasn't been given a life of her own but only a role as loving friend and exploited friend in a drama of bereavement which is Brittain's not hers. The self-centredness of Brittain's grief diminishes Holtby who appears a pitiful saint ...'

338 'I always regard': VB to PhB, 27 September 1939. McM.

338 'the book': St John Ervine to Annie Swan, 15 February 1940, *The Letters of Annie S. Swan*, 243.

338 'no two people ...': Lady Rhondda, *Time and Tide*, 6 January 1940. Virginia Woolf thought *TF* 'a scrambling, gasping, affectionate book: and W.H. deserved a better.' Virginia Woolf to Ethel Smyth, 16 January 1940, Virginia Woolf, *Letters*, vol. 6, 379. Ethel Smyth wrote to VB asking for the 'naked truth' about Harry Pearson. Ethel Smyth to VB, 31 December 1939. McM.

339 'Dear V.': Harry Pearson to VB, 2 January 1940. McM.

339 'I have dedicated': VB to SW, 30 December 1965. McM.

340 'There are no words': VB manuscript note, 20 January 1938. McM.

CHAPTER 12: THE COMBATIVE PACIFIST

341 'Winifred in dying': 31 December 1935, *CF*, 235–6.

341 'It hurts': VB to MSJ, 17 October 1935. McM.

341 'It is difficult': VB to Winifred Horrabin, n.d. NCCL archive, University of Hull.

341 'cruel stupidity of fate': 21 October 1935, *CF*, 228.

342 'after such a devastating': VB to GC, 5 January 1936. McM.

342 'the main business': VB, 'What Is the Main Business of Life?', *Good Housekeeping*, November 1935.

342 'cold & mean': VB to GC, 7 November 1937. McM.

342 'practically wringing': Interview with Bill and Dorothy Page.

342 'You preferred her': GC to VB, 11 October 1937. McM.

343 'a doughty antagonist': VB to Alice Holtby, 25 October 1935. McM.

343 'gradually ossifying': VB to MSJ, 17 October 1935. McM.

343 '... Your life lately': Clare Leighton to VB, 17 November [1935]. McM.

343 'some rather bitter': *TE*, 138.

343 'integrity would indeed': Alice Holtby to VB, 4 February 1936. McM.

344 'all day ... even progress': VB to MSJ, 6 January 1936. McM.

344 'like a penitent': 28 March 1936, *CF*, 268.

345 'I've promised ... high speed': VB to Eric Gillett, 26 June 1936. Copy in PBC.

345 'It was intended': VB to George Brett, 17 July 1936. McM.

345 'the cycle': *TE*, 160.

345 feminist critics: For instance, Kennard, *Vera Brittain and Winifred Holtby*, 191, 'many better-known writers have never written anything as good as either *Testament of Youth* or *Honourable Estate*'. See also Mellown, 'Reflections on Feminism and Pacifism in the Novels of Vera Brittain', 217–23.

345 'one of the greatest': VB, *Honourable Estate*, 13–14.

346 'makes it the more': Ibid., 15.

346 Her notebooks: In the possession of SW.

347 'The author's': Cadogan and Craig, *Women and Children First*, 57. The influence of George Eliot, VB's favourite novelist as an adolescent, is discernible in the novel's heavy tone of moral earnestness.

347 'So often one': VB to Sarah Gertrude Millin, 19 June 1937. Sarah Gertrude Millin Papers, University of the Witwatersrand.

348 'It was pretty grossly': GC to PB, 20 April 1970. PBC.

348 'a fine': *Manchester Guardian*, 30 October 1936.

348 'passionate sincerity': *The Times*, 24 November 1936. See also *Times Literary Supplement*, 7 November 1936.

348 'It must be admitted': Alfred Kazin, *New York Times Book Review*, 15 November 1936.

348 25,000 copies: The actual figure was 25,580. Livia Gollancz to VB, 17 June 1965. PBC. *Honourable Estate* was at the top of the fiction bestsellers for four weeks in Britain, and also appeared on the *Herald-Tribune* list in the United States.

349 'that it might bring': MS notebook in possession of SW.

349 '& much admired it': 3 February 1937, *CF*, 304.

349 'It was written': VB to Sarah Gertrude Millin, 14 December 1936. Sarah Gertrude Millin Papers, University of the Witwatersrand.

349 'a close season': VB to Dr Pugh, 3 June 1936. McM.

349 'A thunderstorm': VB to GC, 19 June 1936. McM.

349 At least ten: The headline in the *Dorset County Chronicle and Somersetshire Gazette*, 25 June 1936, read '8,000 gather at Maumbury. Orators speak in Grilling Heat.' *Peace News*, 11 July 1936, described ten thousand people 'Streaming in on bicycles and motorbuses ... from all over Dorset, Somerset, Devon, Wiltshire, and even South Wales.' VD in *TE*, 164, writes that the amphitheatre could seat fifteen thousand.

350 Canon Dick Sheppard: Lord Soper recalls, 'I can see Dick Sheppard now. He had a bit of an asthma attack during the meeting, and I remember him sitting with his head in his hands to recover his breath.'

350 'non-political': *Dorset County Chronicle*, 25 June 1936.

350 'her customary': *TE*, 165. VB's five pages of notes for her speech at the rally are at McM. These may have been jotted down as an *aide-memoire* after she had spoken. *Peace News*, 11 July 1936, reports that VB invited women to join the Peace Pledge Union, and recorded that more than 600 signatures were obtained on that day alone. The success of the rally led to the founding of the Dorset Peace Council with the writer Sylvia Townsend Warner as its secretary.

350 'I travelled back': VB to GC, 21 June 1936. McM.

350 'the complete pacifist outlook': The complex etymology of the words 'pacifist' and 'pacifism' has often given rise to confusion and requires clarification here. During the Thirties the older, vaguer usage of 'pacifism', defined in the 1933 edition of the *Shorter Oxford English Dictionary* as 'the doctrine or belief that it is desirable and possible to settle international disputes by peaceful means', was slowly being superseded by a more precise meaning, that war is always wrong and should never be resorted to under any circumstances. Although VB used the word indiscriminately, she cannot in fact be said to have become a pacifist ('the complete pacifist outlook' she refers to here) until 1937 when she joined the Peace Pledge Union. Prior to that, her support for the League of Nations makes 'internationalist' the most accurate description of her position. For a rigorous discussion of these definitions, see Ceadel, *Pacifism in Britain 1914–45*, a seminal work, to which this

551

chapter is heavily indebted, and the same author's *Thinking About Peace and War* (Oxford University Press, 1987).

350 'the brave new': VB, 'No Compromise with War', *World Review of Reviews*, 1937; *TG*, 223.

351 'the collective ownership': VB, 'Peace and the Public Mind', *Challenge to Death?*, 1934, 40–66. The other contributors included GC, WH, J.B. Priestley, Rebecca West, Edmund Blunden, and Philip Noel Baker.

351 'a real uniformed peace': VB, 'Why Not A Real Peace Crusade?', 'The Lighter Side of Peacemaking', *Quarterly News*, 1934; *TG*, 220–2.

352 Vice-President of the Youth Movement: VB to Mr Judd, 11 January 1935. McM.

352 the League's policy on collective security: See Birn, *The League of Nations Union*, and J.A. Thompson, 'Lord Cecil and the Pacifists in the League of Nations Union', *Historical Journal*, 20, 1977.

352 'a kind of eunuch organization': GC, *For God's Sake Go!*, 286.

352 Vice-President of the WILPF· At a December 1933 meeting of the WILPF VB had put forward an idea for a Peace Army. However, although it was conceded that the idea had 'many excellent features', including the wearing of a 'fairly conspicuous' peace badge when taking part in processions, the WILPF considered that it 'was hardly the body to carry them out', and recommended that Maude Royden's Peace Army might be more appropriate for the purpose. Minutes of Executive Committee of Women's International League for Peace and Freedom, 12 December 1933, 9 January 1934. British Library of Political and Economic Science.

352 'I have a little': VB to Dorothy Woodman, 25 May 1934. McM. For further details of Woodman and the UDC, see K. Martin, *Editor*, 171–6.

352 'The great thing': VB to Miss Nathan, 20 June 1935. Copy in PBC.

353 'wide moral division': *TE*, 168.

353 upheaval in the peace movement: Ceadel, *Pacifism in Britain 1914–1945*, 193–221.

353 'what . . . does duty': H.R.L. Sheppard, *The Impatience of a Parson*, 62.

354 'Up to now': Sheppard's appeal appeared in *Time and Tide*, 20 October 1934.

354 the Peace Pledge Union: On the early history of the PPU, see Ceadel, *Pacifism in Britain 1914–1945*, and Sybil Morrison, *I Renounce War*.

354 'He had a genius': *What Can We Believe? Letters exchanged between Dick Sheppard and L.H.*, ed. Laurence Housman (Jonathan Cape, 1939), 7.

355 'I fear War': 16 March 1936, *CF*, 256.

355 'Because what the pacifists': VB to GC, 21 June 1936. McM.

355 'how really delighted': Dick Sheppard to VB, 22 June 1936. McM.

356 'after our conversation . . . will be finished': VB to Dick Sheppard, 3 July 1936. McM. Sheppard replied saying that he understood her position, and adding that 'I do regret the fact that these Peace Rallies are opened with prayer or

Bible-reading. I am sure it is the wrong note, and I am doing my best to scotch it. It so often chokes off just the right fellow.' Dick Sheppard to VB, 6 July 1936. McM.

356 'wipe myself out': GC to VB, 25 June 1936. McM.

356 'apparently unattainable': VB to MSJ, 16 March 1936. McM.

356 'revolutionary principle': *TE*, 170. VB's account in *TE* of her conversion to pacifism is viewed through the distorting prism of her Second World War experiences. We are given an impression of a conversion that was more religiously-inspired than was in fact the case. In reality her decision to support the PPU was at once tentative, more pragmatic, and more politically motivated than it appears in her autobiography. Only with the outbreak of war in 1939 would a Christian basis to her pacifism start to develop.

357 This brief tour: e.g. at Matlock, on 5 September 1936, VB spoke on the 'Task Before a Labour Party', and called for 'a real League of Nations' in which collective security would mean 'exactly what is says'. MS McM.

357 'It had become': *TE*, 171.

357 'I need hardly say': VB to Philip Mumford, 28 October 1936. McM.

357 'decent, agreeable'· 5 January 1937, *CF*, 303.

358 'too little tempered': Ryan, *Bertrand Russell*, 149.

358 PPU's New Year campaign: Calendar of Speakers, signed by F.P. Crozier. PPU archive.

358 'seemed an epitome': VB to MSJ, 17 January 1937. McM.

358 'shouted with joy': Dick Sheppard to VB, 27 January 1937. McM. VB wrote to Sheppard on 28 January asking that her name be considered as a Sponsor.

358 'can lead us': VB, 'No Compromise with War', *World Review of Reviews*, May 1937; *TG* 228.

358 'practical and effective methods': VB to Mr Silkin, 21 April 1937. McM.

358 'stands for such': VB to Miss Stancer, 27 January 1937. McM.

359 'professed agnosticism . . . here and now': VB to Mr Glanville, 13 September 1934. McM.

359 'I am not a pacifist': VB, 'Why I Stand for Peace', 1937. TS McM.

359 'that warlike champion': VB, 'One Voice', unpublished Foreword to 'Letters to Peace-Lovers'. McM.

359 'inherited temperament': VB to GC, 11 January 1945. McM.

359 'Good for you': Dick Sheppard to VB, 29 January 1937. McM. On 2 February he wrote to her confirming her unanimous election to the Sponsors.

359 'A proposal . . .': PPU minutes. PPU archive. For VB and the PPU, see Y.A. Bennett, 'Testament of a Minority in Wartime' and the same author's *Vera Brittain*. VB remained a member of the League of Nations Union up to 1938, largely because of its work in co-ordinating nations' responses to humanitarian causes, but also because

she hoped that the machinery of Geneva might one day be employed in administering a true community of nations. Shortly after joining the PPU in 1937 VB became a member of the Fellowship of Reconciliation, the British section of the international Christian pacifist movement.

359 **Margaret Storm Jameson:** MSJ appears as a frail presence in 'Peace or War', a newsreel made for Armistice Week 1933. British Movietone News 6468:08719.

359 'Since the death . . .': VB to W. Colston Leigh, 16 March 1936. McM.

360 'I was immensely': VB to MSJ, 23 April 1940. McM.

360 **appointing Storm as her literary executor:** Apparently within a fortnight of WH's death: see *CF*, 227.

360 **Herbert Gray . . . once remarked:** VB to MSJ, 23 April 1940. McM.

361 'I give it away': MSJ, *Journey from the North*, vol. 1, 94. For information about MSJ see her autobiography, and the excellent introductions by Elaine Feinstein to the Virago editions of her novels.

361 'profound admiration': Grant Richards to VB, 28 August 1923. Grant Richards Archive, University of Illinois.

361 **two breakdowns:** For instance, in July 1936 MSJ suffered a breakdown and was forbidden letters. VB to Guy Chapman, 23 July 1936. McM. MSJ's output was prodigious. As she used to say of herself, she was a better writer than she gave herself time to be. Between 1919 and 1979, she published forty-five novels as well as several works of criticism, and two volumes of autobiography, *Journey from the North*, were reprinted by Virago in the Eighties, but sales were disappointing. Her work is long overdue for a revival.

361 'add a little variety': VB to MSJ, 6 January 1936. McM.

362 'you are the best friend': VB to GC, 22 February 1937. McM.

362 'You have always': VB to MSJ, 23 April 1940. McM.

362 'The last thing': VB to MSJ, 17 October 1935. McM.

362 'It does seem': VB to MSJ, 4 May 1936. McM.

362 'very little use': VB to Dr Jenks, 16 March 1934. McM.

363 'I was interested': VB to MSJ, 2 July 1936. McM.

363 'If I believe': MSJ, *Journey from the North*, vol. 1, 341-2.

363 'dubious': VB to GC, 28 June 1938. McM. From the outset MSJ warned Sheppard that she would be unable to take on any committee work, and she appears not to have addressed any public meetings for him. Before long, her name was the most that she was prepared to lend the cause.

363 'at the mercy': VB, 'Pacifism versus Literature'. MS PBC.

363 'a recent notable': *Peace News*, 6 March 1937.

363 'literary and aesthetic': VB to GC, 28 February 1937. McM.

364 'It was very nice': VB to Sybil Morrison, 2 March 1937. McM.

364 'Rearmament Insanity': 'Rearmament Insanity', February 1937. TS McM.

364 'a sportsman': Dick Sheppard to VB, 1 March 1937. McM.

364 'the inconvenient protest': VB, 'Pacifism versus Literature'. MS PBC.

364 'a trifling': *CF*, 303.

364 **lacked 'the common touch':** Nora Page, Imperial War Museum Sound Archive.

364 'possibly instinctive': ?, *CF*, ?

364 'If I always . . . Buxton upbringing': VB, 'Vigils & Peace Witness', 29 September 1967. TS PBC.

365 'My life': 19 April 1937, *CF*, 310.

365 'the impertinence': VB to MSJ, 25 August 1937. McM.

365 'If . . . I am': VB to Dorothy Plowman, 5 February 1938. McM.

365 **It has been calculated:** *TG*, 32.

366 'coherent plans': VB to PhB, 19 March 1933. McM.

366 'Black Decade'. Foreword to 'Black Decade'. Notebook in possession of SW.

366 'Panorama': Introduction to holograph of *TY*. McM.

366 'the perpetual requests': VB, 'Pacifism versus Literature'. MS PBC.

366 'There is no book': VB to Lovat Dickson, 4 June 1940. BL.

366 'Quite obviously': VB to Lovat Dickson, 7 July 1940. BL.

367 'youth, adventure': VB to MSJ, 13 October 1941. McM. VB also intended to include Amy Johnson in a book called 'Six Portraits' or 'Makers of Yesterday'. VB to Harold Macmillan, 14 July 1941. BL. *A Life of George Lansbury* written by his son-in-law, the socialist historian, Raymond Postgate, was published in 1951. Betty Johnson's memoir of her sister was never completed, and it was not until 1967 that Constance Babington Smith's biography of Amy Johnson appeared.

367 'terrible, inert': VB, 'Women and the Next War', *British Legion Journal*, April 1936.

367 'infinite capacity': VB, 'Women and Disarmament', *Highway*, February 1934.

367 **chief shortcoming:** See Y.A. Bennett, *Vera Brittain*.

367 'the struggle against war': VB, 'Women and Pacifism', *Peace News*, 15 August 1941.

368 'the shadow of death': VB, letter to *Daily Herald*, 19 March 1937.

368 'all that is left': VB, 'Notes for The PPU', n.d. McM.

368 'a sensitive responsiveness': The description is Ruth Colby's. Ruth Colby to VB, 21 November 1940. McM.

368 'Dear love': 20 February 1939, *CF*, 338.

368 'half-concealed': *TF*, 310. JC's enduring affection for WH is one of the most striking features of his memoir of his family, *Family Quartet*.

369 'I think you': VB to JC, 23 September 1937. McM. 'A letter for you to read when I am no longer here to talk to you.'

369 **Poppy**: Named after the Shirley poppy.

369 **'Her affectionate nature'**: Shirley Catlin, School Report, Chelsea Open Air Nursery, 1934. McM.

369 **'our unnatural system'**: VB, letter to the *Daily Express*, 13 December 1930.

370 **Footnote**: *Freedom's Daughter. Letters between Indira Gandhi and Jawaharlal Nehru 1922–39*, ed. Sonia Gandhi (Hodder & Stoughton, 1989), 262. 'A Childhood: Mary Soames', *The Times*, 10 November 1990.

371 **'uppish'**: 19 April 1936. *CF*, 286.

371 **'came, went'**: SW, 'Remembering My Mother'.

371 **'metallic efficiency'**: VB to GC, 14 November 1937. McM.

371 **'If they wish'**: VB, letter to *Daily Herald*, 15 July 1938.

371 **'I'd like to go'**: VB to GC, 28 July 1938. McM.

371 **'getting my head bashed'**: SW, *Sunday Times*, 5 April 1981.

371 **'calling her'**: SW, 'Remembering My Mother'.

372 **'as a genuine symbol'**: GC, *For God's Sake, Go!*, 184.

372 **'Every scrap'**: VB to MSJ, 24 March 1939. McM.

373 **'his sense'**: VB to GC, 9 November 1936. McM.

373 **'take yourself off'**: GC to VB, 12 November 1936. McM.

373 **'For all my'**: VB to GC, 25 September 1937. McM.

373 **'... What matters most ... 1937 – normality'**: VB to MSJ, 30 November 1937. McM.

374 **'might make anything'**: VB to GC, 23 November 1937. McM.

374 **'illusory'**: *TS*, 298.

374 **'Go to'**: VB to GC, 20 October 1937. McM.

374 **'Perhaps you ought'**: VB to GC, 21 October 1937. McM.

374 **'lucid & as little'**: VB to GC, 20 October 1937. McM.

374 **'What you said'**: VB to GC, 7 November 1937. McM.

375 **'It was as though'**: Quoted in *TS*, 272.

375 **'feeling rather forlorn'**: VB to GC, 18 September 1937. McM.

375 **'Bless you'**: Dick Sheppard to VB, 25 October 1937. McM.

375 **'Damn Archie Macdonell'**: VB to GC, 25 November 1937. McM.

375 **'I can't visualize'**: VB to GC, 27 November 1937. McM.

376 **'Police holding ... vision'**: GC to VB, 6 November 1937. McM.

376 **'When the spirit'**: Quoted in *TS*, 317.

376 **'Be sure'**: VB to GC, 29 November 1937. McM.

376 **'genial informality'**: *TS*, 342.

376 **'His real story'**: VB to GC, 14 November 1937. McM.

377 **'a nice fellow'**: GC to VB, 6 December 1937. McM.

377 **'an emotional'**: VB to MSJ, 29 April 1940. McM.

377 **what Sheppard would have done**: As many of Sheppard's friends had done. See Matthews, *Dick Sheppard*, 48. Maude Royden said that 'she could never discover that Dick had any policy in the event of war'; Canon J.M.C. Crum was of the opinion that 'Had he lived till 1939 Dick would assuredly have died of a broken heart.'

377 **'begrudging'**: Cunningham, *British Writers of the Thirties*, 439. An often brilliant, though strangely androcentric, survey of Thirties' writing.

378 **'Our movement'**: VB, *Peace News*, 4 December 1937.

378 **'I do see coming'**: VB to Stuart Morris, 21 March 1938. McM. For the difficulties faced by the PPU after Sheppard's death, see Ceadel, *Pacifism in Britain*, 266ff.

378 **'historical retribution'**: VB, 'Pacifism after Munich', *Fellowship (US)*, November 1938; *TG*, 228.

378 **'economic appeasement'**: Ceadel, *Pacifism in Britain*, 274. See also David Lukowitz, 'British Pacifists and Appeasement: The Peace Pledge Union', *Journal of Contemporary History*, 9 (1), 1974.

379 **'all the services possible'**: VB to MSJ, 30 November 1937. McM.

379 **'... The time'**: VB to George Brett, 13 March 1938. McM.

379 **'the hoydenish'**: *TS*, 278.

380 **'I am off'**: VB to Norman Ginsbury, 24 September 1938. Copy in PBC.

380 **'I shall bring them'**: VB to MSJ, 6 October 1938. McM.

380 **'an inglorious peace'**: VB 'Pacifism after Munich'; *TG*, 229–30.

381 **'pro-Nazi'**: MSJ to VB, 6 August 1940. McM. In this letter MSJ says that she resigned 'after Munich'. In November 1938 she had told VB that she felt that she should resign as a Sponsor because 'The P.P.U. is not a thing one can go into with one foot.' MSJ to VB, 10 November 1938. McM.

381 **'My refuge'**: MSJ to VB, 14 May 1941. McM.

381 **'literally running'**: VB to Sarah Gertrude Millin, 12 November 1938. Sarah Gertrude Millin Papers, University of the Witwatersrand.

381 **'not only because'**: VB to Sarah Gertrude Millin, 15 November 1938. Sarah Gertrude Millin Papers, University of the Witwatersrand. Like many of her class and generation, VB had been guilty of the occasional mildly anti-semitic remark, but as soon as the Nazis' persecution of the Jews became known, she did all that she could to assist the flight of Jewish refugees into this country.

381 **'anti campaigns'**: VB to Ethel Mannin, 30 January 1939. McM.

381 **'the present PPU line'**: VB to MSJ, 18 January 1939. McM. The more militant members of the PPU staff had produced a leaflet arguing that pacifists should decline to take part in ARP to show that they were not prepared to cooperate in the organization of war.

382 **'so tired'**: VB to MSJ, 21 March 1939. McM.

382 **'Never since'**: 20 March 1939, *CF*, 347.

382 'The passionate conviction': VB, letter to *New Statesman and Nation*, 8 April 1939.

382 'I have the greatest': Victor Gollancz, letter to *New Statesman and Nation*, 15 April 1939.

383 'caddish': 14 April 1939, *CF*, 358.

383 'Vera Brittain's sales': Monthly Report, Lovat Dickson to Harold Macmillan, November 1938. Lovat Dickson Papers, Public Archive of Canada.

383 'would rather lose': VB to Harold Macmillan, 25 April 1940. BL.

383 'more vehemently': VB to GC, 3 March 1939. McM.

384 'Complete sang-froid': 27 April 1939, *CF*, 359.

384 'with 20 miles': 17 April 1939, *CF*, 358.

384 'like a puppy': 3 September 1939, *WC*, 28.

385 'and to set': VB, 'Lift Up Your Hearts!', *Peace News*, 8 September 1939; *TG*, 234.

CHAPTER 13: HUMILIATION WITH HONOUR

386 'It was so quiet': *TE*, 214.

386 'To write a weekly': VB to MSJ, 5 September 1939. McM.

387 'What I do want': 'Vera Brittain's Personal Letter to Peace-Lovers', 4 October 1939. Reprinted in *Testament of a Peace Lover*, 1–4.

387 'a shoal . . . to stop': VB, 'One Voice', unpublished foreword to 'Letter to Peace-Lovers'. McM.

387 'It does seem': VB to MSJ, 12 October 1939. McM.

387 'A Cabinet memorandum: Memorandum on Anti-War publications, 4 May 1940. Public Record Office, Kew, CAB 75/7 HPC (40), 103.

388 'an attractive girl': VB, 'One Voice'. For Mrs Eden-Green's reminiscences of working with Vera on the Letter, see her Foreword to the Fontana edition of *England's Hour*, 1–10, and her Introduction to *Testament of a Peace Lover*, and her 'A Wartime Letter to Peace Lovers', unpublished TS in PRC.

388 'his influence': EB to VB, 31 October [1937]. McM.

388 'for fellowship': VB, 'One Voice'.

388 'punchy style': Y.A. Bennett, *Vera Brittain*, 8.

389 'I would rather soil': VB, 'Letter to Peace-Lovers', 8 May 1941.

389 'spiritual havoc': Ibid., 23 May 1940.

389 'better for our': Ibid., 29 February 1940.

390 'valuable': 7 September 1939, *WC*, 29.

390 'I shall be happy': VB to Ministry of Information, 10 September 1939. McM.

390 'colossal cables . . . it is now': VB to PhB, 19 September 1939. McM.

391 'As an individual . . . dear Phyllis': VB to PhB, 23 September 1939. McM.

391 a luncheon party: *The Times*, 2 January 1940.

391 'No English publisher': VB to Harold Macmillan, 2 January 1940. BL.

392 'Lady Rhondda came to see me': Foreign Office Minute from Charles Peake to Mr Scott, 2 January 1940. File: Visit of Miss Brittain to the United States. Public Record Office, Kew, FO 371/24245.

393 'is of the kind': Ibid. The coded telegram from the Foreign Office to Lord Lothian was sent on 10 January 1940, and advised that 'You may think it desirable to represent the facts in the proper quarter before Miss Brittain arrives in Washington.'

393 'with respect': VB to Frank Darvall, 23 January 1940. Public Record Office, Kew, FO 371/24227.

393 Miss Brittain: Response to above. Public Record Office, Kew, FO 371/24227.

393 'not done any': Frank Darvall to E. Rowe-Dutton, 18 May 1940. Public Record Office, Kew, FO 371/24227.

393 the most successful: W. Colston Leigh to VB, 16 April 1940. BL.

393 'intolerable difficulties . . . get home': VB to Harold Macmillan, 2 April 1940. BL.

394 'change of life': VB to GC, 25 February 1940. McM.

394 question in the House of Commons: *Hansard Parliamentary Debates*, 5th series, vol. 357, 6 February to 1 March 1940.

394 'nightmare of a voyage': VB to MSJ, 22 April 1940. McM.

395 'from different angles': MSJ, *Journey from the North*, vol. 2, 13.

395 'a portrait': VB to MSJ, 22 April 1940. McM.

395 ' "It's foolish" ': MSJ, *Europe to Let*, 171.

395 'Please do not destroy': Ibid., 127.

395 'to the point . . . thoroughly': VB to MSJ, 22 April 1940. McM.

396 'I am just': MSJ to PB, 30 April 1974. PBC.

396 'I don't know': VB to MSJ, 22 April 1940. McM.

396 'cold hard . . . properly': VB to MSJ, 23 April 1940. McM.

397 'behaved like a fool': VB to MSJ, 29 April 1940. McM.

397 'Since I dictated': VB to Sarah Gertrude Millin, 15 May 1940. Sarah Gertrude Millin Papers, University of the Witwatersrand.

397 'Fascists': Quoted in Calder, *The Myth of the Blitz*, 111.

397 'So long': VB, 'Letter to Peace-Lovers', 15 February 1940.

397 Poster Trial: See *Pacifism at Bow Street A Full Report of Proceedings under the Defence Regulations against Officers and members of the Peace Pledge Union*, May 9– June 6 1940 (PPU, 1940).

398 Dick Sheppard had once predicted: According to Sybil Morrison, *I Renounce War*, 52.

398 'cleverly furthered': VB to MSJ, 26 June 1940. McM.

398 'was rooted': Hayes, *Challenge of Conscience*, 66.

398 'Unless we have': John Barclay, *Peace News*, 14 June 1940. Quoted in Ceadel, *Pacifism in Britain*, 297.

398 'It has no hope': VB, 'Letter to Peace-Lovers', 23 May 1940.

398 the Forethought Committee: The Forethought Committee was 'dominated by

religious-minded advocates of community living', and included John Middleton Murry, Max Plowman, Wilfred Wellock and Canon Raven. It was guided by four 'affirmations': 1) To conduct educational work based on a positive analysis of the social and political roots of war and its consequences. 2) Definite activity in assisting victims of war. 3) The creation of nucleii of resistance to tyranny. 4) The adoption of a mode of living in simplicity and the renunciation of economic privilege.

The opposing faction in the PPU was the Forward Movement, formed by the younger militants who argued that the PPU should be more active in stopping the war. Although VB was a member of the Forethought Committee, she retained sympathy for a militant activist like Roy Walker, with whom she would work closely later in the war on the campaign for Food Relief in Occupied Europe.

399 'I went': VB to MSJ, 18 May 1940. McM.
399 'Attempted invasion': 28 May 1940, *WC*, 43.
399 'We should have been': VB to Jim and Mannie Putnam, 30 June 1940. McM.
400 'It was the most terrible': VB to MSJ, 27 June 1940. McM.
400 'The cause of peace': MSJ to VB, 24 June 1940. McM.
400 'The point is . . . my life': VB to MSJ, 27 June 1940. McM.
401 'nightmare-ridden darkness': VB, *England's Hour*, 83.
401 'full blast': VB to MSJ, 4 August 1940. McM.
401 'a wartime variety': VB, *England's Hour*, vii.
402 'point-blank': VB to MSJ, 4 August 1940. McM. However, through the good offices of Arthur Creech Jones, Ernest Bevin's Parliamentary Private Secretary at the Ministry of Labour, VB was permitted to inspect a training centre for women engineers for a chapter entitled 'The Training Centres Carry On'.
402 'I can also': VB to MSJ, 7 August 1940. McM.
402 'even he can . . . indefinite years': VB to MSJ, 4 August 1940. McM.
403 'Of course I shall fight': VB to MSJ, 7 August 1940. McM.
403 'If I had wished . . . different treatment': VB to MSJ, 4 August 1940. McM.
403 'in perfect good faith': VB to MSJ, 7 August 1940. McM.
404 'Half-dead': 9 September 1940, *WC*, 53.
405 'If I dropped . . . in London': VB to George Brett, 30 September 1940. McM.
405 'pitiless': MSJ, *Journey from the North*, vol. 1, 331.
405 'small north room': VB, 'Relations M.S.J. 1941'. MS McM.
406 'now a general': VB to George Brett, 30 September 1940. McM.
406 'reckless irresponsibility': VB to GC, 10 October 1940. McM.

406 'He is far too': VB to Ruth Colby, 28 October 1940. McM.
406 'He is like': VB to George Brett, 12 November 1940. McM.
406 'or Robin': Ruth Colby to George Brett, 23 October 1940. McM.
406 'Shirley is going': Ruth Colby to VB, 10 October 1940. McM.
407 'is already getting': Ruth Colby to VB, 21 November 1940. McM.
407 'secretly regards': Ruth Colby to VB, 10 December 1940. McM.
407 'I do love . . . and distrust': Ruth Colby to VB, 20 August 1940. McM.
407 'I never allow': Ruth Colby to George Brett, 4 December [1940]. McM.
407 'their own sad': VB to Ruth Colby, 7 January 1941. McM.
407 Pethick-Lawrence: VB wrote to Pethick-Lawrence on 28 February 1941. McM.
408 'I have a hunch': VB to Arthur Creech Jones, 27 May 1941. McM.
408 'I have never': VB to GC, 26 April 1942. McM.
408 'Only this afternoon': VB to GC, 19 October 1940. McM.
408 'You write': VB to GC, 22 October 1940. McM.
408 'which you usually': VB to MSJ, 27 October 1940 McM.
409 'with the vigilance': VB to MSJ, 28 December 1940. McM.
409 'and *such* months': VB to Sybil Morrison, 25 November 1940. PPU.
409 'some reviewers': VB to MSJ, 6 February 1941. McM.
409 'than a method': VB to MSJ, 12 April 1941. McM.
409 'this attitude': Lorna Lewis, *Time and Tide*, 1 March 1941.
409 'A stranger': Quoted in *Me Again: Uncollected writings of Stevie Smith*, ed. A. London (Virago, 1981), 176–7.
409 'The individuality': E.M. Delafield, *Time and Tide*, 22 February 1941.
410 'a kind': VB to MSJ, 23 August 1941. McM.
410 'rather specially sinister': VB to Lovat Dickson, 17 February 1941. BL.
410 'frightfully keen': VB to MSJ, 6 February 1941. McM.
411 'someday to help you': VB to Dorothy Hogg, 12 December 1940. PBC.
411 'one stood': 7 February 1941, *WC*, 69.
411 'Except for': VB to MSJ, 12 April 1941. McM.
411 'It seems to me': Max Plowman to VB, 25 February 1941, Plowman, *Bridge into the Future*, 761.
412 'a possible society': Quoted in Ceadel, *Pacifism in Britain*, 307.
412 'a bit like living . . . interesting': VB to GC, [?] March 1941. McM.
412 'I know that': Max Plowman to VB, 25 February 1941, *Bridge into the Future*, 761.
412 'who not only forgave': VB, 'Letter to Peace-Lovers', 19 June 1941.

412   'organizationally': Ceadel, *Pacifism in Britain*, 308.

412   'latent antagonism ... towards women': VB to Andrew Dakers, 9 November 1942. McM.

412   'a masculine *Herrenvolk*': 21 February 1942, *WC*, 130.

413   'adorable ... serene': MSJ to VB, 5 May 1941. McM.

413   'a sort of dishonour': MSJ to VB, 5 February 1941. McM.

414   'perhaps more': MSJ, *Journey from the North*, vol. 2, 38; 95–7 on the writing of *The End of This War*.

414   'I think it was probably': MSJ to VB, 5 May 1941. McM.

414   'Please don't ... future': VB to MSJ, 10 May 1941. McM.

415   'Despair': MSJ to VB, 14 May 1941. McM.

415   All India Women's Conference: For VB's interest in Indian affairs and her attempts to travel to India during the war, see Y.A. Bennett and F.E. Montgomery, 'Vera Brittain and India', paper given at 'A Testament to Vera Brittain', Centenary Conference, McMaster University, Hamilton, Ontario, 16 October 1993.

415   'owing to': 16 July 1941, *WC*, 106.

416   'You have': MSJ to VB, 19 August 1941. McM.

416   'in order to prove': VB to MSJ, 23 August 1941. McM.

416   'bridge back': MSJ to VB, 4 September 1941. McM.

416   'Anything that promises': VB to MSJ, 5 September 1941. McM.

416   'even the mild': MSJ to VB, 6 September 1941. McM.

417   'What in effect': VB to GC, 9 September 1941. McM.

417   'isolation': VB to GC, 10 March 1942. McM.

417   'Your style': VB to MSJ, 10 November 1941. McM.

417   'a letter': MSJ, *The End of This War*, 12–13.

417   'most unfair ... in America': VB to MSJ, 10 November 1941. McM.

417   'These slanging ... and say so': VB to MSJ, 13 November 1941. McM. A terrible sadness hangs over the termination of VB's correspondence with MSJ. Before her death VB attached the following note to the letters: 'To be taken care of by my literary executors after my death for publication at some much later date. I hope that there may be an introduction showing that the sad deterioration of our relationship after 1939 was mainly due to the different attitudes we took increasingly towards the war, which drove a wedge between us. It might be better not to publish any of the 1941 letters, except so far as they describe impersonal matters. Paragraphs inspired purely by irrational emotion on either side would be best omitted.'

418   'in a very clear': VB to GC, 10 March 1942. McM.

418   'Personal differences': 21 February 1942, *WC*, 130.

418   'I realize': Ruth Colby to VB, 13 January 1941. McM.

418   Footnote: VB, 'Winifred Holtby in Life and Literature'. Lecture at the Guildhall, Hull, 28 September 1960.

419   'a complete tomboy': George Brett to VB, 25 August 1941. McM.

419   'a disintegrating': VB, to GC, 26 March 1942. McM.

419   Phyllis Bentley mentioned: PhB to VB, 11 December 1940. McM.

419   'It does seem': VB to Miss Acland (NCCL), 12 April 1942. McM.

419   a copy of one intercepted letter: Postal and Telegraph Censorship, Public Record Office, Kew, V8481/180/70.

420   'and said': Winifred Eden-Green to VB, n.d. [February 1942]. Copy in NCCL Archive, University of Hull.

420   'Although, obviously ...': BBC Internal Circulating Memo, 23 August 1940. BBC Written Archives.

420   'immense damage': GC to John Bush, 5 May 1977. PBC. 'The notion at Cabinet level that, because Vera was a *well-known* pacifist, therefore by association *I* must be an ardent pacifist also is a complete lie; but did me immense damage during the 1940–47 period.'

420   'He has ... found': 'Professor Catlin's scheme for an Anglo-American Institute of Cultural Relations', 27 July 1942. Public Record Office, Kew, FO 371/30656.

421   'holding and dominating': VB to GC, 15 August 1941. McM.

421   'a good deal': MSJ to VB, 6 September 1941. McM.

421   'an inconvenient': VB, 'Letter to Peace-Lovers', 20 November 1941.

422   'I am afraid': VB to M.L. Moll, 8 December 1941. McM.

422   'small book': VB to PB, 24 October 1942. PBC.

422   'Once we can': VB, *Humiliation with Honour*, 46–7.

422   'I need hardly': Ibid., 7.

423   'they said': VB to PB, 24 October 1942. PBC.

423   'as the fundamental': VB, 'One Voice', unpublished Foreword to 'Letters to Peace-Lovers'. McM.

424   'The pacifist tries': VB, 'Letter to Peace-Lovers', 18 December 1941.

CHAPTER 14: ONE VOICE

425   'to the conscience': VB, 'Food Relief in Europe', speech at the Aeolian Hall in London, 24 January 1942, published as 'Has Pity Forsaken Us?', *Fellowship (US)*, April 1942.

425   'the sacredness': VB, 'Letter to Peace-Lovers', 28 December 1944.

425   the PPU's Food Relief Campaign: For VB's involvement in Food Relief, see two important papers on which we have relied heavily in this chapter, Y.A. Bennett, 'A Question of Respectability

and Tactics', and Y.A. Bennett (with F.E. Montgomery), 'Morality, Humanity, Law and War'.

425 'humanizing war': VB's arguments are summarized in VB, 'Should we Humanize War?', *Christian Pacifist*, July 1944.

426 'It's war': VB, 'Should We Blockade Germany? It's war on babies says Vera Brittain', *Daily Herald*, 15 November 1939.

426 the blockade: See W.N. Medlicott, *The Economic Blockade* (2 vols, HMSO, 1952 and 1959).

426 'strong and sustained': Peace Pledge Union, Executive Committee Minutes, 2 December 1941. PPU archive.

427 'I am not a defeatist': VB, 'Food Relief in Europe'.

427 'harrowing': W.N. Medlicott, *The Economic Blockade*, vol. 2, 278.

427 a mass demonstration in Trafalgar Square: A photograph of VB speaking at this rally is reproduced on the back cover of this book.

427 a forty-eight-hour fast: According to a letter from VB to Roy Walker, 27 September 1943. McM. Seven hundred people took part in the Famine Relief fast which, by January 1944, had raised £100.

427 'to be [an] unwise': *Peace News*, 19 June 1942.

427 'middle-class mentality': 3 October 1943, *WC*, 237.

427 one such altercation: 23 February 1943, *WC*, 216.

428 'bishops, headmasters': *TE*, 299.

428 'friendly touch': George Bell to William Temple, Archbishop of Canterbury, 1 May 1942. Temple Papers, Lambeth Palace Library. Quoted in Bennett, 'A Question of Respectability and Tactics . . .', 8.

428 'necessary or advisable': Peace Pledge Union, Executive Committee Minutes, 14 June 1942. PPU archive.

428 'one of Miss Brittain's': Public Record Office, Kew, FO 837/1224, 13 October 1942. 'Eight of these effusions came by second post today and they are no doubt, only the first taste of the wrath to come . . .'

428 'a kind of spearhead': VB to Emile Cammaerts, 21 May 1943. McM.

428 'a large non-pacifist': 21 January 1943, *WC*, 208.

429 'a little too': Edith Pye to VB, 9 February 1943. McM.

429 'dreadful willingness': 4 February 1943, *WC*, 212.

429 Footnote: *TE*, 303. Bennett, 'A Question of Respectability and Tactics . . .', 24, concludes, however, that 'These concessions were probably not so much the result of organized pressure outside the government – nor of questioning within – so much as the result of the bold intervention of the Prime Minister's friend, the Minister of State in Cairo, Oliver Lyttelton. The grounds on which Lyttelton made his appeal, and the arguments he advanced in a telegram to Churchill in January 1942, however, richly echoed many of the arguments – pragmatic, humanitarian and moral –

made by Vera Brittain throughout the course of the war.'

429 'a signal contribution': Bennett, 'A Question of Respectability and Tactics . . .', 14.

429 arguments . . . continue unabated: And never more heatedly than on the occasion of the unveiling of a statue to Sir Arthur Harris, the former Air Officer Commander-in-Chief, in May 1992. For an account of the controversy, see John Ezard, 'The Firestorm Rages On', *Guardian*, 18 May 1992. Two years later, in the summer of 1994, the controversy was revived again – almost as violently – when *Death by Moonlight*, a Canadian drama-documentary sharply critical of Harris, was shown in Britain.

430 The Bombing Restriction Committee: See Hughes, *Indomitable Friend*, 175–84.

430 'We are bombing': Quoted in Hughes, 179.

430 'more like': Quoted by Max Hastings, *Bomber Command* (Michael Joseph, 1979), 148.

431 'the passionate': VB, 'Approach of old age'. MS note in PBC.

431 'Has any nation': VB, 'Letter to Peace-Lovers', 2 December 1943.

431 Bishop Bell: See Frank Field, 'What of the unsung hero?' *The Independent*, 25 May 1992. This is useful reassessment of Bell which, unfortunately, omits all mention of VB and the other members of the Bombing Restriction Committee, and erroneously states that 'George Bell stood alone against area bombing in the Second World War.'

431 'very fond . . . difficult or worrying': VB to GC, 27 September 1952. McM.

432 'the affair Neave': VB to GC, 18 September 1952. McM.

432 'collective social conscience': VB, 'My Religious Beliefs'. MS note in PBC.

432 'quite the right home': VB to Miss Perry, 11 May 1948. Copy in PBC.

432 'denominational hybrid': VB, 'My Debt to Friends', *Reynard*, March 1956; *TG*, 337.

433 'Believe me': VB, *'One of These Little Ones* . . .', 10.

433 'something is in train': 26 June 1942, *WC*, 157.

433 'inward agitation': *WC*, 203.

433 'Poor John': 15 January 1943, *WC*, 206.

434 'like a Trojan': 30 April 1943, *WC*, 231.

434 'scrummed in': Quoted in Hughes, *op. cit.*, 174.

434 'I first started': Hugh Maw to PB, 31 March 1983. PBC.

434 'You will realise': VB to Madame Lowndes-Marques, 15 June 1943. McM.

435 'feelings of malaise . . . outward signs': JC, *Family Quartet*, 149.

435 'It is a great comfort': VB to Madame Lowndes-Marques, 8 October 1943. McM.

435 'a tiny fair-haired': 17 October 1943, *WC*, 238.

435 'in a surge': *TE*, 322.

436 'final appeal': *TE*, 327.

436 'the City': Max Hastings, op. cit., 145–6.

436 'Our plans': *TE*, 325.

437 '*first*, that there is': VB, *Seed of Chaos*, 8–10.

437 **The section on Arthur Harris**: 2 January 1944, *WC*, 239.

437 Footnote: Corder Catchpool to VB, 26 February 1943. McM.

438 'he not only': Frank Field, op. cit.

438 'a lamentable lapse': Macaulay, *Letters to a Sister*, 128.

438 'article': 10 March 1944, *WC*, 245–6.

439 'Christian people': Preface to VD, *Massacre by Bombing. The Facts Behind the British-American Attack on Germany*, *Fellowship US*, February 1944.

439 'rather as if': VB to George Brett, 1 May 1944. McM.

439 'a more remarkable': *TE*, 332.

439 'Attacks on Miss Brittain': Martin, 'The Bombing and Negotiated Peace Questions – in 1944', 59. Dr Martin's article, which offered a historical perspective on America's bombing of Vietnam in the late Sixties, provides a thorough review of the printed condemnations of *Massacre by Bombing*.

439 'Revolt Against Bombs': *Newsweek*, 20 March 1944. *Newsweek*'s own editorial proclaimed that 'The military necessity of mass bombing must be left to the decision of Allied military leaders.'

439 'There is no other': Reverend Koslowski, letter to *Christian Century*, 22 March 1944. One journalist in San Francisco denied that mass bombing was taking place and implied that VB's pamphlet was a hoax.

439 'The question': 'Obliteration Bombing', *Christian Century*, 22 March 1944.

439 'British Woman Pacifist': Dorothy Thompson, *Sunday Chronicle*, 17 March 1944. See also Thompson's 'The Pacifists', *Montreal Gazette*, 13 March 1944, which argued that 'The pacifist lives, like the rest of us, in this world. But by rejecting equal moral responsibility for its failures, he invests himself with a righteousness he does not deserve.'

440 'It is much what one': VB to GC, 19 April 1944. McM.

440 'a stinging rebuke': 'F.D.R. Defends Mass Raids', *News Chronicle*, 27 April 1944.

440 'disturbed and horrified': 'Mass Bombing Foes Rebuked by Roosevelt', *New York Herald Tribune*, 26 April 1944.

441 'all sentimental nonsense'. *New York Times*, 31 May 1944. For the background to the Roosevelt administration's reaction to *Massacre by Bombing*, see R. Schaffer, *Wings of Judgement: American Bombing in World War II* (Oxford University Press, 1985), 69.

441 'rebellion': *Times Literary Supplement*, 17 June 1944.

441 'limiting': George Orwell, 'As I Please', *The Tribune*, 19 May 1944. Orwell's other *Tribune* piece, in which he stated that he had received a number of letters – 'some of them quite violent ones' – about his attack on *Seed of Chaos*, appeared on 14 July 1944. Both are reprinted in the Penguin edition of Orwell's collected journalism.

441 'seems to assume': VB, 'Humanizing War?', letter to *Tribune*, 23 June 1944; *TG*, 244.

441 'To walk through': *TE*, 384.

441 'Regarding the furore': VB to PB, 14 April 1944. PBC.

441 'And you had': VB to GC, 19 April 1944. McM.

442 'profound respect': Basil Liddell Hart to VB, 25 July 1944, McM.

442 'For better': VB to George Brett, 1 May 1944. McM.

442 Vera's contribution . . . has sometimes been overlooked: One exception is Charles Messenger, *'Bomber' Harris and the Strategic Bombing Offensive, 1939–45* (Arms & Armour Press, 1984), 209–11.

442 **History has tended to vindicate her position**: See, for instance, Sir Charles Webster and Noble Frankland, *History of the Second World War – The Strategic Air Offensive Against Germany 1939–1945. Volume III: Victory* (HMSO, 1961), 228. 'Huge areas in many great towns all over Germany were severely stricken and some were devastated, but the will of the German people was not broken or even significantly impaired and the effect on war production was remarkably small.'

442 'with complete confidence': VB, *Seed of Chaos*, 116.

442 'more & more upset . . . window again': VB to PB, 14 April 1944. PBC.

443 'other warlike noises': *TE*, 337.

443 'I agree with you': VB to Sarah Gertrude Millin, 4 February 1945. McM.

444 'much better . . . V.G.': VB to GC, 11 January 1945. McM.

444 'deeper than this': Victor Gollancz, Foreword to *Abuse All Nations*.

444 'a bravely': John Betjeman, *Daily Herald*, 16 May 1945.

445 'remarkable & timely': 16 May 1945, *WC*, 266.

445 'The conventional': John Middleton Murry, 'Lublin', *Peace News*, 22 September 1944.

445 **often drawn attention**: She had, however, received the first reports of the Nazi death camps with a measure of scepticism. See, for instance, her diary for 20 December 1942, *WC*, 200, in which she comments that the newspaper reports of the Nazi treatment of the Jews '. . . get more & more fantastic.'

445 'neither from deep': *TE*, 363.

445 *Sonderfahndungsliste GB*: On the 'Black Book', see Charman, ' " . . . And, if necessary, to carry it out" '. As Charman notes, 'Misinformation abounds' on the list, and the address given for VB was already two years out of date when the book was compiled. As well as the obvious names of politicians like Churchill, Eden, and Duff Cooper, the list also contains the names of authors like Virginia Woolf, Rebecca West, E.M. Forster, and H.G. Wells. As West commented to another prospective arrestee, Noël Coward, 'My dear, the people we should have been seen dead with!' VB's name received additional publicity because, cross-referenced under Catlin, she appeared on the same page as

Churchill and Chamberlain. A facsimile reprint was published by the Imperial War Museum in 1990.

446 'once & for all': VB, 'Reflections on being a Prominent Name on the Gestapo's List', *WC*, 271.

446 *'Because* God exists': VB, 'One Voice', unpublished foreword to 'Letters to Peace-Lovers'. McM.

CHAPTER 15: 'BUT THE PRESTIGE GOES TO HELL'

447 'adverse criticism ... face ...': VB to GC, 7 January 1945. McM.

447 'the complete unquestioning': *TE*, 367.

447 'No my husband': VB to PB, 23 June 1945. PBC.

448 'You are well out': VB to GC, 3 September 1951. McM.

448 'In Europe': VB, 'After the Cease Fire', *Christian Pacifist*, June 1945; *TG*, 246

448 'to describe': *TE*, 382.

448 'a thin dark woman': *TE*, 408.

449 'bitter ... narky': VB to GC, 7 and 11 January 1945. McM.

449 'American readers': VB to GC, 29 August 1949. McM.

449 'I caught the mood': VB to GC, 21 May 1951. McM.

449 'not wishing': VB, Inaugural Address to the PPU as Chairman, 23 April 1949, *PPU Journal*, June 1949.

449 'left everyone': Morrison, *I Renounce War*, 65.

449 recorded membership: Figures from Ceadel, *Pacifism in Britain*, 312.

450 'As your Chairman': VB, Inaugural Address to the PPU as Chairman, 23 April 1949.

450 'My Seaside Tour': VB to GC, 6 October 1949. McM.

450 'Can't make out': VB to GC, 11 October 1949. McM.

450 'very frank young pacifist': VB to GC, 19 July 1950. McM.

450 'turgid and superficial': VB to GC, 8 October 1949. McM.

450 'Rebecca has involved me': VB to GC, 13 October 1949. McM.

450 'a much respected': VB to GC, 13 October 1949. McM.

451 'After thinking over': VB to GC, 14 October 1949. McM.

451 'moral turpitude ... in such a cause': VB to GC, 15 October 1949. McM.

452 'a trumpeting ass': Quoted in Glendinning, *Rebecca West*, 138.

452 'Rebecca's present values': VB to GC, 8 September 1949. McM.

452 'a figure-head chairman': VB to GC, 2 August 1950. McM.

452 'I do recognise': VB to GC, 16 August 1950. McM.

452 '... I have done my share': VB to GC, 9 August 1950. McM.

453 'I can hardly believe': VB to GC, 19 October 1949. McM.

454 'I think it is more ... inhuman': VB to A.C. Barrington, 24 January 1950. PBC.

454 'devout, sober-minded': A.C. Barrington to VB, 4 September 1950. PBC.

454 'What do you expect': VB, *Search After Sunrise*, 140.

454 'The light of my life': A.C. Barrington to VB, 26 January 1950. PBC.

455 'The chapters I wrote': VB to GC, 28 September 1950. McM.

455 'the first book': VB to GC, 30 August 1950. McM.

455 'Some accidental likeness': VB to GC, 28 and 30 September 1950. McM.

455 'Few people': VB to GC, 19 July 1950. McM.

455 'a blur': Horace G. Alexander, *Peace News*, 30 November 1951.

455 'But I would not be downed': VB to A.C. Barrington, 6 January 1952. PBC.

456 'to save': VB, *On Becoming a Writer*, 10.

456 'his predecessors': VB, *The Story of St Martin's*.

456 'her next long novel': Contracts for *Account Rendered*, Macmillan and Co. London, and The Macmillan Co. of N.Y. PBC.

456 'all bubbling & surging': 15 October 1942, *WC* 184.

457 'the final collapse of the artist': James Gray, *On Second Thought* (University of Minneapolis Press, 1946), 210.

457 'the novel about Dick Sheppard': VB to GC, 20 October 1965. McM.

458 'It is and it isn't': VB to JC, 23 June 1947. McM.

458 'I want to': VB to PB, 23 June 1945. PBC.

458 'More and more': VB to GC, 29 August 1949. McM.

458 'What is one to do': VB to GC, 21 May 1951. McM.

459 'I hope to finish my novel': VB to Elin Wagner, 15 August 1946. McM.

459 'the Independents': VB to Elin Wagner, 31 October 1948. McM.

459 'no sooner do I get down': VB to PB, 21 February 1949. PBC.

459 'absolutely bogged': VB to PB, 13 October 1948. PBC.

459 'plus the price': VB to GC, 19 July 1950. McM.

459 'having written': VB to GC, 16 August 1950. McM.

459 'What a result': VB to GC, 19 July 1950. McM.

459 'new generations': VB to GC, 15 April 1950. McM.

460 'the NEW STATESMAN': VB to GC, 1 September 1949. McM.

460 'violently anti-pacifist': VB to GC, 29 August 1949. McM.

460 'But I can now be': VB to GC, 7 September 1952. McM.

460 'I don't know': Lovat Dickson to VB, 17 November 1960. PBC.

460 'Of course I read': VB to Lovat Dickson, 20 November 1960. PBC.

SOURCE NOTES

460   'How few': VB to SW, 17 February 1952. McM.

CHAPTER 16: FAMILY QUARTET
461   'spiritual not physical': VB to SW, 9 September 1951. McM.
461   'shyly opened': VB, MS note, 22 May 1968. PBC.
461   'an arrangement': VB to GC, 11 January 1945. McM.
462   'To break': VB to PB, 27 June 1948. PBC.
462   'found myself': TE, 446.
462   'I miss my mother': VB to PB, 22 July 1948. PBC.
462   'loathed . . . definitely come': VB to GC, 26 August 1950. McM.
463   'you attribute': VB to GC, 16 August 1952. McM.
463   'never quite': VB to GC, 15 September 1952. McM.
463   'not for anyone': VB to GC, 23 September 1952. McM.
464   'Your remark': VB to GC, 2 August 1950. McM.
464   'cumulative achievements': VB to GC, 16 August 1952. McM.
464   'tolerable only': GC to VB, 25 August 1949. McM.
464   'I adore': VB to GC, 29 August 1949. McM.
464   'yet the fact': GC to VB, 30 August 1949. McM.
464   'I still prefer': VB to GC, 29 August 1949. McM.
464   'in a condition': TE, 475.
465   'that our life': Ibid. 479.
465   'enjoyed many a dinner': Latham, My Life in Publishing, 155.
465   'I definitely . . . a point': VB to GC, 8 September 1949. McM.
466   'Mrs Catlin is a pacifist': The Diary of Hugh Gaitskell 1945–56, ed. Williams, 534.
466   'my world': GC, For God's Sake, Go! 134.
466   'almost always': VB to PB, 13 May 1963. PBC.
466   'which you could not adopt': VB to GC, 8 September 1949. McM.
467   'any protest': VB to Doris Lessing, 19 December 1952. McM.
467   'to our astonishment': VB to PB, 30 June 1950. PBC.
467   'complete religious': VB to JC, 16 February 1948. McM.
467   'now a Protestant': VB to PB, 23 December 1950. PBC.
468   'for I think': VB to SW, 5 September 1966. McM.
468   'that he has neither': VB to GC, 7 January 1945. McM.
468   'as an adventure': JC, Family Quartet, 140.
469   'persistently pin-pricks': VB to GC, 4 August 1950. McM.
469   'The richest . . . deepened': VB to GC, 7 January 1945. McM.
469   'Of course I didn't': VB to GC, 11 January 1945. McM.
470   'excruciating': JC, Family Quartet, 159.

470   'though I know I must': VB to PB, 2 February 1946. PBC.
471   'because after all . . . do our best': VB to JC, 8 October 1946. McM.
471   'this would at least': JC, Family Quartet, 164.
471   'exchanged the golden treasures': TE, 413.
471   'thoughtful': VB to JC, 6 December, 1946. McM.
471   'I think I can honestly': VB to JC, 3 December 1946. McM.
471   'My problem is': VB to GC, 1 September 1949. McM.
472   'We have already': VB to PB, 22 January 1947. PBC.
472   'and will therefore': VB to JC, 2 May 1947. McM.
472   'but she may be wrong': 7 May 1947. McM.
472   'John and Shirley': VB to PB, 13 October 1948. PBC.
473   'His continued adolescent': VB to GC, 2 August 1950. McM.
473   'Perhaps she would': VB to GC, 21 July 1951. McM.
473   'Better a house': VB to JC, 3 December 1946. McM.
474   'on the nail': VB to GC, 2 August 1952. McM.
474   'when I see how': VB to GC, 18 August 1949. McM.
474   'is trying to squeeze': VB to GC, 2 August 1950. McM.
475   'and he sees': VB to GC, 26 August 1951. McM.
475   'and proposing . . . professions': VB to PB, 19 July 1951. PBC.
476   'my feelings': VB to PB, 25 December 1951. PBC.
476   'I want to wrap him': VB to GC, 20 February 1952. McM.
476   'ready to turn': VB to GC, 6 February 1952. McM.
476   'as cheerful': VB to GC, 8 February 1952. McM.
477   'not talking much': VB to GC, 20 February 1952. McM.
477   'This I forbade': VB to GC, 20 February 1952. McM.
477   'You are better': VB to GC, 20 February 1952. McM.
477   'but I wonder': SW to VB, 10 October 1952. McM.
478   'one of the most gifted': VB to Maurice Richardson, 13 February 1958. Copy in PBC.
478   'for her black': VB to GC, 26 August 1949. McM.
478   'an intense private': VB, MS note, 29 November 1966. PBC.
478   'untidiness': VB, MS note. PBC.
478   'Surely this . . . in himself': VB, MS note, 12 June 1968. PBC.
478   'can look . . . three months!': VB to JC, 2 May 1947. McM.

479 'better and better': VB to GC, 12 July
1949. McM.
479 'When he wrote ... deep waters': VB to
GC, 10 August 1949. McM.
480 'the most incredible': SW to VB, 2
August 1950, VB MS note. PBC.
480 'working like crazy ... at all': SW to VB,
3 January 1950, VB, MS note. PBC.
480 'was the rawest ... mention me': SW to
M. Bostridge, 28 June 1989. PBC.
480 'I forgave her': VB, MS note, 31 May
1968. PBC.
480 '... so that particularly': SW to VB,
summer term 1950, VB, MS note, n.d. PBC.
481 'as her period': Somerville Treasurer to
VB, VB, MS note, 12 October 1950. PBC.
481 'she had contributed': Janet Vaughan to
VB, VB, MS note, n.d. PBC.
481 'at having to face': VB to SW, 23 January
1952. McM.
481 'but was now regarded ...': VB to GC, 5
October 1952. TS PBC.
481 'I am amused ... little money': VB to
GC, 2 September 1952. McM.
482 'I am afraid': VB to GC, 17 July 1952. McM.
482 'but how one could': VB to GC, 4
September 1952. McM.
482 'the solitary sojourn':VB to GC, 29
January 1952. McM.
482 'the dark empty house': VB to GC, 10
February 1952. McM.
482 'up clearing ... many stairs': VB to GC,
2 May 1952. McM.
482 'They will all expect me': VB to GC, 26
February 1952. McM.
482 'quite worn out ... you are in America':
VB to GC, 29 March 1952. McM.
483 'the horrible solitary nights': VB to GC,
29 June 1952. McM.
483 'daring to go off ... an hour later': VB to
GC, 6 August 1952. McM.
483 'One fights and fights': GC to VB, 7 July
1952. TS PBC.
483 'What I have': GC to VB, 9 October 1952,
VB, note. PBC.
484 'absolutely normal again': VB to GC, 16
August 1952. McM.
484 'which makes me': VB to GC, 15
September 1952. McM.
484 'Your suggestion ... tea shops ...': VB
to GC, 4 September 1952. McM.
484 'relived your desolation ... never
again': VB to GC, 23 September 1952. McM.
484 'I could weep': VB to GC, 14 August 52.
McM.
484 'pushed me down ... system': VB to
GC, 15 September 1952. McM.
485 'that from the standpoint': VB to GC, 16
August 1952. McM.
485 'Although I am not': VB to GC, 15
September 1952. McM.
485 'What I hate': VB to GC, 9 September
1952. McM.
485 'The woman question': VB to GC, 4
September 1952. McM.
485 'I believed': VB, MS note, n.d. PBC.

485 'I believe it to be ... equality': VB, Lady
into Woman', xiii, xiv, 'Dedication to my Daughter'.
486 'I would like to feel': VB to GC, 15
March 1953. McM.
486 'You are everything': VB to SW, 25
August 1952. McM.
486 'by charm, vitality':VB to PB, 12 July
1952. PBC.
486 'Emotionally': VB to SW, 25 August 1952.
McM.
486 'So far as love goes' ... wholly without
affection': VB to GC, 2 August 1950. McM.
486 'I am very scared ... to one of the arts':
SW to VB, 24 September 1952. McM.
487 'I suffered poignantly ... short socks':
VB, MS note, n.d. PBC.
487 'made an enchanting bride': VB to PB, 4
July 1955. PBC.
487 'clear, full-toned voice': VB to Bernard
Williams, 6 July 1955. McM.
487 'is quite an Adonis': VB to PB, 4 July
1955. PBC.
487 'For if this is the truth ... achievement
justice': VB to GC, 26 September 1952. McM.

CHAPTER 17: THE WORLD WIDENS
489 'the pre-war period ... of the First ...':
VB to Sybil Morrison, 15 April 1951. PBC.
489 'a little sententious ... enduring love
...': VB to GC, 15 September 1952. McM.
490 'put her literary standing': GC, For God's
Sake, Go!, 291.
490 'Victor ... recently announced': VB to
SW, 9 August 1952. McM.
491 'my imagination ... "achievement" ':
VB to PB, 7 June 1957. PBC.
491 'very good but I thought': VB to A.C.
Barrington, 10 September 1957. PBC.
491 'But because of that': Dennis Gray Stoll,
Aryan Path, January 1958.
491 'are all my friends': VB to PB, 7 June
1957. PBC.
491 'suggesting at its worst': Unidentified
review in VB's papers, signed N.M.R, dated August
1957. PBC.
491 'Funnily enough': Nancy Spain, Daily
Express, 15 June 1957.
492 'went all out': VB to A.C. Barrington, 10
September 1957.
492 'Miss Brittain has assumed': N.R.
Longmate, Books and Bookmen, August 1957.
492 'I have been prevailed on': VB to A.C.
Barrington, 10 September 1957. PBC.
492 'Partly to vindicate': VB to PB, 17 January
1958. PBC.
492 'I sometimes wonder': VB to PB, 7 July
1957. PBC.
492 'would distribute': The Times, 24 January
1958.
492 'to go apart from them': Clare Leighton
to PB, 7 October 1976. PBC.
493 'an elderly chorus girl': TE 106.
493 'It represented': VB, The Women at Oxford,
16.

493 '. . . The most sensible': Marghanita Laski, *Observer*, 17 May 1960.

494 'As we have no children': F. Pethick-Lawrence to VB, 28 September 1935. McM.

494 'while I was waiting': VB to GC, 20 October 1965. McM.

494 'vague and inaccessible': VB to Ruth Colby, 15 October 1963. Copy in PBC.

494 'not one review . . . goes to war': VB to GC, 9 September 1965. McM.

494 'I finally gave way': VB to Ruth Colby, 22 December 1964. Copy in PBC.

495 'a kind of crazy': VB to Ruth Colby, 7 November 1963. Copy in PBC.

495 '. . . At one period': VB to A.J. Muste, 17 November 1964. PBC.

495 'appears to conduct': Mrs E.M. Sidebottom to Fellowship of Reconciliation, 14 December 1964. Copy in PBC.

495 'Favour McGill': VB, 'The Canadian Years – 1956–59'. PBC.

495 'the roughest': VB to PB, 24 November 1956. PBC.

496 'he added . . . she didn't know': Professor James Mallory to PB, 28 October 1982. PBC.

497 'the main purpose': Dr E.G. Malherbe to VB, 18 February 1960. PBC.

498 'just making a few odd': VB to SW, 8 August 1960. McM.

498 'a conscious effort': VB, 'The Expanding Horizons of Twentieth Century Women'. TS McM.

498 'Those were our cups': VB Diary, 3 July 1960. McM.

499 'Presumably': Ibid.

499 'When I speak . . . was herself': Sarah Gertrude Millin to VB, 15 January 1940. McM.

499 '. . . I have pain': Rubin, *Sarah Gertrude Millin*, 266.

499 'began to scold me': VB Diary, 3 July 1960. McM.

500 'more like': VB Diary, 4 July 1960. McM.

500 'exactly like St Anne's': VB Diary, 5 July 1960. McM.

500 'are names like Brighton': VB Diary, 6 July 1960. McM.

500 'These hills are': Paton, *Cry, The Beloved Country*, 62.

500 'the contrast': VB Diary, 4 July 1960. McM.

500 '. . . By making a': VB Diary, 12 July 1960. McM.

501 'the racially bigoted': Huxley, *Memories II*, 73.

501 'In the first place': Sir Julian Huxley, *The Natal Mercury*, 13 July 1960.

501 'We (the overseas speakers)': VB Diary, 12 July 1960. McM.

501 'One would not dare': Dennis Henshaw to PB, 14 October 1983. PBC.

501 'this "wind of change"': *Education and our Expanding Horizons*, ed. R.G. Macmillan, 33.

502 'I had a splendid . . . crowd': VB Diary, 13 July 1960. McM.

502 'She is quite clearly': VB Diary, 21 July 1960. McM.

503 'I was now too tired': VB Diary, 28 July 1960. McM.

503 'I was more interested': VB Diary, 29 July 1960. McM.

503 'we decided to tackle': VB Diary, 1 August 1960. McM.

503 'extensively catechized . . . opposition collapsed': VB, 1 August 1960, private notebook. PBC.

503 'a mild-looking': VB Diary, 2 August 1960. McM.

503 'Luthuli was very . . . "that can't be helped"': VB to SW, 8 August 1960. McM.

504 'he thought him': VB Diary, 1 August 1960. McM.

504 'Don't go to Bloemfontein': VB, 'Hier Rus . . .' *The Friend*, 25 November 1960.

505 'a shortish, very lined': VB Diary, 9 August 1960. McM.

505 'and at the end of the evening': VB, Hull Guildhall, 28 September 1960.

505 'put too much emphasis': Morrison, *I Renounce War*, 91.

506 'while leaving warfare': Ibid., 90.

506 'Nuclear disarmament': *The Christian Century*, 19 November 1958, 1355.

506 'as this would': VB to Bertrand Russell, 9 October 1960. McM.

506 'I want to see you': VB to SW, 13 September 1961. Original in the possession of SW.

507 'indignantly and a little': Mister, 'Vera Brittain', 154.

507 'I enclose a donation': VB to Bertrand Russell, 4 August 1962. McM.

507 'The meaning of Aldermaston': VB, *The Meaning of Aldermaston*, 7.

507 'If you don't succeed': VB to PB, 6 April 1962. PBC.

508 'amazed . . . recent years': VD to PB, 20 July 1962. PBC.

508 'Don't be worried . . . not to make her nervous': Eileen Brock to PB, 8 March 1986. PBC.

508 'a charming, unspoilt girl': VB Diary, 12 March 1965. McM.

509 'She was too much': VB, MS note, 1959. PBC.

509 'But small and': *Guardian*, 18 April 1960.

509 'in some difficult . . . not support him': VB, MS note, 1966. PBC.

509 'Here's a Labour gain . . . attractive': VB, MS n.d. PBC.

510 'Could she be . . . Prime Minister': *Daily Mail*, 4 November 1964.

510 'the apotheosis': VB Diary, 6 October 1966. McM.

510 'We will achieve this . . . speak': VB, MS note. PBG.

510 'my brilliant and beloved': VB to SW, date indecipherable [late December 1967]. McM.

510 'I wish that Shirley': VB to Ruth Colby, 26 September 1967. PBC.

511 'After all . . . and never could': VB to SW, 2 July 1967. McM.

511 'She will go': VB, MS note, 1965. PBC.

511 'I couldn't write': VB to GC, 11 October 1965. McM.

512 'only fair that money': VB to JC, 13 March 1965. McM.

512 'he has been': VB to SW, 5 February 1965. McM.

512 'a house which': VB to JC, 13 March 1965. McM.

512 'I hope this is true': VB to SW, date indecipherable [late December 1967]. McM.

512 'it was not only useless': VB to SW, 5 September 1966. McM.

512 'quite heartbreaking': Ibid.

512 'was sitting in her own room': From *The Pink Fairy Book*, ed. Andrew Lang. Quoted in Preface to *TY* Part I.

513 'they only want you': VB to PB, 4 June 1963. PBC.

513 'I write as always': VB to GC, 1 October 1965. McM.

513 'How I miss you!': VB to GC, 15 October 1965. McM.

513 'It was sad': VB to PB, 6 October 1965. PBC.

513 'three weeks on and off': VB to PB, 8 October 1965. PBC.

513 'I still think . . . and Heaven knows who else': VB to GC, 15 October 1965. McM.

514 'endeavouring to begin': VB to Dr Fassbinder, 22 August 1966. PBC.

CHAPTER 18: 'A PRAYER FOR THE CLOSE OF LIFE'

515 'a kind young man': VB Diary, 2 November 1966. McM.

515 'the strange experience': VB, memorandum on 'Loss of a Mind', 23 April 1968. PBC.

516 ' "Goodbye Vera" ': VB Diary, 17 December 1966. McM.

516 'I felt as though': VB Diary, 10 February 1967. McM.

516 'Darling Shirley': VB to SW, 21 March 1967. McM.

516 'my leaden legs': VB to PB, 23 April 1968. PBC.

516 'longing to get back to writing': VB to PB, 29 December 1966. PBC.

516 'boring in the extreme': VB Diary, 26 February 1967. McM.

516 'first incarnation': VB Diary, 11 April 1967. McM.

516 'relatively famous': VB Diary, 2 April 1967. McM.

516 'Lovely St George's': VB Diary, 7 April 1967. McM.

517 '. . . Rely on your daughter': Patrick Monkhouse to VB, 24 July 1967. PBC.

517 'endless boring research': VB to PB, 20 July 1967. PBC.

517 'the Pecksniffian': C.H. Rolph, Introduction, VB, *Radclyffe Hall*, 25.

517 'I really didn't': VB to PB, 10 July 1968. PBC.

517 'suddenly decided': VB Diary, 20 September 1967. McM.

518 'my mind seems': VB Diary, 2 November 1967. McM.

518 'but I have to': VB Diary, 10 November 1967. McM.

518 'a rather special request': VB to SW, 9 December 1967. McM.

518 'I am just longing': VB to Amy Burnett, 11 January 1968. PBC.

518 'I shan't swim': VB to SW, date indecipherable [late December 1967]. McM.

519 'My mind varies': VB to PB, 14–15 March 1968. PBC.

519 'exactly nothing': GC to Anne Hewitt, 30 July 1970. PBC.

519 'if ever the time': Winifred de Colleville to SW, 2 April 1970. PBC.

519 'I am unlikely': VB to Sybil Morrison, 24 April 1968. PBC.

520 'I certainly do not': VB to Sybil Morrison, 30 April 1968. PBC.

520 'According to those': VB, 'Loss of a Mind', 23 April 1968. PBC.

520 'Please . . .': VB to JC, 22 March 1967. McM.

521 'The fact': VB to GC, 26 April 1968. PBC.

521 'had always represented': VB, 'Italian Notes – Fiesole', July 1968. MS note. PBC.

522 '. . . I am just too tired': GC to Anne Hewitt, 1 February 1970. PBC.

522 'Indeed': SW, 'Remembering My Mother'.

523 'controversial causes': *The Times*, 30 March 1970.

523 'a much better book': *Daily Telegraph*, 30 March 1970.

523 'I want someone': VB to SW, 21 March 1967. McM. GC asked that the urn and a token residue of VB's ashes be brought back to England. On 4 December 1970, after a short committal service, the urn was interred in the Holy Trinity churchyard, Old Milverton, Warwickshire. In 1979 GC was buried there beside his father.

Select Bibliography

1 MAJOR PUBLISHED WORKS BY VERA BRITTAIN

Verses of a VAD (Erskine MacDonald, 1918) Facsimile edition with an introduction by Paul Berry and Mark Bostridge (Arts and Literature Series, General Editor Martin Taylor, Imperial War Museum, 1995)
The Dark Tide (Grant Richards, 1923, Cheap Edition, 1935)
Not Without Honour (Grant Richards, 1924)
Women's Work in Modern England (Noel Douglas, 1928)
Halcyon, or the Future of Monogamy (Kegan Paul, Trench, Trübner and Co., 1929.
Testament of Youth. An Autobiographical Study of the Years 1900–1925 (Gollancz, 1933, Virago, 1978, Fontana, 1979)
Poems of the War and After (Gollancz, 1934)
Honourable Estate. A Novel of Transition (Gollancz, 1936)
Thrice a Stranger. New Chapters of Autobiography (Gollancz, 1938)
Testament of Friendship. The Story of Winifred Holtby (Macmillan, 1940, Virago, 1980, Fontana, 1981)
War-Time Letters to Peace Lovers (Peace Book Company, 1940)
England's Hour. An Autobiography 1939–1941 (Macmillan, 1941, Futura, 1981)
Humiliation with Honour (Andrew Dakers, 1942)
'One of These Little Ones . . .' A Plea to Parents and Others for Europe's Children (Andrew Dakers, 1943)
Seed of Chaos. What Mass Bombing Really Means (The Bombing Restriction Committee, 1944)
Account Rendered (Macmillan, 1945, Virago, 1982)
Above All Nations. An Anthology, compiled by George Catlin, Vera Brittain and Sheila Hodges (Gollancz, 1945)
On Becoming a Writer (Hutchinson, 1947)
Born 1925. A Novel of Youth (Macmillan, 1948, Virago, 1982)
In the Steps of John Bunyan. An Excursion into Puritan England (Rich and Cowan, 1950)
Search After Sunrise (Macmillan, 1951)
The Story of St Martin's. An Epic of London (Pitkin Pictorials, 1951)
Lady into Woman. A History of Women from Victoria to Elizabeth II (Andrew Dakers, 1953)
Testament of Experience. An Autobiographical Story of the Years 1925–1950 (Gollancz, 1957, Virago, 1979, Fontana, 1980)
The Women at Oxford. A Fragment of History (Harrap, 1960)
Selected Letters of Winifred Holtby and Vera Brittain 1920–1935, edited by Vera Brittain and Geoffrey Handley-Taylor (A. Brown & Sons Ltd, 1960)
Pethick-Lawrence. A Portrait (George Allen & Unwin, 1963)
The Rebel Passion. A Short History of Some Pioneer Peacemakers (George Allen & Unwin, 1964)
Envoy Extraordinary. A Study of Vijaya Lakshmi Pandit and her Contribution to Modern India (George Allen & Unwin, 1965)
Radclyffe Hall. A Case of Obscenity? (Femina Books, 1968)
Chronicle of Youth. Vera Brittain's War Diary 1913–1917, edited by Alan Bishop with Terry Smart (Gollancz, 1981, Fontana, 1982)
Chronicle of Friendship. Vera Brittain's Diary of the Thirties 1932–1939, edited by Alan Bishop (Gollancz, 1986)
Wartime Chronicle. Vera Brittain's Diary 1939–1945, edited by Alan Bishop and Y. Aleksandra Bennett (Gollancz 1989)
Testament of a Generation. The Journalism of Vera Brittain and Winifred Holtby, edited and introduced by Paul Berry and Alan Bishop (Virago, 1985)
Testament of a Peace Lover. Letters from Vera Brittain, edited by Winifred and Alan Eden-Green (Virago, 1988)

2 BOOKS AND ARTICLES

The place of publication is London unless otherwise stated.

'Authors Take Sides on the Spanish Civil War', *Left Review*, December 1937
Gillian Avery, *The Best Kind of Girl. A History of Girls' Independent Schools*, André Deutsch, 1991
Hilary Bailey, *Vera Brittain*, Penguin, 1987
Margaret Ballinger, *From Union to Apartheid: A Trek to Isolation*, Bailey Bros & Swiffen, 1969
Albert Beale, *Against all War: Fifty Years of Peace News 1936–1986*, Peace News, 1986
Nicola Beauman, *A Very Great Profession: The Woman's Novel 1914–1939*, Virago, 1983
Deirdre Beddoe, *Back to Duty: Women Between the Wars, 1918–1939*, Pandora, 1989
Y.A. Bennett, 'Vera Brittain: Feminism, Pacifism and Problem of Class, 1900–1953', *Atlantis*, Vol. 12, No. 2, Spring 1987
Y.A. Bennett, *Vera Brittain: Women and Peace*, Peace Pledge Union, 1987
Phyllis Bentley, *Inheritance*, Gollancz, 1932
Phyllis Bentley, *O Dreams, O Destinations*, Gollancz, 1962
Donald Birn, *The League of Nations Union 1918–1945*, Oxford, Clarendon Press, 1981
Alan Bishop, 'With Suffering and Through Time: Olive Schreiner, Vera Brittain and the Great War' in *Olive Schreiner and After*, edited by M. Van Wyle and David Macleiman, Cape Town, David Phillip, 1983
Alan Bishop, 'The Battle of the Somme and Vera Brittain' in *English Literature of the Great War Revisited*, edited by Michel Roucoux, University of Picardy, 1986
Gail Braybon, *Women Workers in the First World War: The British Experience*, Croom Helm, 1981
Timothy Brittain-Catlin, 'Aspects of the Novelist', *The Spectator*, 29 August 1987
Gertrude Bussey and Margaret Tims, *Women's International League for Peace and Freedom 1915–1965*, George Allen & Unwin, 1965

Muriel St Clare Byrne and Catherine Hope Mansfield, *Somerville College, 1879–1921*, Oxford, Oxford University Press, 1922

Mary Cadogan and Patricia Craig, *Women and Children First: The Fiction of the Two World Wars*, Gollancz, 1978

Angus Calder, *The Myth of the Blitz*, Jonathan Cape, 1991

Harry Carter, *Wolvercote Mill: A Study of Papermaking at Oxford*, Oxford Bibliographical Society, 1957

George Catlin, *For God's Sake Go!*, Gerrards Cross, Colin Smythe, 1972

John Catlin, *Family Quartet*, Hamish Hamilton, 1987

Martin Ceadel, *Pacifism in Britain 1914–1945: The Defining of a Faith*, Oxford, Clarendon Press, 1980

Allan Chappelow, *Shaw – The Chucker-Out*, George Allen & Unwin, 1969

Terry Charman, ' "... And, if necessary, to carry it out": Operation Sealion and the Black Book, fact and fiction', *Imperial War Museum Review*, 5, 1990

Sally Craddock, *Retired Except on Demand: The Life of Dr Cicely Williams*, Green College, Oxford, 1983

Valentine Cunningham, *British Writers of the Thirties*, Oxford, Oxford University Press, 1988

Lovat Dickson, *The Ante-Room*, Macmillan, 1959

Lovat Dickson, *The House of Words. Reminiscences with a Portrait*, Macmillan, 1963

F.W. Dillistone, *Charles Raven: Naturalist, Historian, Theologian*, Hodder & Stoughton, 1975

Carol Dyhouse, *Girls Growing Up in Late Victorian and Edwardian England*, Routledge and Kegan Paul, 1981

Carol Dyhouse, 'Mothers and Daughters in the Middle-Class Home, c.1870–1914' in *Labour and Love. Women's Experience of Home and Family*, edited by Jane Lewis, Oxford, Basil Blackwell, 1986

Carol Dyhouse, *Feminism and the Family in England, 1880–1939*, Oxford, Basil Blackwell, 1989

Ruth Dudley Edwards, *Victor Gollancz. A Biography*, Gollancz 1987

Modris Eksteins, *Rites of Spring. The Great War and the Birth of the Modern Age*, Bantam Press, 1989

Lillian Faderman, *Surpassing the Love of Men: Romantic Friendship and Love Between Women from the Renaissance to the Present*, New York, William Morrow, 1981

Vera Farnell, *A Somervillian Looks Back*, privately printed at Oxford University Press, 1948

Fascists at Olympia, Statements from the Injured, Doctors who attended the Injured, and from eyewitnesses including Mr Geoffrey Lloyd MP, Mr Gerald Barry, Mr A.E. Coppard, Mr A.J. Cummings, the Very Rev. H.R.L. Sheppard, Miss Vera Brittain, Gollancz, 1934

Michael Fethney, *The Absurd and the Brave. CORB – The True Account of the British Government's World War II Evacuation of Children Overseas*, Lewes, The Book Guild Ltd, 1990

Ruth First and Ann Scott, *Olive Schreiner*, André Deutsch, 1980

Sheila Fletcher, *Maude Royden: A Life*, Oxford, Basil Blackwell, 1989

Percy Fryer, *The Men from the Greenwood: Being the War History of the 11th (Service) Battalion Sherwood Foresters*, Nottingham, Cresswell & Oaksford, 1921

Paul Fussell, *The Great War and Modern Memory*, Oxford, Oxford University Press, 1975

Stephen A. Garrett, *Ethics and Airpower in World War II*, New York, St Martin's, 1993

Douglas Gill and Gloden Dallas, 'Mutiny at Étaples Base in 1917', *Past and Present*, 69, 1975

Victoria Glendinning, *Rebecca West: A Life*, Weidenfeld and Nicolson, 1987

Dorothy Goldman (editor), *Women and World War 1. The Written Response*, Macmillan Press, 1993

Deborah Gorham, ' "Have We Really Rounded Seraglio Point?": Vera Brittain and Inter-War Feminism' in *British Feminism in the Twentieth Century*, edited by Harold L. Smith, Edward Elgar, 1990

Deborah Gorham, 'The Education of Vera and Edward Brittain: Class and Gender in an upper-middle-class family in late Victorian and Edwardian England', *History of Education Review*, Spring 1990

Deborah Gorham, 'A Woman at Oxford: Vera Brittain's Somerville Experience', *Historical Studies in Education*, vol. 3, no. 1, Spring 1991

Deborah Gorham, 'The Friendships of Women: Friendship, Feminism and Achievement in Vera Brittain's life and work in the interwar decades', *Journal of Women's History*, vol. 3, Winter 1992

Joy Grant, *Stella Benson. A Biography*, Macmillan, 1987

Robert Graves and Alan Hodge, *The Long Week-end: A Social History of Great Britain, 1918–1939*, Faber & Faber, 1940

Brian Harrison, *Prudent Revolutionaries: Portraits of British Feminists Between the Wars*, Oxford, Oxford University Press, 1987

Christopher Harvie, *The Centre of Things: Political Fiction in Britain From Disraeli to the Present*, Unwin Hyman, 1991

Denis Hayes, *Challenge of Conscience. The Story of the Conscientious Objectors of 1939–1949*. George Allen & Unwin, 1949

David Higham, *A Literary Gent*, Jonathan Cape, 1978

Margaret Randolph Higonnet et al (editors), *Behind the Lines. Gender and the Two World Wars*, Yale University Press, 1987

The History of the University of Oxford, Volume VIII, The Twentieth Century, edited by Brian Harrison, Oxford, Clarendon Press, 1994

Sheila Hodges, *Gollancz: The Story of a Publishing House 1928–1978*, Gollancz, 1978

Winifred Holtby, *Anderby Wold*, John Lane, 1923, Virago, 1981

Winifred Holtby, *The Crowded Street*, John Lane, 1924, Virago, 1983

Winifred Holtby, *The Land of Green Ginger*, Jonathan Cape, 1927, Virago, 1983

Winifred Holtby, *A New Voter's Guide to Party Programmes: Political Dialogues*, Kegan Paul, Trench, Trubner & Co., 1929

Winifred Holtby, *Poor Caroline*, Jonathan Cape, 1931, Virago, 1983

Winifred Holtby, *Mandoa, Mandoa!*, Collins, 1933, Virago, 1982

Winifred Holtby, *Women and a Changing Civilisation*, John Lane, 1934

Winifred Holtby, *The Frozen Earth and Other Poems*, Collins, 1935

Winifred Holtby, *South Riding*, Collins, 1936, Virago, 1988

Winifred Holtby, *Pavements at Anderby*, edited by H.S. Reid and Vera Brittain, Collins, 1937

Winifred Holtby, *Take Back Your Freedom*, revised by Norman Ginsbury, Jonathan Cape, 1939

William R. Hughes, *Indomitable Friend. The Life of Corder Catchpool 1883–1952*, George Allen & Unwin, 1956

Julian Huxley, *Memories II*, George Allen & Unwin, 1973

Samuel Hynes, *A War Imagined. The First World War and English Culture*. Bodley Head, 1990

Storm Jameson, *No Time Like the Present*, Cassell, 1932

Storm Jameson (editor), *Challenge to Death*. Foreword to the American edition by Vera Brittain, New York, E.P. Dutton, 1935

Storm Jameson, *Europe to Let*, Macmillan, 1940

Storm Jameson, *The End of This War*, PEN Books, George Allen & Unwin, 1941

Storm Jameson, *Journey from the North*, 2 volumes, Collins, 1969, 1970, Virago, 1984

Storm Jameson, *A Kind of Survivor. The Autobiography of Guy Chapman*, Gollancz, 1975

Sheila Jeffreys, *The Spinster and Her Enemies: Feminism and Sexuality, 1880–1930*, Pandora, 1985

Maroula Joannou, 'Vera Brittain's *Testament of Youth* revisited', *Literature and History*, 2, 1993

John Jolliffe (editor), *Raymond Asquith: Life and Letters*, Collins, 1980

Helen Joseph, *If This be Treason*, André Deutsch, 1963

Jean E. Kennard, *Vera Brittain and Winifred Holtby: A Working Partnership*, New Hampshire, University Press of New England, 1989

R.E. Kennedy, *The Heart of a City: A History of the Johannesburg Public Library*, Juuard Company, 1970

Issac Kramnick and Barry Sheerman, *Harold Laski: A Life on the Left*, Hamish Hamilton, 1993

Harold S. Latham, *My Life in Publishing*, New York, E.P. Dutton, 1965

F.A. Lea, *The Life of John Middleton Murry*, Methuen, 1959

Clare Leighton, *Tempestuous Petticoat. The Story of an Invincible Edwardian*, Gollancz, 1947

Marie Leighton, *Convict 99. A True Story of Penal Servitude*, Grant Richards, 1898

Marie Leighton, *Boy of My Heart*, published anonymously, Hodder and Stoughton, 1916

Roland Leighton, *Poems*, privately printed by David Leighton (n.d.)

Susan J. Leonardi, *Dangerous by Degrees. Women at Oxford and the Somerville College Novelists*, Rutgers University Press, 1989

F.M. Leventhal, *H.N. Brailsford and His World*, Oxford, Clarendon Press, 1985

Jane Lewis, *Women in England, 1870–1950*, Brighton, Wheatsheaf, 1984

Jill Liddington, *The Long Road to Greenham. Feminism and Anti-militarism in Britain since 1820*, Virago, 1989

Albert Luthuli, *Let My People Go: An Autobiography*, Collins, 1962.

Rose Macaulay, *Letters to a Sister*, edited by Constance Babington Smith, Collins, 1964.

Lyn Macdonald, *The Roses of No Man's Land*, Michael Joseph, 1980

John Marriott, *Memories of Four Score Years. The Autobiography of the late Sir John Marriott*, Blackie & Son. 1946

James J. Martin, 'The Bombing and Negotiated Peace Questions – in 1944', *Rampart Journal*, vol. IV, no. 1, Spring 1968, Colorado

Kingsley Martin, *Editor: 'New Statesman' Years, 1931–1945*, Hutchinson, 1968

F.S. Marvin, *The Evolution of World Peace*, Oxford, Oxford University Press, 1921

Arthur Marwick, *The Deluge. British Society and the First World War*, Macmillan, 1965

Arthur Marwick, *Women and War, 1914–1918*, Croom Helm, 1977

Charles H.S. Matthews, *Dick Sheppard: Man of Peace*, James Clarke & Co., 1948

Muriel Mellown, 'Reflections on Feminism and Pacifism in the Novels of Vera Brittain', *Tulsa Studies in Women's Literature*, 2, 1983

Muriel Mellown, 'Vera Brittain: Feminist in a New Age (1893–1970)', *Feminist Theorists: Three Centuries of Key Women Thinkers*, edited by Dale Spender, The Women's Press, 1983

Muriel Mellown, 'The Development of Vera Brittain's Pacifism', *Frontiers*, 8, 1985

Martin Middlebrook, *The First Day on the Somme*, Allen Lane, 1971

Harry Mister, 'Vera Brittain' in *Peace is the Way. A Guide to Pacifist Views and Actions*, edited by Cyril Wright and Tony Augarde, The Lutterworth Press, 1990

Caroline Moorehead, *Troublesome People. Enemies of War 1916–1986*. Hamish Hamilton, 1987

Charles Morgan, *The House of Macmillan*, Macmillan, 1943

Sybil Morrison, *I Renounce War: The Story of the Peace Pledge Union*, Sheppard Press, 1962

George L. Mosse, *Fallen Soldiers: Reshaping the Memory of the World Wars*, Oxford, Oxford University Press, 1990

C.R.W. Nevinson, *Paint and Prejudice*, Methuen, 1937

Robert Nichols, *Ardours and Endurances*, Chatto & Windus, 1917

George A. Panichas (editor), *Promise of Greatness: The War of 1914–1918*, Cassell, 1968

Peter Parker, *The Old Lie: The Great War and the Public School Ethos*, Constable, 1987

Alan Paton, *Cry, The Beloved Country*, Jonathan Cape, 1948

Ruth Roach Pierson (editor), *Women and Peace: Theoretical, Historical and Practical Perspectives*, Croom Helm, 1987

Max Plowman, *Bridge into the Future: Letters of Max Plowman*, Andrew Dakers, 1944

Violet Powell, *The Life of a Provincial Lady: A Study of E.M. Delafield and her Works*, Heinemann, 1988

Martin Pugh, *Women and the Women's Movement in Britain 1914–1959*, Macmillan, 1952

William Purcell, *Odd Man Out. A Biography of Lord Soper of Kingsway*, Mowbray, 1983

Julian Putkowski, 'Toplis, Étaples & "The Monocled Mutineer" ', *Stand To!: The Journal of the Western Front Association*, 18, 1986

Irene Rathbone, *We That Were Young*, Chatto & Windus, 1932, Virago, 1988.

Vanessa Redgrave, *Vanessa Redgrave: An Autobiography*, Hutchinson, 1991

Catherine Reilly (editor), *Scars upon my Heart. Women's Poetry and Verse of the First World War*, Virago, 1981

Margaret, Viscountess Rhondda, *This Was My World*, Macmillan 1933

Grant Richards, *Author Hunting, By an Old Literary Sportsman, Memories of Years Spent Mainly in Publishing, 1897–1925*, Hamish Hamilton, 1934

Joanna Richardson, *Enid Starkie*, John Murray, 1973

Martin Rintala, 'Chronicler of a Generation: Vera Brittain's Testament', *Journal of Political and Military Sociology*, vol. 12, Spring 1984

R. Ellis Roberts, *H.R.L Sheppard: Life and Letters*, John Murray, 1942

Martin Rubin, *Sarah Gertrude Millin: A South African Life*, Johannesburg and London, A.D. Donker, 1977

Bertrand Russell, *Which Way to Peace?*, Michael Joseph, 1936

Alan Ryan, *Bertrand Russell: A Political Life*, Penguin, 1988

Sylvia Scaffardi, *Fire Under the Carpet: Working for Civil Liberties in the Thirties*, Lawrence and Wishart, 1986

Sylvia Scaffardi, *Finding My Way*, Quartet Books, 1988

Olive Schreiner, *The Story of an African Farm*, Chapman and Hall, 1883, Penguin 1982

Olive Schreiner, *Woman and Labour*, Unwin, 1911, Virago, 1978

Carolyn Scott, *Dick Sheppard: A Biography*, Hodder and Stoughton, 1977

Geoffrey Shakespeare, *Let Candles Be Brought In*, Macdonald, 1949

Marion Shaw, ' "A Noble Relationship": Friendship, Biography and Autobiography in the Writings of Vera Brittain and Winifred Holtby' in *The Representation of the Self in Women's Autobiography*, edited by Vita Fortunati and Gabriella Morisco, University of Bologna, 1993

H.R.L. Sheppard, *The Impatience of a Parson. A plea for the recovery of vital Christianity*, Hodder & Stoughton, 1927

R.C. Sherriff and Vernon Bartlett, *Journey's End*, Gollancz, 1930

A.H. Shorter, *Paper Making in the British Isles. An Historical and Geographical Survey*, Newton Abbot, David & Charles, 1971

Elaine Showalter, *A Literature of their Own. British Women Novelists from Brontë to Lessing*, revised edition, Virago, 1984

Helen Zenna Smith, *'Not so Quiet . . .' Stepdaughters of War*, Albert E. Marriott, 1930, Virago, 1988

Edith Summerskill, *A Woman's World*, Heinemann, 1967

Peter Sutcliffe, *The Oxford University Press: An Informal History*, Oxford, Oxford University Press, 1978

The Letters of Annie S. Swan, edited by Mildred Robertson Nicoll, Hodder & Stoughton, 1945

H.M. Swanwick, *I Have Been Young*, Gollancz, 1935

Martin Taylor, *Lads. Love Poetry of the Trenches*, Constable, 1989

John Tebbel, *A History of Book Publishing in the United States*, 4 volumes, New York, R.R. Bowker, 1972–81

Malcolm Tozer, *Physical Education at Thring's Uppingham*, Uppingham School, 1976

Claire M. Tylee, *The Great War and Women's Consciousness. Images of Militarism and Womanhood in Women's Writings, 1914–1964*, Macmillan, 1990

Martha Vicinus, *Independent Women. Work and Community for Single Women, 1850–1920*, Virago, 1985

Martha Vicinus, 'Distance and Desire: English Boarding School Friendships, 1870–1920', in *Hidden from History: Reclaiming the Gay and Lesbian Past*, edited by Martin Bauml Duberman, Martha Vicinus and George Chauncey Jr, Penguin, 1991

Beatrice Webb, *Diary*, vol. 4, 1924–43, edited by W. and J. Mackenzie, Virago, 1985

Evelyne White, *Winifred Holtby As I Knew Her: A Study of the Author and her works*, Collins, 1938

Katharine Whitehorn, 'Life with the Minister's Mother', *The Observer*, 13 April 1978.

Lis Whitelaw, *The Life and Rebellious Times of Cicely Hamilton*, The Women's Press, 1990

P.L. Wickins, *The Industrial and Commercial Workers' Union of Africa*, Cape Town, Oxford University Press, 1978

Philip M. Williams (editor), *The Diary of Hugh Gaitskell 1945–56*, Jonathan Cape, 1983

Shirley Williams, 'My Mother and Her Friend', *The Listener*, 21 November 1985.

Shirley Williams, 'Remembering My Mother', paper given at 'A Testament to Vera Brittain', Centenary Conference, McMaster University, Hamilton, Ontario, 15 October 1993. Abridged version, 'Testament to the Touchstone of My Life' in *The Independent*, 29 December 1993

Trevor Wilson, *The Myriad Faces of War: Britain and the Great War*, Oxford, Polity Press, 1986

J.M. Winter, 'Britain's "Lost Generation" of the First World War', *Population Studies*, 31, 1977

J.M. Winter, *The Great War and the British People*, Macmillan, 1986

Robert Wohl, *The Generation of 1914*, Weidenfeld and Nicolson, 1979

Virginia Woolf, *Letters*, vol. 5, *The Sickle Side of the Moon 1932–1935*, edited by Nigel Nicolson and Joanne Trautmann, Hogarth Press, 1979

Virginia Woolf, *Diary*, vol. 4, 1931–1935, edited by Anne Oliver Bell assisted by Andrew McNeillie, Hogarth Press, 1982

Barbara Wootton, *In a World I Never Made. Autobiographical Reflections*, George Allen & Unwin, 1967

3 UNPUBLISHED ARTICLES AND THESES

Y.A. Bennett, 'Testament of a Minority in Wartime: The Peace Pledge Union and Vera Brittain, 1939–1945', Ph.D thesis, McMaster University, Hamilton, Ontario, 1984

Y.A. Bennett, 'A Question of Respectability and Tactics: Vera Brittain and Food Relief for Occupied Europe, 1941–1944', paper given at the University of Toronto, International Conference on the Pacifist Impulse in Historical Perspective, 4–12 May 1991

Y.A. Bennett (with F.E. Montgomery) 'Morality, Humanity, Law and War: Vera Brittain and Food Relief for Occupied Europe, 1939–1945', Paper given at The Western Conference on British Studies, Tucson, Arizona, 17–18 October 1991

Mark Bostridge, 'An Autobiographer's Life: Problems and Approaches', paper given at 'A Testament to Vera Brittain', Centenary Conference, McMaster University, Hamilton, Ontario, 15 October 1993

Philip Brooke, 'Winifred Holtby: Her Novels and their Context,' Malet Lambert Local History Originals, 1985

Constance A. Brown, 'The Literary Aftermath: English Literary Response to the First World War', Chapter 4, 'Vera Brittain: Testament of Hope', Ph.D thesis, Columbia University, 1978

David Doughan, 'Lobbying for Liberation. British Feminism, 1918–1968', the Vera Douie Memorial Lecture 1979, City of London Polytechnic, 1980

Deborah Gorham, 'Vera Brittain and the Great War', Paper given at the Canadian Historical Association, May 1985

Rita Kissen, 'Vera Brittain: Writing A Life', Ph.D thesis, Massachusetts University, 1986

Pat Kulisheck, 'Ruth Gage-Colby', 1984

Robert Milner, 'Brittains Limited. Cheddleton and Hanley Paper Mills in the context of the history of paper making in England', Certificate in Local History, Keele University, 1987

Margaret Waley, 'Winifred Holtby: A Short Life', 1976

4 RECORDINGS AND BROADCASTS

Vera Brittain introducing Dame Ethel Smyth and the 'March of the Women' from the BBC's 'Scrapbook for 1912'. Recorded on 9 March 1937. Reference LP 1279

Vera Brittain reading short extracts from *Testament of Youth* in 'Scrapbook for 1918', transmitted on BBC's Home Service on 7 April 1959. Recorded on 9 September 1958. Reference T 51641

Vera Brittain lecturing on 'Winifred Holtby in Life and Literature' at the Guildhall, Hull, East Yorkshire, 28 September 1960. Private recording

Vera Brittain interviewed on the BBC for 'Greek in the Kitchen. An Enquiry into the Education of Girls'. Recorded on 26 May 1961. Reference LP 26841

Sir George Catlin, Shirley Williams, and Gillian Tindall discussing Vera Brittain and *Testament of Youth* on BBC Radio 4's 'Woman's Hour', 20 April 1978

'Testament of Youth', a BBC-TV production in association with London Film Productions Ltd. Dramatized in five parts by Elaine Morgan. Directed by Moira Armstrong, produced by Jonathan Powell, and starring Cheryl Campbell as Vera Brittain. First transmitted on BBC2 in October and November 1979

INDEX

Abbott, Elizabeth 510
Adelphi magazine 412
Adshead, Captain Harry 92–3
Agate, James 263
Aldington, Richard: *Death of a Hero* 239
Aldom, Alice (headmistress) 29
Alexander, King of Yugoslavia 298
Alexander, Horace 455
All-India Women's Conferences 415, 453, 494
Allum Green Cottage 384–5, 386, 394, 410, 442–3, 457, 464
American Friends Service Committee 448, 495
Amery, John 450
Amery, Leo 415
Anderson, Sir John 402
Andrews, Henry 390, 452
Anglo-Netherlands Association 344
Answers (weekly newpaper) 52, 53
Anthony, Robert ('Roy') 150–1, 187
Aranyi, Jelly d' 272
Arnim, Elizabeth von: *The Enchanted April* 288
Ash Hall, nr Hanley 12, 317
Ashley, Margery Corbett 415
Asquith, Raymond 131*n*
Asturias (hospital ship) 106
Auden, W. H. 377, 417

Baillie-Stewart, Norman 450
Ballinger, Margaret 339
Ballinger, William 290, 316
Bannister, Roger 481
Barber, Marjorie 68, 79, 80
Barclay, John 365, 398
Barrington, A. C. 454, 455
Barthou, Louis 298
Bateman, Lady 31, 171
Battey, Patricia 474
Baylis, Lilian 221
Beale, Dorothea 36
Beechman, N. A. 153
Bell, George, Bishop of Chichester 389, 425, 428, 430, 431, 438
Bennett, Aleksandra 429
Bennett, Arnold 11, 14; *Clayhanger* 247
Bennett, Robert Sterndale 29, 30
Benson, Stella 276, 283, 334
Bentley, Norman 248
Bentley, Phyllis 247–51, 252, 253–4, 259–61, 271, 274, 276, 296, 308, 336, 338, 347, 366, 391, 396, 419, 460, 482, 491 *Carr* 250; *Inheritance* 247, 248, 254, 294; *Trio* 248
Bentley-Carr, Arthur 21
Bentley-Carr, Lillie (*née* Bervon) 21, 30, 404, 406, 416, 483
Berdahl, Professor Clarence 518
Berengaria (liner) 290, 291, 292
Beresford, J. D. 172

Bergner, Elisabeth 286
Berry, Paul 458, 462, 471, 492, 517, 522, 523
Bervon, Charles ('Charlie') 22
Bervon, Emma Jane (*née* Hampson) 15, 16, 17, 70, 127
Bervon, Florence 21–2, 30, 31, 33, 34, 47, 60, 170, 171, 172, 286, 322, 483
Bervon, Isabel ('Belle') 21, 22, 70, 71, 286, 409, 483
Bervon, John (Bladder) Inglis 15, 16
Bervon, Lillie *see* Bentley-Carr, Lillie
Bervon, William ('Bill') 22
Best, Edna 331
Betjeman, John 444–5
Birkett, Norman 228
Biron, Sir Chartres 228, 517
Blackwell, Basil 156
Blackwell, Miss 156
Bleichenbach, Fräulein 242–3, 289, 318, 319
Blunden, Edmund 156, 264; *Undertones of War* 239
Books and Bookmen 492
Book Society, The 331
Boult, Sir Adrian 481
Bowen, Elizabeth 255
Bowen, Marjorie 448
Box, Muriel 514
Bracken, Brendan 436
Brailsford, H. N. 262
Brett, Bruce 295
Brett, George Platt I 294, 295, 373
Brett, George Platt II 294–6; VB stays with 292, 293, 294, 296; relationship with VB 296, 297, 301–4, 305, 308–9, 310–11, 312–16; and Winifred's death 341; and *Honourable Estate* 308, 345, 347, 348–9; discusses VB's next book 373–4; as guardian to VB's children 314, 379, 400, 413, 419; mentioned 402, 405, 406, 407, 410, 439, 442, 449, 472
Brett, George Platt III 295
Brett, Isabel 292–3, 295, 296, 301, 304, 312, 316, 345, 413
Brett-Young, Mrs Francis 498
Bridges, Robert: *The Testament of Beauty* 241
Bridoux, André 88
Britannic (hospital ship) 106
British Broadcasting Corporation (BBC) 284, 388, 420
Brittain, (Thomas) Arthur (father): birth 14; schooling 14, 29; starts work 14; marriage 15, 16–17; character 22–3, 26; and VB 11, 12, 22, 24, 27, 36, 37, 38, 39–40, 43, 45; life in Buxton 28, 41–2; and Edward 29, 42; dislikes Reverend Ward 45, 46; opposes VB's Oxford ambitions 47–8, and Edward's enlistment 60, 62, 64; welcomes Roland as a future-son-in-law 85; manoeuvred out of the Mill 91–2; disapproves of VB's nursing 102; approves of

Assembly 230–1; produces *Halcyon, or the Future of Monogamy* 231–2; her views on marriage and George's affairs 232–5; begins *Testament of Youth* (q.v.) 235; the birth of her daughter (*see* Williams, Shirley) 242–3; relationship with Phyllis Bentley 247–51, 253–4; and George's objections to *Testament of Youth* 256–9; quarrels with Phyllis Bentley 259–60; with Winifred in France 262; savours fame to the full 269–71; her relationship with Winifred 272–9, 280–1, 369; George resentful of 280–1, 284–5; her financial affairs 285–6; begins *Honourable Estate* (*see below*) 287; Italian holiday with George 288; her indecision about American lecture tour 287, 288–91

1934–9

the tour and her relationship with George Brett 292–305, 308–9, 310–11, 312–16; domestic trials 306–7; at home for George 309; a week of lectures 309; with Winifred in Hornsea 309; exhaustion and depression 309–10; self-deception over Winifred's illness 316–17; visits Buxton 317; and her father's suicide 318–20; nurses George 320–1; and Winifred's death 322–8, 341–2; writes *Testament of Friendship* (*see below*) 333–40; quarrels with George 342; canvasses for him 342–3; flags over *Honourable Estate* 343–4; in Germany and Holland 344; and the publication of *Honourable Estate* 345, 348–9; speaks at the Dorchester Peace Rally 349–50, 355; her affiliation to peace organizations 350–3; becomes Sponsor of the Peace Pledge Union (q.v.) 350, 355–9; her friendship with Margaret Storm Jameson 359–63; her sympathy for George 373–4; on tour in America 373–6; meets Eleanor Roosevelt 376; pacifist activities 378–9, 380–1; to America with the children 380, 383; breaks with Gollancz 381–2; buys cottage 384; and outbreak of war 384–5

1939–45

begins 'Letter to Peace-Lovers' (*see below*) 386–7; a third lecture-tour in USA 390–2, 393–4; her movements monitored 392–3; quarrels with Storm Jameson 395–7; sends the children to America 399–401; works for Children's Overseas Reception Board 401; begins *England's Hour* (*see below*) 401; is refused exit permit 402–3, 407–8; in the blitz 403–5; joins Storm Jameson in Mortimer 405–6; is taught to value George 408; Christmas at Carbis Bay 409; flat-hunting in London 410; 'war work' 411–12; estrangement from Storm Jameson 413–15, 416–18; faces hostility and official disapproval 419–22; rejected by BBC 420; writes *Humiliation with Honour* (*see below*) 422–3; her work for food relief 422, 425–9, 433, and against 'saturation bombing' 422, 425, 429–32, 436–42; writes *Seed of Chaos* (*see below*) 436–7; reopens Allum Green 442–3; plans *Above All Nations* (*see below*) 443; her name on Gestapo list 425, 445–6

1945–70

dispirited and exhausted 447; misjudges political climate 447–8; European tours 448; her sales slump in America 448–9; and Peace Pledge Union (q.v.) 450–1; and her mother's death 461–2; addresses Oxford Labour Club 480; marital problems 463–7; visits India 450, 453–5, 464–5, 480; writes *Account Rendered* 456, *Born 1925* 457–8, and *In the Steps of John Bunyan* 459 (*see below*); admits her limitations as an author 460; Silver Wedding celebrations 467; pleased at John's marriage 475, 476; moves to Whitehall Court 481, 483; besieged with commitments 482; illnesses and loneliness 483–4; writes *Lady into Woman* (*see below*) 485–6, and *Testament of Experience* (*see below*) 487, 488; sues *Books and Bookmen* for libel 492; alienates Clare Leighton 492–3; brings out *The Women at Oxford* 493, biographies 493–4, and *The Rebel Passion* 494–5; with George in Montreal 495–6; in South Africa 497–505; supports CND 506–8; and Shirley's political career 508–10; her pleasure in her grandchildren 487, 511; lectures at the National Liberal Club 513–14; falls 514, 515; last meeting with Gollancz 515–16; continues to write 517; her health deteriorates 517, 518, 519–20, 521; with George in Illinois 517–18, Fiesole 521, and Marrakech 521–2; death and funeral 522; obituaries 523

character and personality 18, 20, 40–1, 67–8, 144, 145, 149–50, 155, 169–70, 215–16, 270–1, 364–5, 465–6

views on:

autobiography 241, 270, 498

feminism and equal rights for women 30, 35–7, 40, 61, 68, 152–4, 160, 172, 176–7, 180, 220, 221, 230, 273–4, 345, 346, 367, 369–70; *see also* marriage

internationalism 121–2, 203

marriage 218–19, 221–3, 230, 231–5, 241–2

pacifism 121–3, 155, 180, 203, 350–3, 355–9, 364, 367, 368, 377–8, 380–3, 385, 397–9, 419, 420–4, 445, 457, 466–7, *see also* 'Letter to Peace-Lovers' (*below*)

religion 27, 43, 45, 67, 94, 100, 356, 359, 423–4, 429, 432, 457, 466

sexuality 201–2, 211–12, 213, 273–4

war memoirs 239–41

World War I 59–60, 61–2, 63–4, 69, 78, 88–9, 446

WORKS (*see also Testament of Youth*):

Above All Nations 443–5, 451, 515

Account Rendered 11, 436, 448–9, 456–7

'America and the Marriage Problem' 217

'Authors Take Sides on the Spanish War' 341, 377

'Boar's Hill' 156

Born 1925 11, 377, 457–8, 459, 462

'Celibate Professions' 230

The Dark Tide 143–4, 145, 148, 156, 165, 166, 172, 173, 174, 180–1, 182–5, 189, 200, 219, 224, 237, 270, 361

England's Hour 267, 401–2, 404, 406, 409–10

Envoy Extraordinary 493, 494

'The Evils of Good Fellowship' 215

'Extracts from a Bride's Diary' 216–17

'Good Citizenship and the League' 179

www.virago.co.uk

To find out more about Paul Berry, Mark Bostridge
and other Virago authors, visit
www.virago.co.uk

Visit the Virago website for:

- News of author events and forthcoming titles
- Features and interviews with authors, including
  Margaret Atwood, Maya Angelou, Sarah Waters,
  Nina Bawden and Gillian Slovo
- Free extracts from a wide range of titles
- Discounts on new publications
- Competitions
- The chance to buy signed copies
- Reading group guides

PLUS
Subscribe to our free monthly newsletter